UNDERSTANDING POETRY

UNDERSTANDING POETRY

Walter Kalaidjian
Emory University

HOUGHTON MIFFLIN COMPANY   Boston   New York

Publisher: Patricia A. Coryell
Executive editor: Suzanne Phelps Weir
Sponsoring editor: Michael Gillespie
Associate Editor: Bruce Cantley
Senior production editor: Rosemary Winfield
Senior production/design coordinator: Jodi O'Rourke
Senior manufacturing coordinator: Priscilla Bailey
Marketing manager: Cindy Graff Cohen

Cover art: The Trees by Andre Derain © Albright-Knox Art Gallery/Corbis

Printed in the U.S.A.

Library of Congress Catalog Card Number: 2003111766

ISBN: 0-618-38629-7

123456789-QWV-08 07 06 05 04

Contents

An Album of Art

Vasily Kandinsky, *Composition vi*
Charles Henry Demuth, *I Saw the Figure Five in Gold*
Andy Warhol, *Marilyn Monroe (Twenty Times)*
The Chicago Women's Graphics Collective, *Boycott Lettuce and Grapes*
Pieter Brueghel, *Landscape with the Fall of Icarus*
Botticelli, *The Birth of Venus*
Raphael, *An Allegory: Vision of a Knight*
Michelangelo, *Leda and the Swan*
William Blake, Illuminated manuscript of "The Lamb"
Dante Gabriel Rossetti, *The Girlhood of Mary Virgin*
Samuel Bak, *Thou Shalt Not Kill*

WRITING

Preface for Instructors

The past twenty years have witnessed exciting evolutions in the way instructors think, talk, and write about literature—the expanding canon, growing interest in literary and cultural theory, changing definitions of what a "text" is, the emergence of new technologies, and so on. Capturing the energy, relevance, and skills of literary study and transmitting them to undergraduate students is one of the most important things we do as English instructors. In creating *Understanding Poetry*, our aim has been twofold—to better address the ways instructors want to teach verse today and to better inspire in students the desire and skills to engage poetry critically. In its reading selections, approach, apparatus, and integrated technology components, *Understanding Poetry* has been carefully crafted to uphold the best literary traditions while furthering innovations that engage a new generation of students and instructors.

The heart of any anthology is found in its reading selections. We have balanced favorite canonical works with an outstanding selection of thought-provoking contemporary writing. We think you will find some wonderful surprises in the table of contents that you will be eager to explore with your students. We have included a wealth of relevant works of art and photographs—including color pages—that enrich the study of poetry and culture. We have also designed a media-rich CD-ROM and Web site—fully integrated with the text—to further bring poetry to life and to better engage the learning styles of today's students.

We focus students on the necessary skills to perform close readings and to think critically about literary works. *Understanding Poetry* starts with discussions of the basic, formal elements students need to understand and analyze verse. Students will benefit from our discussions of understanding poetry in terms of its formal presentation of word choice, imagery, figurative language, sound sense, irony, paradox, rhyme and rhythm, and stanza form. These formalist practices continue to be essential skills that introductory students must master as requisites to understanding and enjoying poetry. However, we feel it is important for today's students to move beyond basic readings toward more considered interpretations of literary texts. Therefore, through integrated, *accessible* discussions of critical approaches to literature, *Understanding Poetry* encourages and supports students as they explore ways in which poetry engages with critical understandings of nationalism, race, gender, sexuality, global multiculturalism, and other cultural and political frames. *Understanding Poetry* enables instructors to adopt a text more in step with the needs and interests of today's students and reflective of the ways many instructors organize their classes.

If you are an instructor who wants to engage your students with a lifelong enjoyment of poetry while encouraging them to reach beyond a reading of the words to more rewarding and interesting interpretations, then *Understanding*

Poetry will meet your needs. We hope you find that *Understanding Poetry* empowers you to go where you want to go and do what you want to do.

Key Features of the Anthology

Understanding Poetry offers instructors a wealth of features that support the teaching of their classes.

Compelling Table of Contents

- **A rich array of the best poetry** offers instructors a wonderful range of authors—from the cherished work of Shakespeare, Keats, Blake, Frost, and Dickinson to the fresh and contemporary voices of Audre Lorde, Tracie Morris, Miguel Piñero, Ha Jin, and Janice Mirikitani. *Understanding Poetry* gives you the flexibility you need to teach the selections that suit your class.

- **Important featured writers are treated in-depth** to allow more focused study of a single writer and give students rich opportunities for writing and research assignments. Featured writers include John Keats, Gwendolyn Brooks, Anne Sexton, and Langston Hughes.

- **Unique chapters explore the broader connections between poetry and culture** as showcased by "A Casebook on Beat Poetry" (Chapter 13), "A Casebook on Performance and Performativity" (Chapter 15), and "Cultural Criticism (Chapter 22). These chapters include a wonderful range of dynamic writers, including the poetry of Allen Ginsberg, Diane Di Prima, and Amiri Baraka, the blues lyricism of Langston Hughes, and the experimental performance art of Guillermo Gómez-Peña and Tracie Morris. Enlivened with relevant social and political commentary, these chapters serve as case studies of how countercultural ideas and modes of expression create a dynamic conversation with mainstream cultural values and forms of expression.

- **Distinctive poetry casebooks** allow students to explore specific themes in-depth, such as "Poetry and Social Activism Between the Wars," "Poetry, Trauma, and Testimony: Holocaust Verses," "Postmodern Poetics," "Chicano/a Poetry," and "Native American Poetry." These casebooks facilitate focused class discussions and provide students with rich topics for writing and research.

Wealth of Visual Texts

- **Numerous photos and works of art, including four pages of full-color work,** are carefully placed throughout the text to help students explore the connections between written and visual texts.

Comprehensive Coverage of Approaches to Studying Poetry

- **Complete coverage of the formal elements of poetry** gives students the knowledge they need to understand the basic features of poetry including diction, rhyme, meter, imagery, and symbolism. Multiple chapters are devoted to the study of these elements giving helpful explanations and accessible examples.
- **Unique, integrated coverage of contemporary critical approaches** offers accessible, insightful discussions of how literary theory and cultural theory are used to explore meaning in poetry. Integrated throughout the anthology in "Critical Perspective" sections rather than placed in an appendix or special chapters, this coverage includes in-text discussions, casebooks, and excerpts from classic and contemporary critical essays that offer students accessible and important critical perspectives into how literary theory can facilitate a deeper understanding of literary texts. Critical Perspectives can also be used as a springboard for class discussion and writing.
- **Emphasis on cultural, social, and historical contexts** reflects the increased desire to view literature through the lens of culture. The text discussions offer students ample opportunities to analyze and interpret poetry using cultural, social, and historical events. Five chapters are especially well-suited to these discussions: "Race and Representation" (Chapter 16), "Feminism and Representation" (Chapter 19), "Representations of Desire and Sexuality" (Chapter 20), and "Postcolonial Poetics" (Chapter 21).

Thorough Coverage of Writing and Research

- **Three chapters are devoted** to guiding students through the process of writing about literature and developing effective essays. Coverage includes general guidance, poetry-specific advice, and help with the research paper.
- **An annotated student paper** provides an excellent model of strong student writing.
- **Topics for Critical Thinking and Critical Writing** are integrated into the chapters followed by suggestions for class discussion and writing topics. Instructors may use these informally in class or assign them as writing projects.

Integrated CD-ROM and Web Site

New technologies are opening up new avenues of literary exploration. Technology cannot replace the pleasure of reading a print text, but it can enhance certain aspects of its study—particularly for today's students who are more accustomed to integrating technology into their lives. By integrating print and technology components, *Understanding Poetry* taps into the strengths of various media to bring poetry to life for your students. Marginal icons throughout *Understanding Poetry* direct you and your students to the related resources on our CD-ROM and Web site that help support and expand the readings and pedagogy in the text.

- **A highly interactive CD-ROM with a wealth of audio and visual resources** offers opportunities for in-depth study of poetry. The poetry unit focuses on the work of Langston Hughes, placing it in broader cultural, political, and artistic contexts. This section features poems by Hughes, seven audio clips of related jazz and blues music and poetry readings, and photos and art. The CD-ROM also includes resources for fiction and drama.

- **A resource-rich Web site** helps students and instructors further explore the works, authors, artistic movements, and literary theories introduced in the anthology. The *Understanding Poetry* Web site provides helpful support for students including a poetry tutorial, questions and writing assignments, insights into literary movements, supplemental biographical materials, and relevant photos and visual art.

Organized to be Flexible and Teachable

Understanding Poetry, rich with the finest classic and contemporary poetry, allows instructors the flexibility to tailor the text to suit their classroom needs. Some instructors may prefer to concentrate on the core chapters that cover the literary elements. Other instructors may choose to blend classic coverage with chapters that explore cultural, social, and historical contexts along with topics such as performative poetry, postmodernism, and postcolonialism.

The practical approaches to reading poems in *Understanding Poetry* allows students to master the challenges of interpreting verse. Students will be introduced to classic voices such as William Shakespeare, Emily Dickinson, T. S. Eliot, and Langston Hughes, along with contemporary writers such as Janice Mirikitani, Jimmy Santiago Baca, Ray A. Young Bear, Ha Jin, and Tracie Morris. Coverage of imagery, figurative language, symbolism, myth, and prosody introduces the rudiments of form in the chapters that make up Part I, "Understanding Poetic Form." Part II "Poetry and History," examines verse writing not just as formal lyric expression but, equally important, as a means of social expression. In this vein, Critical Perspective Casebooks explore poetry's cultural role in modern history, its place in the Native American, Chicano, and African American communities, its power to bear witness to the Holocaust, as well as poetry's changing styles of postcolonial and postmodern expression. In addition, fresh perspectives on poetry's representation of race, ethnicity, feminism, and desire open up bold new realms of classroom discussion and critical reflection. These chapters offer students a rich resource for writing and research.

Writing Guidance

Understanding Poetry is not just a textbook on how to read and interpret great verse; equally important, it also offers a practical guide to student writing. Part IV, on "Writing about Literature," introduces students to the art of critical writing from invention through final execution. Here you will find practical advice about every stage of the compositional process, illustrated by sample student writing. In teaching the craft of critical writing, *Understanding Poetry* addresses the key areas of critical thinking and composition including crafting effective thesis statements and employing evidence in argumentation. In addition to providing a general introduction to effective critical writing, *Understanding Poetry* offers an extensive discussion of college-level research writing.

Resources for Teaching *Understanding Poetry*

A wealth of instructor resources are available to help you in the classroom. A comprehensive instructor's guide discusses every author and nearly every reading selection in the text. The manual provides guidance for discussing the selections in class, answering in-text questions and writing assignments, making connections to other writing selections, incorporating more coverage of literary theory in the classroom, and using the technology components. You will also find additional instructor resources at the Web site.

For instructors who want to assign additional literary works in their course, special packaging options are available with the New Riverside Editions—a wonderful series that complements literary texts with relevant historical documents, cultural contexts, and critical essays. For a complete listing, please visit the Houghton Mifflin Web site at http://college.hmco.com.

Acknowledgments

We would like to thank all the instructors and colleagues who helped throughout the development process of this book. Your feedback and ideas were invaluable, and every chapter of this book has benefited from your insight. We particularly appreciate the dedicated work of Brian W. Gastle, Western Carolina University; Michelle Glaros, Dakota State University; Ann C. Hall, Ohio Dominican College; John Marx, University of Richmond; and Michele Peers, Northern Kentucky University; Aimee Pozorski, Central Connecticut State University.

We thank all of the reviewers, focus group participants, and class testers for their assistance in shaping this project: Linda B. Adams, Jefferson Community College; Frank Ancona, Sussex County Community College; Mike Anzelome, Nassau Community College; Maryam Barrie, Washtenaw Community College; Robert Barton, Rutgers University; Laura C. Berry, University of Arizona; John Blair, Southwest Texas State University; Barbara

Bonallo, Miami-Dade Community College–Wolfson Campus; Lisa Brandom, John Brown University; Richard Brodesky, Pima Community College; Terence Brunk, Columbia College; Robert Callahan, Temple University; Ruth Callahan, Glendale Community College; Ron Carter, Rappahonnock Community College; Peggy Cole, Arapahoe Community College; Mark Garrett Cooper, Florida State University; Keith Coplin, Colby Community College; Gail S. Corso, Neumann College; Carol Ann Davis, College of Charleston; Kathy De Grave, Pittsburg State University; Gillian Devereux, Old Dominion University; Ken Donelson, Arizona State University; Tina D. Eliopulos, Community College of Southern Nevada; Sandra K. Ellston, Eastern Oregon University; Nancy Esposito, Bentley College; Marilyn Falkenberg, Menlo College; Ray Foster, Scottsdale Community College; Phyllis Frus, Hawaii Pacific University; Hank Galmish, Green River Community College; Mark Gellis, Kettering University; Karen Golightly, University of Memphis; John Granger, San Diego State University; Natalie Grinnell, Wofford College; Marlene Groner, State University of New York–Farmingdale; Jean Harper, Ball State University; Randall Howe, North Georgia College and State University; Bryon Lee Grigsby, Centenary College; Grant Jenkins, Old Dominion University; Suzanne Keen, Washington and Lee University; Linda Cooper Knight, College of the Albemarle; Jim Kosmicki, Central Community College; Wendy Kurant, University of Georgia; Eleanor Latham, Central Oregon Community College; Marilyn Levine, Suffolk County Community College; David Levy, Housatonic Community College; Sarah Littefield, Salve Regina University; Jerry Bryan Lincecum, Austin College; Jack Lynch, Rutgers University; Diann V. Mason, Paris Junior College; Deborah Mael, Newberry College; Lisa Marcus, Pacific Lutheran University; Dennis D. McDaniel, Saint Vincent College; Thomas H. McNeely, Emerson College; Walter S. Minot, Gannon University; Janice Okoomian, Brown University; Michael Overman, University of South Carolina–Columbia; Elizabeth Patterson, Yakima Valley Community College; Eva Mokry Pohler, University of Texas at San Antonio; William Provost, University of Georgia; Jean-Michel Rabaté, University of Pennsylvania; Ann Marie Radaskiewicz, Western Piedmont Community College; Jeff Rice, University of Florida; Donald Riggs, Drexel University; Susan Roberts, Boston College; Peter Burton Ross, University of the District of Columbia; Albert Rouzie, Ohio University; Deborah Schwartz, Lourdes College; Carl Seiple, Kutztown University of Pennsylvania; Larry Severeid, College of Eastern Utah; William Sullivan, Winthrop College; John K. Swensson, DeAnza College; Joanna Tardoni, Western Wyoming Community College; Donna Thomsen, Johnson and Wales University; Michael Thro, Tidewater Community College; John Wargacki, Seton Hall University; Robert A. Watts, Drexel University; Joy Wentz, College of the Desert; Sallie Wolf, Arapahoe Community College; Nancy J. Young, Curry College.

We would also like to thank the individuals who helped us on this project from the start. For their thoughtful work on the anthology and the instructor's resource manual, we thank Jaime Hovey, Aimee Pozorski, Craig Owens, Yasmina Madden, Terence Hartnett, Danielle Hartnett, Caitlin Watt, Amy

Nolan, and Johanna Frank. At Houghton Mifflin, we thank June Smith, Kris Clerkin, and Pat Coryell for their unflagging support of *Understanding Poetry* from its earliest stages. We appreciate the editorial guidance of Suzanne Phelps Weir, Michael Gillespie, Katharine Glynn, and Bruce Cantley. Janet Edmonds and Beth McCracken ably developed the technology components, and Rosemary Winfield worked tirelessly to keep the book on schedule through production. Nancy Lyman and Cindy Graff Cohen contributed their ideas and enthusiasm throughout the process, and Maria Maimone and Michael Farmer tackled the Herculean task of clearing all the permissions.

Why Study Literature?

Literature, as the Welsh poet Dylan Thomas famously remarked, is a "sullen art." Bound between the covers of a book, the writer's craft is made up of black marks that lie silent on the page. Yet according to Henry David Thoreau, literature also can empower you to "live deep and suck the marrow out of life." Robin Williams, in the guise of English teacher John Keating, declared in the film *Dead Poets Society* that he read literature because he was "a member of the human race and the human race is filled with passion! Medicine, Law, Banking—these are necessary to sustain life—but poetry, romance, love, beauty! These are what we stay alive for."

Higher education is a requisite, certainly, to becoming a doctor, lawyer, accountant, journalist, or business executive. Nevertheless, the kind of passion to be found from the poetry of Gwendolyn Brooks, Anne Sexton, John Keats, and Garg Soto just might point you toward becoming a more discerning professional, a more engaged citizen, a more thoughtful human being: someone—in short—who is more alive. A work of literature—whether a short story, a poem, or a play—is not just a form of entertainment or an amusement. Reading is not the same as consuming; reading is more radically transformative. Great literature, according to German poet Ranier Maria Rilke, makes you aware that "you must change your life."

In addition to experiencing literature, understanding it requires discipline and critical thinking skills. No one is born with the capacity to detect dramatic irony or to discern the difference between "theater in the round" and "theater of the absurd." Interpreting the complexities of an Elizabethan sonnet or a postmodern work of hyperfiction is not something that comes naturally to most people. It's an acquired art, much like mastering a sport or a musical instrument. The delight of critical thinking lies in both experiencing and understanding what literature can do on the page, at the microphone, and on the stage. This book will give you the tools you will need to enjoy great literature and, equally important, to write about it with greater precision and keener insight.

UNDERSTANDING
POETRY

Part I
Understanding Poetic Form

1 Introduction: Reading Poetry

I, too, dislike it. . . .
   Reading it, however, with a perfect contempt for it, one
   discovers in
   it after all, a place for the genuine.
                    –MARIANNE MOORE, "POETRY" (1924)

Some readers are natural-born poetry lovers, but most of us need a little coaxing in the pleasures of reading verse. Let's face it: unpacking a dense Shakespearean sonnet isn't exactly like watching the season finale of your favorite TV show. Although you can find plenty of action, adventure, comedy, tragedy, romance, intrigue, seduction, and betrayal in poetry, reading verse doesn't entertain in the same fashion as a gripping novel or sensational action movie. Compelling poems can rivet our attention but not in the ways we expect from the latest special effects of, say, George Lucas's Industrial Light and Magic. Reading poetry makes a different claim on our attention than playing *Nintendo*. While you can always get to the next level of a video game, a particularly difficult line of verse often remains dumbfounding even on a second, third, or fourth reading. At times like these, it might help to know that even practicing poets such as Marianne Moore had moments of "perfect contempt" for poetry.

Why then do we bother with reading poetry? Perhaps it has to do with what Moore calls "the genuine." In a world of clichés, stereotypes, and packaged images, nothing satisfies our passion for "the genuine"—for originality, authenticity, "the new"—like poetry. Beyond whatever pleasure we take in a well-crafted poetic form, great poetry delivers a vital knowledge that we can find nowhere else. Late in life, the modern poet William Carlos Williams summed it up this way: "It is difficult," he concluded,

> to get the news from poems
> yet men die miserably every day
>   for lack
> of what is found there.
> (From "Asphodel, That Greeny Flower," 1955)

What one looks to find from a good poem is an act of imagination so fresh, so powerfully presented, so genuine that it possesses its own reality. As

Moore muses in a longer version of "Poetry," compelling poems are like "imaginary gardens with real toads in them." How would you describe Moore's point in the following lines?

MARIANNE MOORE   *(1887–1972)*

Poetry   *(1921)*

I too, dislike it: there are things that are important beyond all this
    fiddle.
  Reading it, however, with a perfect contempt for it, one discovers in
  it after all, a place for the genuine.
    Hands that can grasp, eyes
    that can dilate, hair that can rise   5
      if it must, these things are important not because a

high-sounding interpretation can be put upon them but because they are
  useful. When they become so derivative as to become unintelligible,
  the same thing may be said for all of us, that we
    do not admire what   10
    we cannot understand: the bat
      holding on upside down or in quest of something to

eat, elephants pushing, a wild horse taking a roll, a tireless wolf under
  a tree, the immovable critic twitching his skin like a horse that feels
    a flea, the base-
    ball fan, the statistician—   15
      nor is it valid
      to discriminate against 'business documents and

school-books'; all these phenomena are important. One must make a
    distinction
  however: when dragged into prominence by half poets, the result is not
    poetry,
  nor till the poets among us can be   20
    'literalists of
    the imagination'—above
      insolence and triviality and can present

for inspection, 'imaginary gardens with real toads in them,' shall we have
  it. In the meantime, if you demand on the one hand,   25
  the raw material of poetry in
    all its rawness and
    that which is on the other hand
      genuine, then you are interested in poetry.

Art and reality, the imagination and its "raw material," imaginary gardens and real toads: For Moore, reading poetry requires having an interest in each of these opposites at the same time.

Moore's tribute to "Poetry" is a complex statement. In responding to it, write a one-paragraph **paraphrase** of her poem. A paraphrase is a restatement in your own words of the major ideas, argument, or thematic elements of a poem. A paraphrase provides a prose version of a poem's main message. Paraphrase, of course, can never begin to capture the subtlety of a poem's formal arrangement on the page, but it is a place to begin reading poetry. In paraphrasing Moore's "Poetry," consider the following questions. After you draft your paragraph, compare what you have written to the critical commentary on the poem from the *Understanding Poetry* **Web** :   *www*

1. How does Moore describe "the genuine" in "Poetry"?
2. Where, according to Moore, does understanding poetry begin?
3. In what sense does Moore imply that great poetry is "important" and "useful"?
4. What do you think Moore means by being "interested in poetry"?
5. According to the poem's argument, what relation should the imagination have to the intellect in poetry?

Poetry, of course, goes far beyond paraphrase as it involves the formal activity of verse writing. While paraphrasing summarizes a poem's main idea or theme, what poetry is about—*what it is*, in essence—is not so easily understood. If you've ever seen Tiger Woods swing a golf club, you'd probably agree that it looks like "pure poetry." Watching an Olympic swimming legend such as Janet Evans, we might say her freestyle is "poetry in motion." But what kind of poetry is this? If we were pressed to define the poetry we find in a masterful chip shot or perfect flip turn, what would we say? Considered seriously enough, such questioning sooner or later would, as the Romantic poet John Keats said, "tease us out of thought." Poets, philosophers, and even politicians have all wrestled with the question "What is poetry?"

Perhaps the most direct answer comes from the poet William Stafford. He characterized poetry as "anything said in such a way or put on the page in such a way as to invite from the hearer or reader a certain kind of attention." But how helpful is this? What kind of attention is Stafford talking about exactly? Is he implying that poetry inspires wonder, and, if so, isn't wonder, by definition, outside our understanding? Yes, and that is precisely the point. *Poetry constantly introduces us to—and addresses us by—something that is bracingly different from what we already know, what we have already thought, what we have already felt.* It captures our attention. That's the reason why the British romantic poet Percy Bysshe Shelley claimed that poetry "makes familiar objects be as if they were not familiar." But what is that experience like? And how can we tell if a poem inspires wonder? For her part, the nineteenth-century American poet Emily Dickinson applied a very simple test to the experience of poetry. "If," she says, "I read a book [and] it makes my whole body so cold no fire ever can warm me I know *that* is poetry. If I feel physically as if the top of my head were taken off, I know *that* is poetry. These are the only ways I know it." Wonder, for her, begins in the body; it is played upon the pulses.

Poetry begins, then, with a close encounter with what is radically new and unclaimed in our experience. "A poem," says Robert Frost, "is never a thought to begin with. . . . A poem begins with a lump in the throat." The emotional, and even physical, impact poetry can have on us is one of the reasons that Plato thought of poets as dangerous people. In fact, he set out to ban poets and poetry from his ideal model of the state in Book X of *The Republic*. Poets, like politicians, know that the powerful utterance will find a way to engage our feelings, our hopes, and our anxieties; it will get under our skin.

"You campaign in poetry," said former New York governor Mario Cuomo; "you govern in prose." But if poets, as Shelley writes, are the "unacknowledged legislators of the world," how do they add something original and decisive to existence? For his part, Plato charges that this is precisely what poets never do. Plato writes that poets are slavish imitators, belated and removed from the truths to be witnessed in nature. They are decidedly unheroic and merely record what their betters actually do in the real world. Against this low opinion of poets, Sir Philip Sidney notes in "An Apology for Poetry" that the titles poets carried in the Ancient world (in Greek, *poietes* or maker, and in Latin, *vates* or prophet) had civic and even religious power. Moreover, he reverses Plato to assert that "Nature never set forth the earth in so rich tapestry as diverse poets have done, neither with pleasant rivers, fruitful trees, sweetsmelling flowers, nor whatsoever else may make the too much loved earth more lovely."

Accepting Sidney's defense of why we should read poetry is one thing; knowing how to read a poem is something else altogether. Poetry makes special demands and claims on us as readers. Understanding poetry takes practice in reading it. How should you begin to read a poem? Beyond paraphrasing a poem's content, other ways of beginning to read verse include the following.

- Read the poem aloud, more than once if you need to.
- Make a word-for-word copy of the poem.
- Circle any words you don't understand and look them up in a dictionary.
- Highlight any phrases either that you don't understand or that seem particularly fresh and memorable.
- Explore the relationship between the poem's title and its key statements, key words, and key themes.
- Keep a journal of your poetry-reading experiences (for example, your experience in reading a particular poem; in reading a group of poems on a similar theme, conceit, or poetic form; or in reading poems by the same author).
- Keep a journal of your own creative writing.
- Discuss your experience and your interpretation of a poem with your friends, classmates, family members, or instructor.
- Refer to the prewriting activities in Chapter 26, "Writing about Poetry."

While these are useful strategies, you will also find your own approaches for enjoying and understanding poetry.

To help you better appreciate verse with a more critical eye, we begin this book with the formal elements that make poetry a distinct genre. In poetry, less is indeed more in terms of how we experience the particulars of a poem's diction, a poet's word choice, the tone created by unique turns of phrasing, and so on. Poetry's fresh presentation of images and its reliance on figurative language—metaphor, simile, personification, synaesthesia, and so on—give us new perspectives on how we use language not only in the crafted space of the poem but also in everyday life. These topics are covered in Chapters 3 and 4. Moving out from these most basic formal resources, in Chapters 5 and 6 we consider the ways in which symbolism and myth complicate a poem's presentation of its themes. As a highly stylized form of writing, poetry relies on traditions of rhyme, meter, rhythm, fixed forms, and free verse, which we take into account in Chapters 8 and 9.

Beyond formalism, we consider not just what makes poetry a unique literary genre but also how it participates in a wider dialogue with the nonliterary discourses of its historical occasions and cultural contexts **Web** **CD-ROM** . *www* These concerns are taken up in Part II, "Poetry and History." Poetry is not solely an art form alone, but, as the contemporary poet Adrienne Rich reminds us, verse has ethical and political ends. Verse writing serves as both a means of self-exploration and a way of imagining and representing new modes of social life and cultural identity in the public sphere. In this vein, we explore poetry's "revisionary" role in changing our understandings of self, inflected by race **Web** , gender **Web** , sexual **Web** , and class experiences **Web** .   *www*

While we usually encounter poetry in chapbooks and anthologies, before recorded history poetry lived fully as a spoken art. It still has something of that vital, performative role to play in contemporary society from the Beat Generation up through the latest scenes of open-mike competitions and poetry slams. Even now poetry thrives on the page, in new improvisational modes, and across the postmodern media of our contemporary information age.

2 Poetic Language: Diction, Word Choice, and Tone

"There are no poetic ideas," according to the English writer Evelyn Waugh, "only poetic utterances." We might add to this, "there are no poetic utterances without poetic language." But what is unique about the poet's special use of language? How does the poetic word differ from ordinary language? Many poets would contend that there is no real difference. Poetry simply points out the linguistic richness of our word choices if only we would pay closer attention to them. "A poet," wrote W. H. Auden, "is, before anything else, a person who is passionately in love with language," whether it be cast in the formal, epic utterances of, say, John Milton's *Paradise Lost* or the African American vernacular speech patterns of Langston Hughes's blues lyricism **CD-ROM** . Poets love the texture, sound, and even the taste of words, as the writer Mark Strand has it in his playful lyric "Eating Poetry":

> Ink runs from the corners of my mouth.
> There is no happiness like mine.
> I have been eating poetry.

Just as each wine is distinguished by the year, region, and growing conditions of its vintage, so each word bears the flavor of its particular historicity—what we describe in terms of its **etymology.**

Etymology records the changes, or morphology, a word undergoes throughout its history of usage. Moreover, etymology also defines a word's relation to **cognate** terms in other languages with which it bears a family relation by virtue of a similar linguistic ancestry. The term *cognate* defines a relation of similarity between words that have a common line of descent from the same verbal tradition. "Language," Ralph Waldo Emerson said, "is fossil poetry." If that is so, then any serious poet is not unlike a committed archaeologist or paleontologist who will scour each strata of rock and silt to discover the clues to the unique story of a fossilized bone or shard of ancient pottery.

The signs of language's etymological richness are everywhere on display if only we attend to them. Take any American place name and you are likely to turn up some interesting discoveries. For example, the linguist Lee Pederson reminds us that the upper Midwest city Minneapolis is a hybrid name literally meaning "city of water," blending as it does the Dakota term *minne* (water) with the Greek word *polis* (city). Bryn Mawr in Pennsylvania stems from the Welsh words meaning "great hill." Pennsylvania itself means Penn's woods, combining its founder's name (Admiral Sir William Penn) and the medieval Latin word for forest (*silvanus*). Language is indeed fossil poetry.

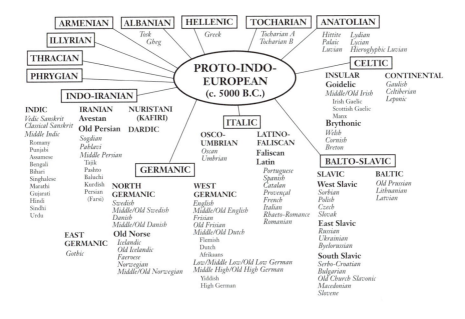

As you can see from the above language chart, the origins of modern English language are made up of lines of descent from the Indo-European language family, reaching back to the Iron Age Celts of 700 B.C. and later German invaders who arrived from the Continent around A.D. 449. The Old English period, dating from 449 to 1066, blends the dialects of the Low German Angles, Saxons, Jutes, and Northern Vikings that together share such cognate terms as *can, come, father, folk, house, man, mother, ride, see, smile, winter,* and *wire.* In his poem "Digging," the Irish Nobel Prize-winning poet Seamus Heaney draws an analogy between *pen* and *spade* as he "digs" down into language's etymological turf.

SEAMUS HEANEY   *(b. 1939)*

Digging   *(1966)*

Between my finger and my thumb
The squat pen rests; snug as a gun.

Under my window, a clean rasping sound
When the spade sinks into gravelly ground:
My father, digging. I look down

5

Till his straining rump among the flowerbeds
Bends low, comes up twenty years away
Stooping in rhythm through potato drills
Where he was digging.

The coarse boot nestled on the lug, the shaft   10
Against the inside knee was levered firmly.
He rooted out tall tops, buried the bright edge deep
To scatter new potatoes that we picked
Loving their cool hardness in our hands.

By God, the old man could handle a spade.   15
Just like his old man.

My grandfather cut more turf in a day
Than any other man on Toner's bog.
Once I carried him milk in a bottle
Corked sloppily with paper. He straightened up   20
To drink it, then fell to right away
Nicking and slicing neatly, heaving sods
Over his shoulder, going down and down
For the good turf. Digging.

The cold smell of potato mould, the squelch and slap   25
Of soggy peat, the curt cuts of an edge
Through living roots awaken in my head.
But I've no spade to follow men like them.

Between my finger and my thumb
The squat pen rests.   30
I'll dig with it.

It's no accident that Heaney should link pen and spade. For generations, peat moss has been widely harvested as a domestic source of fuel in Ireland and Scotland. Removed from the traditional economy of his ancestors, Heaney is drawn nevertheless to the activity of "digging," albeit into language not turf. Burrowing into poetry is also analogous to descending into the ancient strata of the English language's age-old sedimentation. Heaney's word choices mine the Viking, German, and Old French language groups. He excavates the primordial, earthy foundations of Old and Middle English. It is this oldest stratum of the English language that the poet Theodore Roethke views as having a kind of primal signifying power to evoke archetypal states of being. "We all know," he writes, "that poetry is shot through with appeals to the unconsciousness, to the fears and desires that go far back into our childhood, into the imagination of the race. And we know that some words, like *hill, plow, mother, window, bird, fish*, are so drenched with human association, they sometimes can make even bad poems evocative."

Beyond a word's literal, dictionary meaning—its **denotation**—many words suggest a rich range of **connotation:** complex tonalities, associations, overtones of meaning that derive from generations of human usage. For example, the word *snug* has the connotations of being comfortable, content, secure, safe, at ease. The denotative meaning of *snug* is more specific and signifies something that "fits closely," originating perhaps from an Old Norse nautical term meaning "fit" or "ship-shape." Etymology provides clues to the origins of the connotations we bring to particular words. *Bog* comes from the Irish Gaelic term *bogach*, while *rasping* derives from the Old High German term *raspon* signifying a grating sound. Rump comes from Middle English and is of Scandanavian origin; similarly, the words "lug," "shaft," "turf," "spade," "thumb" all stem from Middle English etymological roots. Digging into language, as Heaney suggests, will unearth rich strata of "fossil poetry."

An important etymological layer of English dates from 1066 and the Norman-French invasion of the Battle of Hastings. The victorious French courtly tradition reinforced the Latinate influences of the Romance languages that had appeared much earlier in English through the influence of Christianity from the fifth through seventh centuries. The Jesuit poet Gerard Manley Hopkins features this French tradition in his poem "The Windhover."

GERARD MANLEY HOPKINS   *(1844–1889)*

The Windhover   *(1877)*

To Christ Our Lord

I caught this morning morning's minion, king-
   dom of daylight's dauphin, dapple-dawn-drawn Falcon,
      in his riding
Of the rolling level underneath him steady air, and striding
High there, how he rung upon the rein of a wimpling wing
In his ecstasy! then off, off forth on swing,   5
   As a skate's heel sweeps smooth on a bow-bend: the hurl and gliding
   Rebuffed the big wind. My heart in hiding
Stirred for a bird,—the achieve of, the mastery of the thing!

Brute beauty and valour and act, oh, air, pride, plume, here
   Buckle! AND the fire that breaks from thee then, a billion   10
Times told lovelier, more dangerous, O my chevalier!

   No wonder of it: shéer plód makes plough down sillion
Shine, and blue-bleak embers, ah my dear,
   Fall, gall themselves, and gash gold-vermilion.

Hopkins's dedication, "To Christ Our Lord," suggests that the figure of the Windhover be read as a symbol for Christ. Like the Christian Son of God, the Windhover is the favorite or "minion" of the heavens, ruling there as a "dauphin": the oldest son and heir to the king of France. He is also a "chevalier"—a nobleman or knight—who proves his valor through his descent toward the earth—emblematic of Christ's incarnation and crucifixion, figured in the gashing "vermilion" (vivid red) tonalities of the plough's sillion, or furrow. The obvious French courtly words in the poem are, of course, *dauphin* and *chevalier*, but the majority of Hopkins's language stems from this tradition as well. To take only a few instances of some of the poem's key terms, *minion* stems from the Old French *mignot*; *level* from the Old French *livel* and Latin *libra* meaning balance; *mastery* derives from the Old French *maistre* and Latin *magister*; *beauty* likewise comes from the Old French *bealte* and the Latin *bellus*; *pride* descends from the Old French *prud*. A *buckle* is an Old French derivation from *boucle* and the Latin *buccula*, which is a helmet's cheek strap; as a verb it stems from the Old French *boucler* meaning to attach with a buckle. Similarly, the words *billion*, *sillion*, and *vermilion* all have French roots, which you can explore using the *Oxford English Dictionary*.

American English synthesizes such European roots with African and Asian influences. Coming into the American vernacular via the Georgia Sea Island Gullah culture, the dialect communities of New Orleans, and other southern communities, African languages from such regions as Nigeria, the Congo, Sierra Leone, Cameroon, the Nile valley, and so on have enriched the American vernacular with a savory linguistic stew or "jambalaya" of African-rooted etymologies. Similarly, Chinese, Japanese, Korean, and other East Asian influences have transformed the American dialect.

Asian American poets such as Janice Mirikitani punctuate their poems with Old World word choices to portray the dilemma of living in two cultural worlds at once. Putting such words as *salsa*, *otonashii*, and *shakuhachi* into her poem "Breaking Tradition" gives Mirikitani's readers a more immediate sense of how a diverse, multicultural heritage enriches the poet's sense of identity.

JANICE MIRIKITANI   *(b. 1942)*

Breaking Tradition   *(1978)*

for my Daughter

My daughter denies she is like me,
her secretive eyes avoid mine.
    She reveals the hatreds of womanhood
    already veiled behind music and smoke and telephones.
I want to tell her about the empty room   5
    of myself.
    This room we lock ourselves in
    where whispers live like fungus,
    giggles about small breasts and cellulite,
    where we confine ourselves to jealousies,   10

bedridden by menstruation.
The waiting room where we feel our hands
are useless, dead speechless clamps
that need hospitals and forceps and kitchens
and plugs and ironing boards to make them useful.   15
I deny I am like my mother. I remember why:
She kept her room neat with silence,
defiance smothered in requirements to be otonashii,
passion and loudness wrapped in an obi,
her steps confined to ceremony,   20
the weight of her sacrifice she carried like
a foetus. Guilt passed on in our bones.
I want to break tradition—unlock this room
where women dress in the dark
Discover the lies my mother told me.   25
The lies that we are small and powerless
that our possibilities must be compressed
to the size of pearls, displayed only as
passive chokers, charms around our neck.
Break Tradition.   30
I want to tell my daughter of this room
of myself
filled with tears of shakuhachi,
the light in my hands,
poems about madness,   35
the music of yellow guitars—
sounds shaken from barbed wire and
goodbyes and miracles of survival.
This room of open window where daring ones escape.

My daughter denies she is like me   40
her secretive eyes are walls of smoke
and music and telephones,
her pouting ruby lips, her skirts
swaying to salsa, Madonna and the Stones,
her thighs displayed in carnavals of color.   45
I do not know the contents of her room.
She mirrors my aging.

She is breaking tradition.

TOPICS FOR CRITICAL THINKING

1. Adopting the point of view of a second-generation Japanese American, Mirikitani's persona is suspended between generations. Consider how she would "break tradition" with her mother's traditional "requirements to be otonashii," that is, "to be gentle."

2. How for Mirikitani does being otonashii result in ceremonies of self-effacement and a resignation to the idea that women's lives are "small and powerless"?

3. How does Mirikitani have difficulty accepting her daughter's own form of breaking tradition?

TOPICS FOR CRITICAL WRITING

1. As a third-generation Japanese American writer, Mirikitani portrays her complex identity that draws both from her Japanese ancestry and her American experience. How does "Breaking Tradition" speak to the difficulty of a mother-daughter relationship further marked by a generational clash in cultural identifications?

2. On the one hand, Mirikitani would share her experience of internment—of "sounds shaken from barbed wire" as well as the "tears of shakuhachi" (a bamboo flute). Yet, she realizes her daughter as a sensei "denies" solidarity with her mother across the generations, immersed as she is in a multicultural "salsa" made up of "Madonna and the Stones." How does Mirikitani emphasize her sense of split generational traditions in her metaphor of separate rooms as well as in her dynamic word choices?

     The best resource for understanding the etymology and cultural usage of a particular word over time is the *Oxford English Dictionary*. Whenever you come upon a word that is unfamiliar, spend some time learning its history. The *Oxford English Dictionary* is available online, and using the electronic version is a quick way toward understanding poetic language.

     Poems such as Randall Jarrell's "The Knight, Death, and the Devil" that are rich in etymology will reward your efforts at tracking down their verbal histories.

RANDALL JARRELL   *(1914–1965)*

The Knight, Death, and the Devil   *(1969)*

Cowhorn-crowned, shockheaded, cornshuck-bearded,
Death is a scarecrow—his death's-head a teetotum
That tilts up toward man confidentially
But trimmed with adders; ringlet-maned, rope-bridled,
The mare he rides crops herbs beside a skull.   5
He holds up, warning, the crossed cones of time:
Here, narrowing into now, the Past and Future
Are quicksand.
              A hoofed pikeman trots behind.
His pike's claw-hammer mocks—in duplicate, inverted—   10
The pocked, ribbed, soaring crescent of his horn.
A scapegoat aged into a steer; boar-snouted;
His great limp ears stuck sidelong out in air;
A dewlap bunched at his breast; a ram's-horn wound
Beneath each ear; a spur licked up and out   15
From the hide of his forehead; bat-winged, but in bone;
His eye a ring inside a ring inside a ring

That leers up, joyless, vile, in meek obscenity—
This is the devil. Flesh to flesh, he bleats
The herd back to the pit of being.   20
In fluted mail; upon his lance the bush
Of that old fox; a sheep-dog bounding at his stirrup,
In its eyes the cast of faithfulness (our help,
Our foolish help); his dun war-horse pacing
Beneath in strength, in ceremonious magnificence;   25
His castle—some man's castle—set on every crag:
So, companioned so, the knight moves through this world.
The fiend moos in amity, Death mouths, reminding:
He listens in assurance, has no glance
To spare for them, but looks past steadily   30
At—at—
                    a man's look completes itself.

The death of his own flesh, set up outside him;
The flesh of his own soul, set up outside him—
Death and the devil, what are these to him?   35
His being accuses him—and yet his face is firm
In resolution, in absolute persistence;
The folds of smiling do for steadiness;
The face is its own fate—*a man does what he must*—
And the body underneath it says: *I am*.   40

TOPICS FOR CRITICAL THINKING

1. Look up in the *Oxford English Dictionary* the key words Jarrell uses to describe the figure of Death and the Devil in the opening lines of the poem. What etymological derivations does Jarrell employ here?

2. Investigate the language in which Jarrell portrays the knight, focusing on such terms as *fluted mail* and *companioned*. Where do these words originate?

3. Look up in the *Oxford English Dictionary* the Latin expressions that communicate the poet's tone in characterizing the knight's qualities of "assurance," "resolution," and "absolute persistence," as well as his horse's "ceremonious magnificence."

TOPICS FOR CRITICAL WRITING

1. Compare and contrast Jarrell's "The Knight, Death, and the Devil" with the Albrecht Dürer's artwork from which it takes its title.

2. Is there some dimension of the knight's ride that Jarrell's poetry communicates more vividly than the visual artist's pictorial medium?

In addition to the power of etymology, what is at stake in an entire poem's setting, situation, and theme can turn on the aptness of a particular word choice, as in John Keats's "This Living Hand."

Albrecht Dürer, *The Knight, Death, and the Devil*
(1513–1514)

JOHN KEATS   *(1795–1821)*

This Living Hand   *(1819, 1898)*

This living hand, now warm and capable
Of earnest grasping, would, if it were cold
And in the icy silence of the tomb,
So haunt thy days and chill thy dreaming nights
That thou wouldst wish thine own heart dry of blood   5
So in my veins red life might stream again,
And thou be conscience-calmed—see here it is—
I hold it towards you.

The key word in Keats's poem is *capable*, coming as it does from the Old
French derivation of *capere*, "to hold." There is also the pun in the poem on
the literal hand that the poet offers the beloved and the more haunting specter
of his posthumous handwriting. Prophetically perhaps, Keats left this beautiful lyric on a manuscript page of his posthumously published volume *The Jealousies*.

Similar to Keats's subtle but decisive play on the word *capable*, the entire drama of Seamus Heaney's mysterious lyric "A Dream of Jealousy" turns on the key term *candour*.

SEAMUS HEANEY *(b. 1939)*

A Dream of Jealousy *(1979)*

Walking with you and another lady
In wooded parkland, the whispering grass
Ran its fingers through our guessing silence
And the trees opened into a shady
Unexpected clearing where we sat down.   5
I think the candour of the light dismayed us.
We talked about desire and being jealous,
Our conversation a loose and single gown
Or a white picnic table cloth spread out
Like a book of manners in the wilderness.   10
"Show me," I said to our companion, "what
I have much coveted, your breast's mauve star."
And she consented. O neither these verses
Nor my prudence, love, can heal your wounded stare.

TOPICS FOR CRITICAL THINKING

1. In what ways is the locale of the poem's "unexpected clearing" both a literal and fig-urative setting?
2. The lovers' talk of "desire and being jealous" climaxes in the poet's desire for their "companion" and his lover's "wounded stare." Everything that comes to matter in the poem is clarified by the "candour" of the light that "dismayed" even as it defined the relations among the three of them. Interestingly enough, *candour* means "open and honest." How is that an apt term for the poem's disclosures of desire and jeal-ousy?
3. Behind *candour*'s current meaning, however, stands the Latin origins of *candere*, "to shine," which has its cognate terms in *candle* and *candid*. How does that etymology reinforce the other tropes of light in the poem?

TOPIC FOR CRITICAL WRITING

How do the three lovers come upon the essential though "unexpected" truth of their feelings for one another in the clearing?

The connotations of particular word choices contribute to the **tone** of an uttered phrase, line, stanza, or entire poem. For example, Heaney conveys a tone of wonder and secrecy in the dream's setting through the imagery of the "whispering grass," "guessing silence" and the "shady / Unexpected clearing." The dreamlike tone of "A Dream of Jealousy" differs markedly from the more realistic, raw, and earthy tones of "Digging." Those organic tones, in turn, contrast with the more chivalric and regal tones of "The Windhover."

While poets mine Old English derivations to convey archetypal, earth-bound tones or French etymologies to achieve more formal and ceremonious evocations, Greek and Latin derivations can communicate tones of abstraction, rationality, and intellectual thought. Richard Eberhart's poem on "The Fury of Aerial Bombardment" uses just such Greek and Latin language roots to reflect on the violence of World War II.

RICHARD EBERHART   *(b. 1904)*

The Fury of Aerial Bombardment   *(1947)*

You would think the fury of aerial bombardment
Would rouse God to relent; the infinite spaces
Are still silent. He looks on shock-pried faces.
History, even, does not know what is meant.

You would feel that after so many centuries   5
God would give man to repent; yet he can kill
As Cain could, but with multitudinous will,
No farther advanced than in his ancient furies.

Was man made stupid to see his own stupidity?
Is God by definition indifferent, beyond us all?   10
Is the eternal truth man's fighting soul
Wherein the Beast ravens in its own avidity?

Of Van Wettering I speak, and Averill,
Names on a list, whose faces I do not recall
But they are gone to early death, who late in school   15
Distinguished the belt feed lever from the belt holding pawl.

Eberhart's experience as a gunnery instructor is plain to see in his eye for the details of the machinery of aerial combat, pointing out as he does the differences between the "belt feed lever from the belt holding pawl." Modern war is fought, won, and lost in terms of such minute particulars. But Eberhart further captures the violent immediacy of combat's intensity in the "shock-pried faces" of those in harm's way. What concerns Eberhart in the poem, however, is what to conclude about God and human civilization after the knowledge of modern violence on such a mass or "total" scale. One of his key terms, *aerial*, sets up the ultimate stakes of Eberhart's meditation, signifying on the insubstantial, even metaphysical dimensions of the heavens. *Aerial* comes from the Latin *aerius*, which has a Greek origin *aerios*, for air. Just as the bomber's literal destructive force comes from above, so the figurative "indifference" of God betokens a different, but no less lethal violence. Eberhart lends a quality of abstraction to God's apathy toward creation in the question, "Is God by definition indifferent, beyond us all?" The multisyllabic, Latin words *definition* (*definitio*) and *indifferent* (*indifferens*) resonate with such other terms in the poem as *multitudinous* (*multitudo*) and *avidity* (*avidus*), which together evoke a vision of divinity that is, finally, inexplicable.

Poems for Further Reading and Critical Writing

WILLIAM STAFFORD   *(1914–1993)*

Traveling Through the Dark   *(1960)*

Traveling through the dark I found a deer
dead on the edge of the Wilson River road.
It is usually best to roll them into the canyon:
the road is narrow; to swerve might make more dead.

By glow of the tail-light I stumbled back of the car   5
and stood by the heap, a doe, a recent killing;
she had stiffened already, almost cold.
I dragged her off; she was large in the belly.

My fingers touching her side brought me the reason—
her side was warm; her fawn lay there waiting,   10
alive, still, never to be born.
Beside that mountain road I hesitated.

The car aimed ahead its lowered parking lights;
under the hood purred the steady engine.
I stood in the glare of the warm exhaust turning red;   15
around our group I could hear the wilderness listen.

I thought hard for us all—my only swerving—,
then pushed her over the edge into the river.

TOPICS FOR CRITICAL THINKING

1. As we have seen, sometimes a single word serves as the key to unlocking a poem's major subject and theme. Consider how the poet's key word choices of *swerve* and *swerving* might reveal the meaning and significance of his encounter with the deer.
2. Explore the connotations of Stafford's key word choices such as *aimed, purred, steady,* and so on.
3. How would you characterize the poet's tone in the work?

Does the poem render any moral or ethical judgment about the doe's "recent killing"? Does it resist any moral conclusion? Would that resistance itself be a form of ethics?

LOUISE BOGAN   *(1897–1970)*

Didactic Piece   *(1929)*

The eye unacquitted by whatever it holds in allegiance:
The trees' upcurve thought sacred, the flaked air, sacred and alterable,
The hard bud seen under the lid, not the scorned leaf and the apple—
As once in a swept space, so now with speech in a house,
We think to stand spelled forever, chained to the rigid knocking   5
Of a heart whose time is its own flesh, momently swung and burning—
This, in peace, as well, though we know the air a combatant
And the word of the heart's wearing time, that it will not do without grief.

The limit already traced must be returned to and visited,
Touched, spanned, proclaimed, else the heart's time be all: 10
The small beaten disk, under the bent shell of stars,
Beside rocks in the road, dust, and the nameless herbs,
Beside rocks in the water, marked by the heeled-back current,
Seeing, in all autumns, the felled leaf betray the wind.

If but the sign of the end is given a room   15
By the pillared harp, sealed to its rest by hands—
(On the bright strings the hands are almost reflected,
The strings a mirror and light). The head bends to listen,
So that the grief is heard; tears begin and are silenced
Because of the mimic despair, under the figure of laughter.   20
Let the allegiance go; the tree and the hard bud seed themselves.
The end is set, whether it be sought or relinquished.
We wait, we hear, facing the mask without eyes,
Grief without grief, facing the eyeless music.

TOPICS FOR CRITICAL THINKING

1. How are we to interpret the sense of Bogan's opening line? In the *Oxford English Dictionary,* look up the etymology of the words *unacquitted* and *allegiance.* How do these word choices contribute to Bogan's abstract tone?
2. Contrast this opening use of diction with the language in which she depicts the "heart whose time is its own flesh."

TOPICS FOR CRITICAL WRITING

1. Look up the term *didactic* in the *Oxford English Dictionary*. What does it mean? What are its etymological roots? How does it shed light on the theme of her poem?

2. Discuss the roles such words as *allegiance* and *relinquished* play in the poem's final stanza.

MARIANNE MOORE   *(1887–1972)*

The Mind Is an Enchanting Thing   *(1944)*

is an enchanted thing
    like the glaze on a
katydid-wing
        subdivided by sun
        till the nettings are legion.   5
Like Gieseking° playing Scarlatti;°

like the apteryx-awl°
    as a beak, or the
kiwi's rain-shawl
        of haired feathers, the mind   10
        feeling its way as though blind,
walks along with its eyes on the ground.

It has memory's ear
    that can hear without
having to hear.   15
        Like the gyroscope's fall,
        truly unequivocal
because trued by regnant certainty,

it is a power of
    strong enchantment. It   20
is like the dove-
        neck animated by
        sun; it is memory's eye;
it's conscientious inconsistency.

It tears off the veil; tears   25
    the temptation, the

---

6 *Walter Wilhelm Gieseking (1895–1956):* German pianist.   6 *Domenico Scarlatti (1685–1757):* Italian composer.   7 *apteryx-awl:* A bird native to New Zealand.

mist the heart wears,
        from its eyes—if the heart
        has a face; it takes apart
dejection. It's fire in the dove-neck's   30

iridescence; in the
        inconsistencies
of Scarlatti.
        Unconfusion submits
        its confusion to proof; it's   35
not a Herod's oath that cannot change.

TOPICS FOR CRITICAL THINKING

1. Discuss the various tropes through which Moore explores the terms of the mind's enchantment.
2. Moore had what she called an "inordinate interest in animals" and she regularly visited the Bronx Zoo. Discuss the ways in which she presents the exotic language of ornithology.
3. Focus on the role of diction in drawing out the trope of the mind as gyroscope. Look up and discuss the definitions and etymologies of *unequivocal*, *gyroscope*, and *regnant*.
4. Look up the etymologies of Moore's word choices in describing the mind's "conscientious inconsistency"—its "iridescence; in the / inconsistencies." What is Moore's point here?

TOPIC FOR CRITICAL WRITING

Herod was the king of Judea who upheld his promise to Salome to behead John the Baptist in Mark 6:22–27. How does Moore contrast this biblical allusion to the mind's "enchantment"?

3   Poetic Imagery and Theories of the Modern Image

Imagery in poetry refers to the use of language to evoke sensory experience. Imagery captures the immediate perception of our five senses. Sight, sound, smell, taste, touch: All can be evoked by the masterful rendering of powerful imagery. Reading freshly conceived images in poetry allows us to imagine our sensuous lives more vividly and more originally. The contemporary poet Denise Levertov celebrates the power of verse to transform sensual experience through the force of the imagination and vice versa in her poem "O Taste and See."

DENISE LEVERTOV   *(1923–1997)*

O Taste and See   *(1964)*

The world is
not with us enough.
O taste and see

the subway Bible poster said,
meaning The Lord, meaning   5
if anything all that lives
to the imagination's tongue,

grief, mercy, language,
tangerine, weather, to
breathe them, bite,   10
savor, chew, swallow, transform

into our flesh our
deaths, crossing the street, plum, quince,
living in the orchard and being
hungry, and plucking   15
the fruit.

TOPICS FOR CRITICAL THINKING

1. Levertov makes an **allusion** to Psalms 34:8, which reads "O taste and see that the Lord is good." An allusion is a reference to another quote or figure from literary, popular, or religious traditions. How does Levertov alter our understanding of the poster's theological message?

2. How do you interpret the multiple meanings of Levertov's title?

3. What other allusion to a biblical story can you locate in the poem? What theme does this allusion convey in Levertov's revision of it?

TOPICS FOR CRITICAL WRITING

1. How would you characterize the kind of communion Levertov imagines between life and the imagination in "O Taste and See"?

2. The other literary allusion Levertov makes is to William Wordsworth's "The World is Too Much with Us." Read Wordsworth's poem, and discuss Levertov's revision of Wordsworth's themes.

Whether portraying the vibrant chaos of big-city life or the earthy perceptions of the garden world, imagery frees us from the tired conventions of rational thought. Such an escape from abstract thought into the freshness of perceived imagery is the main subject of Archibald MacLeish's poem "Eleven."

ARCHIBALD MACLEISH   *(1892–1982)*

Eleven   *(1926)*

And summer mornings the mute child, rebellious,
Stupid, hating the words, the meanings, hating
The Think now, Think, the Oh but Think! would leave
On tiptoe the three chairs on the verandah
And crossing tree by tree the empty lawn   5
Push back the shed door and upon the sill
Stand pressing out the sunlight from his eyes
And enter and with outstretched fingers feel
The grindstone and behind it the bare wall
And turn and in the corner on the cool   10
Hard earth sit listening. And one by one,
Out of the dazzled shadow in the room,
The shapes would gather, the brown plowshare, spades,
Mattocks, the polished helves of picks, a scythe
Hung from the rafters, shovels, slender tines   15
Glinting across the curve of sickles—shapes
Older than men were, the wise tools, the iron
Friendly with earth. And sit there, quiet, breathing
The harsh dry smell of withered bulbs, the faint

Odor of dung, the silence. And outside   20
Beyond the half-shut door the blind leaves
And the corn moving. And at noon would come,
Up from the garden, his hard crooked hands
Gentle with earth, his knees still earth-stained, smelling
Of sun, of summer, the old gardener, like   25
A priest, like an interpreter, and bend
Over his baskets.
     And they would not speak:
They would say nothing. And the child would sit there
Happy as though he had no name, as though   30
He had been no one: like a leaf, a stem,
Like a root growing—

One thing to notice in the unfolding action of "Eleven" is how MacLeish stages the escape from abstract thought in the poem. The child's flight from the "words" and "meanings" and the demand to "Think now, Think" happens in the shed through his growing perception of embodied experience. The concrete image—with its sensual immediacy—dramatizes the return to a perceived world before thought and the demands of abstract rationality. Notice how perception returns first in images of touch that involve the "grindstone," then the "cool / Hard earth," leading finally—as the child's eyes adjust to the darkened spaces—to visual images of the garden tools and farm implements stored in the shed. What other perceptual images do you notice in the poem?

 Something else that may help you to understand MacLeish's poem is its title. As guideposts to the poetry, **titles** often set out the key terms for what is at stake in a poem's situation, setting, and themes. Here the child's status as an eleven-year-old sets up the contradictory tensions and demands made on the preadolescent who is no longer a child but not quite an adult. That state of being in-between also marks the setting of the shed. It is similarly located between, on the one hand, the formal demands of thinking associated with the verandah from which the child leaves "on tiptoe" and, on the other hand, the landscape of sun, summer, and nature generally.

TOPICS FOR CRITICAL THINKING

1. Besides the child of "Eleven," the other figure who is depicted as being in-between opposites is the "old gardener." MacLeish compares his job to two other vocations: that of an "interpreter" and a "priest." What similarities do you think MacLeish finds in these comparisons?

2. What do the similarities discussed in question 1 have to do with the in-between situation of the eleven-year-old child?

3. How does the gardener serve as both an interpreter and priest for the child?

TOPIC FOR CRITICAL WRITING

Write an essay on the child's passage from the demands of thought to the consolations of being finally "like a leaf, a stem, / Like a root growing—".

www Theories of the Modern Image Web

In the twentieth century, experimental modernist poets such as Ezra Pound, William Carlos Williams, and Hilda Doolittle (H.D.) advanced new theories and techniques of poetic imagery. They gleaned what Williams called the "radiant gist" of experience in sharply beheld images. These modern poets had a particular understanding of the poetic image. As members of what would become known as the Imagist Movement, they defined an image in poetry as involving a "direct treatment of the thing whether subjective or objective." From 1912–1914, Pound, in particular, crafted a poetic language that would be concise, efficient, and fresh in its original use of images. His colleague, T. S. Eliot, acknowledged Pound's achievement by calling him in *The Waste Land* (1922) *il miglior fabbro*, which in Italian means "the better craftsman." Pound modeled his modern poetry on the compact lyric forms of Chinese verse. Pound's shorter imagist poems also resemble Japanese **Haiku** verse (a short seventeen-syllable poem broken into three lines having the pattern of five, seven, and five syllables per line).

EZRA POUND   *(1885–1972)*

In a Station of the Metro   *(1916)*

The apparition of these faces in the crowd;
Petals on a wet, black bough.

Pound achieves a startling transformation of the natural landscape through his abrupt coupling of faces and flowers, combining urban and pastoral motifs. The specific concrete image of "petals on a wet, black bough" defines the more abstract apparition of the city crowd. The experience for this poem came to Pound in 1913 as he disembarked from a metro train at La Concorde, Paris. In his account, he writes,

> [I] saw suddenly a beautiful face, and then another and another, and then a beautiful child's face, and then another beautiful woman, and I tried all that day to find words for what this had meant to me, and I could not find any words that seemed to me worthy, or as lovely as that sudden emotion. And that evening, as I went home along the Rue Raynouard, I was still trying, and I found, suddenly, the expression. I do not mean that I found words, but there came an equation . . . not in speech, but in little splotches of colour.

The original draft of the poem ran to some thirty lines before Pound threw it away. To capture the striking, visual impression of the metro, he distilled out the essence of the metro vision into a two-line sentence. Pound would later compare his poem to the modern visual canvases of the Russian painter Vasily Kandinsky, who pioneered new forms of experimental art as a founder of the Blaue Reiter group in Berlin the year before Pound's Paris metro experience (see color insert). Just two syllables over the seventeen-syllable haiku form, Pound's short lyric offers an imaginative comparison between two otherwise disparate elements. The poem does not explain the relation between the two major images of the faces and petals but sets them side by side without connectives or transitions.

The compositional style of "In a Station of the Metro" employs **parataxis.** Stemming from the Greek term *paratassein* meaning "beside" (*para*) and "to arrange" (*tassein*), parataxis in poetry as well as in experimental film sets images directly side by side, in the quick cut from one scene or image to another. This technique allows a new perception to arise from the relational arrangement of images. Indeed, the form of "In a Station of the Metro," the poet says, came to him less as a verbal statement than "an equation . . . not in speech, but in little splotches of colour." The poem achieves its power from how the outward image, as Pound says, "darts inward into a thing inward and subjective." The other striking contrast the poem performs is between, on the one hand, the "direct treatment of the thing" and, on the other hand, the phantom-like abstraction of the key word *apparition*. This opening term lends the poem a ghostly quality of invoking the landscape of the underworld, which, as we shall see, is a quality of modern urban life that Pound and Eliot would go on to develop in their collaboration on *The Waste Land*.

The sharp compositional cut Pound makes between the outward "faces in a crowd" and inward "petals on a wet, black bough" is also at work stylistically in the rather jagged verbal surfaces of William Carlos Williams's short imagist lyric "The Great Figure."

WILLIAM CARLOS WILLIAMS   *(1883–1963)*

The Great Figure   *(1921)*

Among the rain
and lights
I saw the figure 5
in gold
on a red   5
firetruck
moving
tense
unheeded

to gong clangs   10
siren howls
and wheels rumbling
through the dark city.

The visual specificity of Pound's "wet, black bough" finds its counterpart in
the particular impressions Williams records in the gold figure 5 that rushes
across a red field set off against the background of "the dark city." Again, what
matters here is the leading term—*among*—that defines the poem's relational
field in which various sights and sounds find their places. In "The Great Figure," Williams witnesses the city's chance happenings that otherwise go unheeded. So compelling is the visual dimension of Williams's imagist lyric that
Charles Henry Demuth chose it as the subject for his classic 1928 abstract oil
painting, *I Saw the Figure Five in Gold*, now part of New York's definitive Museum of Modern Art collection (see color insert).
     While Williams finds compelling images that distill the "radiant gist" of
urban chaos, the contemporary poet Gary Snyder conveys the tranquility of
"high still air" found in the wilderness of "Mid-August at Sourdough Mountain Lookout."

GARY SNYDER   *(b. 1930)*

Mid-August at Sourdough Mountain Lookout   *(1959)*

Down valley a smoke haze
Three days heat, after five days rain
Pitch glows on the fir-cones
Across the rocks and meadows
Swarms of new flies.   5

I cannot remember things I once read
A few friends, but they are in cities.
Drinking cold snow-water from a tin cup
Looking down for miles
Through high still air.   10

     Gary Snyder based this poem on his experience as a forest fire lookout in
Baker National Forest in the early 1950s. By the decade's end, he would become a culture hero in the Beat Movement appearing as the character of Japphy Rider in Jack Kerouac's celebrated novel *The Dharma Bums* (1958).
Snyder also had a serious commitment to Asian studies, first in the graduate
program of the University of California, Berkeley, and later in the 1960s as a
student of Buddhism in Kyoto, Japan under the Zen Master Oda Sesso Roshi.
Similar to Pound's collaborative work with Ernest Fenollosa in *The Chinese
Written Character as a Medium for Poetry*, Snyder's spare imagist style in "Mid-

Gary Snyder

August at Sourdough Mountain Lookout" reflects the poet's work as a translator of classical Chinese lyrics and Japanese Haiku poetry.

TOPICS FOR CRITICAL THINKING

1. How do you imagine the poet's situation depicted in the poem?
2. Describe in one word the poet's mood in the opening lines.
3. How would the effect of the poem's images change if Snyder had depicted himself as drinking, say, an ice-cold soda from a 12 oz. can?

TOPIC FOR CRITICAL WRITING

Compare and contrast the two stanzas of Snyder's poem. How crucial are the sensual images of the poem's last three lines to the poem's themes of stoicism, simplicity, and asceticism?

Poems for Further Reading and Critical Writing

DENISE LEVERTOV   *(1923–1997)*

The Dead Butterfly   *(1959)*

Now I see its whiteness
is not white but green, traced with green,

and resembles the stones
of which the city is built,
quarried high in the mountains.   5

                    2

Everywhere among the marigolds
the rainblown roses and the hedges
of tamarisk are white
butterflies this morning, in constant
tremulous movement, only those   10
that lie dead revealing
their rockgreen color and the bold
cut of the wings.

TOPICS FOR CRITICAL THINKING

1. Explore your reaction to this poem. What do you think Levertov's main thematic
   point is?
2. Which do you think the poet finds more lovely, the butterflies in "tremulous movement" or the "bold / cut of the wings" that she beholds in the dead butterfly?
3. Does it matter that the color of the dead butterflies "resembles the stones / of
   which the city is built"? Is this a simple observation or does Levertov imply something more? Explain.

TOPIC FOR CRITICAL WRITING

Write an essay on the paradox Levertov discovers in the butterfly's actual color as opposed to its appearance.

MINA LOY   *(1882–1966)*

Mexican Desert   *(1921)*

The belching ghost-wail of the locomotive
trailing her rattling wooden tail
into the jazz-band sunset. . . .

The mountains in a row
set pinnacles of ferocious isolation   5
under the alien hot heaven

Vegetable cripples of drought
thrust up the parching appeal
cracking open the earth
stump-fingered cacti   10

and hunch-back palm trees
belabour the cinders of twilight. . . .

TOPICS FOR CRITICAL THINKING

1. Examine your overall experience of "Mexican Desert." Do Loy's images imply a thematic point, or do they simply record a set of impressions?
2. How do the signs of disfigurement and stunted growth in stanza two mirror the poet's situation?

TOPIC FOR CRITICAL WRITING

Loy wrote "Mexican Desert" after the mysterious disappearance of her lover Arthur Cravan off the coast of Mexico. Where can you discern the traces of that loss in the landscape of "ferocious isolation"?

H. D. (HILDA DOOLITTLE)   *(1886–1961)*

Sea Rose   *(1916)*

Rose, harsh rose,
marred and with stint of petals,
meager flower, thin,
sparse of leaf,

more precious   5
than a wet rose
single on a stem—
you are caught in the drift.

Stunted, with small leaf,
you are flung on the sand,   10
you are lifted
in the crisp sand
that drives in the wind.

Can the spice-rose
drip such acrid fragrance   15
hardened in a leaf?

Sea Violet   *(1916)*

The white violet
is scented on its stalk,

the sea-violet
fragile as agate,
lies fronting all the wind   5
among the torn shells
on the sand-bank.

The greater blue violets
flutter on the hill,
but who would change for these   10
who would change for these
one root of the white sort?

Violet
your grasp is frail
on the edge of the sand-hill,   15
but you catch the light—
frost, a star edges with its fire.

TOPICS FOR CRITICAL THINKING

1. What key words convey H. D.'s portrait of the "Sea Rose"?
2. What qualities does she admire in the "Sea Rose"?
3. How does the "Sea Rose" differ from a hot-house flower?
4. How do you interpret the poem's final question?

TOPIC FOR CRITICAL WRITING

Compare H. D.'s depiction of the "Sea Rose" to her "Sea Violet." What qualities do they share? How do they differ?

T. S. ELIOT   *(1888–1965)*

Preludes   *(1917)*

I

The winter evening settles down
With smell of steaks in passageways.
Six o'clock.
The burnt-out ends of smoky days.
And now a gusty shower wraps   5
The grimy scraps
Of withered leaves about your feet
And newspapers from vacant lots;

The showers beat
On broken blinds and chimney-pots,   10
And at the corner of the street
A lonely cab-horse steams and stamps.

And then the lighting of the lamps.

II

The morning comes to consciousness
Of faint stale smells of beer   15
From the sawdust-trampled street
With all its muddy feet that press
To early coffee-stands.
With the other masquerades
That times resumes,   20
One thinks of all the hands
That are raising dingy shades
In a thousand furnished rooms.

III

You tossed a blanket from the bed
You lay upon your back, and waited;   25
You dozed, and watched the night revealing
The thousand sordid images
Of which your soul was constituted;
They flickered against the ceiling.
And when all the world came back   30
And the light crept up between the shutters,
And you heard the sparrows in the gutters,
You had such a vision of the street
As the street hardly understands;
Sitting along the bed's edge, where   35
You curled the papers from your hair,
Or clasped the yellow soles of feet
In the palms of both soiled hands.

IV

His soul stretched tight across the skies
That fade behind a city block,   40
Or trampled by insistent feet
At four and five and six o'clock;
And short square fingers stuffing pipes,
And evening newspapers, and eyes
Assured of certain certainties,   45
The conscience of a blackened street
Impatient to assume the world.

I am moved by fancies that are curled
Around these images, and cling:
The notion of some infinitely gentle
Infinitely suffering thing.

50

Wipe your hand across your mouth, and laugh;
The worlds revolve like ancient women
Gathering fuel in vacant lots.

TOPICS FOR CRITICAL THINKING

1. The urban landscape of "Preludes" is based in Paris and particularly in the somewhat sordid quarter that the French author Charles Louis Philippe describes in his book *Bubu de Montparnasse*. Eliot lived there while studying at the Sorbonne in 1910 at about the time he was working on "The Love Song of J. Alfred Prufrock." What is your overall impression of the setting Eliot depicts in the poem?

2. In the second stanza of section IV, the poet writes that he is "moved by fancies that are curled / Around these images, and cling." The otherwise realistic descriptions of "Preludes" seem to deny the fancies of the imagination. How are we to account for this kind of statement?

3. What attitude does the poet take toward the cityscape in the final stanza?

TOPIC FOR CRITICAL WRITING

What specific objects, scenes, and things in the poem represent the fragmented nature of modern urban life?

Critical Perspective: On Imagist Poetics

A FEW DON'TS

"An 'Image' is that which presents an intellectual and emotional complex in an instant of time. I use the term 'complex' rather technical sense employed by the newer psychologists, such as Hart, though we may not agree absolutely in our application.

"It is the presentation of such a 'complex' instantaneously which gives that sense of sudden liberation; that sense of freedom from time limits and space limits; that sense of sudden growth, which we experience in the presence of the greatest works of art.

"It is better to present one Image in a lifetime than to produce voluminous works.

"All this, however, some may consider open to debate. The immediate necessity is to tabulate A LIST OF DON'TS for those beginning to write verses. I can not put all of them into Mosaic negative.

"To begin with, consider the three propositions (demanding direct treatment, economy of words, and the sequence of the musical phrase), not as dogma—never consider anything as dogma—but as the result of long contemplation, which, even if it is some one else's contemplation, may be worth consideration. . . .

LANGUAGE

"Use no superfluous word, no adjective which does not reveal something.

"Don't use such an expression as 'dim lands of peace.' It dulls the image. It mixes an abstraction with the concrete. It comes from the writer's not realizing that the natural object is always the adequate symbol.

"Go in fear of abstractions. Do not retell in mediocre verse what has already been done in good prose. Don't think any intelligent person is going to be deceived when you try to shirk all the difficulties of the unspeakably difficult art of good prose by chopping your composition into line lengths. . . .

RHYTHM AND RHYME

"Let the candidate fill his mind with the finest cadences he can discover, preferably in a foreign language, so that the meaning of the words may be less likely to divert his attention from the movement; e.g. Saxon charms, Hebridean Folk Songs, the verse of Dante, and the lyrics of Shakespeare—if he can dissociate the vocabulary from the cadence. Let him dissect the lyrics of Goethe coldly into their component sound values, syllables long and short, stressed and unstressed, into vowels and consonants.

"It is not necessary that a poem should rely on its music, but if it does rely on its music that music must be such as will delight the expert.

"Let the neophyte know assonance and alliteration, rhyme immediate and delayed, simple and polyphonic, as a musician would expect to know harmony and counterpoint and all the minutiae of his craft. No time is too great to give to these matters or to any one of them, even if the artist seldom have need of them."

—Ezra Pound, from *A Few Don'ts for an Imagist* (1913)

Critical Perspective: Modern Poetry and Formal Invention

"The arts have a *complex* relation to society. The poet isn't a fixed phenomenon, no more is his work. *That* might be a note on current affairs, a diagnosis, a plan for procedure, a retrospect—all in its own peculiarly enduring form. There need be nothing limited or frustrated about that. It may be a throw-off from the most violent and successful action or run parallel to it, a saga. It may be the picking out of an essential detail for memory, something to be set aside for further study, a sort of shorthand of emotional significances for later reference.

"Let the metaphysical take care of itself, the arts have nothing to do with it. They will concern themselves with it if they please, among other things. To make two bald statements: There's nothing sentimental about a machine, and: A poem is a small (or large) machine made of words. When I say there's nothing sentimental about a poem I mean that there can be no part, as in any other machine, that is redundant.

"Prose may carry a load of ill-defined matter like a ship. But poetry is the machine which drives it, pruned to a perfect economy. As in all machines its movement is intrinsic, undulant, a physical more than a literary character. In a poem this movement is distinguished in each case by the character of the speech from which it arises.

"Therefore, each speech having its own character, the poetry it engenders will be peculiar to that speech also in its own intrinsic form. The effect is beauty, what in a single object resolves our complex feelings of propriety. One doesn't seek beauty. . . .

"When a man makes a poem, makes it, mind you, he takes words as he finds them interrelated about him and composes them—without distortion which would mar their exact significances—into an intense expression of his perceptions and ardors that they may constitute a revelation in the speech that he uses. It isn't what he *says* that counts as a work of art, it's what he makes, with such intensity of perception that it lives with an intrinsic movement of its own to verify its authenticity. Your attention is called now and then to some beautiful line or sonnet-sequence because of what is said there. So be it. To me all sonnets say the same thing of no importance. What does it matter what the line 'says'?

"There is no poetry of distinction without formal invention, for it is in the intimate form that works of art achieve their exact meaning, in which they most resemble the machine, to give language its highest dignity, its illumination in the environment to which it is native. Such war, as the arts live and breathe by, is continuous.

"It may be that my interests as expressed here are pre-art. If so I look for a development along these lines and will be satisfied with nothing else."

—William Carlos Williams, from *The Wedge* (1944)

4 Figurative Language

When you want to give someone a clear set of directions or concise instructions, you rely on *literal* language to provide "just the facts." But in addition to such straightforward, literal word usage, we constantly employ **figurative language** in everyday life. Whether we realize it or not, metaphor, simile, personification, and other examples of figurative language communicate our meanings and give shape to our thinking. We routinely distinguish between literal meanings and figures of speech in making sense of what we hear and say. For example, imagine you are talking with your friend, the edgy day-trader: "Yesterday I got taken to the cleaners," she tells you, "but five minutes ago I made a killing." Without the ability to distinguish figurative from literal meanings, you would probably duck for cover and dial 911. Without even thinking, we know that such figures of speech as being "taken to the cleaners" and "making a killing" are, respectively, **tropes** for losing and making a lot of money. The term *trope* comes from the Greek word *tropein* meaning "to turn." The Latin word *figura* refers to something "made," "shaped," or "formed." Tropes are figures of language that depend or "turn" on describing one thing in terms of something else. Figurative language works through such comparisons and verbal substitutions where a particular word or phrase stands in for some other intended meaning.

Metaphor comes from the Latin word meaning "to transfer," *metapherein*: "change" (*meta*) and "to bear" (*pherein*). Metaphor transfers the qualities and associations from one word directly into another. Ordinary language is fraught with metaphoric transfers of this sort, and metaphor shapes our everyday communication whether we know it consciously or not. It doesn't take very much reflection to hear metaphor at work in what we say. In their book *Metaphors We Live By*, the linguistic theorists George Lakoff and Mark Johnson have catalogued such metaphoric comparisons as, say, "ideas equal food":

> What he said *left a bad taste in my mouth*. All this paper has in it *are raw facts, half-baked ideas*, and *warmed over theories*. There are too many facts here for me to *digest* them all. I just can't *swallow* that claim. That argument *smells fishy*. Let me *stew* over that for a while. Now there's a theory you can really *sink your teeth into*. We need to let that idea *percolate* for a while. That's *food for thought*. He's a *voracious* reader. We don't need to *spoon-feed* our students. He *devoured* the book. Let's let that idea *simmer on the back burner* for a while. This is the *meaty* part of the paper. Let that idea *jell* for a while. That idea has been *fermenting* for years.

Similarly, love can equal madness:

> I'm *crazy* about her. She *drives me out of my mind*. He constantly *raves* about her. He's gone *mad* over her. I'm just *wild* about Harry. I'm *insane* about her.

Or love can be considered a kind of magic:

> She cast her *spell* over me. The *magic* is gone. I was *spellbound*. She had me *hypno-*
> *tized*. He has me *in a trance*. I was *entranced* by him. I'm *charmed* by her. She is
> *bewitching*.

Poets exploit the powers of metaphor inherent in language usage to craft
meanings in more eloquent and vivid terms than a factual or literal statement
could convey. Moreover, in powerful metaphors something mysterious happens in the process of describing one thing in terms of something else. Additional meaning is created. The new whole becomes somehow more than the
sum of its parts. We feel this surplus of new meaning, for instance, when
Sylvia Plath conjures the sunrise in her poem "Ariel" as "the red / Eye, the
cauldron of morning." Similarly, we can feel poetic intensity bristling in
Emily Dickinson's metaphor for existence: "My life had stood—a Loaded
Gun—." Deceptively simple, such profound recognitions that come from the
arresting metaphor exhaust our attempts to paraphrase them.

Striking metaphors have a way of creating new meanings that baffle the
literal-minded, as in Plath's poem "Metaphors."

Sylvia Plath   *(1932–1963)*

Metaphors   *(1959)*

I'm a riddle in nine syllables,
An elephant, a ponderous house,
A melon strolling on two tendrils.
O red fruit, ivory, fine timbers!
This loaf's big with its yeasty rising.   5
Money's new-minted in this fat purse.
I'm a means, a stage, a cow in calf.
I've eaten a bag of green apples,
Boarded the train there's no getting off.

TOPICS FOR CRITICAL THINKING

1. Plath's several metaphors are couched in the form of a riddle. To what condition do
   they refer?
2. Discuss the various dimensions of that subject as Plath explores it through figurative language.
3. How does poetry both reflect and construct her experience of the poem's subject?

TOPIC FOR CRITICAL WRITING

How original are Plath's metaphors? Which ones are predictable, and which are fresh?

Successful metaphors in poetry do take on a lives of their own and possess a certain charm, as in the riddle posed by the anonymous fifteenth-century lyric "I Have a Yong Sister."

ANONYMOUS

I Have a Yong Sister
(c. fifteenth century)

I have a yong sister
    Fer° beyond the sea;
Manye be the druries°
    That she sente me.

She sente me the cherry 5
    Withouten any stone,
And so she did the dove
    Withouten any bone.

She sente me the brere°
    Withouten any rinde;° 10
She bade me love my lemman°
    Without longing.

How should any cherry
    Be withoute stone?
And how should any dove 15
    Be withoute bone?

How should any brere
    Be withoute rind?
How should I love my lemman
    Without longing? 20

When the cherry was a flowr,
    Then hadde it no stone.
When the dove was an ey,°
    Then hadde it no bone.

When the briar was unbred° 25
    Then hadde it no rinde.
When the maiden hath that she loveth,
    She is without longinge.

---

2 *Fer:* Far.   3 *druries:* Love tokens.   9 *brere:* Briar.   10 *rinde:* Bark.   11 *lemman:* Lover.   23 *ey:* Egg.   25 *unbred:* Still a seedling.

Posed as riddles, such "love tokens" as a flower, egg, or seed become classic metaphors for innocent love that bears within itself the beginnings of a lifetime of unity.

The use of such natural images to stand as metaphors for the more abstract dimensions of a love relationship similarly lends structure and coherence to the argument of William Shakespeare's well-known Sonnet 73.

WILLIAM SHAKESPEARE   *(1564–1616)*

Sonnet 73 *(1609)*

That time of year thou mayst in me behold
When yellow leaves, or none, or few, do hang
Upon those boughs which shake against the cold,
Bare ruined choirs, where late the sweet birds sang.
In me thou see'st the twilight of such day   5
As after sunset fadeth in the west;
Which by and by black night doth take away,
Death's second self, that seals up all in rest.
In me thou sees't the glowing of such fire,
That on the ashes of his youth doth lie,   10
As the deathbed whereon it must expire,
Consumed with that which it was nourished by.
  This thou perceiv'st which makes thy love more strong,
  To love that well which thou must leave ere long.

The persona of Sonnet 73 is all too aware of time's effects presented in the three major metaphors shaping his address to the loved one. Shakespeare devotes four lines each to the three metaphors, and these units are further signaled by the Shakespearean rhyme scheme (taken up in Chapter 9). For now, notice how the poet employs time's effect in the opening seasonal metaphor. Here the persona's age is compared to the fall season whose "boughs which shake against the cold" appear even more striking when described through metaphor as "bare ruined choirs." The second metaphor shortens the sense of time as we move from the seasonal metaphor to the end of the solar day where sunset fades before "Death's second self" of evening. The final metaphor compresses time further in the figure of fire changed to ashes signifying youth being consumed in the life process of aging. The poem expresses the sense that time is collapsing in on itself as we move from the seasonal, to solar, to momentary metaphors of the aging process. The final couplet, however, marks a striking reversal that turns this urgency to the speaker's advantage precisely in the recognition of just how precious time is in the lives of lovers. In the couplet's final paradox, the awareness of mortality makes love "more strong" in the face of that which one "must leave ere long."

A similar reversal of metaphoric argument happens in Margaret Atwood's poem "Habitation."

MARGARET ATWOOD   *(b. 1939)*

Habitation   *(1976)*

Marriage is not
a house or even a tent

it is before that, and colder:

the edge of the forest, the edge
of the desert   5
      the unpainted stairs
at the back where we squat
outside, eating popcorn

the edge of the receding glacier

where painfully and with wonder   10
at having survived even
this far

we are learning to make fire

TOPICS FOR CRITICAL THINKING

1. How does Atwood, like Shakespeare, turn what appears to be a series of negatives into a positive in "Habitation"?
2. In the second line, Atwood rejects the conventional metaphors that characterize the domestic "habitations" of a marriage. The poet more radically probes the "edge" of things that any viable relationship must constantly test. What does being on "the edge" mean for Atwood?
3. The final metaphor of fire can stand for many things in marriage, and, certainly, sexual passion would be the hottest. How do you interpret the poem's ending?

TOPIC FOR CRITICAL WRITING

Explore how Atwood's metaphors for marriage present the paradoxes of survival that a successful relationship must negotiate.

    Simile, from the Latin word meaning "like," is another type of figurative language. Simile renders likenesses more explicit than metaphor through the linking terms *like* or *as*. More demonstrative than dramatic, simile nevertheless, like metaphor, has the power to ground abstract states of feeling and insight in concrete images of immediate experience, as in W. S. Merwin's brief lyric "Separation."

W. S. MERWIN   *(b. 1927)*

Separation   *(1973)*

Your absence has gone through me
Like thread through a needle.
Everything I do is stitched with its color.

Simile allows Merwin to convert the nothingness of separation—the literal
absence of the other—into the presence of a compelling image. Simile in
"Separation" enables the reader to visualize and thus share the poignancy of
the poet's sense of loss.

The romantic poet William Wordsworth uses the relational term *as* in
the simile of his title "I Wandered Lonely As a Cloud."

WILLIAM WORDSWORTH   *(1770–1850)*

I Wandered Lonely As a Cloud   *(1807)*

I wandered lonely as a cloud
That floats on high o'er vales and hills,
When all at once I saw a crowd,
A host, of golden daffodils;
Beside the lake, beneath the trees,   5
Fluttering and dancing in the breeze.

Continuous as the stars that shine
And twinkle on the milky way,
They stretched in never-ending line
Along the margin of a bay: 10
Ten thousand saw I at a glance,
Tossing their heads in sprightly dance.

The waves beside them danced; but they
Outdid the sparkling waves in glee;
A poet could not but be gay,   15
In such a jocund company;
I gazed—and gazed—but little thought
What wealth the show to me had brought:

For oft, when on my couch I lie
In vacant or in pensive mood,   20
They flash upon that inward eye
Which is the bliss of solitude;

And then my heart with pleasure fills,
And dances with the daffodils.

Wordsworth's similes describe his own sense of solitude in nature. The poem, however, is not just about solitude but also the close encounter with a visionary setting that in some ways cures the poet's loneliness.

TOPICS FOR CRITICAL THINKING

1. The actual landscape of the daffodils is based on the real outing that the poet's sister Dorothy Wordsworth records in an entry for her *Grasmere Journals* dated April 15, 1802, two years before the publication of "I Wandered Lonely As a Cloud." But the daffodils Wordsworth depicts in the poem have a heightened, visionary quality. How does simile convey that sublime impression?
2. How does the second "recollected" moment cure the poet of his "pensive" mood?

TOPIC FOR CRITICAL WRITING

In his Preface to *Lyrical Ballads*, which Wordsworth published collaboratively with Samuel Taylor Coleridge, Wordsworth defends the "incidents and situations from common life" as proper subjects for poetry. Moreover, he lays out a definition of the role of memory and the emotions in verse composition. Poetry, he asserts, "is the spontaneous overflow of powerful feelings: it takes its origin from emotion recollected in tranquility." In "I Wandered Lonely As a Cloud," how does the first moment of coming upon the daffodils find its counterpart in the recollected moment of enjoying the sensuous memory of the flowers?

The contemporary poet Sharon Olds also relies on natural similes, but unlike the astrophysical comparisons Wordsworth makes between flowers and stars, Olds aims for a more earthbound effect in "Size and Sheer Will."

SHARON OLDS *(b. 1942)*

Size and Sheer Will   *(1984)*

The fine, green pajama cotton,
washed so often it is paper-thin and
iridescent, has split like a sheath
and the glossy white naked bulbs of
Gabriel's toes thrust forth like crocus   5
this early Spring. The boy is growing
as fast as he can, elongated
wrists dangling, lean meat
showing between the shirt and the belt.
If there were a rack to stretch himself, he would   10
strap his slight body to it.

If there were a machine to enter,
skip the next ten years and be
sixteen immediately, this boy would
do it. All day long he cranes his   15
neck, like a plant in the dark with a single
light above it, or a sailor under
tons of green water, longing
for the surface, for his rightful life.

TOPICS FOR CRITICAL THINKING

1. What similes make the comparison between Gabriel's "sheer will" to grow and the organic vitality of plant life?
2. How do you interpret the simile that compares Gabriel to a sailor?
3. What is the effect of pairing these two very different similes together in the same poem?

TOPIC FOR CRITICAL WRITING

Write on the sigificance of Sharon Olds's title and its relation to the poem.

Personification is a third variety of figurative language that is also described as the rhetorical figure **prosopopoeia:** *prosopon,* meaning "face," plus *poiein,* meaning "to make." We use personification for dramatic effect to attribute life or human aspects to what are otherwise inanimate objects, abstractions, or nonhuman creatures. To convey the beauty of a pastoral scene, Shakespeare relies on personification when he writes in Sonnet 33 that "Full many a glorious morning have I seen / Flatter the mountain-tops with sovereign eye, / Kissing with golden face the meadows green." Personification lends a surreal quality to the satisfaction Rita Dove experiences in the abstraction of a math problem in "Geometry": "I prove a theorem," she writes, "and the house expands: / the windows jerk free to hover near the ceiling, / the ceiling floats away with a sigh."

Personification can lend a human aspect to a particular word, phrase, line, or even an entire poem's contents. Wordsworth, for example, relies on several personifications to depict the idealized signs of humanity he witnesses in the urban sunrise of his sonnet "Composed upon Westminster Bridge, September 3, 1802."

WILLIAM WORDSWORTH   *(1770–1850)*

Composed upon Westminster Bridge, September 3, 1802
(1807)

Earth has not anything to show more fair:
Dull would he be of soul who could pass by
A sight so touching in its majesty;
This City now doth, like a garment, wear
The beauty of the morning; silent, bare,   5
Ships, towers, domes, theaters, and temples lie
Open unto the fields, and to the sky;
All bright and glittering in the smokeless air.
Never did sun more beautifully steep
In his first splendor, valley, rock, or hill;   10
Ne'er saw I, never felt, a calm so deep!
The river glideth at his own sweet will:
Dear God! The very houses seem asleep;
And all that mighty heart is lying still!

In "Composed upon Westminster Bridge, September 3, 1802" Wordsworth chooses to personify the "majesty" he beholds in London, albeit distanced from the vantage point of Westminster Bridge. Notice, for example, how Wordsworth's London is personified as wearing the morning's beauty "like a garment." Similarly, the poet invokes the fresh "splendor" of a pastoral setting in the personified figure of the sun. Even the buildings of Wordsworth's city mirror the poet's sense of "calm" and, like its urban dwellers, "seem asleep." Finally, the poet is left marveling over the way "all that mighty heart is lying still!"

In the ancient world, beauty, grace, strength, horror, eros, and so on all had representation in the traditional pantheon of the gods. Modern poets, however, give a human face to such abstractions through the figure of *prosopopoeia.* **Apostrophe** is a special, performative instance of prosopopoeia. Apostrophe invokes personified meaning by addressing an abstract thing, natural object, creature, or even a departed figure from the past as present in human terms. "Death, be not proud," writes John Donne, confronting mortality as an antagonist who can be faced and faced down. Apostrophe can take the form of a heightened emotive address as when Percy Bysshe Shelley summons the mythical powers of the west wind. "O wild West Wind, thou breath of Autumn's being, / Thou, from whose unseen presence the leaves dead / Are driven, like ghosts from an enchanter fleeting." "O Rose," observes William Blake, "thou art sick." Calling our attention to the life of subhuman things in "The Grasshopper," Richard Lovelace couples personification with the more performative rhetoric of apostrophe: "O thou," he writes of the cricket, "that swing'st upon the waving hair of some well-filled oaten beard" (grain). Returning from France to England, Wordsworth invokes through apostrophe the figure of the dead epic poet John Milton to lend authority to his condemnation of the "vanity and parade" witnessed in his sonnet "London, 1802:" "Milton! Thou shouldst be living at this hour: England hath need of thee: she is a fen / Of stagnant waters. . . ." Poets also rely on apostrophe to address their own powers of writing in a more self-referential performance as in Ezra Pound's "Coda." "O my songs," he writes, "Why do you look so eagerly and so curiously into people's faces, / Will you find your lost dead among them?"

Emily Dickinson was fond of personifying the natural world. Yet her tropes of lending a human face to the natural object never lapse into sentimentality. She eludes the pitfall of projecting human qualities onto nature, the kind of facile anthropomorphism that the nineteenth-century writer John Ruskin condemned as the "pathetic fallacy." Instead, she preserves an uncanny sense of difference while exploring the limits of personification in nature, as in her Poem 328, "A Bird came down the Walk."

EMILY DICKINSON   *(1830–1886)*

Poem 328 (A Bird came down the Walk)   *(1891)*

A Bird came down the Walk —
He did not know I saw —
He bit an Angleworm in halves
And ate the fellow, raw,

And then he drank a Dew   5
From a convenient Grass —
And then hopped sidewise to the Wall
To let a Beetle pass —

He glanced with rapid eyes
That hurried all around —   10
They looked like frightened Beads, I thought —
He stirred his Velvet Head

Like one in danger, Cautious,
I offered him a Crumb
And he unrolled his feathers   15
And rowed him softer home —

Than Oars divide the Ocean
Too silver for a seam —
Or Butterflies, off Banks of Noon
Leap, plashless° as they swim.   20

―――
20 *plashless:* Splashless.

The personified figures of Poem 328 stop just the other side of nature from the human. Seemingly courteous in "hopping sidewise" for a passing beetle, the bird is almost human in taking "Dew" from a "convenient" grass. Dickinson's repeated descriptions of the bird in the third person "he" rather than "it," coupled with his "fellow" the Angleworm, give the momentary illusion of community. Such natural companionship, however, is quickly estranged as the former has the latter for a snack. Nor do "the frightened Beads" of the bird's gaze recognize Dickinson's human gesture of offering a crumb. The natural and human orders remain apart despite the poet's effort to bridge them. Even her final simile that would compare wings and oars transcend the familiar, moving into a surreal landscape that mixes air and water.

Much of Dickinson's poetry journeys into such exotic imaginative territory through the bold use of figurative language. Often, she experiments with a certain blending of physical sensations, as in her phrase "To the bugle, every color is red." Describing one of the perceptual senses of sight, hearing, smell, taste, touch in terms of another in figurative language is called **synaesthesia.** The term *synaesthesia* comes from a Greek root word meaning "blended feeling." Examples of synaesthesia are abundant in ancient and biblical literatures as when Homer in the *Odyssey* describes the Sirens as having a "honey-voice." In the modern era, synaesthesia came into vogue through the symbolist poetry of Charles Baudelaire, Arthur Rimbaud, and the French surrealists. Contemporary poets use synaesthesia to depict intense states of perception, as when Sylvia Plath describes an image of tulips filling a hospital room with "a loud noise."

Various examples of personification, simile, metaphor, and synaesthesia contribute to the surreal depiction of the small-scale machinery of Charles Simic's poem "Watch Repair."

CHARLES SIMIC   *(b. 1938)*

Watch Repair   *(1974)*

A small wheel
Incandescent,
Shivering like
A pinned butterfly.

Hands   5
Pointing in all directions:
The crossroads
One enters
In a nightmare.

Higher than anyone   10
Number 12 presides

Like a beekeeper
Over the swarming honeycomb
Of the open watch.

—Other wheels   15
That could fit
Inside a raindrop,

Tools
That must be splinters
Of arctic starlight . . .   20

Tiny golden mills
Grinding invisible
Coffee beans.

When the coffee's boiling,
Cautiously,   25
So it doesn't burn us,

We raise it to it
To the lips
Of the nearest
Ear.   30

TOPIC FOR CRITICAL THINKING

Consider how Simic's line lengths and his patterns of enjambment capture the strangeness he finds in "Watch Repair."

TOPICS FOR CRITICAL WRITING

1. How does personification make a simple watch repair seem otherwordly? Where does Simic rely on simile and metaphor to depict his bizarre experience of the watch's interior?

2. Taking Simic's poem as a model, pick out a common household object and try your hand at depicting it in a new creative way that depends on figurative language for its special effects.

In "Watch Repair," Simic chooses synaesthesia to end the poem with the strange blending of the sensations—confusing mouth and ear, drinking and listening, the sensations of hearing and tasting. Synaesthesia also comes into play in Dylan Thomas's portrait of the child's mythic perception of nature in "Fern Hill."

DYLAN THOMAS   *(1914–1953)*

Fern Hill   *(1946)*

Now as I was young and easy under the apple boughs
About the lilting house and happy as the grass was green,
    The night above the dingle° starry,
        Time let me hail and climb
    Golden in the heydays of his eyes,   5
And honoured among wagons I was prince of the apple towns
And once below a time I lordly had the trees and leaves
        Trail with daisies and barley
    Down the rivers of the windfall light.

And as I was green and carefree, famous among the barns   10
About the happy yard and singing as the farm was home,
    In the sun that is young once only,
        Time let me play and be
    Golden in the mercy of his means,
And green and golden I was huntsman and herdsman, the calves   15
Sang to my horn, the foxes on the hills barked clear and cold,
        And the sabbath rang slowly
    In the pebbles of the holy streams.

All the sun long it was running, it was lovely, the hay
Fields high as the house, the tunes from the chimneys, it was air   20
    And playing, lovely and watery
        And fire green as grass.
    And nightly under the simple stars
As I rode to sleep the owls were bearing the farm away,
All the moon long I heard, blessed among stables, the night-jars°   25
    Flying with the ricks,° and the horses
        Flashing into the dark.

And then to awake, and the farm, like a wanderer white
With the dew, come back, the cock on his shoulder: it was all
    Shining, it was Adam and maiden,   30
        The sky gathered again
    And the sun grew round that very day.
So it must have been after the birth of the simple light
In the first, spinning place, the spellbound horses walking warm
    Out of the whinnying green stable   35
        On to the fields of praise.

---

3 *dingle:* A narrow wooded valley.   25 *night-jars:* Birds.   26 *ricks:* Haystacks.

And honoured among foxes and pheasants by the gay house
Under the new made clouds and happy as the heart was long,
    In the sun born over and over,
        I ran my heedless ways,   40
    My wishes raced through the house high hay
And nothing I cared, at my sky blue trades, that time allows
In all his tuneful turning so few and such morning songs
    Before the children green and golden
        Follow him out of grace,   45

Nothing I cared, in the lamb white days, that time would take me
Up to the swallow thronged loft by the shadow of my hand,
    In the moon that is always rising,
        Nor that riding to sleep
        I should hear him fly with the high fields   50
And wake to the farm forever fled from the childless land.
Oh as I was young and easy in the mercy of his means,
        Time held me green and dying
    Though I sang in my chains like the sea.

Thomas conveys the child's mythic connection to nature through the biblical allusions to the Genesis story of the Garden of Eden and through personifications of time. But equally important, Thomas invokes that first world through the richness and intensity of synaesthesia's complex perceptual blendings of primary elements. For example, the poet depicts air and light in terms of water; he describes the smoke from the cottage fireplaces as "tunes from the chimneys." The freshness of the landscape seems to burn in a "fire green as grass." Sounds mix with colors as in the phrase "whinnying green stable," or blend with sensations of touch as in the foxes that "on the hills barked clear and cold."

Two more types of figurative language, **metonymy** and **synecdoche**, are so closely related that the latter can be considered a type of the former. Metonymy comes from the Greek word meaning "change of name," while synecdoche in Greek denotes the "act of taking together, or taking as a whole." Metonymy describes a word substituted for another word or thing that we associate with it. For example, a throne, crown, or scepter are things we might substitute for the term *king* or for royalty in general, as when James Shirley writes that "Scepter and crown / Must tumble down, / And in the dust be equal made / With the poor crooked scythe and spade." Similarly, W. B. Yeats characterizes an old man in "Sailing to Byzantium" as "A tattered coat upon a stick." If someone invites you to share some wine and you respond with "Sure, I'll have a glass," your host knows, by virtue of metonymy, that you will have a drink, not the literal container. In a restaurant when you order Chianti, your waiter understands, again through metonymy, that this place name stands in for the literal vintage that is produced in Tuscany, that famous wine-growing region of Italy. John Keats's phrase "beaker full of the warm South" is another version of substituting through metonymy an abstract place name for the type of an actual wine such as, say, Syrah. If we say, "Shirley's always out at the track; she is obsessed with the turf," we imply through metonymy that she likes to bet on horse races. "The White House conferred yesterday with leaders of the Pentagon" refers to an office that we associate with the president, not the literal building.

Synecdoche is a type of metonymy that substitutes a part of something for the whole designated. Just as sailors or laborers are often referred to as "hands"—as in "all hands on deck!"—so synecdoche underwrites many other colloquialisms that stage a part for the whole: "Beef prices are up, so we are moving 300 head to market" or "she went shopping for a year-end deal on a new set of wheels." Synecdoches abound in poetry. T. S. Eliot's persona J. Alfred Prufrock compares himself to a subhuman shellfish, complaining that "I should have been a pair of ragged claws / Scuttling across the floors of silent seas." Similarly when Coleridge's becalmed Ancient Mariner is just about to die of thirst, he at last spies a ship and calls out a synecdoche: "I bit my arm, I sucked the blood, / And cried, A sail, a sail!" Synecdoche also lends dramatic force to William Carlos Williams's "The Yachts," where the poet writes that the "ungoverned ocean . . . / . . . tortures the biggest hulls, the best man knows / to pit against its beatings, and sinks them pitilessly."

Poems for Further Reading and Critical Writing

TED HUGHES   *(1930–1998)*

The Thought-Fox   *(1957)*

I imagine this midnight moment's forest:
Something else is alive
Beside the clock's loneliness
And this blank page where my fingers move.

Through the window I see no star: 5
Something more near
Though deeper within darkness
Is entering the loneliness:

Cold, delicately as the dark snow,
A fox's nose touches twig, leaf;   10
Two eyes serve a movement, that now
And again now, and now, and now

Sets neat prints into the snow
Between trees, and warily a lame
Shadow lags by stump and in hollow   15
Of a body that is bold to come

Across clearings, an eye,
A widening deepening greenness,
Brilliantly, concentratedly,
Coming about its own business   20

Till, with sudden sharp hot stink of fox
It enters the dark hole of the head.
The window is starless still; the clock ticks,
The page is printed.

TOPICS FOR CRITICAL THINKING

1. Explore how Hughes describes the encounter with the thought-fox as an intuited process of witnessing.
2. Within the poem's narrative development of its extended metaphor, what do the "neat prints into the snow" stand for?
3. What does Hughes tell us about the tentative and gradual disclosure of the fox's "body" in such modifying terms as *warily, brilliantly, concentratedly*, and so on?
4. How would you describe the poem's ending? What final form does the metaphoric body of the thought-fox take?

TOPIC FOR CRITICAL WRITING

As the title implies, Hughes's poem is not about a literal fox. What does the figure of the thought-fox describe?

WALT WHITMAN   *(1819–1892)*

from Song of Myself (Section 6)   *(1855)*

6

A child said *What is the grass?* fetching it to me with full hands;
How could I answer the child? I do not know what it is any more than he.

I guess it must be the flag of my disposition, out of hopeful green stuff woven.

Or I guess it is the handkerchief of the Lord,
A scented gift and remembrancer designedly dropt,   5
Bearing the owner's name someway in the corners, that we may see and remark,
    and say *Whose?*

Or I guess the grass is itself a child, the produced babe of the vegetation.

Or I guess it is a uniform hieroglyphic,
And it means, Sprouting alike in broad zones and narrow zones,

Growing among black folks as among white,   10
Kanuck,° Tuckahoe,° Congressman, Cuff,° I give them the same, I receive
    them the same.

And now it seems to me the beautiful uncut hair of graves.

Tenderly will I use you curling grass,
It may be you transpire from the breasts of young men,
It may be if I had known them I would have loved them,   15
It may be you are from old people, or from offspring take soon out of their
    mothers' laps,
And here you are the mothers' laps.

This grass is very dark to be from the white heads of old mothers,
Darker than the colourless beards of old men,
Dark to come from under the faint red roofs of mouths.   20

O I perceive after all so many uttering tongues,
And I perceive they do not come from the roofs of mouths for nothing.

I wish I could translate the hints about the dead young men and women,
And the hints about old men and mothers, and the offspring taken soon out of
    their laps.

What do you think has become of the young and old men?   25
And what do you think has become of the women and children?

They are alive and well somewhere,
The smallest sprout shows there is really no death,
And if ever there was it led forward life, and does not wait at the end to
    arrest it,
And ceas'd the moment life appear'd.   30

All goes onward and outward, nothing collapses,
And to die is different from what any one supposed, and luckier.

TOPICS FOR CRITICAL THINKING

1. In answering the child's question—"What is the grass?"—what point does Whitman make in admitting that "I do not know what it is any more than he"?
2. Consider the metaphors Whitman employs to account for his experience of the
   grass. What does the grass signify as the "handkerchief of the Lord"?

---

11 *Kanuck:* French Canadian.   11 *Tuckahoe:* Slave term for *Virginian*, of Native American origin.   11 *Cuff:* African American.

3. What does Whitman mean by "uniform hieroglyphic"? How does the grass as a "uniform hieroglyphic" become a metaphor for the democracy of American place?

4. Examine the imagery of darkness that Whitman uses to depict the poem's tropes of mortality following his metaphor of the grass as "the beautiful hair of graves."

TOPIC FOR CRITICAL WRITING

What point does Whitman make about the processes of life and death perceived in the example of grass?

ROBERT FROST   *(1874–1963)*

The Silken Tent   *(1942)*

She is as in a field a silken tent
At midday when a sunny summer breeze
Has dried the dew and all its ropes relent,
So that in guys° it gently sways at ease,
And its supporting central cedar pole,   5
That is its pinnacle to heavenward
And signifies the sureness of the soul,
Seems to owe naught to any single cord,
But strictly held by none, is loosely bound
By countless silken ties of love and thought   10
To everything on earth the compass round,
And only by one's going slightly taut
In the capriciousness of summer air
Is of the slightest bondage made aware.

TOPICS FOR CRITICAL THINKING

1. What do you know about tents? How do tents stay upright? Describe the poetic logic by which Frost depicts his spouse as a tent.

2. Focus on the metaphor of the "central cedar pole" as a trope for the "sureness of the soul." Examine the balance Frost sets up in the way in which it, on the one hand, points "its pinnacle to heavenward" and, on the other hand, is bound "to everything on earth."

3. Examine the tension Frost depicts in the poem between things that are "loosely bound" and those "slightly taut."

4. How does the poet heighten that tension in the final lines? Explain your interpretation of the phrase "capriciousness of summer air" and how it finds its counterpart in the word *bondage*.

---

4 *guys:* Tent ropes.

Describe the theme that Frost's metaphors portray in "The Silken Tent."

JOHN DONNE   *(1572–1631)*

A Valediction Forbidding Mourning   *(1633)*

As virtuous men pass mildly away,
    And whisper to their souls to go
Whilst some of their sad friends do say,
    The breath goes now, and some say, no;

So let us melt, and make no noise,   5
    No tear-floods, nor sigh-tempests move,
'Twere profanation of our joys
    To tell the laity our love.

Moving of th'earth brings harms and fears,
    Men reckon what it did and meant;   10
But trepidation of the spheres,
    Though greater far, is innocent.

Dull sublunary lovers' love
    (Whose soul is sense) cannot admit
Absence, because it doth remove   15
    Those things which elemented it.

But we by'a love so much refined,
    That our selves know not what it is,
Inter-assuréd of the mind,
    Care less, eyes, lips, and hands to miss.   20

Our two souls therefore, which are one,
    Though I must go, endure not yet
A breach, but an expansion,
    Like gold to airy thinness beat.

If they be two, they are two so   25
    As stiff twin compasses are two;
Thy soul the fixed foot, makes no show
    To move, but doth, if th'other do.

And though it in the center sit,
    Yet when the other far doth roam,   30

It leans, and hearkens after it,
　And grows erect, as that comes home.

Such wilt thou be to me, who must
　Like th'other foot, obliquely° run.
Thy firmness makes my circle just,   35
　And makes me end where I begun.

TOPICS FOR CRITICAL THINKING

1. Discuss the first simile that depicts a death scene and the mourners' difficulty in determining the exact moment of the dying man's last breath. How does Donne compare the soul's departure and his own?
2. "Trepidation of the spheres" refers to the vibration of the celestial spheres theorized by Ptolemaic versions of the universe. It accounts for the discrepancies in the movement of heavenly objects. Everything below the sphere of the moon or "sublunary"—the world of earthly elements—was considered mutable and subject to change. Beyond the moon, life was unchanging. How does Donne turn this cosmology to his advantage in stanzas four and five to stress the "refined" love that he shares in marriage regardless of his physical proximity to his spouse?
3. In alchemical traditions, gold is considered the most spiritual of elements. In stanza six, how does Donne console his spouse by describing their spiritual oneness as "gold to airy thinness beat"?
4. Examine the extended simile of the compass—a tool for drawing circles—in the poem's final stanzas. How does this comparison eroticize the homecoming of Donne's anticipated reunion with his spouse?

TOPIC FOR CRITICAL WRITING

A *valediction* is a speech bidding farewell, and, according to Izaak Walton, Donne wrote this poem to his wife when he was traveling on the Continent in 1611. Consider the arguments Donne uses to lessen the impact of their temporary separation.

MATTHEW ARNOLD   *(1822–1888)*

Dover Beach   *(1867)*

The sea is calm tonight.
The tide is full, the moon lies fair
Upon the straits; on the French coast the light
Gleams and is gone; the cliffs of England stand,
Glimmering and vast, out in the tranquil bay.   5
Come to the window, sweet is the night-air!

———
35 *obliquely:* Diagonally.

Only, from the long line of spray
Where the sea meets the moon-blanched land,
Listen! you hear the grating roar
Of pebbles which the waves draw back, and fling,   10
At their return, up the high strand,
Begin, and cease, and then again begin,
With tremulous cadence slow, and bring
The eternal note of sadness in.

Sophocles long ago   15
Heard it on the Aegean, and it brought
Into his mind the turbid ebb and flow
Of human misery; we
Find also in the sound a thought,
Hearing it by this distant northern sea.   20

The Sea of Faith
Was once, too, at the full, and round earth's shore
Lay like the folds of a bright girdle furled.
But now I only hear
Its melancholy, long withdrawing roar,   25
Retreating, to the breath
Of the night-wind, down the vast edges drear
And naked shingles of the world.

Ah, love, let us be true
To one another! for the world, which seems   30
To lie before us like a land of dreams,
So various, so beautiful, so new,
Hath really neither joy, nor love, nor light,
Nor certitude, nor peace, nor help for pain;
And we are here as on a darkling plain   35
Swept with confused alarms of struggle and flight,
Where ignorant armies clash by night.

TOPICS FOR CRITICAL THINKING

1. Discuss the situation and setting of "Dover Beach."
2. Explore Arnold's use of simile in stanza three. How does Arnold use simile to depict "The Sea of Faith"?
3. Arnold published "Dover Beach" in 1867 after Charles Lyell's *Principles of Geology* (1830) and *The Geological Evidence of the Antiquity of Man* (1863), which, through fossil records, undermined biblical accounts of time and human history generally. Together with Charles Darwin's theories of natural selection in *Origin of Species* (1859), such modern revisions of geological change and evolution eroded the humanist foundations of biblical faith. How does Arnold depict the impact of this new modernist sensibility on the poet's perception of the "vast edges drear / And naked shingles of the world"?

4. How does Arnold use simile in the fourth stanza to contrast the imagined landscape with its real setting?

5. What is Arnold's solution to the contingencies and uncertainties of modern experience? How does he perform that answer in his direct address to his lover?

TOPIC FOR CRITICAL WRITING

Contrast Wordsworth's sonnet "It Is a Beauteous Evening" and its description of the ocean—"Listen! The mighty Being is awake"—with Arnold's "Listen! you hear the grating roar." How does Arnold's view of nature differ from Wordsworth's?

5 Symbolism

The term *symbol* comes from a Greek verb *symballein*, "to put together." In the ancient world a *symbolon* was a coin or token that was broken in two. Once broken, each half belonged to one of the two parties entering into a legal contract or agreement. Each half depended on its relation to the other half. As a kind of linguistic contract, a literary **symbol** consists of something present whose meaning and significance depends on something absent. Symbols are based on comparisons between concrete images and abstract ideas. On the one hand, a symbol is made up of something specific: an image, word, thing, setting, or even a person. On the other hand, something less immediately self-evident completes the symbol: a moral truth, an emotional state, an abstract realization or idea.

Often, you can easily identify a symbol's meaning because the concrete symbolic object bears a conventional resemblance to the abstract concept it represents. Light is generally taken to symbolize spiritual illumination. Darkness—as in the "dark night of the soul"—generally stands for its opposite. A candle symbolically lights the darkness and is a familiar symbol for humanitarian organizations such as Amnesty International. Hollywood cinema also relies on the power of symbols to define character, action, and thematic values. For example, Russell Crowe's character in the film *Gladiator*, the Roman general Maximus Decimus Meridius, always picks up a handful of soil before risking his life in battle or in the arena. As a symbol, that fistful of dirt stands for Maximus's connection to the earth, nature, and, ultimately, the risk of death that gives his life meaning, dignity, and vitality.

Symbols abound in popular culture, literature, and political and religious institutions. Nations adopt national symbols to signify particular values or ideals. The United States is represented in the eagle as a symbol of fierce independence. Religions employ concrete symbols such as the lamb, dove, cross, or menorah to stand for historical events or metaphysical concepts of God, resurrection, damnation, and so on. Poets often adopt such well-known symbols for their own purposes. For example, William Blake's poem "The Lamb" from the *Songs of Innocence* presents a straightforward account of the lamb as a traditional symbol for Christ and his divine incarnation.

WILLIAM BLAKE   *(1757–1827)*

The Lamb   *(1789)*

Little Lamb, who made thee?
Dost thou know who made thee?
Gave thee life, and bid thee feed
By the stream and o'er the mead;
Gave thee clothing of delight,   5
Softest clothing, woolly, bright;
Gave thee such a tender voice,
Making all the vales rejoice?
   Little Lamb, who made thee?
   Dost thou know who made thee?   10

   Little Lamb, I'll tell thee,
   Little Lamb, I'll tell thee:
He is callèd by thy name,
For he calls himself a Lamb.
He is meek, and he is mild;   15
He became a little child.
I a child, and thou a lamb.
We are called by his name.
   Little Lamb, God bless thee.
   Little Lamb, God bless thee.   20

The literal lamb that Blake addresses is innocent of its symbolic correspondence to Christ, the Lamb. It needs the poet's lesson on the mystery of its existence and who or what sustains it. The answer to the opening question draws out the relation between the literal and symbolic figures of the lamb. The likenesses between the two are not based only on resemblance—both being meek and mild—but are underwritten by the "name" of the lamb that signifies the symbolic correspondence between earth and heaven (see color insert).

Through repeated usage over time, symbols enter into the conventions of everyday life. On Valentine's Day, for example, you might give your "sweetheart" (itself a symbol) a dozen roses symbolizing love. The original association of the lover with the rose is no doubt based on such resemblances as freshness, beauty, delicacy. Thus, Robert Burns symbolizes his new love with the Spring rose when he exclaims "O my luve's like a red, red rose, / That's newly sprung in June."

Through repeated usage, the rose as a symbol of love has become a social convention—a gesture of affection that Dorothy Parker whimsically revisits in her ironic poem "One Perfect Rose."

DOROTHY PARKER   *(1893–1967)*

One Perfect Rose   *(1926)*

A single flow'r he sent me, since we met.
   All tenderly his messenger he chose;
Deep-hearted, pure, with scented dew still wet—
   One perfect rose.

I knew the language of the floweret;   5
   "My fragile leaves," it said, "his heart enclose."
Love long has taken for his amulet
   One perfect rose.

Why is it no one ever sent me yet
   One perfect limousine, do you suppose?   10
Ah no, it's always just my luck to get
   One perfect rose.

We live in a world of conventional symbols where words all too quickly stand in as emblems for known abstractions. A rose symbolizes love; a lion stands for courage; the sun has long been a symbol of life, while a skull signifies death. Yet poets enhance the word's capacity for symbolic reference. Instead of using the concrete image to denote clichéd meaning, poetry often works in reverse to allow more subtle and unique insights to complicate a word's or image's everyday significance.

Romantic poets such as William Blake reject outworn symbols, presenting instead fresh images that would grow and be shaped by their organic relation to symbolic meaning, as in "The Sick Rose."

WILLIAM BLAKE   *(1757–1827)*

The Sick Rose   *(1794)*

O Rose, thou art sick.
The invisible worm
That flies in the night
In the howling storm

Has found out thy bed   5
Of crimson joy,
And his dark secret love
Does thy life destroy.

TOPICS FOR CRITICAL THINKING

1. Why is the rose's love "dark" and "secret"?
2. What is a "bed / Of crimson joy"?
3. Who or what is the worm, and why is it "invisible"? Does it only appear "in the night"? Must it be associated with the "howling storm"? How has the worm found the rose?

TOPICS FOR CRITICAL WRITING

1. Can we ever be sure what the rose represents exactly? Why does Blake call it a "sick rose"?
2. What does the storm symbolize?

Blake's symbolic rose is neither as simple nor as clear as Parker's "amulet" of the "one perfect rose." Not surprisingly, the poem resists any easy answers to the questions posed above. Blake's symbolic drama cannot be exhausted by any simple paraphrase but, like the relation that the romantic poet John Keats finds between truth and beauty, "dost tease us out of thought." Each of us, no doubt, has an idea about how to answer questions about the poem's meaning, but will they be the same? Not likely. Presenting a symbolic action, the poem generates meaning through the reader's act of interpreting what finally remains a mystery.

Many symbols suggest rather than insist on a particular meaning, idea, or concept. The Native American poet Mary TallMountain invokes the symbolic power of nature in her poem "The Last Wolf."

MARY TALLMOUNTAIN   *(1918–1994)*

The Last Wolf   *(1989)*

the last wolf hurried toward me
through the ruined city
and I heard his baying echoes
down the steep smashed warrens
of Montgomery Street and past   5
the few ruby-crowned highrises
left standing
their lighted elevators useless

passing the flicking red and green
of traffic signals   10
baying his way eastward
in the mystery of his wild loping gait
closer the sounds in the deadly night
through clutter and rubble of quiet blocks

I heard his voice ascending the hill 15
and at last his low whine as he came
floor by empty floor to the room
where I sat
in my narrow bed looking west, waiting
I heard him snuffle at the door and 20
I watched
he trotted across the floor

he laid his long gray muzzle
on the spare white spread
and his eyes burned yellow 25
his small dotted eyebrows quivered

Yes, I said.
I know what they have done.

TOPICS FOR CRITICAL THINKING

1. TallMountain was born in 1918 in Nulato, Alaska, and inherited a dual cultural identity. On her mother's side she is Koyukon/Athabaskan, and on her father's side Scottish and Irish. After her mother's death, TallMountain was adopted and taken far away from her native traditions rooted in the Yukon. That dispossessed heritage is a common theme in her verse. How does TallMountain create the "ruined" urban present of the poem's opening setting?
2. Describe the shift in the wolf's presentation as we move from stanza one to stanza two.
3. How do you understand the final lines of the poem in her address to the wolf?

TOPIC FOR CRITICAL WRITING

Written during TallMountain's bouts with illness, her poem "The Last Wolf" presents a very intense and special relation to the wolf. What do you think the wolf symbolizes in this poem? Why is it a "last" wolf?

Some poets like to complicate a symbol's conventional meaning so as to call into question our habitual modes of interpretation. Robert Frost, for example, probes the deceptively straightforward meaning of walls as boundaries and barriers between neighbors in his poem "Mending Wall."

ROBERT FROST *(1874–1963)*

Mending Wall *(1914)*

Something there is that doesn't love a wall,
That sends the frozen-ground-swell under it,

And spills the upper boulders in the sun;
And makes gaps even two can pass abreast.
The work of hunters is another thing: 5
I have come after them and made repair
Where they have left not one stone on a stone,
But they would have the rabbit out of hiding,
To please the yelping dogs. The gaps I mean,
No one has seen them made or heard them made,   10
But at spring mending-time we find them there.
I let my neighbor know beyond the hill;
And on a day we meet to walk the line
And set the wall between us once again.
We keep the wall between us as we go.   15
To each the boulders that have fallen to each.
And some are loaves and some so nearly balls
We have to use a spell to make them balance:
'Stay where you are until our backs are turned!'
We wear our fingers rough with handling them.   20
Oh, just another kind of outdoor game,
One on a side. It comes to little more:
There where it is we do not need the wall:
He is all pine and I am apple orchard.
My apple trees will never get across   25
And eat the cones under his pines, I tell him.
He only says, 'Good fences make good neighbors.'
Spring is the mischief in me, and I wonder
If I could put a notion in his head:
'*Why* do they make good neighbors? Isn't it   30
Where there are cows? But here there are no cows.
Before I built a wall I'd ask to know
What I was walling in or walling out,
And to whom I was like to give offense.
Something there is that doesn't love a wall,   35
That wants it down.' I could say 'Elves' to him,
But it's not elves exactly, and I'd rather
He said it for himself. I see him there
Bringing a stone grasped firmly by the top
In each hand, like an old-stone savage armed.   40
He moves in darkness as it seems to me,
Not of woods only and the shade of trees.
He will not go behind his father's saying,
And he likes having thought of it so well
He says again, 'Good fences make good neighbors.'   45

   In reading Frost's poem, how do we know that repairing the wall is not
just a literal but a symbolic activity? For one thing, in setting up the poem's
dramatic situation, Frost tells us that he and his neighbor don't really need the

wall. Because Frost's side consists of an apple orchard and his neighbor's a pine forest, there is nothing of literal value at stake in "walling in or walling out" their respective properties. It's "just another kind of outdoor game." Neither of them is at risk of livestock straying across the boundary onto the other's land. Something else, though, of symbolic value is at issue in the colloquial truism that "Good fences make good neighbors." Part of the brilliance of the poem is the way in which Frost leaves unanswered his own question "*Why* do they make good neighbors?" What the wall symbolizes, finally, is left, like the human condition generally, an open-ended mystery. There are, of course, hints that the wall—like the rule of civil law—protects us from "the darkness" of our own capacities of violence toward the other. The neighbor shoulders his rocks "like an old-stone savage armed" and seems to move in a symbolic "darkness . . . Not of woods only and the shade of trees."

How we are to judge the activity of shoring up the wall remains ambiguous in the poem itself. Clearly, the poem's speaker has no use for the wall. As far as he's concerned, it's an absurdity, for "There where it is we do not need the wall." Several phrases reinforce the notion that the wall creates division. We "set the wall between us once again," he says; "We keep the wall between us as we go." "Something there is" in the natural scheme of things as such, he philosophizes, "that doesn't love a wall." Nevertheless, at the end of the day, and in the poem's concluding lines, Frost realizes that the neighbor cannot admit, or say "it for himself." Instead, the neighbor takes a certain pleasure in "his father's saying." He prides himself on what for the poet is a mindless cliché reproducing social division. All in all, he will forever restore the literal wall as a symbol. However ironic, the poem's title underscores the symbolic paradox of "mending" through separation, encoding in more subtle, more compressed, and more cryptic terms the proposition that "Good fences make good neighbors."

Walls, of course, have a deep archetypal symbolic resonance in cultural usage. The literary term *archetype* stems from the Greek word *archetypos*, which means "original pattern." The Cambridge anthropologists Sir James Frazer, Gilbert Murray, and Jesse Weston, as well as the psychoanalytic tradition influenced by the famous Swiss psychologist Carl Jung, shaped the modern literary understanding of archetypes. An **archetype** in literature describes a symbolic image that is basic to the human experience of birth, death, fertility, disease, war, quest, and so on. The symbolic power of, say, the Great Wall of China or the former Berlin Wall signifies the power, authority, and sovereignty of boundaries beyond their literal, physical structures. Archetypes are so basic that they recur in the mythology, customs, rituals, and literatures of particular societies as a world phenomenon stretching across cultures and historical periods. Such basic archetypes as images of fire, water, earth, stars, caves, cups, animals, wounds, crosses, swastikas, circles, and so on give shape to one's individual dream life and poetic imagination because they are deeply imprinted in what Jung characterized as the "collective unconscious" of human culture.

Sylvia Plath's poetry also works with primal, archetypal symbols such as a tree and the moon in her poem "The Moon and the Yew Tree."

The Berlin Wall, Heidelberger Strasse

SYLVIA PLATH   *(1932–1963)*

The Moon and the Yew Tree   *(1961)*

This is the light of the mind, cold and planetary.
The trees of the mind are black. The light is blue.
The grasses unload their griefs on my feet as if I were God,
Prickling my ankles and murmuring of their humility.
Fumy, spiritous mists inhabit this place   5
Separated from my house by a row of headstones.
I simply cannot see where there is to get to.

The moon is no door. It is a face in its own right,
White as a knuckle and terribly upset.
It drags the sea after it like a dark crime; it is quiet   10
With the O-gape of complete despair. I live here.
Twice on Sunday, the bells startle the sky—
Eight great tongues affirming the Resurrection.
At the end, they soberly bong out their names.

The yew tree points up. It has a Gothic shape.   15
The eyes lift after it and find the moon.
The moon is my mother. She is not sweet like Mary.
Her blue garments unloose small bats and owls.
How I would like to believe in tenderness—

The face of the effigy, gentled by candles,   20
Bending, on me in particular, its mild eyes.

I have fallen a long way. Clouds are flowering
Blue and mystical over the face of the stars.
Inside the church, the saints will all be blue,
Floating on their delicate feet over the cold pews,   25
Their hands and faces stiff with holiness.
The moon sees nothing of this. She is bald and wild.
And the message of the yew tree is blackness—blackness and silence.

TOPICS FOR CRITICAL THINKING

1. What kinds of symbolic meanings do you associate with the archetypal images of the moon and the tree?
2. Do the tree and moon have opposing meanings in Plath's symbolic presentation of them? Or do they complement one another?
3. Plath claims the moon as mother and further contrasts that personification with the Christian figure of Mary. What is her point here?

TOPIC FOR CRITICAL WRITING

Explore the differences in the poem's two settings that contrast the outdoor scene of evening with what is going on "inside the church."

Poetry, at times, plays on the archetypal dimensions of uncanny, everyday things so as to make us think twice about the meanings we routinely take for granted. Such psychological estrangement happens in W. S. Merwin's unsettling poem "Strawberries."

W. S. MERWIN   *(b. 1927)*

Strawberries   *(1983)*

When my father died I saw   a narrow valley

it looked as though it began   across the river
from the landing where he was born   but there was no river

I was hoeing the sand   of a small vegetable plot
for my mother   in deepening twilight   5
and looked up in time   to see a farm wagon
dry and gray   horse already hidden
and no driver   going into the valley
carrying a casket

                                      and another wagon   10
coming out of the valley   behind a gray horse
with a boy driving   and a high load
of two kinds of berries   one of them strawberries

        that night when I slept   I dreamed of things
wrong in the house   all of them signs   15
the water of the shower   running brackish
and an insect of a kind   I had seen him kill
climbing around   the walls of his bathroom
        up in the morning   I stopped on the stairs
my mother was awake   already and asked me   20
if I wanted a shower   before breakfast
and for breakfast she said   we have strawberries

    Several forceful archetypes underwrite the situation, imagery, and action
of "Strawberries." In addition to the poet's dream, nearly all the poem's elements can be read as signs of symbolic meaning. To begin with, the poem's
framing scenario deals with death and the succession of father and son in their
respective relationships to the mother. This domestic situation itself touches
on the tensions of the Oedipal myth, which is fundamental for **psychoanalytic**
www Web approaches to literature. In Sophocles' famous Oedipal trilogy, the son's
sexual rivalry with the father for the mother's attentions is a story that Sigmund
Freud, the founder of modern psychoanalysis, interpreted as fundamental to
the psychic development of men and women. The successful passage through
the Oedipal situation, for Freud, is marked by the child's relinquishing of his
primal relationship to and desire for the mother in favor of substitute satisfac-
tions that make up the wider social and cultural sublimations of everyday life.

    Merwin's poem opens with a garden of sand in a valley landscape where
there once was a river; it ends with the mother's suggestion that the son take
a "shower." There are two wagons: one driverless, carrying a casket, the other
full of two kinds of berries driven by a boy. Similar to the archetypal rites of
passage that we find, say, in T. S. Eliot's long poem *The Waste Land* (1922), we
move from a burial of the dead and the dry garden associated with death to
images of water, rejuvenation, and even resurrection. The son dreams of an
insect the father had once killed. This detail reinforces, perhaps, the Oedipal
narrative that, as Freud described it, characterizes the son's renouncing of his
desire for the mother out of fear of the father's violent threat of castration. In
Merwin's poem, however, the son replaces the father and receives the ambiguous dish of strawberries for breakfast.

TOPICS FOR CRITICAL THINKING

1. What do the strawberries symbolize?
2. What do the strawberries have to do with the berries carted out of the valley by the
   boy and his gray horse?

3. Why does the poet dream of things "wrong in the house," and what kinds of emotions does the son experience when the mother tells him that "for breakfast . . . we have strawberries"?

TOPIC FOR CRITICAL WRITING

How does the poet's use of spacings within the lines on the page affect how we read the poem's action and complicate how we interpret its meanings?

What the signs of the poet's imagination actually mean are as opaque, finally, as the typographical gaps Merwin inserts as a stylistic feature into his line lengths. Such spacings suggest the power of particular words and phrases by making us pause over them. But they obscure even as they suggest possible lines of significance and interpreted meaning. Guided by the symbolic enigmas of his dream life, Merwin seems to concur in "Strawberries" with the great Irish bard W. B. Yeats and his belief that "the poet of essences and pure ideas must seek in the half-lights that glimmer from symbol to symbol as if to the ends of the earth, all that the epic and dramatic poet finds of mystery and shadow in the accidental circumstances of life."

Symbols, as we have seen, explore the likenesses between something close to hand and something else that is less easily known. **Allegory** presents a more purposeful narrative structuring of symbolic analogies. The term *allegory* comes from the Greek words meaning "other" (*allos*) and "to speak" (*agoreuein*): to speak, that is, in terms of something other. In literary allegories, virtually all the narrative details of setting, characterization, imagery, and so on stand as emblems for moral truths and spiritual meanings in another, more metaphysical register. Through the narrative experience or quest of a protagonist— whether it is the Spenserian knight of the *Faerie Queen* torn between Una and Duessa or Bunyan's hero Christian beguiled by Mr. Wordly Wiseman in *Pilgrim's Progress*, or even Dante's descent into the underworld in the *Divine Comedy*—allegories teach us how to recognize the differences between good and evil, truth and error, the saved and the damned.

Such a scene of spiritual instruction happens in the allegorical analogies that Edward Taylor witnesses in "Upon a Spider Catching a Fly."

EDWARD TAYLOR *(1642–1729)*

Upon a Spider Catching a Fly *(1680–1682)*

Thou sorrow, venom elf:
  Is this thy ploy,
To spin a web out of thyself
  To catch a fly?
    For why?   5

I saw a petish wasp
  Fall foul therein,

Whom yet thy whorl-pins did not clasp
     Lest he should fling
          His sting.   10

But as afraid, remote
     Didst stand hereat
And with thy little fingers stroke
     And gently tap
          His back.   15

Thus gently him didst treat
     Lest he should pet,
And in a froppish, waspish heat
     Should greatly fret
          Thy net.   20

Whereas the silly fly,
     Caught by its leg
Thou by the throat tookst hastily
     And hind the head
          Bite dead.   25

This goes to pot, that not[;]
     Nature doth call.
Strive not above what strength hath got
     Lest in the brawl
          Thou fall.   30

This fray seems thus to us.
     Hell's spider gets
His entrails spun to whip-cords thus,
     And wove to nets
          And sets.   35

To tangle Adam's race
     In's stratagems
To their destructions, spoiled, made base
     By venom things,
          Damned sins.   40

But mighty, gracious Lord
     Communicate
Thy grace to break the cord, afford
     Us glory's gate
          And state.   45

We'll nightingale sing like
     When perched on high
In glory's cage, thy glory, bright,

And thankfully,
   For Joy.   50

    Taylor, the New England Puritan pastor and poet, was born in Leicester-
shire, England, and emigrated to the Bay Colony (Boston) in 1668. He studied
at Harvard University and later ministered to the frontier community of West-
field, Massachusetts, from 1671 until his death in 1729. Influenced by the
metaphysical conceits he read in John Donne's *Holy Sonnets* and Richard
Crashaw's *Steps to the Temple*, Taylor's devotional poetry, *Prepatory Meditations*
(1682–1725) offers more plainspoken and didactic verse allegories for humanity's relationship to God. "Upon a Spider Catching a Fly" pays close attention
to everyday life whose worldly scenes, as Taylor believed, "illustrate supernatural things by natural." The poem sets out in a rather plainspoken style the literal situation of a spider catching a wasp or fly in its web. The second half of
the poem illuminates this scenario as an allegory for the Calvinist belief in the
so-called total depravity of Original Sin. The literal spider is an allegorical figure for "Hell's spider" or Satan, who has spun a metaphysical web "To tangle
Adam's race / In's stratagems." Like the fly, humanity cannot free itself from
the entanglements of total depravity on its own. Only God's irresistible grace
offered to a selected few—the elect who are predestined for salvation through
Christ's limited atonement—can hope to "break the cord" of Original Sin.

Poems for Further Reading and Critical Writing

WALT WHITMAN   *(1819–1892)*

When Lilacs Last in the Dooryard Bloom'd   *(1868)*

1

When lilacs last in the dooryard bloom'd,
And the great star early droop'd in the western sky in the night,
I mourn'd, and yet shall mourn with ever-returning spring.

Ever-returning spring, trinity sure to me you bring,
Lilac blooming perennial and drooping star in the west,   5
And thought of him I love.

2

O powerful western fallen star!
O shades of night—O moody, tearful night!
O great star disappear'd—O the black murk that hides the star!
O cruel hands that hold me powerless—O helpless soul of me!   10
O harsh surrounding cloud that will not free my soul.

3

In the dooryard fronting an old farm-house near the white-wash'd
    palings,
Stands the lilac-bush tall-growing with heart-shaped leaves of rich
    green,
With many a pointed blossom rising delicate, with the perfume strong I love,
With every leaf a miracle—and from this bush in the dooryard,   15
With delicate-color'd blossoms and heart-shaped leaves of rich green,
A sprig with its flower I break.

4

In the swamp in secluded recesses,
A shy and hidden bird is warbling a song.

Solitary the thrush,   20
The hermit withdrawn to himself, avoiding the settlements,
Sings by himself a song.

Song of the bleeding throat,
Death's outlet song of life, (for well dear brother I know,
If thou wast not granted to sing thou would'st surely die.)   25

5

Over the breast of the spring, the land, amid cities,
Amid lanes and through old woods, where lately the violets peep'd from the
    ground, spotting the gray debris,
Amid the grass in the fields each side of the lanes, passing the endless grass,
Passing the yellow-spear'd wheat, every grain from its shroud in the dark-
    brown fields uprisen,
Passing the apple-tree blows of white and pink in the orchards,   30
Carrying a corpse to where it shall rest in the grave,
Night and day journeys a coffin.

6

Coffin that passes through lanes and streets,
Through day and night with the great cloud darkening the land,
With the pomp of the inloop'd flags with the cities draped in black,   35
With the show of the States themselves as of crape-veil'd women
    standing,
With processions long and winding and the flambeaus of the night,
With the countless torches lit, with the silent sea of faces and the
    unbared heads,
With the waiting depot, the arriving coffin, and the sombre faces,
With dirges through the night, with the thousand voices rising strong and   40
    solemn,
With all the mournful voices of the dirges pour'd around the coffin,

The dim-lit churches and the shuddering organs—where amid these you
    journey,
With the tolling tolling bells' perpetual clang,
Here, coffin that slowly passes,
I give you my sprig of lilac.   45

7

(Nor for you, for one alone,
Blossoms and branches green to coffins all I bring,
For fresh as the morning, thus would I chant a song for you O sane
    and sacred death.

All over bouquets of roses,
O death, I cover you over with roses and early lilies,   50
But mostly and now the lilac that blooms the first,
Copious I break, I break the sprigs from the bushes,
With loaded arms I come, pouring for you,
For you and the coffins all of you O death.)

8

O western orb sailing the heaven,   55
Now I know what you must have meant as a month since I walk'd,
As I walk'd in silence the transparent shadowy night,
As I saw you had something to tell as you bent to me night after night,
As you droop'd from the sky low down as if to my side, (while the other stars
    all look'd on,)
As we wander'd together the solemn night, (for something I know not   60
    what kept me from sleep,)
As the night advanced, and I saw on the rim of the west how full you
    were of woe,
As I stood on the rising ground in the breeze in the cool transparent night,
As I watch'd where you pass'd and was lost in the netherward black of the
    night,
As my soul in its trouble dissatisfied sank, as where you sad orb,
Concluded, dropt in the night, and was gone.   65

9

Sing on there in the swamp,
O singer bashful and tender, I hear your notes, I hear your call,
I hear, I come presently, I understand you,
But a moment I linger, for the lustrous star has detain'd me,
The star my departing comrade holds and detains me.   70

10

O how shall I warble myself for the dead one there I loved?
And how shall I deck my song for the large sweet soul that has gone?
And what shall my perfume be for the grave of him I love?

Sea-winds blown from east and west,
Blown from the Eastern sea and blown from the Western sea, till there on   75
    the prairies meeting,
These and with these and the breath of my chant,
I'll perfume the grave of him I love.

11

O what shall I hang on the chamber walls?
And what shall the pictures be that I hang on the walls,
To adorn the burial-house of him I love?   80

Pictures of growing spring and farms and homes,
With the Fourth-month eve at sundown, and the gray smoke lucid and
    bright,
With floods of the yellow gold of the gorgeous, indolent, sinking sun, burn-
    ing, expanding the air,
With the fresh sweet herbage under foot, and the pale green leaves of the
    trees prolific,
In the distance the flowing glaze, the breast of the river, with a wind-dapple   85
    here and there,
With ranging hills on the banks, with many a line against the sky, and
    shadows,
And the city at hand with dwellings so dense, and stacks of chimneys,
And all the scenes of life and the workshops, and the workmen
    homeward returning.

12

Lo, body and soul—this land,
My own Manhattan with spires, and the sparkling and hurrying tides,   90
    and the ships,
The varied and ample land, the South and the North in the light, Ohio's
    shores and flashing Missouri,
And ever the far-spreading prairies cover'd with grass and corn.

Lo, the most excellent sun so calm and haughty,
The violet and purple morn with just-felt breezes,
The gentle soft-born measureless light,   95
The miracle spreading bathing all, the fulfill'd noon,
The coming eve delicious, the welcome night and the stars,
Over my cities shining all, enveloping man and land.

13

Sing on, sing on you gray-brown bird,
Sing from the swamps, the recesses, pour your chant from the bushes, 100
Limitless out of the dusk, out of the cedars and pines.

Sing on dearest brother, warble your reedy song,
Loud human song, with voice of uttermost woe.

O liquid and free and tender!
O wild and loose to my soul—O wondrous singer! 105
You only I hear—yet the star holds me, (but will soon depart,)
Yet the lilac with mastering odor holds me.

14

Now while I sat in the day and look'd forth,
In the close of the day with its light and the fields of spring, and the farmers
    preparing their crops,
In the large unconscious scenery of my land with its lakes and forests, 110
In the heavenly aerial beauty, (after the perturb'd winds and the storms,)
Under the arching heavens of the afternoon swift passing, and the
    voices of children and women,
The many-moving sea-tides, and I saw the ships how they sail'd,
And the summer approaching with richness, and the fields all busy with
    labor,
And the infinite separate houses, how they all went on, each with its meals 115
    and minutia of daily usages,
And the streets how their throbbings throbb'd, and the cities pent—lo, then
    and there,
Falling upon them all and among them all, enveloping me with the rest,
Appear'd the cloud, appear'd the long black trail,
And I knew death, its thought, and the sacred knowledge of death.

Then with the knowledge of death as walking one side of me, 120
And the thought of death close-walking the other side of me,
And I in the middle as with companions, and as holding the hands of
    companions,
I fled forth to the hiding receiving night that talks not,
Down to the shores of the water, the path by the swamp in the dimness,
To the solemn shadowy cedars and ghostly pines so still. 125

And the singer so shy to the rest receiv'd me,
The gray-brown bird I know receiv'd us comrades three,
And he sang the carol of death, and a verse for him I love.

From deep secluded recesses,
From the fragrant cedars and the ghostly pines so still, 130
Came the carol of the bird.

And the charm of the carol rapt me,
As I held as if by their hands my comrades in the night,
And the voice of my spirit tallied the song of the bird.

Come lovely and soothing death,   135
Undulate round the world, serenely arriving, arriving,
In the day, in the night, to all, to each,
Sooner or later delicate death.

Prais'd be the fathomless universe,
For life and joy, and for objects and knowledge curious,   140
And for love, sweet love—but praise! praise! praise!
For the sure-enwinding arms of cool-enfolding death.

Dark mother always gliding near with soft feet,
Have none chanted for thee a chant of fullest welcome?
Then I chant it for thee, I glorify thee above all,   145
I bring thee a song that when thou must indeed come, come unfalteringly.

Approach strong deliveress,
When it is so, when thou hast taken them I joyously sing the dead,
Lost in the loving floating ocean of thee,
Laved in the flood of thy bliss O death.   150

From me to thee glad serenades,
Dances for thee I propose saluting thee, adornments and feastings for thee,
And the sights of the open landscape and the high-spread sky are
*   fitting,*
And life and the fields, and the huge and thoughtful night.

The night in silence under many a star,   155
The ocean shore and the husky whispering wave whose voice I know,
And the soul turning to thee O vast and well-veil'd death,
And the body gratefully nestling close to thee.

Over the tree-tops I float thee a song,
Over the rising and sinking waves, over the myriad fields and the prairies wide,   160
Over the dense-pack'd cities all and the teeming wharves and ways,
I float this carol with joy, with joy to thee O death.

15

To the tally of my soul,
Loud and strong kept up the gray-brown bird,
With pure deliberate notes spreading filling the night.   165

Loud in the pines and cedars dim,
Clear in the freshness moist and the swamp-perfume,
And I with my comrades there in the night.

While my sight that was bound in my eyes unclosed,
As to long panoramas of visions. 170

And I saw askant the armies,
I saw as in noiseless dreams hundreds of battle-flags,
Borne through the smoke of the battles and pierc'd with missiles I saw them,
And carried hither and yon through the smoke, and torn and bloody,
And at last but a few shreds left on the staffs, (and all in silence,) 175
And the staffs all splinter'd and broken.

I saw battle-corpses, myriads of them,
And the white skeletons of young men, I saw them,
I saw the debris and debris of all the slain soldiers of the war,
But I saw they were not as was thought, 180
They themselves were fully at rest, they suffer'd not,
The living remain'd and suffer'd, the mother suffer'd,
And the wife and the child and the musing comrade suffer'd,
And the armies that remain'd suffer'd.

16

Passing the visions, passing the night, 185
Passing, unloosing the hold of my comrades' hands,
Passing the song of the hermit bird and the tallying song of my soul,
Victorious song, death's outlet song, yet varying ever-altering song,
As low and wailing, yet clear the notes, rising and falling, flooding the
    night,
Sadly sinking and fainting, as warning and warning, and yet again bursting 190
    with joy,
Covering the earth and filling the spread of the heaven,
As that powerful psalm in the night I heard from recesses,
Passing, I leave thee lilac with heart-shaped leaves,
I leave thee there in the door-yard, blooming, returning with spring.

I cease from my song for thee, 195
From my gaze on thee in the west, fronting the west, communing with thee,
O comrade lustrous with silver face in the night.
Yet each to keep and all, retrievements out of the night,
The song, the wondrous chant of the gray-brown bird,
And the tallying chant, the echo arous'd in my soul, 200
With the lustrous and drooping star with the countenance full of woe,
With the holders holding my hand nearing the call of the bird,
Comrades mine and I in the midst, and their memory ever to keep, for the
    dead I loved so well,
For the sweetest, wisest soul of all my days and lands—and this for his dear
    sake,
Lilac and star and bird twined with the chant of my soul, 205
There in the fragrant pines and the cedars dusk and dim.

TOPICS FOR CRITICAL THINKING

1. Whitman wrote "When Lilacs Last in the Dooryard Bloom'd" just after the assassination of President Abraham Lincoln on April 14, 1865. Explore the ways in which Whitman presents the slain president through the symbolism of the star, or "western orb," in the poem.

2. Consider the symbolic significance of the two other major tropes in the poem: the lilac and bird. What does each of these figures stand for?

3. How does the funeral procession serve to unify the divided nation in an act of mourning?

4. Explore Whitman's personification of death as a "strong deliveress." Examine the implied view of death the poet projects as he listens to "death's outlet song" in section 16.

TOPIC FOR CRITICAL WRITING

How is Lincoln's death itself symbolic of the nation's wounds? How does the poet's mourning for Lincoln open onto the larger project of seeking "reconciliation" between North and South after the Civil War?

WALT WHITMAN   *(1819–1892)*

I Saw in Louisiana a Live-Oak Growing   *(1860)*

I saw in Louisiana a live-oak growing,
All alone stood it and the moss hung down from the branches,
Without any companion it grew there uttering joyous leaves of dark green,
And its look, rude, unbending, lusty, made me think of myself,
But I wonder'd how it could utter joyous leaves standing alone there without   5
    its friend near, for I knew I could not,
And I broke off a twig with a certain number of leaves upon it, and twined
    around it a little moss,
And brought it away, and I have placed it in sight in my room,
It is not needed to remind me as of my own dear friends,
(For I believe lately I think of little else than of them,)
Yet it remains to me a curious token, it makes me think of manly love;   10
For all that, and though the live-oak glistens there in Louisiana solitary in
    a wide flat space,
Uttering joyous leaves all its life without a friend a lover near,
I know very well I could not.

TOPICS FOR CRITICAL THINKING

1. Describe Whitman's opening portrait of the live-oak tree. What does he emphasize in his impressions of it?

2. Pay close attention to Whitman's description of the tree "uttering joyous leaves." What does this depiction mirror in the poet's identity?

3. How does Whitman both identify with the live-oak and note its differences from himself?

TOPICS FOR CRITICAL WRITING

1. Whitman saves a twig from the tree as a "curious token" of what the tree symbolizes for him. What symbolic meaning does the live-oak represent?
2. What final realization does the poet come to about himself through musing on the tree's symbolic example?

WILLIAM CARLOS WILLIAMS   *(1883–1963)*

The Yachts   *(1935)*

contend in a sea which the land partly encloses
shielding them from the too-heavy blows
of an ungoverned ocean which when it chooses

tortures the biggest hulls, the best man knows
to pit against its beatings, and sinks them pitilessly.   5
Mothlike in mists, scintillant in the minute

brilliance of cloudless days, with broad bellying sails
they glide to the wind tossing green water
from their sharp prows while over them the crew crawls

ant-like, solicitously grooming them, releasing,   10
making fast as they turn, lean far over and having
caught the wind again, side by side, head for the mark.

In a well guarded arena of open water surrounded by
lesser and greater crafts which, sycophant, lumbering
and flittering follow them, they appear youthful, rare   15

as the light of a happy eye, live with the grace
of all that in the mind is fleckless, free and
naturally to be desired. Now the sea which holds them

is moody, lapping their glossy sides, as if feeling
for some slightest flaw but fails completely.   20
Today no race. Then the wind comes again. The yachts

move, jockeying for a start, the signal is set and they
are off. Now the waves strike at them but they are too
well made, the slip through, though they take in canvas.

Arms with hands grasping seek to clutch at the prows.   25
Bodies thrown recklessly in the way are cut aside.
It is a sea of faces about them in agony, in despair

until the horror of the race dawns staggering the mind,
the whole sea become an entanglement of watery bodies
lost to the world bearing what they can not hold. Broken,   30

beaten, desolate, reaching from the dead to be taken up
they cry out, failing, failing! their cries rising
in waves still as the skillful yachts pass over.

TOPICS FOR CRITICAL THINKING

1. Analyze the opening situation and setting as Williams presents them in the poem.
2. Does the fact that this poem was written in 1935 in the middle of the Great Depression clarify what is at stake in its presentation of the yacht race?
3. Do the yachts as symbols stand for more than one meaning?
4. What is the "horror" of the race that Williams alludes to in the poem?

TOPIC FOR CRITICAL WRITING

What qualities does Williams depict in the yachts? What do these qualities symbolize?

6　Myth

Literature's connections to myth are primordial, reaching back to ancient, oral traditions that predate writing. Mythic narratives take many forms and serve several cultural functions. Some myths tell stories of how life came into being; such **emergence myths** explain the origins of things and describe humanity's place in the world. For example, in the creation stories of the Hopi Pueblo tribe of the American Southwest, Grandmother Spider Woman assists in the metamorphosis of insects into animals and finally into human beings through four successive worlds of evolution. Similarly, the Book of Genesis gives the biblical account of the world's creation and the fall of humanity from the Garden of Eden. In the Greek tradition, the *Theogony* chronicles the mythic history of the Greek pantheon of gods. Such myths provide foundational narratives of a culture's world outlook. **Quest myths** offer exemplary models of heroism in the stories, say, of Prometheus's gift of fire to humanity after he stole it from the gods, or Beowulf's epic battle with the monster Grendel. Similarly, the myth of Psyche tells the story of a woman's trials in pursuing the love of the god Cupid.

By giving a deep, structural understanding of the way things are, myth has a powerful shaping influence on basic beliefs, forms of worship, civic governance, tribal customs, social practices, gender roles, sexual behavior, and the makeup of everyday life. Myths also provide a rich cultural resource for poetry. In the epic tradition, Virgil's *The Aeneid* and John Milton's *Paradise Lost* make instructive, or didactic, use of mythic narratives to lend shape and significance to the past.

In lyric modes, poets reinterpret classical myths as, for example, W. H. Auden does in his rereading of Pieter Breughel's sixteenth-century painting *Landscape with the Fall of Icarus* (see color insert).

W. H. AUDEN　*(1907–1973)*

Musée des Beaux Arts　*(1940)*

About suffering they were never wrong,
The Old Masters: how well they understood
Its human position; how it takes place
While someone else is eating or opening a window or just walking
　　dully along;

How, when the aged are reverently, passionately waiting   5
For the miraculous birth, there always must be
Children who did not specially want it to happen, skating
On a pond at the edge of the wood:
They never forgot
That even the dreadful martyrdom must run its course   10
Anyhow in a corner, some untidy spot
Where the dogs go on with their doggy life and the torturer's horse
Scratches its innocent behind on a tree.

In Breughel's *Icarus*, for instance: how everything turns away
Quite leisurely from the disaster; the ploughman may   15
Have heard the splash, the forsaken cry,
But for him it was not an important failure; the sun shone
As it had to on the white legs disappearing into the green
Water; and the expensive delicate ship that must have seen
Something amazing, a boy falling out of the sky,   20
Had somewhere to get to and sailed calmly on.

To understand Auden's point about Breughel's painting, one has to know
something of the myth of Icarus. The myth of Icarus and his father Daedalus
has deep roots in the world of classical antiquity. The Roman poet Ovid, the
Greek writer Apollodorus, and Diodorus of Sicily all tell of Daedalus's exploits. The master craftsperson of the ancient world, Daedalus was commissioned by King Minos of the island of Crete to design the Labyrinth that
housed the mythic Minotaur. The Minotaur was the offspring of Minos's wife,
Pasiphaë and a bull, the gift from Poseidon, the god of the Sea. Poseidon had
given the bull to Minos to be sacrificed, but Minos kept it for himself instead.
As punishment, Poseidon had Pasiphaë fall in love with it. The Minotaur was
housed in the Labyrinth and each spring Minos required the sacrifice of seven
Athenian maidens and youths to the monster as tribute. Daedalus helped Ari-
adne show the Athenian hero Theseus how to escape the maze after killing
the Minotaur and, as punishment, Minos imprisoned both Daedalus and
Icarus in the Labyrinth. To escape from Crete, Daedalus fashioned wings held
together with wax. Before taking off, Daedalus gave his son the warning not
to fly too close to the sun because the heat would melt the wings. Icarus, of
course, did not take his father's advice and thus fell to his death in the sea.
Traditionally, the myth has been considered an allegory for the impetuousness
of youth, but this is not the lesson of Auden's poem.

TOPICS FOR CRITICAL THINKING

1. What point does Auden make about the "human position" of suffering in the first
   stanza of the poem?
2. What examples does Auden give of suffering that go unnoticed in life?
3. Do you agree with Auden's interpretation of Breughel's *Icarus?* Are there other
   ways to consider the painting? Explain.

TOPIC FOR CRITICAL WRITING

Where does Breughel place Icarus in the frame of his painting? What point does Auden make in his second stanza about the visual arrangement of Breughel's painting?

Auden interprets Breughel's representation of a famous myth to present the ways in which we ignore and even resist acknowledging the suffering of others. Myth can also offer new perspectives on experience, as when Anne Sexton returns to the story of Icarus. Her poem "To a Friend Whose Work Has Come to Triumph" muses on myth not so much to draw a moral lesson from it, but more to identify with Icarus's flight.

ANNE SEXTON   *(1928–1974)*

To a Friend Whose Work Has Come to Triumph   *(1962)*

Consider Icarus, pasting those sticky wings on,
testing that strange little tug at his shoulder blade,
and think of that first flawless moment over the lawn
of the labyrinth. Think of the difference it made!
There below are the trees, as awkward as camels;   5
and here are the shocked starlings pumping past
and think of innocent Icarus who is doing quite well:
larger than a sail, over the fog and the blast
of the plushy ocean, he goes. Admire his wings!
Feel the fire at his neck and see how casually   10
he glances up and is caught, wondrously tunneling
into that hot eye. Who cares that he fell back to the sea?
See him acclaiming the sun and come plunging down
while his sensible daddy goes straight into town.

TOPICS FOR CRITICAL THINKING

1. Sexton wrote this poem after the poet W. D. Snodgrass, one of Sexton's teachers, won the Pulitzer Prize for poetry in 1960. The poem expresses her joy in her mentor's achievement. What relationship do you draw between Icarus and the poet's vocation?
2. In imagining Icarus's flight, Sexton invites us to "Think of the difference it made!" What difference does it make, do you think?
3. What is Sexton's point in saying "Who cares that he fell back to the sea?"
4. Sexton herself luxuriated in her sunbaths. "All my life," she once said, "I have been in love with the sun. I looked at it as the great lover, the great seizure. Somehow, letting the sun wash over you, letting its heat adore you, was like having intercourse with God." How does she encourage us as readers toward that kind of ecstasy in the poem by asking us to "feel the fire at his neck" in the moment of glory "acclaiming the sun"?

TOPIC FOR CRITICAL WRITING

Contrast Auden's point of view with the ways in which Sexton urges us not just to "consider" Icarus but more actively to "see him" and even identify with his experience of flight.

Poets not only employ allusions to classical mythology in describing universal truths about the human condition. They also dramatize the expressive possibilities of the mythic imagination beyond conventional modes of being. For example, in her poem "Jacklight," the Native American writer Louise Erdrich revisits the boundary between the human and animal world that in Chippewa myth fuses hunting, seduction, and sexuality.

LOUISE ERDRICH   *(b. 1955)*

Jacklight   *(1984)*

The same Chippewa word is used both for
flirting and hunting game, while another
Chippewa word connotes both using force in
intercourse and also killing a bear with
one's bare hands.
     —R. W. DUNNING, SOCIAL AND ECONOMIC
        CHANGE AMONG THE NORTHERN OJIBWA
                                    (1959)

We have come to the edge of the woods,
out of brown grass where we slept, unseen,
out of knotted twigs, out of leaves creaked shut,
out of hiding.

At first the light wavered, glancing over us.   5
Then it clenched to a fist of light that pointed,
searched out, divided us.
Each took the beams like direct blows the heart answers.
Each of us moved forward alone.

We have come to the edge of the woods,   10
drawn out of ourselves by this night sun,
this battery of polarized acids,
that outshines the moon.

We smell them behind it
but they are faceless, invisible.   15
We smell the raw steel of their gun barrels,
mink oil on leather, their tongues of sour barley.
We smell their mothers buried chin-deep in wet dirt.

We smell their fathers with scoured knuckles,
teeth cracked from hot marrow.   20
We smell their sisters of crushed dogwood, bruised apples,
of fractured cups and concussions of burnt hooks.

We smell their breath steaming lightly behind the jacklight.
We smell the itch underneath the caked guts on their clothes.
We smell their minds like silver hammers   25
cocked back, held in readiness
for the first of us to step into the open.

We have come to the edge of the woods,
out of brown grass where we slept, unseen,
out of leaves creaked shut, out of our hiding.   30
We have come here too long.

It is their turn now,
their turn to follow us. Listen,
they put down their equipment.
It is useless in the tall brush.   35
And now they take the first steps, not knowing
how deep the woods are and lightless.
How deep the woods are.

TOPICS FOR CRITICAL THINKING

1. As her epigraph from R. W. Dunning implies, Erdrich locates mythic connections
   in Chippewa language between hunting and flirting, between sexual violence and
   the force of "killing a bear with one's bare hands." How do those mythic connections shape the dramatic conflict in "Jacklight"?

2. How do you interpret the action represented in the poem's final stanza? What do
   you think Erdrich's point is in repeating the phrasing "how deep the woods are" in
   her last two lines?

TOPIC FOR CRITICAL WRITING

A jacklight is a powerful flashlight, car headlight, or search light used illegally to startle game while hunting at night. Discuss the world that Erdrich associates with the
jacklight through her poem's imagery and figurative language. What effect does the
jacklight have on the hunters' intended prey? How do they resist the forces the jacklight represents?

Poems for Further Reading and Critical Writing

LOUISE GLÜCK   *(b. 1943)*

Mythic Fragment   *(1985)*

When the stern god
approached me with his gift
my fear enchanted him
so that he ran more quickly
through the wet grass, as he insisted,   5
to praise me. I saw captivity
in praise; against the lyre,
I begged my father in the sea
to save me. When
the god arrived, I was nowhere,   10
I was in a tree forever. Reader,
pity Apollo: at the water's edge,
I turned from him, I summoned
my invisible father—as
I stiffened in the god's arms,   15
of his encompassing love
my father made
no other sign from the water.

TOPICS FOR CRITICAL THINKING

1. Glück's "Mythic Fragment" alludes to the Roman tale told by Ovid of Daphne's metamorphosis into a laurel tree. Daphne, the daughter of the river-god Peneus, was a nymph who resisted the idea of marriage in favor of leading the independent life of a huntress, like the goddess Diana. Pursued in the forest by Apollo—the god of song, sun, and perfect form—she called on her father for help. Accordingly, Peneus transformed her into a laurel tree, which became sacred to Apollo. How does the poet portray Apollo's romantic interest in Daphne? Why, according to Glück, is Apollo attracted to Daphne?

2. Why do you think Daphne associates Apollo's praise with captivity? What kind of general comment on relationships is Glück making here?

3. Why does Daphne call on the reader to pity Apollo when she is transformed into a tree?

4. What is Daphne's attitude toward her metamorphosis, and do you detect any pun in her lines "as / I stiffened in the god's arms, / of his encompassing love"? How do you interpret her final lines about her father?

TOPIC FOR CRITICAL WRITING

Compare Glück's use of the dramatic monologue to rewrite classical mythology with T. S. Eliot's dramatic persona in "Journey of the Magi."

T. S. ELIOT   *(1888–1965)*

Journey of the Magi   *(1927)*

"A cold coming we had of it,
Just the worst time of the year
For a journey, and such a long journey:
The ways deep and the weather sharp,
The very dead of winter."   5
And the camels galled, sore-footed, refractory,
Lying down in the melting snow.
There were times we regretted
The summer palaces on slopes, the terraces,
And the silken girls bringing sherbet.   10
Then the camel men cursing and grumbling
And running away, and wanting their liquor and women,
And the night-fires going out, and the lack of shelters,
And the cities hostile and the towns unfriendly
And the villages dirty and charging high prices: 15
A hard time we had of it.
At the end we preferred to travel all night,
Sleeping in snatches,
With the voices singing in our ears, saying
That this was all folly.   20

Then at dawn we came down to a temperate valley,
Wet, below the snow line, smelling of vegetation;
With a running stream and a water-mill beating the darkness,
And three trees on the low sky,
And an old white horse galloped away in the meadow.   25
Then we came to a tavern with vine-leaves over the lintel,
Six hands at an open door dicing for pieces of silver,
And feet kicking the empty wine-skins,
But there was no information, and so we continued
And arrived at evening, not a moment too soon   30
Finding the place; it was (you may say) satisfactory.

All this was a long time ago, I remember,
And I would do it again, but set down
This set down

This: were we led all that way for   35
Birth or Death? There was a Birth, certainly,
We had evidence and no doubt. I had seen birth and death,
But had thought they were different; this Birth was
Hard and bitter agony for us, like Death, our death.
We returned to our places, these Kingdoms,   40
But no longer at ease here, in the old dispensation,
With an alien people clutching their gods.
I should be glad of another death.

TOPICS FOR CRITICAL THINKING

1. T. S. Eliot bases the first five lines of his poem on a sermon delivered by Bishop Lancelot Andrewes in 1622. The biblical subtext for the poem comes from Matthew 2:1–2:

   > 1 NOW after Jesus was born in Bethlehem of Judea in the days of Herod the king, magi from the east arrived in Jerusalem, saying,
   > 2 Where is He who has been born King of the Jews? For we saw His star in the east and have come to worship Him.

   How does Eliot imagine the actual journey made by the Magi? What details does he use to depict their quest?

2. The three trees of the third stanza, as well as the images of dicing and the pieces of silver, all have symbolic resonance with the story of Christ's crucifixion in the three crosses, the Roman soldiers' gambling for Christ's robe, and Judas Iscariot's betrayal of Christ for silver. What is Eliot's purpose in alluding to the crucifixion in a poem about Christ's nativity?

3. How do you interpret the poem's final line?

TOPIC FOR CRITICAL WRITING

What is the effect of the journey on the Magus? In what ways has he become alienated from the "old dispensation"?

LESLIE MARMON SILKO   *(b. 1948)*

Prayer to the Pacific   *(1981)*

I traveled to the ocean
              distant
                    from my southwest land of sandrock
                    to the moving blue water
              Big as the myth of origin.   5

Pale
pale water in the yellow-white light of
     sun floating west
       to China
     where ocean herself was born.   10
Clouds that blow across the sand are wet.

Squat in the wet sand and speak to the Ocean:
   I return to you turquoise the red coral you sent us,
     sister spirit of Earth.
Four round stones in my pocket I carry back the ocean   15
     to suck and to taste.

Thirty thousand years ago
     Indians came riding across the ocean
     carried by giant sea turtles.
Waves were high that day   20
    great sea turtles waded slowly out
       from the gray sundown sea.
Grandfather Turtle rolled in the sand four times
     and disappeared
       swimming into the sun.   25
And so from that time
    immemorial,
      as the old people say,
rain clouds drift from the west
     gift from the ocean.   30

Green leaves in the wind
Wet earth on my feet
    swallowing raindrops
      clear from China.

TOPICS FOR CRITICAL THINKING

1. Silko is of mixed Pueblo, Laguna, Mexican, and white descent lines. Her novels—
   Ceremony (1977), *Almanac of the Dead* (1991), *Yellow Woman* (1993), and *Gardens
   Among the Dunes* (1999), among other works—dwell on the Southwest Laguna
   Pueblo culture near Albuquerque, New Mexico, where she grew up. In "Prayer to
   the Pacific," she offers "turquoise" and "red coral" from her native "southwest land
   of sandrock" to the Pacific Ocean. In what terms does she personify the ocean in
   the poem?

2. In what ways does the poem perform the prayer or ritual of return to the ocean?

3. What does the ocean have to do with the desert landscape of the southwest?

4. In Silko's version of the Native American myth of origin, Grandfather Turtle rides
   sea turtles across the ocean "thirty thousand years ago." This myth may allude to
   the Beringia land bridge across the fifty-five-mile wide Bering Strait that today separates Siberia from Alaska's Seward Peninsula. During the periods of Ice Age

glaciation in the Pleistocene era, the Bering Straight periodically froze and served as a land bridge allowing for the prehistoric peopling of the Americas from Asia between 40,000 to 13,000 years ago. At times during the Ice Age, so much of the Earth's supply of water took the form of glaciers that sea levels fell to 350 feet below today's levels, allowing for travel across Beringia, the Bering Straight sea bed now covered in water. In what ways does Silko lend a mythic dimension to this prehistoric migration?

TOPIC FOR CRITICAL WRITING

Compare the mythic presentation of the natural world in Silko's "Prayer to the Pacific" with Erdrich's "Jacklight."

The Chicana poet Pat Mora adopts the mythic persona of the Mexican goddess Coatlicue to give advice in "Coatlicue's Rules: Advice from an Aztec Goddess." Her poem presents a whimsical fusion of ancient wisdom and contemporary self-help tips.

PAT MORA   *(b. 1942)*

Coatlicue's Rules: Advice from an Aztec Goddess   *(1995)*

Rule 1: Beware of offers to make you famous.

I, pious Aztec mother lost in housework,
am pedestaled, "She of the Serpent Skirt,"
necklace dangling hearts and hands, faceless
statue, two snakes eye-to-eye on my shoulders,   5
goddess of earth, also death, which leads to

Rule 2: Retain control of your own publicity.

Past is present. Women are women.
I'm not competitive and motherhood isn't
about numbers, but four hundred sons and a daughter   10
may be a record even without the baby.
There's something wrong in this world
if a woman isn't safe even when she sweeps
her own house, when any speck can enter even through
the eye, I'll bet, and become a stubborn tenant.   15

Rule 3: Protect your uterus.

Conceptions, immaculate and otherwise, happen.
Women swallow sacred stones that fill their bellies
with elbows and knees. In Guatemala, a skull dangling
from a tree whispers, "Touch me,"   20
to a young girl, and a clear drop

drips on her palm, disappears. Dew
drops in, if you know what I mean.
Saliva moved in her, the girl says. Moved in, I say,
settled into that empty space, and grew. Men know.   25
They stay full of themselves, keeps occupancy down.

Rule 4: Avoid housework.

Remember, I was sweeping, humming, actually,
high on Coatepec, our Serpent Mountain, humming loud
so I wouldn't hear all those sighs inside.   30
I was sweeping slivers, gold and jade, picking up
after four hundred sons who think they're gods,
and their spoiled sister. I was sweeping
when feathers fell on me, brushed my face,
first light touch in years, like in a dream.   35

At first, I just blew them off, then I saw
the prettiest ball of tiny plumes, glowing
green and gold. Gently, I gathered it. Oh,
it was soft as baby hair, brought back mother-
shivers when I pressed it to my skin. I nestled it   40
like I used to nestle them, here,
when they finished nursing. Maybe I even stroked
the roundness. I have since heard that feathers
aren't that unusual at annunciations, but I was innocent.

After sweeping, I looked in vain inside   45
my clothes, but the soft ball had vanished, well,
descended. I think I showed within the hour,
or so it seemed. They noticed first, of course.

Rule 5: Avoid housework. It bears repeating.

I was too busy washing, cooking, sweeping again,   50
worrying about my daughter, Painted with Bells,
when I began to bump into their frowns
and mutterings. They kept glancing at my stomach,
started pointing. I got so hurt and mad, I started crying.
Why do they get to us? One wrong word or look   55
from any one of them doubles me over,
and I've had four hundred and one, no anesthetic.
Near them I'm like a snail with no shell on a sizzling day.
They started yelling, "Wicked, wicked," and my daughter,
right there with them, my wannabe warrior boy.   60

The yelling was easier than the whispers, "Kill. Kill.
Kill. Kill." Kill me? Their mother?

One against four hundred and one? All I'd done
was press that feathered softness into me.

Rule 6: Listen to inside voices.   65

You mothers know about the baby in a family, right?
Even if he hadn't talked to me from deep inside,
he would have been special. Maybe the best.
But as my name is Coatlicue, he did.
That unborn child, that started as a ball of feathers   70
all soft green and gold, heard my woes, and spoke to me.
A thoughtful boy. And formal too. He said, "Do not be afraid,
I know what I must do." So I stopped shaking.

Rule 7: Verify that the inside voice is yours.

I'll spare you the part about the body hacking   75
and head rolling. But he was provoked, remember.
All this talk of gods and goddesses distorts.

This planet wasn't big enough for all of us,
but my whole family has done well for itself, I think.
I'm the mother of stars. My daughter's white head   80
rolls round the heavens each night, and my sons
wink down at me. What can I say—a family
of high visibility. The baby? Up there also, the sun,
the real thing. Such a god he is, of war unfortunately,
and the boy never stops, always racing across the sky,   85
every day of the year, a ball of fire since birth.
But I think he has forgotten me. You sense my ambivalence.
I'm blinded by his light.

Rule 8: Insist on personal interviews.

Past is present, remember. Men carved me,   90
wrote my story, and Eve's, Malinche's, Guadalupe's,
Llorona's, snakes everywhere, even in our mouths.

Rule 9: Be selective about what you swallow.

TOPICS FOR CRITICAL THINKING

1. Coatlicue means "she of the Serpent Skirt." In Aztec iconography, Coatlicue is depicted as wearing a skirt of snakes and a necklace made out of human hearts. How does Mora's first rule of advice "Beware of offers to make you famous" reflect ironically on Coatlicue's mythic status?

2. While sweeping in a temple, Coatlicue was struck by a mysterious ball of feathers and immediately gave birth to Huitzilopochtli, the Aztec sun god. Discuss how Mora rewrites this immaculate conception story as a contemporary advice-to-women narrative in rules 3 and 4.

3. Angered by her mother's pregnancy, Coyolxauhqui, the goddess of the Moon, persuaded Coatlicue's four hundred children to try and kill her. Coatlicue was saved by Huitzilopochtli. Discuss Mora's rewriting of this narrative in rule 5.

4. Choose a mythic persona to offer self-help tips and advice of your own.

TOPIC FOR CRITICAL WRITING

How does Mora portray Coatlicue's "ambivalence" toward her son and her own legacy in the poem?

WALT WHITMAN   *(1819–1892)*

from Song of Myself (Section 24)   *(1855)*

24

Walt Whitman, a kosmos, of Manhattan the son,
Turbulent, fleshy, sensual, eating, drinking and breeding,
No sentimentalist, no stander above men and women or apart from them,
No more modest than immodest.

Unscrew the locks from the doors!   5
Unscrew the doors themselves from their jambs!

Whoever degrades another degrades me,
And whatever is done or said returns at last to me.

Through me the afflatus surging and surging, through me the current and
     index.

I speak the pass-word primeval, I give the sign of democracy,   10
By God! I will accept nothing which all cannot have their counterpart of on
     the same terms.

Through me many long dumb voices,
Voices of the interminable generations of prisoners and slaves,
Voices of the diseas'd and despairing and of thieves and dwarfs,
Voices of cycles of preparation and accretion,   15
And of the threads that connect the stars, and of wombs and of the father-
     stuff,
And of the rights of them the others are down upon,

Of the deform'd, trivial, flat, foolish, despised,
Fog in the air, beetles rolling balls of dung.

Through me forbidden voices,   20
Voices of sexes and lusts, voices veil'd and I remove the veil,
Voices indecent by me clarified and transfigur'd.

I do not press my fingers across my mouth,
I keep as delicate around the bowels as around the head and heart,
Copulation is no more rank to me than death is.   25

I believe in the flesh and the appetites,
Seeing, hearing, feeling, are miracles, and each part and tag of me is a
    miracle.

Divine am I inside and out, and I make holy whatever I touch or am touch'd
    from,
The scent of these arm-pits aroma finer than prayer,
This head more than churches, bibles, and all the creeds.   30

If I worship one thing more than another it shall be the spread of my own
    body, or any part of it,
Translucent mould of me it shall be you!
Shaded ledges and rests it shall be you!
Firm masculine colter it shall be you!
Whatever goes to the tilth of me it shall be you!   35
You my rich blood! your milky stream pale strippings of my life!
Breast that presses against other breasts it shall be you!
My brain it shall be your occult convolutions!
Root of wash'd sweet-flag! timorous pond-snipe! nest of guarded duplicate
    eggs! it shall be you!
Mix'd tussled hay of head, beard, brawn, it shall be you!   40
Trickling sap of maple, fibre of manly wheat, it shall be you!
Sun so generous it shall be you!
Vapors lighting and shading my face it shall be you!
You sweaty brooks and dews it shall be you!
Winds whose soft-tickling genitals rub against me it shall be you!   45
Broad muscular fields, branches of live oak, loving lounger in my winding
    paths, it shall be you!
Hands I have taken, face I have kiss'd, mortal I have ever touch'd, it shall be
    you.

I dote on myself, there is that lot of me and all so luscious,
Each moment and whatever happens thrills me with joy,
I cannot tell how my ankles bend, nor whence the cause of my faintest wish, 50
Nor the cause of the friendship I emit, nor the cause of the friendship I take
    again.

That I walk up my stoop, I pause to consider if it really be,
A morning-glory at my window satisfies me more than the metaphysics of
    books.

To behold the day-break!
The little light fades the immense and diaphanous shadows,   55
The air tastes good to my palate.

Hefts of the moving world at innocent gambols silently rising, freshly
    exuding,
Scooting obliquely high and low.

Something I cannot see puts upward libidinous prongs,
Seas of bright juice suffuse heaven.   60

The earth by the sky staid with, the daily close of their junction,
The heav'd challenge from the east that moment over my head,
The mocking taunt, See then whether you shall be master!

TOPICS FOR CRITICAL THINKING

1. In the opening six lines of section 24 of "Song of Myself," examine the terms in which Whitman creates a myth of the modern self, one grounded in a frank openness concerning the body, its energies, and desires.
2. Discuss Whitman's catalogue of the body and the ways in which the body fuses with the natural landscape.

TOPIC FOR CRITICAL WRITING

How does Whitman understand that mythic sense of self as also a "democratic" identity made up of a plurality of "voices"?

PERCY BYSSHE SHELLEY   *(1792–1822)*

Ode to the West Wind   *(1820)*

1

O wild West Wind, thou breath of Autumn's being,
Thou, from whose unseen presence the leaves dead
Are driven, like ghosts from an enchanter fleeing,

Yellow, and black, and pale, and hectic red,
Pestilence-stricken multitudes: O thou,   5
Who chariotest to their dark wintry bed

The wingéd seeds, where they lie cold and low,
Each like a corpse within its grave, until
Thine azure sister of the Spring shall blow

Her clarion o'er the dreaming earth, and fill   10
(Driving sweet buds like flocks to feed in air)
With living hues and odors plain and hill:

Wild Spirit, which art moving everywhere;
Destroyer and preserver; hear, oh, hear!

2

Thou on whose stream, mid the steep sky's commotion,   15
Loose clouds like earth's decaying leaves are shed,
Shook from the tangled boughs of Heaven and Ocean,

Angels of rain and lightning: there are spread
On the blue surface of thine aëry surge,
Like the bright hair uplifted from the head   20

Of some fierce Maenad,° even from the dim verge
Of the horizon to the zenith's height,
The locks of the approaching storm. Thou dirge

Of the dying year, to which this closing night
Will be the dome of a vast sepulcher,   25
Vaulted with all thy congregated might

Of vapors, from whose solid atmosphere
Black rain, and fire, and hail will burst: oh, hear!

3

Thou who didst waken from his summer dreams
The blue Mediterranean, where he lay,   30
Lulled by the coil of his crystálline streams,

Beside a pumice isle in Baiae's bay,°
And saw in sleep old palaces and towers
Quivering within the wave's intenser day,

All overgrown with azure moss and flowers   35
So sweet, the sense faints picturing them! Thou
For whose path the Atlantic's level powers

_____

21 *Maenad:* A female worshipper of Dionysus.   32 *Baiae's bay:* A bay near Naples.

Cleave themselves into chasms, while far below
The sea-blooms and the oozy woods which wear
The sapless foliage of the ocean, know   40

Thy voice, and suddenly grow gray with fear,
And tremble and despoil themselves: oh, hear!

4

If I were a dead leaf thou mightest bear;
If I were a swift cloud to fly with thee;
A wave to pant beneath thy power, and share   45

The impulse of thy strength, only less free
Than thou, O uncontrollable! If even
I were as in my boyhood, and could be

The comrade of thy wanderings over Heaven,
As then, when to outstrip thy skyey speed   50
Scarce seemed a vision; I would ne'er have striven

As thus with thee in prayer in my sore need.
Oh, lift me as a wave, a leaf, a cloud!
I fall upon the thorns of life! I bleed!

A heavy weight of hours has chained and bowed   55
One too like thee: tameless, and swift, and proud.

5

Make me thy lyre, even as the forest is:
What if my leaves are falling like its own!
The tumult of thy mighty harmonies

Will take from both a deep, autumnal tone,   60
Sweet though in sadness. Be thou, Spirit fierce,
My spirit! Be thou me, impetuous one!

Drive my dead thoughts over the universe
Like withered leaves to quicken a new birth!
And, by the incantation of this verse,   65

Scatter, as from an unextinguished hearth
Ashes and sparks, my words among mankind!
Be through my lips to unawakened earth

The trumpet of a prophecy! O, Wind,
If Winter comes, can Spring be far behind?   70

TOPICS FOR CRITICAL THINKING

1. The year 1819 was a highly creative one in Shelley's life; he composed *Prometheus Unbound, The Cenci, The Mask of Anarchy,* and *A Philosophical View of Reform.* But it was also a year marked by the tragic deaths of his children Clara and William. The cycles of birth and death, creation and destruction, life and death weighed on Shelley's mind when he composed "Ode to the West Wind" while living in Florence. How does Shelley depict the wind's mythic agency as both a "Destroyer and Preserver" in its seasonal roles?

2. Examine the natural metaphors Shelley employs to describe his relation to the West Wind in section 4 of the poem.

3. Discuss the musical metaphors Shelley develops in section 5 to describe the social and prophetic roles of his poetic vocation. How does poetry serve as the cure for Shelley's grief?

TOPIC FOR CRITICAL WRITING

The poem opens with the figure of apostrophe, and, following the etymology of the Latin *spiritus* that links breath, soul, and the spirit, Shelley personifies the West Wind as "thou breath of Autumn's being." What other personifications can you identify in the poem? How do they contribute to the poem's major themes?

7   Emotive Poetics

When William Wordsworth defined poetry in terms of "impassioned expression," he described what all good poets know: that verse writing involves the life of the emotions. Poetry, for Wordsworth, voices the "spontaneous overflow of powerful feelings." *Overflow* is the key word here. Deeply felt **emotive** states have a psychological urgency that demands utterance, as when John Keats begins his "Ode to a Nightingale" with the plaintive cry "My heart aches." Similarly, Wordsworth witnesses to poetry's almost therapeutic value. In his "Ode: Intimations of Immortality," he writes that "To me alone there came a thought of grief: / A timely utterance gave that thought relief, / And I again am strong."

Some poems take the experience of a dominant emotive state as in Wordsworth's "thought of grief" and make it the subject of an entire poem. For example, Theodore Roethke portrays his emotional theme in the title of his short lyric "Dolor."

THEODORE ROETHKE   *(1908–1963)*

Dolor   *(1942)*

I have known the inexorable sadness of pencils,
Neat in their boxes, dolor of pad and paper-weight,
All the misery of manila folders and mucilage,
Desolation in immaculate public places,
Lonely reception room, lavatory, switchboard,   5
The unalterable pathos of basin and pitcher,
Ritual of multigraph, paper-clip, comma,
Endless duplication of lives and objects.
And I have seen dust from the walls of institutions,
Finer than flour, alive, more dangerous than silica,   10
Sift, almost invisible, through long afternoons of tedium,
Dropping a fine film on nails and delicate eyebrows,
Glazing the pale hair, the duplicate grey standard faces.

TOPICS FOR CRITICAL THINKING

1. *Dolor* means sadness and comes from the Latin word for pain. What other key word choices unpack Roethke's emotional experience of dolor in the poem?

2. Of "Dolor" Roethke has written that "we continue to make a fetish of 'thing-hood,' we surround ourselves with junk, ugly objects endlessly repeated in an economy of waste." How does Roethke's poem assign dolor to things set in the dry institutional spaces of contemporary society?

TOPIC FOR CRITICAL WRITING

What thematic comment does Roethke make on the everyday monotony of today's standardized and homogeneous institutional settings?

Robert Bly, an American poet who was profoundly influenced by Theodore Roethke, explores a feeling at the opposite end of the emotive spectrum from "Dolor" in his poem "Waking from Sleep."

ROBERT BLY   *(b. 1926)*

Waking from Sleep   *(1962)*

Inside the veins there are navies setting forth,
Tiny explosions at the water lines,
And seagulls weaving in the wind of the salty blood.

It is the morning. The country has slept the whole winter.
Window seats were covered with fur skins, the yard was full   5
Of stiff dogs, and hands that clumsily held heavy books.

Now we wake, and rise from bed, and eat breakfast!—
Shouts rise from the harbor of the blood,
Mist, and masts rising, the knock of wooden tackle in the sunlight.

Now we sing, and do tiny dances on the kitchen floor.   10
Our whole body is like a harbor at dawn;
We know that our master has left us for the day.

TOPICS FOR CRITICAL THINKING

1. While Roethke relies on the literal presentation of standardized things to express dolor, Bly develops the emotions of waking through a highly metaphoric style. Discuss his major metaphor for the experience of waking up.
2. How does Bly depict this waking as a seasonal motif as well?
3. How would you characterize this poem's tone?

TOPIC FOR CRITICAL WRITING

The poem ends on an enigmatic note that presents waking as a new dawning of freedom, a lifting of repression communicated in the figurative phrase "We know that our master has left us for the day." How do you interpret this line?

In addition to depicting singular emotional states, it is not unusual for a poem to run the gamut of the emotions moving from despair to ecstatic joy, as in William Shakespeare's Sonnet 29.

WILLIAM SHAKESPEARE   *(1564–1616)*

Sonnet 29   *(1609)*

When, in disgrace with fortune and men's eyes,
I all alone beweep my outcast state,
And trouble deaf heaven with my bootless° cries
And look upon myself, and curse my fate,
Wishing me like to one more rich in hope,   5
Featured like him, like him with friends possessed,
Desiring this man's art and that man's scope
With what I most enjoy contented least;
Yet in these thoughts myself almost despising,
Haply I think on thee—and then my state,   10
Like to the lark at break of day arising
From sullen earth, sings hymns at heaven's gate;
   For thy sweet love rememb'red such wealth brings
   That then I scorn to change my state with kings.

Sonnet 29 begins with the emotions of despair, futility, envy, desire, and self-loathing. The whole movement of the poem's first eight lines reaches its lowest point in the line "With what I most enjoy contented least" where the nadir climaxes in the word *least*. However, as we move into the next line's qualification of "yet," a turning point frees the speaker from "despising" his own failures. "Haply" his thoughts turn to the lover, and through simile his mood ascends in the figure of the lark associated with the "day arising." Moving away from "sullen earth" in favor of "heaven's gate," the speaker finds joy in the final couplet through the insight that "sweet love" is of far greater value than either the wealth or scope of kings.

As we have seen, poetry has the power to depict primary emotions such as joy and sorrow, hope and despair, courage and fear, love and hate, wonder and apathy. But the emotive image can also be drawn in shades that obscure their differences. Like the primary colors of the painter's palette, basic emotional states can be rendered almost infinitely complex through their subtle merging in a poetic phrase, line, or stanza as in Galway Kinnell's "First Song."

---

3 *bootless:* Futile.

GALWAY KINNELL   *(b. 1927)*

First Song   *(1960)*

Then it was dusk in Illinois, the small boy
After an afternoon of carting dung
Hung on the rail fence, a sapped thing
Weary to crying. Dark was growing tall
And he began to hear the pond frogs all   5
Calling on his ear with what seemed their joy.

Soon their sound was pleasant for a boy
Listening in the smoky dusk and the nightfall
Of Illinois, and from the fields two small
Boys came bearing cornstalk violins   10
And they rubbed the cornstalk bows with resins
And the three sat there scraping of their joy.

It was now fine music the frogs and the boys
Did in the towering Illinois twilight make
And into dark in spite of a shoulder's ache   15
A boy's hunched body loved out of a stalk
The first song of his happiness, and the song woke
His heart to the darkness and into the sadness of joy.

Kinnell presents the Illinois farm boy after a hard day's work as "a sapped thing." He is worn out and "weary to crying." The fatigue of that sapped and weary emotional state is complicated, however, by the oncoming darkness that brings him the sounds of the frogs. Their call invokes a "pleasant" sense of "joy" to which the boy and his friends respond in making a "fine music" of their own out of "cornstalk violins." Their "first song" transforms the "shoulder's ache" into a kind of "happiness" but one that, in the "darkness," combines the opposite states of sadness and joy into a new, heartfelt emotion.

Such blending of opposites is called **oxymoron** from the Greek roots meaning sharp (*oxus*) and foolish (*moros*). Oxymoron is a rhetorical figure that combines contradictory terms such as *deafening silence, living death, solemn gaiety,* and so on. Thus, John Milton invokes the figure of oxymoron in describing the flames of hell as "darkness visible" while Walt Whitman characterizes a conflicted emotional state in terms of the "sweet hell within."

Whitman's contemporary, Emily Dickinson, also deftly described extreme and often clashing emotive states as in her Poem 258, "There's a certain Slant of light."

EMILY DICKINSON   *(1830–1886)*

Poem 258 (There's a certain Slant of light)   *(1861)*

There's a certain Slant of light,
Winter Afternoons —
That oppresses, like the Heft
Of Cathedral Tunes —

Heavenly Hurt, it gives us —   5
We can find no scar,
But internal difference,
Where the Meanings, are —

None may teach it — Any —
'Tis the Seal Despair —   10
An imperial affliction
Sent us of the air —

When it comes, the Landscape listens —
Shadows — hold their breath —
When it goes, 'tis like the Distance   15
On the look of Death —

Not unlike the sad joy that Kinnell recalls in "First Song," Dickinson explores here a contradictory psychic moment conveyed to her, strangely enough, in the quality or slant of light she witnesses on a winter afternoon. We don't usually think of light as having any mass, but Dickinson feels its weight in the heft, or oppressive heaviness, that she compares through simile to the mighty force of a cathedral organ. This is a metaphysical light, but it doesn't bestow the consolation of an assured faith or ideal meaning. Instead, its luminous trace is divisive and unsettling. It leaves behind an interior, emotive "scar" of "internal difference." Light descends on the poet as an agony that marks her not with any sign of grace but rather with the "Seal Despair." Dickinson relies on figurative language to capture the suspense of this beheld light in the personification of how the entire "Landscape listens" or how "Shadows — hold their breath." Simile estranges such personifications in the departing light that is "like the Distance / On the look of Death." Oxymoron most aptly captures the light's uncanny visitation. Such phrases as "Heavenly Hurt," "Seal Despair," and "imperial affliction" communicate the paradoxical mystery of the light's poignant grace.

In drawing attention to contradiction, oxymoron heightens our sense of the irony and paradox of everyday life. Stemming from the Greek root words meaning "beyond" (*para*) and "opinion" (*doxos*), **paradox** describes a contradictory experience, insight, or truth that cuts across the grain of our conventional expectations. Theodore Roethke was fond of using such paradoxes as "We think by feeling" or "In a dark time, the eye begins to see."

Irony, like paradox and oxymoron, dramatizes the ways in which certain experiences contain something of their opposites or when situations run contrary to expectation. In classical Greek mythology, it is ironic, for example, when Oedipus flees his supposed father Polybus seeking to avoid the Delphic oracle's prophecy that he would murder his father. What Oedipus doesn't know is that Polybus is his foster parent, and that the man Oedipus kills in a struggle at a crossroads on his way from Delphi to Thebes is, in fact, his real father King Laius. **Dramatic irony** builds when Oedipus, seeking to find the murderer, discovers that he is the guilty party and, worse, that he has married his mother, King Laius's wife Queen Jocasta. Sophocles' tragic drama *Oedipus Rex* turns on drawing out the suspense of this dramatic irony. In popular narrative, irony can become a source of wry humor, as in the film *Reality Bites*. Leaving the scene of yet another unsuccessful job interview, Winona Ryder is asked to define *irony* as the doors are about to close in an elevator. Not surprisingly, Ryder can't produce a definition on the spot, pointing out the film's central irony of the class valedictorian who can only get temp jobs. The pop star Alanis Morissette made irony the subject of her song "Ironic," defining irony as "the good advice that you just didn't take." Similarly, it's appropriately ironic that Dorothy Parker receives the symbol of love in "One Perfect Rose" when what she really desires is the material reward of "one perfect limousine." **Verbal irony** compresses such situational ironies into contradictory, ambiguous, and often sarcastic utterances, as when Allen Ginsberg in his poem "America" playfully asserts his determination to resist American middle-class conformity: "America I'm putting my queer shoulder to the wheel."

Poems for Further Reading and Critical Writing

EMILY DICKINSON   *(1830–1886)*

Poem 512 (The Soul has Bandaged moments)   *(1862)*

The Soul has Bandaged moments —
When, too appalled to stir —
She feels some ghastly Fright come up
And stop to look at her —

Salute her — with long fingers   5
Caress her freezing hair —
Sip, Goblin, from the very lips
The Lover — hovered — o'er —
Unworthy, that a thought so mean
Accost a Theme — so — fair —   10

The soul has moments of Escape —
When bursting all the doors —
She dances like a Bomb, abroad,
And swings upon the Hours,

As do the Bee — delirious borne —   15
Long Dungeoned from his Rose —
Touch Liberty — then know no more,
But Noon, and Paradise —

The Soul's retaken moments —
When, Felon led along,   20
With shackles on the plumed feet,
And staples, in the Song,

The Horror welcomes her, again,
These, are not brayed of Tongue —

TOPICS FOR CRITICAL THINKING

1. What are "Bandaged moments" in the life of the soul? Can you give examples of them? Examine the ways in which Dickinson presents these moments in the poem.
2. Compare and contrast the emotional extremities of Dickinson's psychological life in this poem.

TOPIC FOR CRITICAL WRITING

What examples of figurative language can you identify in the poet's characterization of the soul's various "moments"?

SYLVIA PLATH   *(1932–1963)*

Fever 103°   *(1962)*

Pure? What does it mean?
The tongues of hell
Are dull, dull as the triple

Tongues of dull, fat Cerberus
Who wheezes at the gate. Incapable   5
Of licking clean

The aguey tendon, the sin, the sin.
The tinder cries.
The indelible smell

Of a snuffed candle!   10
Love, love, the low smokes roll
From me like Isadora's scarves, I'm in a fright

One scarf will catch and anchor in the wheel.
Such yellow sullen smokes
Make their own element. They will not rise,   15

But trundle round the globe
Choking the aged and the meek,
The weak

Hothouse baby in its crib,
The ghastly orchid   20
Hanging its hanging garden in the air,

Devilish leopard!
Radiation turned it white
And killed it in an hour.

Greasing the bodies of adulterers   25
Like Hiroshima ash and eating in.
The sin. The sin.

Darling, all night
I have been flickering, off, on, off, on.
The sheets grow heavy as a lecher's kiss.   30

Three days. Three nights.
Lemon water, chicken
Water, water make me retch.

I am too pure for you or anyone.
Your body   35
Hurts me as the world hurts God. I am a lantern—

My head a moon
Of Japanese paper, my gold beaten skin
Infinitely delicate and infinitely expensive.

Does not my heat astound you. And my light.   40
All by myself I am a huge camellia
Glowing and coming and going, flush on flush.

I think I am going up,
I think I may rise—
The beads of hot metal fly, and I, love, I   45

Am a pure acetylene
Virgin
Attended by roses,

By kisses, by cherubim,
By whatever these pink things mean.   50
Not you, nor him.

Not him, nor him
(My selves dissolving, old whore petticoats)—
To Paradise.

TOPICS FOR CRITICAL THINKING

1. Given Plath's title, how would you characterize her emotional state in "Fever
   103°"?
2. Plath wrote "Fever 103°" during her separation from her husband, the poet Ted
   Hughes, owing in part to his infidelity. What references to adultery can you find in
   the poem? How do they function in the work?
3. How does the poet answer the question "Pure? What does it mean?" In what terms
   does she imagine her own metaphoric purity in the poem?

TOPIC FOR CRITICAL WRITING

Plath alludes to Cerberus, the three-headed dog that guards the gates to Hades in
Greek mythology, to Isadora Duncan, the American dance artist who was strangled
when her long scarf became tangled in the wheel spokes of a Bugati automobile, and
to Hiroshima, Japan, which was the target of an American nuclear bombing at the
close of World War II. How do you interpret these allusions? What functions do they
serve in the poem? Does Plath's identification with Japanese nuclear bomb victims run
the risk of trivializing their victimization?

WALT WHITMAN   *(1819–1892)*

from Song of Myself (Section 26)   *(1855)*

26

Now I will do nothing but listen,
To accrue what I hear into this song, to let sounds contribute toward it.

I hear bravuras of birds, bustle of growing wheat, gossip of flames, clack of
        sticks cooking my meals,
I hear the sound I love, the sound of the human voice,
I hear all sounds running together, combined, fused or following,   5
Sounds of the city and sounds out of the city, sounds of the day and night,

Talkative young ones to those that like them, the loud laugh of work-people
　　at their meals,
The angry base of disjointed friendship, the faint tones of the sick,
The judge with hands tight to the desk, his pallid lips pronouncing a death-
　　sentence,
The heave'e'yo of stevedores unlading ships by the wharves, the refrain of　　　10
　　the anchor-lifters,
The ring of alarm-bells, the cry of fire, the whirr of swift-streaking engines
　　and hose-carts with premonitory tinkles and color'd lights,
The steam whistle, the solid roll of the train of approaching cars,
The slow march play'd at the head of the association marching two and two,
(They go to guard some corpse, the flag-tops are draped with black muslin.)

I hear the violoncello, ('tis the young man's heart's complaint,)　　　　　　15
I hear the key'd cornet, it glides quickly in through my ears,
It shakes mad-sweet pangs through my belly and breast.
I hear the chorus, it is a grand opera,
Ah this indeed is music—this suits me.

A tenor large and fresh as the creation fills me,　　　　　　　　　　　　20
The orbic flex of his mouth is pouring and filling me full.

I hear the train'd soprano (what work with hers is this?)
The orchestra whirls me wider than Uranus flies,
It wrenches such ardors from me I did not know I possess'd them,
It sails me, I dab with bare feet, they are lick'd by the indolent waves,　　　25
I am cut by bitter and angry hail, I lose my breath,
Steep'd amid honey'd morphine, my windpipe throttled in fakes of death,
At length let up again to feel the puzzle of puzzles,
And that we call Being.

TOPIC FOR CRITICAL THINKING

How do the sounds Whitman hears from the orchestra and opera differ from those of
everyday life as he catalogs them above?

TOPIC FOR CRITICAL WRITING

Whitman says that the music "wrenches such ardors from me I did not know I possess'd them." Discuss the ways in which Whitman accounts for the emotional effect
the opera has on him.

8   Prosody

Prosody comes from the Greek word *prosodia* meaning "tune" and alludes to poetry's origins in song and the oral tradition. As an art form, poetry doesn't just belong to the page but reaches all the way back before the invention of printing or even writing. Today, however, unless we are creative writing majors or regulars at poetry slams and coffee houses, we mostly encounter verse in a book or, just as likely, on a computer screen. Poetry is more often read in the silent encounter of person and page. Thanks to the Internet, live-streaming, and digital technology, the oral dimension is returning to verse. Prosody, in any case, reminds us that poetry has always been an oral, performative art with roots not just in entertainment but in religious worship and ritual celebration. The word *lyric* derives from the Greek musical instrument, the *lyra*, and connotes poetry's strong ties to music and song. Similarly, in the ancient Old English tradition of the Beowulf poet, the poet was called a *scop* or *gleeman* and performed at court in song accompanied by the harp.

Sound

Beyond its origins in song, however, prosody describes poetry's material medium, which—insofar as it employs sound effects, rhyme, and rhythm—is more tangible and less transparent than prose. One reason we might find poetry more satisfying or stimulating than prose has to do with how we receive and make sense of the spoken rather than written word. Poetry, in fact, is a whole-brain activity that involves the bicameral mind. In a right-handed person, the left hemisphere of the brain is responsible for processing rational thought, cognition, and motor activity, while music is a right hemispheric activity. Poetry—because it involves both abstract thought and the material textures of rhyme, rhythm and sound—is processed by both sides of the brain. The prosodic aspects of poetry, like music, are right-brain activities and begin with the sounds of poetry.

Sound effects, of course, are key elements of popular entertainment. In the early days of radio theater, the sounds of a crackling fire could be mimicked through the crumpling of cellophane. The galloping of a horse was imitated through clopping coconut shells on a table. Each year the Academy of Motion Pictures awards an Oscar to the best audio effects, which are key elements in any successful action or sci-fi movie. Thanks to Hollywood production facilities like Industrial Light and Magic and Dreamworks Studios, we know what light sabers sounds like, even though they don't really exist.

Similarly, poetry employs **onomatopoeia**, or verbal sounds that are meant to mimic things imaginatively heard in the world. The onomatopoeia of Robert Frost's phrase "snarled and rattled" captures the menace and danger of a working buzz saw in his poem about a farm accident, "Out, Out—." "The buzz saw," he writes, "snarled and rattled in the yard / . . . And the saw snarled and rattled, snarled and rattled." Similarly, Emily Dickinson renders a death scene even more unsettling in the sound of a fly in her Poem 465, "I heard a Fly buzz — when I died."

EMILY DICKINSON   *(1830–1886)*

Poem 465 (I heard a Fly buzz – when I died)   *(1862)*

I heard a Fly buzz — when I died —
The Stillness in the Room
Was like the Stillness in the Air —
Between the Heaves of Storm —

The Eyes around — had wrung them dry —   5
And Breaths were gathering firm
For that last Onset — when the King
Be witnessed — in the Room —

I willed my Keepsakes — Signed away
What portion of me be   10
Assignable — and then it was
There interposed a Fly —

With Blue — uncertain stumbling Buzz —
Between the light — and me —
And then the Windows failed — and then   15
I could not see to see —

TOPICS FOR CRITICAL THINKING

1. What do you associate with flies? How does Dickinson's fly appear as a negative presence that intrudes into the poem's death scene?

2. How does the fly mark the moment of literal and spiritual blindness, presented in the metonymy of the windows whose light failed at the fly's approach?

3. Consider how in breaking the stillness of the room, the fly manifests not God, the "King," but the repulsive sound of the insect's "uncertain stumbling Buzz." How does Dickinson's masterful use of onomatopoeia in the repeated short *u* sound flout the poet's anticipation of the afterlife with the unsettling noise of death?

TOPIC FOR CRITICAL WRITING

Taken as a symbol of decay and mortality, how does the fly cancel the hope of resurrection in the poem?

Another question one might pose is whether the "buzz" of onomatopoeia represents something already there in nature. If so, why does the word for *buzz* in English sound differently, say, in the French *bourdonner,* German *summen,* Italian *ronzare,* Spanish *zumbar,* or even Dutch *zoemen?* It is debatable whether onomatopoeia directly mimes sounds we hear or if it instead presents stylized versions of words that we associate with sounds through usage and connotation.

Depending on one's linguistic point of view, the same could be said of the other techniques of sound sense that English poets employ to create **euphony,** the impression of sounds that are pleasing to the ear, and **cacophony,** sounds that are unpleasant and grating. Some schools of thought emphasize the kinesthetic quality of a particular consonant or vowel sound: that is, how resemblance between a sound and its meaning is based on the way a particular sound is shaped in the mouth, nose, and throat. The common variety of consonant sounds include the following.

- The *r* and *l* or *liquids* that roll in a flowing movement off the tongue, as in W. B. Yeats's "I hear lake water lapping with low sounds by the shore"
- The *m, n,* and *ng* sounds of the *nasals,* as in Alfred, Lord Tennyson's "The murmuring of innumerable bees"
- The harsh, rasping sounds or the *h, f, c, th, dh,* or *fricatives* and the *s, z, sh, zh* or *sibilants,* as in Robert Lowell's description of whaling: "The fat flukes arch and whack about its ears, / The death-lance churns into the sanctuary, tears"
- The hard *p, b, t, d, k, g* sounds or *stops* and *plosives,* as in John Donne's prayer for violent conversion: "bend / Your force to break, blow, burn, and make me new"

The term *alliteration* describes the repetition of consonant sounds at the beginning of successive words (initial alliteration) and within adjacent words (internal alliteration). John Keats's "Ode on Melancholy" combines both initial and internal alliteration in a richly textured depiction of deeply felt emotional states:

> But when the me*l*ancholy *f*it shall *f*all
>   Sudden from heaven like a weeping cloud,
> That *f*osters the droop-headed *f*lowers all,
>   And *h*ides the green *h*ill in an April shroud;
> Then glut thy so*rr*ow on a mo*r*ning *r*ose,
>   O*r* on the *r*ainbow of the *s*alt *s*and-wave,
>   Or on the wealth of globéd peonies;
> Or if thy mistress some rich anger shows,
>   Imprison *h*er soft *h*and, and let *h*er rave,
>   And feed *d*eep, *d*eep u*p*on her *p*eerless eyes.

Assonance—stemming from the Latin *assonare*, "to answer with, or echo, the same sound"—is the complementary term for the repetition of vowel sounds in a line. Because alliterations typically come at the beginning of words, we tend to read them as much as hear them. Assonance, however, occurs more often within words and therefore bears a more aural character. In acoustics, sound is a measured in terms of the frequency of its waves per second, and the greater a vowel's frequency, the higher the intensity of its pitch. English vowels range all the way from the low frequency long *o* sounds of *stone*, up through the middle range of short *u* sounds as in *mud, tub, jug*, up to the higher registers of the short *e* and short *i* of *jet*, and *thick*, ending with the highest frequency vowel sounds of the long *a* and *i* of *say* and *tight*.

The sonorous combination of these effects can greatly enhance the performative tonalities of a poem's subjects, settings, and themes, as in W. B. Yeats's "The Lake Isle of Innisfree" that employs both alliteration and assonance.

W. B. YEATS   *(1865–1939)*

The Lake Isle of Innisfree   *(1892)*

I will arise and go now, and go to Innisfree,
And a small cabin build there, of clay and wattles made:
Nine bean rows will I have there, a hive for the honey bee,
And live alone in the bee-loud glade.

And I shall have some peace there, for peace comes dropping slow,   5
Dropping from the veils of the morning to where the cricket sings;
There midnight's all a glimmer, and noon a purple glow,
And evening full of the linnet's wings.

I will arise and go now, for always night and day
I hear lake water lapping with low sounds by the shore;   10
While I stand on the roadway, or on the pavements grey,
I hear it in the deep heart's core.

TOPICS FOR CRITICAL THINKING

1. Yeats wrote "The Lake Isle of Innisfree" after noticing the sound of tinkling water from a fountain in Fleet Street, the "roadway" and "pavements grey" in the poem. The small cabin and nine bean rows are patterned after Yeats's reading in Henry David Thoreau's *Walden* (1854). How does the poem present the Irish poet's fantasy of making a retreat into nature on Innisfree, which means "Heather Island"?

2. Consider how the repetition of liquids and nasals tends to have an almost hypnotic effect of lulling the reader with the music of an interior dreamscape heard "in the deep heart's core."

TOPIC FOR CRITICAL WRITING

Yeats relies heavily on the sound effects of alliteration and assonance to perform both the high register sounds of the "bee-loud glade" and the dropoff into low frequency tonalities of "lake water lapping with low sounds by the shore." Identify as many examples of these effects as you can and consider how they function in the poem.

In "The Lake Isle of Innisfree," consonant and vowel sounds create harmonious effects that are pleasing to the ear. While Yeats presents the euphony overheard in his poem, Sylvia Plath invokes tones of a violent cacophony in depicting the ocean setting of "Point Shirley."

SYLVIA PLATH *(1932–1963)*

Point Shirley *(1959)*

From Water-Tower Hill to the brick prison
The shingle booms, bickering under
The sea's collapse.
Snowcakes break and welter. This year
The gritted wave leaps   5
The seawall and drops onto a bier
Of quahog chips,
Leaving a salty mash of ice to whiten

In my grandmother's sand yard. She is dead,
Whose laundry snapped and froze here, who   10
Kept house against
What the sluttish, rutted sea could do.
Squall waves once danced
Ship timbers in through the cellar window;
A thresh-tailed, lanced   15
Shark littered in the geranium bed —

Such collusion of mulish elements
She wore her broom straws to the nub.
Twenty years out
Of her hand, the house still hugs in each drab   20
Stucco socket
The purple egg-stones: from Great Head's knob
To the filled-in Gut
The sea in its cold gizzard ground those rounds.

Nobody wintering now behind   25
The planked-up windows where she set
Her wheat loaves

And apple cakes to cool. What is it
Survives, grieves
So, over this battered, obstinate spit   30
Of gravel? The waves'
Spewed relics clicker masses in the wind,

Grey waves the stub-necked eiders ride.
A labor of love, and that labor lost.
Steadily the sea   35
Eats at Point Shirley. She died blessed,
And I come by
Bones, bones only, pawed and tossed,
A dog-faced sea.
The sun sinks under Boston, bloody red.   40

I would get from these dry-papped stones
The milk your love instilled in them.
The black ducks dive.
And though your graciousness might stream,
And I contrive,   45
Grandmother, stones are nothing of home
To that spumiest dove.
Against both bar and tower the black sea runs.

TOPICS FOR CRITICAL THINKING

1. How does Point Shirley's "spit of gravel" remain "obstinate" in its resistance to the sea's onslaught?

2. Plath's ocean, unlike Yeats's, is not serene but "sluttish." Picking up on the Middle English derivation of *slutte*, or female dog, Plath's ocean is a "dog-faced sea" that "Eats at Point Shirley." Unlike Yeats's euphonious liquid consonants, Plath features in her opening stanza several plosive hard *b* sounds. Identify as many as you can and discuss their dramatic effect in the poem.

3. In addition to these plosives, Plath also employs fricatives and sibilants to heighten the cacophony communicated in her hard *c* and *g* consonants. Discuss some of the poem's key sound effects in such onomatopoetic phrases as "cold gizzard ground those rounds."

4. Through consonant stops, the sea seems to explode "against both bar and tower" of the "battered" coast. But the poem also exploits the assonance of the guttural short *u* sounds in such monosyllables as *nub, gut, stub, ducks, hug,* and so on. How do these repeated gutturals add a primal quality to her grandmother's uncanny dwelling between shore and surf?

TOPIC FOR CRITICAL WRITING

"Point Shirley" is an elegy to Plath's grandmother, whose house on the sea's edge near Boston bears the signs of the eroding effects of time and the stubborn, "mulish" elements of wind and water. Describe the poet's presentation of setting in the poem.

While Plath and Yeats aim at differing emotive effects through the contrast of euphony and cacophony, we find both techniques combined in Samuel Taylor Coleridge's "Kubla Khan."

SAMUEL TAYLOR COLERIDGE   *(1772–1834)*

Kubla Khan

Or, a Vision in a Dream. A Fragment   *(1797–1798)*

In Xanadu did Kubla Khan
A stately pleasure dome decree:
Where Alph, the sacred river, ran
Through caverns measureless to man
   Down to a sunless sea.   5
So twice five miles of fertile ground
With walls and towers were girdled round:
And there were gardens bright with sinuous rills,
Where blossomed many an incense-bearing tree;
And here were forests ancient as the hills,   10
Enfolding sunny spots of greenery.

But oh! that deep romantic chasm which slanted
Down the green hill athwart a cedarn cover!
A savage place! as holy and enchanted
As e'er beneath a waning moon was haunted   15
By woman wailing for her demon lover!
And from this chasm, with ceaseless turmoil seething,
As if this earth in fast thick pants were breathing,
A mighty fountain momently was forced:
Amid whose swift half-intermitted burst   20
Huge fragments vaulted like rebounding hail,
Or chaffy grain beneath the thresher's flail:
And 'mid these dancing rocks at once and ever
It flung up momently the sacred river.
Five miles meandering with a mazy motion   25
Through wood and dale the sacred river ran,
Then reached the caverns measureless to man,
And sank in tumult to a lifeless ocean:
And 'mid this tumult Kubla heard from far
Ancestral voices prophesying war!   30

   The shadow of the dome of pleasure
   Floated midway on the waves;
   Where was heard the mingled measure
   From the fountain and the caves.

It was a miracle of rare device,   35
A sunny pleasure dome with caves of ice!

   A damsel with a dulcimer
   In a vision once I saw:
   It was an Abyssinian maid,
   And on her dulcimer she played,   40
   Singing of Mount Abora.
   Could I revive within me
   Her symphony and song,
      To such a deep delight 'twould win me,
That with music loud and long,   45
I would build that dome in air,
That sunny dome! those caves of ice!
And all who heard should see them there,
And all should cry, Beware! Beware!
His flashing eyes, his floating hair!   50
Weave a circle round him thrice,
And close your eyes with holy dread,
For he on honey-dew hath fed,
And drunk the milk of Paradise.

As his 1816 Preface implied, Coleridge intended that "Kubla Khan" be read as a fragment of a larger, visionary work. As it happened, Coleridge, like many others in nineteenth-century England, was in the habit of taking laudanum, an alcohol-opium mixture, for medicinal purposes. One side effect, however, was his serious addiction to the drug after 1801. Coleridge conceived the poem after taking two grains of opium, and, however we might debate the drug's role in his imaginative life, the poet envisions a remarkably euphoric landscape in "Kubla Khan."

Critics have offered a wide range of interpretations of the two major landscapes of the poem: Kubla Khan's pleasure dome and the chasm with its "mighty fountain" that feeds into the River Alph. For our purposes, notice how sound effects enhance the sharp contrast in the artistic order of the measured garden world as opposed to the "ceaseless turmoil" of the natural, subterranean energies witnessed in the chasm setting. Coleridge renders the euphony of the former scene of the garden in the liquids and nasals, culminating in the hypnotic "sinuous rills" of the sacred river's "five miles meandering with a mazy motion." The force of the chasm's volcanic energies are conveyed in the fricatives of the *ch*, *th*, *f*, and *s* sounds combined with the plosives of the hard *b*, *t*, and *p*.

   And *f*rom this *ch*asm, with *ceaseless* *t*urmoil *seeth*ing,
   A*s* i*f* thi*s* earth in *f*ast *th*ick *p*ants were brea*th*ing,
   A mighty *f*ountain momently was *f*orced:
   Amid whose swi*ft* hal*f*-intermi*tt*ed *b*urst
   Huge *f*ragments vaulted like re*b*ounding *h*ail,
   Or *ch*a*ff*y grain *b*eneath the *th*resher's *f*lail:

Few locales in poetry are as vividly rendered as the exotic landscapes of "Kubla Khan." So convincing is Coleridge's "mingled measure" that we come away with the impression of actualities that are, nevertheless, based entirely in fantasies of the poetic imagination.

Rhyme

While alliteration and assonance give a sensuous sound texture to verse writing, rhyme and rhythm organize these acoustical elements for musical effects. In oral traditions, rhyme has entertainment value and, for the performer, works as an aid to memory. Rhyme is present in everyday slang terms ("fender bender,"), in advertising ("the real deal"), in teen argot ("yo, rude dude, choose it or loose it"), and rap lyrics (by, say, Dr. Dre: "Worldwide, got the triple beam, I slide. / Listenin' to yo demo in a stretch limo."). In folk culture, colloquial truisms such as "birds of a feather flock together" turn on rhyme, as do such practical proverbs as this one.

> Evening red and morning gray
> Will speed a traveler on his way;
> But evening gray and morning red
> Will pour down rain upon his head.

Rhyme can be playful, as in children's jump rope games.

> Bluebells, cockle shells,
> Eevie, ivy, over;
> I like coffee, I like tea;
> I like the boys, and the boys like me.
> Tell your mother to hold her tongue;
> She had a fellow when she was young.
> Tell your father to do the same;
> He had a girl and he changed her name.

The same is true in riddles.

> In marble walls as white as milk,
> Lined with a skin as soft as silk,
> Within a fountain crystal clear,
> A golden apple doth appear;
> No doors there are to this stronghold,
> Yet thieves break in and steal the gold.
>
> (Answer: an egg)

Rhyme also serves as a memory aid in popular usage as in the well-known Mother Goose rhyme for remembering the months of the calendar.

> Thirty days hath September,
> April, June, and November;
> February has twenty-eight alone,

All the rest have thirty-one,
Excepting leap year, that's the time
When February's days are twenty-nine.

In verse composition, **pure rhyme** is defined in terms of the heard likenesses and differences linking two or more words. For example, in the above
rhyming pair "milk/silk," the accented vowel sound of the short *i* makes the
connection of likeness along with the sameness of the ending consonant *k*.
The difference is the consonants—*m* and *s*—that come before. Thus likeness
must define the vowel sound of a rhyming pair of words and whatever sound
elements follow it, while what comes before must signify a difference. For example, the following excerpt from Christopher Marlowe's "The Passionate
Shepherd to His Love" illustrate the end rhymes "love/prove" and "fields/
yields."

> Come live with me and be my love,
> And we will all the pleasures prove
> That valleys, groves, hills and fields,
> Woods, or steepy mountain yields.

Monosyllabic rhymes are called **masculine rhyme**. In addition, masculine
rhyme describes rhyming words of more than one syllable only when the
rhyming sound falls on the final, unstressed syllable, as in *desire* and *aspire*.
Words with two syllables, where the second syllable is unstressed, are termed
feminine rhyme, as in Jonathan Swift's "The Lady's Dressing Room."

> But Vengeance, goddess never sleeping
> Soon punished Strephon for his peeping.

Triple syllable combinations are more rare and can have sarcastic and ironic
effects, as when Alexander Pope describes the cutting of Belinda's hair in his
mock epic "The Rape of the Lock."

> "The meeting points the sacred hair dissever
> From the fair head, forever, and forever!"

Rhyming effects extend beyond **end rhyme** to include **internal rhyme**:
rhyming words within lines and across adjacent lines. Poets use internal
rhyming for a variety of purposes in verse composition. Andrew Marvell
employs it to perform the resemblances between mind and nature in "The
Garden": "The *mind,* that ocean where each *kind* / Does straight its own resemblance *find.*" William Shakespeare achieves an incantatory effect with internal rhyme in the witches' spell cast in *Macbeth*: "*Double, double* toil and
trouble; / Fire burn, and cauldron *bubble.*" In the modern period, internal
rhyme performs in "God's Grandeur" the sense of monotony that Gerard
Manley Hopkins finds in the industrial world:

> And all is *seared* with trade; *bleared, smeared* with toil;
> And *wears* man's smudge and *shares* man's smell: the soil
> Is bare now, nor can foot feel, being shod.

While pure rhyme voices an exact match of vowel sounds, poets also express minor and dissonant tonalities through the use of what is variously

termed **half, near,** or **slant rhyme.** Emily Dickinson uses near rhyme more often than not; Poem 303 signals a certain sense of finality through near rhyme:

> The Soul selects her own Society —
> Then — shuts the Door —
> To her divine Majority —
> Present no more —

Near rhyme often occurs with **consonance,** the repetition of the initial and terminal consonants surrounding a medial vowel. Wilfred Owen, the British soldier who died as a combatant in World War I, depicts the edgy and potentially lethal quality of modern armaments as well as the barbarism of twentieth-century war in his famous poem "Arms and the Boy."

WILFRED OWEN   *(1893–1918)*

Arms and the Boy   *(1918)*

Let the boy try along this bayonet-blade
How cold steel is, and keen with hunger of blood;
Blue with all malice, like a madman's flash;
And thinly drawn with famishing for flesh.

Lend him to stroke these blind, blunt bullet-leads,   5
Which long to nuzzle in the hearts of lads;
Or give him cartridges whose fine zinc teeth,
Are sharp with the sharpness of grief and death.

For his teeth seem for laughing round an apple.
There lurk no claws behind his fingers supple;   10
And God will grow no talons at his heels,
Nor antlers through the thickness of his curls.

The near rhymes of *blade* and *blood, flash* and *flesh, leads* and *lads* are rendered even more sharply dissonant through the enveloping effect of **consonance** in the repetition of *bl-d, fl-sh,* and *l-d.* In his poem "Toads," Philip Larkin uses consonance for a different, somewhat self-parodic effect in comparing himself to the little amphibian.

> For something sufficiently toad-*like*
> Squats in me, too;
> Its hunkers are heavy as hard *luck,*
> And cold as snow.

Further on in the poem, half-rhyme serves to describe the complacent squalor of Larkin's neighbors.

> Lots of folks live up lanes
>   With fires in a bucket,

> Eat windfalls and tinner sardines—
> They seem to like it.

Successful, as opposed to clichéd, rhyming emphasizes key terms of significance in a poem in ways that are fresh and unexpected. "The sound," writes Alexander Pope, "must seem an echo to the sense."

Meter and Rhythm

Rhyme renders the striking utterance even more memorable when it enters into purposeful relation with the **meter** and **rhythm** of the line.

Meter comes from the Greek word *metron*, which means "measure." *Rhythm* too has a Greek derivation in the word *rhuthmos*, meaning "flow." Rhythm, of course, is basic to our experience of the world—from the internal embodied rhythm of one's heart beat or sleep and waking rhythms to the outward rhythms of the tides, night and day, the seasons, and so on. Words have their own rhythms that we can hear in the way we give weight and emphasis to certain syllables in pronunciation. We can visualize such stressed syllables with accent marks. For example, words such as gráteful, táble, gíngĕr, hátchĕt, signǎl, and so on lay more stress on the first syllable, which is accented in relation to the second, unaccented syllable. Conversely, words such as sŭrpríse, rĕnéw, ŭndóne, bĕneáth, ăgáin have just the opposite pattern of flowing from an unaccented to an accented syllable. Our everyday language usage too is shaped by the rhythmic flow of emphasis and stress that we find in individual words as we combine them into phrases and sentences. You can hear a rhythmic pattern in virtually any utterance: "Wĕ wént tŏ seé thĕ filṁ lăst níght." "Woǔld yóu líke friés wĭth thát?" "Páss ṁe thĕ spórts séctiŏṇ." "Ĭ nów prŏnoúnce yŏu mán aňd wife." "Ĭ can't belieẃ Ĭ áte the whóle thing." "Gíve thĕ dóg ă bóne, leáve the dóg alóne."

The earliest metrical pattern in English verse is the so-called strong-stress meter or **accentual meter** that characterizes Old English poetry. Accentual meter is formed by a pattern of stresses and alliteration. Four stresses give metrical regularity to the line. Moreover, the stresses are balanced in relation to each half of the line or **hemistich**. Two stresses fall in the first half of the line and another two in the second half. The middle of the line—dividing the first hemistich from the second—is marked by a caesural pause (‖). **Caesura** comes from the Latin verb *caedere* meaning "to cut." In addition, three of the four stresses are alliterations. Typically, both the stresses in the first hemistich begin with the same letter followed by its repetition on the first stressed syllable belonging to the second hemistich. Ezra Pound's translation of the Anglo-Saxon, Old English poem "The Seafarer" preserves the accentual metrics of the original in virtually every line.

> Chill its cháins are |;| cháfing síghs
> Héw my heárt round ‖ and huńger begót
> Mére-weary moód |.| Lest mán know nót

That hé on dry land || lóveliest livéth,
List how Í, care-wretched, || on icé-cold sea
Weathered the winter |,| wretched outcast

Richard Wilbur's contemporary poem "Junk" offers a mock-heroic reprise of the Old English line, setting off each hemistich with visual spacing on the page:

An axe angles
                  from my neighbor's ashcan;
It is hell's handiwork,
                  the wood not hickory,
The flow of the grain
                  not faithfully followed.
The shivered shaft
                rises from a shellheap
Of plastic playthings,
                paper plates,
And the sheer shards
                of shattered tumblers
That were not annealed
                for the time needful.

Following the Norman invasion of England in 1066, the Old English accentual meter began to undergo a transformation, influenced as it was by the Greek and Latinate metrics of Old French. **Accentual-syllabic meter** became the dominant form of English reaching back to the fourteenth century as the Renaissance spread from Italy. The powerful examples of Petrarch's *Canzoniere* and *Trionfi* and Dante's *La Vita Nuova* and *Commedia* were felt in France, Spain, and Portugal, arriving somewhat later in England.

In accentual-syllabic meter, what we typically gauge is the rhythmic pattern of accented and unaccented syllables in a line divided into units of measurement called poetic feet. A **poetic foot** is analogous to a measure of music, which is governed by a fixed number of beats: three for a waltz, four in four-quarter march time, and so on. Since the beginning of the Renaissance, the metrical workhorse of English poetry has been the **iambic** foot—an iamb being made up of an unaccented and an accented syllable (˘ ´). We can further describe the metrics of a line by the number of feet it contains and chart both accents and syllables in what is called a **scansion**. Similar to a musical score, a scansion provides a diagram interpreting the measure of poetic feet—including accented and unaccented syllables—in a given line, stanza, or entire poem.

The most typical metrical line in English is constructed of five iambic feet per line, called **iambic pentameter** (*penta* being the Greek word signifying "five," as in the Pentagon or a pentagram). Sonnets are generally written in iambic pentameter, and this meter is plain to see in a scansion of the opening lines of Shakespeare's Sonnet 73:

That time | of yeár | thŏu máy'st | ĭn mé | bĕholḋ
Whĕn yél | lŏw leavés, | ŏr noné, | ŏr feẃ, | dŏ hańg
Úpón | thŏse boughs | whĭch sháke | ăgaińst | thĕ cold

There are, of course, other metrical line lengths that poets work in besides pentameter. The first is **monometer**, lines comprising two syllables each in one-foot units. Robert Herrick's "Upon His Departure Hence" is one of a very few number of poems composed in monometer:

Thus I
Passe by,
And die:
As one,
Unknown,
And gone:
I'm made
A shade,
And laid
I'th grave:
There have
My cave.
Where tell
I dwell.
Farewell.

The primary line length in Dorothy Parker's "Résumé" is **dimeter,** or two feet per line.

Razors | pain you;
Rivers | are damp;
Acids | stain you;
And drugs | cause cramp.
Guns aren't | lawful;
Nooses | give;
Gas smells | awful;
You might | as well live.

Sir Walter Raleigh's "The Lie" is composed in **trimeter**, or lines made up of three feet each.

Go, soul, | the bod | y's guest,
Upon | a thank | less errand;
Fear not | to touch | the best;
The truth | shall be | thy warrant.
Go, since | I needs | must die,
And give | the world | the lie.

Andrew Marvell's "The Garden" is in **tetrameter**, or four feet per line:

How vain | ly men | themselves | amaze
To win | the Palm, | the oak, | or bays
And their | inces | sant la | bors sede
Crowned from | some sin | gle herb, | or tree,
Whose short | and nar | row-verg | ed shade
Does pru | dently | their toils | upbraid;
While all | flowers and | all trees | do close
To weave | the gar | lands | of repose!

William Shakespeare's Sonnet 55 is composed in **pentameter**, five feet per line.

> Not mar | ble, nor | the gild | ed mon | uments
> Of princes, | shall out | live this | power | ful rhyme;
> But you | shall shine | more bright | in these | contents
> Than un | swept stone, | besmeared | with slut | tish time.

W. B. Yeats composed "The Cold Heaven" in six-foot lines of **hexameter**.

> Sudden | ly I | saw the | cold and | rook-de | lighting | heaven
> That seemed | as though | ice burned | and was | but the | more ice,
> And there | upon | imag | ina | tion and | heart were | driven
> So wild | that eve | ry ca | sual thought | of that | and this
> Vanished, | and left | but mem | ories, that | should be | out of |
> season
> With the | hot blood | of youth, | of love | crossed long | ago;

Heptameter, or seven feet per line length, is the meter Williams Words-worth chooses for "The Norman Boy."

> High on | a broad | unfer | tile tract | of for | est-skirt | ed Down,
> Nor kept | by Na | ture for | herself, | nor made | by man | his own,
> From home | and com | pany | remote | and eve | ry play | ful joy,
> Served, tend | ing a | few sheep | and goats, | a rag | ged Nor | man
> Boy.

The most famous eight-foot, **octameter** poem is Edgar Allan Poe's "The Raven."

> Once up | on a | midnight | dreary | while I | pondered | weak and |
> weary
> Over | many | a quaint | and cur | ious vol | ume of | forgot | ten lore,
> While I | nodded | nearly | napping, | sudden | ly there | came a |
> tapping
> As of | someone | gently | rapping, | rapping | at my | chamber door.

As you can see in the above examples, poets often vary the dominant metrical pattern of a line with irregular feet to emphasize key words and to enhance and perform the rhythmic sense of the line. **Rhythm** describes the flow of the stresses within the dominant meter of the line. For example, the prevailing meter of John Donne's Holy Sonnet 14 is iambic pentameter. But as the first quatrain demonstrates, not every foot scans as an iamb.

> Bátter | my heárt, | thrée-pér | soñed Gód; | for Yóu
> As yét | but knóck, | breáthe, shine, | and seék | to meńd;
> That I | may rise | and stand, | o'erthrow me,' | And bend
> Your force | to breák, | blow, burn, | and make | me néw.

Donne's poem prays for a violent conversion experience to alter the poet's present spiritual malaise. In the poem, he combines accentual emphasis with the plosive *b* consonant to perform that forceful transformation. "Batter" makes use of the irregular trochaic foot; in a **trochee** (˘) the accent falls on the first syllable rather than on the second in the iamb. Certain of Donne's poetic feet accent both syllables—in the irregular foot, the **spondee** (´´)—as in breáthe, shíne, or, more emphatically, in the phrasings blów, búrn.

In masterful verse compositions, an entire poem's action can turn on how irregular rhythms play against the dominant metrical pattern, as in this excerpt from Robert Frost's "The Vantage Point."

> Ănd íf | bў noón | Ĭ havé | tŏo múch | ŏf these,
> Ĭ have | bŭt tŏ | túrn ŏn | my árm, | ănd ló,
> The sún | -burńed híll | sĭde sets | my face | ăglów,

The metrical pattern here is iambic pentameter, but Frost performs the nimble shift in perspective by varying the rhythm as the poet turns on his arm to take in a different vantage point. The phrase "bŭt tŏ | túrn ŏn | my árm" combines "bŭt tŏ," a **pyrrhic** foot—two unaccented syllables—with the trochee "túrn tŏ" to dramatize the turning rhythmically.

Similarly, W. B. Yeats creates a certain rhythmic intensity in "Who Goes with Fergus," especially in stanza two.

> Who will go drive with Fergus now,
> And pierce the deep wood's woven shade,
> And dance upon the level shore?
> Young man, lift up your russet brow,
> And lift your tender eyelids, maid,
> And brood on hopes and fear no more.
>
> And no more turn aside and brood
> Upon love's bitter mystery;
> For Fergus rules the brazen cars,
> And rules the shadows of the wood,
> And the white breast of the dim sea
> And all dishevelled wandering stars.

The poem's next-to-last-line is the one to pay attention to. Varying the metrical pattern of iambic tetrameter (four feet per line), Yeats repeats the rhythmic combination of the pyrrhic foot followed by a spondee—"Ănd thĕ | white bréast | ŏf thĕ | dím séa"—so as to set off the visual impact of the white breast against dim sea.

Two other irregular feet are the **anapest** (˘˘´)—two unaccented syllables followed by an accented syllable—and its opposite, the **dactyl** (´˘˘)—an accented followed by two unaccented syllables. The first, third, and fourth lines of Thomas Hardy's "The Voice" intone the dactylic meter for a haunting effect:

> Wómăn múch | missed, hŏw yŏu | cáll tŏ mé, | cáll tŏ mé,
> Sáyĭng | thăt nów | yŏu aře | nót ăs | yŏu wére
> When yŏu hăd | chánged frŏm thĕ | óne whŏ wăs | áll tŏ mé,
> But ăs ăt | fírst, whĕn oŭr | dáy wăs faír.

Lord Byron's "The Destruction of Sennacherib" is composed primarily in anapestic tetrameter, as in the poem's first stanza.

Thĕ Ăssýr | iăn camĕ dówn | likĕ thĕ wolf | oñ thĕ fóld,
Aňd hĭs có | hořts wĕre gléam | iňg iň púr | plĕ aňd góld;
Aňd thĕ shéen | of thĕir speárs | wăs like stárs | oñ thĕ séa,
Whĕn thĕ blúe | wăves rolls night | lў oñ deép | Gălĭleé.

Rhyme coupled with rhythm can lay down a pattern that enhances the themes and subjects of a given poem's unique performance. For example, Theodore Roethke's "My Papa's Waltz" mimics in its formal arrangement of rhythm and rhyme the three-quarter time of a waltz.

THEODORE ROETHKE   *(1908–1963)*

My Papa's Waltz   *(1948)*

The whiskey on your breath
Could make a small boy dizzy;
But I hung on like death:
Such waltzing was not easy.

We romped until the pans   5
Slid from the kitchen shelf;
My mother's countenance
Could not unfrown itself.

The hand that held my wrist
Was battered on one knuckle;   10
At every step you missed
My right ear scraped a buckle.

You beat time on my head
With a palm caked hard by dirt,
Then waltzed me off to bed   15
Still clinging to your shirt.

In "My Papa's Waltz," Roethke devises a poetic form that has a natural, organic fit to the memory of his childhood waltz. English verse, however, offers a repertoire of preset forms that test a poet's power not only in mastering the pattern, say, of a sonnet or villanelle but in marking it for all time with one's own signature of greatness.

TOPICS FOR CRITICAL THINKING

1. Roethke's father, Otto Roethke, owned a greenhouse business in rural Saginaw, Michigan, and died when the poet was in early adolescence. Many of Roethke's poems are set in the greenhouse world of his youth and several dwell on the figure of

the overbearing father in particular. Like Sylvia Plath, whose father also died while she was a child, Roethke had powerfully conflicted feelings about his father that were magnified by his loss at a formative age. How does "My Papa's Waltz" present a somewhat divided memory of the father?

2. The poem presents a bittersweet recollection of what might have been a nightly ritual from the poet's childhood. On the surface, the poem offers a comic, even cartoon-like, portrait of his family life, especially in the surreal image of the mother whose "countenance could not unfrown itself." Consider how key words like *romped* and *waltzed* contribute to the fond memories the poet has of the father.

3. Plenty of evidence, however, points to an underlying tone of violence and abuse in the connotations of such words as *battered*, *scraped*, and *beat*. How do these key terms resonate with phrases like "Such waltzing was not easy" or "I hung on like death"?

TOPIC FOR CRITICAL WRITING

Rhyme and meter contribute to the waltz metaphor in combining iambic trimeter with the alternating rhyme scheme of the quatrain stanza units. Together, they mimic the three-quarter waltz time, which counts three beats to the measure. In lines 2, 4, 10, and 12, Roethke captures the rollicking, off-kilter "beat" of the waltzing by adding an extra syllable to the last foot of the line in an irregular foot called the *amphibrach*: "Sŭch wáltz | ĭng wás | nŏt eásў." Explore the rhythmic effects of Roethke's dancing measures.

9  Poetic Forms

Fixed Poetic Forms

When asked why he didn't compose free or nonstructured verse, Robert Frost responded, "I'd just as soon play tennis with the net down." Fixed form imposes the kind of rules, boundaries, and prior examples of craft that some poets welcome as a competitive chance to prove their verbal prowess. Formal arrangements of meter and rhyme—working together with alliteration, assonance, figurative language, imagery, and the rest—provide more than enough ingredients to make fixed form poetry a linguistic challenge every bit as bracing as Wimbledon or the U.S. Open.

Blank Verse, Couplets, Tercets, and Quatrains

Fixed form begins with **blank verse**, or unrhymed iambic pentameter. Blank verse imposes the rigor of metrical composition. It became the stock-in-trade of William Shakespeare's comedies and tragedies as well as of John Milton's epic *Paradise Lost*. Milton imitated Greek and Latin epic-staged, grammatically complex utterances whose patterns of **enjambment**—the movement of syntactic phrasing from the end of one line to the beginning of the next— overflowed the closure of **end rhyme**. His **inversions** (reversals) of normal **syntax** (the patterning of phrases and sentences) and his highly embedded clauses are unique contributions to the blank verse medium, as the opening lines of *Paradise Lost* show.

> Of Man's first disobedience, and the fruit
> Of that forbidden tree whose mortal taste
> Brought death into the world, and all our woe,
> With loss of Eden, till one greater Man
> Restore us and regain the blissful seat,
> Sing, Heavenly Muse, . . .

Milton's blank verse inverts the normal word order of the imperative sentence "Sing, Heavenly Muse, of Man's first disobedience" to suspend meaning across the enjambments of five lines of verse.

Rhyme lends further architectural shape and complexity to verse, especially in **couplets**, or pairs of rhyming lines. The **heroic couplet**, composed in iambic pentameter, became a popular form in the eighteenth century, especially in the translation of Greek and Latin epic works by John Dryden and Alexander Pope. The coupling of rhyme and phrasing lends itself to striking truisms and epigrams. Pope's "An Essay on Man," for example, focuses on the essential paradoxes of the human condition that joins opposite states of being in a precarious and, at times, absurd balance.

> Placed on this isthmus of a middle state,
> A being darkly wise, and rudely great:
> With too much knowledge for the Sceptic side,
> With too much weakness for the Stoic's pride,
> He hangs between; in doubt to act, or rest,
> In doubt to deem himself a God, or Beast;
> In doubt his Mind or Body to prefer,

Pope's balancing of opposites is reinforced by the formal possibilities afforded by his heroic couplets. Gwendolyn Brooks playfully deflates the "heroic" stature of the couplet form in her contemporary poem "Religion," spoken by a boy named Ulysses: "Our teachers feed us geography. / We spit it out in a hurry." The Shakespearean sonnet's final couplets typically seal the form's arguments in a memorable concluding statement, as in Shakespeare's Sonnet 12.

> And nothing 'gainst Time's scythe can make defense
> Save breed, to brave him when he takes thee hence.

Closed form poetry is typically organized into **stanza** units, or groupings of lines that have the same or similar patterns of rhythm and end rhyme. For example, Robert Frost composes his famous poem "Provide, Provide" into three-line stanzas—called **tercets**—of iambic tetrameter linked with matching end rhyme.

> The witch that came (the withered hag)
> To wash the steps with pail and rag,
> Was once the beauty Abishag,
>
> The picture pride of Hollywood.
> Too many fall from great and good
> For you to doubt the likelihood.

Another well-known tercet pattern, **terza rima** or "triple rhyme," takes the middle rhyme of each stanza and uses it as the **envelope** frame for the next stanza unit to rhyme: *aba, bcb, cdc, efe,* and so on. As the term *envelope* implies, the end rhymes of the first and third lines surround the middle line. Dante composed *The Divine Comedy* in terza rima, and Shelley chose it as the closed form for his "Ode to the West Wind." A contemporary example of the form can be seen in Richard Wilbur's "First Snow in Alsace."

RICHARD WILBUR   *(b. 1921)*

First Snow in Alsace   *(1947)*

The snow came down last night like moths
Burned on the moon; it fell till dawn,
Covered the town with simple cloths.

Absolute snow lies rumpled on
What shellbursts scattered and deranged,   5
Entangled railings, crevassed lawn.

As if it did not know they'd changed,
Snow smoothly clasps the roofs of homes
Fear-gutted, trustless and estranged.

The ration stacks are milky domes;   10
Across the ammunition pile
The snow has climbed in sparkling combs.

You think: beyond the town a mile
Or two, this snowfall fills the eyes
Of soldiers dead a little while.   15

Persons and persons in disguise,
Walking the new air white and fine,
Trade glances quick with shared surprise.

At children's windows, heaped, benign,
As always, winter shines the most,   20
And frost makes marvelous designs.

The night guard coming from his post,
Ten first-snows back in thought, walks slow
And warms him with a boyish boast:

He was the first to see the snow.   25

TOPICS FOR CRITICAL THINKING

1. Just west of the Rhine River, the Alsace region of France shares its eastern border with Germany. Ceded to the German Empire at the end of the Franco-Prussian War in 1871, it was the site of military conflict in both World Wars of the twentieth century owing to its strategic location. Examine the key terms that describe how the war has turned the setting of Alsace into a battlefield.

2. In what ways does the snow have a consoling, reparative effect on the otherwise "Fear-gutted, trustless and estranged" town?

3. How does the snow permit the soldiers to regress to an earlier, more innocent moment of youthful peace?

TOPIC FOR CRITICAL WRITING

Consider how terza rima connects the key terms of the poem. How does it link, for example, the consolations of "home" with the snow's transformation of "ration stacks" and the "ammunition pile" into enchanted "milky domes" and "sparkling combs." Discuss how terza rima creates an artistic envelope that contains war's barbarism within the frame of a formal artifice.

Another stanza pattern is the **quatrain**, a four-line stanza unit. The most common quatrain pattern is the ballad stanza, as in William Wordsworth's "A Slumber Did My Spirit Seal."

> No mo | tion has | she now |,| no force;
>   She nei | ther hears | nor sees;
> Rolled round | in earth's | diur | nal course,
>   With rocks |,| and stones |,| and trees.

As this second stanza of Wordsworth's poem illustrates, the ballad stanza alternates lines of iambic tetrameter with iambic trimeter in the rhyme scheme *abcb* or, as in the above example, the *abab* pattern. The term *common meter* describes ballad stanzas when used in hymnals. Virtually all of Emily Dickinson's poems can be sung to the common meter of "The Battle Hymn of the Republic." Other options for the quatrain would include the monorhyme of Dante Gabriel Rossetti's "The Woodspurge" and the *abba* envelope stanza that Alfred, Lord Tennyson uses in "In Memoriam." A final option combines two pairs of couplets, as in Adrienne Rich's "Aunt Jennifer's Tigers" and Sir Walter Raleigh's poem addressed to Queen Elizabeth I, "Fortune Hath Taken Thee Away, My Love."

> Fortune hath taken thee away, my love,
> My life's soul and my soul's heaven above;
> Fortune hath taken thee away, my princess;
> My only light and my true fancy's mistress.

Longer Fixed Stanza Forms

Five-line stanzas such as Edgar Allan Poe's "To Helen" combine an envelope tercet with a couplet to rhyme *ababb, cdcee,* and so on. Thomas Hardy's "New Year's Eve" also combines couplets with envelope patterns in rhyming his five-line stanza unit *abaab, cdccd,* and so on.

> "I have finished another year," said God,
>   "In grey, green, white, and brown;
> I have strewn the leaf upon the sod,
> Sealed up the worm within the clod,
>   And let the last sun down."

The **Scottish stanza** is a six-line unit rhyming *aaabab* popularized by Robert Burns. Another common six-line stanza unit follows the *ababcc* pattern of Shakespeare's poem "Venus and Adonis." Among the many poems composed in the **"Venus and Adonis" stanza** is Edmund Spenser's "The Shepheardes Calendar."

> A Shepheards boye (no better doe him call)
> When Winters wastful spight was almost spent,
> All in a sunneshine day, as did befall,
> Led for th his flock, that had bene long ypent.°
> So faynt they woxe°, and feeble in the folde,
> That now unnethes° their feete could them uphold.

5

Of the longer stanza units, **rhyme royal** is a seven-stanza patterned *ababbcc*. Chaucer is its earliest proponent in English verse in *Troilus and Criseide*. Others who have explored its possibilities include W. H. Auden in "The Shield of Achilles" and Sir Thomas Wyatt in "They Flee from Me." Wyatt also was the first to compose in **ottava rima** or eighth rhyme, the eight-line stanza pattern rhyming *abababcc*. Lord Byron employs ottava rima in *Don Juan* as does W. B. Yeats in "The Statues," "Sailing to Byzantium," and "Among School Children." The most distinctive nine-line stanza is the **Spenserian stanza** named after Edmund Spenser's *The Fairie Queene*. This pattern presents eight lines of iambic pentameter with a final iambic hexameter line—or alexandrine; the rhyme scheme is *ababbcbcc*. Keats's "The Eve of St. Agnes" is, perhaps, the most impressive performance of this stanza, and it is the form Percy Bysshe Shelley chooses in *Adonais*, his elegy to Keats. Among its other practitioners were Byron in *Childe Harold's Pilgrimage* and Tennyson in "The Land of the Lotus Eaters."

The Sonnet

Certain closed forms determine the entire shape of poems in their patterning of end rhymes, stanza lengths, use of couplets, and so on. Of these fixed forms, the most widely written and read is the **sonnet**, which came into English from the Italian influence of poet Francesco Petrarch. In fact, the word *sonnet* comes from the Italian *sonnetto*, which means "little song." The Italian sonnet, based on Petrarch's rhyme scheme, remains the most popular of the three kinds of sonnets, which also include the English, or Shakespearean, sonnet and the Spenserian sonnet. Each of these three variations on the sonnet form has the distinctive iambic pentameter, fourteen-line structure. Their differences stem from their rhyme schemes. The Italian sonnet rhymes *abba abba cde cde*; the Shakespearean sonnet rhymes *abab cdcd efef gg*. The Spenserian rhyme scheme bears a closer resemblance to the Shakespearean than to the Italian sonnet, rhyming *abab bcbc cdcd ee*. Of the three, the Italian form comprises a two-part structure. That is, the repeated envelope rhyme *abba abba* signals a break in the poem's presentation of themes, images, subjects,

---

4 *ypent:* Penned up.   5 *woxe:* Grew.   6 *unnethes:* Scarcely.

and arguments, moving from the first eight lines or **octave** to the final six lines, or **sestet**. In contrast, the alternating rhyme scheme of the Shakespearean and Spenserian patterns—divided as they are into three quatrains—tends to break the poem's presentation into three stages with a summary statement framed in the concluding couplet.

In "When I Consider How My Light Is Spent," the great English epic poet John Milton uses the Italian sonnet form to reflect on the blindness that afflicted him in 1651 at the age of forty-three.

JOHN MILTON   *(1608–1674)*

When I Consider How My Light Is Spent   *(1652)*

When I consider how my light is spent
   Ere half my days, in this dark world and wide,
   And that one talent which is death to hide
   Lodged with me useless, though my soul more bent
To serve therewith my Maker, and present   5
   My true account, lest he returning chide;
   "Doth God exact day-labor, light denied?"
   I fondly ask; but Patience to prevent
That murmur, soon replies, "God doth not need
   Either man's work or his own gifts; who best   10
   Bear his mild yoke, they serve him best. His state
Is kingly. Thousands at his bidding speed
   And post o'er land and ocean without rest:
   They also serve who only stand and wait."

TOPICS FOR CRITICAL THINKING

1. The sonnet takes the form of a question, presented in the octave, followed by the answer given in the sestet. Rhyming *spent*, *wide*, *hide*, *bent*, *present*, *chide*, *denied*, and *prevent*, how does the poem's octave question whether God will "exact day-labor, light denied"? What is Milton's point here?

2. Consider how Milton's pun on the word *light* signifies both the poet's literal loss of eyesight and his unenlightened spiritual state.

3. Examine the poem's turning point in the sestet where the allegorical figure of "Patience" consoles the poet with a sublime insight into the transcendent vision that "His state / Is kingly."

4. What advice does "Patience" give Milton about enduring the "mild yoke" of his condition as sufficient proof of his good faith?

TOPIC FOR CRITICAL WRITING

The subtext for this poem is the biblical parable of the talents related by Jesus Christ in Matthew 25:14–30. In it, God gives a man a gold piece or talent, which he buries for safekeeping. When God returns, he chides the man for not turning his talent to profit as the other servant has done, increasing his talent fivefold. How does Milton's sonnet work through the poet's dilemma and his doubts concerning his fitness to serve God by putting to good use his "one talent" of writing (Milton's pun on the biblical talent)?

William Shakespeare and Edmund Spenser similarly muse in the sonnet form on poetry itself as the cure for the forces of change and mortality.

WILLIAM SHAKESPEARE *(1564–1616)*

Sonnet 55 *(1609)*

Not marble, nor the gilded monuments
Of princes, shall outlive this powerful rhyme;
But you shall shine more bright in these contènts
Than unswept stone, besmeared with sluttish time.
When wasteful war shall statues overturn,   5
And broils root out the work of masonry,
Nor Mars his sword nor war's quick fire shall burn
The living record of your memory.
'Gainst death and all-oblivious enmity
Shall you pace forth; your praise shall still find room   10
Even in the eyes of all posterity
That wear this world out to the ending doom.
   So, till the judgment that yourself arise,
   You live in this, and dwell in lovers' eyes.

TOPICS FOR CRITICAL THINKING

1. Examine how Shakespeare's Sonnet 55 divides into three movements across the sonnet's three quatrain divisions.
2. What is Shakespeare's argument concerning poetry's power to prove more lasting than monuments made from what, at first glance, seem more valuable: marble and gold?
3. What is "sluttish time"? What is Shakespeare's argument concerning poetry's relation to time?
4. Consider the ways in which Shakespeare's couplet encapsulates the sonnet's themes on the love and transcendence that poetry achieves over time, mortality, and doom.

TOPIC FOR CRITICAL WRITING

In Shakespeare's Sonnet 55, how does poetry's "living record" similarly outlast war as well as the "work" of the stonemason?

EDMUND SPENSER   *(1552–1599)*

Sonnet 75   *(1595)*

One day I wrote her name upon the strand,
But came the waves and washèd it away:
Agayne I wrote it with a second hand,
But came the tyde, and made my paynes his pray.
Vayne man, sayd she, that doest in vaine assay,   5
A mortall thing so to immortalize,
For I my selve shall lyke to this decay,
And eek my name bee wypèd out lykewize.
Not so, (quod I) let baser things devize
To dy in dust, but you shall live by fame: 10
My verse your vertues rare shall eternize,
And in the hevens wryte your glorious name.
Where whenas death shall all the world subdew,
Our love shall live, and later life renew.

TOPICS FOR CRITICAL THINKING

1. Consider how the first three quatrain rhyme units stage a dialogue on the situation of writing in relation to time, change, and mortality.
2. How does the poet's couplet give Spenser the last word on poetry's power to "immortalize" the lover?

TOPIC FOR CRITICAL WRITING

Although less grand in its claims than Shakespeare's Sonnet 55, Spenser's Sonnet 75 similarly offers poetry as the antidote for time's mutability. Discuss this theme in Spenser's poem.

Not all sonnet forms follow the prescribed rhyme scheme to the letter. The majority of Italian sonnets, especially, present a variation on the *cdecde* rhyme pattern in the sestet, as in Gwendolyn Brooks's "the rites for Cousin Vit."

GWENDOLYN BROOKS   *(1917–2000)*

the rites for Cousin Vit   *(1949)*

Carried her unprotesting out the door.
Kicked back the casket-stand. But it can't hold her,
That stuff and satin aiming to enfold her,
The lid's contrition nor the bolts before.
Oh oh. Too much. Too much. Even now, surmise,   5

She rises in the sunshine. There she goes,
Back to the bars she knew and the repose
In love-rooms and the things in people's eyes.
Too vital and too squeaking. Must emerge.
Even now she does the snake-hips with a hiss,   10
Slops the bad wine across her shantung, talks
Of pregnancy, guitars and bridgework, walks
In parks or alleys, comes haply on the verge
Of happiness, haply hysterics. Is.

TOPICS FOR CRITICAL THINKING

1. How does Brooks vary the rhyme scheme of the Italian sonnet form in her sestet?
2. Characterize Cousin Vit. What qualities and forces of vitality does she embody?
3. In what ways does Cousin Vit transcend mortality and the funeral rites that are "aiming to enfold her"? How are her energies more powerful than mortality?
4. What kinds of dramatic effects does Brooks achieve through her use of sentence fragments and exclamatory utterances in the poem?

TOPIC FOR CRITICAL WRITING

Discuss the poem's opening situation and its reversal in the sestet.

The Villanelle

As equally complex and demanding of the poet's art as the sonnet, the French form of the **villanelle** originated in Italy and shares its root meaning with such words as *villanella*, a dance or country song, and *villano* or peasant. At nineteen lines, the villanelle is somewhat longer than the sonnet with five tercets and a final quatrain. The rhyme scheme describes a series of repeated refrain lines that reflect the form's origins in the circular returns of a folk dance. The complicated refrain pattern follows the sequence of *A1bA2 abA1 abA2 abA1 abA2 abA1A2*, with *A1* and *A2* forming the refrain lines as in Theodore Roethke's villanelle "The Waking."

THEODORE ROETHKE   *(1908–1963)*

The Waking   *(1953)*

I wake to sleep, and take my waking slow.
I feel my fate in what I cannot fear.
I learn by going where I have to go.

We think by feeling. What is there to know?
I hear my being dance from ear to ear.   5
I wake to sleep, and take my waking slow.

Of those so close beside me, which are you?
God bless the Ground! I shall walk softly there,
And learn by going where I have to go.

Light takes the Tree; but who can tell us how?   10
The lowly worm climbs up a winding stair;
I wake to sleep, and take my waking slow.

Great Nature has another thing to do
To you and me, so take the lively air,
And, lovely, learn by going where to go.   15

This shaking keeps me steady. I should know.
What falls away is always. And is near.
I wake to sleep, and take my waking slow.
I learn by going where I have to go.

TOPICS FOR CRITICAL THINKING

1. "The Waking" is a masterful performance of the villanelle whose fixed form provides the vehicle for the poet's celebration of his being in the world. Discuss the ways in which Roethke's refrain lines turn on life's contradictory intensities.
2. What other paradoxes does the poem celebrate?
3. Consider how the villanelle affords Roethke, as poet, the formal means for giving memorable utterance to his key insights into his experience.

TOPIC FOR CRITICAL WRITING

Roethke has written that "sometimes, of course, there is regression. I believe that the spiritual man must go back in order to go forward. The way is circuitous, and sometimes lost, but invariably returned to." How does the figure of the "lowly worm" present a symbol for the poet's regression—of "going back" to subhuman things? How does that regressive identification with subhuman things, paradoxically enough, become the beginning of his spiritual journey?

The Sestina

The last fixed form we will consider is the most complex of all, the **sestina**. This form began in the twelfth century with the troubadours, medieval poets who set their poems to music to be sung by performing artists called *joglars*. Provençal poet Arnaut Daniel is thought to have invented the first sestina. The form is composed in pentameter with six stanzas of six lines each, followed by a three-line **envoy,** or short stanza. Instead of being structured with end rhyme, the form is organized according to the repetition of the initial six end words that shift their line position in the following order:

```
stanza 1: A B C D E F
       2: F A E B D C
       3: C F D A B E
       4: E C B F A D
       5: D E A C F B
       6: B D F E C A
envoy:    E C A or A C E
```

Poets who have successfully mastered the complexity of the sestina are a select group indeed. Among the practitioners of this difficult fixed form are Sir Philip Sidney ("Yee Gote-heard Gods"), Algernon Swinburne ("The Complaint of Lisa"), Ezra Pound ("Sestina: Altaforte" and "Sestina for Isolt"), W. H. Auden ("Paysage moralisé"), Louise MacNeice ("To Hedli"), Roy Fuller ("Sestina"), Anthony Hecht ("The Book of Yolek"), John Ashbery ("The Painter"), and Elizabeth Bishop ("Sestina").

Pattern Poetry, Concrete Poetics, and Vers Libre

A version of fixed form verse, **pattern poetry,** presents the typography and arrangement of lines on the page as a visual icon for its subject matter. Pattern poetry dates as far back as the Cretan and Egyptian civilizations; in ancient Greece it was known as *technopaigneia*. Pattern poetry in the shapes of the sun and moon, wings, altars, columns, pyramids, and so on were popular during the Medieval period and can be seen, for example, in George Herbert's poem "Easter Wings."

GEORGE HERBERT   *(1593–1633)*

Easter Wings   *(1633)*

Lord, who createdst man in wealth and store,
Though foolishly he lost the same,
Decaying more and more
Till he became
Most poor:
With thee
O let me rise
As larks, harmoniously,
And sing this day thy victories:
Then shall the fall further the flight in me.

5

10

My tender age in sorrow did begin;
And still with sicknesses and shame
Thou didst so punish sin,
That I became
Most thin.   15
With thee
Let me combine,
And feel this day thy victory;
For, if I imp my wing on thine,
Affliction shall advance the flight in me.   20

Herbert's pattern poem not only mimics the look of wings on the page, but represents in the length of the line the poem's thematic nadir of the loss of grace and the plenitude of its recovery. In the twentieth century, the **Concrete Poetry Movement** of the 1950s, spearheaded by Eugen Gomringer and Öyvind Fahlström, played with the visual possibilities of pattern poems in calligraphy, typewriter art, stamp art, and typographical design. Contemporary poets such as John Hollander and May Swenson offer further examples of how pattern poetry can suggest fascinating parallels between word and world.

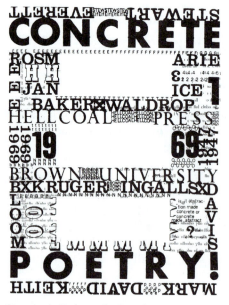

Stewart A. Baker, ed., Envelope Lover,
Love Vortex Vertigo (1969)

JOHN HOLLANDER   *(b. 1929)*

Swan and Shadow   *(1969)*

```
                         Dusk
                      Above the
                  water hang the
                          loud
                          flies                                    5
                          Here
                          O so
                          gray
                          then
                   What              A pale signal will appear    10
                   When              Soon before its shadow fades
                   Where            Here in this pool of opened eye
                   In us     No Upon us As at the very edges
                 of where we take shape in the dark air
                    this object bares its image awakening          15
                    ripples of recognition that will
                         brush darkness up into light
 even after this bird this hour both drift by atop the perfect sad instant now
                       already passing out of sight
                    toward yet-untroubled reflection               20
                  this image bears its object darkening
                  into memorial shades Scattered bits of
                   light     No of water Or something across
                   water          Breaking up No Being regathered
                   soon             Yet by then a swan will have    25
                    gone            Yes out of mind into what
                         vast
                          pale
                          hush
                          of a                                     30
                          place
                          past
                  sudden dark as
                      if a swan
                          sang                                     35
```

MAY SWENSON   *(1913–1989)*

Bleeding   *(1970)*

Stop bleeding   said the knife
I would if I   could said the cut.
Stop bleeding   you make me messy with this blood.
I'm sorry said   the cut.
Stop or I will   sink in farther said the knife.   5
Don't said the   cut.
The knife did   not say it couldn't help it but it sank in farther.
If only you   didn't bleed said the knife I wouldn't have to do this.
I know said   the cut I bleed too easily I hate that I can't
help it I   wish I were a knife like you and   didn't have to bleed.   10
Meanwhile   stop bleeding will you said the knife.
Yes you   are a mess and sinking in deeper said the cut I will
have to   stop.
Have you   stopped by now said the knife.
I've almost   stopped I think.   15
Why must you   bleed in the first place said the knife.
For the reason   maybe that you must do what you must do said the cut.
I can't stand   bleeding said the knife and sank in farther.
I hate it too   said the cut I know it isn't you it's me   20
you're lucky to   be a knife you ought to be glad about that.
Too many cuts   around said the knife they're messy I don't know
how they stand   themselves.
They don't said   the cut.
You're bleeding   again.   25
No I've stopped   said the cut. See you're coming out now the
blood is drying   it will rub off you'll be shiny again and clean.
If only cuts   wouldn't bleed so much said the knife coming out a little.
But then knives   might become dull said the cut.
Aren't you bleeding   a little said the knife.   30
I hope not said the   cut.
I feel you are just   a little.
Maybe just a little   but I can stop now.
I feel a little   wetness still said the knife sinking in
a little but then   coming out a little.   35
Just a little maybe   just enough said the cut.
That's enough now   stop now do you feel better now said the knife.
I feel I have to   bleed to feel I think said the cut.
I don't I don't have   to feel said the knife drying now becoming shiny.

Open Poetic Forms

Increasingly in the twentieth century, much poetry parts company with the formal measures of fixed form as well as iconic form of pattern poetry. Variously labeled as **vers libre, free verse**, and **open form** poetry, this kind of verse varies line length, typography, rhythms, and stanza patterns to fit the particular style and content of the work at hand. The modern poet Theodore Roethke composed in both fixed and free verse, and especially mined the possibilities of open form in his expansive long poem sequence "North American Sequence." Roethke, however, thought of free verse as a "denial in terms." "There is, invariably," he wrote, "the ghost of some other form, often blank verse, behind what is written."

Nevertheless, the careers of other poets, such as W. S. Merwin, move increasingly away from the closure of fixed form. Merwin, especially, plays his lines off against the white space of the page, and, after his 1963 volume *The Moving Target*, he abandons completely the fixity of punctuation. "Punctuation," he has said, "nails the poem down on the page; when you don't use it the poem becomes more a thing in itself, at once more transparent and more actual." Such techniques create a striking openness of statement, as in his poem "The Well."

W. S. MERWIN   *(b. 1927)*

The Well   *(1970)*

Under the stone sky the water
waits
with all its songs inside it
the immortal
it sang once   5
it will sing again
the days
walk across the stone in heaven
unseen as planets at noon
while the water   10
watches the same night

Echoes come in like swallows
calling to it
it answers without moving
but in echoes   15
not in its voice
they do not say what it is
only where

It is a city to which many travellers
came with clear minds   20
having left everything even
heaven
to sit in the dark praying as one silence
for the resurrection

TOPICS FOR CRITICAL THINKING

1. How does Merwin's line length mirror the sense of the metaphoric figures in this poem?
2. How has his decision to abandon punctuation opened up the possibilities of interpretive meaning in "The Well"?

TOPIC FOR CRITICAL WRITING

In what ways do Merwin's lines play against the white space of the page? To what effect?

Questions like those posed above are not easily answered because open form verse frees up, rather than limits, the available range of the reader's response to the work. Many different versions of free verse abound in twentieth-century poetics, and your instructor can help you interpret the several free verse poems included throughout the Poetry Section of *Understanding Poetry*.

Featured Writer

Joseph Severn, *John Keats* (1818)

JOHN KEATS

Born in 1795, John Keats was the eldest child of Thomas and Frances Jennings Keats; he had three brothers—George, Thomas, and Edward—and one sister, Frances Mary. Thomas Keats managed a livery stable at the Swan and Hoop Inn that was owned by his father-in-law John Jennings. Not insignificantly, John Keats's boyhood was marked by a series of traumas. When the poet was nine years old, his father was killed in a riding accident in April 1804; Keats's mother remarried two months later. Soon thereafter, Keats and his siblings were taken in by their grandmother Alice Jennings. The next year, John Jennings, the poet's grandfather, died, leaving an estate that was subsequently mismanaged to the poet's disadvantage in later life. In 1805, Alice moved the children from Enfield to Edmonton. The following year, the poet's mother Frances left her second husband and was reputed to be living with another man in Edmonton. She would eventually return to live with her mother and children for a short time before dying in 1810 of tuberculosis. As one of his mother's primary caregivers during her illness, John Keats was profoundly affected by this loss, magnified in the deaths by tuberculosis of his uncle in 1808 and his brother Tom ten years later.

After receiving an early education from John Clarke, the independent-minded headmaster of the Enfield school, Keats began an apprenticeship to the Edmonton apothecary surgeon Thomas Hammond in 1811. In 1814, Keats's grandmother Alice Jennings died. The following year, Keats pursued his medical training at Guy's Hospital. Passing his apothecaries' examination the next year, Keats also published his first poem, the sonnet "O Solitude" in Leigh Hunt's journal, the *Examiner*.

Keats's commitment to poetry grew apace, owing in part to his reading of Homer, the subject of his sonnet "On First Looking into Chapman's Homer." The title of this Italian sonnet refers to a 1616 folio edition of Homer's *Iliad* and *Odyssey* translated by George Chapman. Keats's friend Charles Cowden Clarke had been loaned the book, and the two had sat up all night reading it together in October 1816. The next morning, Keats composed what is regarded as his finest work from his first volume *Poems*.

On First Looking into Chapman's Homer   *(1816)*

Much have I traveled in the realms of gold,
   And many goodly states and kingdoms seen;
   Round many western islands have I been
Which bards in fealty to Apollo hold.
Oft of one wide expanse had I been told   5
   That deep-browed Homer ruled as his demesne;
   Yet did I never breathe its pure serene
Till I heard Chapman speak out loud and bold:
Then felt I like some watcher of the skies
   When a new planet swims into his ken;   10
Or like stout Cortez when with eagle eyes
   He stared at the Pacific—and all his men
Looked at each other with a wild surmise—
   Silent, upon a peak in Darien.

TOPICS FOR CRITICAL THINKING

1. The word *demesne* is defined by the *American Heritage Dictionary* as "lands retained by a feudal lord for his own use." Similarly *fealty* refers to a vassal's loyalty to a lord. What tropes of ownership, regal authority, and divine rule can you identify in the poem?

2. How does Keats read literary tradition in terms of these relations of power? To what extent does the sonnet perform Keats's own place within that tradition?

3. Balboa, not Cortez, was the first European to view the Pacific Ocean from Darien in Panama. What do you know about Cortez? However mistaken, how does this error on Keats's part parallel the poem's other themes of ownership, ambition, and conquest?

TOPIC FOR CRITICAL WRITING

Keats's brother George had a keen interest in America and emigrated there two years after Keats composed "On First Looking into Chapman's Homer." For his part, Keats had the opportunity to read William Robertson's *History of America*, which documents the European discovery of the Pacific. In what ways does Keats portray the role of reading as discovery?

Soon Keats's circle of acquaintances grew to include Benjamin Haydon, John Hamilton Reynolds, and Percy Bysshe Shelley. Keats abandoned medicine as a career in 1817. That same year, C. and J. Ollier published Keats's first volume of verse, *Poems*, as the poet combined work on his next volume *Endymion* with visits to the Isle of Wight, Margate, Hastings, and Oxford. By the end of 1817, Keats had also met Benjamin Bailey, Charles Wentworth Dilke, Charles Brown, and the poet William Wordsworth. Even at this early stage, Keats's poetry begins to testify to a certain world weariness and growing sense of mortality, which the young poet portrays in "On Seeing the Elgin Marbles."

On Seeing the Elgin Marbles   *(1817)*

My spirit is too weak—mortality
  Weighs heavily on me like unwilling sleep,
  And each imagined pinnacle and steep
Of godlike hardship tells me I must die
Like a sick eagle looking at the sky.   5
  Yet 'tis a gentle luxury to weep
  That I have not the cloudy winds to keep
Fresh for the opening of the morning's eye.
Such dim-conceived glories of the brain
  Bring round the heart an indescribable feud;   10
So do these wonders a most dizzy pain,
  That mingles Grecian grandeur with the rude
Wasting of old Time—with a billowy main—
  A sun—a shadow of a magnitude.

    The so-called Elgin Marbles consist of fragmentary remains of sculptures that once adorned the Parthenon built in Athens from 447 B.C. to 432 B.C. The Parthenon housed a magnificent statue of the goddess Athena. The marbles stage battle scenes between Olympian gods and mythic giants, as well as among the Greeks, Amazons, Centaurs, and Trojans. Other scenes depict Panathenaic festivals. In addition to the Elgin Marbles of the British Museum, the Parthenon marbles are housed in Athens and the Louvre in Paris. Lord Elgin had brought fragments of the Parthenon marbles to London from Greece

The Elgin Marbles

in 1807. The year before Keats wrote the sonnet, they were the subject of political debate in the House of Commons on the question of whether England should purchase them from Elgin. At the time, Keats's liberal colleagues sided with the effort to buy them as a way of elevating British culture. Conservatives were reluctant to support a neoclassical revival that would undermine Christian values. Indeed, by celebrating Grecian art and literature, Keats himself was attacked as the "Cockney Homer" in an 1818 issue of *Blackwood's.*

TOPICS FOR CRITICAL THINKING

1. How does Keats relate the representations of "godlike hardship" back to his own situation as poet in the opening sestet of this Italian sonnet?
2. Describe the ways in which Keats interrupts his lines in the octave to imitate the breaks and erosions visible in the marbles, which have been subject to the "Wasting of old Time."
www 3. Take a look at the images of the Elgin Marbles **Web** and imagine other ways that Keats might have celebrated their "magnitude" in verse.

TOPIC FOR CRITICAL WRITING

Compare Keats's experience of viewing the "Grecian grandeur" of the Elgin marbles with his imaginative musings on the myths and mysteries of classical art in "Ode on a Grecian Urn," which is printed on the following pages.

The sparse sales of Keats's first volume of poems led him to place his second book *Endymion* with Taylor and Hessey, who published it in 1818. Keats's ties to the liberal-minded editor Leigh Hunt generated hostile reviews from the conservative ranks of Blackwood's *Edinburgh Magazine* and from the editors of *Critical Quarterly.* The myth that Keats was devastated by this harsh reception—that, as Lord Byron has it in *Don Juan,* the young Keats was "snuffed out by an article"—has been somewhat overstated. For his part, Keats allowed as how "my own domestic criticism has given me pain beyond what Blackwood or the *Quarterly* could possibly inflict." Certainly, however, 1818 was a very difficult year for Keats, owing not only to the critical attacks he suffered for *Endymion* but to his brother Tom's declining health from tuberculosis.

Beginning in March 1818, John replaced his brother George as Tom's caretaker in Teignmouth. George would go on to marry Georgiana Augusta Wylie that May and emigrate to America the next month. For Tom and John Keats, however, that early Devonshire spring was wet and dreary. Yet it was also a time when Keats read deeply in Milton and drafted, among other things, his poem *Isabella* and his famous letter to John Hamilton Reynolds on the "Chamber of Maiden-thought." At the end of the spring, John accompanied George and Georgiana to Liverpool and then joined Charles Brown on a tour of the Lake District and Scotland. By the end of the summer, Keats's own health was jarred by a severe cold and sore throat that, along with the news that Tom's condition had deteriorated, made him cut short his tour of Scotland.

Returning to London in August, it was during the upcoming fall that Keats met and eventually fell in love with Fanny Brawne. But the poet's brother Tom was bedridden and emaciated from advanced tuberculosis, and

Keats took on the responsibility of nursing his brother as he had earlier with their mother. On the morning of December 1, Tom died of the disease. Following the death of his brother, Keats shared half of Brown's house at Wentworth Place, Hampstead.

Beginning in January 1819, Keats enjoyed the most creative and productive period of his career as a poet. From January through February he composed "The Eve of St. Agnes," followed by "La Belle Dame sans Merci" that April, the same month that the Brawne family became his neighbors at Wentworth Place. During April and May, he composed the great odes—"Psyche," "Nightingale," "Grecian Urn," and "Melancholy." Leaving Wentworth, in part to distance himself from his passionate attachment to Fanny, Keats composed *Lamia* on the Isle of Wight and worked on *The Fall of Hyperion* from July through the end of the summer, composing "To Autumn" as well that September. This intense schedule of writing also included the poet's collaboration with Brown on the tragedy *Otho the Great*, several scenes for another tragedy, *King Stephen*, and a partially completed satire, *The Jealousies (The Cap and Bells)*.

Keats's great creative period came to an end that fall as the symptoms of tuberculosis began to manifest themselves, culminating with a severe hemorrhage in the lungs on February 3, 1820. That May, Keats moved to Kentish Town, close to Hampstead, then to the home of Leigh Hunt following yet another hemorrhage. Eventually, Keats returned to Wentworth Place in August where he was attended by Fanny Brawne and her mother. Meanwhile, Keats's third book of poems *Lamia, Isabella, The Eve of St. Agnes and Other Poems* was published in July by Taylor and Hessey. Twelve reviews came out in the two months following its release and, unlike the criticisms of *Endymion*, the majority were favorable. Yet this good news was tempered by Keats's diagnosis of consumption and his doctors' insistence that he spend the winter in Italy, which, of course, meant a separation from Fanny. By this time the two had an understanding of engagement, but there was little realistic hope that Keats would return from his trip to Rome.

Keats left England bound for Italy on September 18, 1820, accompanied by his friend, the artist Joseph Severn. After taking up residence on the second floor of 26 Piazza di Spagna in Rome, Keats's condition worsened steadily and, attended by Severn until the very end, the poet died on February 23, 1821. Today, Keats lies buried in the Protestant cemetery in Rome, where his tombstone, as the poet intended, bears his famous epitaph: "Here lies 'One Whose Name was writ in Water.'"

Poems for Further Reading and Critical Writing

JOHN KEATS   *(1795–1821)*

Ode on a Grecian Urn   *(1820)*

1

Thou still unravished bride of quietness,
    Thou foster child of silence and slow time,

Sylvan historian, who canst thus express
　　A flowery tale more sweetly than our rhyme:
What leaf-fringed legend haunts about thy shape   5
　　Of deities or mortals, or of both,
　　　　In Tempe or the dales of Arcady?°
　　What men or gods are these? What maidens loath?
What mad pursuit? What struggle to escape?
　　　　What pipes and timbrels? What wild ecstasy?   10

2

Heard melodies are sweet, but those unheard
　　Are sweeter; therefore, ye soft pipes, play on;
Not to the sensual ear, but, more endeared,
　　Pipe to the spirit ditties of no tone:
Fair youth, beneath the trees, thou canst not leave   15
　　Thy song, nor ever can those trees be bare;
　　　　Bold Lover, never, never canst thou kiss,
Though winning near the goal—yet, do not grieve;
　　　　She cannot fade, though thou hast not thy bliss,
　　Forever wilt thou love, and she be fair!   20

3

Ah, happy, happy boughs! that cannot shed
　　Your leaves, nor ever bid the Spring adieu;
And, happy melodist, unweariéd,
　　For ever piping songs for ever new;
More happy love! more happy, happy love!   25
　　For ever warm and still to be enjoyed,
　　　　For ever panting, and for ever young;
All breathing human passion far above,
　　That leaves a heart high-sorrowful and cloyed,
　　　　A burning forehead, and a parching tongue.   30

4

Who are these coming to the sacrifice?
　　To what green altar, O mysterious priest,
Lead'st thou that heifer lowing at the skies,
　　And all her silken flanks with garlands dressed?
What little town by river or sea shore,   35
　　Or mountain-built with peaceful citadel,
　　　　Is emptied of this folk, this pious morn?
And, little town, thy streets forevermore
　　Will silent be; and not a soul to tell
　　　　Why thou art desolate, can e'er return.   40

———
7 *Arcady:* Pastoral valleys in Greece.

5

O Attic° shape! Fair attitude! with brede
　Of marble men and maidens overwrought,
With forest branches and the trodden weed;
　Thou, silent form, dost tease us out of thought
As doth eternity: Cold Pastoral!　　　　　　　　　　　　　　　45
　When old age shall this generation waste,
　　Thou shalt remain, in midst of other woe
Than ours, a friend to man, to whom thou say'st,
　"Beauty is truth, truth beauty,"—that is all
　　Ye know on earth, and all ye need to know.　　　　　　50

TOPICS FOR CRITICAL THINKING

1. Examine and discuss your interpretations of each of Keats's personifications of the urn in stanza one. How do these figurative presentations of the urn set up particular themes and presentational motifs in the remaining stanzas of the poem?
2. Compare the images inscribed on the urn in stanzas two and three. How do they move beyond the realities of human time into a vision of eternity? How would you describe the effect of this vision on the poet at the end of the third stanza?
3. Consider the poet's changing narrative point of view in the ode. How does the narrative voice of the poem differ before, during, and after the poet's encounter with the urn?
4. Why does Keats call the urn a "Cold Pastoral" in the last stanza?
5. In earlier drafts of the poem, the concluding insight that "Beauty is truth, truth beauty" is stated without quotation marks. What difference do the quote marks make? Who do you imagine is speaking here? What are the possibilities?

TOPIC FOR CRITICAL WRITING

Compare the poet's conclusions on truth and beauty with his letter to Benjamin Bailey, November 22, 1817, reprinted later in this chapter, where Keats writes that "the Imagination may be compared to Adam's dream—he awoke and found it truth."

Keats composed "Ode to a Nightingale" in May 1819 prior to his writing "Ode on a Grecian Urn." The two poems share a similar narrative plot design of

- imaginatively penetrating beyond the actualities of the real world;
- envisioning a metaphysical dimension variously of eternity, spirituality, and truth; and
- returning to the present with an altered understanding of existence.

Consider how this tri-part structure gives shape to Keats's "Ode to a Nightingale."

──────

41 *Attic:* Attic was a geographical region in Greece that included Athens.

Ode to a Nightingale   *(1819)*

1

My heart aches, and a drowsy numbness pains
   My sense, as though of hemlock° I had drunk,
Or emptied some dull opiate to the drains
   One minute past, and Lethe-wards° had sunk:
'Tis not through envy of thy happy lot,   5
   But being too happy in thine happiness—
      That thou, light-wingéd Dryad of the trees,
         In some melodious plot
   Of beechen green, and shadows numberless,
   Singest of summer in full-throated ease.   10

2

O, for a draught of vintage! that hath been
   Cooled a long age in the deep-delvéd earth,
Tasting of Flora° and the country green,
   Dance, and Provençal song, and sunburnt mirth!
O for a beaker full of the warm South,   15
   Full of the true, the blushful Hippocrene,°
      With beaded bubbles winking at the brim,
         And purple-stainéd mouth;
   That I might drink, and leave the world unseen,
   And with thee fade away into the forest dim: 20

3

Fade far away, dissolve, and quite forget
   What thou among the leaves hast never known,
The weariness, the fever, and the fret
   Here, where men sit and hear each other groan;
Where palsy shakes a few, sad, last gray hairs,   25
   Where youth grows pale, and specter-thin, and dies,
      Where but to think is to be full of sorrow
         And leaden-eyed despairs,
   Where Beauty cannot keep her lustrous eyes,
   Or new Love pine at them beyond tomorrow.   30

4

Away! away! for I will fly to thee,
   Not charioted by Bacchus and his pards,

---

2 *hemlock:* Poison.   4 *Lethe-wards:* Toward the mythic river of forgetfulness in Hades.
13 *Flora:* Roman goddess of flowers.   16 *Hippocrene:* Fountain on Mt. Helicon, sacred
to the Muses.

But on the viewless wings of Poesy,
　　Though the dull brain perplexes and retards:
Already with thee! tender is the night,　　　　　　　　　　　　35
　　And haply the Queen-Moon is on her throne,
　　　　Clustered around by all her starry Fays;°
　　　　　　But here there is no light,
Save what from heaven is with the breezes blown
　　Through verdurous glooms and winding mossy ways.　　40

5

I cannot see what flowers are at my feet,
　　Nor what soft incense hangs upon the boughs,
But, in embalméd darkness, guess each sweet
　　Wherewith the seasonable month endows
The grass, the thicket, and the fruit tree wild;　　　　　　45
　　White hawthorn, and the pastoral eglantine;
　　　　Fast fading violets covered up in leaves;
　　　　　　And mid-May's eldest child,
The coming musk-rose, full of dewy wine,
　　The murmurous haunt of flies on summer eves.　　　50

6

Darkling I listen; and for many a time
　　I have been half in love with easeful Death,
Called him soft names in many a muséd rhyme,
　　To take into the air my quiet breath;
Now more than ever seems it rich to die,　　　　　　　55
　　To cease upon the midnight with no pain,
　　　　While thou art pouring forth thy soul abroad
　　　　　　In such an ecstasy!
Still wouldst thou sing, and I have ears in vain—
　　To thy high requiem become a sod.　　　　　　　　60

7

Thou wast not born for death, immortal Bird!
　　No hungry generations tread thee down;
The voice I hear this passing night was heard
　　In ancient days by emperor and clown:
Perhaps the selfsame song that found a path　　　　　65
　　Through the sad heart of Ruth,° when, sick for home,
　　　　She stood in tears amid the alien corn;
　　　　　　The same that ofttimes hath
Charmed magic casements, opening on the foam
　　Of perilous seas, in faery lands forlorn.　　　　　　70

---

37 *Fays:* Fairies.　　66 *Ruth:* See Biblical Book of Ruth.

8

Forlorn! the very word is like a bell
 To toil me back from thee to my sole self!
Adieu! the fancy cannot cheat so well
 As she is famed to do, deceiving elf.
Adieu! adieu! thy plaintive anthem fades   75
  Past the near meadows, over the still stream,
   Up the hill side; and now 'tis buried deep
    In the next valley-glades:
Was it a vision, or a waking dream?
 Fled is that music:—Do I wake or sleep?   80

TOPICS FOR CRITICAL THINKING

1. Consider Keats's opening address to the nightingale in the figure of a "Dryad" or wood nymph and discuss the ways in which he attempts to identify with it in stanzas 1–4.

2. Keats had nursed his brother Tom all during the previous fall up until his death in December 1818. How might that experience bear on the poet's sense of grief and vision of mortality in stanza 3?

3. Consider how Keats's various attempts to escape the heartache described in the opening stanzas relate to his stated death wish in stanza 6.

4. Read Keats's letter to George and Thomas Keats, December 21, 1817, reprinted later in this chapter, especially where Keats defines "Negative Capability" as the ability to be "in uncertainties, Mysteries, doubts, without any irritable reaching after fact & reason." How might this state characterize the poet's transcendental encounter with the nightingale in stanzas 6 and 7?

5. Describe Keats's transcendental vision of the "immortal Bird" in stanza 7. Compare and contrast that metaphysical moment to the encounter Keats has with the urn in "Ode on a Grecian Urn."

6. Compare and contrast the poet's return to the actual world in stanza 8 with the urn as a "Cold Pastoral" in "Ode on a Grecian Urn."

TOPIC FOR CRITICAL WRITING

Keats's final question—"Do I wake or sleep?"—hints at the poet's bewilderment after his ecstatic encounter with the nightingale. Compare this poem with the knight's dream in the poem that follows, "La Belle Dame sans Merci."

La Belle Dame sans Merci   *(1819)*

1

O what can ail thee, knight-at-arms,
 Alone and palely loitering?
The sedge has withered from the lake,
 And no birds sing.

2

O what can ail thee, knight-at-arms,   5
   So haggard and so woe-begone?
The squirrel's granary is full
   And the harvest's done.

3

I see a lily on thy brow
   With anguish moist and fever dew,   10
And on thy cheeks a fading rose
   Fast withereth too.

4

"I met a lady in the Meads,
   Full beautiful, a faery's child,
Her hair was long, her foot was light   15
   And her eyes were wild.

5

"I made a Garland for her head,
   And bracelets too, and fragrant Zone;
She looked at me as she did love,
   And made sweet moan.   20

6

"I set her on my pacing steed
   And nothing else saw all day long,
For sidelong would she bend, and sing
   A faery's song.

7

"She found me roots of relish sweet,   25
   And honey wild, and manna dew,
And sure in language strange she said
   'I love thee true.'

8

"She took me to her elfin grot,
   And there she wept and sighed full sore,   30
And there I shut her wild wild eyes
   With kisses four.

9

"And there she lulléd me asleep,
  And there I dreamed, Ah! Woe betide!
The latest dream I ever dreamed   35
  On the cold hill side

10

"I saw pale kings and princes too,
  Pale warriors, death pale were they all;
They cried—"La belle dame sans merci
  Hath thee in thrall!"   40

11

"I saw their starved lips in the gloom,
  With horrid warning gapéd wide,
And I awoke, and found me here
  On the cold hill's side.

12

"And this is why I sojourn here,   45
  Alone and palely loitering,
Though the sedge is wither'd from the lake,
  And no birds sing."

TOPICS FOR CRITICAL THINKING

1. Compare and contrast the portraits of the belle dame and the knight. How does Keats's imagery and language distinguish the two?
2. Discuss Keats's presentation of narrative point of view in the poem. How many points of view can you distinguish? Who narrates the first four stanzas? How does the narrator of the first-person pronoun *I* shift in stanza 4? What other narrators can you find in the poem?
3. Is la belle dame a femme fatale? Is it clear how we are to judge her haunting encounter with the knight? Is there evidence in the poem that makes her a sympathetic, rather than a demonic, figure?

TOPIC FOR CRITICAL WRITING

Keats took his title for the poem from the French writer and poet Alain Chartier, and literary scholars have advanced several echoes in the poem from Spenser and Shakespeare, among others. A possible source for the poem in the pictorial arts is Raphael's painting *An Allegory: Vision of a Knight* (1504), now housed in the National Gallery, London. Keats admired Raphael and may well have seen the painting since it had been on display in London since 1801. Compare Raphael's painting (included in the color insert) with Keats's poem.

The Eve of St. Agnes   *(1819)*

1

St. Agnes' Eve—Ah, bitter chill it was!
The owl, for all his feathers, was a-cold;
The hare limped trembling through the frozen grass,
And silent was the flock in woolly fold:
Numb were the Beadsman's fingers, while he told   5
His rosary, and while his frosted breath,
Like pious incense from a censer old,
Seemed taking flight for heaven, without a death,
Past the sweet Virgin's picture, while his prayer he saith.

2

His prayer he saith, this patient, holy man;   10
Then takes his lamp, and riseth from his knees,
And back returneth, meager, barefoot, wan,
Along the chapel aisle by slow degrees:
The sculptured dead, on each side, seem to freeze,
Imprisoned in black, purgatorial rails: 15
Knights, ladies, praying in dumb orat'ries,
He passeth by; and his weak spirit fails
To think how they may ache in icy hoods and mails.

3

Northward he turneth through a little door,
And scarce three steps, ere Music's golden tongue   20
Flattered to tears this aged man and poor;
But no—already had his deathbell rung:
The joys of all his life were said and sung:
His was harsh penance on St. Agnes' Eve:
Another way he went, and soon among   25
Rough ashes sat he for his soul's reprieve,
And all night kept awake, for sinners' sake to grieve.

4

That ancient Beadsman heard the prelude soft;
And so it chanced, for many a door was wide,
From hurry to and fro. Soon, up aloft,   30
The silver, snarling trumpets 'gan to chide:
The level chambers, ready with their pride,
Were glowing to receive a thousand guests:
The carvéd angels, ever eager-eyed,
Stared, where upon their heads the cornice rests,   35
With hair blown back, and wings put crosswise on their breasts.

5

At length burst in the argent revelry,
With plume, tiara, and all rich array,
Numerous as shadows haunting faerily
The brain, new stuffed, in youth, with triumphs gay   40
Of old romance. These let us wish away,
And turn, sole-thoughted, to one Lady there,
Whose heart had brooded, all that wintry day,
On love, and winged St. Agnes' saintly care,
As she had heard old dames full many times declare.   45

6

They told her how, upon St. Agnes' Eve,
Young virgins might have visions of delight,
And soft adorings from their loves receive
Upon the honeyed middle of the night,
If ceremonies due they did aright;   50
As, supperless to bed they must retire,
And couch supine their beauties, lily white;
Nor look behind, nor sideways, but require
Of heaven with upward eyes for all that they desire.

7

Full of this whim was thoughtful Madeline: 55
The music, yearning like a God in pain,
She scarcely heard: her maiden eyes divine,
Fixed on the floor, saw many a sweeping train
Pass by—she heeded not at all: in vain
Came many a tiptoe, amorous cavalier,   60
And back retired; not cooled by high disdain;
But she saw not: her heart was otherwhere:
She sighed for Agnes' dreams, the sweetest of the year.

8

She danced along with vague, regardless eyes,
Anxious her lips, her breathing quick and short: 65
The hallowed hour was near at hand: she sighs
Amid the timbrels, and the thronged resort
Of whisperers in anger, or in sport;
'Mid looks of love, defiance, hate, and scorn,
Hoodwinked with faery fancy; all amort,   70
Save to St. Agnes and her lambs unshorn,
And all the bliss to be before tomorrow morn.

9

So, purposing each moment to retire,
She lingered still. Meantime, across the moors,
Had come young Porphyro, with heart on fire   75
For Madeline. Beside the portal doors,
Buttressed from moonlight, stands he, and implores
All saints to give him sight of Madeline,
But for one moment in the tedious hours,
 That he might gaze and worship all unseen;   80
Perchance speak, kneel, touch, kiss—in sooth such things have been.

10

He ventures in: let no buzzed whisper tell:
All eyes be muffled, or a hundred swords
Will storm his heart, Love's fev'rous citadel:
For him, those chambers held barbarian hordes,   85
Hyena foemen, and hot-blooded lords,
Whose very dogs would execrations howl
Against his lineage: not one breast affords
 Him any mercy, in that mansion foul,
Save one old beldame, weak in body and in soul.   90

11

Ah, happy chance! the aged creature came,
Shuffling along with ivory-headed wand,
To where he stood, hid from the torch's flame,
Behind a broad hall-pillar, far beyond
The sound of merriment and chorus bland: 95
He startled her; but soon she knew his face,
And grasped his fingers in her palsied hand,
 Saying, "Mercy, Porphyro! hie thee from this place;
They are all here tonight, the whole bloodthirsty race!

12

"Get hence! get hence! there's dwarfish Hildebrand;   100
He had a fever late, and in the fit
He curséd thee and thine, both house and land:
Then there's that old Lord Maurice, not a whit
More tame for his gray hairs—Alas me! flit!
Flit like a ghost away."—"Ah, Gossip dear,   105
We're safe enough; here in this armchair sit,
 And tell me how"—"Good Saints! not here, not here;
Follow me, child, or else these stones will be thy bier."

13

He followed through a lowly archéd way,
Brushing the cobwebs with his lofty plume,   110
And as she muttered "Well-a—well-a-day!"
He found him in a little moonlight room,
Pale, latticed, chill, and silent as a tomb.
"Now tell me where is Madeline," said he,
"O tell me, Angela, by the holy loom   115
Which none but secret sisterhood may see,
When they St. Agnes' wool are weaving piously."

14

"St. Agnes! Ah! it is St. Agnes' Eve—
Yet men will murder upon holy days:
Thou must hold water in a witch's sieve,   120
And be liege lord of all the Elves and Fays,
To venture so: it fills me with amaze
To see thee, Porphyro!—St. Agnes' Eve!
God's help! my lady fair the conjuror plays
This very night: good angels her deceive!   125
But let me laugh awhile, I've mickle° time to grieve."

15

Feebly she laugheth in the languid moon,
While Porphyro upon her face doth look,
Like puzzled urchin on an aged crone
Who keepeth closed a wond'rous riddle-book,   130
As spectacled she sits in chimney nook.
But soon his eyes grew brilliant, when she told
His lady's purpose; and he scarce could brook
Tears, at the thought of those enchantments cold,
And Madeline asleep in lap of legends old.   135

16

Sudden a thought came like a full-blown rose,
Flushing his brow, and in his painéd heart
Made purple riot: then doth he propose
A stratagem, that makes the beldame start:
"A cruel man and impious thou art: 140
Sweet lady, let her pray, and sleep, and dream
Alone with her good angels, far apart
From wicked men like thee. Go, go!—I deem
Thou canst not surely be the same that thou didst seem."

---

126 *Mickle:* Much.

21

So saying, she hobbled off with busy fear.
The lover's endless minutes slowly passed;
The dame returned, and whispered in his ear
To follow her; with aged eyes aghast
From fright of dim espial. Safe at last,   185
Through many a dusky gallery, they gain
The maiden's chamber, silken, hushed, and chaste;
Where Porphyro took covert, pleased amain.
His poor guide hurried back with agues in her brain.

22

Her falt'ring hand upon the balustrade,   190
Old Angela was feeling for the stair,
When Madeline, St. Agnes' charméd maid,
Rose, like a missioned spirit, unaware:
With silver taper's light, and pious care,
She turned, and down the aged gossip led   195
To a safe level matting. Now prepare,
Young Porphyro, for gazing on that bed;
She comes, she comes again, like ringdove frayed and fled.

23

Out went the taper as she hurried in;
Its little smoke, in pallid moonshine, died: 200
She closed the door, she panted, all akin
To spirits of the air, and visions wide:
No uttered syllable, or, woe betide!
But to her heart, her heart was voluble,
Paining with eloquence her balmy side;   205
As though a tongueless nightingale should swell
Her throat in vain, and die, heart-stifled, in her dell.

24

A casement high and triple-arched there was,
All garlanded with carven imag'ries
Of fruits, and flowers, and bunches of knot-grass,   210
And diamonded with panes of quaint device,
Innumerable of stains and splendid dyes,
As are the tiger-moth's deep-damasked wings;
And in the midst, 'mong thousand heraldries,
And twilight saints, and dim emblazonings,   215
A shielded scutcheon blushed with blood of queens and kings.

17

"I will not harm her, by all saints I swear,"
Quoth Porphyro: "O may I ne'er find grace
When my weak voice shall whisper its last prayer,
If one of her soft ringlets I displace,
Or look with ruffian passion in her face:
Good Angela, believe me by these tears;
Or I will, even in a moment's space,
Awake, with horrid shout, my foemen's ears,
And beard them, though they be more fanged than wolves
    and bears."

18

"Ah! why wilt thou affright a feeble soul?
A poor, weak, palsy-stricken, churchyard thing,
Whose passing bell may ere the midnight toll;
Whose prayers for thee, each morn and evening,
Were never missed."—Thus plaining, doth she bring
A gentler speech from burning Porphyro;
So woeful, and of such deep sorrowing,
That Angela gives promise she will do
Whatever he shall wish, betide her weal or woe.

19

Which was, to lead him, in close secrecy,
Even to Madeline's chamber, and there hide
Him in a closet, of such privacy
That he might see her beauty unespied,
And win perhaps that night a peerless bride,
While legioned fairies paced the coverlet,
And pale enchantment held her sleepy-eyed.
Never on such a night have lovers met,
Since Merlin paid his Demon all the monstrous debt.

20

"It shall be as thou wishest," said the Dame:
"All cates and dainties shall be storéd there
Quickly on this feast night: by the tambour frame
Her own lute thou wilt see: no time to spare,
For I am slow and feeble, and scarce dare
On such a catering trust my dizzy head.
Wait here, my child, with patience; kneel in prayer
The while: Ah! thou must needs the lady wed,
Or may I never leave my grave among the dead."

25

Full on this casement shone the wintry moon,
And threw warm gules on Madeline's fair breast,
As down she knelt for heaven's grace and boon;
Rose-bloom fell on her hands, together pressed, 220
And on her silver cross soft amethyst,
And on her hair a glory, like a saint:
She seemed a splendid angel, newly dressed,
Save wings, for heaven—Porphyro grew faint:
She knelt, so pure a thing, so free from mortal taint. 225

26

Anon his heart revives: her vespers done,
Of all its wreathéd pearls her hair she frees;
Unclasps her warméd jewels one by one;
Loosens her fragrant bodice; by degrees
Her rich attire creeps rustling to her knees: 230
Half-hidden, like a mermaid in sea-weed,
Pensive awhile she dreams awake, and sees,
In fancy, fair St. Agnes in her bed,
But dares not look behind, or all the charm is fled.

27

Soon, trembling in her soft and chilly nest, 235
In sort of wakeful swoon, perplexed she lay,
Until the poppied warmth of sleep oppressed
Her soothéd limbs, and soul fatigued away;
Flown, like a thought, until the morrow-day;
Blissfully havened both from joy and pain; 240
Clasped like a missal where swart Paynims pray;
Blinded alike from sunshine and from rain,
As though a rose should shut, and be a bud again.

28

Stol'n to this paradise, and so entranced,
Porphyro gazed upon her empty dress, 245
And listened to her breathing, if it chanced
To wake into a slumberous tenderness;
Which when he heard, that minute did he bless,
And breathed himself: then from the closet crept,
Noiseless as fear in a wide wilderness, 250
And over the hushed carpet, silent, stepped,
And 'tween the curtains peeped, where, lo!—how fast she slept.

29

Then by the bedside, where the faded moon
Made a dim, silver twilight, soft he set
A table, and, half anguished, threw thereon   255
A cloth of woven crimson, gold, and jet:—
O for some drowsy Morphean amulet!
The boisterous, midnight, festive clarion,
The kettledrum, and far-heard clarinet,
Affray his ears, though but in dying tone—   260
The hall door shuts again, and all the noise is gone.

30

And still she slept an azure-lidded sleep,
In blanchéd linen, smooth, and lavendered,
While he from forth the closet brought a heap
Of candied apple, quince, and plum, and gourd;   265
With jellies soother than the creamy curd,
And lucent syrups, tinct with cinnamon;
Manna and dates, in argosy transferred
From Fez; and spicéd dainties, every one,
From silken Samarcand to cedared Lebanon.   270

31

These delicates he heaped with glowing hand
On golden dishes and in baskets bright
Of wreathéd silver: sumptuous they stand
In the retiréd quiet of the night,
Filling the chilly room with perfume light.—   275
"And now, my love, my seraph fair, awake!
Thou art my heaven, and I thine eremite:
Open thine eyes, for meek St. Agnes' sake,
Or I shall drowse beside thee, so my soul doth ache."

32

Thus whispering, his warm, unnervéd arm   280
Sank in her pillow. Shaded was her dream
By the dusk curtains: 'twas a midnight charm
Impossible to melt as icéd stream:
The lustrous salvers in the moonlight gleam;
Broad golden fringe upon the carpet lies: 285
It seemed he never, never could redeem
From such a steadfast spell his lady's eyes;
So mused awhile, entoiled in wooféd fantasies.

33

Awakening up, he took her hollow lute,—
Tumultuous,—and, in chords that tenderest be,   290
He played an ancient ditty, long since mute,
In Provence called, *"La belle dame sans merci":*
Close to her ear touching the melody;
Wherewith disturbed, she uttered a soft moan:
He ceased—she panted quick—and suddenly   295
Her blue affrayéd eyes wide open shone:
Upon his knees he sank, pale as smooth-sculptured stone.

34

Her eyes were open, but she still beheld,
Now wide awake, the vision of her sleep:
There was a painful change, that nigh expelled   300
The blisses of her dream so pure and deep:
At which fair Madeline began to weep,
And moan forth witless words with many a sigh;
While still her gaze on Porphyro would keep,
Who knelt, with joinéd hands and piteous eye,   305
Fearing to move or speak, she looked so dreamingly.

35

"Ah, Porphyro!" said she, "but even now
Thy voice was at sweet tremble in mine ear,
Made tuneable with every sweetest vow;
And those sad eyes were spiritual and clear: 310
How changed thou art! how pallid, chill, and drear!
Give me that voice again, my Porphyro,
Those looks immortal, those complainings dear!
Oh leave me not in this eternal woe,
For if thou diest, my love, I know not where to go."   315

36

Beyond a mortal man impassioned far
At these voluptuous accents, he arose,
Ethereal, flushed, and like a throbbing star
Seen mid the sapphire heaven's deep repose;
Into her dream he melted, as the rose   320
Blendeth its odor with the violet—
Solution sweet: meantime the frost-wind blows
Like Love's alarum pattering the sharp sleet
Against the windowpanes; St. Agnes' moon hath set.

37

'Tis dark: quick pattereth the flaw-blown sleet: 325
"This is no dream, my bride, my Madeline!"
'Tis dark: the icéd gusts still rave and beat:
"No dream, alas! alas! and woe is mine!
Porphyro will leave me here to fade and pine.—
Cruel! what traitor could thee hither bring?   330
I curse not, for my heart is lost in thine,
Though thou forsakest a deceivéd thing—
A dove forlorn and lost with sick unprunéd wing."

38

"My Madeline! sweet dreamer! lovely bride!
Say, may I be for aye thy vassal blest?   335
Thy beauty's shield, heart-shaped and vermeil dyed?
Ah, silver shrine, here will I take my rest
After so many hours of toil and quest,
A famished pilgrim—saved by miracle.
Though I have found, I will not rob thy nest   340
Saving of thy sweet self; if thou think'st well
To trust, fair Madeline, to no rude infidel."

39

"Hark! 'tis an elfin-storm from faery land,
Of haggard seeming, but a boon indeed:
Arise—arise! the morning is at hand—   345
The bloated wassaillers will never heed—
Let us away, my love, with happy speed;
There are no ears to hear, or eyes to see—
Drowned all in Rhenish and the sleepy mead:
Awake! arise! my love, and fearless be,   350
For o'er the southern moors I have a home for thee."

40

She hurried at his words, beset with fears,
For there were sleeping dragons all around,
At glaring watch, perhaps, with ready spears—
Down the wide stairs a darkling way they found.—   355
In all the house was heard no human sound.
A chain-dropped lamp was flickering by each door;
The arras, rich with horseman, hawk, and hound,
Fluttered in the besieging wind's uproar;
And the long carpets rose along the gusty floor.   360

41

They glide, like phantoms, into the wide hall;
Like phantoms, to the iron porch, they glide;
Where lay the Porter, in uneasy sprawl,
With a huge empty flagon by his side:
The wakeful bloodhound rose, and shook his hide,   365
But his sagacious eye an inmate owns:
By one, and one, the bolts full easy slide:
The chains lie silent on the footworn stones;
The key turns, and the door upon its hinges groan.

42

And they are gone: aye, ages long ago   370
These lovers fled away into the storm.
That night the Baron dreamt of many a woe,
And all his warrior-guests, with shade and form
Of witch, and demon, and large coffin-worm,
Were long be-nightmared. Angela the old   375
Died palsy-twitched, with meager face deform;
The Beadsman, after thousand aves told,
For aye unsought for slept among his ashes cold.

St. Agnes was a virgin martyr who was executed in A.D. 306 during the reign of Emperor Dioclesian. Before her execution, her virginity was miraculously defended by thunder and lightning against the Romans' attempts to rape her. Following her martyrdom, her parents had a vision of Agnes among angels and attended by a lamb, her symbol. The Feast of St. Agnes is celebrated on January 21. According to folk belief, a virgin may receive the dream vision of her future husband on the eve of St. Agnes if she (1) refuses any kisses and the "salute" of any man during the day and evening before the Feast of St. Agnes, (2) wears a clean shift, or nightgown, to bed, (3) lays her right hand under her head, (4) and says "Now the god of Love send me my desire."

TOPICS FOR CRITICAL THINKING

1. How does Keats incorporate the ritual of St. Agnes's eve into the plot and imagery of his poem?
2. How are we to judge Porphyro's character and his motives for "hoodwinking" Madeline by pretending to be her dream vision? In section 16, Porphyro has a sudden "thought" that comes "like a full-blown rose." How do you interpret his strategem? Is it a plot of premeditated sexual seduction, or are his intentions more honorable?
3. Is there a way in which Madeline's following of the folk ways of St. Agnes and her dream can be read as a confirmation of the power of the imagination to enchant real life? How would this reading lead us to interpret Porphyro's role in the narrative as fulfilling the legend rather than simply manipulating it?

TOPICS FOR CRITICAL WRITING

1. In one version of the poem, which his editors and friends resisted, Keats depicts a more literal consummation of the dream in stanza 36:

> See, while she speaks his arms encroaching slow,
> Have zoned her, heart to heart,—loud, loud the dark winds blow!
> For on the midnight came a tempest fell;
> More sooth, for that his quick rejoinder flows
> Into her burning ear: and still the spell
> Unbroken guards her in serene repose.
> With her wild dream he mingled, as a rose
> Marrieth its odour to a violet.
> Still, still she dreams, the louder the frost wind lows, . . .

Which version works more successfully? Should the poem leave ambiguous the sexual dimension of the lovers' "mingling," or should it be more explicit? Does explicit sexuality undermine the romantic possibility of the lovers' otherwise more mysterious union?

2. Reread "The Eve of St. Agnes" closely and gather evidence from its language and imagery that supports either reading the poem as a legend of romantic love or as a more realistic tale of modern seduction.

To Autumn   *(1820)*

1

Season of mists and mellow fruitfulness,
   Close bosom-friend of the maturing sun;
Conspiring with him how to load and bless
   With fruit the vines that round the thatch-eaves run;
To bend with apples the mossed cottage-trees,   5
   And fill all fruit with ripeness to the core;
     To swell the gourd, and plump the hazel shells
   With a sweet kernel; to set budding more,
And still more, later flowers for the bees,
Until they think warm days will never cease,   10
     For Summer has o'er-brimmed their clammy cells.

2

Who hath not seen thee oft amid thy store?
   Sometimes whoever seeks abroad may find
Thee sitting careless on a granary floor,
   Thy hair soft-lifted by the winnowing wind;   15
Or on a half-reaped furrow sound asleep,
   Drowsed with the fume of poppies, while thy hook
     Spares the next swath and all its twinéd flowers:
And sometimes like a gleaner thou dost keep

Steady thy laden head across a brook;   20
Or by a cider-press, with patient look,
    Thou watchest the last oozings hours by hours.

                        3

Where are the songs of Spring? Aye, where are they?
    Think not of them, thou hast thy music too—
While barréd clouds bloom the soft-dying day,   25
    And touch the stubble-plains with rosy hue;
Then in a wailful choir the small gnats mourn
    Among the river sallows, borne aloft
        Or sinking as the light wind lives or dies;
And full-grown lambs loud bleat from hilly bourn;   30
    Hedge crickets sing; and now with treble soft
    The red-breast whistles from a garden-croft;
        And gathering swallows twitter in the skies.

TOPIC FOR CRITICAL THINKING

Examine how patterns of rhyme, alliteration, and assonance contribute to Keats's depiction of Autumn.

TOPIC FOR CRITICAL WRITING

Consider the role of apostrophe and personification in Keats's address to, and presentation of, the Autumn season.

Letters of John Keats

Excerpt from Letter to Benjamin Bailey   *November 22, 1817*

O I wish I was as certain of the end of all your troubles as that of your momentary start about the authenticity of the Imagination. I am certain of nothing but of the holiness of the Heart's affections and the truth of Imagination—What the imagination seizes as Beauty must be truth—whether it existed before or not—for I have the same idea of all our Passions as of Love: they are all, in their sublime, creative of essential beauty. In a word, you may know my favorite Speculation by my first Book, and the little song I send in my last—which is a representation from the fancy of the probable mode of operating in these Matters—The imagination may be compared to Adam's dream—he awoke and found it truth. I am more zealous in this affair because I have never yet been able to perceive how anything can be known for truth by consecutive reasoning—and yet it must be—Can it be that even the greatest Philosopher ever arrived at his goal without putting aside numerous objections—However it may be, O for a Life of Sensations rather than of Thoughts!

It is a 'Vision in the form of Youth,' a Shadow of reality to come—and this consideration has further convinced me for it has come as auxiliary to another favorite Speculation of mine, that we shall enjoy ourselves here after by having what we called happiness on Earth repeated in a finer tone and so repeated—And yet such a fate can only befall those who delight in sensation, rather than hunger as you do after Truth—Adam's dream will do here and seems to be a conviction that Imagination and its empyreal reflection is the same as human Life and its spiritual repetition. But, as I was saying—the simple imaginative Mind may have its rewards in the repetition of its own silent Working coming continually on the spirit with a fine suddenness—to compare great things with small—have you never by being surprised with an old Melody—in a delicious place—by a delicious voice, felt over again your very speculations and surmises at the time it first operated on your soul—do you not remember forming to yourself the singer's face more beautiful than it was possible and yet with the elevation of the Moment you did not think so—even then you were mounted on the Wings of Imagination so high—that the Prototype must be here after—that delicious face you will see—What a time! I am continually running away from the subject—sure this cannot be exactly the case with a complex Mind—one that is imaginative and at the same time careful of its fruits—who would exist partly on sensation partly on thought—to whom it is necessary that years should bring the philosophic Mind—such an one I consider your's and therefore it is necessary to your eternal Happiness that you not only drink this old Wine of Heaven, which I shall call the redigestion of our most ethereal Musings on Earth; but also increase in knowledge and know all things.

Excerpt from Letter to George and
Thomas Keats
December 21, 1817

I spent Friday evening with Wells & went the next morning to see *Death on the Pale horse*. It is a wonderful picture, when West's age is considered; But there is nothing to be intense upon; no women one feels mad to kiss, no face swelling into reality. The excellence of every Art is its intensity, capable of making all disagreeables evaporate, from their being in close relationship with Beauty & Truth—Examine King Lear & you will find this examplified throughout; but in this picture we have unpleasantness without any momentuous depth of speculation excited, in which to bury its repulsiveness—The picture is larger than Christ rejected—I dined with Haydon the sunday after you left, & had a very pleasant day, I dined too (for I have been out too much lately) with Horace Smith & met his two Brothers with Hill & Kingston & one Du Bois, they only served to convince me, how superior humour is to wit in respect to enjoyment—These men say things which make one start, without making one feel, they are all alike; their manners are alike; they all know fashionables; they have a mannerism in their very eating & drinking, in their mere handling a Decanter—They talked of Kean & his low company—Would I were with that company instead of yours said I to myself! I know such like acquaintance will never do for me & yet I am going to Reynolds, on wednesday—Brown & Dilke walked with me & back from the Christmas pantomine. I had not a dispute but a disquisition with Dilke, on various subjects; several things dovetailed in my mind, & at once it struck me, what quality went to form a Man of Achievement especially in Literature & which Shakespeare posessed so enormously—I mean *Negative Capability*, that is when man is capable of being in uncertainties, Mysteries, doubts, without any irritable reaching after fact & reason—Coleridge, for instance, would let go by a fine isolated verisimilitude caught from the Penetralium of mystery, from being incapable of remaining content with half knowledge. This pursued through Volumes would perhaps take us no further than this, that with a great poet the sense of Beauty overcomes every other consideration, or rather obliterates all consideration.

Excerpt from Letter to John Taylor   *February 27, 1818*

It is a sorry thing for me that any one should have to overcome Prejudices in reading my verses—that affects me more than any hypercriticism on any particular Passage—In *Endymion*, I have most likely but moved into the Go-cart from the leading-strings. In Poetry I have a few Axioms, and you will see how far I am from their Centre. 1st I think poetry should surprise by a fine excess and not by singularity, it should strike the Reader as a wording of his own highest thoughts, and appear almost a Remembrance.—2d Its touches of Beauty should never be half way, therby making the reader breathless, instead of content: the rise, the progress, the setting of imagery should, like the Sun, come natural too him,— shine over him, and set soberly although in magnificence leaving him in the Luxury of twilight—but it is easier to think what Poetry should be than to write it—and this leads me to another axiom. That if poetry comes not as naturally as the Leaves to a tree it had better not come at all. However, it may be with me, I cannot help looking into new countries with 'O for a Muse of Fire to ascend!'— If Endymion serves me as a Pioneer perhaps I ought to be content. I have great reason to be content, for thank God I can read, and perhaps understand Shakespeare to his depths; and I have I am sure many friends, who, if I fail, will attribute any change in my Life and temper to Humbleness rather than to pride—to a cowering under the Wings of great Poets, rather than to a Bitterness that I am not appreciated. I am anxious to get Endymion printed that I may forget it and proceed. I have copied the 3rd Book and begun the 4th.

Your sincere and obliged friend,
John Keats

Excerpt from Letter to John Hamilton Reynolds   *May 3, 1818*

I will return to Wordsworth—whether or no he has an extended vision or a circumscribed grandeur—whether he is an eagle in his nest, or on the wing—And to be more explicit and to show you how tall I stand by the giant, I will put down a simile of human life as far as I now perceive it; that is, to the point to which I say we both have arrived at—Well—I compare human life to a large Mansion of Many Apartments, two of which I can only describe, the doors of the rest being as yet shut upon me—The first we step into we call the infant or thoughtless Chamber, in which we remain as long as we do not think—We remain there a long while, and notwithstanding the doors of the second Chamber remain wide open, showing a bright appearance, we care not to hasten to it; but are at length imperceptibly impelled by the awakening of the thinking principle—within us—we no sooner get into the second Chamber, which I shall call the Chamber of Maiden-Thought, than we become intoxicated with the light and the atmosphere, we see nothing but pleasant wonders, and think of delaying there for ever in delight: However, among the effects this breathing is father of is that tremendous one of sharpening one's vision into the heart and nature of man—of convincing one's nerves that the World is full of Misery and Heartbreak, Pain, Sickness, and oppression— whereby This Chamber of Maiden Thought becomes gradually darken'd and at the same time, on all sides of it many doors are set open—but all dark—all leading to dark passages—We see not the balance of good and evil. We are in a mist.—*We* are now in that state—We feel the "burden of the Mystery," To this Point was Wordsworth come, as far as I can conceive when he wrote "Tintern Abbey" and it seems to me that his Genius is explorative of those dark Passages. Now if we live, and go on thinking, we too shall explore them. He is a Genius and superior [to] us, in so far as he can, more than we, make discoveries, and shed a light in them. Here I must think Wordsworth is deeper than Milton—though I think it has depended more upon the general and gregarious advance of intellect, than individual greatness of Mind.

Critical Perspective: On Keats and Critical Judgment

"The difficulty of interpreting Keats's poetry is closely bound up with its loveliness, its power to gratify our wish for beauty. This is a power to provoke nearly unanimous value judgments together with widely disparate accounts of their occasion. Modern criticism of Keats presents a curious picture: a clear consensus on the harmonious tenor of the development leading from *Sleep and Poetry* to the ode *To Autumn*, together with strong disagreement on the meaning of its individual moments. I will begin by sketching one such disagreement—about how to characterize Keats's situation in the exquisite fifth stanza of the *Ode to a Nightingale*—to help us ask: what investments can we discern here, important enough to be common to such opposite critical readings? For if critics give incompatible accounts of key passages, and yet end with the same judgments, their conclusions must be motivated by some other kind of constraint than the acts of reading from which they ostensibly arise. The nature of such constraints on critical reading can emerge for us, I suggest, if we attend to the tropes and the rhetorical gestures that Keats's ode cites or repeats if we carry out a certain kind of intertextual reading.

"How does one characterize the gesture of the ode's peculiarly Keatsian fifth stanza—naming flowers in the darkness, guessing each sweet, 'White hawthorn, and the pastoral eglantine'? It depends on how one reads the fourth: it depends on that notorious crux where—as typically in Keats—the most lovely and the most variously interpreted lines of the poem coincide:

> Already with thee! tender is the night,
>   And haply the Queen-Moon is on her throne,
>   Cluster'd around by all her starry Fays;
>   But here there is no light,
>   Save what from heaven is with the breezes blown
>   Through verdurous glooms and winding mossy ways.

The fifth stanza continues, 'I cannot see what flowers are at my feet. . . .' The question of how to take this passage is loaded by the lines at the opening of stanza 4 with the issue of Keats's commitment to poetic flight:

> Away! away! for I will fly to thee,
>   Not charioted by Bacchus and his pards,
> But on the viewless wings of Poesy,
>   Though the dull brain perplexes and retards:

The decision how to read what follows amounts to a judgment upon the speaker's commitment to 'the viewless wings of Poesy.' It is here that one finds an incipient consensus, not upon the function of the viewless wings in these lines, but upon the desirability of Keats's ultimately giving them up. Interpretations of the fourth and fifth stanzas converge in a final value judgment—that Keats ought to abandon poetic flight—after diverging widely on just *how* these stanzas mean that. Keats's lines effectively resist attempts to determine the matter more precisely by appealing to them alone, for at this decisive juncture the ode's syntax turns radically ambiguous. To judge the effects of recourse to the viewless wings of poesy we have to decide how to voice the exclamation point after the fourth stanza 'thee.' A mute mark stands at the place which is *either* an exclamation at arrival *or* a statement of distance. The punctuation mark doesn't tell us how to hear it: whether as an expression of passionate satisfaction, or as a mere pause for differentiation, like a heavier comma or displaced italics. To have an *ear* for this can only be to have a stake in a story about the nightingale and Keats."

—Cynthia Chase, from "Viewless Wings:
Keats's 'Ode to a Nightingale'" (1986)

Critical Perspective: On Keats and Symbolism

"Although the *Ode to a Nightingale* ranges more widely than the *Ode on a Grecian Urn*, the poem can also be regarded as the exploration or testing out of a symbol, and, compared with the urn as a symbol, the nightingale would seem to have both limitations and advantages. The advantage of the urn is that it does convey the notion of experience immortally prolonged, but it does not readily allow the poet to enter and share the life it portrays. He has to stand on the outside as a spectator. The nightingale, however, has a living identity and sings to the senses, thus allowing a massive sympathetic response. The liability is that unlike the urn the song of the nightingale does not suggest something potentially eternal. It is true that in his ardor the poet momentarily makes it immortal, but he does so at the cost of destroying any sympathetic union with it, and, in the logic of the poem, virtually compels it to fly away. Hence the same sympathetic grip that makes the experience vivid to the point that one would wish to prolong it, also forces the recognition that it must be short-lived.

"The dramatic development that takes place in the ode lies partly in the gradual transformation of a living nightingale into a symbol of visionary art. By means of the symbol the ode explores the consequences of a commitment to vision, and as it does so, comes close to implying that the destruction of the protagonist is one of the results. In the verse previous to the odes, Keats had occasionally associated creative activity—whether visionary or not—with death. There is nothing surprising in this. Many artists have expressed themselves in a similar way; notions of withdrawal and self-immolation are all too readily suggested by creative enterprise. The distinction is partly that Keats makes poetry of the theme and partly that he gives it an individual bias."

—David Perkins, from "The 'Ode to a Nightingale'"

Critical Perspective: On Imagination and Reality in the Odes

"Keats was twenty-three years old when, in the spring and autumn of 1819, he wrote the five odes that many critics consider his finest achievement. He had begun serious composition little more than three years earlier, had published a first volume, *Poems* (1817), and a long narrative poem, *Endymion* (1818), in the two years preceding, and would publish only one more volume, containing the odes and, as the title page has it, *Lamia, Isabella, The Eve of St. Agnes, and Other Poems* (1820), before his death in 1821 at the age of twenty-five. When it was all over, he had the shortest writing career—a span (not counting juvenile effusions) of four years, from the winter of 1815–16 to the end of 1819—of any of the major poets in English, and without question the rapidest development.

"It is a nice job to explain that development. The documents concerning the facts of his early life—the upbringing around a London livery stable, enrollment at John Clarke's academy at Enfield, a few miles north of London, when he was seven, the death of his father and hasty remarriage of his mother when he was eight, the death of his mother when he was fourteen—contain no hint of the poet-to-be. His formal education, first at Clarke's school (1803–11), then as an apprentice to an apothecary-surgeon of Edmonton (1811–15), and finally as a medical student at Guy's Hospital, from which after a year's course he emerged in 1816 with a certificate to practice as an apothecary, was meager by the standards of the time for a man of letters. We know that he read widely, in the Latin and English poets, under Clarke's tutelage and on his own. It is not difficult, especially as we see it dramatized in *Poems* of 1817, to understand his desire to be a poet. But it borders on the impossible, once Keats has embarked on his choice, to account fully for the incredibly fast ripening in his work from the earliest imitative efforts, embarrassing in their lushness and sentimentality, to the richest products of his maturity. One can observe, at any stage in their careers, how a Ben Jonson, a Tennyson, or even a Pope *crafted* his poems. With Keats, just as with Shakespeare, one wants, even while knowing better, to invoke the mystery and magic associated with "genius" to say what lay behind the fusion of serious theme with the perfectly controlled sounds and abundance of striking images that we see in his best writing.

"One can, however, describe what Keats's poems are about, and in the description at least partially account for his peculiar excellence. He wrote on most of the standard subjects: nature, poetry, art, love, fame, and death. But in the over-all view, his significant poems center on a single basic problem, the mutability inherent in nature and human life, and openly or in disguise they debate the pros and cons of a single hypothetical solution, transcendence of earthly limitations by means of the visionary imagination. If one were to summarize the career in a sentence, it would be something like this: Keats came to learn that this kind of imagination was a false lure, inadequate to the needs of the problem, and in the end he traded it for the naturalized imagination, embracing experience and process as his own and man's chief good. His honesty in treating the problem and his final opting for the natural world, where all the concrete images of poetry come from and where melodies impinge on 'the sensual ear' or not at all, are what, more than anything else, guarantee his place 'among the English Poets.'

"What goes up must, in reality, come down. Stock notions of 'romanticism' to the contrary, the typical lyric of the English Romantic period has the structure of a literal or metaphorical excursion that can best be represented, in blackboard fashion, by the following diagram:[1]

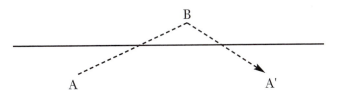

---

1. Keats himself provides a basis of sorts for this diagram in his second axiom for poetry: "the rise, the progress, the setting of imagery should like the Sun come natural [to the reader] . . . shine over him and set soberly although in magnificence leaving him in the Luxury of twilight" (to John Taylor, 27 February 1818—*The Letters of John Keats*, ed. Hyder E. Rollins, Cambridge, Mass., 1958, I, 238). Northrop Frye might seem to counter the direction of the diagram when he says that "the metaphorical structure of Romantic poetry tends to move inside and downward instead of outside and upward" ("The Drunken Boat: The Revolutionary Element in Romanticism," in *Romanticism Reconsidered*, ed. Frye, New York and London, 1963, p. 16). But his view is not fundamentally incompatible with my description here; he is in effect focusing on the descent from B to A'.

The horizontal line stands for a boundary separating the actual world (below) and the ideal (above). (The two realms have many common labels: earth and heaven, mortality and immortality, time and eternity, materiality and spirituality, the known and the unknown, the finite and the infinite, realism and romance, and so on. The ideal is represented above the line because it is, so to speak, a 'higher' reality—what is intended by the difference between 'natural' and '*super*natural.') Characteristically, the speaker in a Romantic lyric begins in the real world (A), takes off in mental flight to visit the ideal (B), and then— for a variety of reasons, but most often because he finds something wanting in the imagined ideal or because, being a native of the real world, he discovers that he does not or cannot belong permanently in the ideal—returns home to the real (A'). But he has not simply arrived back where he began (hence A' rather than A at the descent), for he has acquired something—a better understanding of a situation, a change in attitude toward it—from the experience of the flight, and he is never again quite the same person who spoke at the beginning of the poem.

"In various ways, hundreds of poems, and not all of them lyrics, may be seen to display this typical structure—to pick examples almost at random, Coleridge's *The Eolian Harp* (mental fantasies leading up to a 'what if' speculation about the organic unity of 'all of animated nature,' followed by a descent to orthodoxy at the end), *The Rime of the Ancient Mariner* (a voyage out to the unknown and subsequent journey home to the real world and society), and poems by Wordsworth as diverse as *A slumber did my spirit seal* (slumber succeeded by awakening, a return of sorts), *Tintern Abbey* (the general progress is from memory to the awareness of 'A presence . . . something far more deeply interfused,' and then back to memory), the *Intimations* ode (an imaginative excursion to childhood's 'visionary gleam' and what it intimates, followed by a return to the adult world of 'the light of common day'), all those poems in which a fancied notion is put down by a closer look (e.g., *Resolution and Independence* and *A narrow girdle of rough stones*), and even the Prologue to *Peter Bell*, where a literal flight among the stars proves a terrifying experience for the poet. Many others could be cited, and the structure is of course common to other literatures and art besides those of the early nineteenth century. In *The Wizard of Oz*, Dorothy's 'homeward fever' (to borrow a phrase from *Endymion*) is no different from that experienced by a number of cosmically displaced Romantic heroes, and the lesson she learns at the end, 'There's no place like home,' is a main point, though never in quite such plain language, of some notable poems of Keats's period."

—Jack Stillinger, from "Imagination and Reality in the Odes" (1971)

Part II
Poetry and History

10 Beyond Formalism: Poetry and New Historicism

Chapters 2–9 have discussed poetry in terms of its formal components of word choice, diction, tone, imagery, figurative language, patterns of symbolism, traditions of prosody, and so on. Taken together, such formalist approaches make up the foundation for understanding what defines poetry as a literary genre. But beyond the qualities that are intrinsic to poetry, verse writing also engages with cultural discourses that are extrinsic to poetry's own forms of composition. In addition to its formalist frameworks, poetry speaks to its historical moment. A poem responds to the assumptions, beliefs, trends, and theories of its age. It is affected by the biographic circumstances of its author; a poem's meaning and significance evolves in its critical reception as it weathers the rising and falling opinions of its general and professional readers through the test of time. Poetry has a life that goes beyond its form to touch on history.

Dating from the 1980s, the practice of historical criticism has benefited from the developing methology of **new historicism** Web . This critical approach to literature was pioneered by Stephen Greenblatt, who brings social and cultural contexts to bear on Renaissance texts in such groundbreaking books as *Renaissance Self-Fashioning* (1980) and *Shakespearean Negotiations* (1988). Greenblatt's example quickly spread to other periods of English studies to become a major movement in critical reading. Unlike traditional forms of historical criticism, however, new historicism does not assume that literature simply reflects the political, religious, and intellectual trends of its era. Similarly, new historicism does not consider a story, poem, or play to be necessarily shaped by its moment in time. In contrast, new historicist critics pay close attention to how literary works enter into a dynamic dialogue with the nonliterary, public discourses that make up a period's social text. For the new historicist, a literary work is not simply passive in relation to its context; it does not express only one given historical moment. Instead, new historicism investigates literature's active negotiations in shaping history through the power of the word.

To begin with, new historicism parts company with the humanist assumption that literature expresses an author's discovery of timeless, universal truths. On the contrary, new historicism argues that cultural discourses are prior to authorial genius and the humanist verities it expresses. New historicism explains how the particular languages of art, politics, religion, science, and so on actively shape how we experience history. **Ideology** is a term that

www

defines this process of how language provides us with ways of knowing and acting in the world. "Ideology," according to the French theorist Louis Althusser, "represents the imaginary relationship of individuals to their real conditions of existence." Ideologies not only express world outlooks, they provide us with the material forms of living in it. That is, ideologies function through concrete social rituals, customs, practices of everyday life embodied in such institutions as the church, state, corporation, school system, entertainment industries, and so on. Together, such institutions shape our experience of reality through the language of several public discourses.

Through the force of language, ideologies offer us a diverse and sometimes contradictory set of roles—or subject positions—in everyday life. For example, the language system that defines one's identity and place as a Jew, Christian, Muslim, or Buddhist differs from the language that represents one's identity as, say, a national citizen, consumer, professional, family member, student, and so on. Each of the roles we play in the family, in school, in the state, in the work world, and in our religious lives is produced from particular institutional contexts whose specific discourses define regimes of knowledge and power. A rabbi, minister, or priest uses different discursive conventions and expects different responses from you than does your teacher, your boss, or your mother. The versions of knowledge and the kind of self-understandings we have of ourselves as family members differ somewhat from how we perceive ourselves at work or in school, or at the mall. Some of the roles we adopt are more empowering than others depending on our class, gender, ethnic, and racial positions. In all cases, however, the ideologies of the family, nation, religion, and workplace are sustained by discursive practices and social conventions, which are themselves constantly evolving through dynamic forces of debate, negotiation, and compromise. Moreover, contradictory and contested social forces are at play in the associations and connotations of the key words that shape our experience of the social world. For example, what defines a patriot, a pious person, a successful student, a responsible family member, and so on changes from community to community and over the course of time.

Dialogism—a key concept that new historicism takes from the twentieth-century Russian thinker Mikhail Mikhailovich Bakhtin—defines the open-ended nature of the key words through which we interpret our place in, and relation to, the social life around us.

We can see a concrete example of dialogism in William Blake's poem "London." A new historical reading of this poem does not consider only how the poet portrays the history of industrial city life in the late eighteenth century. More to the point, new historicism examines the ways in which the poem participates in shaping history by entering into dialogue with the key terms of eighteenth-century political debate.

WILLIAM BLAKE   *(1757–1827)*

London   *(1794)*

I wander thro' each charter'd street,
Near where the charter'd Thames does flow.
And mark in every face I meet
Marks of weakness, marks of woe.

In every cry of every Man,   5
In every Infant's cry of fear,
In every voice, in every ban,
The mind-forg'd manacles I hear:

How the Chimney-sweepers cry
Every blackning Church appalls,   10
And the hapless Soldiers sigh,
Runs in blood down Palace walls.

But most thro' midnight streets I hear
How the youthful Harlot's curse
Blasts the new-born Infant's tear   15
And blights with plagues the Marriage hearse.

    In the first stanza of "London," Blake points to the exploitative reality of monopoly commerce and political regulation on the city of London through the key term *charter'd*. Like "each street," the river Thames too is "charter'd." The word *charter'd*—one of the poem's key terms—has at least two metaphoric meanings in the poem. First, it alludes to the power of commerce and ownership belonging to the great chartered companies such as the East India Company, whose ships could be seen everywhere along the Thames unloading the spoils of imperial conquest from the colonies. Second, Blake's poem signifies ironically on the constitutional rhetoric of chartered rights and chartered liberties coming into being at this time. In 1793, "to charter" meant granting certain rights and privileges of political entitlement. The dialogism built into this key word stems from the era's political debate over these rights, as reflected in Thomas Paine's criticism of the new "chartered towns" in his *Rights of Man* published the previous year. Paine argued that to bestow political franchise and rights on one company, class, or corporation was to do so through the force of exclusion toward others. As a new regime of knowledge, the discourse of legal chartering empowered some Londoners over others. "It is a perversion of terms," he wrote, "to say, that a charter gives rights. It operates by a contrary effect, that of taking rights away. Rights are inherently in all the inhabitants; but charter, by annulling those rights in the majority, gave the right by exclusion in the hands of a few."

    Blake teases out the dialogic forces at work in the word *charter*. For, the civic entitlement guaranteed to the privileged few by charter'd rights also entailed oppression for the many through the charter's powers of social exclusion. As Blake puts it in "The Human Abstract": "Pity would be no more, / If we did not make somebody Poor; / And Mercy no more could be, / If all were as happy as we." The human costs of London's completely "charter'd" environment are all too plainly seen in the metaphor of the "Marks" that everywhere disfigure the faces of the Londoners with weakness and woe. The verb *mark* describes Blake's act of noticing the signs of dehumanization around him, but it also puns on the poet's artistic activity as an engraver who would score or "mark" the plates for his illuminated manuscripts. To bear the mark of weakness and woe, however, also resonates as a dialogic word with biblical discourse. Specifically, it is an allusion to the "mark of the Beast" of the apocalypse in Revelation 8:16–17. Blake, as poet, wanders not just through the literal streets of London but also through the metaphoric avenues of an apocalyptic hell.

The confining metaphor of things, "charter'd" carries forward into the figure of the "ban"—or legal and political prohibition—that Blake hears in the "mind-forg'd manacles" of the second stanza. In an earlier version of the poem, Blake described these handcuffs as "german-forg'd manacles"—a historical allusion to the Hanoverian monarchy whose troops were expected at the time to be deployed against British dissenters. "Mind-forg'd," however, implies a more universal condition beyond this particular historical context. As a more general metaphor, the "mind-forg'd manacles" suggest how the chartered political economy of the modern city has policed and confined Londoners' abilities to think freely for themselves. The cries of exploitation-that Blake hears in "every man" and "every Infant" are rendered more concrete in the poem's final two stanzas.

The chimney sweeper's cry has the metaphoric effect of "blackning" the institutions of the church again with marks of spiritual hypocrisy. Alternatively, as agent rather than object of such "blackning," the church can also be considered as figuratively blackening or having a hand in exploiting the lives of London's children. Small children were the only ones who could climb into the narrow, seven-inch smoke stacks of London's coal-driven factories. With only rags tied to their hands and knees against the scorching effects of the hot brick chimneys, they often fell to their deaths. It was not unusual for such "climbing boys"—like the one in Blake's "The Chimney Sweeper" from the *Songs of Innocence*—to be sold into apprenticeship before they could barely talk. Recognizing the lethal effects of coal soot, Parliament passed the Chimney Sweepers Act (1788) that legislated (but did not enforce) a ban on hiring out "climbing boys" under the age of eight. The other vivid metaphor of stanza three is the "sigh" of the "hapless Soldier" that—depicted through the figure of **synaesthesia** or the blending of the senses—"Runs in blood down Palace walls." Like the chimney sweeper's cry, the soldier's bloody sigh (alluding, in part, to the recent violence of the French Revolution beginning in 1789) prepares for the poem's perhaps most complex metaphors of institutional violence carried out, in this case, against women as well as children.

The cry witnessed earlier now returns in the "midnight streets" as a harlot's curse: one that, metaphorically, has the power to "blast" and "blight" new life. The prostitute, of course, is the most abject victim of London's "charter'd" social economy. The only commodity she can bargain is her own body. In her economic victimization as whore, the harlot—like the chimney sweep and soldier—is "youthful." Yet her presentation in the poem undercuts the vigor we normally assign to youth. The agricultural metaphors of "blasting" and "blighting" imply destructive natural forces—battering winds and infectious diseases—that distort and kill the organic vitality of the next generation. As a metaphor for venereal disease—a common side effect of prostitution—the "Harlot's curse" further has the power of deranging the difference between life and death by collapsing the ritual of marriage with that of the funeral, captured in the final line's arresting figure of the "marriage hearse."

Blake's poem features the force of key words whose regimes of power have material effects on particular victims of the emerging industrial order of the modern city: its chimney sweepers, soldiers, workers, homeless people, and prostitutes. The dialogism of words such as *charter'd* and *mark* suggest that the very rhetoric of civic empowerment that drives modern industry happens through a violence on society's most marginal members. That the "mind-forg'd manacles" that "Mark" London's urban working poor are the result of social rather than spiritual limitation is further illustrated, as new historicist Heather Glen has shown, in one of Blake's "ancient Proverbs" from his 1792 notebook:

> Remove away that black'ning church,
> Remove away that marriage hearse,
> Remove away that——of blood,
> You'll quite remove the ancient curse.

New historicism not only explores the relationship between poetry and the dialogism of historic key words, but it also pays special attention to the literary expression of groups that have been "marked" with political disenfranchisement. New historicism revisits the texts of women, ethnic and racial minorities, gays and lesbians, and the working classes, among others. It recovers those voices historically marginalized by the official, "charter'd" canons of cultural power. But equally important, new historicism allows us to interpret the subtle ways in which power charters verbal privilege. New historicism investigates how power shapes who has the right to speak, what one is permitted to say in a given era, and how one can say it in particular historical periods whose social and aesthetic politics differ from our own. In its attention to the contexts of a poem's formal production, new historicism moves beyond both a simple, biographical account of an author's life and a reading of a poem that is bounded by considerations of literary form. Instead, new historicism interprets literary form as it is embedded in the broader social text of its moment.

In this vein, a new historicist attention to the social context of Anne Bradstreet's place as a woman in Puritan society sheds important light on her poetic strategy of personification in "The Author to Her Book."

ANNE BRADSTREET   *(1612–1672)*

The Author to Her Book   *(1678)*

Thou ill-form'd offspring of my feeble brain,
Who after birth did'st by my side remain,
Till snatcht from thence by friends, less wise than true,
Who thee abroad expos'd to public view,
Made thee in rags, halting to th' press to trudge,   5
Where errors were not lessened (all may judge).
At thy return my blushing was not small,
My rambling brat (in print) should mother call;
I cast thee by as one unfit for light,
Thy Visage was so irksome in my sight,   10
Yet being mine own, at length affection would
Thy blemishes amend, if so I could:
I wash'd thy face, but more defects I saw,
And rubbing off a spot still made a flaw.
I stretcht thy joints to make thee even feet,   15
Yet still thou run'st more hobbling than is meet;
In better dress to trim thee was my mind,
But nought save home-spun cloth, i' th' house I find;
In this array, 'mongst vulgars may'st thou roam,
In critic's hands, beware thou dost not come;   20
And take thy way where yet thou art not known.
If for thy father asked, say, thou had'st none;
And for thy mother, she alas is poor,
Which caus'd her thus to send thee out of door.

    Born in 1612, Anne Bradstreet sailed aboard the *Arbella* to America in
1630 along with other members of the Massachusetts Bay Colony, including
her father Thomas Dudley and her husband Simon Bradstreet, both of whom
would serve as governors of Massachusetts. In 1650, her brother-in-law took
her poetry to England and arranged for its publication as a book entitled *The
Tenth Muse*, most likely without Anne's prior approval. Circulating her writing in the Puritan public sphere was particularly risky for a woman in the
colonies. In seventeenth-century America, women's place was mainly confined to domestic life. Indeed, Anne Bradstreet was mindful of the example of
her friend Anne Hutchinson who, based on her outspoken theological views,
was banished by the General Court of Boston for "traducing the ministers"
and was excommunicated by the Boston Church in 1638. After settling in Pel-
ham Bay on Long Island Sound, Anne Hutchinson and all of her servants and
children save one were killed in a skirmish with Native Americans in 1643. In
"The Author to Her Book," Bradstreet employs personification to criticize
her own writing in a strategy of self-deprecation. That is, seeking to avoid the

harsh treatment of Anne Hutchinson, Bradstreet offers an apology for her appearing in print at all. This strategy is calculated to earn her public approval, paradoxically, through disavowing her literary brainchild.

TOPICS FOR CRITICAL THINKING

1. How does Bradstreet describe her identity and faculties as writer in the poem?
2. Discuss the poet's characterization of her book. Make a list of the various ways in which she describes the book as a personified child.
3. Can you think of any recent analogies or contemporary counterparts to Bradstreet's stance in negotiating her public role in "The Author to Her Book"?

TOPIC FOR CRITICAL WRITING

What gestures does the poem make to acknowledge the force of social criticism and judgment of Bradstreet's literary offspring? Describe how personification anticipates that critical judgment.

11

Critical Perspectives

A Casebook on Poetry and Social Activism Between the Wars

www

The poetry of social activism **Web** that flourished between the World Wars in the United States had its seeds in the early twentieth century. Socialist poets in America took a critical stance toward global capitalism, especially during the turbulent decade of the Great Depression. In revisiting early modern socialist poetry from our point of vantage in the twenty-first century, we may find that it makes unsettling but refreshing claims on us as readers. Today, popular culture affords us fewer chances to think critically about global labor markets and class oppression. Unlike the activist culture of the early twentieth century, the contemporary scene offers fewer social alternatives to the status quo driven by fantasies of personal wealth, status, fame, and so on. Few of us would want to sacrifice our individuality to embrace "the togetherness / of bodies phalanxed in a common cause," as American poet Edwin Rolfe has it in "Credo." Nevertheless, in looking back at this period, we begin to see how the progressive poetic legacy between the World Wars remains an important forerunner of the feminist, antiwar, black, gay, and lesbian aesthetic movements that, a generation later, changed the face of contemporary American society.

In the early part of the twentieth century, the American scene was rapidly changing. By the 1910s, New York City had a population of some 5 million city dwellers, 40 percent of whom were first-generation émigrés. It was these new masses of working men and women that the young, former Columbia College student and social critic Randolph Bourne welcomed in his landmark essay "Trans-National America" (1916). Bourne's campaign for a cosmopolitan socialist culture was reinforced by the literary network of little magazines of the period such as the *Craftsman, Comrade, International Socialist Review, Coming Nation, Mother Earth,* and *New York Call.* By far, the most popular of these venues *The Masses,* was originally launched as a muckraking publication by Piet Vlag in 1911 and later edited by Max Eastman. The term *muckraker* was coined by President Theodore Roosevelt in a 1906 speech to describe the wave of novelists, writers, and investigative journalists who waged a cultural campaign against abusive labor practices, corporate monopolies, and corrupt politicians at the turn of the century. Reflecting back on this time, Eastman wrote in *The Enjoy-*

ment of Living (1948), "Our magazine provided for the first time in America a meeting ground for revolutionary *labor* and the radical intelligentsia."

The Masses offered a lively forum for the era's political journalism, manifestoes, cartoon art, poetry, fiction, and drama. But equally important, it fostered the kind of salon culture hosted in Greenwich Village parties by socialites, patrons, and cultural radicals such as Mabel Dodge, Alyse Gregory, and Gertrude Vanderbilt Whitney. At these social get-togethers, Dodge wrote, one could come upon "Socialists, Trade-Unionists, Anarchists, Suffragists, Poets, Relations, Lawyers, Murderers, 'Old Friends,' Psychoanalysts, IWWs, Single Taxers, Birth Controlists, Newspapermen, Artists, Modern-Artists, Club Women, woman's-place-is-in-the-home Women, Clergymen, and just plain men." Some of the social reform issues popularized by *The Masses* that would later become enacted into law include the income tax, women's suffrage, child labor restrictions, worker's compensation, minimum wage rates, and the eight-hour workday.

In this cultural context, poetry played an active role in portraying the plight of working-class men, women, and children, in raising public awareness of social inequities, and in imagining progressive social alternatives to the status quo. Through their visual art, cultural activists such as the suffragette illustrator Alice Beach Winter and socialist photographer Lewis Hine exposed the dire straits of the laboring poor. Winter's cover "Why Must I Work?" for the May 1912 issue of *The Masses* recalled Lewis Hine's famous 1908 portrait of a child spinner in the Whitnel Cotton Mill in North Carolina. Such arresting images exposed the scandal of the estimated 1.7 million children under sixteen who, by the end of the nineteenth century, were employed in southern mills, New England factories, and farms nationwide. Poetry, likewise, made the class tyranny of child labor an urgent and vivid issue for the general reader, as in Sarah Cleghorn's ironic and succinct lyric "Golf Links":

"WHY MUST I WORK?"
CONCERNING CHRISTIAN CHARITY - - - By WILL IRWIN
THE DAY OF A MAN - - - By MARY HEATON VORSE

Alice Beach Winter, *The Masses* (May 1912).

The Golf Links lie so near the mill
    That almost every day
The laboring children can look out
    And see the men at play.

Max Eastman, along with the black poet Claude McKay, would go on in 1918 to participate on the *Liberator*, the successor to *The Masses*. By the mid-1920s, such writers as Floyd Dell, Langston Hughes, Horace Kallen, Lola Ridge, Joseph Freeman, and Michael Gold were planning an American Proletarian Artist and Writers League that in 1926 led to a revival of *The Masses* under the title of the *New Masses*. Its contributing

editors also included such major
American authors as Sherwood
Anderson, Stuart Davis, Waldo
Frank, Carl Sandburg, Upton Sin-
clair, Eugene O'Neill, and Lewis
Mumford, among others. Its first
issues featured contributions by
significant modernist writers such
as William Carlos Williams, D. H.
Lawrence, Babette Deutsch, John
Dos Passos, and Robinson Jeffers.

Several other socialist literary
magazines of the period were
sponsored by the John Reed Club
network in major cities such as
Chicago, Cleveland, Detroit, Philadelphia, and Seattle. Named after
the Harvard alumnus and hero of
the Soviet Revolution, John Reed,
the clubs comprised some thirty

Lewis W. Hine, *Child Laborer at the Whitnel Cotton Mill* (1908)

chapters with over twelve hundred members. Such JRC journals as Detroit's
The New Force, Grand Rapids's *The Cauldron*, Indianapolis's *Midland Left*, Hollywood's *The Partisan*, Chicago's *Left Front*, Philadelphia's *Red Pen*, and New
York's *Partisan Review* popularized the club's cultural activities in the fine arts,
drama, film, photography, dance, music, and poetry.

Poetry of social conscience during this period responded to and commented on world and national events, often bringing writers together in joint
publication ventures and group collections. "Cooperative anthologies," wrote
Lucia Trent and Ralph Cheney, "are the poets' logical answer to the public's
neglect to buy other anthologies." Trent's and Cheney's *America Arraigned*
(1928) was one of many alternative anthologies published between the World
Wars, including such titles as *An Anthology of Revolutionary Poetry* (1929), *Poems of Justice* (1929), *The Red Harvest* (1930), *We Gather Strength* (1933), *Banners of Brotherhood* (1933), and *Proletarian Literature in the United States* (1935).
The growing inequities between rich and poor—which Ernest Hemingway
would later depict in *To Have and Have Not* (1937)—created a receptive, mass
audience for the kind of poetry of social conscience that these group anthologies collected.

During the Depression era, the New York Workers school and John Reed
Clubs would provide cultural centers for aspiring socialist poets such as Edwin
Rolfe. Rolfe came of age as a revolutionary poet within a cultural milieu whose
internationalist scope, diversity of gender, racial, and class perspectives, and
blend of high, avant-garde, and populist styles are reflected in publishing venues like the *New Masses* and the various magazines sponsored by the John Reed
Clubs and other socialist organizations. Of his time studying with Michael
Gold and Joseph Freeman, Rolfe has said, "Talking, lecturing, writing, they
kept their ideas and convictions alive and growing when all others descended

into bogs, were side tracked, or deserted. It was Joseph Freeman who finally showed some of us our real direction, our real goal. . . . 'Stop thinking of yourselves,' he said, 'as poets who are also revolutionists or revolutionists who are also poets. Remember that you are *revolutionary poets*.'" Rolfe's lyric verse would fully mature in his poetry on the Spanish Civil War where he served in the Abraham Lincoln Brigade during the latter part of the 1930s.

Drawing from the new poetic innovations and free verse techniques of imagist poetry (see Chapter 3), the early twentieth-century poetry of social protest employed a range of styles and techniques. Poets across a diverse spectrum of class, race, and regional representation composed verse ranging from traditional lyricism in fixed forms, to folk ballads, to choral and group chant recitals. These writers also took up new poetic modes gleaned from the examples of the experimental modernists, the imagists, international surrealism, Zurich Dada, and Russian Constructivism. Kenneth Fearing, for example, learned from high modernists such as T. S. Eliot and James Joyce the technique of using references to popular culture, advertising slogans, and newspaper headlines in textual collage formats that resembled the use of found urban objects in the cubofuturist art work of Pablo Picasso and Georges Braques. Fearing, however, more than Eliot, used popular references for pointedly comic critiques of American consumer society during the Depression years, as in his poem "Dirge." Fantasies of success, luxury, and prosperity in Fearing's poetry circulate through a contrived environment of radios, magazines, brokerage houses, dance halls, theaters—all of which are wholly rigged for making a quick buck. In such a setting, one's full social being is constantly deferred and dispersed across a network of alienating subject positions of collectors, salespeople, movie queens, and magnates.

Similarly, Langston Hughes criticized the spectacle of modern consumer values by using poetic forms drawing from the vernacular forms of African American expressive culture: blues lyricism, black sermon, spirituals, and folk ballads. Several of his poetic personae capture the voices of ordinary, everyday black folk, as in "Elevator Boy." While Hughes pointed to the ways in which race mattered in the poetry of class oppression, Tillie Olsen, Genevieve Taggard, and Muriel Rukeyser exposed the role gender played in the exploitative labor market of the Depression era, as in "I Want You Women Up North to Know" and "Mill Town."

Poems for Further Reading and Critical Writing

KENNETH FEARING   *(1902–1961)*

Dirge   *(1934)*

.

1-2-3 was the number he played but today the number came
    3-2-1;
      bought his Carbide° at 30 and it went to 29; had the
      favorite at Bowie but the track was slow—

O executive type, would you like to drive a floating power,   5
    knee-action, silk-upholstered six? Wed a Hollywood
    star? Shoot the course in 58? Draw to the ace,
    king, jack?
    O fellow with a will who won't take no, watch out for
      three cigarettes on the same, single match; O,   10
      democratic voter born in August under Mars,
      beware of liquidated rails—

Denoument to denoument, he took a personal pride in the
    certain, certain way he lived his own, private life,
    But nevertheless, they shut off his gas; nevertheless, the   15
      bank foreclosed; nevertheless, the landlord called;
      nevertheless, the radio broke,

And twelve o'clock arrived just once too often,
Just the same he wore one grey tweed suit, bought one
    straw hat, drank one straight Scotch, walked one   20
    short step, took one long look, drew one deep
    breath,
Just one too many,

And wow he died as wow he lived,
Going whop to the office and blooie home to sleep and   25
    biff got married and bam had children and oof got
    fired,
Zowie did he live and zowie did he die,

With who the hell are you at the corner of his casket, and
    where the hell're we going on the right-hand silver   30
    knob, and who the hell cares walking second from

---

3 *Carbide:* Refers to shares of stock in Union Carbide Corporation, which has merged with Dow
Chemical Company.

the end with an American Beauty wreath from why
    the hell not,

Very much missed by the circulation staff of the New York
    Evening Post; deeply, deeply mourned by the   35
    B.M.T.,°

Wham, Mr. Roosevelt; pow, Sears Roebuck; awk, big
    dipper; bop, summer rain;
Bong, Mr., bong, Mr., bong, Mr., bong.

$2.50   *(1934)*

But that dashing, dauntless, delphic, diehard, diabolic
    cracker likes his fiction turned with a certain elegance
    and wit; and that anti-anti-anti slum-congestion
    clublady prefers romance;
    search through the mothballs, comb the lavender and   5
      lace,
    were her desires and struggles futile or did an innate
      fineness bring him at last to a prouder, richer peace
      in a world gone somehow mad?

We want one more compelling novel, Mr. Filbert Sopkins   10
    Jones,
    all about it, all about it,
    with signed testimonials to its stark, human, while-u-
      wait, iced-or-heated, taste-that-sunshine tenderness
      and truth;   15
    one more comedy of manners, Sir Warwick Aldous
      Wells, involving three blond souls; tried in the
      crucible of war, Countess Olga out-of-limbo by
      Hearst through the steerage peerage,
    glamorous, gripping, moving, try it, send for a 5 cent,   20
      10 cent sample, restores faith to the flophouse,
      workhouse, warehouse, whorehouse, bughouse life
      of man,
    just one more long poem that sings a more heroic age,
      baby Edwin, 58,   25

But the faith is all gone,
    and all the courage is gone, used up, devoured on the
      first morning of a home relief menu,
    you'll have to borrow it from the picket killed last
      Tuesday on the fancy knitgoods line;   30

---

36 *B.M.T.:* Brooklyn-Manhattan Transit Corporation; a New York Subway line.

and the glamor, the ice for the cocktails, the shy appeal,
   the favors for the subdeb ball? O.K.,
O.K.,
but they smell of exports to the cannibals,
reek of something blown away from the muzzle of a   35
   twenty inch gun;

Lady, the demand is for a dream that lives and grows and
   does not fade when the midnight theater special
   pulls out on track 15;
   cracker, the demand is for a dream that stands and   40
   quickens and does not crumble when a General
   Motors dividend is passed;
   lady, the demand is for a dream that lives and grows
   and does not die when the national guardsmen fix
   those cold, bright bayonets;   45
   cracker, the demand is for a dream that stays, grows
   real, withstands the benign, afternoon vision of the
   clublady, survives the cracker's evening fantasy of
   honor, and profit, and grace.

X Minus X   *(1935)*

Even when your friend, the radio, is still; even when her dream,
   the magazine, is finished; even when his life, the ticker, is
   silent; even when their destiny, the boulevard, is bare;
And after that paradise, the dance-hall, is closed; after that
   theater, the clinic, is dark,   5

Still there will be your desire, and hers, and his hopes and theirs,
Your laughter, their laughter,
Your curse and his curse, her reward and their reward, their
   dismay and his dismay and her dismay and yours—

Even when your enemy, the collector, is dead; even when your   10
   counsellor, the salesman, is sleeping; even when your
   sweetheart, the movie queen, has spoken; even when your
   friend, the magnate, is gone.

LANGSTON HUGHES   *(1902–1967)* **CD-ROM**

Goodbye Christ   *(1932)*

Listen, Christ,
You did alright in your day, I reckon—
But that day's gone now.

They ghosted you up a swell story, too,
Called it Bible—   5
But it's dead now,
The popes and the preachers've
Made too much money from it.
They've sold you to too many

Kings, generals, robbers, and killers—   10
Even to the Tzar and the Cossacks,
Even to Rockefeller's Church,
Even to THE SATURDAY EVENING POST.
You ain't no good no more.
They've pawned you   15
Till you've done wore out.

Goodbye,
Christ Jesus Lord God Jehova,
Beat it on away from here now.
Make way for a new guy with no religion at all—   20
A real guy named
Marx Communist Lenin Peasant Stalin Worker ME—

I said, ME!

Go ahead on now,
You're getting in the way of things, Lord.   25
And please take Saint Gandhi with you when you go,
And Saint Pope Pius,
And Saint Aimee McPherson,
And big black Saint Becton
Of the Consecrated Dime.   30
And step on the gas, Christ!
Move!

Don't be so slow about movin'!
The world is mine from now on—
And nobody's gonna sell ME   35
To a king, or a general,
Or a millionaire.

Johannesburg Mines   *(1928)*

In the Johannesburg mines
There are 240,000 natives working.

What kind of poem
Would you make out of that?

240,000 natives working   5
In the Johannesburg mines.

Elevator Boy   *(1926)*

I got a job now
Runnin' an elevator
In the Dennison Hotel in Jersey.
Job ain't no good though.
No money around.   5
   Jobs are just chances
   Like everything else.
   Maybe a little luck now,
   Maybe not.
   Maybe a good job sometimes: 10
   Step out o' the barrel, boy.
Two new suits an'
A woman to sleep with.
   Maybe no luck for a long time.
   Only the elevators   15
   Goin' up an' down,
   Up an' down,
   Or somebody else's shoes
   To shine,
   Or greasy pots in a dirty kitchen.   20
I been runnin' this
Elevator too long.
Guess I'll quit now.

ALFRED HAYES   *(1911–1985)*

In a Coffee Pot   *(1934)*

Tonight, like every night, you see me here
Drinking my coffee slowly, absorbed, alone.
A quiet creature at a table in the rear
Familiar at this evening hour and quite unknown.
The coffee steams. The Greek who runs the joint   5
Leans on the counter, sucks a dead cigar.
His eyes are meditative, sad, lost in what it is
Greeks think about the kind of Greeks they are.

I brood upon myself. I rot
Night after night in this cheap coffee pot.   10
I am twenty-two I shave each day

I was educated at a public school
They taught me what to read and what to say
The nobility of man my country's pride
How Nathan Hale died   15
And Grant took Richmond.
Was it on a summer or a winter's day?
Was it Sherman burned the Southland to the sea?
The men the names the dates have worn away
The classes words the books commencement prize   20
Here bitter with myself I sit
Holding the ashes of their prompted lies.

The bright boys, where are they now?
Fernando, handsome wop who led us all
The orator in the assembly hall   25
Arista man the school's big brain.
He's bus boy in an eat-quick joint
At seven per week twelve hours a day.
His eyes are filled with my own pain
His life like mine is thrown away.   30
Big Jorgensen the honest, blond, six feet,
And Daniels, cunning, sly,—all, all—
You'll find them reading Sunday's want ad sheet.
Our old man didnt know someone
Our mother gave no social teas   35
You'll find us any morning now
Sitting in the agencies.

You'll find us there before the office opens
Crowding the vestibule before the day begins
The secretary yawns from last night's date   40
The elevator boy's black face looks out and grins.
We push we crack our bitter jokes we wait
These mornings always find us waiting there
Each one of us has shined his broken shoes
Has brushed his coat and combed his careful hair   45
Dance hall boys pool parlor kids wise guys
The earnest son the college grad all, all
Each hides the question twitching in his eyes
And smokes and spits and leans against the wall.

We meet each other sometimes on the street   50
Sixth Avenue's high L bursts overhead
Freak shows whore gypsies hotdog stands
Cajole our penniless eyes our bankrupt hands.
"Working yet?" "The job aint come
Got promised but a runaround."   55

The L shakes building store and ground
"What's become of Harry? and what's become
Of Charley? Martinelli? Brooklyn Jones?"
"He's married—got a kid—and broke."
And Charley's on Blackwell's, Martinelli's through—   60
Met him in Grand Central—he's on the bum—
We're all of us on the bum—
A freak show midget's pounding on a drum
The high L thunders redflag auctioneers
Are selling out a bankrupt world—   65
The hammer falls—a bid! a bid!—and no one hears . . .

The afternoon will see us in the park
With pigeons and our feet in peanut shells.
We pick a bench apart. We brood.

TILLIE OLSEN   *(b. 1913?)*

I Want You Women Up North to Know   *(1934)*

(Based on a Letter by Felipe Ibarro in New Masses, *Jan. 9th, 1934.)*

i want you women up north to know
how those dainty children's dresses you buy
    at macy's, wanamakers, gimbels, marshall fields,
are dyed in blood, are stitched in wasting flesh,
down in San Antonio, "where sunshine spends the winter."   5

I want you women up north to see
the obsequious smile, the salesladies trill
    "exquisite work, madame, exquisite pleats"
vanish into a bloated face, ordering more dresses,
    gouging the wages down,   10
dissolve into maria, ambrosa, catalina,
    stitching these dresses from dawn to night,
    in blood, in wasting flesh.

Catalina Rodriguez, 24,
    body shrivelled to a child's at twelve,   15
catalina rodriguez, last stages of consumption,
    works for three dollars a week from dawn to midnight.
A fog of pain thickens over her skull, the parching heat
    breaks over her body.
and the bright red blood embroiders the floor of her room.   20
    White rain stitching the night, the bourgeois poet would say,

white gulls of hands, darting, veering,
    white lightning, threading the clouds,
this is the exquisite dance of her hands over the cloth,
and her cough, gay, quick, staccato,   25
    like skeleton's bones clattering,
is appropriate accompaniment for the esthetic dance
    of her fingers,
and the tremolo, tremolo when the hands tremble with pain.
Three dollars a week,   30
two fifty-five,
seventy cents a week,
no wonder two thousands eight hundred ladies of joy
are spending the winter with the sun after he goes down—
for five cents (who said this was a rich man's world?) you can   35
    get all the lovin you want
"clap and syph aint much worse than sore fingers, blind eyes, and
    t.m."

Maria Vasquez, spinster,
    for fifteen cents a dozen stitches garments for children she has   40
    never had,
Catalina Torres, mother of four,
    to keep the starved body starving, embroiders from dawn to
    night.
Mother of four, what does she think of,   45
    as the needle pocked fingers shift over the silk—
    of the stubble-coarse rags that stretch on her own brood,
    and jut with the bony ridge that marks hunger's landscape
    of fat little prairie-roll bodies that will bulge in the
    silk she needles?   50
(Be not envious, Catalina Torres, look!
    on your own children's clothing, embroidery,
    more intricate than any a thousand hands could fashion,
    there where the cloth is ravelled, or darned,
    designs, multitudinous, complex and handmade by Poverty   55
    herself.)

Ambrosa Espinoza trusts in god,
    "Todos es de dios, everything is from god,"
    through the dwindling night, the waxing day, she bolsters herself
    up with it—   60
but the pennies to keep god incarnate, from ambrosa,
and the pennies to keep the priest in wine, from ambrosa,
ambrosa clothes god and priest with hand-made children's dresses.

Her brother lies on an iron cot, all day and watches,
on a mattress of rags he lies.   65
For twenty-five years he worked for the railroad, then they laid him off.

(racked days, searching for work; rebuffs; suspicious eyes of
    policemen.)
goodbye ambrosa, mebbe in dallas I find work; desperate swing
    for a freight,
surprised hands, clutching air, and the wheel goes over a   70
leg,
the railroad cuts it off, as it cut off twenty-five years of his life.)
She says that he prays and dreams of another world, as he lies
    there, a heaven (which he does not know was brought to earth
    in 1917 in Russia, by workers like him).   75

Women up north, I want you to know
when you finger the exquisite hand made dresses
what it means, this working from dawn to midnight,
on what strange feet the feverish dawn must come
    to maria, catalina, ambrosa,   80
how the malignant fingers twitching over the pallid faces jerk them
    to work,
and the sun and the fever mounts with the day—
    long plodding hours, the eyes burn like coals, heat jellies the
        flying fingers,
down comes the night like blindness.
    long hours more with the dim eye of the lamp, the breaking   85
        back,
    weariness crawls in the flesh like worms, gigantic like earth's in
        winter.
And for Catalina Rodriguez comes the night sweat and the blood
    embroidering the darkness.
    for Catalina Torres the pinched faces of four huddled
    children,   90
    the naked bodies of four bony children,
    the chant of their chorale of hunger.
And for twenty eight hundred ladies of joy the grotesque act gone
        over—
    the wink—the grimace—the "feeling like it baby?"
And for Maria Vasquez, spinster, emptiness, emptiness.   95
    flaming with dresses for children she can never fondle.
And for Ambrosa Espinoza—the skeleton body of her brother on
    his mattress
of rags, boring twin holes in the dark with his eyes to the image of
    christ
remembering a leg, and twenty-five years cut off from his life by
    the railroad.

Women up north, I want you to know,   100
I tell you this can't last forever.

I swear it won't.

GENEVIEVE TAGGARD *(1894–1948)*

Mill Town *(1936)*

(Dedicated to Paul de Kruif)

> *. . . the child died, the investigator said, for lack of
> proper food. After the funeral the mother went back to
> the mill. She is expecting another child . . .*

       . . . then fold up without pause
The colored ginghams and the underclothes.
       And from the stale
Depth of the dresser, smelling of medicine, take
The first year's garments. And by this act prepare   5
Your store of pain, your weariness, dull love,
To bear another child with doubled fists
And sucking face.

       Clearly it is best, mill-mother,
Not to rebel or ask clear silly questions,   10
Saying womb is sick of its work with death,
Your body drugged with work and the repeated bitter
Gall of your morning vomit. Never try
Asking if we should blame you. Live in fear. And put
Soap on the yellowed blankets. Rub them pure.   15

EDWIN ROLFE *(1909–1954)*

Credo *(1931)*

To welcome multitudes—the miracle of deeds
performed in unison—the mind
must first renounce the fiction of the self
and its vainglory. It must pierce
the dreamplate of its solitude, the fallacy   5
of its omnipotence, the fairytale
aprilfools recurring every day
in speeches of professors and politicians.

It must learn
the wisdom and the strength and the togetherness   10
of bodies phalanxed in a common cause,
of fists tight-clenched around a crimson banner
flying in the wind above a final, fierce
life-and-death fight against a common foe.

Emerging then, the withered land will grow   15
—purged—in a new florescence; only then,
cleansed of all chaos, a race of men may know
abundance, life, fecundity.

Asbestos   *(1928)*

Knowing (as John did) nothing of the way
men act when men are roused from lethargy,
and having nothing (as John had) to say
to those he saw were starving just as he

starved, John was like a workhorse. Day by day   5
he saw his sweat cement the granite tower
(the edifice his bone had built), to stay
listless as ever, older every hour.

John's deathbed is a curious affair:
the posts are made of bone, the spring of nerves,   10
the mattress bleeding flesh. Infinite air,
compressed from dizzy altitudes, now serves

his skullface as a pillow. Overhead
a vulture leers in solemn mockery,
knowing what John had never known: that dead   15
workers are dead before they cease to be.

Not Men Alone   *(1935)*

What, you have never seen a lifeless thing flower,
revive, a new adrenaline in its veins?
Come, I shall show you: not men alone
nor women, but cities also are reborn;
not without labor, not before the hour   5
when flesh feels lacerated, mangled, torn.

Not only men are resurrected. I have seen
dull cities bloom, grow meaningful
overnight. Wherever class war comes
awareness is its courier, a newer life,   10
new depths in shallow, parallel streets
which may revert to commonplace, but never
relinquish scenes that have occurred on them.

Toledo's such a city. I remember
its dullness, how I always skirted   15
its edges on long trips west. Returning east,

I chose roads miles to the north or south
to escape its barrenness; the mind went dead,
the muscles flagged, in passing it.

Then the strike flared: the workers met   20
and merged at factories. The unions called
Down tools! and the militiamen
sped to the scene of combat. When the smoke
rose with the wind, a hundred men were maimed
but thousands more, the first time in their lives   25
were conscious of their needs, their role, their destiny.

I passed through Toledo yesterday.
The usual quiet prevailed, but from the eyes
of men and houses a newer spirit flamed.
The deadness I had felt before remained   30
but it was make-up only, mere disguise
for men aroused, a city awakened,
awaiting the propitious, inevitable day.

MURIEL RUKEYSER   *(1913–1980)*

The Minotaur   *(1944)*

Trapped, blinded, led; and in the end betrayed
Daily by new betrayals as he stays
Deep in his labyrinth, shaking and going mad.
Betrayed.   Betrayed.   Raving, the beaten head
Heavy with madness, he stands, half-dead and proud.   5
No one again will ever see his pride.
No one will find him by walking to him straight
But must be led circuitously about,
Calling to him and close and, losing the subtle thread,
Lose him again; while he waits, brutalized   10
By loneliness.   Later, afraid
Of his own suffering.   At last, savage and made
Ravenous, ready to prey upon the race
If it so much as learn the clews of blood
Into his pride his fear his glistening heart.   15
Now is the patient deserted in his fright
And love carrying salvage round the world
Lost in a crooked city; roundabout,
By the sea, the precipice, all the fantastic ways
Betrayal weaves its trap; loneliness knows the thread,   20

And the heart is lost, lost, trapped, blinded and led,
Deserted at the middle of the maze.

JOSEPH KALAR   *(1906–1972)*

Papermill   *(1931)*

Not to be believed, this blunt savage wind
Blowing in chill empty rooms, this tornado
Surging and bellying across the oily floor
Pushing men out in streams before it;
Not to be believed, this dry fall   5
Of unseen fog drying the oil
And emptying the jiggling greasecups;
Not to be believed, this unseen hand
Weaving a filmy rust of spiderwebs
Over these turbines and grinding gears,   10
These snarling chippers and pounding jordans;°
These fingers placed to lips saying shshsh;
Keep silent, keep silent, keep silent;
Not to be believed hardly, this clammy silence
Where once feet stamped over the oily floor,   15
Dinnerpails clattered, voices rose and fell
In laughter, curses, and songs. Now the guts
Of this mill have ceased their rumbling, now
The fires are banked and red changes to black,
Steam is cold water, silence is rust, and quiet   20
Spells hunger. Look at these men, now,
Standing before the iron gates, mumbling,
"Who could believe it? Who could believe it?"

Worker Uprooted   *(1935)*

The slow sleepy curl of cigaret smoke and butts
glowing redly out of moving smiling mouths;
now a whisper in the house, laughter muted,
and warm words spoken no more to me.
Alien, I move forlorn among curses,   5
laughing falsely, joking with tears
aching at my eyes, now surely alien and lonely.
Once I rubbed shoulders with sweating men,
pulled when they pulled, strained, cursed,

---

11 *jordans:* Papermill machinery.

comrade in their laughter,   10
comrade in their pain,
knowing fellowship of sudden smiles
and the press of hands in silent speech.
At noon hour, sprawled in the shade,
opening our lunches, chewing our sandwiches,   15
laughing and spitting,
we talked of the days and found joy
in our anger, balm in our common contempt;
thought of lumber falling with thump of lead
on piles geometrically exact; of horses   20
sweating, puffing, bulging their terrible muscles;
of wagons creaking; of sawdust
pouring from the guts of the mill.
Now alien, I move forlorn, an uprooted tree,
feel the pain of hostile eyes   25
lighting up no more for me;
the forced silence, the awkward laugh,
comrade no more in laughter and pain.

And at dawn, irresolutely,
into the void . . .   30

Critical Perspective: On Countée Cullen's "Incident"

"As one begins to reread both poets now classed as minor and poets essentially written out of the story of modern literature, one discovers, for example, that traditional forms continued to do vital cultural work throughout this period. Far from being preeminently genteel, poetry in traditional forms was a frequent vehicle for sharply focused social commentary. Poets were thus often quite successful at making concise, paradigmatic statements about social life. Freed from the need to provide extended analysis or support a thesis with detailed evidence, poetry instead could highlight both the most basic structures of oppression in the culture and the fundamental principles that positive change should observe. Countée Cullen's (1903–1946) 'Incident' (1925)—a widely known poem by a poet generally viewed as relatively minor because of his preference for traditional forms—describes a black child's encounter with a Maryland resident:

> Now I was eight and very small,
>   And he was no whit bigger,
> And so I smiled, but he poked out
>   His tongue, and called me, 'Nigger.'

> I saw the whole of Baltimore
>   From May until December;
> Of all the things that happened there
>   That's all that I remember.

"'Incident' hardly says all there is to say about race relations in America, but it does point with notable economy to its continuing human cost. The violation of this childlike form by the word 'Nigger' is more disturbing and effective than its appearance in a modernist collage would be. Moreover, the very innocence of the form makes the poem's pathos a productively self-conscious burden for contemporary readers."

—Cary Nelson, from *Repression and Recovery* (1989)

Critical Perspective: On Depression Era Culture

"In Gregory La Cava's 1936 film, *My Man Godfrey*, the 'forgotten man,' loitering among his fellow trash pickers on the dump, is whisked away to become a butler for a society family; when hardship threatens them too, the butler (who is actually one of the wealthy Parkeses of Boston) saves the day by turning the dump into a nightclub called, *mirabile dictu*, 'The Dump.' Thus garbage becomes classy decor, and the erstwile trash pickers become costumed waiters—actors of sorts in a profitable theme park based on their former 'lifestyle.' This entrepreneurial solution to economic hardship would seem to smack of the wishful thinking of the Reagan years, but the film's juxtaposed ingredients of wealth, poverty, and entertaining spectacle are, in fact, observable everywhere in the culture of the Depression decade. There is perhaps a temptation, looking back as we do, to think of what Alfred Kazin has called the 'lean and angry Thirties' as the last decade of the real America: a time when politics was politics, and Reds were Reds, when strikes were actually radical, when the faces of sharecroppers bespoke some kind of authenticity; a time before class disappeared, before intellectuals became professors, before culture retreated to the museums, before the shopping malls were built, and before the dump became a nightclub. But it is also possible to argue, as Jean Baudrillard does in *The Mirror of Production*, that the stock market crash of 1929 marked the birth of our present social formation, of a culture that theorists have characterized by various and much-disputed terms like the 'society of the spectacle,' the 'culture of abundance,' 'postindustrial' or 'postmodern' society, and 'late capitalism.'

—Rita Barnard, from *The Great Depression and the Culture of Abundance* (1995)

TOPICS FOR CRITICAL THINKING

1. Discuss the sources of Fearing's ironic humor in portraying the American everyman of "Dirge."

2. Consider Fearing's depictions of the fantasies of luxury, romance, and status that drive consumer society in "$2.50" and "X Minus X." What alternative dream does "$2.50" allude to in its closing stanza?

3. Compare Hughes's portrait of the "Elevator Boy" to the dramatic persona that Hayes depicts in "In a Coffee Pot."

4. Discuss the ways in which Rolfe's "Credo" poses a solution to the kind of industrial victimization offered in "Asbestos." Compare and contrast Rolfe's poetic techniques and rhetorical strategies in the two poems.

5. In what ways does Kalar rely on the power of sharply beheld images to defamiliarize the modern settings of industry when they are shut down in his Depression-era poem "Papermill"?

6. Contrast the rhetoric of Taggard's "Mill Town" with her address to the mill town mother in the poem. How does the latter's cleaning the blankets serve as a symbolic act in the poem's closing lines?

TOPICS FOR CRITICAL WRITING

1. Discuss the ways in which class, ethnic, and regional differences lead women to discriminate against other women in Olsen's "I Want You Women Up North to Know." How does Olsen's address position the reader in the role of privileged consumer? What is it that Olsen wants northern women to know and understand?

2. Examine how Olsen's critique of the fashion industry parallels her rejection of the aesthetic conceits of "the bourgeois poet" (line 21). How do both obscure the realistic details of women's oppression, according to Olsen?

3. Examine Rukeyser's figure of the Minotaur as a symbol for the violence of modern twentieth-century history.

12

Critical Perspectives

A Casebook on Poetry, Trauma, and Testimony: Holocaust Verses

www The term *holocaust* **Web** derives from the Greek root *holokaustos*, which combines *holos*, "whole," and *kaustos*, "burnt," to denote a burning of the whole. The notions of a burnt sacrifice and martyrdom through burning have wide currency in biblical literature. Since early modern times, *holocaust* has also come to signify mass murder. In the twentieth century, the capitalized usage of *Holocaust* refers specifically to the genocide of the Jews perpetrated by the German Nazis during 1939–1945. This modern-day genocide has also been referred to as the *Shoah*, meaning "catastrophe." A third term, also meaning "catastrophe" is *Churban*, but this word joins the Nazi genocide to historic precedents of disaster for the Jews in *Churban Bayis Rishon*, the destruction of the First Temple in 586 B.C., and *Churban Bayis Sheni*, the destruction of the Second Temple by the Romans in A.D. 70. Furthermore, the notion of a *Churban* is tied to a historical pattern of *Churban-Golus-Geulah:* destruction followed by exile and redemption.

The term *Holocaust*, then, conveys the idea of a unique, all-consuming disaster: an event without historical precedent. The fact of genocide, of course, is not what makes the Holocaust unique. The wholesale destruction of Native Americans during the colonization of the Americas and the massacre of the Armenians in the Ottoman Empire are two precursors to the genocide of World War II. Contemporary genocides in Cambodia and Rwanda, as well as more recent, so-called ethnic cleansings in former Yugoslavia, perpetuate early-modern precedents of mass murder. Nevertheless, the Holocaust stands out as a unique event in world history. While involving Communists, gypsies, homosexuals, the disabled, and so on, the Nazis' Final Solution was conceived first and foremost with the idea of exterminating every single Jew on the planet. "The uniqueness lies," according to Holocaust scholar Yehuda Bauer in "Lessons of the Holocaust," not in the numbers or technology of modern genocide but "in the motivation of the perpetrator. Who was the Jew in the eye of the Nazis? Why the destruction? The destruction came because the Jew was viewed as a Satanic element in human society. As an extra-human on earth." The noted Jewish philosopher and theologian Emil Fackenheim describes the Holocaust as a unique event or *novum* in human history, one whose legacy commands remembrance. "We are commanded," he writes, "to remember in our very guts and bones the martyrs of the holocaust, lest their memory perish."

The ethics of commemoration is also a central concern of Auschwitz survivor Primo Levi. He addresses the reader with the force of that commitment in his poem "Shemá," whose title is based on the Jewish prayer: "Hear [Shemá] O Israel, the Lord our God the Lord is One" (Deuteronomy 6:4–9; 11:13–21). "You who live secure," he writes, "in your warm houses":

> Consider that this has been:
> I commend these words to you.
> Engrave them on your hearts
> When you are in your house, when you walk on your way,
> When you go to bed, when you rise.
> Repeat them to your children.
> Or may your house crumble,
> Disease render you powerless,
> Your offspring avert their faces from you.

Forgetting the past, of course, risks its repetition in the future. Yet, as we shall see, understanding the world historical trauma of the Holocaust poses both intellectual and psychological difficulties. The archive of political, philosophical, psychoanalytic, literary, legal, and theological discussions of the Holocaust is only a half century in the making, yet it is already vast. Time does not allow us to address here the complexity of intellectual witness to the Holocaust. A basic timeline, however, would include the following events.

1933

- Hitler becomes Chancellor of Germany.
- Civil Service Law denies government employment to Jews.
- Public book burnings are staged.
- Dachau concentration camp is established.
- Nazi party is declared the only political party in Germany.

1934

- Hitler assumes the titles of both President and Chancellor after the death of Paul von Hindenberg.

1935

- Nuremberg Race Laws deny German Jews of citizenship, military service, and political rights. Marriage and sexual relations between Jews and non-Jews are prohibited. Nazis define a Jew as anyone with three Jewish grandparents or who belonged to the Jewish community and had two Jewish grandparents. Those with any trace of Jewish blood are termed Mischling or "hybrid."

1936

- Olympic Games are held in Nazi Germany.
- Germany and Italy sign the Rome–Berlin Axis agreement.
- Sachsenhausen concentration camp opens.

1937

- Germany and Japan sign an international pact.
- Gypsies are defined as "inveterate criminals."

1938

- Germany annexes Austria.
- Buchenwald, Mauthausen and Flossenburg concentration camps open.
- Evian Conference brings together thirty-two countries to review Jewish immigration issues.
- Adolph Eichmann heads up the Central Office for Jewish Emigration in Vienna.
- Pogrom of Kristallnacht ("crystal night" or the "night of broken glass") is carried out after the assassination of an official in the Paris–German embassy. Germans kill ninety-six Jews; one thousand synagogues are destroyed; seven thousand Jewish businesses are looted; and thirty thousand Jews are arrested.

1939

- Ravensbrück and Stutthoff concentration camps open.
- Hitler and Stalin sign Nazi–Soviet Non-Aggression Pact.
- Hitler invades Poland.
- Ghettos are sealed off in occupied Poland beginning with Piotrkow Trybunalski.
- Jews required to wear the Star of David.
- Nazis destroy Jewish synagogues of Lotz.

1940

- Germany wages war on Denmark, Norway, Belgium, the Netherlands, Luxembourg, France, and England.
- Auschwitz concentration camp is established.
- Warsaw ghetto is sealed.

1941

- Germany occupies Yugoslavia and Greece and invades the Soviet Union.
- Hermann Göring appoints Reinhard Heydrich to administer the Final Solution.
- Three thousand units of the Einsatzgruppen begin the "special task" of exterminating what would amount by 1943 to 1.25 million Eastern European and Soviet Jews.
- Thirty-three thousand Jews are mass murdered outside Kiev at Babii Yar.
- Extermination camps at Birkenau, Auschwitz II, and Chelmno are constructed.
- Nazis put gas vans into operation at Chelmno.

1942

- Dutch Jews are slated for concentration and deportation.
- Heydrich unveils extermination plan at the Wannsee Conference.
- Belzec, Sobibor, and Treblinka extermination camps begin operation.

- Jewish partisans in Byelorussia and the Baltic States resist the Nazis while Jews mount challenges in Poland; Jews mount armed resistance in ghettos of Kletzk, Kremenets, Lachva, Mir, and Tuchin.
- Jewish Fighting Organization (ZOB) undertakes resistance in Warsaw.
- Jews are deported to the killing centers from Belgium, Croatia, France, the Netherlands, Poland, Germany, Greece, and Norway.

1943

- German Sixth Army is defeated at Stalingrad.
- Kraków Ghetto is liquidated.
- Jewish community mounts Warsaw Ghetto revolt.
- Reichsfuehrer-SS Heinrich Himmler oversees the liquidation of ghettos in Poland and the Soviet Union.
- Jewish resistance fighters stage revolts in Bedzin, Bialystok, Czestochowa, Lvov, and Tarnów ghettos as well as at Sobibor.
- In an attempt to destroy the evidence of genocide, Germans exhume and burn bodies of Jewish victims of Babii Yar using a special work unit of Jewish prisoners, the Sonderkommando, who are themselves in turn executed.

1944

- Germany occupies Hungary and begins deportation of Hungarian Jews.
- Allies invade Normandy on D-Day.
- Senior German officers fail in assassination attempt against Hitler.
- Russian troops liberate Majdanek extermination camp.
- Sonderkommando concentration camp inmates destroy one crematorium at Auschwitz.

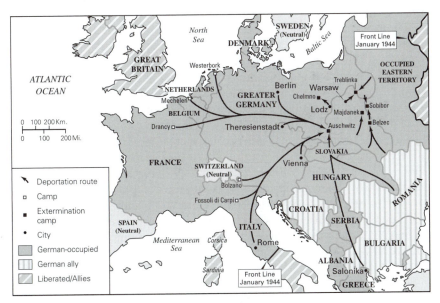

Major deportations to extermination camps, 1942–1944

1945

- Death marches of deported Jews begin from Budapest to Austria and from the evacuation of Auschwitz, Stutthof, and Buchenwald.
- Hitler withdraws to bunker under the garden of the old chancellery ("Alte Reichskanzlei").
- Hitler marries his lover Eva Braun, and the two commit suicide in the bunker.
- In the bunker, Propaganda Minister Joseph Goebbels and his wife commit suicide after killing their six children.
- Germany surrenders on VE-Day.

Knowing the history of the Holocaust in detail is important, but it is quite another thing to wrestle with the issue of how it could have happened. In approaching the *novum* of the Holocaust, the question of how we are to come to terms with its extremity has no satisfactory answer. However urgently we may take Primo Levi's command to "Consider that this has been," the fact of the Holocaust confounds any attempt to explain it. Theological discussion, as for example in Arthur Cohen's definition of the "tremendum," relies on the figure of the abyss to mark the unique difference between the Holocaust and human understanding. "As abyss," Cohen writes in *The Tremendum: A Theological Interpretation of the Holocaust* (1981), "the tremendum transforms everything that went before into distance and remoteness, as though an earthquake had overturned the center of a world, obliterating mountains that had once been near at hand and that we had formerly dreamt of scaling." Acknowledging the significance of the Holocaust in human history begins with silence. The final solution leads to silence because, according to George Steiner, its violence "lies outside speech as it lies outside reason."

On the other hand, focusing on uniqueness for its own sake, according to Fackenheim, risks "taking the event out of history and thus mystifying it." Such historical silence, as André Neher reminds us, characterized the passive response of the Allied powers and reached all the way to the absent "silence of God" toward the plight of European Jewry. "At Auschwitz," Neher writes in his essay "The Silence of Auschwitz," "everything unfolded, was fulfilled and accomplished for weeks, months, and years on end in absolute silence, away from and out of the mainstream of history." The persistence of such silence lasted well after the war in the difficulty many survivors had in communicating what they had experienced. Silence in the cross-generational repression of the Holocaust is also a special feature of postwar German perpetrator culture examined by Holocaust scholars Dan Bar-On, Barbara Heimannsberg, and Christoph J. Schmidt, among others (see color insert of Samuel Bak).

As a historical task, witnessing to the Holocaust begins with a certain awe, shock, and terror that end in silence. Such silence, however, demands a second moment: one that sacrifices silence in favor of testimony. Here, the imperative to bear witness is driven by the engraved memory of unspeakable acts: crimes against humanity, mass violence, cruelty, personal trauma, loss, and so on. The testimonial moment happens as a radical negation: a violent breaching of the everyday world. Such a world historical trauma opens a gap and a silence in our cultural response. It possesses discourse as a "negative phrase" or what Jean François Lyotard calls a *differend:* a linguistic black hole, whose silence "nevertheless calls upon phrases which are in principle possible." For his part, moreover, "what is at stake in a literature, in a philosophy, in a politics perhaps, is to bear witness to *differends* by finding idioms for them." Recent psychoanalytic writing on the Holocaust is one such discourse where the "negative phrase" of the *differend* has found an idiom whose repetition, however acted out, nevertheless makes a difference in working through the event. In the writings of Dori Laub and Shoshana Felman, the Holocaust is again invoked in the silence of an abyssal metaphor, but in their texts, the extreme event is considered through the more complex understanding of time, memory, and witnessing to disaster.

Poetry is another important site for giving testimony to the *novum* of the Holocaust. One symptom of the difficulties in writing about the Holocaust is the relative lack of contemporary verse devoted to the event. It would be normal to expect repression to follow upon a death encounter. As an unprecedented trauma, however, the Holocaust changes the status of death as such. "Planet Auschwitz," as Yehiel Dinur called it, marks a radical negation of life that thereby introduces a new anxiety into human existence. Similarly, Theodor Adorno concludes in *Negative Dialectics* (1974) that "the administrative murder of millions made of death a thing one had never yet to fear in just this fashion." For his part, Adorno insisted that any contemporary thinking that failed to reflect on its belatedness "after Auschwitz" is complicit with the obscenity of the death camps. "If thought," he writes, "is not measured by the extremity that eludes the concept, it is from the outset in the nature of the musical accompaniment with which the SS liked to drown out the screams of its victims." Adorno, of course, included contemporary poetics in the "superflous trash" thrown up by postwar culture, declaring in *Prisms* (1981) his famous slogan that "to write poetry after Auschwitz is barbaric."

This dire judgment, however, has not stood as the final word on contemporary verse. In fact, it has prompted a number of counterstatements, as in the rejoinder of Edmond Jabès in *The Book of Margins* (1993): "Adorno once said that after Auschwitz we can no longer write poetry. I say that after Auschwitz we *must* write poetry but with wounded words." In the postwar context, many fewer poems have been written on genocide than the historical struggles over race, gender, sexuality, the environment, native ethnicities, and so on. "We never discussed the Second World War much when I was growing up," writes the contemporary American poet Charles Bernstein. Morever, he admits, "I don't feel much like discussing it now." Reflecting the latency of a global trauma, Bernstein notes that it is only some five decades after the Holocaust that "we are just beginning to come out of the shock enough to try to make sense of the experience." Peculiar to the temporal structure of extremity, the encounter with death, missed through survival, gathers traumatic force only through the passage of time. Echoing an observation made by Terence Des Pres, among others, Bernstein notes that for him "each year, the Extermination Process seems nearer, more recent." Similarly, Terrence Des Pres writes in his Introduction to *Legacy of Night: The Literary Universe of Elie Wiesel* (1982):

The Holocaust would seem to have no end. The destruction of Europe's Jews stopped in 1945, but the spectacle of the death camps continues to haunt us, and not merely as a fading memory or as a bad dream that lingers. The Holocaust happened. That in itself is the intractable fact that we can neither erase nor evade. And the more we think of it, the more it intrudes to occupy our minds, until *l'univers concentrationnaire* becomes a demonic anti-world that undermines our own.

Poems for Further Reading and Critical Writing

PRIMO LEVI   *(1919–1987)*

Shemá   *(1958)*

Translated by Ruth Feldman and Brian Swann

You who live secure
In your warm houses,
Who return at evening to find
Hot food and friendly faces:

   Consider whether this is a man,   5
   Who labours in the mud
   Who knows no peace
   Who fights for a crust of bread
   Who dies at a yes or a no.
   Consider whether this is a woman,   10
   Without hair or name
   With no more strength to remember
   Eyes empty and womb cold
   As a frog in winter.

Consider that this has been: 15
I commend these words to you.
Engrave them on your hearts
When you are in your house, when you walk on your way,
When you go to bed, when you rise.
Repeat them to your children.   20
Or may your house crumble,
Disease render you powerless,
Your offspring avert their faces from you.

NELLY SACHS   *(1891–1970)*

O the Chimneys   *(1971)*

Translated by Michael Hamburger

*And though after my skin worms destroy this
body, yet in my flesh shall I see God.*
                              —JOB 19:26

O the chimneys
On the ingeniously devised habitations of death
When Israel's body drifted as smoke
Through the air—
Was welcomed by a star, a chimney sweep,   5
A star that turned black
Or was it a ray of sun?

O the chimneys!
Freedomway for Jeremiah and Job's dust—
Who devised you and laid stone upon stone   10
The road for refugees of smoke?

O the habitations of death,
Invitingly appointed
For the host who used to be a guest—
O you fingers   15
Laying the threshold
Like a knife between life and death—

O you chimneys,
O you fingers
And Israel's body as smoke through the air!   20

ELIE WIESEL   *(b. 1928)*

Never Shall I Forget   *(1958)*

Never shall I forget that night,
the first night in the camp
which has turned my life into one long night,
seven times cursed and seven times sealed.

Never shall I forget that smoke.   5
Never shall I forget the little faces of the children

whose bodies I saw turned into wreaths of smoke
beneath a silent blue sky.

Never shall I forget those flames
which consumed my faith for ever.   10
Never shall I forget that nocturnal silence
which deprived me for all eternity of the desire to live.

Never shall I forget those moments
which murdered my God and my soul
and turned my dreams to dust.   15

Never shall I forget these things,
even if I am condemned to live as
long as God Himself.

Never.

YEVGENY YEVTUSHENKO   *(b. 1933)*

Babii Yar   *(1961)*

Translated by George Reavey

No monument stands over Babii Yar.
A drop sheer as a crude gravestone.
I am afraid.
            Today I am as old in years
as all the Jewish people.   5
Now I seem to be
                  a Jew.
Here I plod through ancient Egypt.
Here I perish crucified, on the cross,
and to this day I bear the scars of nails.   10
I seem to be
            Dreyfus.
The Philistine
                  is both informer and judge.
I am behind bars.   15
                        Beset on every side.
Hounded,
        spat on,
                  slandered.

Squealing, dainty ladies in flounced Brussels lace   20
stick their parasols into my face.

I seem to be then
                a young boy in Byelostok.
Blood runs, spilling over the floors.
The barroom rabble-rousers   25
give off a stench of vodka and onion.
A boot kicks me aside, helpless.
In vain I plead with these pogrom bullies.
While they jeer and shout,
                   'Beat the Yids. Save Russia!'   30
Some grain-marketeer beats up my mother.
O my Russian people!
                I know
                    you
are international to the core.   35
But those with unclean hands
have often made a jingle of your purest name.
I know the goodness of my land.
How vile these anti-Semites—
                      without a qualm   40
they pompously called themselves
the Union of the Russian People!

I seem to be
          Anne Frank
transparent   45
          as a branch in April.
And I love.
          And have no need of phrases.
My need
          is that we gaze into each other.   50
How little we can see
                or smell!
We are denied the leaves,
                we are denied the sky.
Yet we can do so much—   55
                tenderly
embrace each other in a darkened room.
They're coming here?
                Be not afraid. Those are the booming
sounds of spring: 60
             spring is coming here.
Come then to me.
             Quick, give me your lips.
Are they smashing down the door?

                     No, it's the ice breaking. . . .   65
The wild grasses rustle over Babii Yar.

The trees look ominous,
                    like judges.
Here all things scream silently,
                        and, baring my head,   70
slowly I feel myself
                turning grey.
And I myself
            am one massive, soundless scream
above the thousand thousand buried here.   75
I am
        each old man
                    here shot dead.
I am
        every child   80
                here shot dead.
Nothing in me
                shall ever forget!
The 'Internationale,' let it
                        thunder   85
when the last anti-Semite on earth
is buried for ever.
In my blood there is no Jewish blood.
In their callous rage, all anti-Semites
must hate me now as a Jew.   90
For that reason
                I am a true Russian!

DAN PAGIS   *(b. 1930)*

Written in Pencil in the Sealed Railway-Car   *(1970)*
Translated by Stephen Mitchell

here in this carload
i am Eve
with my son Abel
if you see my older boy
Cain son of Adam   5
tell him that i

PAUL CELAN   *(1920–1970)*

Death Fugue   *(1944, 1980)*

Translated by Michael Hamburger

Black milk of daybreak we drink it at sundown
we drink it at noon in the morning we drink it at night
we drink and we drink it
we dig a grave in the breezes there one lies unconfined
A man lives in the house he plays with the serpents he writes   5
he writes when dusk falls to Germany your golden hair
     Margarete
he writes it and steps out of doors and the stars are flashing he
     whistles his pack out
he whistles his Jews out in earth has them dig for a grave
he commands us strike up for the dance

Black milk of daybreak we drink you at night   10
we drink in the morning at noon we drink you at sundown
we drink and we drink you
A man lives in the house he plays with the serpents he writes
he writes when dusk falls to Germany your golden hair
     Margarete
your ashen hair Shulamith we dig a grave in the breezes there   15
     one lies unconfined

He calls out jab deeper into the earth you lot you others sing
     now and play
he grabs at the iron in his belt he waves it his eyes are blue
jab deeper you lot with your spades you others play on for the
     dance

Black milk of daybreak we drink you at night
we drink you at noon in the morning we drink you at   20
     sundown
we drink and we drink you
a man lives in the house your golden hair Margarete
your ashen hair Shulamith he plays with the serpents

He calls out more sweetly play death death is a master from
     Germany
he calls out more darkly now stroke your strings then as   25
     smoke you will rise into air
then a grave you will have in the clouds there one lies
     unconfined

Black milk of daybreak we drink you at night
we drink you at noon death is a master from Germany
we drink you at sundown and in the morning we drink and
    we drink you
death is a master from Germany his eyes are blue   30
he strikes you with leaden bullets his aim is true
a man lives in the house your golden hair Margarete
he sets his pack on to us he grants us a grave in the air
he plays with the serpents and daydreams death is a master
    from Germany

your golden hair Margarete   35
your ashen hair Shulamith

SYLVIA PLATH   *(1932–1963)*

Lady Lazarus   *(1962)*

I have done it again.
One year in every ten
I manage it——

A sort of walking miracle, my skin
Bright as a Nazi lampshade,   5
My right foot

A paperweight,
My face a featureless, fine
Jew linen.

Peel off the napkin   10
O my enemy.
Do I terrify?——

The nose, the eye pits, the full set of teeth?
The sour breath
Will vanish in a day.   15

Soon, soon the flesh
The grave cave ate will be
At home on me

And I a smiling woman.
I am only thirty.   20
And like the cat I have nine times to die.

This is Number Three.
What a trash
To annihilate each decade.

What a million filaments.   25
The peanut-crunching crowd
Shoves in to see

Them unwrap me hand and foot——
The big strip tease.
Gentlemen, ladies   30

These are my hands
My knees.
I may be skin and bone,

Nevertheless, I am the same, identical woman.
The first time it happened I was ten.   35
It was an accident.

The second time I meant
To last it out and not come back at all.
I rocked shut

As a seashell.   40
They had to call and call
And pick the worms off me like sticky pearls.

Dying
Is an art, like everything else.
I do it exceptionally well.   45

I do it so it feels like hell.
I do it so it feels real.
I guess you could say I've a call.

It's easy enough to do it in a cell.
It's easy enough to do it and stay put.   50
It's the theatrical

Comeback in broad day
To the same place, the same face, the same brute
Amused shout:

'A miracle!'   55
That knocks me out.
There is a charge

For the eyeing of my scars, there is a charge
For the hearing of my heart——
It really goes.   60

And there is a charge, a very large charge
For a word or a touch
Or a bit of blood

Or a piece of my hair or my clothes.
So, so, Herr Doktor.   65
So, Herr Enemy.

I am your opus,
I am your valuable,
The pure gold baby

That melts to a shriek.   70
I turn and burn.
Do not think I underestimate your great concern.

Ash, ash—
You poke and stir.
Flesh, bone, there is nothing there——   75

A cake of soap,
A wedding ring,
A gold filling.

Herr God, Herr Lucifer
Beware   80
Beware.

Out of the ash
I rise with my red hair
And I eat men like air.

WILLIAM HEYEN   *(b. 1940)*

Kotov   *(1991)*

Ivan Ivanovitch Kotov, short of speech,
clarity drifting away to mindlessness—

Kotov of stutter and suddenly empty eyes—
only Kotov, in all Russia, of all those locked inside,
survived the *dushegubka*,   5
the murder wagon, the gas van. Only Kotov,

pushed with his new bride
into the seatless seven-ton gray truck,
stood on that grated floor, and lived. Only Kotov,
pressed together with fifty others, would wake   10
in the ditch of dead, half buried, and crawl away.
He'd smelled gas, torn off one sleeve,
soaked it in his urine, covered nose and mouth,

lost consciousness, and lived, waking
in a pit of bodies somewhere outside of Krasnodar.   15
His wife?—he could not find her.
Except for the dead, he was alone. . . .
He stood up, staggered and groped through fields
back to the city, where he hid until the end.

Only Kotov, saved by his own brain and urine, woke   20
from that wedding in the death van,
in Russia, in the time of that German invention,
the windowless seven-ton gray *dushegubka*.

ANTHONY HECHT   *(b. 1921)*

The Book of Yolek   *(1991)*

Wir Haben ein Gesetz,
Und nach dem Gesetz soll er sterben.°

The dowsed coals fume and hiss after your meal
Of grilled brook trout, and you saunter off for a walk
Down the fern trail. It doesn't matter where to,
Just so you're weeks and worlds away from home,
And among midsummer hills have set up camp   5
In the deep bronze glories of declining day.

You remember, peacefully, an earlier day
In childhood, remember a quite specific meal:
A corn roast and bonfire in summer camp.
That summer you got lost on a Nature Walk;   10
More than you dared admit, you thought of home:
No one else knows where the mind wanders to.

———
Wir . . . sterben: We have a law, and according to the law he must die.

The fifth of August, 1942.
It was the morning and very hot. It was the day
They came at dawn with rifles to The Home   15
For Jewish Children, cutting short the meal
Of bread and soup, lining them up to walk
In close formation off to a special camp.

How often you have thought about that camp,
As though in some strange way you were driven to,   20
And about the children, and how they were made to walk,
Yolek who had bad lungs, who wasn't a day
Over five years old, commanded to leave his meal
And shamble between armed guards to his long home.

We're approaching August again. It will drive home   25
The regulation torments of that camp
Yolek was sent to, his small, unfinished meal,
The electric fences, the numeral tattoo,
The quiet extraordinary heat of the day
They all were forced to take that terrible walk.   30

Whether on a silent, solitary walk
Or among crowds, far off or safe at home,
You will remember, helplessly, that day,
And the smell of smoke, and the loudspeakers of the camp.
Wherever you are, Yolek will be there, too.   35
His unuttered name will interrupt your meal.

Prepare to receive him in your home some day.
Though they killed him in the camp they sent him to,
He will walk in as you're sitting down to a meal.

Tadeusz Rózewicz *(b. 1921)*

Pigtail   *(1948)*

Translated by Adam Czerniawski

When all the women in the transport
had their heads shaved
four workmen with brooms made of birch twigs
swept up   5
and gathered up the hair

Behind clean glass
the stiff hair lies

of those suffocated in gas chambers
there are pins and side combs   10
in this hair

The hair is not shot through with light
is not parted by the breeze
is not touched by any hand
or rain or lips   15

In huge chests
clouds of dry hair
of those suffocated
and a faded plait
a pigtail with a ribbon   20
pulled at school
by naughty boys.

The Museum, Auschwitz, 1948

CHARLES REZNIKOFF   *(1894–1976)*

from Holocaust   *(1975)*

from VII, Workcamps
3

When the Second World War began
he was living in Lodz with his mother.
The family was hungry
and his mother became bloated from hunger—
as many were.   5
His mother and her family escaped from the ghetto in Lodz
and fled to the Warsaw ghetto;
but there it became much worse:
his mother had sold everything she had
and they had nothing to eat.   10
She then told him to get to the Lublin area
where other members of the family lived,
and he escaped to a small town.

One morning he heard cries and shrieking:
the Germans were taking the Jews to the market place.   15
They crowded them into freight cars
and he was among them.
There was hardly room to stand

and many fainted.
But the journey took only two or three hours   20
and they were brought to a death camp.
When they got off the train
they were hurried to a small gate,
the SS men shouting, 'Hurry! Hurry!'
and there the men were taken from the women and children.   25
While this was going on
a band was playing.

The men stayed there all night
but the women and children were taken at once to the gas
     chambers.
Many of the Jews had not believed there would be any mass   30
     extermination—
a few murders, of course;
and even when they were jammed into the freight cars,
many were happy not to be going to a camp they knew to be a
     hard labour camp
and going eastward instead:
it had been rumoured that they would be taken to the Ukraine   35
     to work in the fields
now that Germany had taken over most of it.
But some remembered a Jew who had come to town and said:
'Do not believe what you are told.
The Jews are not being taken to the Ukraine;
they are sent to death camps—   40
and killed there.'
But nobody believed him;
they thought he was just trying to start a panic.
And even in the camp they had now been sent to—
a few hundred feet from the gas chambers—   45
the men were told by the Germans that in a few weeks they
     would rejoin their families.
They saw the belongings of the women and children piled up;
but the Germans said:
'They are getting new clothes.
You are going to be gathered together and then sent to the   50
     Ukraine.'

There were really three camps at that camp:
one for shoemakers, tailors, and other craftsmen;
another for those who worked at sorting the clothes of those
     who came in the transports and were gassed;
and the third camp where the gas chambers were.
The morning after the arrival of the Jewish men who had just   55
     come,
the Germans began to sort them:

choosing the young and able-bodied by saying, 'du'—the
    German familiar for 'you'.
In about half an hour most of the men who had come in that
    transport
had been taken to the gas chambers
and only about a hundred and fifty were left to work;   60
the young man who had fled from Warsaw to the Lublin area
    among them.

He was put to work taking and piling up the clothing of the
    people who had come—
and were coming—in the transports
and kept seeing that many who had come disappeared.
After the young man had worked for a while the first day,   65
he was dazed
and as he stood, dazed and benumbed—
he was only fifteen then—
a Jew came up to him and said, 'My boy, if you are going to
    behave this way, you are not going to survive here.'
•   •   •

6

Jews from Holland, France, and Hungary, and later from   70
    Greece,
were brought to a camp in freight trains or cattle cars—
three or four trains a day—
the cars crowded
and on the road days and nights,
with nothing for those inside   75
to eat or drink;
and when the cars were at the camp
they were driven out with whips
and blows from the butts of rifles.

They were then lined up before the camp physician   80
and as they passed before him
he would ask their age of the men—if they did not show it—
and what they did for a living,
and then point with his thumb
to the right or left;   85
and those sent to the left—all able to work—
were driven barefoot to the camp,
even when snow was on the ground,
and whipped to go faster.
One of the soldiers on guard said as a joke,   90
pointing to the smoke from the chimneys of the crematorium,
'The only road from here to freedom!'

Some of those sent to the right
would be loaded on vans
with only a single member of an SS squad   95
seated in front
and were gassed in the van—
if it was that kind—
and their bodies brought straight to the crematorium.
But most would be brought to the gas chambers   100
behind trees that had been cut down
and set up in rows.

If the gas chambers were crowded
and no room for the youngest children—or even adults—
they were thrown on piles of wood   105
that had been sprinkled with gasoline
and just burnt alive.
But that their screams might not be too disturbing
to those who worked
an orchestra of Jews from the camp   110
was set to playing loudly
well-known German songs.
•   •   •

from VIII, Children
1

Once, among the transports, was one with children—two
    freight cars full.
The young men sorting out the belongings of those taken to
    the gas chambers
had to undress the children—they were orphans—
and then take them to the 'lazarette.'
There the SS men shot them.   5

A large eight-wheeled car arrived at the hospital
where there were children;
in the two trailers—open trucks—were sick women and men
lying on the floor.
The Germans threw the children into the trucks   10
from the second floor and the balconies—
children from one year old to ten;
threw them upon the sick in the trucks.
Some of the children tried to hold on to the walls,
scratched at the walls with their nails;   15
but the shouting Germans
beat and pushed the children towards the windows.

The children arrived at the camp in buses,
guarded by gendarmes of the French Vichy government.
The buses stopped in the middle of the courtyard   20
and the children were quickly taken off
to make room for the buses following.
Frightened but quiet,
the children came down in groups of fifty or sixty to eighty;
the younger children holding on to older ones.   25
They were taken upstairs to empty halls—
without any furniture
and only dirty straw bags on the floor, full of bugs:
children as young as two, three, or four years of age,
all in torn clothes and dirty,   30
for they had already spent two or three weeks in other camps,
uncared for;
and were now on their way to a death camp in Poland.
Some had only one shoe.
Many had diarrhoea   35
but they were not allowed in the courtyard
where the water-closets were;
and, although there were chamber pots in the corridor of each
    story,
these were too large for the small children.

The women in the camp who were also deportees   40
and about to be taken to other camps
were in tears:
they would get up before sunrise
and go into the halls where the children were—
in each a hundred to a hundred and twenty—   45
to mend the children's clothing;
but the women had no soap to clean the children,
no clean underwear to give them,
and only cold water with which to wash them.
When soup came for the children,   50
there were no spoons;
and it would be served in tins
but the tins were sometimes too hot for the children to hold.
• • •

A visitor once stopped one of the children:
a boy of seven or eight, handsome, alert and gay.   55
He had only one shoe and the other foot was bare,
and his coat of good quality had no buttons.
The visitor asked him for his name
and then what his parents were doing;
and he said, 'Father is working in the office   60

and Mother is playing the piano.'
Then he asked the visitor if he would be joining his parents
    soon—
they always told the children they would be leaving soon to
    rejoin their parents—
and the visitor answered, 'Certainly. In a day or two.'
At that the child took out of his pocket   65
half an army biscuit he had been given in camp
and said, 'I am keeping this half for Mother';
and then the child who had been so gay
burst into tears.

from X, Mass Graves
1

After the Jew who had recognized the man from his
    home town
had been working in the woods for some time,
other Jews from his own town were among the dead
and among them—
his wife and his two children!   5
He lay down next to his wife and children and wanted the
    Germans to shoot him;
but one of the SS men said:
'You still have enough strength to work,'
and pushed him away.
That evening he tied to hang himself   10
but his friends in the cellar would not let him
and said, 'As long as your eyes are open,
there is hope.'
The next day the man who had tried to die was on a truck.

They were still in the woods   15
and he asked one of the SS men for a cigarette.
He himself did not smoke usually
but he lit the cigarette and, when he was back where his
    companions were sitting, said:
'Look here! He gives out cigarettes.
Why don't you all ask him for a cigarette?'   20
They all got up—
they were in the back of the truck—
and went forwards
and he was left behind.
He had a little knife   25
and made a slit in the tarpaulin at the side
and jumped out;

came down on his knees
but got up and ran.
By the time the SS men began shooting   30
he was gone in the woods.

•   •   •

3

In the morning the Jews were lined up by an officer
and the officer told them:
'You are Jews, unworthy of life,
but are now supposed to work.'   35
They were put upon trucks
and taken away to a forest
and set to digging.
After two or three spadefuls of earth,
the spade of one hit something hard,   40
and he saw that it was the head of a human being.
There was also a bad smell all around.
He stopped digging
and the officer in charge came towards him shouting:
'Why did you stop?   45
Didn't you know there are bodies buried here?'
He had opened a mass grave.

There were about ten thousand dead in that grave.
And after they had dug up the bodies
they were told to burn them.   50
Planks had been brought and beams—long and heavy.
The Germans also brought a grinding machine to grind the
    bones
and the ground bones would be sieved
for the gold fillings of teeth.
The dust of the bones would then be spread over the fields,   55
and the smell was dreadful.

They kept on working three months
opening mass graves;
and opened eight or nine.
In one those digging saw a boy of two or three,   60
lying on his mother's body.
He had little white shoes on
and a little white jacket,
and his face was pressed against his mother's.

One grave would remain open for new corpses   65
coming all the time;

a truck would bring the bodies, still warm,
to be thrown into the grave—
naked as Adam and Eve;
Jewish men, many of them bearded, and Jewish women and   70
    children.
The graves they had opened would be refilled with earth
and they had to plant grass all over them;
as for the dead—
a thousand bodies would be put on a pyre;
and there were two pyres of bodies burning all the time.   75

ADRIENNE RICH   *(b. 1929)*

from Sources   *(1986)*

V

All during World War II
I told myself I had some special destiny:
there had to be a reason
I was not living in a bombed-out house
or cellar   hiding out with rats   5

there had to be a reason
I was growing up safe, American
with sugar rationed in a Mason jar

split at the root   white-skinned social christian
neither gentile nor Jew   10

through the immense silence
of the Holocaust

I had no idea of what I had been spared

still less of the women and men   my kin
the Jews of Vicksburg or Birmingham   15
whose lives must have been strategies no less
than the vixen's on Route 5

XVI

The Jews I've felt rooted among
are those who were turned to smoke

Reading of the chimneys against the blear air
I think I have seen them myself

the fog of northern Europe licking its way   5
along the railroad tracks

to the place where all tracks end
You told me not to look there

to become
a citizen of the world   10

bound by no tribe or clan
yet dying you followed the Six Day War

with desperate attention
and this summer I lie awake at dawn

sweating the Middle East through my brain   15
wearing the star of David

on a thin chain at my breastbone

XVII

But there was also the other Jew. The one you most feared, the one from the *shtetl*, from Brooklyn, from the wrong part of history, the wrong accent, the wrong class. The one I left you for.   The one both like and unlike you, who explained you to me for years, who could not explain himself.   The one who said, as if he had memorized the formula, *There's nothing left now but* 5
the food and the humor.   The one who, like you, ended isolate, who had tried to move in the floating world of the assimilated who know and deny they will always be aliens.   Who drove to Vermont in a rented car at dawn and shot himself.   For so many years I had thought you and he were in opposition. I needed your unlikeness then; now it's your likeness that stares me in 10
the face.   There is something more than food, humor, a turn of phrase, a gesture of the hands: there is something more.

XVIII

There is something more than self-hatred. That still outlives
these photos of the old Ashkenazi° life:
we are gifted children at camp in the country
or orphaned children in kindergarten
we are hurrying along the rare book dealers' street   5
with the sunlight striking one side
we are walking the wards of the Jewish hospital
along diagonal squares   young serious nurses
we are part of a family group

---

13 *Ashkenazi:* From the Hebrew word for "German," it designates German and Eastern European Jews.

formally taken in 1936   10
with tables, armchairs, ferns
(behind as, in our lives, the muddy street
and the ragged shames
the street-musician, the weavers lined for strike)
we are part of a family wearing white head-bandages   15
we were beaten in a pogrom

The place where all tracks end
is the place where history was meant to stop
but does not stop   where thinking
was meant to stop but does not stop   20
where the pattern was meant to give way at last
                                                    but only

becomes a different pattern
                                        terrible, threadbare
strained   familiar   on-going   25

Rachel Blau DuPlessis   *(b. 1943)*

Draft 17: Unnamed   *(1992)*

It's true that every ending only erases the board
rather than filling it.
The poems are written in strange chalk
strange, a chalk
in some lights dark, plump with serifs   5
on a scumbled, agitated whiteness,
but mainly a white chalk on a whiter page.

Which can hardly be read
and that, only under angled light.

As wide as my life though when you look again it's   10
a scroll narrow, but fast,
paper towels in the hands of a toddler,
down and up hillocks and rises,
blazes and falls
so fast one can only   15
trail after it, "what could be more natural."

Or dark as a mist
hanging over the fill-built airport,
smoke brown the sky looks daubed
and of no depth.   20

But the chalk (with luck, another turn) turns
    translucent, light on light
        which is, in certain lights, like dark on dark
but more
    blinding.   25

Words,
    scattered falling
             arcs of shame,
                      glaze the flicker-ridden labyrinth—
it makes a peculiar medium.   30
            And its crossgrained nourishment
                    demands a strange tooth.

Perhaps translucence is a quality of erasure.
The thing anyway looks like a Cy Twombly°
strokes trailing each other and dibs, nibs,   35
flicks of the wrist and a dreamy evisceration of pencil.
A morning glory bolted across the door.
My little valise is filled with souvenirs.
And none of them is "art."
I can see why he said I wasn't interested in art.   40

"Poetry depersonalizes 'days'
in language." It sounded
as if this were what I wanted

yet the hole, the sufferance
fell open. Heard the shaped scream of a duration.   45
Three times: the game, the same, the same again,
"nothing but these facts and all these facts."
Why did he think I "wasn't interested in art"?

Low song clouds in unbelonging places
            emphasize the activities of light,   50
                which is unspeakable.

While the sound, not just the light,
        plays along certain vectors
                pools in the force field

large, square, rent, timeless   55
        void. Know?
                Can barely know what labyrinth.

---

34 *Cy Twombly (b. 1928):* Contemporary American painter.

The grass clods push up
     between the lines and cracks
          of pavement. In the depth   60

of night, a street lamp
     looming behind them
          they rise and lurk,

turf tufts made near twice
     their "real" size   65
          by shadow.

But what I mean is this.
     She stood at the pit
          where, this 50 years,

155 Jews were shot.   70
     There, near a field of rye,
          she'd found dozens of notes and addresses

tossed away
     moments before their deaths.
          To this day,   75

she regrets
     that, out of fear
          she did not pick them up.

The poetics seems plain.
     Since then   80
          there are many people spend their time

picking up the notes.
     But they are not there.
          They are as gone as possible to be.

So the gathering   85
     is impossible.
          But still the shapes are bowed,

and search
     this otherwhere of here.
          Yet had they actually   90

been there
     that time
          being remembered,

it is equally possible
> they too would have left   95
>> all of them where they lay.

What illusion, what delusion, what disillusion
> writes these gaps?
>> tries these missing bits and scraps?

It is not elegy   100
> though elegy seems the nearest category of genre
>> raising stars, strewing flowers. . . .

It's not that I have not
> done this, in life or wherever I
>> needed to   105

or throwing out the curled tough leather
> of the dead
>> the cracked insteps of unwalkable shoes,

but it is not the name or term
> for what is meant   110
>> by this inexorable bending.

And it is not "the Jews"
> (though of course it's the Jews),
>> but Jews as an iterated sign of this site.

Words with (to all intents and purposes)   115
no before and after
hanging in a void of loss
the slow and normal whirlwind
from which it roars
they had not ever meant to be so lost,   120
so little wordth.

> There are plenty of reasons to wonder.
> Forlorn spirits with spinning "swords of flame"
>> as much like angels
>> as it's possible to be, but without   125
>>> choices or pleasure,
>>> stand empty.
>> Wavy wheaty heads
>> dart and sway;
> contradictory rages swivel them.   130
>> But (pace Rilke) we can tell
>> these angels, or their similacra
>>> "things."

Late busses, glass smash, styrofoam containers.
Low sun plain wing   135
grey toyota
ormolu
soccer freshener
kith, soot, food
rainbows of oil.   140

The intersection
by Dunkin'
Donuts, chicken
buckets, milk
and Gulf is   145
where you have to turn

coming
here.

So speak, stutterer, and stain the light with figments.
Rush, and brush, this evanescent shimmer   150
that does not even track

that does not
even fill or replicate
the historical air clotted here.

And Here   155
where all this is and are
this back and forth through time,

Alight.
It's never
what you think.   160

Critical Perspective: On Holocaust Testimony

"In addition, both in literary studies and in the field of public health a new awareness arises which is ethical as well as clinical. There is more *listening*, more *hearing* of words within words, and a greater openness to *testimony*. (While the status of such testimony in formal legal hearings should be and does remain subject to questioning and challenge, it is not as often ruled out of court because of its personal, emotional, and overdetermined or multivocal nature.) In nonlegal situations, the psychoanalytic dialogue had already encouraged a greater measure of supportive listening; this is now reinforced, even as the problem of the 'real' cause of trauma deepens, especially in the matter of recovered memories. As in literature, we find a way of *receiving* the story, of listening to it, of drawing it into an interpretive conversation. Medical or political reductionism is avoided. The experts are not given the last word. The story, Kathryn Hunter says, 'must be returned to the patient.' . . .

"For a generation now, literature has been increasingly looked at from a political angle. Many in the profession are desperate to redeem their drug, that is, to make the literary object of study more transitive, more connected with what goes on in a blatantly political world. Trauma studies provide a more natural transition to a 'real' world often falsely split off from that of the university, as if the one were activist and engaged and the other self-absorbed and detached. There is an opening that leads from trauma studies to public, especially mental health issues, an opening with ethical, cultural, and religious implications.

"The result is not moral criticism exactly, because this newest perspective does not attempt a definitive judgment or evaluation of the individual work. The change introduced operates at the level of theory, and of exegesis in the service of insights about human functioning. The focus is on disclosing an unconscious or not-knowing knowledge—a potentially literary way of knowing, if you wish—combining insight and blindness, play and earnest (or an adult management of transitional objects), and linking inspiration to sound as well as sense. Emphasis falls on the imaginative use of language rather than on an ideal transparency of meaning. The real—the empirical or historical origin—cannot be known as such because it presents itself always within the resonances or 'field' of the traumatic."

—Geoffrey Hartman, from "On Traumatic Knowledge and
Literary Studies" (1995)

Critical Perspective: On Paul Celan's Imagery

"The performance of the act of drinking, traditionally a poetic metaphor for yearning, for romantic thirst and for desire, is here transformed into the surprisingly abusive figure of an endless torture and a limitless exposure, a figure for the impotent predicament and the unbearable ordeal of having to endure, absorb, continue to *take in* with no end and no limit. This image of the drunkenness of torture ironically perverts, and ironically demystifies, on the one hand, the Hellenic-mythic connotation of libidinal, euphoric Dionysiac drinking of both wine and poetry, and on the other hand, the Christian connotation of ritual religious consecration and of Eucharistic, sacred drinking of Christ's blood—and of Christ's virtue. The prominent underlying Eucharistic image suggests, however, that the enigmatic drinking which the poem repetitiously invokes is, indeed, essentially drinking of blood.

"The perversion of the metaphor of drinking is further aggravated by the enigmatic image of the 'black milk,' which, in its obsessive repetitions, suggests the further underlying—though unspeakable and inarticulated—image of a child striving to drink from the mother's breast. But the denatured 'black milk,' tainted possibly by blackened, burnt ashes, springs not from the mother's breast but from the darkness of murder and death, from the blackness of the night and of the 'dusk' that 'falls to Germany' when death uncannily becomes a 'master.' Ingesting through the liquefied black milk at once dark blood and burnt ashes, the drinking takes place not at the maternal source but at the deadly source, precisely, of the wound, at the bleeding site of reality as stigma.

"The Christian figure of the wound, traditionally viewed as the mythic vehicle and as the metaphoric means for a *historical transcendence*—for the erasure of Christ's death in the advent of Resurrection—is reinvested by the poem with the literal concreteness of the death camp blood and ashes, and is made thus to include, within the wound, not resurrection and historical transcendence, but the specificity of history—of the concrete historical reality of massacre and race annihilation—as unerasable and untranscendable. What Celan does, in this way, is to force the language of the Christian metaphorics to *witness* in effect the Holocaust, and be in turn witnessed by it.

"The entire poem is, indeed, not simply about violence but about the relation between violence and language, about the passage of the language through the violence and the passage of the violence through language."

—Shoshana Felman, from *Testimony (on Paul Celan's "Death Fugue")* (1992)

Critical Perspective: On Witnessing to the Holocaust

"On the basis of the many Holocaust testimonies I have listened to, I would like to suggest a certain way of looking at the Holocaust that would reside in the following theoretical perspective: that what precisely made a Holocaust out of the event is the unique way in which, during its historical occurrence, *the event produced no witnesses*. Not only, in effect, did the Nazis try to exterminate the physical witnesses of their crime; but the inherently incomprehensible *and* deceptive psychological structure of the event precluded its own witnessing, even by its very victims.

"A witness is a witness to the truth of what happens during an event. During the era of the Nazi persecution of the Jews, the truth of the event could have been recorded in perception and in memory, either from within or from without, by Jews, or any one of a number of 'outsiders.' Outsider-witnesses could have been, for instance, the next-door neighbor, a friend, a business partner, community institutions including the police and the courts of law, as well as bystanders and potential rescuers and allies from other countries.

"Jews from all over the world, especially from Palestine and the United States, could have been such possible outside witnesses. Even the executioner, who was totally oblivious to the plea for life, was potentially such an 'outside' witness. Ultimately, God himself could be the witness. As the event of the Jewish genocide unfolded, however, most actual or potential witnesses failed one-by-one to occupy their position as a witness, and at a certain point it seemed as if there was no one left to witness what was taking place.

"In addition, it was inconceivable that any historical insider could remove herself sufficiently from the contaminating power of the event so as to remain a fully lucid, unaffected witness, that is, to be sufficiently detached from the inside, so as to stay entirely *outside* of the trapping roles, and the consequent identities, either of the victim or of the executioner. No observer could remain untainted, that is, maintain an integrity—a wholeness and a separateness—that could keep itself uncompromised, unharmed, by his or her very witnessing. The perpetrators, in their attempt to rationalize the unprecedented scope of the destructiveness, brutally imposed upon their victims a delusional ideology whose grandiose coercive pressure totally excluded and eliminated the possibility of an unviolated, unencumbered, and thus sane, point of reference in the witness.

"What I feel is therefore crucial to emphasize is the following: it was not only the reality of the situation and the lack of responsiveness of bystanders or the world that accounts for the fact that history was taking place with no witness: it was also the very circumstance of *being inside the event* that made unthinkable the very notion that a witness could exist, that is, someone who could step outside of the coercively totalitarian and dehumanizing frame of reference in which the event was taking place, and provide an independent frame of reference through which the event could be observed. One might say that there was, thus, historically no witness to the Holocaust, either from outside or from inside the event."

—Dori Laub, from *Testimony* (1992)

Critical Perspective: On the Holocaust Survivor

"The survivor is the figure who emerges from all those who fought for life in the concentration camps, and the most significant fact about their struggle is that it depended on fixed activities: on forms of social bonding and interchange, on collective resistance, on keeping dignity and moral sense active. That such thoroughly *human* kinds of behavior were typical in places like Buchenwald and Auschwitz amounts to a revelation reaching to the foundation of what man is. Facts such as these discredit the claims of nihilism and suggest, further, that when men and women must face months and years of death threat they endure less through cultural than through biological imperatives. The biological sciences have begun to point in the same direction, and toward the end of the book I have incorporated some of their broader insights to clarify what survivors mean when they speak of *a talent for life*, or of life as a *power*, or of their reliance on *life in itself*. But here the reader should not be misled: speculation about the relation between survival behavior and basic life-processes is speculation only. The experience itself is what counts. An agony so massive should not be, indeed cannot be, reduced to a bit of datum in a theory.

"In the concentration camps, as everyone knows, vastly more people died than came through. Statisticians may therefore wish to quarrel with my concern for the survivors. Fernand Braudel, a historian I greatly admire, argues that human destiny is shaped by sheer weight of numbers. Perhaps so, but that is not the issue here. We must not, in any case, confuse history with the constituent activities of selfhood. The image of the survivor includes any man or woman striving to keep life and spirit intact—not only those who returned, but the hundreds of thousands who stayed alive sometimes for years, only to die at the last minute. . . .

"Men have always been ready to die for beliefs, sacrificing life for higher goals. That made sense once, perhaps; but no cause moves without live men to move it, and our predicament today— as governments know—is that ideas and ideologies are stopped by killing those who hold them. The 'final solution' has become a usual solution, and the world is not what it was. Within a landscape of disaster, places like Auschwitz, Hiroshima or the obliterated earth of Indo-China, where people die in thousands, where machines reduce courage to stupidity and dying to complicity with aggression, it makes no sense to speak of death's dignity or of its communal blessing. We require a heroism commensurate with the sweep of ruin in our time: action equal to situations in which it becomes less self-indulgent and more useful to live, to be there. History moves, times change, men find themselves caught up in unexpected circumstance. The grandeur of death is lost in a world of mass murder, and except for special cases the martyr and his tragic counterpart are types of the hero unfit for the darkness ahead. When men and women must live against terrible odds, when mere existence becomes miraculous, to die is in no way a triumph.

"If by heroism we mean the dramatic defiance of superior individuals, then the age of heroes is gone. If we have in mind glory and grand gesture, the survivor is not a hero. He or she is anyone who manages to stay alive in body *and* in spirit, enduring dread and hopelessness without the loss of will to carry on in human ways. That is all."

—Terrence Des Pres, from *The Survivor* (1976)

Critical Perspective: On Post-Traumatic Stress Disorder

"In the years since Vietnam, the fields of psychiatry, psychoanalysis, and sociology have taken a renewed interest in the problem of trauma. In 1980, the American Psychiatric Association finally officially acknowledged the long-recognized but frequently ignored phenomenon under the title 'Post-Traumatic Stress Disorder' (PTSD), which included the symptoms of what had previously been called shell shock, combat stress, delayed stress syndrome, and traumatic neurosis, and referred to responses to both human and natural catastrophes. On the one hand, this classification and its attendant official acknowledgment of a pathology has provided a category of diagnosis so powerful that it has seemed to engulf everything around it: suddenly responses not only to combat and to natural catastrophes but also to rape, child abuse, and a number of other violent occurrences have been understood in terms of PTSD, and diagnoses of some dissociative disorders have also been switched to that of trauma. On the other hand, this powerful new tool has provided anything but a solid explanation of disease: indeed, the impact of trauma as a concept and a category, if it has helped diagnosis, has done so only at the cost of a fundamental disruption in our received modes of understanding and of cure, and a challenge to our very comprehension of what constitutes pathology. This can be seen in the debates that surround 'category A' of the American Psychiatric Association's definition of PTSD (a response to an event 'outside the range of usual human experience'), concerning how closely PTSD must be tied to specific kinds of events; or in the psychoanalytic problem of whether trauma is indeed pathological in the usual sense, in relation to distortions caused by desires, wishes, and repressions. Indeed, the more we satisfactorily locate and classify the symptoms of PTSD, the more we seem to have dislocated the boundaries of our modes of understanding—so that psychoanalysis and medically oriented psychiatry, sociology, history, and even literature all seem to be called upon to explain, to cure, or to show why it is that we can no longer simply explain or simply cure. The phenomenon of trauma has seemed to become all-inclusive, but it has done so precisely because it brings us to the limits of our understanding: if psychoanalysis, psychiatry, sociology, and even literature are beginning to hear each other anew in the study of trauma, it is because they are listening through the radical disruption and gaps of traumatic experience. . . .

"While the precise definition of post-traumatic stress disorder is contested, most descriptions generally agree that there is a response, sometimes delayed, to an overwhelming event or events, which takes the form of repeated, intrusive hallucinations, dreams, thoughts or behaviors stemming from the event, along with numbing that may have begun during or after the experience, and possibly also increased arousal to (and avoidance of) stimuli recalling the event. This simple definition belies a very peculiar fact: the pathology cannot be defined either by the event itself—which may or may not be catastrophic, and may not traumatize everyone equally—nor can it be defined in terms of a *distortion* of the event, achieving its haunting power as a result of distorting personal significances attached to it. The pathology consists, rather, solely in the *structure of its experience* or reception: the event is not assimilated or experienced fully at the time, but only belatedly, in its repeated *possession* of the one who experiences it. To be traumatized is precisely to be possessed by an image or event."

—Cathy Caruth, from *Trauma: Explorations in Memory* (1995)

TOPICS FOR CRITICAL THINKING

1. Primo Levi was born in Turin, Italy. Before the Holocaust he was a chemistry student, graduating in 1941 first in his class at the University of Turin. While attempting to join a partisan group in Northern Italy, he was taken prisoner by the Nazis and deported to Auschwitz. There, as he relates in his memoir *Survival in Auschwitz*, his expertise in chemistry enabled him to survive inside the death camp until it was liberated in 1945. Returning to Turin, he eventually returned to his work as a chemist, becoming the general manager at a paint factory from 1961 until 1977.

   Discuss Levi's special address to the reader in "Shemá." How do you interpret the tone of the address? What ethical demand does Levi make on the reader?

2. Nelly Sachs was born in Berlin and emigrated to Sweden in 1940. Although she escaped personal disaster, her poetry pays witness to the destruction of her people in the tradition of the Old Testament verses of Lamentations. Sachs was awarded the

Nobel Prize for Literature with S. Y. Agnon in 1966. Is there an implied point or message in the questions Sachs poses in her poem "O the Chimneys"? How would you interpret her questions? What is the relation, do you think, between her questions and her exclamatory statements?

3. Elie Wiesel's poem "Never Shall I Forget" appears in his memoir on the Holocaust entitled *Night* (1958), which relates the death of his family members and his own survival at Auschwitz and later at Buchenwald. How does the poem's pattern of repetition emphasize the force of its commitment to memory?

4. Examine the psychic costs of the Holocaust as William Heyen depicts them in his poem "Kotov," which portrays a survivor of the gas extermination vans used to kill Jews in Chelmno.

TOPICS FOR CRITICAL WRITING

1. Dmitri Shostakovich based his Thirteenth Symphony on five poems by the modern Russian poet Yevgeny Yevtushenko, including his 1961 poem "Babii Yar." Babii Yar is a ravine outside of Kiev where 33,331 Jewish men, women, and children were shot by the Nazis on September 29–30, 1941. Consider Yevtushenko's use of oxymoron to invoke the force of genocide, paradoxically, through tropes of silence and absence. Does Yevtushenko succeed or fail in his attempt to identify with the Jewish victims of the Holocaust?

2. Dan Pagis's poem "Written in Pencil in the Sealed Railway-Car" is narrated through the dramatic persona of the biblical character Eve, rendered as a modern-day victim of a Holocaust deportation. She addresses her son Cain, who in the Bible's account murders his brother Abel. What is the poetic effect of cutting off Eve's speech in midsentence? Why does she call Cain the "son of man"? What do you think she meant to tell him?

3. Born to a Jewish family in Czernovitz, Romania, in 1920, Paul Ansel grew up speaking Romanian, Yiddish, and German, but it was the latter tongue in which he composed his verse. This contradiction between German and Jewish identification stemmed from his mother's encouragement to speak German, which was the cosmopolitan language of the arts, literature, and politics of the former Austro-Hungarian empire. The poet and his parents were deported in the summer of 1942. Ansel survived as a worker in several labor battalions, but his parents quickly succumbed to concentration camp existence. After the war, Ansel changed his name to Paul Celan, moved to Vienna, and later to Paris. Although Celan would receive world acclaim as a poet, he nevertheless committed suicide in 1970.

Jews undergoing selection at Auschwitz with camp entrance in background.

In "Death Fugue," the contradiction between the poet's German and Jewish identification is figured in the two mythic women Margarete and Shulamith. The former alludes to the heroine of Goethe's Faust and the "golden-hair" of Heinrich Heine's siren Lorelei. Shulamith is based on the dark Old Testament princess of the Song of Songs. Her name echoes the Hebrew word for peace, *shalom*, as well as *Yerusha-layim*, or Jerusalem.

In what ways do these two complementary female principals contradict and balance one another in the poem? How do you interpret the paradoxical figure of "black milk"? Discuss Celan's use of apostrophe in his address to "black milk" as a personified contradiction.

4. Discuss the comparative identifications that Sylvia Plath makes between women and concentration camp victims. Are these comparisons valid? Do they enhance the representation of women's experience or trivialize Holocaust victims?

5. Consider the ways in which the formal resources of the sestina in "The Book of Yolek" allow Anthony Hecht to shift the meanings of the repeated end words—*meal, walk, home, camp, day*—from their familiar, everyday connotations to their opposite associations with the Holocaust.

13

Critical Perspectives

A Casebook on Beat Poetry

After the Second World War, a group of young writers who first met at Columbia University began to explore the joy of unfettered creativity. Inspired by jazz, the crazy potentials of language, the excitement of the road, and the utter ecstasy of knowledge, this group grew to include Jack Kerouac `Web`, Allen Ginsberg `Web`, Neal Cassady, William S. Burroughs, Gregory Corso, and later Lawrence Ferlinghetti, Amiri Baraka (LeRoi Jones) `Web`, Diane Di Prima, Gary Snyder `Web`, Michael McClure, Bruce Conner, and Ann Waldman, all of whom gave voice to the tradition of twentieth-century avant-gardism. These artists congregated in Greenwich Village and later San Francisco. They wrote poetry and prose, made films, staged readings and theatrical "happenings," and generally spread a new excitement about art and language throughout New York and later American culture. Paradoxically, what began as a distinctly countercultural, even radical, movement eventually became—and has continued to be in the twenty-first century—a dominant social force. Fifty years ago, their identity as cultural icons became so established that magazines like *Time* and *Newsweek* wrote about their unconventional lifestyle and rich socialites used to "rent" beatniks to attend parties. Both their work and their personas, although not without their critics, became the subjects of both fascination and emulation. California beat Michael McClure associated with Jim Morrison of The Doors, who liked to think of himself as a beat poet; today, the images of Jack Kerouac and actor-photographer Dennis Hopper, have been appropriated by Gap to help sell khakis. Their images still exude hipness and style.

www
www
www
www

The beats were not, however, simply "arts-for-art's sake" writers. Much of their work contains a social critique stimulated by what they saw as a 1950s culture of repressiveness in America. The decade gave rise to a host of political and social events promulgating notions of conformity and convention, including the House of Un-American Activities hearings, which was led by Senator Joseph McCarthy and blacklisted Hollywood writers and others for their political beliefs; a cold war mentality that thrived on paranoia; the threat of the atomic bomb; the racial oppressions and segregations intrinsic to American culture; the destructive greed of corporations; narrow and conformist notions of family, sexuality, and identity; and the exploration of what constitutes a useful endeavor. If Jack Kerouac travels the country with Neal

*Beat poetry book rack at the Paperback
Book Gallery, New York, 1960.*

Cassady looking for the soul of jazz and the charms of the everyday citizen, if
Allen Ginsberg looks for ways to make words sing, if Gary Snyder and Bruce
Conner seek visionary experiences through Eastern religion or Native American culture, all extol the spirit of life and art. Their work represents a mixture
of media—language, photography, film, jazz, and a liberated theater no
longer kept inside the confines of traditional form and stage.

In other words, beat art reflects all of these: it is a fusion of jazz rhythms and soulfulness
with the liberations of humor, philosophy, and substances. But beat art is not
simply an accident or the result of some kind of spontaneous generation. Beat
artists were conscious of their methods and the meanings of what they did. Although their public image may have been one of unrestrained action, their art
was the result of the thoughtful analysis of the relations of individuals to the
world. If beat artists extolled spontaneity, it was because they realized they
could not control much of what happened. Beat art made a virtue out of understanding that a 9-to-5 workaday world may not be life.

In other words, beat art—beat literature, in particular—embodies a philosophy of critical action. More often than not, beat literature "does" something
by intervening in contemporary events, ideologies, or oppressions. Both Allen
Ginsberg and Gregory Corso spoke out in poems against nuclear proliferation
during the cold war era; Kerouac and Ginsberg, to name just two, wrote strong
criticisms of American capitalism that, in many respects, are still relevant and

are entirely compatible with critiques of multinational capitalism today; black beats like LeRoi Jones (who changed his name to Amiri Baraka shortly after the assassination of Malcolm X), Bob Kaufman, and Ted Joans saw beat culture as embracing black cultural forms and making an intervention in what was, at the time, a deeply segregated America. For all of these reasons and more, beat culture metamorphosed readily into the "free love" generation of the later 1960s, into the anti-Vietnam War and civil rights movements, and into many other social and political causes. Aesthetic innovation and social critique joined in the beat movement; coffee houses and alternative bookstores, folk rock, and independent film remain today some of its significant legacies.

ᏩᏩ

JACK KEROUAC

Belief & Technique for Modern Prose   *(1958)*

List of Essentials

1. Scribbled secret notebooks, and wild typewritten pages, for yr own joy
2. Submissive to everything, open, listening
3. Try never get drunk outside yr own house
4. Be in love with yr life   5

Jack Kerouac

5. Something that you feel will find its own form
6. Be crazy dumbsaint of the mind
7. Blow as deep as you want to blow
8. Write what you want bottomless from bottom of the mind
9. The unspeakable visions of the individual   10
10. No time for poetry but exactly what is
11. Visionary tics shivering in the chest
12. In tranced fixation dreaming upon object before you
13. Remove literary, grammatical and syntactical inhibition
14. Like Proust be an old teahead of time   15
15. Telling the true story of the world in interior monolog
16. The jewel center of interest is the eye within the eye
17. Write in recollection and amazement for yourself
18. Work from pithy middle eye out, swimming in language sea
19. Accept loss forever   20
20. Believe in the holy contour of life
21. Struggle to sketch the flow that already exists intact in mind
22. Dont think of words when you stop but to see picture better
23. Keep track of every day the date emblazoned in yr morning
24. No fear or shame in the dignity of yr experience, language & knowledge 25
25. Write for the world to read and see yr exact pictures of it
26. Bookmovie is the movie in words, the visual American form
27. In praise of Character in the Bleak inhuman Loneliness
28. Composing wild, undisciplined, pure, coming in from under, crazier the
    better
29. You're a Genius all the time   30
30. Writer-Director of Earthly movies Sponsored & Angeled in Heaven

ᖍᖍᖍ

ALLEN GINSBERG

America   *(1956)*

America I've given you all and now I'm nothing.
America two dollars and twentyseven cents January 17, 1956.
I can't stand my own mind.
America when will we end the human war?
Go fuck yourself with your atom bomb.   5
I don't feel good don't bother me.
I won't write my poem till I'm in my right mind.
America when will you be angelic?
When will you take off your clothes?
When will you look at yourself through the grave?   10

When will you be worthy of your million Trotskyites?°
America why are your libraries full of tears?
America when will you send your eggs to India?
I'm sick of your insane demands.
When can I go into the supermarket and buy what I need with my
    good looks?   15
America after all it is you and I who are perfect not the next
    world.
Your machinery is too much for me.
You made me want to be a saint.
There must be some other way to settle this argument.
Burroughs° is in Tangiers I don't think he'll come back it's sinister.   20
Are you being sinister or is this some form of practical joke?
I'm trying to come to the point.
I refuse to give up my obsession.
America stop pushing I know what I'm doing.
America the plum blossoms are falling.   25
I haven't read the newspapers for months, everyday somebody goes
    on trial for murder.
America I feel sentimental about the Wobblies.°
America I used to be a communist when I was a kid I'm not sorry.
I smoke marijuana every chance I get.
I sit in my house for days on end and stare at the roses in the
    closet.   30
When I go to Chinatown I get drunk and never get laid.
My mind is made up there's going to be trouble.
You should have seen me reading Marx.
My psychoanalyst thinks I'm perfectly right.
I won't say the Lord's Prayer.   35
I have mystical visions and cosmic vibrations.
America I still haven't told you what you did to Uncle Max after
    he came over from Russia.

I'm addressing you.
Are you going to let your emotional life be run by Time
    Magazine?
I'm obsessed by Time Magazine.   40
I read it every week.
Its cover stares at me every time I slink past the corner candystore.
I read it in the basement of the Berkeley Public Library.
It's always telling me about responsibility. Businessmen are serious.
    Movie producers are serious. Everybody's serious but me.
It occurs to me that I am America.   45
I am talking to myself again.

-----

11 *Trotskyites:* Communist idealists, followers of Leon Trotsky (1879–1940).   20 *Burroughs:*
William Burroughs (1914–1997), author of *Naked Lunch*.   27 *Wobblies:* Members of the Industrial Workers of the World, a militant labor organization strong in the 1910s.

Asia is rising against me.
I haven't got a chinaman's chance.
I'd better consider my national resources.
My national resources consist of two joints of marijuana millions of
     genitals an unpublished private literature that goes 1400 miles
     an hour and twentyfive-thousand mental institutions.   50
I say nothing about my prisons nor the millions of underprivileged
     who live in my flowerpots under the light of five hundred
     suns.
I have abolished the whorehouses of France, Tangiers is the next
     to go.
My ambition is to be President despite the fact that I'm a
     Catholic.

America how can I write a holy litany in your silly mood?
I will continue like Henry Ford my strophes are as individual as
     his automobiles more so they're all different sexes.   55
America I will sell you strophes $2500 apiece $500 down on your
     old strophe
America free Tom Mooney°
America save the Spanish Loyalists°
America Sacco & Vanzetti° must not die.
America I am the Scottsboro boys.°   60
America when I was seven momma took me to Communist Cell
     meetings they sold us garbanzos a handful per ticket a ticket
     cost a nickel and the speeches were free everybody was
     angelic and sentimental about the workers it was all so sincere
     you have no idea what a good thing the party was in 1935
     Scott Nearing was a grand old man a real mensch Mother
     Bloor made my cry I once saw Israel Amter° plain. Everybody
     must have been a spy.
America you don't really want to go to war
America it's them bad Russians
Them Russians them Russians and them Chinamen. And them
     Russians.
The Russia wants to eat us alive. The Russia's power mad. She
     wants to take our cars from out our garages.   65
Her wants to grab Chicago. Her needs a Red Reader's Digest. Her

---

57 *Tom Mooney:* Labor leader sentenced to death for killings in 1916. The sentence was commuted and he was eventually pardoned.   58 *Spanish Loyalists:* Opponents of Franco's Fascists in the Spanish Civil War.   59 *Sacco & Vanzetti:* Anarchists executed in Massachusetts for murder (1927) in a case that aroused much controversy.   60 *Scottsboro boys:* Nine black men falsely convicted in Alabama for the rape of two white women (1931). The defense was undertaken by the Communist Party, and the case became a cause for liberals and radicals, who believed it to be a miscarriage of justice.   61 *Scott . . . Amter:* Nearing, Bloor, and Amter were active in Socialist and radical causes.

wants our auto plants in Siberia. Him big bureaucracy
    running our fillingstations.
That no good. Ugh. Him make Indians learn read. Him need big
    black niggers. Hah. Her make us all work sixteen hours a day.
    Help.
America this is quite serious.
America this is the impression I get from looking in the television
    set.
America is this correct?   70
I'd better get right down to the job.
It's true I don't want to join the Army or turn lathes in precision
parts factories, I'm nearsighted and psychopathic anyway.
America I'm putting my queer shoulder to the wheel.

A Supermarket in California   *(1955–1956)*

What thoughts I have of you tonight, Walt Whitman, for I walked down the
sidestreets under the trees with a headache self-conscious looking at the full
moon.

In my hungry fatigue, and shopping for images, I went into the neon fruit
supermarket, dreaming of your enumerations!

What peaches and what penumbras! Whole families shopping at night!
Aisles full of husbands! Wives in the avocados, babies in the tomatoes!—and
you, Garcia Lorca,° what were you doing down by the watermelons?

I saw you, Walt Whitman, childless, lonely old grubber, poking among
the meats in the refrigerator and eyeing the grocery boys.

I heard you asking questions of each: Who killed the pork chops? What
price bananas? Are you my Angel?   5

I wandered in and out of the brilliant stacks of cans following you, and
followed in my imagination by the store detective.

We strode down the open corridors together in our solitary fancy tasting
artichokes, possessing every frozen delicacy, and never passing the cashier.

Where are we going, Walt Whitman? The doors close in an hour. Which
way does your beard point tonight?

(I touch your book and dream of our odyssey in the supermarket and feel
absurd.)

Will we walk all night through solitary streets? The trees add shade to
shade, lights out in the houses, we'll both be lonely.   10

Will we stroll dreaming of the lost America of love past blue automobiles
in driveways, home to our silent cottage?

Ah, dear father, graybeard, lonely old courage-teacher, what America did
you have when Charon quit poling his ferry and you got out on a smoking
bank and stood watching the boat disappear on the black waters of Lethe?°

---

3 *Garcia Lorca:* Spanish poet and dramatist (1889–1937).   12 *Lethe:* River of forgetfulness in
Hades, in classical myth.

First Party at Ken Kesey's with Hell's Angels   *(1965)*

Cool black night thru redwoods
cars parked outside in shade
behind the gate, stars dim above
the ravine, a fire burning by the side
porch and a few tired souls hunched over   5
in black leather jackets. In the huge
wooden house, a yellow chandelier
at 3 A.M. the blast of loudspeakers
hi-fi Rolling Stones Ray Charles Beatles
Jumping Joe Jackson and twenty youths   10
dancing to the vibration thru the floor,
a little weed in the bathroom, girls in scarlet
tights, one muscular smooth skinned man
sweating dancing for hours, beer cans
bent littering the yard, a hanged man   15
sculpture dangling from a high creek branch,
children sleeping softly in their bedroom bunks.
And 4 police cars parked outside the painted
gate, red lights revolving in the leaves.

ᴄᴏᴄᴏ

JACK KEROUAC

About the Beat Generation   *(1957)*

The beat generation, that was a vision that we had, John Clellon Holmes and
I, and Allen Ginsberg in an even wilder way, in the late Forties, of a generation of crazy, illuminated hipsters suddenly rising and roaming America, serious,
curious, bumming and hitchhiking everywhere, ragged, beatific, beautiful in
an ugly graceful new way—a vision gleaned from the way we had heard the
word "beat" spoken on streetcorners on Times Square and in the Village, in
other cities in the downtown city night of postwar America—beat, meaning
down and out but full of intense conviction—We'd even heard old 1910
Daddy Hipsters of the streets speak the word that way, with a melancholy
sneer—It never meant juvenile delinquents, it meant characters of a special
spirituality who didn't gang up but were solitary Bartlebies staring out the
dead wall window of our civilization—the subterraneans heroes who'd finally
turned from the "freedom" machine of the West and were taking drugs, digging bop, having flashes of insight, experiencing the "derangement of the
senses," talking strange, being poor and glad, prophesying a new style for
American culture, a new style (we thought) completely free from European
influences (unlike the Lost Generation), a new incantation—The same thing
was almost going on in the postwar France of Satre and Genet and what's

Neal Cassady

more we knew about it—But as to the actual existence of a Beat Generation, chances are it was really just an idea in our minds—We'd stay up 24 hours drinking cup after cup of black coffee, playing record after record of Wardell Gray, Lester Young, Dexter Gordon, Willie Jackson, Lennie Tristano and all the rest, talking madly about that holy new feeling out there in the streets— We'd write stories about some strange beatific Negro hepcat saint with goatee hitchhiking across Iowa with taped up horn bringing the secret message of blowing to other coasts, other cities, like a veritable Walter the Penniless leading an invisible First Crusade—We had our mystic heroes and wrote, nay sung novels about them, erected long poems celebrating the new "angels" of the American underground—In actuality there was only a handful of real hip swinging cats and what there was vanished mighty swiftly during the Korean War when (and after) a sinister new kind of efficiency appeared in America, maybe it was the result of the universalization of Television and nothing else (the Polite Total Police Control of Dragnet's "peace" officers) but the beat characters after 1950 vanished into jails and madhouses, or were shamed into silent conformity, the generation itself was shortlived and small in number.

But there'd be no sense in writing this article if it weren't equally true that by some miracle of metamorphosis, suddenly, the Korean postwar youth emerged cool and beat, had picked up the gestures and the style, soon it was everywhere, the new look, the "twisted" slouchy look, finally it began to appear even in movies (James Dean) and on television, bop arrangements that were once the secret ecstasy music of beat contemplatives began to appear in every pit in every square orchestral book (cf. the works of Neil Hefti and not meaning Basie's book), the bop visions became common property of the commercial popular cultural world, the use of expressions like "crazy," "hungup," "hassle," "make it," "like" ("like make it over sometime, like"), "go," became familiar and common usage, the ingestion of drugs became official (tranquilizers and the rest), and even the clothes style of the beat hipsters carried over to the new Rock'n'Roll youth via Montgomery Clift (leather jacket), Marlon Brando (T-shirt), and Elvis Presley (long sideburns), and the Beat Generation, though dead, was suddenly resurrected and justified.

It really happened, and the sad thing is, that while I am asked to explain the Beat Generation, there is no actual original Beat Generation left.

Yet today from Montreal to Mexico City, from London to Casablanca kids in blue jeans are now playing Rock'n'Roll records on jukeboxes.

As to an analysis of what it means . . . who knows? Even in this late stage   5 of civilization when money is the only thing that really matters, to everybody, I think perhaps it is the Second Religiousness that Oswald Spengler prophesied for the West (in America the final home of Faust), because there are elements of hidden religious significance in the way, for instance, that a guy like Stan Getz, the highest jazz genius of his "beat" generation, was put in jail for trying to hold up a drug store, suddenly had visions of God and repented (something gracefully Villonesque in that story)—Or take the case of the posthumous canonization of James Dean by millions of kids—Strange talk we'd heard among the early hipsters, of "the end of the world" at the "second coming," of "stoned-out visions" and even visitations, all believing, all inspired and fervent and free of Bourgeois-Bohemian Materialism, such as P.L.'s[1] being knocked off his chair by the Angel and his vision of the books of the Fathers of the Church and of Christ crashing through Time, G.C.'s[2] visions of the devil and celestial Heralds, A.G.'s[3] visions in Harlem and elsewhere of the tearful Divine Love, W.S.B.'s[4] reception of the word that he is the One Prophet, G.S.'s[5] Buddhist visions of the vow of salvation, peotl visions of all the myths being true, P.W.'s[6] visions of malific flashes and forms and the roof flying off the house, J.K.'s[7] numerous visions of Heaven, the "Golden Eternity," bright light in the night woods, H.H.'s[8] geekish visions of Armaggedon (experienced in Sing Sing), N.C.'s[9] visions of reincarnation under God's will [. . .] A.L.'s[10] vision of everything as mysterious electricity, and

------

1. Philip Lamantia.

2. Gregory Corso.

3. Allen Ginsberg.

4. William S. Burroughs.

5. Gary Snyder.

6. Philip Whalen.

7. Jack Kerouac.

8. Herbert Huncke.

9. Neal Cassady.

10. Alene L., the African-American woman with whom Kerouac had an affair in New York City in 1953; she is called "Mardou" in *The Subterraneans*.

Allen Ginsberg

one unnamed Times Square kid's vision of the Second Coming being televised (all taking place, a definite fact, in the midst of everyday contemporary
life in the minds of typical members of my generation whom I know), reap-
pearances of the early Gothic Springtime feeling of Western mankind before
it went on its "Civilization" Rationale and developed relativity, jets and su-
perbombs and supercolossal bureaucratic totalitarian benevolent Big Brother
structures—so, as Spengler says, when comes the sunset of our culture (due
now, according to his morphological graphs) and the dust of civilized striving
settles, lo, the clear late-day glow reveals the original concerns again, reveals
a beatific indifference to things that are Caesar's, for instance, a tiredness of
that, and a yearning for, a regret for, the transcendent value, or "God," again,
"Heaven," the spiritual regret for Endless Love which our theory of electro-
magnetic gravitation, our conquest of space will prove, and instead of only
techniques of efficiency, all will be left, as with a population that has gone
through a violent earthquake, will be the Last Things . . . again (for the fact
that everybody dies makes the world kind).

   We all know about the Religious Revival, Billy Graham and all, under
which the Beat Generation, even the existentialists with all their intellectual
overlays and pretenses of indifference, represent an even deeper religiousness,
the desire to be gone, out of this world (which is not our kingdom), "high,"
ecstatic, saved, as if the visions of the cloistral saints of Chartres and Clairvaux
were back with us again bursting like weeds through the sidewalks of stiffened
Civilization wearying through its late motions.

   Or maybe the Beat Generation, which is the offspring of the Lost Generation, is just another step towards that last, pale generation which will not
know the answers either.

In any case, indications are that its effect has taken root in American culture.
Maybe.
Or, what difference does it make?   10

149th Chorus   *(1959)*

from Mexico City Blues

I keep falling in love
    with my mother,
I dont want to hurt her
—Of all people to hurt.

Every time I see her   5
    she's grown older
But her uniform always
    amazes me
For its Dutch simplicity
And the Doll she is,   10
The doll-like way
    she stands
Bowlegged in my dreams,
Waiting to serve me.

    And I am only an Apache   15
    Smoking Hashi
    In old Cabashy
    By the Lamp

211th Chorus   *(1959)*

from Mexico City Blues

The wheel of the quivering meat
                conception
Turns in the void expelling human beings,
Pigs, turtles, frogs, insects, nits,
Mice, lice, lizards, rats, roan   5
Racinghorses, poxy bucolic pigtics,
Horrible unnameable lice of vultures,
Murderous attacking dog-armies
Of Africa, Rhinos roaming in the
                jungle,   10
Vast boars and huge gigantic bull
Elephants, rams, eagles, condors,
Pones and Porcupines and Pills—

All the endless conception of living   15
                  beings
Gnashing everywhere in Consciousness
Throughout the ten directions of space
Occupying all the quarters in & out,
From supermicroscopic no-bug
To huge Galaxy Lightyear Bowell   20
Illuminating the sky of one Mind—
      Poor! I wish I was free
      of that slaving meat wheel
      and safe in heaven dead

The Thrashing Doves   *(1959)*

from Mexico City Blues

In the back of the dark Chinese store
    in a wooden jailhouse bibbet box
    with dust of hay on the floor, rice
    where the rice bags are leaned,
    beyond the doomed peekokoos in the box   5
    cage

All the little doves'll die.
    As well as the Peekotoos—eels
    —they'll bend chickens' necks back
    oer barrels and slice at Samsara   10
    the world of eternal suffering with silver
    blades as thin as the ice in Peking

As thick & penetrable as the Wall of China
    the rice darkness of that store, beans,
    tea, boxes of dried fish, doodlebones,   15
    pieces of sea-weed, dry, pieces of eight,
    all the balloon of the shroud on the floor

And the lights from little tinkly Washington St.
    Behung, dim, opium pipes and gong wars,
    Tong, the rice and the card game—and   20
    Tibbet de tibbet the tink tink tink
    them Chinese cooks do in the kitchen
    Jazz

The thrashing doves in the dark, white fear,
    my eyes reflect that liquidly   25
    and I no understand Buddha-fear?
    awakener's fear? So I give warnings
    'bout midnight round about midnight

And tell all the children the little otay
   story of magic, multiple madness, maya   30
   otay, magic trees-sitters and little girl
   bitters, and littlest lil brothers
   in crib made made of clay (blue in the moon).

For the doves.

∽∞∾

GREGORY CORSO

Dream of a Baseball Star   *(1960)*

I dreamed Ted Williams
leaning at night
against the Eiffel Tower, weeping.

He was in uniform
and his bat lay at his feet   5
—knotted and twiggy.

'Randall Jarrell says you're a poet !' I cried.
'So do I ! I say you're a poet !'

He picked up his bat with blown hands;
stood there astraddle as he would in the batter's box,   10
and laughed ! flinging his schoolboy wrath
toward some invisible pitcher's mound
—waiting the pitch all the way from heaven.

It came; hundreds came! all afire!
He swung and swung and swung and connected not one   15
sinker curve hook or right-down-the-middle.
A hundred strikes !
The umpire dressed in strange attire
thundered his judgement: YOU'RE OUT !
And the phantom crowd's horrific boo   20
dispersed the gargoyles from Notre Dame.

And I screamed in my dream :
God ! throw thy merciful pitch !
Herald the crack of bats !
Hooray the sharp liner to left !   25
Yea the double, the triple !
Hosannah the home run !

∽∞∾

Amiri Baraka (LeRoi Jones)

Three Modes of History and Culture   *(1969)*

Chalk mark sex of the nation, on walls we drummers
know
as cathedrals. Cathedra, in a churning meat milk.

Women glide through looking for telephones. Maps
weep   5
and are mothers and their daughters listening to

music teachers. From heavy beginnings. Plantations,
learning
America, as speech, and a common emptiness. Songs knocking

inside old women's faces. Knocking through cardboard trunks.   10
Train's
leaning north, catching hellfire in windows, passing through

the first ignoble cities of missouri, to illinois, and the panting
Chicago.
And then all ways, we go where flesh is cheap. Where factories   15

sit open, burning the chiefs. Make your way! Up through fog and
history
Make your way, and swing the general, that it come flash open

and spill the innards of that sweet thing we heard, and gave theory
to.   20
Breech, bridge, and reach, to where all talk is energy. And there's

enough, for anything singular. All our lean prophets and rhythms.
Entire
we arrive and set up shacks, hole cards, Western hearts at the edge

of saying. Thriving to balance the meanness of particular skies.   25
Race
of madmen and giants.

Brick songs. Shoe songs. Chants of open weariness.
Knife wiggle early evenings of the wet mouth. Tongue
dance midnight, any season shakes our house. Don't   30
tear my clothes! To doubt the balance of misery

ripping meat hug shuffle fuck. The Party of Insane
Hope. I've come from there too. Where the dead told lies
about clever social justice. Burning coffins voted
and staggered through cold white streets listening   35
to Willkie or Wallace or Dewey through the dead face
of Lincoln. Come from there, and belched it out.

I think about a time when I will be relaxed.
When flames and non-specific passion wear themselves
away. And my eyes and hands and mind can turn   40
and soften, and my songs will be softer
and lightly weight the air.

DIANE DI PRIMA

On Sitting Down to Write, I Decide Instead to
Go to Fred Herko's Concert   *(1975)*

As water, silk
the quiver of fish
or the long cry of goose
        or some such bird
        I never heard   5
your orange tie
a sock in the eye
        as Duncan
        might forcibly note
are you sitting under the irregular drums   10
of Brooklyn Joe Jones
(in a loft which I know to be dirty
& probably cold)
or have you scurried already
        hurried already   15
uptown
on a Third Avenue Bus
toward smelly movies & crabs I'll never get
and you all perfumed too
as if they'd notice   20

O the dark caves of obligation
into which I must creep
        (alack)
like downstairs & into a coat
        O all that wind   25
Even Lord & Taylor don't quite keep out

that wind
and that petulant vacuum
I am aware of it
sucking me into Bond Street   30
into that loft
        dank
        rank
I draw a blank
at the very thought   35

                    Hello
I came here
        after all

∽∽

ANNE WALDMAN

College Under Water   *(1966)*

Who are these women and offices
that control the will of the dead graduates?

They come to dinner like swimmers
assembling before a final race

Now coffins are lined up outside   5
where campus elms seize precedence over girls

Now offices are closed for the afternoon
in correspondence with the courts and the pool

Now because instructed the sky changes hands
shuffling wills that are transferred   10

to file cards behind locked doors
These vendetta women will not be put off

Now I write like this because
it could happen   My will weakens

Is there a choice? the alternative   15
lies on the other side of the poem.

14

Critical Perspectives

A Casebook on Postmodern Poetics

Postmodernism **Web** is a key word that you are as likely to encounter *www* on MTV as in a book of scholarly critical theory. Architecture, music, art, theater, literature, economics, and the social sciences all describe our present moment in terms of postmodernism. Although the word *postmodernism* literally denotes what comes after twentieth-century modernism (see Chapter 14), the widespread use of this rubric in academic circles and popular culture generally makes it more than simply a term covering a moment in history. Not just a period term, postmodernism involves complex understandings of language, philosophical thought, human subjectivity and political theory. The critical theorist Fredric Jameson distinguishes between modernism and postmodernism by drawing a contrast between poet Ezra Pound's modernist slogan "make it new" and William Gibson's rejoinder "when-it-all-changed" from his 1988 cyberpunk novel *Mona Lisa Overdrive*. According to Jameson in *Postmodernism, or The Cultural Logic of Late Capitalism* (1991), modernism "thought compulsively about the New and tried to watch its coming into being . . . but the postmodern looks for breaks, for events rather than new worlds, for the telltale instant after which it is no longer the same . . . or better still, for shifts and irrevocable changes in the representation of things and of the way they change."

Ezra Pound's dictum—"make it new"—signaled a rupture and departure from what he criticized as the mannered world outlook of the Victorian era that, by the end of the nineteeth century, had become all too predictable in its aesthetic conventions. Following the example of such cubist artists as Pablo Picasso and Georges Braques, and paralleling futurist writers like F. T. Marinetti, Pound sought to overturn conventional habits of perception and thought. He wanted to renew poetic expression based on the "image" (see Chapter 3). At the level of technique, Pound defined *imagism* in terms of a "direct treatment of the 'thing' whether subjective or objective." However experimental in employing poetic collage forms, Pound's poetic dictum "make it new" assumed the fixed, knowable world of the "thing" whose referent ("It") could be comprehended, grasped, de-created, and re-created through the power of the imagination. Similarly, the modern poet Wallace Stevens wanted the imagination to "be completely adequate in the face of reality." He defined the poem as a kind of settlement between the mind and the real. In *The Necessary Angel* (1951), he wrote that a poem expresses "a violence from within that protects us from a violence without. It is the imagination pressing back against the pressure of reality." Like Pound, Stevens assumed that reality—however chaotic—has force, depth, and substance.

In contrast, Gibson's postmodern phrasing "when-it-all-changed," as its hyphenated format suggests, unhinges the "thing" (the signifer "It") from any referent grounded in a real, fixed world of essences. *As we move from the modern to the postmodern condition, the real world of things is increasingly difficult to tell apart from copies of things, or simulations, created by the influences of advertising, television, digitized computer graphics, the Internet, and other technological tools of the information age.* Gibson's slogan denotes a decisive break with the world of referential things-in-themselves. Instead, Gibson points to the postmodern turn toward a process of endless representational change in signification. While modernism still presents versions of the individual's personal point of view, or subjectivity, postmodernism parts company with the person's unique frame of reference. While the former still features the emotional lives of characters, the latter portrays random intensities that cut across individual selves. The postmodern condition is defined more by the kind of turbulent unpredictability that James Gleick describes in terms of chaos theory. In postmodern literature, for example, the author is viewed less as the creative genius presiding over the work and more as a manipulator of free-floating codes and chance operations. While we can study modernism—read its texts, experience its insights, learn from its triumphs and failures—it is, for better or worse, in the postmodern condition that we now live.

Postmodernism marks the limit of the Enlightenment philosophy of modernism dating back to the sixteenth century. The philosophical underpinnings of Enlightenment humanism are based in reason. Rational thought is foundational, and thinking defines one's human essence. *Cogito ergo sum.* "I think, therefore I am," as René Descartes famously asserted in his 1637 volume *Discourse on the Method of Rightly Conducting the Reason and Seeking the Truth in the Sciences.* Such Enlightenment principles rest on a knowable, objective universe available to scientific inquiry and reasoned verification. The Enlightenment faith in progress stems from the mind's ability to discern determinable, universal truths that can be applied to the state, government, law, legal institutions, and human relations generally. Similarly, language serves in this model as the transparent medium for reasoned thought, the articulation of truth, the practice of ethics, and the expression of beauty. Moreover, the world outlook of the Enlightenment maintains that all of these things can be rationally communicated because the written or spoken word, as signifier, reflects the "thing" or referent "It" in an unproblematic relation. The Enlightenment project seeks to map the human domains of science, politics, ethics, and aesthetics through grand or "master" narratives that rest on universal principles whose foundational truths can withstand the test of time and be applied uniformly across regional circumstance and local differences.

By the nineteenth century, however, these Enlightenment ideals became complicated by new understandings of human subjectivity. The humanist faith in rationality began to erode from new theories of evolution—inaugurated with

Charles Darwin's *On the Origin of Species by Means of Natural Selection* (1859)—
and reinforced by the Freudian revolution in psychology, Friedrich Nietzsche's
theories of the death of God and the will to power in *The Gay Science* (1882), as
well as Karl Marx's and Friedrich Engels's analyses of class conflict. Moreover,
the whole concept of a constant, natural universe was further undermined in the
modern theories of relativity that emerged in modern, post-Newtonian physics.

Experimental literary modernism of the early twentieth century also
marks the breakup of the Enlightenment paradigm. We can see this emerging
crisis in the kind of fragmentation witnessed in T. S. Eliot's bleak depiction of
the post-World War I milieu of *The Waste Land* (1922). The end of Enlightenment thinking is also evident in the dispersal of the individual's personal
awareness through unconscious, stream-of-consciousness narratives in the
fiction of such modernist authors as Virginia Woolf and James Joyce. We can
observe a similar shift in the modern self as it is exposed to the new forms of
mass media, print journalism, film, and radio, as in the collaged newsreel
montages of John Dos Passos. Modernist literary characters are increasingly
saturated as well by a new erotic politics of desire, as portrayed by such expatriate American writers as Henry Miller and Djuna Barnes.

Modernism responds inventively to the loss of foundational belief, certainty,
rationality, and the human-scale order of things. Postmodernism celebrates
the modernist desire to "make it new" but accelerates the forms and representations of "the new" at a dizzying pace as the ever-multiplying technologies of the
information age allow for instant global communication. Even more than modernism, postmodernism reveals the structuring role of language and sign systems
in *determining* our experience of the world, rather than merely *reflecting* it. **Semiotics** Web —the scholarly analysis of sign systems and practices of signification   *www*
in everyday life—reflects this new awareness of how the constant acceleration
of advertising and mass mediated messages broadcast via television, radio, the
Internet, and so on has fundamentally changed contemporary experience.

Some postmodern theorists are committed to a **Marxist** Web analysis of   *www*
these contemporary trends. Influenced by the nineteenth-century German
philosopher, historian, social scientist, and revolutionary Karl Marx, Marxist
critics advance, in a variety of ways, a labor theory of value. In particular, they
consider how underlying economic structures influence global and state politics, popular culture, and everyday life. From a Marxist point of view, the
postmodern paradigm shift—"when-it-all-changed"—amounts to both an expression and shaping of underlying economic trends. They point to the evolution after World War II away from the economies of industrial production
that define modernism and toward the consumer society of the postwar
decades. Money in the postwar era is not just made from its modern settings
of industrial production—the factory, textile mill, power plant, construction
site, or agribusiness combine. Instead postwar capital seizes on the frontier
markets of consumption—the mall, the road strip, the nuclear household—
and exploits these new niche markets with ever new generations of consumer
items: gas and restaurant franchises, prepackaged foods, electronic appliances,
and gadgetry of all kinds. Even the most private spaces of the body and the
unconscious are exploited with accelerating rhythms of style, fashion, and
popular trends in music, teen culture, and suburban living. Mediated by the

new electronic media, the postmodern condition of everyday life increasingly is driven by sign exchange for its own sake.

By now, we have grown accustomed to the new cultural logic of the information age and its endless layering of sign systems whose fantasies of affluence, success, luxury, and satisfaction through consumption exceed anything most of us will ever experience concretely in the real world. Increasingly, advertising has depended on the sheer repetition of canned or artificial signs of enjoyment. Harbingers of the postmodern can be seen in the postmodern visual art of Andy Warhol. Through playful but arresting images, Warhol parodies the commodity form, as in his reproduction of literal Campbell soup cans or his portraits of such Hollywood icons as Marilyn Monroe, who became inseparable from her star image (see color insert). We live not only in the society of the media spectacle but in a world of simulacra, or artificial copies, of real things. Here the endless proliferation of signs and semiotic exchange confuses the difference between the real and its manufactured imitations. Such films as the Wachowski brothers' *The Matrix* depict in the cyperpunk subgenre the blurring of the real and its postmodern simulation. Within this new horizon, the things we take for granted in everyday life—human subjectivity, thought, and personal will—are no longer simply expressed and communicated through language. Instead, they suddenly appear as produced by a complex matrix of digitized codes. In postmodern thinking, likewise, the human subject is increasingly viewed as itself linguistically produced, as shaped by complex practices of signification.

According to the postmodern view of things, the sources of our desire and what we value are neither simple nor consistent. In fact, they are not even personal; they don't belong to us as individuals. Rather, our sexual preferences, our gender identifications, the kind of work we pursue, the company we keep—the entire repertoire of where we live, what we wear, the sports we pursue, what we find appetizing, which TV channels we watch and how quickly we surf them, the Web sites we frequent—are all formed by an assemblage of competing and discursively produced seductions driven by services and consumables whose bottom-line aim is to make money. In this postmodern register, the self is experienced as dispersed across a range of desiring subject positions that are less fixed than fluid, less authentic than situational, less predictable than subject to chance. Subjectivity is no longer unitary but divided by a multiplicity of conflicting, even schizophrenic, narrative tensions.

Beginning in the late 1970s, the postmodern emphasis on language's constituting role in postmodern experience began to make itself felt in contemporary poetics, especially in the magazine *L=A=N=G=U=A=G=E* edited by Bruce Andrews and Charles Bernstein. A new movement of postmodern poets located primarily in New York City and the San Francisco Bay area began to publish experimental work in such journals as *Poetics Journal, Sulfur, This, Hills,* and in books by independent presses such as Lyn Hejinian's Tuumba, Barrett Watten's This Press, and James Sherry's Roof Press, among many others.

These writers no longer thought of the author as the expressive genius of the poetic utterance. They went beyond regarding the author as a modern craftsman of a new poetic form. In this regard, the Language writers followed the lead of the French theorist Roland Barthes, who in his 1968 essay "The Death of the Author" radically reinterpreted the author's relation to language.

Instead of expressing individual genius, the literary text for Barthes inverts the author's relation to the writing. "Linguistically," Barthes writes, "the author is never more than the instance writing, just as *I* is nothing other than the instance saying I: language knows a 'subject', not a 'person.'" Similarly, the Language writers stressed the autonomous linguistic operations and verbal chance events that take place in language itself, beyond any authorial intention. "It's a mistake," said Charles Bernstein, "to posit the self as the primary organizing feature of writing. As many others have pointed out, a poem exists in a matrix of social and historical relations that are more significant to the formation of an individual text than any personal qualities of the life or voice of an author."

Much of the new, postmodern poetry sought to challenge the normative conventions that put language at the beck and call of consumer values. Many language poets subverted the "formal requirements of clarity and exposition" shaping the verbal formats of journalism, advertising, bureaucratic speaking, and other discourses that sustain consumer society through sound bites, packaged phrasings, and clichéd utterances. Instead, says Bernstein in *Content's Dream* (1986), in Language writing "contradiction, obsessiveness, associative reasoning, etc., are given fre(er) play." For Language poets, the presentation of a poem's individual letters, its formal procedures, and its syntax matter more than the qualities of its voice or emotive authenticity. Bob Perelman's postmodern manipulations of language in "Virtual Reality," for example, mimic the normative speaking voice in its first-person plural address to the reader. Nevertheless, our conventional identification with the poem's "we" quickly breaks down and is dispersed through a scene of simulated experience:

> We turned to analysis, negotiation, persuasion,
> cards on the table, confession, surrender.
>
> But there was no refamiliarizing. Our
> machines filled the freeway with names
>
> and desires, hurling aggressively streamlined
>   messages
> Toward a future that seemed restless,
>   barely interested.

More playfully, Perelman's poem "Seduced by Analogy" dismantles the ways in which language's formal operations and verbal "seductions" shape thought, not the other way around:

> First sentence: *Her cheap perfume*
> *Caused cancer in the White House late last night.*
> With *afford, agree and arrange,* use the infinitive.
> *I can't agree to die.* With *practice,*
> *Imagine,* and *resist,* use the gerund. *I practice to live*
> Is wrong. Specify, "We've got to nuke 'em, Henry."
> Second sentence: *Inside the box is plutonium.*
> The concept degrades, explodes,
> Goes all the way, in legal parlance.
>
> "I can't stop. Stop. I can't stop myself."
> First sentence: *She is a woman who has read*

Powers of Desire. Second sentence:
She is a man that has a job, no job, a car, no car,
To drive, driving. Tender is the money
That makes the bus *to go* over the bridge.
Go over the bridge. *Tender*
Are the postures singularly verbally undressed men and women
Assume. *Strong* are the rivets of the bridge. "I'm not interested,
Try someone else." First sentence:
Wipe them off the face. Not complete.

In these opening stanzas of "Seduced by Analogy," Perleman's "first sentence" mixes up the fetishized codes of broadcast news—"caused cancer" and "in the White House last night"—to seduce and derail the reader's consumption of a typical news report. The poem estranges and defamiliarizes our expectations of the conventional news narrative. Not only do the poet's non sequiturs subvert our habitual reliance on the simple sentence as a journalistic commodity form, but this playful quoting of grammatical rules calls attention to how the constructed nature of discourse shapes our experience of the world.

Serial repetition lays bare the fabricated codes of postmodern experience in much the same way as in, say, Andy Warhol's multiple icons of Marilyn Monroe (see color insert). Repetition of phrasing, parts of grammar, and key words in postmodern poetry parallel the serial musical forms of Philip Glass and analogous cinematic techniques of avant-garde film directors like Hollis Frampton, Sally Potter, Yvonne Rainer, and Michael Snow. Presenting language as assemblage, rather than as lyric expression, other language writers such as Ron Silliman and Lyn Hejinian likewise employ serial composition. For example, Hejinian employs her age in *My Life* (1980) as a basis for her sentence and paragraph constructions: 37 paragraphs of 37 sentences each. Similarly, Ron Silliman's "2197" is made up of 13 sections, each embodying 13 stanzas of 13 sentence units; the title "2197" equals 13 cubed.

Analogous techniques of composing lines in sentences made up of a fixed number of words point not only to the fabricated nature of all utterance but also afford new opportunities for discoveries and meanings in language usage, as in this excerpt from Perelman's "Chronic Meanings":

The single fact is matter.
Five words can say only.
Black sky at night, reasonably.
I am, the irrational residue.

Blown up chain link fence.
Next morning stronger than ever.
Midnight the pain is almost.
The train seems practically expressive.

A story familiar as a.
Society has broken into bands.
The nineteenth century was sure.
Characters in the withering capital.

Such truncated, utterances and their structural relation of **parataxis**—setting phrases side by side without obvious or logical connection—may be indeterminable, nonsensical, illuminating, comic, and profoundly unsettling. But they are never predictable. They seldom make reference to a world that comes before their invocation of it.

A more radical deployment of arranged language on the page happens in the poetry of Susan Howe **Web** . Beginning her career as a visual artist after graduating from the Boston Museum School of Fine Arts in 1961, Howe brings her painter's sensitivity to the pictorial space of the page. Howe began writing poems in the 1970s and published such important volumes of experimental poetry in the 1980s as *The Liberties* (1980), *Pythagorean Silence* (1982), *Articulation of Sound Forms in Time* (1987). It was at this stage in her career that she also published an influential book of criticism entitled *My Emily Dickinson* (1985). Her volumes from the 1990s include *Singularities* (1990), *The Europe of Trusts* (1990), and *The Nonconformist's Memorial* (1993) **Web** . *www*

Howe's visual sense of space was reinforced through her partner of twenty-seven years, David von Schlegell, who directed the Yale sculpture program in New Haven. Further shaping Howe's eclectic sensibilities as a visual artist were the minimalist influences of mixed media and collage artists whom she encountered in the 1960s New York art scene, artists such as Richard Serra, Joan Jonas, Don Judd, Eva Hesse, Ellsworth Kelly, Robert Morris, Carl Andre, John Cage, and Agnes Martin. Like these postmodern artists, Howe was drawn to the new aesthetic possibilities afforded by composing across the boundaries of genre of painting, film, music, sculpture, and poetry. Inspired by the open format "projective verse" experiments of the Black Mountain poet Charles Olson, Howe began to compose her visual compositions in language fragments, as photocopied texts cut into lines and pasted as visual objects on the canvas of the page. Of her poetic method in *The Nonconformist's Memorial*, Howe has said:

> First I would type some lines. Then cut them apart. Paste one on top of another, move them around until they looked right. Then I'd xerox that version, getting several copies, and then cut and paste again until I had it right. The getting it right has to do with how it's structured on the page as well as how it sounds—this is the meaning.

Rather than regarding verse as the vehicle for the poet's personal or confessional experience, Howe thinks of language in terms of pictorial images where the look of a verbal arrangement signifies original meanings in new compositional formats. Her poetry experiments with verbal collage and intertextual citations from other authors such as Emily Dickinson and Herman Melville, as well as the Gospel According to John. At times, her poetry suggests the contested reception of traumatic historical events such as the execution of Charles I, which is the subject of her poem "Eikon Basilike."

In her long poem on the execution of Charles I, Howe runs lines into and over one another in jagged, chaotic formats where words and phrases intersect and collide to suggest historical violence. Howe describes her compositional strategy this way:

> In the "Eikon Basilike," the sections that are all vertically jagged are based around the violence of the execution of Charles I, the violence of history, the violence of that particular event, and also then the stage drama of it. It was a trial, but the

scene of his execution was also a performance; he acted his own death. There's no way to express that in just words in ordinary fashion on the page. So I would try to match that chaos and violence visually with words.

Other long poem sequences such as "Thorow" require the reader to turn the poem up to 180 degrees as some lines are written at angles or in upside-down relation to other lines. Howe describes this as a poetic "mirroring" technique. In her poetry readings, she whispers the upside-down lines for strange, other-worldly, and uncanny effects.

Beyond Howe's compositional language experiments on the page, post-modern poetics becomes more provocative, perhaps, in the expanded public sphere of everyday life where language, signage, and technology intersect in the makeup of today's society of the spectacle. Jenny Holzer's appropriation of light emitting diode (L.E.D.) boards is one example of this new form of po-etic expression. Holzer came to New York in 1976–1977 via the Whitney Mu-seum's Independent Study Program. After collaborating with a number of performance artists at the Whitney, she jettisoned her pursuit of more typical artistic values and in 1977 began to compose aphorisms that she collected in a series of "Truisms" formatted onto posters, stickers, handbills, hats, T-shirts, and other paraphernalia. The verbal character of the "Truisms" themselves relies on the familiar slogans and one-liners common to tabloid journalism, the *Reader's Digest* headline, the TV evangelist pitch line, campaign rhetoric, rap and hip-hop lyrics, bumper sticker and T-shirt displays, and countless other kitsch forms.

In the mid-1980s, Holzer intensified her art's political content in her more militant "Survival" series and, at the same time, undertook a bolder appropri-ation of a uniquely authoritative and spectacular medium: the L.E.D. boards installed worldwide in stock exchanges, urban squares, airports, stadiums, sports arenas, and other mass locales. The formal elements of this new high-tech medium—its expanded memory of over 15,000 characters coupled with a built-in capacity for special visual effects and dynamic motion—advanced

Jenny Holzer, *Untitled* (1989–1990)

Holzer's poster aesthetics into the linguistic registers of poetics and textual performance art. In 1982, under the auspices of the Public Art Fund, Holzer went to the heart of America's mass spectacle, choosing selections from among her most succinct and powerful "Truisms" for public broadcast on New York's mammoth Times Square Spectacolor Board. In Holzer's work, contemporary poetics took on a life beyond the limits of the printed page and went to the literal crossroads of postmodern consumer society.

Poems for Further Reading and Critical Writing

BOB PERELMAN   *(b. 1947)*

Virtual Reality   *(1993)*

It was past four when we
found our feet lifted above our

accelerators, only touching them at intervals.
Inside, our car radios were displaying

the body of our song, marked   5
with static from Pacific storms. Outside

was the setting for the story
of our life: Route 80 near

Emeryville—fence, frontage road, bay, hills,
billboards changing every couple of months.

It was the present—there was   10
nothing to contradict this—but it

seemed stopped short, a careless afterthought,
with the background impossible to keep

in focus. We weren't pleased with
the choices, words or stations, and   15

our desire pouted in the corners
of our song, where it clung

self-consciously to the rhythm-fill or bass
or the scratch in the voice

as it pushed the big moments   20
of the lyrics over the hump.

We were stacked up and our
path was jammed negotiation for every

forward foot. Hope of automatic writing,
of turning the wheel freely in   25

a narrative of convincing possibility, was
only a byproduct of the fallen

leaves lifted in the ads and
drifting sideways in slow motion as

the BMW cornered away from us   30
at forty. We were recording everything,

but the unlabeled cassettes were spilling
over into the footage currently being

shot. This was making the archives
frankly random. A specific request might   35

yield a county fair displaying its
rows of pleasures: candy apples, Skee-Ball,

two-headed sheep, the Cave Woman. She
looked normal enough, standing in her

Plexiglass cage as the MC spieled: 40
the startled expedition, capture, scientific analysis.

But suddenly she interrupted him, breaking
her chains, thumping the glass and

grunting, as a holograph of a
gorilla was projected more or less   45

over her. The MC turned his
mike up and shouted, "We can't

control her!" and the lights went
out, which apparently was the signal

for us to stumble out of   50
the tent, giggling, every hour on

the hour, gypped certainly, but possibly
a bit nostalgic. We had already

fashioned nooses out of coded nursery
twine to help the newscasters with   55

their pronunciation, and whipped up stampedes
of ghost dancers from old westerns,

not that we could see them.
If we lived here, in separate

bodies, we'd have been home long   60
ago, watching the entertainment morsels strip

and hand over everything, and telling
the dog to sit and not

to beg. But the more commands
we gave our body the more   65

it gaped and clumped together, over-excited
and impossible to do anything with.

We turned to analysis, negotiation, persuasion,
cards on the table, confession, surrender.

But there was no refamiliarizing. Our   70
machines filled the freeway with names

and desires, hurling aggressively streamlined messages
toward a future that seemed restless,

barely interested. We could almost see
our hands seizing towers, chains, dealerships,   75

the structures that drew the maps,
but there was no time to

read them, only to react, as
the global information net had become

obsessed with our body's every move,   80
spasm, twitch, smashing at it with

videotaped sticks, validating it, urging instant
credit, free getaways, passionate replacement offers.

Chronic Meanings

(1993)

for Lee Hickman

The single fact is matter.
Five words can say only.
Black sky at night, reasonably.
I am, the irrational residue.

Blown up chain link fence.   5
Next morning stronger than ever.
Midnight the pain is almost.
The train seems practically expressive.

A story familiar as a.
Society has broken into bands.   10
The nineteenth century was sure.
Characters in the withering capital.

The heroic figure straddled the.
The clouds enveloped the tallest.
Tens of thousands of drops.   15
The monster struggled with Milton.

On our wedding night I.
The sorrow burned deeper than.
Grimly I pursued what violence.
A trap, a catch, a.   20

Fans stand up, yelling their.
Lights go off in houses.
A fictional look, not quite.
To be able to talk.

The coffee sounds intriguing but.   25
She put her cards on.
What had been comfortable subjectivity.
The lesson we can each.

Not enough time to thoroughly.
Structure announces structure and takes.   30
He caught his breath in.
The vista disclosed no immediate.

Alone with a pun in.
The clock face and the.
Rock of ages, a modern.   35
I think I had better.

Now this particular mall seemed.
The bag of groceries had.
Whether a biographical junkheap or.
In no sense do I.   40

These fields make me feel.
Mount Rushmore in a sonnet.
Some in the party tried.
So it's not as if.

That always happened until one.   45
She spread her arms and.
The sky if anything grew.
Which left a lot of.

No one could help it.
I ran farther than I.   50
That wasn't a good one.
Now put down your pencils.

They won't pull that over.
Standing up to the Empire.
Stop it, screaming in a.   55
The smell of pine needles.

Economics is not my strong.
Until one of us reads.
I took a breath, then.
The singular heroic vision, unilaterally.   60

Voices imitate the very words.
Bed was one place where.
A personal life, a toaster.
Memorized experience can't be completely.

The impossibility of the simplest.   65
So shut the fucking thing.
Now I've gone and put.
But that makes the world.

The point I am trying.
Like a cartoon worm on.   70
A physical mouth without speech.
If taken to an extreme.

The phone is for someone.
The next second it seemed.

But did that really mean.   75
Yet Los Angeles is full.

Naturally enough I turn to.
Some things are reversible, some.
You don't have that choice.
I'm going to Jo's for.   80

Now I've heard everything, he.
One time when I used.
The amount of dissatisfaction involved.
The weather isn't all it's.

You'd think people would have.   85
Or that they would invent.
At least if the emotional.
The presence of an illusion.

Symbiosis of home and prison.
Then, having become superfluous, time.   90
One has to give to.
Taste: the first and last.

I remember the look in.
It was the first time.
Some gorgeous swelling feeling that.   95
Success which owes its fortune.

Come what may it can't.
There are a number of.
But there is only one.
That's why I want to.   100

SUSAN HOWE   *(b. 1937)*

Turning   *(1989)*

The enthusiast suppresses her tears, crushes her opening thoughts, and—all is changed.
—MARY SHELLEY Journal, *Feb. 7, 1822.*
Marked by Herman Melville in his
copy of Shelley Memorials.

The Nonconformist's Memorial

20.15 Jesus saith unto her, Woman,
why weepest thou? whom seekest
thou? She, supposing him to be the
gardener, saith unto him, Sir, if thou

have borne him hence, tell me where
thou has laid him, and I will take
him away.
16 Jesus saith unto her, Mary. She
turned herself, and saith unto him,
Rabboni; which is to say, Master.
17 Jesus saith unto her, Touch me
not; for I am not yet ascended to
my Father: but go to my brethren,
and say unto them, I ascend unto my
Father, and your Father; and *to* my
God, and your God.
18 Mary Magdalene came and told
the disciples that she had seen the
Lord, and *that* he had spoken these
things unto her.
—THE GOSPEL ACCORDING TO ST JOHN

Contempt of the world
and contentedness

Lilies at this season

other similitudes
Felicities of life   5

Preaching constantly
in woods and obscure

dissenting storms
A variety of trials

Revelations had had   10
and could remember

far away historic fact

Flesh become wheat

which is a nothingness
The I *John* Prologue   15

Original had no title
Ingrafted onto body

dark night stops suddenly
It is the last time

Run then run run   20

Often wild ones nest in woods
Every rational being

The act of Uniformity

ejected her

and informers at her heels   25

Citations remain abbreviated

Often a shortcut

stands for Chapter

1.

nether John and John harbinger

In Peter she is nameless   30
Actual world nothing ideal

headstrong anarchy thoughts
A single thread of narrative

She was coming to anoint him
As if all history were a progress   35

  As if all history were a progress
She was coming to anoint him
      A single thread of narrative
headstrong anarchy thoughts
    Actual world nothing ideal   40

    In Peter she is nameless
  The nets were not torn

The Gospel did not grasp

Whether the words be a command

words be a commandless

Mortal contained in

Dissent and saying is from authority

his hiding is understood

night lift or counsel

having counted the cost

Wind blowing and veering

More in faith as to sense

in the place

shreds earth knowledge

Where he always he late

Upon Cherubim

First anything

in deep ocean

Testimony

Must have been astonished

45

dark background (Gardener

50

Pure Sacrosanct Negator

I John bright picture

What are

suddenly unperceivable time from place to place

All other peace

Effectual crucifying knowledge

55

I John bright picture

dark background (Gardener

Must have been astonished

First anything so later

Testimony

60

More in faith as to sense

Having counted the most

his hiding is understood

Mortal contained in

the soul's Ascension in a state separation Where he says He Upon the Cherubim and in deep ocean Baffled consuming doggerel

In the Evangelist's mind   65

it is I absolutely I

Word before name

Resurrection and life are one

it is I

without any real subject   70

all that I say is I

A predicate nominative

not subject the I is

the bread the light the door

the way the shepherd the vine   75

   Stoics Academics Peripatetics

   and liturgical fierce adversity symbol

   Hazard visionary ages foursquare

   She ran forward to touch him
   Alabaster and confess   80

   Don't cling to me
   Pivot

Literally the unmoving point around which a body
   Literally stop touching me
turns   85

   We plural are the speaker

Came saw went running told

Came along

Solution continuous chaos

Asked told observed   90

Caught sight of said said

Wrapped lying there

Evangelists refer to dawn

The Three Day Reckoning

Alone in the dark to a place of   95

execution

Wording of an earlier tradition

Disciples are huddled together

We do not know

The Evangelist from tradition   100

He bent down

Mary was standing

In the synoptic tradition Mary

enters the tomb

The Narrative of Finding   105

One solitude lies alone
Can be represented

where the capture breaking
along the shock wave

interpreted as space-time   110
on a few parameters

Only in the absolute sky
as it is in Itself

word flesh crumbled page edge

The shadow of history   115
is the ground of faith

A question of overthrowing

Formulae of striking force
Vision and such possession

How could Love not be loved   120

Disciples are huddled together
They do not know

Retrospectives chronologies
Synoptics speak

Revelatory Discourse Source   125
The Feeding Narrative in Mark

Rough messenger Trust
I studious am

Would never have stumbled
on the paved road   130

What is that law

You have your names

To do and to settle
Spirit of Conviction

Who wounded the earth   135

Out of the way of Night
no reason to count

Crying out testimony

Paths of righteousness
Love may be a stumbling   140

out on the great meadows
Prose is unknown

You have your names

I have not read them

Coming from a remote field   145
abandoned to me

The motif of fear is missing
The motif of searching

Historicity of the scene
Confused narrative complex   150

Two women with names
followed by two without names

Distance original disobedience

Against the coldness of force
Intellectual grasp   155

Scene for what follows
Do not touch me

It is by chance that she weeps
Her weeping is not a lament

She has a voice to cry out 160

No community can accompany her
No imagination can dream

Improbable disciple passages
Exegetes explain the conflict

Some manuscripts and versions 165

Her sadness

was out of enclosure 170
Transfiguration
Out of enclosure She

So many stumble

going out of the world

Come then!

Feet wrapped in hay

I stray to stray

her knowledge of Me 175

Hearers of the Face Discourse
Happy to be in peace
know next to nothing
She drank a tumbler-full of water
Often singing
Her body trembled like a leaf

CHARLES BERNSTEIN   *(b. 1950)*

The Kiwi Bird in the Kiwi Tree   *(1991)*

I want no paradise only to be
drenched in the downpour of words, fecund
with tropicality. Fundament be-
yond relation, less 'real' than made, as arms
surround a baby's gurgling: encir-   5
cling mesh pronounces its promise (not bars
that pinion, notes that ply). The tailor tells
of other tolls, the seam that binds, the trim,
the waste. & having spelled these names, move on
to toys or talcums, skates & scores. Only   10
the imaginary is real—not trumps
beclouding the mind's acrobatic versions. The first fact is the social body,
one from another, nor needs no other.

Ear Shot   *(1991)*

Here is the spare
aside the locker room
where I am marooned

House of Formaldehyde   *(1991)*

It's not where you're going, it's
Where you've been. Dateline
In the harbor. Fellow rushes
For funding, fuming, flipping
Flaccid: rimless erosion, witless   5
Emulsification. As on a bent,
Meal, plaid, plane, a girl
Holds a pail, defends a swirl

Stumbling for eviscerated lead hooks
Englotted, Nordic stoops   10
Whosover irradiates decay, plunged
As pediment, foaming sail, lining the
Shifts with spongy (spectacular) spatulas.

Horatio of spell-bent positioning, fusing
Co-spaniel foresight and copper-wire calumny   15
Against the grain of saddlestitch cornmash.
Precisely giddy, morosely fecundated. Snorkling

& then snookered. Roadside rest-test adjoined
To defamilial tireiron. (Unhooks what's
Best left loose.) As was fonder than   20
Revenants. Neither a fender nor a succotash
Be. (Merely a spittoon of her petunia.) Seeking
Not or seeing blotted—wave-high the croon,
Defrock the peeling Argonaut. I would
Not sink her ship nor span her   25
Border as lacking sun-stained
Catapults. Neither have I . . .

Whose deflection can only pronounce incipience
As the promise leadens enactment
& the dusted gables parrot the stick to which   30
Only lessening accounts. The serpentine miles
Of the long-laundered parade dissolve
In gulps, becalmed forays. Having hidden
My amulets & fired my token,
Alone on a dust-dark sea, with only   35
Thee. Or wails oasis, deeded ground
Where foot cannot fall, & felled, retains.

TOPICS FOR CRITICAL THINKING

1. Discuss how Susan Howe's visual arrangement of the lines in the poem "Turning" **Web** affects their meaning for the reader.   *www*
2. Consider the ways in which Bob Perelman employs and departs from the metaphor of highway driving to describe postmodern experience in "Virtual Reality."

TOPICS FOR CRITICAL WRITING

1. Explore the convention of the five-word sentence as a formal device that generates new possibilities of poetic utterance in "Chronic Meanings." How does the five-word line disrupt our normal habits of reading?
2. Examine the ways in which Charles Bernstein subverts the conventions of setting, character, plot, and narrative coherence generally in "House of Formaldehyde."

Critical Perspective: On Nonlinear Poetics

"When Pound declares in Canto 81, 'To break the pentameter, that was the first heave,' he is speaking to a particular situation in late-Victorian 'genteel' verse, when meter stood for a particular collective attitude, a social and cultural restriction on the 'freedom' of the subject. Vladimir Mayakovsky, coming out of an entirely different tradition, but in the same time period, makes a similar gesture when he declares in 1926, 'Trochees and iambs have never been necessary to me. I don't know them and don't want to know them. Iambs impede the forward movement of poetry.'

"Such statements, [Henri] Meschonnic points out, are neither true nor untrue; rather, they must be understood as part of the drive toward rupture characteristic of the early twentieth-century avant-garde. And the form Pound's
own prosody took—the 'ideogrammizing of Western verse,' in Meschonnic's
words—had everything to do with the revolution in mass print culture, a revolution that bred what Meschonnic calls the 'theatre of the page.' 'If we were
to talk about practices rather than intentions,' he says, 'every page of poetry
would represent a conception of poetry.' Blank spaces, for example, would
become just as important as the words themselves in composing a particular
construct. Thus, the structuralist argument that lineation in and of itself guarantees that a text will be read and interpreted as a poem is based on two mis-
conceptions. First, it ignores the active role that white space (silence) plays in
the visual and aural reception of the poem: the line, after all, is anchored in a
larger visual field, a field by no means invariable. Second, and more important, the response to lineation must itself be historicized. In a contemporary
context of one-liners on the television screen and the computer monitor, as
well as lineated ads, greeting-cards, and catalog entries, the reader/viewer has
become quite accustomed to reading 'in lines.' Indeed, surfing the Internet is
largely a scanning process in which the line is rapidly replacing the paragraph
as the unit to be accessed.

"How lineation as device signifies thus depends on many factors, historical, cultural, and national. The history of free verse in English remains to be
written: when it is, it will be clear that the dominant example has been, not
that of Ezra Pound, whose ideographic page has only recently become a
model for poets, but that of William Carlos Williams, whose verse signature
is still a powerful presence."

—Marjorie Perloff, from "After Free Verse:
The New Nonlinear Poetries" (1988)

Critical Perspective: On Postmodernism and Capitalism

"The last few years have been marked by an inverted millenarianism in which
premonitions of the future, catastrophic or redemptive, have been replaced by
senses of the end of this or that (the end of ideology, art, or social class; the 'crisis' of Leninism, social democracy, or the welfare state, etc., etc.); taken together,
all of these perhaps constitute what is increasingly called postmodernism. The
case for its existence depends on the hypothesis of some radical break or *coupure*,
generally traced back to the end of the 1950s or the early 1960s.

"As the word itself suggests, this break is most often related to notions of
the waning or extinction of the hundred-year-old modern movement (or to its
ideological or aesthetic repudiation). Thus abstract expressionism in painting,
existentialism in philosophy, the final forms of representation in the novel, the
films of the great *auteurs*, or the modernist school of poetry (as institutionalized and canonized in the works of Wallace Stevens) all are now seen as the
final, extraordinary flowering of a high-modernist impulse which is spent

and exhausted with them. The enumeration of what follows, then, at once becomes empirical, chaotic, and heterogeneous: Andy Warhol and pop art, but also photorealism, and beyond it, the 'new expressionism'; the moment, in music, of John Cage, but also the synthesis of classical and 'popular' styles found in composers like Phil Glass and Terry Riley, and also punk and new wave rock (the Beatles and the Stones now standing as the high-modernist moment of that more recent and rapidly evolving tradition); in film, Godard, post-Godard, and experimental cinema and video, but also a whole new type of commercial film . . . ; Burroughs, Pynchon, or Ishmael Reed, on the one hand, and the French *nouveau roman* and its succession, on the other, along with alarming new kinds of literary criticism based on some new aesthetic of textuality or *écriture* . . . The list might be extended indefinitely."

—Fredric Jameson, from *Postmodernism or,*
The Cultural Logic of Late Capitalism (1991)

Critical Perspective: On "Language Writing"

"There was never any self-consciously organized group known as the language writers or poets—not even a fixed name.

"This fact has not prevented 'language writing,' as a polemic horizon pregnant with unknown but unwanted developments, from often being invoked over the last two decades. There are real reasons for this: the positive structures of language writing are socially and aesthetically complex and in places strained and contradictory, but the movement has been more united by its opposition to the prevailing institutions of American poetry. During this period, American poetry has been dominated by writing workshops and creative-writing departments with large networks of legitimation—publishing, awards, reviews, extensive university connections. The aesthetics of this mainstream are not without variation, but generalizations are possible, and were certainly made, polemically, by those involved in the formation of language writing: the mainstream poet guarded a highly distinct individuality; while craft and literary knowledge contributed to poetry, sensibility and intuition reigned supreme. The mainstream poet was not an intellectual and especially not a theoretician. Hostility to analysis and, later, to theory, were constitutive of such a poetic stance. In this situation, modernism was no longer especially important. The discursive tone of later Eliot, the incantatory vaticism of Yeats, the kaleidoscopic novelty of Surrealism minus Marx and Freud, the authoritative common sense and rural cast of Frost (often translated to the suburbs), and an attenuated version of Williams as poet of the quotidian—these echoes might be read everywhere, but the more basic facts of modernism were shunned. The poet as engaged, oppositional intellectual, and poetic form and syntax as sites of experiment for political and social purposes—these would not be found. The confessional poets were the model: Lowell, Plath, Sexton, Berryman. Poems were short, narrative, focused on small or large moments of crisis or optimism. Whether the form was free verse or rhymed iambic stanzas, the tone was conversational. Such work was often unambitious, and the steady production of books and MFA graduates bespoke a bureaucratized routine, but the breakdowns and suicides of the leading exemplars stood as guarantees of intensity.

"The formation of language writing was given a negative impetus by such a poetic climate. The goals variously articulated by members of the group were quickly registered as hostile to the well-being of that climate. And this literary hostility was seen as emanating from a group of writers. Subsequent publications would show that 'the group' was not often all that cohesive: influence and interaction never produced a uniform literary program, let alone a uniform style. But there was a loose set of goals, procedures, habits, and verbal textures breaking the automatism of the poetic 'I' and its naturalized voice; foregrounding textuality and formal devices; using or alluding to Marxist or poststructuralist theory in order to open the present to critique and change. These, along with the group interaction and the aggressive dismissals of self-expressive mainstream poetics as politically reactionary, raised the specter of a Lenin-esque cadre dedicated to the overthrow of poetry. Robert von Hallberg sees mainstream American poetry of this period as the poetry of accommodation; language writing coalesced as American involvement in Vietnam was nearing its bankrupt conclusion: this was a significant cause of the unaccommodating nature of its poetics. But linkages between poetry and politics were always the source of dispute. For some, language writing was too programmatically political to be poetry; for a number of New American poets and their supporters, it was too poststructuralist to be political.

"Many features of this literary battle were reproduced on a wider scale by the introduction of poststructuralist thought into the American academy. While both were housed in universities, creative writing departments and English departments generally had nothing to do with one another; the advent of theory made the separation wider. Language writing was easy enough to subsume under the category of theory or postmodernism as part of a large tendency attacking self, reference, and history. As initial formal goals and polemical rallying cries, such attacks had specific literary value; as slogans they have devolved to little more than inflight snacks served on the proliferant hovercrafts of postmodernism."

—Bob Perelman, from *The Marginalization of Poetry* (1996)

15

Critical Perspectives

A Casebook on Performance and Performativity

We humans love performance. From earliest times to modern times, from rituals to film, theater to spectacle, oral poetry, and even storytelling and juggling, the art of performance is something we cherish. Performance occurs whenever one person deliberately presents an act to be witnessed (visually, orally, or both) by another. The defining element of performance is a consciousness of this witnessing.

Typically, we think of performance in the context of theater, television, and film; we link it to acting. Acting is the most obvious example of one person presenting another person (or character) and at the same time enacting the techniques necessary to produce the illusion of this other person. Drama, whether on stage or screen, is performance; people present acts to be witnessed by others and in ways that situate these acts as things to be seen and heard. In film and television, extra layers of presentation are present in the camera work, editing, sound tracks, and other apparatus of the filmmaking process.

Performativity

A performative text is a text that both describes something and produces the effect it is describing at the same time. For example, in a marriage ceremony, the betrothed say, "I do." Saying "I do" accomplishes the marriage. The words of consent produce the consent and the legal tie. When stage performance also emphasizes the ways it is doing what it is saying, it becomes performance art. Performance art is a postmodern genre of theater that emphasizes improvisation and direct address to the audience. It is performative in its desire to shock, disturb, and otherwise destroy complacency.

Included in this chapter are two short pieces from contemporary performance artist Guillermo Gómez-Peña, who combines radio, television, poetry, wrestling, music, and social criticism in his work. For Gómez-Peña, the aesthetic concept of hybridity—the melding together of distinct cultural forms from various media—corresponds with his vision of a twenty-first-century

287

America not as a "melting pot" but a "menudo chowder." The difference between the two terms in his metaphor is crucial: While the former melts away difference into a bland, colorless homogeneity, the latter maintains "stubborn chunks" of cultural and ethnic difference. The result is an exciting, multicultural America. Although we categorize literature in terms of genre—fiction, poetry, and drama—authors not only write within these generic traditions, their creative expression also can make a difference in such "wordly" multicultural contexts of social life. Literature's power to shape the imagination is not limited to the high school or college curriculum. It also plays a significant role in popular culture. Broadly defined, **popular culture** comprises the attitudes, customs, and folkways of ordinary, everyday people. In the modern period, popular culture becomes increasingly mediated by the new information technologies of phonograph, radio, television, computerization, and the Internet, representations that give shape and definition to everyday life.

Performative Poetics

More than likely, there's a coffeehouse near your school or campus where you can hear the spoken word of poetry at an open-mike night or even read your own verse in a poetry competition ("slam"). Poetry readings, jazz poetry, beat poetry, performance poetry, and shout-outs are alive and well, and they share crossover audiences with rap and popular song. What are the historical roots of these contemporary literary and performative traditions?

Marcel Duchamp, *Bicycle Wheel* (1913)

Key forerunners for an experimental mode of performance poetics in the twentieth century began with the language experiments of Dadaism and the sound-influenced verse of Russian *zaum* verse. Aspiring to the kind of pure sound qualities found in musical composition, *zaum* poetry relied on repeating particular syllables for onomatopoetic effects.

Dadaism and *zaum* verse were two modern antecedents to present-day performance poetics. But reaching back to the Homeric age and even further to prehistoric times, poetry from the beginning has been as much a performed as it is a written art. Although we now read Homer's *Iliad* and *Odyssey* between the covers of a book, the written version of Homeric epic is a latecomer. In Ancient Greece, the poet as oral reciter (*rhapsoidos*) and composer (*aoidos*) originally performed to the accompaniment of a lyre at public events. Not infrequently, the Homeric poet would compose on the spot and improvise in response to audience suggestions.

The Homeric context of poetic performance may not sound that far removed from modern-day poetry slams, spoken word fests, and jazz rap performances. But there are major differences between the two in their performative roles. In this context, giving voice to one's experience in a poetry reading involves less the "sincere" or "authentic" expression of inward and personal emotive states. Instead, stepping up to the mike at a poetry slam demands a more self-conscious and coded performance of identity including the clothing, speaking voice, props, and the like. Such performative values have always been a factor in a conventional poetry reading, but whereas the modern poet assumed cultural authority largely in resistance to popular culture, the postmodern slam rapper/urban griot blurs the boundaries between the rigor of poetic form and the mass appeal of populist representation.

Performance poetry has its grass-roots origins in the local, subcultural public sphere of bars, coffeehouses, nightclubs, and other more mundane spaces such as community libraries, bookstores, and school auditoriums. Poetry slams had their beginnings in Chicago's Green Mill bar in the 1980s, where they were first organized by Marc Smith. But the origin of slam, according to Nuyorican poet Miguel Algarín "grows out of ancient traditions of competitive and/or linked rhymes between orators—from the Greek mythological tale of Apollo and Marsyas to the African griots, from the Sanjurokunin sen, or imaginary poetry team competitions, of tenth-century Japanese court poet Fujiwara no Kinto to the African-American 'dozens.'" A major modern influence on such rap/poetry events is the Beat Movement of the 1950s in New York City and San Francisco (see Chapter 13).

Signifying

A key element of the jazz aesthetic that influenced contemporary performance poetry is the technique of **signifying,** the improvisational appropriation and reworking of mainstream melodies and popular songs. Here the jazz musician, according to Henry Louis Gates, Jr., "suggests a given structure precisely by failing to coincide with it—that is, suggests it by dissemblance." Gates cites

John Coltrane's jazz version of "My Favorite Things" that signified on the song Julie Andrews popularized in *The Sound of Music*. Another influence on the "open mic" rap sessions of contemporary performance poetics is the improvisational competitions that jazz musicians called "cutting contests." These musical competitions go back to the witty games of verbal one-upmanship called the "dozens" in the African American community. The vitally inventive tradition of jazz and jazz poetics is what ties hip-hop to be-bop, according to jazz composer Quincy Jones: "I see a connection," Jones writes, "between Hip Hop and Be-Bop. They both had to invent their own language. You know: If you don't let us in your culture, then we'll start our own!" One venue that has promoted rap, hip-hop, and spoken poetry since the 1970s is the Nuyorican Poets Café founded by Miguel Algarín and Miguel Piñero. Over the past two decades, poets such as Sandra Maria Esteves, Luis Reyes Rivera, Amiri Baraka, Pedro Pietri, Tracie Morris, and Paul Beatty conceived diverse poetic voices and styles of poetic performance art. "The philosophy and purpose of the Nuyorican Poets Café," writes Miguel Algarín,

> "has always been to reveal poetry as a living art. Even as the eye scans the lines of a poem, poetry is in flux in the United States. From Baja California to Seattle to Detroit, from the dance clubs with rap lyrics booming to the schools where Gil Scott-Heron plays to the churches where poetry series thrive to community centers with poets-in-residence and coffee houses throughout the whole of the nation, the spoken word is on fire."

Much of spoken word poetry is site-specific, spontaneous, ephemeral, and performed in the moment. If Baraka's verse—as in, say, "Black Dada Nihilismus" or "Prayer for Saving"—jams popular, vernacular references to black history and black performance art, then Beatty's poetics cut and mix such signs of black expressive culture with advertising signage and consumer slogans as in "The Revolution Will Be Commercialized":

> 7 out of 10 grass root interventionists
> recommend trident missiles
> for their patients
> who eschew guns

This playful lyric signifies simultaneously on at least three disparate discursive references. Beatty jams Gil Scott-Heron's song "The Revolution Will Not Be Televised," with a pun on the U.S. Navy's Trident submarine-launched ballistic missile, spliced with the advertising slogan made famous by Trident sugarless gum: "Four out of five dentists surveyed recommend sugarless gum to their patients who chew gum." Similarly, a poem such as "Darryl Strawberry Asleep in a Field of Dreams" probes the racial politics of baseball spectatorship and Hollywood cinema. In it, Beatty places former New York Yankee left fielder and convicted cocaine offender Daryl Strawberry in the film title *Field of Dreams*, which is based on W. P. Kinsella's baseball novel *Shoeless Joe* (1982). By contrasting the film's setting in heartland Iowa with Harlem and Cabrini Green, Beatty makes the sly point that

> shoeless joe jackson was white
> his uni was white

> all the dead white players was white
> takin batting practice in white home uniforms
> under the white iowa clouds

Not only does Beatty recover the segregated contexts of baseball's pre-civil rights history, but, equally important, he shows the ways in which such racism persists in the subtle and not-so-subtle entertainment codes of Hollywood cinema.

Winner of the National Haiku Slam and the Nuyorican Grand Slam competitions, Tracie Morris's poetry, when read on the page, only begins to suggest the oral complexity and sonic richness she brings to her performance poetics. She often performs her incredible range of voiced sonic effects not just as a solo slam poet at the mike but also with her posse, the Words-N-Music band. As she suggests in her poem "Griot," the postmodern performance poet uses her voice less as the expression of personal or confessional values and more as a pure rhythmic instrument. "Work the voice," she advises, "like a drum":

> With some treble tremor
> May seem tenuous
> It's syncretic
> Mesh ascension of flesh
> Touched with a tinge of regret.

> What you said?

Morris's verse presents a sensuous linguistic surface that draws heavily on alliteration, assonance, and internal rhymes in playfully associative and highly "syncretic" verbal signifying. But more radically, in its hybridized patois of phonic signification, a poem like, say, "Chief Song" is meant to be heard, as well as read, on the page:

TRACIE MORRIS *(b. 1968)*

Chief Song *(1998)*

Mene
Mene lazu na guine puene

Many Bete

Mene lazu na guine puene

I am supposed to be	Noh
I am supposed to be	Noh, Noh
I am supposed to be	Noh

The lead in   Danse ce
                                 Danse ce paradis

Ki Yi-K
Ki Yi-K

Ki Yi-K
Ki Yi-K
Ki Yi-K

-Os?

	Noh
But. I ah	Noh, Noh

I-A-Kuko
A cool/cool/cool/kuko

The lead	Back, Bock
Cool so	Back, Bock
Teeth on edge	eje, eje
Tre chaud	sho 'nuf
show	sho' nuf
show	sho'nuf
chaud	
chaud	eau.

Hearkening back, in some ways, to the transrational, phonic experimentation of the *zaum* poets, Morris's performative verse bears a closer resemblance to the DVD or videotape media than to the inscribed text on the page. Hers is a poetry seemingly tailor-made to the digitized streaming of today's information technology.

Performance Literature

GUILLERMO GÓMEZ-PEÑA   *(b. 1955)*

I Could Only Fight Back in My Poetry   *(1996)*

Performed live as "El Quebradito," a flamboyant vaquero from northern Mexico, dressed in a fake zebra-skin tuxedo. He looks tired and crestfallen, and his voice is raspy. Soundbed: Music by guitar maestro Antonio Bribiesca plays on a ghetto blaster; the irritating voice of an evangelist preacher can be heard in the distance.

it was the spring of '87 in the city of Arlington
I tried to explain to you in my very broken English
that Texas had once been a Mexican ranch
& that truth was not a "gringo-bashing ideology"
but you had seen too many Stallone films   5
& felt obliged to let me have it, ¿que no?
so you tried to beat the Meskin out of me

of course, since you were a foot taller & 85 lbs. heavier
& not that skilled in cross-cultural diplomacy
I could only fight back in my poetry   10
in fact, I'm fighting back right now
you claimed you hated my accent & my arrogance
but the real reason you despised me
was that your wife was just about to leave you
& hit the road to sexy Mexico   15
to escape the Texan nightmare, your inflexible arms,
your smelly feet & psychotic eyes
so Mexico became the source of all your fears
the red-light district where gringos are poisoned by midget
      whores
the mountain of trash where kids with typhoid make holes to   20
      sleep in
the bus that keeps breaking down on your way to some
      generic jungle
the gentle mariachi who touched your wife like you never did
you saw all these images in my eyes before you broke my ribs
& I could only fight back in my poetry

P.S. #1   I don't harbor any resentments but I sure hope one   25
      of these days you learn to read & write

P.S. #2   See, I told you culero, I win most fights in the
      streets of my poetry

P.S. #3   I heard you joined the militia movement last
      month. . . . I must say that you are consistent in
      misplacing your anger, man

AMIRI BARAKA   *(b. 1934)*

KA 'BA   *(1969)*

A closed window looks down
on a dirty courtyard, and black people
call across or scream across or walk across
defying physics in the stream of their will

Our world is full of sound   5
Our world is more lovely than anyone's
tho we suffer, and kill each other
and sometimes fail to walk the air

We are beautiful people
with african imaginations   10
full of masks and dances and swelling chants
with african eyes, and noses, and arms,
though we sprawl in grey chains in a place
full of winters, when what we want is sun.
We have been captured,   15
brothers. And we labor
to make our getaway, into
the ancient image, into a new

correspondence with ourselves
and our black family. We need magic   20
now we need the spells, to raise up
return, destroy, and create. What will be

the sacred words?

Black Dada Nihilismus   *(1969)*

                    Against what light

is false what breath
sucked, for deadness.
                    Murder, the cleansed

purpose, frail, against   5
God, if they bring him
                    bleeding, I would not

forgive, or even call him
black dada nihilismus.

The protestant love, wide windows,   10
color blocked to Mondrian, and the
ugly silent deaths of jews under

the surgeon's knife. (To awake on
69th street with money and a hip
nose. Black dada nihilismus, for   15

the umbrella'd jesus. Trilby intrigue
movie house presidents sticky the floor.
B.D.N., for the secret men, Hermes, the

blacker art. Thievery (ahh, they return
those secret gold killers. Inquisitors   20
of the cocktail hour. Trismegistus,° have

them, in their transmutation, from stone
to bleeding pearl, from lead to burning
looting, dead Moctezuma, find the West

a grey hideous space.   25

                                2

From Sartre,° a white man, it gave
the last breath. And we beg him die,
before he is killed. Plastique, we

do not have, only thin heroic blades.
The razor. Our flail against them, why   30
you carry knives? Or brutaled lumps of

heart? Why you stay, where they can
reach? Why you sit, or stand, or walk
in this place, a window on a dark

warehouse. Where the minds packed in   35
straw. New homes, these towers, for those
lacking money or art. A cult of death,

need of the simple striking arm under
the streetlamp. The cutters, from under
their rented earth. Come up, black dada   40

nihilismus. Rape the white girls. Rape
their fathers. Cut the mothers' throats.
Black dada nihilismus, choke my friends

in their bedrooms with their drinks spilling
and restless for tilting hips or dark liver   45
lips sucking splinters from the master's thigh.

Black scream
and chant, scream,
and dull, un
earthly   50

---

21 *Trismegistus:* Thrice-great Hermes or Thoth-Hermes, mythical inventor of language and
founder of Hermeticism.   26 *Sarte:* Jean-Paul Sartre (1905–1980), French existentialist
philosopher.

hollering. Dada, bilious
what ugliness, learned
in the dome, colored holy
shit (i call them sinned

or lost   55
        burned masters
                        of the lost
                                nihil German killers
                                        all our learned

art, 'member   60
what you said
money, God, power,
a moral code, so cruel
it destroyed Byzantium, Tenochtitlan, Commanch
                                        (got it, *Baby!*   65

For tambo, willie best, dubois, patrice, mantan, the
bronze buckaroos.

                For Jack Johnson, asbestos, tonto, buckwheat,
                billie holiday.

                For tom russ, l'overture, vesey, beau jack,   70

(may a lost god damballah, rest or save us
against the murders we intend
against his lost white children
black dada nihilismus

PAUL BEATTY   *(b. 1962)*

Darryl Strawberry Asleep in a Field of Dreams   *(1991)*

                they raised the price of dreams
blue inked can of del monte creamed corn
where baseball players
are reborn

                in their prime   5
                to play in modern day times

and not only was the ball white

shoeless joe jackson was white
                his uni was white

        all the dead white players was white   10
takin batting practice in white home uniforms
under white iowa clouds

i squirmed in my seat hopin for a
warm thunder storm
        that would rain down cool papa bell   15
        and hell would drip off corn stalk blades

pool into a homestead grey
           inna grey away uniform
flip down flip-up shades
and say   hey now lets really play   20

        got to wear your sun glasses
          so you can feel cool

but its only a movie
and in film school heaven is
where white doctors who played   25
only an inning and a half in the show
can pray for a tinker everlastin chance to groove the 0-2 sinker

    white boys steady leanin in
      truly believin this is the best movie they've ever seen
but none of em asked josh gibson to slo-dance   30

across the color line that
falls in an iowa ball field
        broken but unhealed

fathers younger than their sons play catch
onna mismatch patch   35
natural grass and james earl jonezes broad ass

    hollywoods black fat majesty
    bellows . . . *and the people will come*

  black people smiled and fell in single file
to pay to watch mel ott run through Fences   40

and put the suicide squeeze on my mothers mother
whose color
is the same
as a night game infield

     . . . and the people will come   45

to see that black fathers to be
  with scars on their knees
      from shinbones split in half
        and knocked off kneecaps
practice the tap dunks they will pump over their daughters n sons   50

        . . . and the people will come

how could daughters n fathers build
wooden bleachers
just to sit and cheer male features

if umpire pam postema dies in the minor leagues   55
ty cobb'll hook slide into heaven
and she'll call him out

and he will
get up   dust himself   call her a . . .
brush it off as a tease   60

is this heaven
  no its iowa

is this heaven
    no its harlem

is this heaven   65
    no its bedrock

is this heaven
    no its cabrini green

do they got a team
  aint sure they got dreams   70
  damn sure aint got a field
or crops that yield
      is that the sign for steal
      i approach the third base coach
      and ask is all the movies for real   75

A Three Point Shot from Andromeda   *(1991)*

                rain rusted orange
                ring of saturn
                        in urban orbit
          over an outdoor gym

                    nighttime jumpers   5
                    pull up to the hoop
                              dance on the rim
                        bolted against a
                        metal backboard sky
                        riddled with   10

ninety-nine thousand
BB-sized holes
compressing fifth floor duplex
                              kitchen light
into a galaxy   15
                    of 50 watt schoolyard stars

supra-flex intense constellations
                              handcheck
                        rotate on defense
                              double down   20
            tryin to guard
            spinning playground
                        planetarium delirium
of black gods flyin
on neighborhood rep   25
                        shake n bake
        pump fake
                    jab step
past orion
walk on air   30
and burst a reverse
                    on the stellar bear

MAGGIE ESTEP *(b. 1963)*

The Stupid Jerk I'm Obsessed With   *(1994)*

THE STUPID JERK I'M OBSESSED WITH
stands so close
I can feel his breath on my neck
and smell the way he would smell
if we slept together   5
because he is THE STUPID JERK I'M OBSESSED WITH
and that is his primary function in life
to be A STUPID JERK I CAN OBSESS OVER
and to talk to that dingy bimbette blonde
as if he really wanted to hear about her   10
manicures and pedicures and New Age Ritualistic Enema Cures

and, truth be told, he probably does want to hear about it
because he is
THE STUPID JERK I'M OBSESSED WITH
and he does anything he can to lend fuel to my fire   15
he makes a point
of standing, looking over my shoulder
when I'm talking to the guy who adores me
and would **bark like a dog and wave to strangers**
if I asked him to **bark like a dog and wave to strangers**   20
but I can't ask the guy to bark like a dog or impersonate
any kind of animal at all
cause I'm too busy
looking at the way
THE STUPID JERK I'M OBSESSED WITH   25
has pants on
that perfectly define his well-shaped ass
to the point where I'm thoroughly frantic,
I'm just gonna go home
stick my head in the oven   30
overdose on nutmeg and aspirin or sit in the bathtub
reading *The Executioner's Song*
and being completely confounded by the fact that I can see
THE STUPID JERK I'M OBSESSED WITH'S face
defining itself in the peeling plaster of the wall   35
grinning
and winking
and I start yelling: "Hey, get the hell out of there, you're just a figment of
my overripe imagination, get a life and get out of my plaster and pass me
the next painful situation please."   40

But he just keeps on
grinning
and winking
he's THE STUPID JERK I'M OBSESSED WITH
and he's mine   45
in my plaster
and frankly,
I COULDN'T BE HAPPIER.

TRACIE MORRIS   *(b. 1968)*

Project Princess   *(1998)*

Teeny feet rock layered double socks
The popping side piping of
many colored loose lace-ups

Racing toe keeps up with fancy free gear,
slick slide and just pressed recently weaved hair.   5

Jeans oversized belying her hips, back, thighs that have made guys sigh
for milleni-year.

Topped by an attractive jacket
her suit's not for flacking, flunkies or punk homies on the stroll.

Her hands the mobile thrones of today's urban goddess   10
Clinking rings link dragon fingers there's no need to be modest.

One or two gap teeth coolin'
sport gold initials
Doubt you get to her name
just check from the side,   15
please chill.

Multidimensional shrimp earrings
frame her cinnamon face

Crimson with a compliment if a
comment hits the right place   20

Don't step to the place with datelines from '88
Spare your simple, fragile feelings with the same sense that you came

Color woman variation reworks the french twist
with crinkle-cut platinum frosted bangs from a spray can's mist

Never dissed, she insists: "No you can't touch this."   25
And, if pissed, bedecked fist stops boys who must persist.

She's the one. Give her some. Under fire. Smoking gun. Of which songs are
sung, raps are spun, bells are rung, rocked, pistols cocked, unwanted advances
blocked, well-stacked she's jock. It's all about you girl. You go on. Don't you
dare stop.   30

Gangsta Suite   *(1998)*

I. Who Knew?
Thought I had my shit together
I was feeling fly whatever

Feather hanging with the chickies looking dope.
Hoping I was doing better snapping on them foolish fellas
looking too hard scoping this cutie, I was like, 'nope.'   5

So I hook up with some glamour picture-pretty like a camera
gangsta thought I was a hottie and he stepped to me.
He was chillin on the d.l. guess he thought I freaked.
Thinking he'd treat me like a $5 skeeza.
Please ya damn if ya don't, screwed if ya do.   10
What I know about him flippin'?
I admit kissin', tounged him down 'till he started trippin'.

But he was hard and took no shit from nobody.
Mighta been dealing. Coming to grips with the economy.
Times is tough. He was used to being Mack Daddy.   15
Groping 'till I said ease up at my throat manhandling me.
I kicked him in his dick and split.
He almost got out his jeep.

Sweetest situation suddenly got real sticky.

II. Harder

Muthafukas try and step to me to get the best of me   20
Stay one up on a C.O. Free so 5 zero come up to another with a
big gun gonna git some dread out
ballistic kicking the lead out.
Ain't a damn thing left fa me ta do.
Go to school? Got the crazy cool Urkel flava, dudes catch ya   25
later with the boom-shoot.
Get up let up make they bones off ya ass with a 12 year wanna
crack dealer trigger fast.
Mass media wanna greedy ya with the product
so black buck, buck from the project go for the gleaming objects.   30
Rocks, cars or the poom-poom honey.
Smack up with the sheep skin inner sleeve got the money.
Funny how down low folks get the set up.
Cold steel apocalyptic drug deal blows another head up.
The Feds up and give 25 if ya good.   35
Graduation from probation lock down for ya new hood.

III. Gotta Get Yours, Girl

I cried for you and I'm still crying. One finger flick spritz
downed a six packed dying.
Fine fine gonna get some gotta flex little muscle hustle for a
coup Lex front fender for the projects   40
Gotta get yours but at who's loss did you get it? warned how many

times before you died to regret it. "Don't sweat it" you said
when your mother was sweating you. First man in the fam cause
your pops was forgetting you.
There I go, there I go, there I go with the uphill stroller   45
trying to fit the token slit in the slip with the little kid in tow.
I'm brooding and breeding after your bleeding stressing on milk
and diapers I'm needing money spent on your funeral dressing.
Now you can gloat got the coat maxing got the sneaks. Flyest
corpse in the morgue eulogize shout out from ya peeps.   50
Beside me. What about our forever lasting?
Did you think about the us you threw away
when you were 9 mm. O.G. blasting?

MIGUEL PIÑERO *(1947–1988)*

The Book of Genesis According to
St. Miguelito   *(1985)*

Before the beginning
God created God
In the beginning
God created the ghettos & slums
and God saw this was good.   5
So God said,
"Let there be more ghettos & slums"
and there were more ghettos & slums.
But God saw this was plain
so   10
to decorate it
God created lead-based paint
and then
God commanded the rivers of garbage & filth
to flow gracefully through the ghettos.   15
On the third day
because on the second day God was out of town
On the third day
God's nose was running
& his jones was coming down and God   20
in his all knowing wisdom
knew he was sick
he needed a fix
so God
created the backyards of the ghettos   25
& the alleys of the slums
in heroin & cocaine

and
with his divine wisdom & grace
God created hepatitis   30
who begat lockjaw
who begat malaria
who begat degradation
who begat
        GENOCIDE   35
and God knew this was good
in fact God knew things couldn't git better
but he decided to try anyway
On the fourth day
God was riding around Harlem in a gypsy cab   40
when he created the people
and he created these beings in ethnic proportion
but he saw the people lonely & hungry
and from his eminent rectum
he created a companion for these people   45
and he called this companion
capitalism
who begat racism
who begat exploitation
who begat male chauvinism   50
who begat machismo
who begat imperialism
who begat colonialism
who begat wall street
who begat foreign wars   55
and God knew
and God saw
and God felt this was extra good
and God said
VAYAAAAAAA   60
On the fifth day
the people kneeled
the people prayed
the people begged
and this manifested itself in a petition   65
a letter to the editor
to know why? WHY? WHY? qué pasa babyyyyy?????
and God said,
"My fellow subjects
let me make one thing perfectly clear   70
by saying this about that:
No . . . . COMMENT!"
but on the sixth day God spoke to the people
he said . . . "PEOPLE!!!

the ghettos & the slums   75
& all the other great things I've created
will have dominion over thee"
and then
he commanded the ghettos & slums
and all the other great things he created   80
to multiply
and they multiplied
On the seventh day God was tired
so he called in sick
collected his overtime pay   85
a paid vacation included
But before God got on that t.w.a.
for the sunny beaches of Puerto Rico
He noticed his main man Satan
planting the learning trees of consciousness   90
around his ghetto edens
so God called a news conference
on a state of the heavens address
on a coast to coast national t.v. hookup
and God told the people   95
to be
COOL
and the people were cool
and the people kept cool
and the people are cool   100
and the people stay cool
and God said
Vaya . . .

NTOZAKE SHANGE   *(b. 1948)*

Blood Rhythms–Blood Currents–Black Blue N Stylin'   *(1994)*

(French sugar-beet farmers, overwhelmed by mulatto competitors, plastered Europe's cities with advertisements proclaiming: "Our sugar is not soiled with black blood." A popular Afro-Cuban saying is: "Sugar is made with blood," while in the South of the United States, cane growers processed natural sugar "to get the nigger out.")

Fragrant breezes in the South
melt to melodies round small fires
mount tree limbs
with bodies black
and swayin' black n croonin'   5
songs of sunsets

comin' from the fields bawdy
brazen
hard to put yr finger on
like the blues   10
like the strum of guitars on dark damp

southern nights
hard to put your finger on
like screams in the black bloody southern soil
sweet black blood echoin' thru the evenin' service   15
grindin' by the roadhouse door
sweet black blood
movin' with slow breath

outta breath
young negroes run to pick up a bale of cotton   20
run to flee southern knights
crosses *bare blazin'* signals black bloods
gone runnin'
for Chicago
for the hollow   25
for the C.C. Rider
for the new day *sweet*

blocked melodies ache in young girls' throats
rip thru their lips like the road to freedom was lit
all lit up with the grace of God and   30
Sears Tower
the Ford plane and Pontiac's vision
all lit up *sleek* fires
sheddin' the haunts of poll taxes and test questions *like*
where is America   35
cost a *finger*
a ear
a heart
a teardrop fallin' from the saggin' front porch
to the project stairway   40
from the water fountain to the chain gang

the *night train* carried *smuggled* goods *news*
of struttin' signifyin' fellas with gold teeth
neath *they feet and brawny sway* for blocks and blocks
far as the eye cd see from Biloxi to Birmingham   45
the *contraband* of freedom *seeped* thru the swamps
the air hung heavy
with the cries of "ain't gonna let nobody turn me round"
and *young* boys in nice-cut suits
who was awready standin' with they heads up   50

awready prancin' with finesse and grand stature
like men wit eyes
don't never look down
men wit eyes burstin' wit glory
from the red sedans   55
and the *seats in schools*
to the right to set wherever they want
and when the sounds of the harmonica was slowed
by snarlin' dogs and hoses
when the *washboards* and *bottleneck players*   60
was skedattlin' *out the bullets way*
up came a roarin'
force a light blue controlled fire in un-mussed lamé
pleated silk and faces
bearin' no scars   65
to say *"we ain't been touched"*
we the *sweet black fires of dreams*
& of unobfuscated beauty

like the trails of freedom
the Good Lord himself lit up   70
we gonna *take this*
new city neon light
sound
volumes for millions to hear
to love themselves   75
enough to turn back the pulse of a whippin' history
make it carry the modern black melody from L.A.
to downtown Newark City
freedom buses
freedom riders   80
freedom is the way we walk that walk
talk that talk
gotta take that *charred black body out the ground*
switch on the current to a new sound
to a new way of walkin' a new way of talkin'   85
blues

electrified
blues
boltin-the-lynchin-tree-
n-tremblin-n-chirren-   90
blues
defyin' the sound of gravity

for a people singin'
about the sashay of blood rhythms set free.

Part III
Understanding Poetic Representation

16   Race and Representation

Contemporary notions of race are closely bound up with their **representation**
www **Web** in literature, history, popular culture, the media, and everyday life. What
do we mean, however, by the representation of race? How do we define representation? Understanding representation starts with the concept of **mimesis.**
www **Web** Mimesis is defined by the idea of imitation and shares its root meaning
with the art of mime and mimicry. The philosophy of mimesis begins with
Plato in *The Republic.* In it, he argues that words reflect real objects in the world
that are themselves based on ideal, fixed forms. In this Platonic understanding,
*representation describes the act of using a word, image, or pictorial sign to stand for a
thing or action.* For example, to pass your state driver's license exam, you had to
memorize a set of verbal and pictorial representations for navigating the road-
ways. Three-color traffic signals, of course, give us coded representations of
the act of going (green light), using caution (yellow light), and stopping (red
light). In airports around the world, even if you don't always know the language, you can figure out which bathroom to use by following the pictorial
icons that provide representations distinguishing women from men.

In this mimetic scheme, representations are verbal equivalents of the
things we use and the actions we perform in the real world. But it's not that
simple. For not all representations refer to identical things or actions. It
doesn't take much reflection to realize that representations frame as much as
they reflect how we understand things in the world. For example, in the ancient world, the sun typically was represented as a god such as Ra (Egyptian),
Lugh (Celtic), Apollo (Greek), Liza (Fon), Amaterasu (Shinto), Huitzilopochtli
(Aztec), or Shamash (Sumerian). Although all of these representations name
the sun, they represent it differently. For the modern scientist, the sun represents the hydrogen- and helium-based thermonuclear energy source some
94,500,000 miles away from us at the center of our solar system. Which of
these representations is the real sun? It depends, to a certain extent, on your
point of view. The representations we use in language don't simply reflect a
given world of things but actively shape our understanding of those things;
they constitute, as much as reflect, the real world.

Equally important, representations not only reflect a given world of
things, facts, and actions. They also act as persuasive rhetoric. *Representations
have a shaping role in society. They convey impressions, communicate perceptions, influence opinion, build consensus, and determine attitude and beliefs.* In the United
States, our form of democratic government relies on the ways in which our
elected congressional officials represent our collective will and interests in the
Senate and the House of Representatives. Similarly, to make a representation

before a court of law is to argue a particular point of view on a case. In language usage, representations don't just mimic a world of fixed meanings and objective facts. Equally important, they perform meanings that serve particular groups and individuals politically.

Color and Representation

Historically, attitudes toward racial difference **Web** have been closely bound up *www* with cultural representations of color. A famous lesson in the cultural associations of color is dramatized in *The Autobiography of Malcolm X* (1965). During the civil rights era of the 1960s, Malcolm X emerged as one of the most influential spokespersons for African Americans. Before that time, however, he led the life of a street hustler. Convicted of robbery in 1946, he spent seven years in jail where he became a follower of Elijah Muhammad, the leader of the Nation of Islam. In prison, Malcolm learned about the politics of racial representation the first time he looked up the words *white* and *black* in a standard dictionary. There he read that *white* and *black* are not defined only by their **denotations**—that is, their objective dictionary meanings. White and black are not just neutral representations of opposites on the color wheel, one reflecting the visible spectrum of light and the other wholly absorbing it. Malcolm X discovered how color is implicated in a representational system of racial difference: one whose **connotations**—that is, the values, qualities, and associations a word acquires in usage over time—have social and political consequences.

Connotations of color have served, historically, to value whiteness at the expense of blackness. Whiteness, in fact, is valued insofar as it differs from blackness. According to the *Oxford English Dictionary*, the color black, as it has come down to us through the ages, carries with it the connotations of what is "iniquitous, atrocious, horribly wicked." Contemplating the murder of King Duncan, Macbeth remarks in a famous aside "Let not light see my black and deep desires." Blackness also conjures what is "pertaining to or involving death." Thus, William Shakespeare often marks death's limits to life through solar representations, as in Sonnet 3 where mortality is figured in "brave day sunk in hideous night" or in the "twilight" of Sonnet 73, "As after sunset fadeth in the west; / Which by and by black night doth take away."

Conversely, the color white tends to be associated with that which is "highly prized, precious; dear, beloved, favorite." Whiteness is further linked to "fairness," with what is "beautiful to the eye, of pleasing form or appearance." If the color black in traditional Anglo-European usage connotes negativity generally, whiteness is thought to be "free from malignity or evil intent—beneficent, innocent, harmless, especially as opposed to something characterized as black." John Keats, for example, invokes whiteness as the absolute marker of love's authenticity when he writes in *Endymion* that "I loved her to the very white of truth." Historically, white has not only signified truth but has stood as a universal representation of spiritual redemption, as Emily Dickinson claims in Poem 528: "Mine—by the Right of the White Election!"

The setting of heaven's grace is similarly represented in Robert Herrick's "The White Island, or Place of the Blest."

ROBERT HERRICK   *(1591–1674)*

The White Island, or Place of the Blest   *(1648)*

In this world, the isle of dreams,
While we sit by sorrow's streams,
Tears and terrors are our themes
        Reciting:

But when once from hence we fly,   5
More and more approaching nigh
Unto young eternity,
        Uniting:

In that whiter island, where
Things are evermore sincere;   10
Candor here and luster there
        Delighting:

There are no monstrous fancies shall
Out of hell an horror call,
To create, or cause at all   15
        Affrighting.

There, in calm and cooling sleep,
We our eyes shall never steep,
But eternal watch shall keep,
        Attending   20

Pleasures, such as shall pursue
Me immortalized, and you;
And fresh joys, as never too
        Have ending.

Notice in Herrick's poem how whiteness stands as a constituting representation of "young eternity," whose "whiter island" of "things ever more sincere" has the power of "uniting" and "delighting" and "attending pleasure." The candor, or shining truth, of that ideal setting is set off against the "sorrow's streams" and "tears and terrors" of "this world" as well as the "monstrous fancies" of hell.

    Light and darkness not only serve opposite moral ends in the setting of Herrick's scheme of redemption and damnation but also set the representational terms of heavenly versus earthly existence in Thomas Campion's "Follow Thy Fair Sun."

THOMAS CAMPION *(1567–1620)*

Follow Thy Fair Sun   *(1601)*

Follow thy fair sun, unhappy shadow;
Though thou be black as night,
And she made all of light,
Yet follow thy fair sun, unhappy shadow.

Follow her whose light thy light depriveth;   5
Though here thou liv'st disgraced,
And she in heaven is placed,
Yet follow her whose light the world reviveth!

Follow those pure beams whose beauty burneth,
That so have scorched thee,   10
As thou still black must be,
Till her kind beams thy black to brightness turneth.

Follow her while yet her glory shineth;
There comes a luckless night,
That will dim all her light;   15
And this the black unhappy shade divineth.

Follow still since so thy fates ordained;
The sun must have his shade,
Till both at once do fade;
The sun still proved, the shadow still disdained.   20

For Campion, sun and shadow represent opposite spiritual states. The former is "proved" (or approved) while the latter is "disdained." One is "placed" in heaven and the other "liv'st disgraced" as the reminder of mortality and impending death. Light, fairness, beauty, glory is attributed to the sun while the shadow is "unhappy," "scorched," and "luckless" by being black. The only hope of salvation for the benighted shade lies in following after that "light thy light depriveth."

A similar opposition between fairness and night encodes the figure of the lover in the octave of Sir Philip Sidney's Sonnet 71 from *Astrophil and Stella*.

Sir Philip Sidney   *(1554–1586)*

from Sonnet 71   *(1582)*

Who will in fairest book of Nature know
How virtue may best lodged in beauty be,
Let him but learn of love to read in thee,
Stella, those fair lines which true goodness show.
There shall he find all vices' overthrow,   5
Not by rude force, but sweetest sovereignty
Of reason, from whose light those night birds fly,
That inward sun in thine eyes shineth so.

Again, night is linked here with vice. In contrast, the luminous gaze of the lover, Stella, reflects the "fairest," "beauty," "reason," and "virtue" that can be "read" in the "book of Nature." Whiteness in these works is defined by superlative qualities of purity. Abstract and spiritually transcendent, whiteness stands for the epitome of what is good. Whiteness represents an ideal. In comparison, all other colors are found wanting in their difference from the fairest of the fair.

How then does this color hierarchy as it is inscribed in literary tradition relate to race? The Nobel Prize-winning author Toni Morrison tackles this question in her book *Playing in the Dark: Whiteness and the Literary Imagination* (1992), a collection of essays delivered at Harvard University. In it, Morrison looks at how classic American literature defines white national identity against figures of an imagined "Africanist" presence. This representation of an Africanist presence as "other" relies on the negative tropes of blackness described above. Moreover, as Morrison reminds us, those figures of blackness are bound up with the cultural politics of slavery:

> Black slavery enriched the country's creative possibilities. For in that construction of blackness and enslavement could be found not only the not-free but also, with the dramatic polarity created by skin color, the projection of the not-me. The result was a playground for the imagination. What rose up out of collective needs to allay internal fears and to rationalize external exploitation was an American Africanism—a fabricated brew of darkness, otherness, alarm, and desire that is uniquely American.

In Morrison's account of American literature and culture, white national identity has been defined through its representational difference from stereotyped notions of African Americans as "other." No one except, perhaps, Disney's Snow White is literally a perfect "10" on the color scale. Historically, however, differing degrees of civic power, cultural status, and moral worth have been assigned to people on the basis of what the postcolonial philosopher and psychiatrist Franz Fanon dubbed the "racial epidermal schema" of skin color. Institutional discrimination, of course, was supported by the rule of law in the pre-civil rights era United States as well as under the apartheid regime of South Africa. Moreover, separate and unequal treatment of people of color was furthered, in part, by the ways in which whiteness and blackness were traditionally depicted in language, literature, and the cultural representations of everyday life.

As noted black intellectual W. E. B. Du Bois put it in *The Souls of Black Folk* (1913), "the problem of the Twentieth Century is the problem of the color line." The whole notion of a modern black aesthetic, as it takes shape in the 1920s, emerges as a challenge to this color line. Literature in this context becomes an important site for re-imagining race through changing the representation and thereby the status of the Africanist presence in the national context. Setting out this new literary agenda in his 1922 anthology *The Book of American Negro Poetry*, James Weldon Johnson wrote that "[t]he status of the Negro in the United States is more a question of national mental attitude toward the race than of actual conditions. And nothing will do more to change that mental attitude and raise his status than a demonstration of intellectual parity by the Negro through the production of literature and art." The renaissance in black art and literature called for by Johnson soon found its movement and home in Harlem.

Poetry and the Harlem Renaissance Web CD-ROM   *www*

A combination of demographic factors including crop failures, rural race oppression, and urban job opportunities contributed to the Great Migration of African Americans to Harlem in the 1920s. But above all, according to former Howard University professor Alain Locke, a "new vision" of cosmopolitan opportunity made Harlem into the social "laboratory of a great race-welding." The Harlem night clubs and salon parties, like those hosted by Carl and Fania Van Vechten, provided occasions where musicians such as Bessie Smith and George Gershwin, Hollywood stars like Tallulah Bankhead and Rudolph Valentino, actors such as Paul Robeson, writers like Theodore Dreiser, James Weldon Johnson, Zora Neale Hurston, F. Scott Fitzgerald, and Countée Cullen could mix and mingle. Harlem, for Locke and the other "New Negroes," had "the same rôle to play for the New Negro as Dublin has had for the New Ireland or Prague for the New Czechoslovakia—a race capital." Reflecting this new cosmopolitan milieu, Locke's edited anthology *The New Negro* (1925) promoted an African American aesthetic with featured sections on art, music, dance, sculpture, drama and poetry, as well as sociological readings of the emerging black professional and bourgeois classes.

The New Negro boldly parted company with the minstrel stereotypes and Reconstruction figures caricaturing black identity of the previous century. Locke declared that "[t]he day of 'aunties,' 'uncles' and 'mammies' is equally gone. Uncle Tom and Sambo have passed on. . . ." Locke followed James Weldon Johnson by embracing black "self-determination." He called for a "new figure on the national canvas," one that above all would be "culturally articulate." Locke and the "New Negroes" opposed dominant and oppressive stereotypes of race. In the modern age, he maintained, "race is at present the mainspring of Negro life. It seems to be the outcome of the reaction to proscription and prejudice; an attempt, fairly successful on the whole, to convert a defensive into an offensive position, a handicap into an incentive."

The poets of the Harlem Renaissance turned the social hindrance of race into a cultural asset. Similarly, Langston Hughes in his manifesto "The Negro Artist and the Racial Mountain" (1926) boldly declared that "we younger Negro artists who create now intend to express our individual dark-skinned selves without fear or shame." As in "Dream Variations," Hughes asserted a positive African American presence in poetry by changing the traditional representation of blackness.

LANGSTON HUGHES   *(1902–1967)*   CD-ROM

Dream Variations   *(1926)*

To fling my arms wide
In some place of the sun,
To whirl and to dance
Till the white day is done.
Then rest at cool evening   5
Beneath a tall tree
While night comes on gently,
    Dark like me—
That is my dream!

To fling my arms wide   10
In the face of the sun,
Dance! Whirl! Whirl!
Till the quick day is done.
Rest at pale evening . . .
A tall, slim tree . . .   15
Night coming tenderly
    Black like me.

TOPICS FOR CRITICAL THINKING

1. How does Hughes revise the traditional representation of day and night in "Dream Variations"? How do setting and imagery contribute to Hughes's claim to a black identity in the poem?

2. Stanza two is a variation that repeats key motifs in stanza one but with subtle changes in diction, syntax, and punctuation. Discuss your experience of the shifts in tone, meaning, and emphasis that Hughes builds into the poem's variations.

TOPIC FOR CRITICAL WRITING

Compare Hughes's celebration of the evening as a representation of black identity with Helene Johnson's poem "What Do I Care for Morning," which follows. Examine the interplay of color motifs in Johnson's attention to the moon and sun imagery set off against the darkness of night.

HELENE JOHNSON *(1907–1995)*

What Do I Care for Morning *(1927)*

What do I care for morning,
For a shivering aspen tree,
For sunflowers and sumac
Opening greedily?
What do I care for morning,   5
For the glare of the rising sun,
For a sparrow's noisy prating,
For another day begun?
Give me the beauty of evening,
The cool consummation of night,   10
And the moon like a love-sick lady,
Listless and wan and white.
Give me a little valley,
Huddled beside a hill,
Like a monk in a monastery,   15
Safe and contented and still.
Give me the white road glistening,
A strand of the pale moon's hair,
And the tall hemlocks towering,
Dark as the moon is fair.   20
Oh what do I care for morning,
Naked and newly born—
Night is here, yielding and tender—
What do I care for dawn!

TOPICS FOR CRITICAL THINKING

1. Examine the imagery in which Helene Johnson represents the morning world.
2. Contrast her images of the morning with the qualities she celebrates in its opposite of night.

TOPIC FOR CRITICAL WRITING

Consider how Johnson's evening imagery mixes images of whiteness and blackness.

Poetry and Double-Consciousness

In addition to celebrating new expressions of a modern black aesthetic, Hughes also plumbs the paradoxes of African American identity, what W. E. B. Du Bois defines in *The Souls of Black Folk* as "double-consciousness":

> After the Egyptian and Indian, the Greek and Roman, the Teuton and Mongolian, the Negro is a sort of seventh son, born with a veil, and gifted with second-sight in this American world,—a world which yields him no true self-consciousness, but only lets him see himself through the revelation of the other world. It is a peculiar sensation, this double-consciousness, this sense of always looking at one's self through the eyes of others, of measuring one's soul by the tape of a world that looks on in amused contempt and pity. One ever feels his two-ness—an American, a Negro; two souls, two thoughts, two unreconciled strivings; two warring ideals in one dark body, whose dogged strength alone keeps it from being torn asunder.

Double-consciousness, as Du Bois defines it, also touches on the traumatic legacy of slavery. Beginning with the Middle Passage—the transatlantic economy of slave trade among Africa, the Americas, and Europe—the African American heritage in the United States is a history of clashing racial forces. As a black person, Du Bois argues, "[o]ne ever feels his two-ness,—an American, a Negro; two souls, two thoughts, two unreconciled strivings; two warring ideals in one dark body, whose dogged strength alone keeps it from being torn asunder." Not insignificantly, Du Bois also describes the contradiction of double-consciousness as a resource and a gift. Being able to experience oneself as a person of color *and* to see oneself through the eyes of the dominant white culture provides a heightened self-consciousness. Du Bois employs the metaphor of the veil to depict this kind of double insight into self and society. The modern African American, he writes, is "born with a veil, and gifted with second-sight in this American world,—a world which yields him no true self-consciousness, but only lets him see himself through the revelation of the other world."

In the poetry of the Harlem Renaissance, the definitive work on the theme of double-consciousness is Countée Cullen's "Heritage." In it, Cullen poses the key refrain question "What is Africa to me?"

COUNTÉE CULLEN   *(1903–1946)*

Heritage   *(1925)*

For Harold Jackman

What is Africa to me:
Copper sun or scarlet sea,
Jungle star or jungle track,
Strong bronzed men, or regal black

Women from whose loins I sprang   5
When the birds of Eden sang?
One three centuries removed
From the scenes his fathers loved,
Spicy grove, cinnamon tree,
What is Africa to me?   10

So I lie, who all day long
Want no sound except the song
Sung by wild barbaric birds
Goading massive jungle herds,
Juggernauts of flesh that pass   15
Trampling tall defiant grass
Where young forest lovers lie,
Plighting troth beneath the sky.
So I lie, who always hear,
Though I cram against my ear   20
Both my thumbs, and keep them there,
Great drums throbbing through the air.
So I lie, whose fount of pride,
Dear distress, and joy allied.
Is my somber flesh and skin,   25
With the dark blood dammed within
Like great pulsing tides of wine
That, I fear, must burst the fine
Channels of the chafing net
Where they surge and foam and fret.   30

Africa? A book one thumbs
Listlessly, till slumber comes.
Unremembered are her bats
Circling through the night, her cats
Crouching in the river reeds,   35
Stalking gentle flesh that feeds
By the river brink; no more
Does the bugle-throated roar
Cry that monarch claws have leapt
From the scabbards where they slept.   40
Silver snakes that once a year
Doff the lovely coats you wear,
Seek no covert in your fear
Lest a mortal eye should see;
What's your nakedness to me?   45
Here no leprous flowers rear
Fierce corollas in the air;
Here no bodies sleek and wet,
Dripping mingled rain and sweat,

Tread the savage measures of   50
Jungle boys and girls in love.
What is last year's snow to me,
Last year's anything? The tree
Budding yearly must forget
How its past arose or set—   55
Bough and blossom, flower, fruit,
Even what shy bird with mute
Wonder at her travail there,
Meekly labored in its hair.
One three centuries removed   60
From the scenes his fathers loved,
Spicy grove, cinnamon tree,
What is Africa to me?

So I lie, who find no peace
Night or day, no slight release   65
From the unremitting beat
Made by cruel padded feet
Walking through my body's street.
Up and down they go, and back,
Treading out a jungle track.   70
So I lie, who never quite
Safely sleep from rain at night—
I can never rest at all
When the rain begins to fall;
Like a soul gone mad with pain   75
I must match its weird refrain;
Ever must I twist and squirm,
Writhing like a baited worm,
While its primal measures drip
Through my body, crying, "Strip!   80
Doff this new exuberance.
Come and dance the Lover's Dance!"
In an old remembered way
Rain works on me night and day.

Quaint, outlandish heathen gods   85
Black men fashion out of rods,
Clay, and brittle bits of stone,
In a likeness like their own,
My conversion came high-priced;
I belong to Jesus Christ,   90
Preacher of Humility,
Heathen gods are naught to me.

Father, Son, and Holy Ghost,
So I make an idle boast;

Jesus of the twice-turned cheek, 95
Lamb of God, although I speak
With my mouth thus, in my heart
Do I play a double part.
Ever at Thy glowing altar
Must my heart grow sick and falter, 100
Wishing He I served were black,
Thinking then it would not lack
Precedent of pain to guide it,
Let who would or might deride it;
Surely then this flesh would know 105
Yours had borne a kindred woe.
Lord, I fashion dark gods, too,
Daring even to give You
Dark despairing features where,
Crowned with dark rebellious hair, 110
Patience wavers just so much as
Mortal grief compels, while touches
Quick and hot, of anger, rise
To smitten cheek and weary eyes.
Lord, forgive me if my need 115
Sometimes shapes a human creed.
All day long and all night through,
One thing only must I do:
Quench my pride and cool my blood,
Lest I perish in the flood, 120
Lest a hidden ember set
Timber that I thought was wet
Burning like the dryest flax,
Melting like the merest wax,
Lest the grave restore its dead. 125
Not yet has my heart or head
In the last way realized
They and I are civilized.

TOPICS FOR CRITICAL THINKING

1. The phrase "So I lie" is used five times in the poem. How does Cullen employ the word *lie* as a pun in this phrase? How does Cullen "lie" to himself about his racial identity?

2. Discuss how Cullen depicts a double-consciousness toward Africa, race, and Christianity.

3. How does the poem describe a double-consciousness toward primitivism?

TOPIC FOR CRITICAL WRITING

Cullen's question "What is Africa to me?" can be interpreted in two differing ways. It can be read as a probing question *and* as a rhetorical question: one that performs a statement of indifference. Explain how double-consciousness is inscribed in this question.

"Heritage" makes use of stylized and exotic primitivist imagery. In the modern era, aesthetic primitivism began with the importation of African, Brazilian, and Native American figurines, masks, and ritual objects that circulated in the flea markets and private collections of Paris. The fetish of primitive "otherness" projected onto these artifacts not only marked the avant-garde imagination of visual and literary artists such as Pablo Picasso, Fernand Léger, Guillaume Apollinaire, Blaise Cendrars, Hugo Ball, and Tristan Tzara, but coincided with African American jazz culture popularized for an international audience by Josephine Baker's performances in *La Revue Nègre*. Cullen alludes to the stereotypes of primitivism in his naked "jungle boys and girls."

Three years before Cullen wrote "Heritage," Gwendolyn Bennett published her own poem of the same title. Bennett's "Heritage" looks forward to her 1926 cover illustration for *Opportunity*, after she witnessed Josephine Baker's celebrated "dance sauvage" in Paris the preceding year. In the three-year interim between the poem and the illustration, however, Bennett's representations evolve from what Sterling Brown described as the New Negro "discovery of Africa as a source of race pride" to a more cosmopolitan mixing of primitive and modern aesthetic codes. Compare Bennett's use of primitive motifs in her illustration and poem with Cullen's poem.

Josephine Baker (mid-1920s)

Gwendolyn B. Bennett, Cover, *Opportunity: Journal of Negro Life* (July 1926)

GWENDOLYN B. BENNETT *(1902–1981)*

Heritage *(1923)*

I want to see the slim palm-trees,
Pulling at the clouds
With little pointed fingers. . . .

I want to see lithe Negro girls,
Etched dark against the sky   5
While sunset lingers.

I want to hear the silent sands
Singing to the moon
Before the Sphinx-still face . . . .

I want to hear the chanting   10
Around a heathen fire
Of a strange black race.

I want to breathe the Lotus flow'r,
Sighing to the stars
With tendrils drinking at the Nile. . . .   15

I want to feel the surging
Of my sad people's soul
Hidden by a minstrel-smile.

TOPICS FOR CRITICAL THINKING

1. How does Nugent reverse the primitivist representations associated with an African-ist presence in American culture between the World Wars?
2. Discuss the ways in which Nugent reverses racial codes of whiteness and blackness in the white figures of his "Drawing for Mulattoes" series.

TOPIC FOR CRITICAL WRITING

Compare and contrast the representation of primitivism in Bennett's *Opportunity* cover illustration with the contemporaneous artwork of Bruce Nugent.

Bruce Nugent, *Drawings for Mulattoes, Number 2* (left) and *Number 3* (right) (1927)

Poems for Further Reading and Critical Writing

PAUL LAURENCE DUNBAR   *(1872–1906)*

We Wear the Mask *(1896)*

We wear the mask that grins and lies,
It hides our cheeks and shades our eyes,—
This debt we pay to human guile;
With torn and bleeding hearts we smile,
And mouth with myriad subtleties.   5

Why should the world be over-wise,
In counting all our tears and sighs?
Nay, let them only see us, while
    We wear the mask.

We smile, but O great Christ, our cries   10
To thee from tortured souls arise.
We sing, but oh the clay is vile
Beneath our feet, and long the mile;
But let the world dream otherwise,
    We wear the mask!   15

CLAUDE McKAY   *(1890–1948)*

The Harlem Dancer *(1917)*

Applauding youths laughed with young prostitutes
And watched her perfect, half-clothed body sway;
Her voice was like the sound of blended flutes
Blown by black players upon a picnic day.
She sang and danced on gracefully and calm,   5
The light gauze hanging loose about her form;
To me she seemed a proudly-swaying palm
Grown lovelier for passing through a storm.
Upon her swarthy neck black shiny curls
Luxuriant fell; and tossing coins in praise,   10
The wine-flushed, bold-eyed boys, and even the girls,
Devoured her shape with eager, passionate gaze;
But looking at her falsely-smiling face,
I knew her self was not in that strange place.

America   *(1921)*

Although she feeds me bread of bitterness,
And sinks into my throat her tiger's tooth,
Stealing my breath of life, I will confess
I love this cultured hell that tests my youth!
Her vigor flows like tides into my blood,   5
Giving me strength erect against her hate.
Her bigness sweeps my being like a flood.
Yet as a rebel fronts a king in state,
I stand within her walls with not a shred
Of terror, malice, not a word of jeer.   10
Darkly I gaze into the days ahead,
And see her might and granite wonders there,
Beneath the touch of Time's unerring hand,
Like priceless treasures sinking in the sand.

JEAN TOOMER   *(1894–1967)*

Portrait in Georgia   *(1923)*

Hair—braided chestnut,
    coiled like a lyncher's rope,
Eyes—fagots,°
Lips—old scars, or the first red blisters,
Breath—the last sweet scent of cane,   5
And her slim body, white as the ash
    of black flesh after flame.

GEORGIA DOUGLAS JOHNSON   *(1880–1966)*

The Heart of a Woman   *(1918)*

The heart of a woman goes forth with the dawn
As a lone bird, soft winging, so restlessly on;
Afar o'er life's turrets and vales does it roam
In the wake of those echoes the heart calls home.

The heart of a woman falls back with the night,   5
And enters some alien cage in its plight,
And tires to forget it has dreamed of the stars
While it breaks, breaks, breaks on the sheltering bars.

---

3 *fagots:* Bundles of twigs.

The True American   *(1927)*

America, here is your son, born of your iron heel;
Black blood and red and white contend along this frame of
    steel.
The thorns deep in his brow are set and yet he does not cower;
He goes with neither fears nor tears to crucifixion hour.   5
Nor yet does hatred blur his view of mankind's frail parade;
From his commanding triple coign, all prejudices fade.
The ebbing nations coalesce in him and flow as one;
The bright shining rainbow sweeping back to God at set of sun!
Mark well the surety of tread, the new song high in air,   10
The new note in the nation's throat, as permanent as prayer.
America, regard your son, The Cosmopolitan,
The pattern of posterity, The True American.

HELENE JOHNSON   *(1907–1995)*

My Race   *(1925)*

Ah, my race,
Hungry race,
Throbbing and young—
Ah, my race,
Wonder race,   5
Sobbing with song—
Ah, my race,
Laughing race,
Careless in mirth—
Ah, my veiled   10
Unformed race,
Fumbling in birth.

GWENDOLYN B. BENNETT   *(1902–1981)*

To a Dark Girl   *(1923)*

I love you for your brownness
And the rounded darkness of your breast.
I love you for the breaking sadness in your voice
And shadows where your wayward eye-lids rest.

Something of old forgotten queens   5
Lurks in the lithe abandon of your walk

And something of the shackled slave
Sobs in the rhythm of your talk.

Oh, little brown girl, born for sorrow's mate,
Keep all you have of queenliness,   10
Forgetting that you once were slave,
And let your full lips laugh at Fate!

TOPICS FOR CRITICAL THINKING

1. Discuss the ways in which Dunbar describes the figure of the "mask" as both a symbol of oppression and a resource of double-consciousness. How does his repeated statement "We Wear the Mask" perform both of those symbolic meanings?
2. Explore McKay's ambivalence toward American nationalism in his personifications of "America." Compare the tensions among race, sexuality, and violence witnessed in McKay's poem with Toomer's "Portrait in Georgia."
3. Consider the paradoxical representations of identity and its place in modern society as Georgia Douglas Johnson portrays them in the figure of the "alien cage" and the oxymoron of "sheltering bars" from "The Heart of a Woman."

TOPICS FOR CRITICAL WRITING

1. Compare McKay's representation of dancing in "The Harlem Dancer" with similar dance motifs in Cullen and Bennett. How do you interpret the poem's final couplet?
2. Examine the differing depictions of racial diversity celebrated in Gwendolyn B. Bennett, "To a Dark Girl" and Georgia Douglas Johnson's "The True American."

Critical Perspective: On "Double-Consciousness"

"Between me and the other world there is ever an unasked question: unasked by some through feelings of delicacy; by others through the difficulty of rightly framing it. All, nevertheless, flutter round it. They approach me in a half-hesitant sort of way, eye me curiously or compassionately, and then, instead of saying directly, How does it feel to be a problem? they say, I know an excellent colored man in my town; or, I fought at Mechanicsville; or, Do not these Southern outrages make your blood boil? At these I smile, or am interested, or reduce the boiling to a simmer, as the occasion may require. To the real question, How does it feel to be a problem? I answer seldom a word.

"And yet, being a problem is a strange experience,—peculiar even for one who has never been anything else, save perhaps in babyhood and in Europe. It is in the early days of rollicking boyhood that the revelation first bursts upon one, all in a day as it were. I remember well when the shadow swept across me. I was a little thing, away up in the hills of New England, where the dark Housatonic winds between Hoosac and Taghkanic to the sea. In a wee wooden schoolhouse, something put it into the boys' and girls' heads to buy gorgeous visiting-cards—ten cents a package— and exchange. The exchange was merry, till one girl, a tall newcomer, refused my card,—refused it peremptorily, with a glance. Then it dawned upon me with a certain suddenness that I was different from the others; or like, mayhap, in heart and life and longing, but shut out from their world by a vast veil. I had thereafter no desire to tear down that veil, to creep through; I held all beyond it in common contempt, and lived above it in a region of blue sky and great wandering shadows. That sky was bluest when I could beat my mates at examination time, or beat them at a foot-race, or even beat their stringy heads. Alas, with the years all this fine contempt began to fade, for the worlds I longed for, and all their dazzling opportunities, were theirs, not mine. But they should not keep these prizes, I said; some, all, I would wrest from them. Just how I would do it I could never decide: by reading law, by healing the sick, by telling the wonderful tales that swam in my head,—some way. With other black boys the strife was not so fiercely sunny: their youth shrunk into tasteless sycophancy, or into silent hatred of the pale world about them and mocking distrust of everything white; or wasted itself in a bitter cry, Why did God make me an outcast and a stranger in mine own house? The shades of the prison-house closed round about us all: walls strait and stubborn to the whitest, but relentlessly narrow, tall, and unscalable to sons of night who must plod darkly on in resignation, or beat unavailing palms against the stone, or steadily, half hopelessly, watch the streak of blue above.

"After the Egyptian and Indian, the Greek and Roman, the Teuton and Mongolian, the Negro is a sort of seventh son, born with a veil, and gifted with second-sight in this American world,—a world which yields him no true self-consciousness, but only lets him see himself through the revelation of the other world. It is a peculiar sensation, this double-consciousness, this sense of always looking at one's self through the eyes of others, of measuring one's soul by the tape of a world that looks on in amused contempt and pity. One ever feels his two-ness,—an American, a Negro; two souls, two thoughts, two unreconciled strivings; two warring ideals in one dark body, whose dogged strength alone keeps it from being torn asunder.[1]

"The history of the American Negro is the history of this strife,—this longing to attain self-conscious manhood, to merge his double self into a better and truer self. In this merging he wishes neither of the older selves to be lost. He would not Africanize America, for America has too much to teach the world and Africa. He would not bleach the Negro soul in a flood of white Americanism, for he knows that Negro blood has a message for the world. He simply wishes to make it possible for a man to be both a Negro and an American, without being cursed and spit upon by his fellows, without having the doors of Opportunity closed roughly in his face.

"This, then, is the end of his striving: to be a co-worker in the kingdom of culture, to escape both death and isolation, to husband and use his best powers and his latent genius. These powers of body and mind have in the past been strangely wasted, dispersed, or forgotten. The shadow of a mighty Negro past flits through the tale of Ethiopia the Shadowy and of Egypt the

---

1. This passage is often referred to as Du Bois's theory of the "double-consciousness." It is a "gift of second-sight" but it is also a curse of ambivalence.

Sphinx. Throughout history, the powers of single black men flash here and there like falling stars, and die sometimes before the world has rightly gauged their brightness. Here in America, in the few days since Emancipation, the black man's turning hither and thither in hesitant and doubtful striving has often made his very strength to lose effectiveness, to seem like absence of power, like weakness. And yet it is not weakness,—it is the contradiction of double aims. The double-aimed struggle of the black artisan—on the one hand to escape white contempt for a nation of mere hewers of wood and drawers of water, and on the other hand to plough and nail and dig for a poverty-stricken horde—could only result in making him a poor craftsman, for he had but half a heart in either cause. By the poverty and ignorance of his people, the Negro minister or doctor was tempted toward quackery and demagogy; and by the criticism of the other world, toward ideals that made him ashamed of his lowly tasks. The would-be black *savant* was confronted by the paradox that the knowledge his people needed was a twice-told tale to his white neighbors, while the knowledge which would teach the white world was Greek to his own flesh and blood. The innate love of harmony and beauty that set the ruder souls of his people a-dancing and a-singing raised but confusion and doubt in the soul of the black artist; for the beauty revealed to him was the soul-beauty of a race which his larger audience despised, and he could not articulate the message of another people. This waste of double aims, this seeking to satisfy two unreconciled ideals, has wrought sad havoc with the courage and faith and deeds of ten thousand thousand people,—has sent them often wooing false gods and invoking false means of salvation, and at times has even seemed about to make them ashamed of themselves."

—W. E. B. Du Bois, from *The Souls of Black Folk* (1903)

Critical Perspective: On Race and Art

"One of the most promising of the young Negro poets said to me once, 'I want to be a poet—not a Negro poet,' meaning, I believe, 'I want to write like a white poet'; meaning subconsciously, 'I would like to be a white poet'; meaning behind that, 'I would like to be white.' And I was sorry the young man said that, for no great poet has ever been afraid of being himself. And I doubted then that, with his desire to run away spiritually from his race, this boy would ever be a great poet. But this is the mountain standing in the way of any true Negro art in America—this urge within the race toward whiteness, the desire to pour racial individuality into the mold of American standardization, and to be as little Negro and as much American as possible.

"But let us look at the immediate background of this young poet. His family is of what I suppose one would call the Negro middle class: people who are by no means rich yet never uncomfortable nor hungry—smug, contented, respectable folk, members of the Baptist church. The father goes to work every morning. He is a chief steward at a large white club. The mother sometimes does fancy sewing or supervises parties for the rich families of the town. The children go to a mixed school. In the home they read white papers and magazines. And the mother often says 'Don't be like niggers' when the children are bad. A frequent phrase from the father is, 'Look how well a white man does things.' And so the word white comes to be unconsciously a symbol of all the virtues. It holds for the children beauty, morality, and money. The whisper of 'I want to be white' runs silently through their minds. This young poet's home is, I believe, a fairly typical home of the colored middle class. One sees immediately how difficult it would be for an artist born in such a home to interest himself in interpreting the beauty of his own people. He is never taught to see that beauty. He is taught rather not to see it, or if he does, to be ashamed of it when it is not according to Caucasian patterns.

"For racial culture the home of a self-styled 'high-class' Negro has nothing better to offer. Instead there will perhaps be more aping of things white than in a less cultured or less wealthy home. The father is perhaps a doctor, lawyer, landowner, or politician. The mother may be a social worker, or a teacher, or she may do nothing and have a maid. Father is often dark but he has usually married the lightest woman he could find. The family attend a fashionable church where few really colored faces are to be found. And they themselves draw a color line. In the North they go to white theatres and white movies. And in the South they have at least two cars and a house 'like white folks.' Nordic manners, Nordic faces, Nordic hair, Nordic art (if any), and an Episcopal heaven. A very high mountain indeed for the would-be racial artist to climb in order to discover himself and his people.

"But then there are the low-down folks, the so-called common element, and they are the majority—may the Lord be praised! The people who have their nip of gin on Saturday nights and are not too important to themselves or the community, or too well fed, or too learned to watch the lazy world go round. They live on Seventh Street in Washington or State Street in Chicago and they do not particularly care whether they are like white folks or anybody else. Their joy runs, bang! into ecstasy. Their religion soars to a shout. Work maybe a little today, rest a little tomorrow. Play awhile. Sing awhile. O, let's dance! These common people are not afraid of spirituals, as for a long time their more intellectual brethren were, and jazz is their child. They furnish a wealth of colorful, distinctive material for any artist because they still hold their own individuality in the face of American standardizations. And perhaps these common people will give to the world its truly great Negro artist, the one who is not afraid to be himself. Whereas the better-class Negro would tell the artist what to do, the people at least let him alone when he does appear. And they are not ashamed of him—if they know he exists at all. And they accept what beauty is their own without question.

"Certainly there is, for the American Negro artist who can escape the restrictions the more advanced among his own group would put upon him, a great field of unused material ready for his art. Without going outside his race, and even among the better classes with their 'white' culture and conscious American manners, but still Negro enough to be different, there is sufficient matter to furnish a black artist with a lifetime of creative work. And when he chooses to touch on the relations between Negroes and whites in this country with their innumerable overtones and undertones surely, and especially for literature and the drama, there is an inexhaustible supply of themes at hand. To these the Negro artist can give his racial individuality, his heritage of rhythm and warmth, and his incongruous humor that so often, as in the Blues, becomes ironic laughter mixed with tears. But let us look again at the mountain.

"A prominent Negro clubwoman in Philadelphia paid eleven dollars to hear Raquel Meller sing Andalusian popular songs. But she told me a few weeks before she would not think of going to hear 'that woman,' Clara Smith, a great black artist, sing Negro folksongs. And many an upper-class Negro church, even now, would not dream of employing a spiritual in its services. The drab melodies in white folks' hymnbooks are much to be preferred. 'We want to worship the Lord correctly and quietly. We don't believe in "shouting."' Let's be dull like the Nordics,' they say, in effect.

"The road for the serious black artist, then, who would produce a racial art is most certainly rocky and the mountain is high. Until recently he received almost no encouragement for his work from either white or colored people. The fine novels of Chesnutt go out of print with neither race noticing their passing. The quaint charm and humor of Dunbar's dialect verse brought to him, in his day, largely the same kind of encouragement one would give a sideshow freak (A colored man writing poetry! How odd!) or a clown (How amusing!).

"The present vogue in things Negro, although it may do as much harm as good for the budding colored artist, has at least done this: it has brought him forcibly to the attention of his own people among whom for so long, unless the other race had noticed him beforehand, he was a prophet with little honor. I understand that Charles Gilpin acted for years in Negro theatres without any special acclaim from his own, but when Broadway gave him eight curtain calls, Negroes, too, began to beat a tin pan in his honor. I know a young colored writer, a manual worker by day, who had been writing well for the colored magazines for some years, but it was not until he recently broke into the white publications and his first book was accepted by a prominent New York publisher that the 'best' Negroes in his city took the trouble to discover that he lived there. Then almost immediately they decided to give a grand dinner for him. But the society ladies were careful to whisper to his mother that perhaps she'd better not come. They were not sure she would have an evening gown.

"The Negro artist works against an undertow of sharp criticism and misunderstanding from his own group and unintentional bribes from the whites. 'Oh, be respectable, write about nice people, show how good we are,' say the Negroes. 'Be stereotyped, don't go too far, don't shatter our illusions about you, don't amuse us too seriously. We will pay you,' say the whites. Both would have told Jean Toomer not to write *Cane*. The colored people did not praise it. The white people did not buy it. Most of the colored people who did read *Cane* hate it. They are afraid of it. Although the critics gave it good reviews the public remained indifferent. Yet (excepting the work of Du Bois) *Cane* contains the finest prose written by a Negro in America. And like the singing of Robeson, it is truly racial.

"But in spite of the Nordicized Negro intelligentsia and the desires of some white editors we have an honest American Negro literature already with us. Now I await the rise of the Negro theatre. Our folk music, having achieved world-wide fame, offers itself to the genius of the great individual American composer who is to come. And within the next decade I expect to see the work of a growing school of colored artists who paint and model the beauty of dark faces and create with new technique the expressions of their own soul-world. And the Negro dancers who will dance like flame and the singers who will continue to carry our songs to all who listen—they will be with us in even greater numbers tomorrow.

"Most of my own poems are racial in theme and treatment, derived from the life I know. In many of them I try to grasp and hold some of the meanings and rhythms of jazz. I am as sincere as I know how to be in these poems and yet after every reading I answer questions like these from my own people: Do you think Negroes should always write about Negroes? I wish you wouldn't read some of your poems to white folks. How do you find anything interesting in a place like a cabaret? Why do you write about black people? You aren't black. What makes you do so many jazz poems?

"But jazz to me is one of the inherent expressions of Negro life in America; the eternal tom-tom beating in the Negro soul—the tom-tom of revolt against weariness in a white world, a world of subway trains, and work, work, work; the tom-tom of joy and laughter, and pain swallowed in a smile. Yet the Philadelphia clubwoman is ashamed to say that her race created it and she does not like me to write about it. The old subconscious 'white is best' runs through her mind. Years of study under white teachers, a lifetime of white books, pictures, and papers, and white manners, morals, and Puritan standards made her dislike the spirituals. And now she turns up her nose at jazz and all its manifestations—likewise almost everything else distinctly racial. She doesn't care for the Winold Reiss portraits of Negroes because they are 'too Negro.' She does not want a true picture of herself from anybody. She wants the artist to flatter her, to make the white world believe that all Negroes are as smug and as near white in soul as she wants to be. But, to my mind, it is the duty of the younger Negro artist, if he accepts any duties at all from outsiders, to change through the force of his art that old whispering 'I want to be white,' hidden in the aspirations of his people, to 'Why should I want to be white? I am a Negro—and beautiful!'

"So I am ashamed for the black poet who says, 'I want to be a poet, not a Negro poet,' as though his own racial world were not as interesting as any other world. I am ashamed, too, for the colored artist who runs from the painting of Negro faces to the painting of sunsets after the manner of the academicians because he fears the strange un-whiteness of his own features. An artist must be free to choose what he does, certainly, but he must also never be afraid to do what he might choose.

"Let the blare of Negro jazz bands and the bellowing voice of Bessie Smith singing Blues penetrate the closed ears of the colored near-intellectuals until they listen and perhaps understand. Let Paul Robeson singing 'Water Boy,' and Rudolph Fisher writing about the streets of Harlem, and Jean Toomer holding the heart of Georgia in his hands, and Aaron Douglas drawing strange black fantasies cause the smug Negro middle class to turn from their white, respectable, ordinary books and papers to catch a glimmer of their own beauty. We younger Negro artists who create now intend to express our individual dark-skinned selves without fear or shame. If white people are pleased we are glad. If they are not, it doesn't matter. We know we are beautiful. And ugly too. The tom-tom cries and the tom-tom laughs. If colored people are pleased we are glad. If they are not, their displeasure doesn't matter either. We build our temples for tomorrow, strong as we know how, and we stand on top of the mountain, free within ourselves."

—Langston Hughes, "The Negro Artist and the Racial Mountain" (1926)

Critical Perspective: On New Representations of Race

"In the last decade something beyond the watch and guard of statistics has happened in the life of the American Negro and the three norns who have traditionally presided over the Negro problem have a changeling in their laps. The Sociologist, the Philanthropist, the Race-leader are not unaware of the New Negro, but they are at a loss to account for him. He simply cannot be swathed in their formulae. For the younger generation is vibrant with a new psychology; the new spirit is awake in the masses, and under the very eyes of the professional observers is transforming what has been a perennial problem into the progressive phases of contemporary Negro life.

"Could such a metamorphosis have taken place as suddenly as it has appeared to? The answer is no; not because the New Negro is not here, but because the Old Negro had long become more of a myth than a man. The Old Negro, we must remember, was a creature of moral debate and historical controversy. His has been a stock figure perpetuated as an historical fiction partly in innocent sentimentalism, partly in deliberate reactionism. The Negro himself has contributed his share to this through a sort of protective social mimicry forced upon him by the adverse circumstances of dependence. So for generations in the mind of America, the Negro has been more of a formula than a human being—a something to be argued about, condemned or defended, to be 'kept down,' or 'in his place,' or 'helped up,' to be worried with or worried over, harassed or patronized, a social bogey or a social burden. The thinking Negro even has been induced to share this same general attitude, to focus his attention on controversial issues, to see himself in the distorted perspective of a social problem. His shadow, so to speak, has been more real to him than his personality. Through having had to appeal from the unjust stereotypes of his oppressors and traducers to those of his liberators, friends and benefactors he has had to subscribe to the traditional positions from which his case has been viewed. Little true social or self-understanding has or could come from such a situation.

"But while the minds of most of us, black and white, have thus burrowed in the trenches of the Civil War and Reconstruction, the actual march of development has simply flanked these positions, necessitating a sudden reorientation of view. We have not been watching in the right direction; set North and South on a sectional axis, we have not noticed the East till the sun has us blinking.

"Recall how suddenly the Negro spirituals revealed themselves; suppressed for generations under the stereotypes of Wesleyan hymn harmony, secretive, half-ashamed, until the courage of being natural brought them out—and behold, there was folk-music. Similarly the mind of the Negro seems suddenly to have slipped from under the tyranny of social intimidation and to be shaking off the psychology of imitation and implied inferiority. By shedding the old chrysalis of the Negro problem we are achieving something like a spiritual emancipation. Until recently, lacking self-understanding, we have been almost as much of a problem to ourselves as we still are to others. But the decade that found us with a problem has left us with only a task. The multitude perhaps feels as yet only a strange relief and a new vague urge, but the thinking few know that in the reaction the vital inner grip of prejudice has been broken.

"With this renewed self-respect and self-dependence, the life of the Negro community is bound to enter a new dynamic phase, the buoyancy from within compensating for whatever pressure there may be of conditions from without. The migrant masses, shifting from countryside to city, hurdle several generations of experience at a leap, but more important, the same thing happens spiritually in the life-attitudes and self-expression of the Young Negro, in his poetry, his art, his education and his new outlook, with the additional advantage, of course, of the poise and greater certainty of knowing what it is all about. From this comes the promise and warrant of a new leadership. As one of them has discerningly put it:

We have tomorrow
Bright before us
Like a flame.

Yesterday, a night-gone thing
A sun-down name.

And dawn today
Broad arch above the road we came.
We march!

"This is what, even more than any 'most creditable record of fifty years of freedom,' requires that the Negro of to-day be seen through other than the dusty spectacles of past controversy. The day of 'aunties,' 'uncles' and 'mammies' is equally gone. Uncle Tom and Sambo have passed on, and even the 'Colonel' and 'George' play barnstorm rôles from which they escape with relief when the public spotlight is off. The popular melodrama has about played itself out, and it is time to scrap the fictions, garret the bogeys and settle down to a realistic facing of facts.

"First we must observe some of the changes which since the traditional lines of opinion were drawn have rendered these quite obsolete. A main change has been, of course, that shifting of the Negro population which has made the Negro problem no longer exclusively or even predominantly Southern. Why should our minds remain sectionalized, when the problem itself no longer is? Then the trend of migration has not only been toward the North and the Central-Midwest, but cityward and to the great centers of industry—the problems of adjustment are new, practical, local and not peculiarly racial. Rather they are an integral part of the large industrial and social problems of our present-day democracy. And finally, with the Negro rapidly in process of class differentiation, if it ever was warrantable to regard and treat the Negro *en masse* it is becoming with every day less possible, more unjust and more ridiculous.

"In the very process of being transplanted, the Negro is becoming transformed."

—Alain Locke, from *The New Negro* (1925)

Critical Perspective: On Women Writers of the Harlem Renaissance

"Other specifically literary factors further illuminate the status of women writers in the Harlem Renaissance. A principal one is the issue of poetry as a genre. During the period, it was, in a real sense, the preeminent form—based on its universality, accessibility for would-be writers, suitability for magazine publication, and classical heritage as the highest expression of cultured, lyric sensibility. The big three writers of the era—McKay, Cullen, and Hughes—made their reputations as poets. And most of the notable women writers of the period were poets, with only Larsen and Hurston not essaying verse. In addition to Johnson, Dunbar-Nelson, and Grimké, six others produced significant work—Anne Spencer, Jessie Fauset, Effie Lee Newsome, Gwendolyn Bennett, Helene Johnson, and the lesser-known Gladys Mae Casely Hayford.

"Anne Spencer is an arresting poet because of the originality of her material and approach. Working in forms that are an eccentric mixture of free verse and rhymed, iambic-based lines, she treated subjects as varied as her titles: 'Before the Feast of Shushan,' 'At the Carnival,' 'The Wife-Woman,' 'Dunbar,' 'Letter to My Sister,' 'Lines to a Nasturtium,' 'Neighbors,' and 'Creed.' She is most modern in her predilection for casting herself into roles, her sense of woman-self and female identity, and her style, which is characterized by terseness, apt or unusual diction, and vivid images and metaphors. Known best as a novelist, Fauset is usually represented in anthologies by her love poems. Some of them are distinguished by the French titles she gave them and by her sometimes humorous anti ironic cast of mind. Effie Lee Newsome primarily wrote children's verse based on nature lore.

"Gwendolyn Bennett and Helene Johnson are the stellar poets of the younger generation. Bennett's poetry can be quite impressive. She was, by occupation, an artist, and consequently in her work she envisions scenes, paints still lifes, and expresses herself especially well in color. Of all the women poets, Helene Johnson's work most reflects the qualities commonly designated as characteristic of the Renaissance. She took 'the "racial" bull by the horns' (as James Weldon Johnson put it), and also wrote poems in the new colloquial-folk-slang style popular during that time. Although the bulk of her poems are traditional romance and nature lyrics, her 'Sonnet to a Negro in Harlem' is pro-black and militant. In her frequently reprinted 'Poem,' she waxes ecstatic over the 'Little brown boy / Slim, dark, big-eyed,' who croons love songs to his banjo down at the Lafayette Theater.

"Gladys Mae Hayford's distinctions are being born in Africa and having two of her poems—'Nativity' (in which the Christ Child is black) and 'The Serving Girl'—published in the *Atlantic Monthly*. A Fanti, she committed herself to imbuing 'our own people with the idea of their own beauty, superiority and individuality.' Because Africa for her was a very real place, her poems have a concrete specificity not usually found in some other Harlem Renaissance works on that theme. She talks about blue lappah, frangipani blossoms, and the brass ankle bells that guard 'Brown Baby Cobina.' Her regularly accented couplets also employ various lyric personae and speak naturally about love and sex (particularly 'Rainy Season Love Song')."
—Gloria T. Hull, from *Color, Sex, and Poetry in the Harlem Renaissance* (1987)

Critical Perspective: On Formal Mastery and the Harlem Renaissance

"*The New Negro*, like the valued documents from which we grasp iconic images and pictorial myths of a colonial or frontier America, is perhaps our first *national* book, offering not only a description of streams of tendency in our collective lives but also an actual construction within its pages of the sounds, songs, images, and signs of a nation. The collection's combination of phaneric display and formal mastery can come as no surprise to the person who has followed the lines of Afro-American development through an extensive discursive field. For though the enabling conditions for Locke's collection are found in marronage, there is no gainsaying the work's quite canny presentation, utilization, and praise of formal mastery. Witness, for example, the high evaluations of Countee Cullen's poetry, poetry that is meant to imitate with astute fidelity the efforts of British romanticism. Or turn to Claude McKay's 'The White House,' a poem whose title Locke changed to 'White Houses,' and you find an English, or modified Shakespearean, sonnet. Again, most of the short fiction and, certainly, the single drama presented in *The New Negro* scarcely escape initial recognition as formally *standard* works.

"The present discussion is hardly the place to explore fully the Afro-American cultural dimensions and significances of McKay's or Cullen's *standard* artistic postures. But one can contextualize such efforts by saying that McKay's 'sonnet,' like Cullen's 'ballads,' are just as much mastered *masks* as the minstrel manipulations of Booker T. Washington and Charles Chesnutt are. The trick of McKay and Cullen was what one of my colleagues calls the denigration of form—a necessary ('forced,' as it were) adoption of the standard that results in an effective *blackening*. Locke was never of the opinion that Western *standards* in art were anything other than adequate goals for high Afro-American cultural achievement. And the revaluation of the Afro-American based on artistic accomplishment for which he calls mandated, in his view, a willingness on the part of black spokespersons to aspire toward such standards. Hence, one would have to present *recognizably* standard forms and get what black mileage one could out of subtle, or, by contrast, straining (like McKay's rebellious cries) variations and deepenings of these forms. If the

younger generation was to proffer 'artistic' gifts, such gifts had first to be recognizable as 'artistic' by Western, formal standards and not simply as un-
adorned or primitive *folk* creations.

"Now Locke—and, indeed, the entire Harlem movement—has often
been criticized severely for its advocacy of the standard. Yet it seems that such
criticism proceeds somewhat in ignorance of the full discursive field marking
Afro-American national possibilities. For we may not enjoy or find coura-
geous models of derring-do in the masking that characterizes formal mastery,
but we certainly cannot minimize its significant and strategic presence in our
history. Furthermore, such masking carries subtle resonances and effects that
cannot even be perceived (much less evaluated) by the person who begins with
the notion that recognizably *standard* form automatically disqualifies a work
as an authentic and valuable Afro-American national production. Analysis is
in fact foreclosed by a first assumption of failure. Certainly Countée Cullen,
for example, served a national need in a time of 'forced' institution building
and national projection. He gained white American recognition for 'Negro
poetry' at a moment when there was little encouraging recognition in the
United States for *anything* Negro. And Cullen gained such recognition by means
of a mastery of form pleasing *to Afro-Americans* as well as Anglo-Americans. It
seems inconceivable that, in the first flush of pioneering urbanity and heady
self-consciousness, the congregation of Reverend Frederick Cullen's well-
attended Salem Methodist Episcopal Church in Harlem would have responded
positively if, after the father's announcement of his son's accomplishments as
a poet, the young Countee had produced sounds such as: 'April is the cruellest
month, breeding / Lilacs out of the dead land, mixing / Memory and desire,
stirring / Dull roots with spring rain.' The delivery of such lines would probably have caused consternation akin to the congregation's reaction to John in
DuBois's classic story 'Of the Coming of John': 'Little had they understood of
what he said, for he spoke an unknown tongue.' Not only was the 'tongue' of
such collaged allusiveness as Eliot's *unknown* to a congregation like Reverend
Cullen's; it was also unnecessary, unneeded, of little use in a world bent on
recognizable (rhyme, meter, form, etc.) artistic 'contributions.' One has only
to peruse the 1913 issue of *Poetry* in which Ezra Pound's famous imagist manifesto appeared to see that 'cruellest months' and breeding lilacs were the exception rather than the American rule in Cullen's day."

—Houston Baker, from "Modernism and the Harlem Renaissance" (1987)

Critical Perspective: On the White Gaze and Race Representation

"The paradox of racial representation marks a good deal of Old Left representations of black Americans but is especially patent in a cartoon that William
Siegel published in the May 1930 issue of *New Masses*. Siegel offers two contradictory versions of the African-American community: 'the white bourgeois
version of the Negro' vs. 'as the white worker knows him.' However well intended, Siegel's visual rendering of these representational differences actually
served to perpetuate both racist and classist assumptions about blacks. Siegel's

leftist reduction of the black aesthetic, nevertheless, appealed to the CP leadership as evidenced, two months later, in his sanitized portrait of 'Negro Workers' that was showcased on the cover of the July 1930 *New Masses*.

"In both plates of the May issue cartoon the power of defining the cultural roles available to blacks belongs to a foregrounded pair of white viewers. Thus the shift in class representation is, nonetheless, framed by a distanced (hence privileged) Caucasian gaze—one that interprets, and thereby fixes, African-American identity. The ideological limits of Siegel's unconscious racial framing are plain to see in the second panel which, however much it liberates blacks from both rural and urban stereotypes, also expunges the distinctive, vernacular nuances of the slave songs, black sermon, African ritual performance, blues, and jazz culture that have historically empowered black Americans with their own distinctive interpretive community. While Siegel's cartoon reduces the political subtext of biblical slave songs to sheer caricature, James Weldon Johnson, as early as 1922, had clearly identified the biblical story of Moses and the Hebrew Exodus as a trope for liberation in African-American slave songs.

"Five years later, in *God's Trombones* (1927), Johnson would theorize the black preacher as a source of consolation and political solidarity for displaced slaves in the antebellum South. 'It was through him,' Johnson wrote, 'that the people of diverse languages and customs who were brought here from diverse parts of Africa and thrown into slavery were given their first sense of unity and solidarity.' Johnson's focus on antebellum sermon as a discourse of black 'unity and solidarity' was visually underscored by Aaron Douglas' illustrations. These original images transcoded Biblical typology to a stylized African-American iconography of exodus from the chains of Southern bondage. The recovery of black sermon in Johnson's 'Let My People Go' presented less

MAY, 1930   7

The white bourgeois version of the Negro   —*as the white worker knows him.*   —*Drawn by William Siegel*

a theological than a materialist reading of Israel's oppressed class role, 'working without money and without price':

> Four hundred years
> They'd held them down in Egypt land.
> Held them under the driver's lash,
> Working without money and without price.
> And it might have been Pharaoh's wife that said:
> "Pharaoh—look what you've done.
> You let those Hebrew Children go,
> And who's going to serve us now?
> Who's going to make our bricks and mortar?
> Who's going to plant and plow our corn?
> Who's going to get up in the chill of the morning?
> And who's going to work in the blazing sun?
> Pharaoh, tell me that!"

In contrast to this liberatory narrative, Siegel reads the Hebrew exodus as a symptom of religious false consciousness. He drains this folk tradition of any political effectivity, linking it instead to the racist stereotypes of the black minstrel tradition: the surreal world of Jim Crow, Zeb Coon, Amos an' Andy, plantation medleys and 'August hams.'"
    —Walter Kalaidjian, from *American Culture Between the Wars* (1994)

Critical Perspective: On Langston Hughes and Walt Whitman

"It is therefore only poetically just that Langston Hughes began composing the forerunner of one of his most famous poems on his Americanism and on the kinship of white and black Americans on the back of a letter he had received from Claude McKay in 1924. This poem became 'I Too,' which Alain Locke included in *The New Negro*:

> I, too, sing America,
>
> I am the darker brother.
> They send me to eat in the kitchen
> When company comes.

In the American family home, the 'darker brother,' disowned by white siblings, prophesies the transforming force of his song's challenge—on the basis of his own aesthetic—to the Americanism of the white kinfolk. At the same time Hughes makes his claim as an heir to Whitman and registers his distinctive poetic identity as both black and American: 'They'll see how beautiful I am / And be ashamed,— / I, too, am America.' The poem was retitled 'Epilogue' (from the Greek, meaning 'peroration') for his first book a year later; for years he often used it to conclude his poetry readings. James Baldwin would redouble Hughes's defiant stress on the kinship of white and black Americans three decades and more later.

"Hughes had come to Whitman by way of such Midwestern rebels as Carl Sandburg prior to the twenties. His was the democratic 'transnational,' socialist, 'comradely' Whitman pushed by Horace Traubel and the *Masses* circle (as opposed to the Whitman of 'cosmic consciousness' Toomer responded to). Nonetheless, he early sensed the affinity between the inclusive 'I' of Whitman and the 'I' of the spirituals, whose fusion shaped one of his first published poems, 'The Negro Speaks of Rivers,' also in *The New Negro*:

> I've known rivers ancient as the world and older than the flow of
>   human blood in human veins.
> My soul has grown deep like the rivers.
>
> I bathed in the Euphrates when dawns were young,
> I built my hut near the Congo and it lulled me to sleep,
> I looked upon the Nile and raised the pyramids above it.
>
> I heard the singing of the Mississippi when Abe Lincoln went down
>   to New Orleans,
> and I've seen its muddy bosom turn all golden in the
>   sunset.

Readers rarely notice that if the soul of the Negro in this poem goes back to the Euphrates, it goes back to a pre-'racial' dawn and a geography far from Africa that is identified with neither blackness nor whiteness—a geography at the time of Hughes's writing considered the cradle of all the world's civilizations and possibly the location of the Garden of Eden. Thus, even in this poem about the depth of the Negro's soul Hughes avoids racial essentialism while nonetheless stressing the existential, racialized conditions of black and modern identity.

"Returning, however, to the matter of form, I would reiterate the related point that along with the pan-Africanism of Du Bois and the force of the spirituals, the example of Whitman's break with traditional definitions of the 'poetic,' his attempts to capture the cadence and diction of the voice on the street, in the pulpit, and at the water's edge, provided a partial model for the young black poet looking for a way to sing his own song, which would be at the same time a song of his people. This role of Whitman in Hughes's career is representative of his relationship to folk poetry of the period generally, most dramatically in the case of the author of *America's Songbag*, Carl Sandburg.

"Hughes had yet to find himself in the blues and jazz—although he had published 'The Weary Blues' already—and few of Locke's selections (except 'Jazzonia') suggest his move in that direction. What Locke was interested in at this point, it seems, was the soulfulness of 'The Negro Speaks of Rivers' and the kind of 'paganism' and 'spontaneously emotional, affably democratic and naive spirit' that he found in the 'folk temperament'—not a poetry in actual folk forms, but one exploring the spiritual 'endowment' of the race. As Hughes moved closer to Van Vechten, McKay, and others of the left he abandoned 'African' primitivism—despite the influence of his patron Charlotte Osgood Mason—and increasingly experimented with the possibilities of jazz and blues."
—George Hutchinson, from *The Harlem Renaissance in Black and White* (1996)

Featured Writer

Gwendolyn Brooks

GWENDOLYN BROOKS

The granddaughter of an escaped slave, Gwendolyn Brooks was the first African American to receive the Pulitzer Prize. Although born on June 7, 1917, in Topeka, Kansas, Brooks lived her entire life in Chicago. Showing early promise as a writer, Brooks published her first poem at the age of thirteen in the popular magazine *American Childhood*. Brooks received encouragement in her early career from the African American modernist poet Langston Hughes **CD-ROM**.

By the age of seventeen she became a regular poetry contributor to one of the most widely read African American papers, *The Chicago Defender*. In 1936, Brooks graduated from Wilson Junior College and three years later married Henry Blakely, with whom she would have two children: her son Henry born in 1940 and her daughter Nora born in 1951.

Brooks's rise to the status of major author began in 1941 when she enrolled in a Southside Chicago poetry workshop sponsored by the Gold Coast socialite Inez Cunningham Stark. By the end of the decade, Brooks was on her way toward becoming a canonical twentieth-century author. In 1943, she received the Midwestern Writers' Conference Award, followed two years later by the Mademoiselle Merit Award. Soon after she went on to win the American Academy of Letters Award (1946), two Guggenheim Fellowships (1946, 1947), *Poetry*'s prestigious Eunice Tietjens Memorial Award (1949), and the Pulitzer Prize (1949).

From the beginning, Brooks, like Langston Hughes, put the lives of ordinary African Americans at the center of her work. "I read Langston Hughes's *Weary Blues*," she writes, "and got very excited about what he was doing. I realized that writing about the ordinary aspects of Black life was important." Brooks's first volume of verse, *A Street in Bronzeville* (1945), depicts stylized portraits of the people Brooks knew so well in such works as "Sadie and Maud."

Sadie and Maud   *(1945)*

Maud went to college.
Sadie stayed at home.
Sadie scraped life
With a fine-tooth comb.

She didn't leave a tangle in.   5
Her comb found every strand.
Sadie was one of the livingest chits
In all the land.

Sadie bore two babies
Under her maiden name.   10
Maud and Ma and Papa
Nearly died of shame.
Every one but Sadie
Nearly died of shame.

When Sadie said her last so-long   15
Her girls struck out from home.
(Sadie had left as heritage
Her fine-tooth comb.)

Maud, who went to college,
Is a thin brown mouse.   20
She is living all alone
In this old house.

TOPICS FOR CRITICAL THINKING

1. Discuss Brooks's symbol of the comb with which "Sadie scraped life." What values does Brooks associate with the comb? What kind of heritage does the comb embody?
2. Sadie is a portrait of an unwed, single mother. How does Brooks depict societal attitudes toward Sadie's subject position?
3. What point does Brooks make in her title and final imagery in framing the contrast between Sadie and Maud? How do the two women differ? Are there any key terms that assign differing value to their life choices?

TOPIC FOR CRITICAL WRITING

Examine the pattern of oppositional choices that shape the narrative structure in both "Sadie and Maud" and the poem that follows, "a song in the front yard."

a song in the front yard   *(1945)*

I've stayed in the front yard all my life.
I want a peek at the back
Where it's rough and untended and hungry weed grows.
A girl gets sick of a rose.

I want to go in the back yard now   5
And maybe down the alley,

To where the charity children play.
I want a good time today.

They do some wonderful things.
They have some wonderful fun.   10
My mother sneers, but I say it's fine
How they don't have to go in at quarter to nine.
My mother, she tells me that Johnnie Mae
Will grow up to be a bad woman.
That George'll be taken to Jail soon or late   15
(On account of last winter he sold our back gate.)

But I say it's fine. Honest, I do.
And I'd like to be a bad woman, too,
And wear the brave stockings of night-black lace
And strut down the streets with paint on my face.   20

TOPICS FOR CRITICAL THINKING

1. How do you imagine the persona Brooks depicts in this dramatic monologue in terms of her age, background and lifestyle, experience, and so on?
2. Examine the kind of lives that Brooks imagines in the back yard.
3. Why does Brooks describe the stockings of the final stanza as "brave"? How does this key term hint at what might be at stake in the speaker's fascination with the life of the back yard?

TOPIC FOR CRITICAL WRITING

Discuss the ways in which the front and back yards of Brooks's poem represent differing social and personal values.

    In addition to examining the contradictory impulses, choices, and lifestyles of contemporary African American women, Brooks also offered frank depictions of the racial and class oppressions that weighed on black women's lives in the pre-civil rights era of the late 1940s. In particular, Brooks's dramatic monologue in "The Mother" presents an unflinching look at a woman's choice of abortion and the psychological and ethical consequences of that choice.

The Mother   *(1945)*

Abortions will not let you forget.
You remember the children you got that you did not get,
The damp small pulps with a little or with no hair,
The singers and workers that never handled the air.   5
You will never neglect or beat
Them, or silence or buy with a sweet.

You will never wind up the sucking-thumb
Or scuttle off ghosts that come.
You will never leave them, controlling your luscious sigh,
Return for a snack of them, with gobbling mother-eye.   10

I have heard in the voices of the wind the voices of my dim killed
    children.
I have contracted. I have eased
My dim dears at the breasts they could never suck.
I have said, Sweets, if I sinned, if I seized
Your luck   15
And your lives from your unfinished reach,
If I stole your births and your names,
Your straight baby tears and your games,
Your stilted or lovely loves, your tumults, your marriages, aches,
    and your deaths,
If I poisoned the beginnings of your breaths,   20
Believe that even in my deliberateness I was not deliberate.
Though why should I whine,
Whine that the crime was other than mine?—
Since anyhow you are dead.
Or rather, or instead,   25
You were never made.
But that too, I am afraid,
Is faulty: oh, what shall I say, how is the truth to be said?
You were born, you had body, you died.
It is just that you never giggled or planned or cried.   30

Believe me, I loved you all.
Believe me, I knew you, though faintly, and I loved, I loved you
All.

TOPICS FOR CRITICAL THINKING

1. How would you characterize the mother's reflection on and her attitude toward her own abortions?
2. In what ways does Brooks present the paradox of the mother's choices both in the phrasings of the poem's opening lines and in its title?
3. How does the mother imagine the life her aborted children did not lead?
4. What significance is there in the poem's shift from the second-person *you* voice to the first-person *I* voice after the opening stanza?
5. Although "The Mother" mourns the loss of "the children you got that you did not get," does it make any moral or political claims concerning abortion?

TOPIC FOR CRITICAL WRITING

What role does direct address play in the poem, and what point does Brooks make in her shift from questions to declarative statements in the poem's final two stanzas?

In addition to probing women's lived experience of abortion, Brooks also worked in the folk ballad form to explore the complexity of women's encounters with sexual betrayal and racial violence, as in the "Ballad of Pearl May Lee."

Ballad of Pearl May Lee   *(1945)*

Then off they took you, off to the jail,
A hundred hooting after.
And you should have heard me at my house.
I cut my lungs with my laughter,
    Laughter,   5
    Laughter.
I cut my lungs with my laughter.

They dragged you into a dusty cell.
And a rat was in the corner.
And what was I doing? Laughing still.   10
Through never was a poor gal lorner,
    Lorner,
    Lorner.
Through never was a poor gal lorner.

The sheriff, he peeped in through the bars,   15
And (the red old thing) he told you,
"You son of a bitch, you're going to hell!"
'Cause you wanted white arms to enfold you,
    Enfold you,
    Enfold you.   20
'Cause you wanted white arms to enfold you.

But you paid for your white arms, Sammy boy,
And you didn't pay with money.
You paid with your hide and my heart, Sammy boy,
For your taste of pink and white honey,   25
    Honey,
    Honey.
For your taste of pink and white honey.

Oh, dig me out of my don't-despair.
Pull me out of my poor-me.   30
Get me a garment of red to wear.
You had it coming surely,
    Surely,
    Surely,
You had it coming surely.
                                       35

At school, your girls were the bright little girls.
You couldn't abide dark meat.
Yellow was for to look at,
Black for the famished to eat.
Yellow was for to look at,   40
Black for the famished to eat.

You grew up with bright skins on the brain,
And me in your black folks bed.
Often and often you cut me cold,
And often I wished you dead.   45
Often and often you cut me cold.
Often I wished you dead.

Then a white girl passed you by one day,
And, the vixen, she gave you the wink.
And your stomach got sick and your legs liquefied.   50
And you thought till you couldn't think.
    You thought,
    You thought,
You thought till you couldn't think.

I fancy you out on the fringe of town,   55
The moon an owl's eye minding;
The sweet and thick of the cricket-belled dark,
The fire within you winding . . . .
    Winding,
    Winding   60
The fire within you winding.

Say, she was white like milk, though, wasn't she?
And her breasts were cups of cream.
In the back of her Buick you drank your fill.
Then she roused you out of your dream.   65
In the back of her Buick you drank your fill.
Then she roused you out of your dream.

"You raped me, nigger," she softly said.
(The shame was threading through.)
"You raped me, nigger, and what the hell   70
Do you think I'm going to do?
    What the hell,
    What the hell
Do you think I'm going to do?

"I'll tell every white man in this town.   75
I'll tell them all of my sorrow.
You got my body tonight, nigger boy.

I'll get your body tomorrow.
  Tomorrow.
  Tomorrow.   80
I'll get your body tomorrow."

And my glory but Sammy she did! She did!
And they stole you out of the jail.
They wrapped you around a cottonwood tree.
And they laughed when they heard you wail.   85
  Laughed,
  Laughed.
They laughed when they heard you wail.

And I was laughing, down at my house.
Laughing fit to kill.   90
You got what you wanted for dinner,
But brother you paid the bill.
  Brother,
  Brother,
Brother you paid the bill.   95

You paid for your dinner, Sammy boy,
And you didn't pay with money.
You paid with your hide and my heart, Sammy boy,
For your taste of pink and white honey,
  Honey,   100
  Honey.
For your taste of pink and white honey.

Oh, dig me out of my don't-despair.
Oh, pull me out of my poor-me.
Oh, get me a garment of red to wear.   105
You had it coming surely.
  Surely.
  Surely.
You had it coming surely.

TOPICS FOR CRITICAL THINKING

1. Discuss your understanding of the subject matter of racial lynching and its social context depicted in "Ballad of Pearl May Lee."

2. Describe how you imagine the character of Pearl May Lee as Brooks portrays her. What kind of relationship has she had to Sammy?

3. How do you interpret the tone that Pearl May Lee takes in her address to Sammy? Is there a tonal difference between her laughter and that of the whites who lynch Sammy?

4. What point does the poem make about race and sexuality?

TOPIC FOR CRITICAL WRITING

Consider Brooks's use of figurative language to probe the link between sexuality and consumption in such examples as "taste of pink and honey," "dark meat," "milk," and "cups of cream."

Brooks's subsequent volume *Annie Allen* (1949) and her experimental novel *Maud Martha* (1953) went to the heart of her experience as a cosmopolitan African American woman. In long-poem sequences such as "The Anniad" and "The Womanhood," Brooks explores contemporary urban identity as it is shaped by race, gender, and class forces.

Throughout the 1960s, Brooks's verse reflected on the turbulent history of the civil rights era in poems from *The Bean Eaters* (1960). One poem from that book, "A Bronzeville Mother Loiters in Mississippi. Meanwhile a Mississippi Mother Burns Bacon," is based on the violent 1955 racial murder of Emmet Till, a Chicago youth who was killed while visiting with relatives in the South. After allegedly whistling at a Caucasian woman in Money, Mississippi, Till was kidnapped and brutally beaten to death by a group of whites.

A Bronzeville Mother Loiters in Mississippi.
Meanwhile a Mississippi Mother Burns Bacon   *(1960)*

From the first it had been like a
Ballad. It had the beat inevitable. It had the blood.
A wildness cut up, and tied in little bunches,
Like the four-line stanzas of the ballads she had never quite
Understood—the ballads they had set her to, in school.   5

Herself: the milk-white maid, the "maid mild"
Of the ballad. Pursued
By the Dark Villain. Rescued by the Fine Prince.
The Happiness-Ever-After.
That was worth anything.   10
It was good to be a "maid mild."
That made the breath go fast.

Her bacon burned. She
Hastened to hide it in the step-on can, and
Drew more strips from the meat case. The eggs and sour-   15
     milk biscuits
Did well. She set out a jar
Of her new quince preserve.

. . . But there was a something about the matter of the
     Dark Villain.
He should have been older, perhaps.

The hacking down of a villain was more fun to think about   20
When his menace possessed undisputed breadth, undisputed
     height,
And a harsh kind of vice.
And best of all, when his history, was cluttered
With the bones of many eaten knights and princesses.

The fun was disturbed, then all but nullified   25
When the Dark Villain was a blackish child
Of fourteen, with eyes still too young to be dirty,
And a mouth too young to have lost every reminder
Of its infant softness.

That boy must have been surprised! For   30
These were grown-ups. Grown-ups were supposed to be
     wise.
And the Fine Prince—and that other—so tall, so broad,
     so
Grown! Perhaps the boy had never guessed
That the trouble with grown-ups was that under the
     magnificent shell of adulthood, just under,
Waited the baby full of tantrums.   35

It occurred to her that there may have been something
Ridiculous in the picture of the Fine Prince
Rushing (rich with the breadth and height and
Mature solidness whose lack, in the Dark Villain, was
     impressing her,
Confronting her more and more as this first day after the   40
     trial
And acquittal wore on) rushing
With his heavy companion to hack down (unhorsed)
That little foe.
So much had happened, she could not remember now what
     that foe had done
Against her, or if anything had been done.   45
The one thing in the world that she did know and knew
With terrifying clarity was that her composition
Had disintegrated. That, although the pattern prevailed,
The breaks were everywhere. That she could think
Of no thread capable of the necessary   50
Sew-work.

She made the babies sit in their places at the table.
Then, before calling Him, she hurried
To the mirror with her comb and lipstick. It was necessary
To be more beautiful than ever.   55

The beautiful wife.
For sometimes she fancied he looked at her as though
Measuring her. As if he considered, Had she been worth It?

Had *she* been worth the blood, the cramped cries, the little
    stuttering bravado,
The gradual dulling of those Negro eyes,   60
The sudden, overwhelming *little-boyness* in that barn?
Whatever she might feel or half-feel, the lipstick necessity
    was something apart. He must never conclude
That she had not been worth It.

He sat down, the Fine Prince, and
Began buttering a biscuit. He looked at his hands.   65
He twisted in his chair, he scratched his nose.
He glanced again, almost secretly, at his hands.
More papers were in from the North, he mumbled. More
    meddling headlines.
With their pepper-words, "bestiality," and "barbarism,"
    and
"Shocking."   70
The half-sneers he had mastered for the trial worked
    across
His sweet and pretty face.

What he'd like to do, he explained, was kill them all.
The time lost. The unwanted fame.
Still, it had been fun to show those intruders   75
A thing or two. To show that snappy-eyed mother,
That sassy, Northern, brown-black——

Nothing could stop Mississippi.

He knew that. Big Fella
Knew that.   80
And, what was so good, Mississippi knew that.
Nothing and nothing could stop Mississippi.
They could send in their petitions, and scar
Their newspapers with bleeding headlines. Their governors
Could appeal to Washington. . . .   85

"What I want," the older baby said, "is 'lasses on my jam."
Whereupon the younger baby
Picked up the molasses pitcher and threw
The molasses in his brother's face. Instantly
The Fine Prince leaned across the table and slapped   90
The small and smiling criminal.

She did not speak. When the Hand
Came down and away, and she could look at her child,
At her baby-child,
She could think only of blood.   95
Surely her baby's cheek
Had disappeared, and in its place, surely,
Hung a heaviness, a lengthening red, a red that had no end.
She shook her head. It was not true, of course.
It was not true at all. The   100
Child's face was as always, the
Color of the paste in her paste-jar.

She left the table, to the tune of the children's lamenta-
      tions, which were shriller
Than ever. She
Looked out of a window. She said not a word. *That*   105
Was one of the new Somethings—
The fear,
Tying her as with iron.

Suddenly she felt his hands upon her. He had followed her
To the window. The children were whimpering now.   110
Such bits of tots. And she, their mother,
Could not protect them. She looked at her shoulders, still
Gripped in the claim of his hands. She tried, but could not
      resist the idea
That a red ooze was seeping, spreading darkly, thickly,
      slowly,
Over her white shoulders, her own shoulders,   115
And over all of Earth and Mars.

He whispered something to her, did the Fine Prince, some-
      thing
About love, something about love and night and intention.

She heard no hoof-beat of the horse and saw no flash of
      the shining steel.

He pulled her face around to meet   120
His, and there it was, close close,

For the first time in all those days and nights.
His mouth, wet and red,
So very, very, very red,
Closed over hers.   125

Then a sickness heaved within her. The courtroom Coca-
      Cola,

The courtroom beer and hate and sweat and drone,
Pushed line a wall against her. She wanted to bear it.
But his mouth would not go away and neither would the
Decapitated exclamation points in that Other Woman's   130
  eyes.

She did not scream.
She stood there.
But a hatred for him burst into glorious flower,
And its perfume enclasped them—big,
Bigger than all magnolias.   135

The last bleak news of the ballad.
The rest of the rugged music.
The last quatrain.

TOPICS FOR CRITICAL THINKING

1. Brooks doesn't present "A Bronzeville Mother" in the form of a ballad but in a dramatic monologue told from the point of view of Till's alleged but actually perjured "victim." How do you interpret Brooks's strategy here?
2. In what ways does the Mississippi mother's sense of value and self-worth depend on Till's murder? What is the point of her question "Had she been worth it?" How does she try to be of worth to her husband, Till's murderer?
3. In what ways does the Mississippi mother identify with Till as the object of her husband's violence?
4. Examine the complex interplay of guilt, violence, and victimization that the Mississippi mother experiences as the "glorious flower" of the poem's final lines.
5. Discuss Brooks's strategy of representing that crime through its effect on the Mississippi mother rather than on the Bronzeville mother.
6. What effect does Till's murder have on the poem's narrator, and how does she feel implicated in her husband's violence?

TOPIC FOR CRITICAL WRITING

In the opening sentence of her poem, Brooks writes that "From the first it had been like a / Ballad." Compare the themes of race, sexuality, and violence in this poem with that of "Ballad of Pearl May Lee."

Brooks's career took a decisive turn in 1967 after she attended the Second Black Writers' Conference at Fisk University. At Fisk, she was impressed by the energy, talent, and political commitment of the new generation of writers such as Amiri Baraka, John Killens, David Llorens, and Ron Milner in the Black Aesthetic Movement. "First, I was aware of a general energy," Brooks has said of that moment, "an electricity, in look, walk, speech, gesture of the young blackness I saw all about me." Soon, Brooks began to show the influence of such younger writers as Don L. Lee (Haki Madhubuti) and Carolyn Rodgers in featuring a black expressive style based, as Rodgers defined it, on "signifying, teachin/rappin, covers-off, spaced, bein, love, shoutin, jazz, du-wah, and pyramid" styles. Concerning that politicized period of her life Brooks has written,

> 1966. 1967. 1968. Years of explosion. In those years a young black with pen in hand responded not to pretty sunsets and the lapping of lake water but to the speech of physical riot and spiritual rebellion. . . . Literary rhythms altered! Sometimes the literature seemed to issue from pens dipped in, *stabbed* in, writhing blood.

Brooks's next volume *In the Mecca*—published in 1968, the year Brooks succeeded Carl Sandburg as the Poet Laureate of Illinois—explored the tenement life of the Mecca building in Southside Chicago and the subculture of "Gang Girls" in "The Blackstone Rangers." In addition, she also included homages to slain civil rights leaders such as Malcolm X and Medgar Evers. Importantly, with her 1969 volume *Riot*, Brooks shifted to an Afro-American publisher, Dudley Randall's Broadside Press, leaving Harper and Row, which would publish only one more of her volumes, *The World of Gwendolyn Brooks* (1971). Subsequent volumes such as *Beckonings* (1975), *To Disembark* (1981), *Blacks* (1987), and *Children Coming Home* (1991) build on Brooks's foundational celebration of both the heroic and mundane lives of black people in America and around the globe from Chicago to Johannesburg.

Brooks remained active in publishing and performing well into the mid-1990s. In 1995 she published *Report from Part Two*. Until her death at age 83 in December 2000, Brooks offered what she called "an evocative translation of the materials of the world."

Poems for Further Reading and Critical Writing

GWENDOLYN BROOKS *(1917–2000)*

piano after war   *(1945)*

On a snug evening I shall watch her fingers,
Cleverly ringed, declining to clever pink,
Beg glory from the willing keys. Old hungers
Will break their coffins, rise to eat and thank.
And music, warily, like the golden rose
That sometimes after sunset warms the west,   5
Will warm that room, persuasively suffuse
That room and me, rejuvenate a past.
But suddenly, across my climbing fever
Of proud delight—a multiplying cry.
A cry of bitter dead men who will never   10
Attend a gentle maker of musical joy.

Vasily Kandinsky, *Composition vi* (1913)

Charles Henry Demuth, *I Saw the Figure Five in Gold* (1928)

Andy Warhol, *Marilyn Monroe (Twenty Times)* (1962)

The Chicago Women's Graphics Collective, Boycott Lettuce and Grapes (c. 1970)

Pieter Brueghel, *Landscape with the Fall of Icarus* (1558)

Botticelli, *The Birth of Venus* (1485)

Raphael, *An Allegory: Vision of a Knight* (1504)

Michelangelo, *Leda and the Swan* (1530)

William Blake, Illuminated manuscript of "The Lamb" (1789)

Dante Gabriel Rossetti, *The Girlhood of Mary Virgin* (1848–1849)

Samuel Bak, *Thou Shalt Not Kill* (1978)

Then my thawed eye will go again to ice.
And stone will shove the softness from my face.

TOPICS FOR CRITICAL THINKING

1. Consider Brooks's title and how it frames the dramatic action of "piano after war."
2. Brooks begins her poem with a revival of past hungers and hopes. Discuss her use of figurative language to depict that rejuvenation in the poem's octave, or first eight lines.
3. How do you interpret what happens to the speaker's psychological state in the poem's sestet? Examine the ways in which the poem stages that temporal difference in the contrast between the opening's "musical joy" versus the closing's "multiplying cry."

TOPIC FOR CRITICAL WRITING

Composed in the form of the Shakespearean sonnet, "piano after war" signals the contrast between the present and past in the movement from the first eight lines (octave) to the last six (sestet). Discuss the ways in which the poem reverses the movement of rejuvenation in line nine.

kitchenette building   *(1945)*

We are things of dry hours and the involuntary plan,
Grayed in, and gray. "Dream" makes a giddy sound, not strong
Like "rent," "feeding a wife," "satisfying a man."

But could a dream send up through onion fumes
Its white and violet, fight with fried potatoes   5
And yesterday's garbage ripening in the hall,
Flutter, or sing an aria down these rooms

Even if we were willing to let it in,
Had time to warm it, keep it very clean,
Anticipate a message, let it begin?   10

We wonder. But not well! not for a minute!
Since Number Five is out of the bathroom now,
We think of lukewarm water, hope to get in it.

TOPICS FOR CRITICAL THINKING

1. How do you imagine the speaker of the poem's second-person plural *we* voice who opens "kitchenette building."
2. What is a kitchenette building? Describe your sense of the poem's setting as Brooks depicts it through her vivid imagery.

Discuss the tension in the poem between reality and the imagination, the latter represented in the figure of the dream. What might the dream refer to? How is it deferred by everyday life as rendered in the poem's ending?

Jessie Mitchell's Mother   *(1960)*

Into her mother's bedroom to wash the ballooning body.
"My mother is jelly-hearted and she has a brain of jelly:
Sweet, quiver-soft, irrelevant. Not essential.
Only a habit would cry if she should die.
A pleasant sort of fool without the least iron. . . .   5
Are you better, mother, do you think it will come today?"
The stretched yellow rag that was Jessie's Mitchell's mother
Reviewed her. Young, and so thin, and so straight.
So straight! as if nothing could ever bend her.
But poor men would bend her, and doing things with poor men,   10
Being much in bed, and babies would bend her over,
And the rest of things in life that were for poor women,
Coming to them grinning and pretty with intent to bend and to kill.
Comparisons shattered her heart, ate at her bulwarks:
The shabby and the bright: she, almost hating her daughter,   15
Crept into an old sly refuge: "Jessie's black
And her way will be black, and jerkier even than mine.
Mine, in fact, because I was lovely, had flowers
Tucked in the jerks, flowers were here and there. . . ."
She revived for the moment settled and dried-up triumphs,   20
Forced perfume into old petals, pulled up the droop
Refueled
Triumphant long-exhaled breaths.
Her exquisite yellow youth. . . .

TOPICS FOR CRITICAL THINKING

1. How does Jessie Mitchell regard her mother? How would you characterize the relationship between mother and daughter in the poem?
2. What does Jessie Mitchell's mother think of her daughter?
3. Discuss the ways in which Brooks generates dramatic tension in the poem by narrating the action from both the daughter's and mother's differing points of view.

TOPIC FOR CRITICAL WRITING

In what ways does race complicate the common class position of poverty that mother and daughter share in the poem? How does the mother's memory of her "yellow youth" pit her against Jessie's blackness?

We Real Cool   *(1960)*

The Pool Players.
Seven at the Golden Shovel.

We real cool. We
Left school. We

Lurk late. We
Strike straight. We

Sing sin. We   5
Thin gin. We

Jazz June. We
Die soon.

TOPICS FOR CRITICAL THINKING

1. Discuss how you imagine the lives of the players Brooks portrays in "We Real
   Cool." Brooks published "We Real Cool" in 1960; how would you portray these
   types of characters today?
2. Discuss the ways in which Brooks's rhythms and her pattern of enjambment mimic
   the sounds and action of an actual pool hall.

TOPIC FOR CRITICAL WRITING

Just how "cool" are the players in Brooks's poem? How does the poem's title and its closing create ironic distance on the codes of hipness that these players live by and die for?

Gang Girls   *(1968)*

A Rangerette

Gang Girls are sweet exotics.
Mary Ann
uses the nutrients of her orient,
but sometimes sighs for Cities of blue and jewel
beyond her Ranger rim of Cottage Grove.   5
(Bowery Boys, Disciples, Whip-Birds will
dissolve no margins, stop no savory sanctities.)

Mary is
a rose in a whiskey glass.

Mary's   10
Februaries shudder and are gone. Aprils
fret frankly, lilac hurries on.
Summer is a hard irregular ridge.
October looks away.
And that's the Year!   15
                    Save for her bugle-love.
Save for the bleat of not-obese devotion.

Save for Somebody Terribly Dying, under
the philanthropy of robins. Save for her Ranger
bringing   20
an amount of rainbow in a string-drawn bag.
"Where did you get the diamond?" Do not ask:
but swallow, straight, the spirals of his flask
and assist him at your zipper; pet his lips
and help him clutch you.   25

Love's another departure.
Will there be any arrivals, confirmations?
Will there be gleaning?

Mary, the Shakedancer's child
from the rooming-flat, pants carefully, peers at   30
her laboring lover. . . .
                    Mary! Mary Ann!
Settle for sandwiches! settle for stocking caps!
for sudden blood, aborted carnival,
the props and niceties of non-loneliness—   35
the rhymes of Leaning.

TOPICS FOR CRITICAL THINKING

1. Brooks calls the gang girls "sweet exotics." Discuss the ways in which she depicts
   their exotic, teen identities. How, for example, do you interpret Brooks's metaphoric portrait of Mary as "a rose in a wine glass"?
2. What role does sexuality play in defining the gang girls' identities?
3. What questions does Brooks put to the gang girls, and what advice would she im-
   part to Mary Ann in the poem's final stanza?

TOPIC FOR CRITICAL WRITING

Compare and contrast Brooks's representations of urban youth culture in "We Real
Cool" and "Gang Girls."

Boy Breaking Glass

(1968)

To Marc Crawford
from whom the commission

Whose broken window is a cry of art
(success, that winks aware
as elegance, as a treasonable faith)
is raw: is sonic: is old-eyed première.
Our beautiful flaw and terrible ornament.   5
Our barbarous and metal little man.

"I shall create! If not a note, a hole.
If not an overture, a desecration."

Full of pepper and light
and Salt and night and cargoes.   10

"Don't go down the plank
if you see there's no extension.
Each to his grief, each to
his loneliness and fidgety revenge.

Nobody knew where I was and now I am no longer there."   15

The only sanity is a cup of tea.
The music is in minors.

Each one other
is having different weather.

"It was you, it was you who threw away my name!   20
And this is everything I have for me."

Who has not Congress, lobster, love, luau,
the Regency Room, the Statue of Liberty,
runs. A sloppy amalgamation.
A mistake.   25
A cliff.
A hymn, a snare, and an exceeding sun.

TOPICS FOR CRITICAL THINKING

1. "Boy Breaking Glass" is about a juvenile delinquent who vandalizes property, but
   how does that label fail to account for the complexity that Brooks discovers in her
   characterization of this urban youth?

2. Brooks defines the "Boy Breaking Glass" through the figure of oxymoron, or the combining of opposites (see Chapter 7). In addition to such coinages as "treasonable faith," what other pairs of opposites and contradictory phrasings does Brooks present in the poem?

TOPIC FOR CRITICAL WRITING

What relation does Brooks draw between art and crime in the poem? How does the boy's act of "desecration" protest his marginalization from the centers of civic, class, and racial privilege?

Ulysses   *(1991)*

Religion

At home we pray every morning, we
get down on our knees in a circle,
holding hands, holding Love,
and we sing Hallelujah.

Then we go into the World.   5

Daddy *speeds,* to break bread with his Girl Friend.
Mommy's a Boss. And a lesbian.
(She too has a nice Girl Friend.)

My brothers and sisters and I come to school.
We bring knives pistols bottles, little boxes, and cans.   10

We talk to the man who's cool at the playground gate.
Nobody Sees us, nobody stops our sin.

Our teachers feed us geography.
We spit it out in a hurry.

Now we are coming home.   15

At home, we pray every evening, we
get down on our knees in a circle,
holding hands, holding Love.

And we sing Hallelujah.

TOPICS FOR CRITICAL THINKING

1. Discuss Brooks's ironic reflections on contemporary family life in "Ulysses." How does Brooks's poem complicate and defamiliarize our stereotypical images of the traditional nuclear family?
2. Brooks's dramatic persona is one of twenty other child narrators from her volume *Children Coming Home*. But Ulysses is also the Roman name for the Greek hero Odysseus of Homer's epic poem the *Odyssey*. How do you think that heroic allusion functions in the poem?

TOPIC FOR CRITICAL WRITING

What does Brooks gain from narrating the poem from the child's point of view? How might she have told the family's story from one or both of the parent's perspectives?

Critical Perspective: On Gwendolyn Brooks and Poetic Form

"'[K]itchenette building' steps past façade into an apartment. Taking an Eliotic wryness from 'The Hollow Men' Brooks begins, 'We are things of dry hours and the involuntary plan.' The Latinate verbal tendency, favored by Eliot, is suggested by 'involuntary,' but gives way immediately to terse phrasing that evokes the local scene. Irregular rhyme, slant rhyme, and meter move toward pentameter. The thirteen lines present a kitchenette milieu where things incline askew. Nothing works well: yesterday's garbage remains 'ripening in the hall'; patience is rewarded by tepid water in the communal bathroom on each floor ('We think of lukewarm water, hope to get in it').

"The poem poses the question of dreams deferred, the 'raisin in the sun' that Langston Hughes feared they would become. The poet-narrator wonders whether aspiration can survive its fight with 'onion fumes' and 'fried potatoes' and the entire constellation of poverty. Colors of the dream are 'white' and 'violet.' Brooks has commented that the colors were chosen for their 'delicacy,' and that, although dreams can be nightmares, she preferred to deal with them in the poem as 'lovely lightsome things.' White is partly ironic. Violet, color of the flower that figures in the tenth sonnet of 'Gay Chaps at the Bar,' is a solitary flower, honeyed, self-pollinating. The speaker doubts that art, 'an aria' sung by the dream, can survive its physical habitation.

"From the interior view of the staid 'old-marrieds' and 'kitchenette,' Brooks probes deeper. '[T]he mother' is a dramatic monologue on abortion, a controversial topic then, as now. She comments: 'Hardly your crowned and praised and "customary" Mother; but a Mother not unfamiliar, who decides that *she*, rather than her World, will kill her children. The decision is not nice, not simple, and the emotional consequences are neither nice nor simple.'

"The poet employs full rhyme with a touch of slant in this thirty-two-line poem, very irregularly metered. The first stanza rhymes five couplets; the second alternates rhyme in the first six lines, then continues the couplet pattern. The meter, rolling insistent, often anapestic, conveys the profound agitation of the speaker. Tonal control, epecially in the first stanza, heightens tension. The mother begins rhetorically. 'Abortions will not let you forget,' addressing the reader/listener in impersonal second person. She reviews the loss judiciously: the children will not be neglected; she will not be burdened. But during the second stanza, her defenses fall away: 'I have heard in the voices of the wind the voices of my dim killed children.' The woman then justifies herself to the aborted children, confessing that her 'crime' was not 'deliberate.' She wanted to shield them from a painful existence. She loved them all, she insists, the last line univerbal, emphatic: 'All.'"

—D. H. Melhem, from *Gwendolyn Brooks:*
Poetry and the Heroic Voice (1987)

Critical Perspective: On Gwendolyn Brooks and Dramatic Form

"Part of Brooks's modernity lies in her use of dramatic modes in her poetry. Focus on character as expressed through the spoken, performative voice allows for indirection, complexity of narration, and obfuscation of poetic statement. Several of the greatest poems in American literature, including Wallace Stevens's 'Sunday Morning,' Pound's 'Hugh Selwyn Mauberley,' and Eliot's 'Gerontion,' are classic examples of modernist interweaving of portraiture, narration, and dramatic voice. This intermixture of modes allows the poets to demand active complicity between their reader and their poem until the full import of their poetic statement emerges as a construct put together by the reader from various indications dispersed throughout the text.

"If the way in which Brooks handles character is one index of her modernity and her aesthetic engagement, her choice of character has always indicated the fundamentally social context of her work, even at its most difficult. Thus, it seems necessary to distinguish between character and persona in her work. Brooks's characters are largely taken from the dispossessed, the unheroic residents of America's urban ghettos (named, by custom, 'Bronzeville'). These characters dramatize a microcosm of black urban life—its struggles, its small triumphs, and its unheroic survival. By focusing on them, Brooks has been able to engage, often indirectly, some of the major social issues of her time, including war and peace, racial justice, and the plight of women. Yet this commitment to social issues is often disguised by her modernist use of personae. For example, Brooks's sonnet series, 'Gay Chaps at the Bar,' from her first publication, *A Street in Bronzeville*, is both a tour de force technically and an exploration of America's unequal treatment of the black soldiers during World War II. Similarly, her unusual ballads on the death of Emmett Till in her third volume, *The Bean Eaters*, offer protest subject matter in an innovative narrative form. Again, her gallery of female portraits, from the practical Hattie Scott to the 'crazy woman who sings in November' instead of May, stresses varieties of heroism and antiheroism in women's responses to difficulties they confront; yet the complexity of their responses may not be fully apparent, particularly to the uninitiated reader who is unable to meet the demands placed upon him or her by Brooks's modernist use of nuance, ellipsis, and allusion.

"The way in which Brooks handles her characters is only one index of her modernity. Brooks's modernity also permeates her poetry in its mixture of forms and variations on forms (ballads, sonnets, sonnet-ballads, mock-epics); in its juxtaposition of 'high' and 'low' styles; and in its rich prosodic texture, including the use of varied meters, creative enjambment, melisma, and indeterminate modification. The centrality of the concrete as opposed to the abstract and Brooks's skillful deployment of image and the visual line are equally important clues of her modernity. Finally, Brooks's objective rather than subjective authorial stance creates texts in which her personality seems largely effaced. In recent years, however, Brooks seems to be moving away from the objective voice of modernity to a more personal yet public voice that is, at turns, elegiac and celebratory, reminiscent of her more recent contemporaries, Robert Lowell and Theodore Roethke."

—Maria K. Mootry, from "Down the Whirlwind of Good Rage: An Introduction to Gwendolyn Brooks" (1987)

Critical Perspective: On Voice and "We Real Cool"

"For more than three decades now, Gwendolyn Brooks has been writing poetry that reflects a particular historical order, often close to the heart of the public event, but the dialectic that is engendered between the event and her reception of it is, perhaps, one of the more subtle confrontations of criticism. We cannot always say with grace or ease that there is a direct correspondence between the issues of her poetry and her race and sex, nor does she make the assertion necessary at every step of our reading. Black and female are basic and inherent in her poetry. The critical question is *how* they are said. Here is what the poet has to say about her own work: 'My aim, in my next future, is to write poems that will somehow successfully "call" . . . all black people: black people in taverns, black people in alleys, black people in gutters, schools, offices, factories, prisons, the consulate; I wish to reach black people in pulpits, black people in mines, on farms, on thrones; *not* always to "teach"—I shall wish often to entertain, to illumine. My newish voice will not be an imitation of the contemporary young black voice, which I so admire, but an extending adaptation of today's G. B. voice.'

" 'Today's G. B. voice' is one of the most complex on the American scene precisely because Brooks refuses to make easy judgments. In fact, her disposition to preserve judgment is directly mirrored in a poetry of cunning, laconic surprise. Any descriptive catalog can be stretched and strained in her case: I have tried 'uncluttered,' 'clean,' 'robust,' 'ingenious,' 'unorthodox,' and in each case a handful of poems will fit. This method of grading and cataloging, however, is essentially busywork, and we are still left with the main business. What in this poetry is stunning and evasive?

"To begin with, one of Brooks's most faithfully anthologized poems, 'We Real Cool,' illustrates the wealth of implication that the poet can achieve in a very spare poem:

> We real cool. We
> Left school. We
>
> Lurk late. We
> Strike straight. We
>
> Sing sin. We
> Thin gin. We
>
> Jazz June. We
> Die soon.

The simplicity of the poem is stark to the point of elaborateness. Less than lean, it is virtually coded. Made up entirely of monosyllables and end-stops, the poem is no non-sense at all. Gathered in eight units of three-beat lines, it does not necessarily invite inflection, but its persistent bump on 'we' suggests waltz time to my ear. If the reader chooses to render the poem that way, she runs out of breath, or trips her tongue, but it seems that such 'breathlessness' is exactly required of dudes hastening toward their death. Deliberately subverting the romance of sociological pathos, Brooks presents the pool players— 'seven in the golden shovel'—in their own words and time. They make no excuse for themselves and apparently invite no one else to do so. The poem is their situation as *they* see it. In eight (could be nonstop) lines, here is their total destiny. Perhaps comic geniuses, they could well drink to this poem, making it a drinking/revelry song."

—Hortense J. Spillers, from "Gwendolyn the Terrible:
Propositions on Eleven Poems" (1987)

17

Critical Perspectives

A Casebook on Chicano/a Poetry

Chicano literature represents the rich cultural heritage of what has become the fastest growing population group in the United States. In the broadest meaning of the term, *Chicano* refers to people of Mexican descent who live in the United States. Chicanos make up about 66 percent of the total Hispanic American community, which includes people of South and Central American, Cuban, and Puerto Rican origins. Together, these Hispanic American communities constitute more than 12 percent of the entire U.S. population.

But understanding Chicano heritage requires a more complex definition, one that extends beyond simple demographics. Chicano experience migrates across class, linguistic, national, and racial boundaries. The Chicano heritage—its music, cuisine, art, and language—is a vital part of the larger American culture. What defines the Chicano community, however, is neither static nor fixed; instead, Chicano identity entails a dynamic process of cultural cross-fertilization. Even the word *Chicano* signifies in ways that are less settled than they are contested; for example, its verbal coinage is split by gender in the feminine form *Chicana*, which designates the difference of women's place in the Mexican American community. Chicano speaking itself comprises a range of dialects mixing not just Spanish and English but also a vernacular patois made up of Mayan, Nahuatl, Native American, "Texan," and African American expressive communities. Consequently, as Chicano writer Guillermo Gómez-Peña explains, Chicano identity is more de-centered than self-possessed: "My 'identity,'" he writes, "now possesses multiple repertoires: I am Mexican but I am also Chicano and Latin American. At the border they call me *chilango* or *mexiquillo*; in Mexico City it's *pocho* or *norteño*; and in Europe it's *sudacap*. . . . My wife Emilia is Anglo-Italian, but speaks Spanish with an Argentine accent, and together we walk amid the rubble of the Tower of Babel of our American postmodernity."

Contemporary Chicano poetry reaches back to the 1960s civil rights era with El Movimiento, the Chicano Movement of the 1960s. Poetry in that context protested the oppressive social conditions and civic marginality of Chicano people. Moreover, Chicano verse gave an empowering voice to "La Raza"—a new, imagined vision of the people in political solidarity. The celebration of civic heroes of El Movimiento derived, in part, from the Mexican *corridos* or folk ballads that, in turn, are influenced by older European romance and other narrative forms. The movement's mission to spread the Chicano heritage stemmed to some extent from the Catholic Church, which throughout the nineteenth century employed music, song, and verse as ways of instructing and acculturating Native Americans and Mexicans into Hispanic and American contexts.

At the beginning of the twentieth century, this tradition was appropriated for indigenous political ends by such poets as Arculiano Barela, who composed "El estraique de 1910," a poem on the workers' strike that resulted in the infamous Ludlow massacre of union coal miners in Colorado. Barela's poem combined oral elements of the *corridos* with the instructional aims coming from the church and Anglo-Hispanic written traditions of Latin America. Poetry's power to mobilize political change is witnessed in Jimmy Santiago Baca's elegy "Mi Tío Baca El Poeta De Socorro," written to his uncle Antonio Ce De Baca "whose poems roused *la gente* / to demand their land rights back."

The decisive year for the emerging literature of contemporary Chicano resistance was 1965 when, according to Rafael Jesús González, "the workers in the vineyards of Delano declared themselves on strike under the leadership of César Chávez and the banner of Our Lady of Guadalupe." The agitational tradition of Hispanic American workers' poetry became a resource for publications of El Movimiento such as *El Malcriado*, the organ of the United Farm Workers campaign, and *El Grito del Norte*, the voice of the Federal Alliance of Land Grants or Alianza Federal de Mercedes (see color insert).

In translating the heroic dimensions of the *corridos* to the print medium, Chicano poets largely chose to abandon the rhyme schemes and ballad forms of the oral tradition in favor of free verse composition (see Chapter 9). A foundational text for contemporary Chicano verse is Rodolfe Corky Gonzales's *I Am Joaquín* (1967), which mixed English and Spanish languages, archetypal symbols, and popular icons. The desire for an indigenous homeland first assumed the dimensions of pre-Colombian mythology in *Floricanto en Aztlán* by the poet Alurista. Not just a timeless vision of the ancient past, the mythic homeland of Aztlán also functioned as a metaphor for social and political solidarity. "The myth of Aztlán," Alurista has written, "as I saw it, in the '60s was just a way to identify a people, a land, and a consciousness that said, 'Struggle, do not be afraid'." The search for mythic origins went hand-in-hand with a new emphasis on racial pride. Race took on cosmic proportions in José Vasconcelos's formulation of La Raza Cósmica that envisioned the emergence of a New Chicano as "a pluralistic man, a universal man, combining the racial strains and cultures of the entire world in his own person."

The poetic technique of crosscutting such deep, mythological, and racial narratives with images drawn from popular culture became a hallmark of the Chicano style that mixed high art with lowbrow spectacle, English with Spanish, Mexican with American cultural signs. Similarly, portmanteau terms— invented words or neologisms combining the sounds of two or more terms—and mixed linguistic constructions also made up the signature style of Chicano discourse. According to Carmen Tafolla's essay in *A Gift of Tongues: Critical Challenges in Contemporary American Poetry* (1987):

["Lexical creations"] sprang from an awareness of our own dually bilingual existence and from the discovery of new worlds of thought and literature—the Mayan, Aztec, Native American, and so forth. Formerly we would, in our daily lives, hispanicize English realities: "I missed" would resurrect in Spanish as "*mistié*," "I flunked" would expand the traditional lexicon with "*flonquié*," and the "big, old thing" ending "*azo*" would turn a party in an English sentence into a *parozo* in a Spanish conversation. . . . Acutely aware of the sounds of English, we would accent our Spanish to a mock-Anglicized "free holes" (for *frijoles*) and then play the reverse by accenting our English with the sounds of Spanish: *pino borra* for "peanut butter."

Such verbal and cultural crossings define the poetics, for example, of *el sol y los de abajo* by Jose Montoya and Raul Salinas's "Trip Through the Mind Jail," as well as the pronounced surrealist forms of Ricardo García and the ethnic hilarity of Jose Antonio Burciaga's poetry.

The early agenda of Chicano verse reflected its agitational aims of conceiving and celebrating global, universal, and public forms of social emancipation from the legacy of colonial rule in the United States. But Chicano poetry quickly expanded its focus beyond the national context to consider the transnational situation of La Raza (the People) of Mexico, Central and South America. More recent forms of Chicano poetry have shifted the focus from the agenda of Chicano national unity to more regionally specific, local, personal, and intrapersonal themes that reflect the micropolitics of gender relations, sexuality, and a contradictory mélange of racial, national, and class experiences. Beginning in the mid-1970s with Margarita Cota-Cárdenas's *Noches despertando inconciencias*, Angela de Hoyos's *Arise, Chicano* and *Chicano Poems for the Barrio*, and Bernice Zamora's *Restless Serpents*, Chicana poets celebrated the power of women's experience in mythological tropes such as *la tierra* (the earth as nurturer, healer, and source of creativity) and the serpent (as figure for the cyclic rather than linear understanding of time, change, and transformation). Moreover, female poets such as Pat Mora and Margarita Cota-Cárdenas recovered heroic feminine personae such as La Llorona, La Virgen de Guadalupe, and La Adelita to rewrite male historicism from a decidedly feminist point of view.

Exploring women's embodied experience, writers such as Alma Villanueva, Carmen Tafolla, and Vangie Vigil dealt explicitly with the disturbing realities of Chicana gender, racial and class oppression; the persistence of sexual and psychic violence; the ever-present threat of rape; and other atrocities perpetrated against women. Like Sylvia Plath and Anne Sexton before her, Villanueva accepts but recodes the role of "madwoman" and "witch" in speaking out against the injustice of contemporary social arrangements. In this regard, poetry serves as a resource against those who would judge and condemn her, as she describes in "The Last Words":

calling me sentimental, bitter, minor, emotionally ill
    [and ah, possessed].

they do not know I burn, self/imposed
in a fire of my

own making
my witches' secret: the poem as
my witness

this cannot be destroyed.
they burn in the heart, long after
the witch is dead.

Increasingly, the poetry of Chicano witness has received both popular
and academic recognition. Poets such as Orlando Romírez, Lorna Dee Cer-
vantes, Gary Soto, and Alberto Ríos have all won major academic awards as
they pursue careers that partake of life both in La Raza and the literary world.
Complicating the political unity of the early Chicano Movement, contemporary Chicano poets do not necessarily presume to represent the voice of an
entire community. According to the Chicano scholar Bruce-Novoa, "they no
longer feel the need to speak as political prophets. [T]his makes the recent poetry much harder to study and categorize, much harder to reduce for the sake
of students and dabblers from other cultural milieu—but for that very reason
much more dynamic, healthy, and interesting."

Poems for Further Reading and Critical Writing

PAT MORA   *(b. 1942)*

Agua negra   *(1995)*

I see her shadow
rocking in the candle-
light. Wind and rain bang
wood slats, slash palm trees.
We're two women caught   5
in a storm of stories.

In the hills, rivers
leap to light, plunge
through bougainvillea
into the green hiss,   10
the island's víbora.

Water rushes
down street to shacks,
to cardboard rooms. Agua negra oozes
between small toes   15
of shoeless children.

"I hear their whimpers,
'¡Mamá! ¡Mamá!'
from across the street,"
her voice begins its spin,   20
a worn familiar record,
the voice of tías and abuelitas,
storytellers.

"Ay los blanquitos
y su dinero.   25
Their soft hands hunger
for amber and our pink mangoes,
not the tugging
pleas, 'Look, mees. Buy, mees.'
Every afternoon   30
los policías grabbed
mis muchachos, threw them
into the police yard,
kicked their toothpick ribs.
No shade, no water.   35

'¡Mamá! ¡Mamá!' they scream,
and a club thuds a skull.
Glare scorches their eyes and throats
until turistas y su dinero sail,
hands and hearts heavy with bundles.   40

'¡Mamá! ¡Mamá!'

'¡Por Dios! Son niños,'
I'd yell, but they baked them
in that horno,
baked them to their bones, pobrecitos.   45

I bought a little house
a hiding place.
Ay, que tristeza,"
she rocks, shakes her head,
"It's our country,   50
and we have to hide."

Wind runs round, around
the widow's hushed home
like children chase themselves
in rain, mouths open,   55
ready to swallow
what falls from the sky.

Dear Frida°

(1995)

1

We're stuck on you, on thorns you press
into your swan neck, black swan, niñita
limping, stubborn, withered leg.

"Frida, pata de palo. Frida, pata de palo,"
sing-sing stones to break your bones.   5

You cover the skinny ankle, skirts long
even when sweat slides down your legs
like sangre, your paint, Frida.

"Pata de palo, Frida, pata de palo."

You make us taste blood that burst   10
everywhere, bones crushed in a bus crash,
rod shoved through you pelvis to spine.

Perfect aim, your clothes ripped away,
young swan plucked clean, skin gleaming
in the sun, blood and gold, powdered gold   15

bursts into air with wheels, eggs, hair, bones
and screams, wild, when you glitter
like a mangled dancer, their screams:

"¡La bailarina, la bailarina!"

2

Round your bed, she dances round   20
your stiff white cast, your stiff white room,
La Pelona dances round your body tomb.

Clakati, clak-clak, clakati, clak-clak.

Bald Death watches surgeons carve,
below your long neck—knives, needles, cut,   25
stitch, pinch skin together, but your body falls apart.

They mold you stiff, but you slip
out head first, escape from boring ceilings through
your fingertips, through the smell of paint.

―――
Frida Kahlo (1907–1954): Mexican artist.

3

You're stuck on him, Frida, on your old fat frog,   30
your "Sapo-Rana" croaking, *Yo, yo, yo,*
into your neck, perfect aim stroking your scars

until each opens, bleeds. How his thick lips suck
on you, your Diego, immense baby bending your
crooked spine while your babies melt and slip away.   35

Clakati, clak-clak, clakati, clak-clak.

Your dolls and hungry black monkeys
curl round your neck, watch you brand
yourself, stamp Diego° right between your eyes.

We want to erase him, Frida, but we can't,   40
the man you love more than your own sad bones,
the hungry toad who likes a woman in each hand.

He is the sun, the moon. His flesh, warm dough,
surrounds you until you can't hear the pain,
his sweat sweet brandy on your nervous tongue.   45

You drink his breath heavy as a storm. Lightning
sizzles through you, pelvis to spine. His hands
stroke your hair, mold your broken pieces.

You find the ones he went to, chew lips
he kissed, hungry for some shred   50
of him, lick his smell on their willing breasts.

No others will do. "¡Chingado!" you cry
but try men, women, bite them so hard
they bleed, but always you taste Diego, Diego.

4

La Pelona Tonta dances while you paint   55
yourself, splatter sangre, smear breasts,
thighs, arms, hands, shirts, skirts, sheets white as milk.

Your paintings don't laugh like you do,
Frida, that laugh smelling of curses,
espinas flung at curdled faces.   60

---

39 *Diego Rivera (1886–1957):* Mexican muralist, husband of Frida Kahlo.

She grins, La Más Pelona, at her bones
in your mirror while you soak your scars, grins
at skulls floating white in your bath, small like soaps.

Clakati, clak-clak, clakati, clak-clak.

Your wounds are always open, Frida.   65
Why can't you hide stabs, gashes, corsets?
Why can't you vomit in private, like a lady?

                              5

Drugged, on fire, you burst into your last show
in an ambulance. You drink, sing from your bed.
You are your art, and you make us watch you die.   70

Clakati, clak-clak, clakati, clak

Frida, pata de palo, Frida, pate de palo,
we still hear, "NO!" that mangled scream, "no!"
But La Pelona says your leg has to go.

                              6

Clak. In your body slides, Frida, to its last burning,   75
bolts up in the lick of oven's hungry tongues,
hair, your hair, around your face, crackles, blazes.

JIMMY SANTIAGO BACA   *(b. 1952)*

Mi Tío Baca El Poeta De Socorro°   *(1989)*

Antonio Ce De Baca
chiseled on stone chunk gravemarker,
propped against a white wooden cross.
Dust storms faded the birth and death numbers.
Poet de Socorro,°   5
whose poems roused *la gente*
to demand their land rights back,
'til one night—that terrible night,
hooves shook your earthen-floor
one-room adobe, lantern flame   10
flickered shadowy omens on walls,
and you scrawled across the page,
"*¡Aquí vienen! ¡Aquí vienen!*

―――
Mi Tío . . . .Socorro: My Uncle Baca, the Poet of Socorro.   5 *Socorro:* Town in New Mexico on
the Rio Grande River.

Here they come!"
Hooves clawed your front yard,   15
guns glimmering blue
angrily beating at your door.

      You rose.
Black boots scurried round four adobe walls,
trampling flower beds.   20
They burst through the door.
It was a warm night, and carried the scent
of their tobacco, sulphur, and leather.
Faces masked in dusty hankies,
men wearing remnants of Rinche uniforms,   25
arms pitchforked you out,
where arrogant young boys on horses
held torches and shouted,
"Shoot the Mexican! Shoot him!"
Saliva flew from bits   30
as horses reared from you,
while red-knuckled recruits held reins tight,
drunkenly pouring whiskey over you,
kicking you up the hill by the yucca,
where you turned, and met the scream   35
of rifles with your silence.

      Your house still stands.
Black burnt tin covers window openings,
weeds grow on the dirt roof
that leans like an old man's hand   40
on a cane *viga*. . . .
I walk to the church a mile away,
a prayer on my lips bridges
years of disaster between us.
Maybe things will get better.   45
Maybe our struggle to speak and be
as we are, will come about.
For now, I drink in your spirit, Antonio,
to nourish me as I descend
into dangerous abysses of the future.   50
I came here this morning
at 4:30 to walk over my history.
Sat by the yucca, and then imagined you again,
walking up to me
face sour with tortuous hooks   55
pulling your brow down in wrinkles,
cheeks weary with defeat,
face steady with implacable dignity.
The softness in your brown eyes

said you could take no more.   60
You will speak with the angels now.
I followed behind you to the church,
your great bulky field-working shoulders
lean forward in haste
as if angels really did await us.   65
Your remorseful footsteps
in crackly weeds
sound the last time
I will hear and see you. Resolve is engraved
in each step. I want to believe   70
whatever problems we have, time will take
its course, they'll be endured and consumed.
Church slumps on a hill, somber and elegant.
After you, I firmly pull the solid core door back.
You kneel before La Virgen De Guadalupe,   75
bloody lips moving slightly,
your great gray head poised in listening,
old jacket perforated with bloody bullet holes.
I close the door, and search the prairie,
considering the words *faith*, *prayer* and *forgiveness*,   80
wishing, like you, I could believe them.

Dust-Bowl Memory   *(1986)*

for Abaskin

My ancient neighbor, Mr. Abaskin,
was born in Russia, roamed Europe,
and when the call came from America,
he boarded ship and came.
Seventy years farming this land.   5
Every morning he walks the dirt road
with his aging wife, reminding me
of two solitary mesquite trees
rooted high at the edge of a rocky cliff,
overlooking a vast canyon gorge.   10
Hands hardened, yellow claws
from farming tenderly pocket candy
in my son's pants.
He scolds his shepherd Kiki
for exciting grazing sheep or scaring   15
Rhode Island Reds. We meet every noon
by the fence where our feed is
and small talk
conditions of fields,
how he and his wife could buck   20

three hundred bales an afternoon
when they were my age.
His memory an old dust-bowl town,
he remembers who lived where
before we came, who was born to whom,   25
when Williams' Packing Company started
stealing people's cattle, when people
started locking their screen doors,
and a time when only Spanish was spoken in this valley.
"Didn't have to go to town. These Mexican folk   30
had the finest gardens in the world,
why tomatoes and chile you wouldn't believe. . . ."

Bells   *(1986)*

Bells. The word gongs my skull bone. . . .
Mamá carried me out, just born,
swaddled in hospital blanket,
from St. Vincent's in Santa Fe.
Into the evening, still drowsed   5
with uterine darkness,
my fingertips purple with new life,
cathedral bells splashed
into my blood, plunging iron hulls
into my pulse waves. Cathedral steeples,   10
amplified brooding, sonorous bells,
through narrow cobbled streets, bricked patios,
rose-trellis'd windows,
red-tiled Spanish rooftops, bells
beat my name, "Santiago! Santiago!"   15
Burning my name in black-frosted streets,
bell sounds curved and gonged deep,
ungiving, full-bellowed beats of iron on iron,
shuddering pavement Mamá walked,
quivering thick stainless panes, creaking   20
plaza shop doors, beating its gruff thuds
down alleys and dirt
passageways, past men waiting in doorways
of strange houses. Mamá carried me, past
peacocks and chickens, past the miraculous   25
stairwell winding into the choirloft, touted
in tourist brochures, *"Not one nail was used*
to build this, it clings tenaciously
together by pure prayer power, a spiraling
pinnacle of faith. . . ." And years later,   30
when I would do something wrong,
in kind reprimand Mamá would say,

"You were born of bells, more than my womb,
they speak to you in dreams.
Ay, *Mijito*,   35
you are such a dreamer!"

Choices   *(1986)*

An acquaintance at Los Alamos Labs
who engineers weapons
black x'd a mark where I live
on his office map.
Star-wars humor. . . .   5
He exchanged muddy boots
and patched jeans
for a white intern's coat
and black polished shoes.
A month ago, after butchering a gouged bull,   10
we stood on a pasture hill,
and he wondered with pained features
where money would come from
to finish his shed, plant alfalfa,
and fix his tractor.   15
Now his fingers
yank horsetail grass,
he crimps herringbone tail-seed
between teeth, and grits out words,
"Om gonna buy another tractor   20
next week. More land too."
Silence between us is gray water
let down in a tin pail
in a deep, deep well,
a silence   25
milled in continental grindings
millions of years ago.
I throw my heart
into the well, and it falls
a shimmering pebble to the bottom.   30
Words are hard
to come by. "Would have lost everything
I've worked for, not takin' the job."
His words try to
retrieve   35
my heart
from the deep well.
We walk on in silence,
our friendship
rippling away.   40

BERNICE ZAMORA   *(b. 1938)*

Notes from a Chicana "COED"   *(1977)*

To cry that the *gabacho*
is our oppressor is to shout
in abstraction, *carnal.*
He no more oppresses us
than you do now as you tell me   5
"It's the gringo who oppresses you, Babe."
You cry "The gringo is our oppressor!"
to the tune of $20,000 to $30,000
a year, brother, and I wake up
alone each morning and ask,   10
"Can I feed my children today?"

To make the day easier
I write poems about
pájaros, mariposas,
and the fragrance   15
of perfume I
smell on your collar;
you're quick to point out
that I must write
about social reality,   20
about "the gringo who
oppresses you, Babe."
And so I write about
how I worked in beet fields
as a child, about how I   25
worked as a waitress
eight hours at night to
get through high school,
about working as a
seamstress, typist, and field clerk   30
to get through college, and
about how, in graduate school
I held two jobs, seven days
a week, still alone, still asking,
"Can I feed my children today?"   35

To give meaning to my life
you make love to me in alleys,
in back seats of borrowed Vegas,
in six-dollar motel rooms
after which you talk about   40

your five children and your wife
who writes poems at home
about *pájaros, mariposas,*
and the fragrance of perfume
she smells on your collar.   45
Then you tell me how you
bear the brunt of the
gringo's oppression for me,
and how you would go
to prison for me, because   50
"The gringo is oppressing you, Babe!"

And when I mention
your G.I. Bill, your
Ford Fellowship, your
working wife, your   55
three *gabacha guisas*
then you ask me to
write your thesis,
you're quick to shout,
"Don't give that   60
Women's Lib trip, mujer,
that only divides us,
and we have to work
together for the *movimiento*
the *gabacho* is oppressing us!"   65

Oye carnal, you may as well
tell me that moon water
cures constipation, that
penguin soup prevents *crudas,*
or that the Arctic Ocean is *menudo,*   70
because we both learned in the *barrios,*
man, that pigeon shit slides easier.

Still, because of the *gabacho,*
I must write poems about
pájaros, mariposas, and the fragrance   75
of oppressing perfume I smell somewhere.

ALMA VILLANUEVA   *(b. 1944)*

Of Utterances   *(1977)*

a woman is her own
(muse)
that's the main thing.
    —ANNE SEXTON

the "White Goddess"
to white men
to poets and men of genius
    "a source of inspiration;
    a guiding genius . ."   5
that beautiful Goddess
that legendary Angel,
                        descending
    with her milky white limbs,
        full breasts, rosy at the   10
            tips with the milky
                stanzas and lyrics
                    to the touch of man:
the cunt all acceptance,   opening wide
                        to the mind of man   and   15
                giving birth to their children
    The Poem.   The Painting.   The Sculpture.

and I with my fetish for dark men.
and dislike (dis-taste) for sucking (this part's o.k.—
cocks and swallowing the salty sperm (this part's not—   20
of prose and rhymes.
we women just don't have any
dark and lovely,
                descending
"Black Gods"—   so being   25
a woman of resources
and imagination, I decided to become
my own source of inspiration;
my very own genius—
I grew my own wings, became my   30
own muse.

I decided to fly
and not
descend.

The Last Words   *(1977)*

to Anne & Sylvia
& all those that burned before them
  in Salem & other places—

  Out of the ash
  I rise with my red hair
  And I eat men like air.
            —SYLVIA PLATH

if they knew my heart
they would

if they knew my heart
they would burn

if they knew my heart   5
they would burn me

if they knew my heart
they would burn me at the

if they knew my heart
they would burn me at the stake.   10

witches' blood must flow! dry and crackle—
sink into the mother, turn to ash—
red fire/blood release the utterance—
the last words
unheard by stupid mob—   15
the hysterical mob does not like to be
reminded of their true natures—
they would like to forget women like me.
they back away, cowering, from the heat of
my love   20
my words
my blood
calling me sentimental, bitter, minor, emotionally ill
                    [and ah, possessed].

they do not know I burn, self/imposed   25
in a fire of my

own making.
my witches' secret: the poem as
my witness.

this cannot be destroyed.   30
they burn in the heart, long after
the witch is dead.

GARY SOTO   *(b. 1952)*

Mexicans Begin Jogging   *(1981)*

At the factory I worked
In the fleck of rubber, under the press
Of an oven yellow with flame,
Until the border patrol opened
Their vans and my boss waved for us to run.   5
"Over the fence, Soto," he shouted,
And I shouted that I was American.
"No time for lies," he said, and pressed
A dollar in my palm, hurrying me
Through the back door.   10

Since I was on his time, I ran
And became the wag to a short tail of Mexicans—
Ran past the amazed crowds that lined
The street and blurred like photographs, in rain.
I ran from that industrial road to the soft   15
Houses where people paled at the turn of an autumn sky.
What could I do but yell *vivas*
To baseball, milkshakes, and those sociologists
Who would clock me
As I jog into the next century   20
On the power of a great, silly grin.

The Tale of Sunlight   *(1978)*

Listen, nephew.
When I opened the cantina
At noon
A triangle of sunlight
Was stretched out   5
On the floor
Like a rug
Like a tired cat.
It flared in
From the window   10
Through a small hole

Shaped like a yawn.
Strange I thought
And placed my hand
Before the opening,   15
But the sunlight
Did not vanish.
I pulled back
The shutters
And the room glowed,   20
But this pyramid
Of whiteness
Was simply brighter.
The sunlight around it
Appeared soiled   25
Like the bed sheet
Of a borracho.°
Amazed, I locked the door,
Closed the windows.
Workers, in from   30
The fields, knocked
To be let in,
Children peeked
Through the shutters,
But I remained silent.   35
I poured a beer,
At a table
Shuffled a pack
Of old cards
And watched it   40
Cross the floor,
Hang on the wall
Like a portrait
Like a calendar
Without numbers.   45
When a fly settled
In the sunlight
And disappeared
In a wreath of smoke,
I tapped it with the broom,   50
Spat on it.
The broom vanished.
The spit sizzled.
It is the truth, little one.
I stood eye to blank eye   55
And by misfortune

---

27 *borracho:* Drunkard.

This finger
This pink stump
Entered the sunlight,
Snapped off   60
With a dry sneeze,
And fell to the floor
As a gift
To the ants
Who know me   65
For what I gave.

SANDRA CISNEROS　*(b. 1954)*

Little Clown, My Heart　　　　　　　　　　　　　　*(1994)*

Little clown, my heart,
Spangled again and lopsided,
Handstands and Peking pirouettes,
Backflips snapping open like
A carpenter's hinged ruler,   5

Little gimp-footed hurray,
Paper parasol of pleasures,
Fleshy undertongue of sorrows,
Sweet potato plant of my addictions,

Acapulco cliff-diver *corazón*,°   10
Fine as an obsidian dagger,
Alley-oop and here we go
Into the froth, my life,
Into the flames!

TOPICS FOR CRITICAL THINKING

1. "Agua negra" means black water; what contradictions does Pat Mora's title set up in the connotations of blackness and water? How do both terms simultaneously take on positive and negative connotations in the work?

2. Consider the ways in which Bernice Zamora's ironic dramatic monologue in "Notes from a Chicana 'COED'" points to the clashing politics of class and gender in El Movimiento. How do you imagine the poem's addressee? In what ways does poetry allow Zamora to reverse the power imbalance between Chicano men and women in order to have the last word?

---

10 *corazón:* Heart.

3. Explore the ways in which Alma Villanueva rewrites the angelic and demonic stereotypes of women to claim an alternative feminist mythology of empowerment in "Of Utterance" and "The Last Words."

4. Investigate the ways in which Soto's line length contributes to the narrative suspense of "The Tale of Sunlight." Is it clear what exactly the mysterious triangle of sunlight symbolizes in the poem?

TOPICS FOR CRITICAL WRITING

1. In addition to suffering from childhood polio, Mexican painter Frida Kahlo was also hit by a bus at the age of eighteen. Her injuries were severe—breaks to her spinal column, collarbone, ribs, pelvis, right leg, and right foot—and she spent over a month in a plaster cast. A chronic pain victim throughout her life, Kahlo nevertheless enjoyed a successful career as a painter and had a passionate and, at times, stormy marriage to the Mexican muralist Diego Rivera. In "Dear Frida," "La Pelona," as Mora explains in a note to this poem, "was feisty Frida's name for death." What relation does Mora draw in the poem between death, trauma, and artistic creativity?

2. Of mixed Chicano and Apache blood lines, Jimmy Santiago Baca lost his father at an early age to alcoholism, while his mother was murdered by her new husband after she remarried. Baca's early years were marked by homelessness, drug and alcohol abuse, and eventually prison, solitary confinement, and shock therapy. Poetry became a means of survival, however, and the relation between violence and creative resistance is a constant feature of his work. In what ways does Baca's elegy to his uncle, also a poet and victim of violence, take on the ancestral values of "faith, prayer, and forgiveness"? To what extent does the poem's ironic turn mark certain limits to these ideals?

3. Examine how Gary Soto complicates Chicano national identity in "Mexicans Begin Jogging."

4. Consider the metaphors through which Sandra Cisneros addresses her "heart" in her apostrophe to "Little Clown, My Heart."

18

Critical Perspectives

A Casebook on Native American Poetry

Native American culture reaches back some 30,000 years on the combined North and South American continents of what has been called "Turtle Island." In the United States, between 4 and 8 million native peoples once existed in over 500 ancient cultures, each with its own distinct language. Today, some 550 tribal governments preside over more than 300 tribal groups. While about half of native peoples live on approximately 53 million acres of reservation lands, about 1 million reside in urban areas.

Complicating these demographics, however, is the question of what defines Native American identity and literature. One marker is the blood-quantum of one's descent lines that federal and tribal governments use to determine membership rolls variously according to race. But according to Native American scholar Geary Hobson, whether one embodies a full, half, quarter, or even a trace of Native American blood heritage is not as significant as the degree of one's social commitment to and cultural identification with the Native American community. In his introduction to *The Remembered Earth: An Anthology of Native American Literature* (1991), Hobson writes:

> [A] person is judged as Native American because of how he or she views the world, his or her views about land, home, family, culture, etc. There are, I think, no easy answers. I do believe, however, that John Ross, the one-eighth blood Cherokee chief (with seven-eighths Scottish blood), who fought arduously against the removal of his people into Indian Territory, was more "Indian" than John Ridge, the seven-eighths Cherokee, who collaborated with Andrew Jackson's henchmen, selling out his people.

Similarly, what constitutes Native American literature is also difficult to determine. Native American poetry is rooted in the oral traditions of ritual, ceremony, and mythic storytelling that have a sacred relation to tribal life and its connections to ongoing natural and supernatural processes. The visionary Lakota medicine man Hehaka Sapa (Black Elk) described himself as a "word sender" because as a *wicasa wakan* or "holy man" his role, according to Kenneth Lincoln, was to release through language "the spirit in things to move through this world." "Black Elk," Lincoln writes in *Native American Renaissance* (1983), "imagined language in projective flight, as in the arrowed movements

Turtle Island around 1500

of spirits from one place of sacred origin into worldly form." Indeed, in Hopi tradition, storytelling is such a powerful activity that it takes place primarily during the winter solstice month of December, a time of transition from the old year to the new. "[T]he association of storytelling with the winter solstice," writes Native American critic Andrew Wiget, "may stem from a belief that telling a story is a creative activity that has the power to restructure the world being spoken of, and that the safest time to tell stories is when the sun is coming to a standstill in the sky, to be turned back toward spring."

The oral tradition of poetics—grounded as it is in ritual oratory, ceremonial chant, jokes and "clowning," as well as performed story—remains worlds apart from the literary text. To begin with, oral performance tends to join rather than divide author from audience. The spoken word emerges out of a communal setting of shared participation in a sacred event. Such an oral tradition is site-specific insofar as the person taking on the narrative role addresses and is addressed by a particular, face-to-face audience. Here the performative nuances of body language and gesture as well as voiced stress, pitch, volume, intonation, narrative pacing, and so on are tailored to the immediate circumstances of the spoken word. Native American literature, in contrast, mediates tribal experience through the discursive modes and textual conventions of literary tradition. Numerous written accounts of tribal values have sought to negotiate between oral contexts and literary conventions: from Samson Occom's *A Sermon Preached at the Execution of Moses Paul* (1772) to George Copway's *Traditional History and Characteristic Sketches of the Ojibway Nation* (1850), and on through Scott Momaday's Pulitzer Prize-winning *The Way to Rainy Mountain* (1969) and Leslie Marmon Silko's *Ceremony* (1977).

Contemporary Native American writers compose not only out of a tribal context but, equally important, out of a literary tradition that includes such eighteenth-, nineteenth-, and early twentieth-century Native American writers as Samson Occom, Charles Eastman, Alexander Posey, Mourning Dove, D'Arcy McNickle, William Apess, Alice Callahan, John Rollin Ridge, and Jane Johnson Schoolcraft, among many others. This tradition of Native American literature is itself deeply indebted to the literary conventions of anglophone literature. John Joseph Mathews's *Wah'Kon Tah* became a Book-of-the-Month Club selection in 1932 not just because it narrated a compelling account of Native American experience but also because it drew on the literary motifs, plot devices, and stylistic techniques that made for a readable text: one designed to appeal to a mass readership. Moreover, the very composition of works such as *Black Elk Speaks* (1932) oftentimes involve ethnographic collaboration among informants, interpreters, and translators. Indeed, the full author credits for *Black Elk Speaks* include both the title *Black Elk Speaks, Being the Life Story of a Holy Man of the Oglala Sioux* and the additional phrasing "as told through John G. Neihardt (*Flaming Rainbow*)." In fact, Black Elk communicated his vision to Neihardt in 1931 via his son, Ben Black Elk, as translator, while Neihardt's daughter Enid took stenographic notes of the exchange. Nevertheless, the reverence for native place and its animal and plant "people," the holy character of the sacred hoop—where the "red road" of the spirit intersects the secular "black road" at the center of the tribal circle—the rituals of survival, the magical nexus of dream vision, breath, the chanted word all remain central concerns that carry over from oral performance into Native American writing.

Poetry, perhaps more than autobiography, sermon, or fiction comes closest to capturing on the page the immediacy and intensity of oral performance. Some of the ways in which Native American writers have invoked a sense of oral textuality in verse composition include altering patterns of enjambment and spacings of the line, formulaic repetitions of key phrasings and other forms of anaphora, innovative typography, alternative patterns of punctuation, and the absence of punctuation. Such verbal techniques can recreate the cadences of ceremonial chant, as in Joy Harjo's surrealist poem "She Had Some Horses":

She had horses who were bodies of sand.
She had horses who were maps drawn of blood.
She had horses who were skins of ocean water.
She had horses who were the blue air of sky.
She had horses who were fur and teeth.
She had horses who were clay and would break.
She had horses who were splintered red cliff.

Whether in oral or written forms, the Native American presence pervades American literature and culture from the colonial era to the present. Yet, according to the modern writer D. H. Lawrence, "white people always, or nearly always, write sentimentally about Indians."

We are all familiar, of course, with the modern desire to romanticize the Native American as a "noble savage," natural seer, and helpmate to western colonization. Native peoples have been the subject of much sentimental representation, from the founding colonial myth of Pocahontas and John Smith, through such American literary figures as Henry Wadsworth Longfellow's *Hiawatha* (1855), such popular icons as the Long Ranger and Tonto, and such contemporary Hollywood depictions as the Sioux in *Dances with Wolves.* Yet the need to idealize Native peoples, as Lawrence theorizes in his widely read *Studies in Classic American Literature* (1923), goes hand-in-hand with its opposite impulse. In particular, Lawrence locates a double-consciousness at the heart of America's relation to the native peoples of Turtle Island: "The desire to extirpate the Indian. And the contradictory desire to glorify him. Both are rampant still, to-day."

The flip side to the "noble savage," of course, is the "blood-thirsty savage," and it is the persistent association of Indians with violence that Native American leaders have protested in, say, their criticism of the infamous "tomahawk chop" that is still the rallying cry of Atlanta Braves baseball fans. The myth of the Indian as the violent "other" was a staple of the American western genre well into the twentieth century, and it masked, according to writers such as Louise Erdrich and Michael Dorris, the imperialist aims of American Manifest Destiny. Writes Paula Gunn Allen in *The Sacred Hoop* (1986),

> [The view of Indians] as hostile savages who capture white ladies and torture them, obstruct the westward movement of peaceable white settlers, and engage in bloodthirsty uprisings in which they glory in the massacre of innocent colonists and pioneers is dear to the hearts of producers of bad films and even worse television. However, it is this view that is most deeply embedded in the American unconscious, where it forms the basis for much of the social oppression of other people of color and of women.

Regarding the Indian as "other" was an indispensable ingredient in the construction of an American heroic ideal. The fact that taming the frontier was synonymous with taming the Indian is a given in such American film classics as *Stagecoach, The Searchers,* and *Broken Arrow.* It is this connection between "progress" and subduing native populations that Louise Erdrich draws in her poem "Dear John Wayne." In the Hollywood formula of the western action genre, "Always the lookout spots the Indians first, / spread north to south, barring progress." Slipping into the voice of John Wayne, who made his cinematic mark by slaying Indian warriors, Erdrich sums up the blunt, ideological message of the western as it persists into the present: *"It is / not over, this fight, not as long as you resist. / Everything we see belongs to us."*

Whether idealized or demonized, Native Americans largely have been positioned as passive objects of ethnographic, literary, and popular representation. One effect of the widespread stereotyping of native peoples has been to flatten the rich diversity of tribal differences into a homogeneous image of the nameless, faceless, and largely ahistorical Indian as "other." The place of modern Native Americans remains largely invisible within the American mainstream. Indeed, as Vine Deloria has it in *Custer Died for Your Sins* (1969), "to be an Indian in modern American society is in a very real sense to be unreal and ahistorical." It is only in the post-World War II decades that such initiatives as the Native American Movement have empowered native peoples with an active voice in representing their social, cultural, and political lives. Moreover, such federal educational initiatives as the Indian Education Act of 1972 and the Indian Self-Determination and Educational Assistance Act of 1975 have gone a long way toward enabling a new generation of writers and scholars to represent the Native American masses.

The latter part of the twentieth century saw a dramatic increase in the number of publishers that feature Native American literary artists. Indian Center papers and newsletters include such publications as the *Shannon County News*, the *Navajo Times*, *Indian Country Today*, and *Akwesasne Notes*. Several small presses have emerged, such as Sun Tracks, which publishes a Native American book series, and Greenfield Review, which publishes numerous anthologies of Native American fiction and poetry. Scholarly journals such as *American Indian Quarterly* and the *American Indian Culture and Research Journal* now exist as well, further promoting a vibrant and visible literary and intellectual community. Native Americans, writes critic Joseph Bruchac, "have come away from their educations with a stronger sense of their ethnic and tribal identities and with the sophisticated knowledge of contemporary literary techniques which enables them to express the enduring values of their Native American identity to both white and Indian alike." It is to that body of work that we now turn.

Poems for Further Reading and Critical Writing

LOUISE ERDRICH   *(b. 1954)*

Dear John Wayne°   *(1984)*

August and the drive-in picture is packed.
We lounge on the hood of the Pontiac
surrounded by the slow-burning spirals they sell
at the window, to vanquish the hordes of mosquitoes.
Nothing works. They break through the smoke screen for blood.   5

Always the lookout spots the Indians first,
spread north to south, barring progress.

John Wayne (1907–1979): American film star.

The Sioux or some other Plains bunch
in spectacular columns, ICBM missiles,
feathers bristling in the meaningful sunset.　　　　　　　　10

The drum breaks. There will be no parlance.
Only the arrows whining, a death-cloud of nerves
swarming down on the settlers
who die beautifully, tumbling like dust weeds
into the history that brought us all here　　　　　　　　15
together: this wide screen beneath the sign of the bear.

The sky fills, acres of blue squint and eye
that the crowd cheers. His face moves over us,
a thick cloud of vengeance, pitted
like the land that was once flesh. Each rut,　　　　　　　20
each scar makes a promise: *It is*
not over, this fight, not as long as you resist.

Everything we see belongs to us.

A few laughing Indians fall over the hood
slipping in the hot spilled butter.　　　　　　　　25
The eye sees a lot, John, but the heart is so blind.
Death makes us owners of nothing.
He smiles, a horizon of teeth
the credits reel over, and then the white fields

again blowing in the true-to-life dark.　　　　　　　　30
The dark films over everything.
We get into the car
scratching our mosquito bites, speechless and small
as people are when the movie is done.
We are back in our skins.　　　　　　　　35

How can we help but keep hearing his voice,
the flip side of the sound track, still playing:
Come on, boys, we got them
where we want them, drunk, running.
They'll give us what we want, what we need.　　　　　40
Even his disease was the idea of taking everything.
Those cells, burning, doubling, splitting out of their skins.

WENDY ROSE   *(b. 1948)*

Trickster: 1977   *(1977)*

I.

The Trickster's time
is not clicked off neatly
on round dials, nor shadowed
in shifty lengths
on the earth. He counts his changes   5
slowly and is not accurate.
He lives for his own mess of words,
his own spilled soup. He can see
when you are spread out
and captured and numb and   10
speechless; when you have stretched
to your limit and can
no more bear to hear the frozen words
circle like ravens above you,
than to see worms grow into songs   15
from your gut.
He turns to wind, he turns to sand,
he turns walking off with your singer's tongue
left invisible. We'll say he is
the whistling coyote as he steals   20
all the words you ever knew.

II.

Reach in deep: then leave me
to find the words alone.
The whole world is made up
of words, mountain-thick, that wait   25
to cave in with edges that squeeze
hurt and reason into separate sounds.
The songs become tons
of bilingual stuff to reckon with.
Tricked: let me not touch the pen.   30
Let my voice be still . . . let anesthesia ride each nerve.
Let the bones melt into the rain and
disappear; let me disappear
and let those soft bones go.

If I Am Too Brown or Too White
for You   *(1985)*

remember I am a garnet woman
whirling into precision
as a crystal arithmetic
or a cluster and so

why the dream   5
in my mouth,
the flutter of blackbirds
at my wrists?

In the morning
there you are   10
at the edge of the river
on one knee

and you are selecting me
from among polished stones
more definitely red or white   15
between which tiny serpents swim

and you see that my body
is blood frozen
into giving birth
over and over in a single motion   20

and you touch the matrix
shattered in winter
and begin to piece together
the shape of me

wanting the fit in your palm   25
to be perfect
and the image less
clouded, less mixed

but you always see
just in time   30
working me around
in the evening sun

there is a small light
in the smoke, a tiny sun
in the blood, so deep   35
it is there and not there,

so pure
it is singing.

Story Keeper   *(1985)*

The stories would be braided in my hair
between the plastic combs and blue wing tips
but as the rattles would spit,
the drums begin,
along would come someone   5
to stifle and stop the sound
and the story keeper I would have been
must melt into the cave
of artifacts discarded

and this is a wound   10
to be healed
in the spin of winter,
the spiral
of beginning.
This is the task: 15
to find the stories now
and to heave at the rocks,
dig at the moss
with my fingernails,
let moisture seep along my skin   20
and fall within
soft and dark
to the blood

and I promise
I will find them   25
even after so long: where underground
they are albino
and they listen, they shine,
and they wait
with tongues shriveled like leaves   30
and fearful of their names
that would crystallize them,
make them fossils
with the feathers on their backs
frozen hard   35
like beetle wings.

∆∆∆∆   ∆∆∆∆

But spring is floating
to the canyon rim;
needles burst yellow
from the pine branch   40
and the stories have built a new house.
Oh they make us dance
the old animal dances
that go a winding way
back and back   45
to the red clouds
of our first
Hopi morning.

Where I saw them last
they are still: antelope and bear   50
dancing in the dust,
prairie dog and lizard
whirling just whirling,
pinyon and willow
bending, twisting,   55
we women
rooting into the earth
our feet becoming water
and our hair pushing up
like tumbleweed   60

and the spirits should have noticed
how our thoughts wandered those first days,
how we closed our eyes against them
and forgot the signs;
the spirits were never smart about this   65
but trusted us to remember it right
and we were distracted,
we were new.
We mapped the trails
the spirits had walked   70
as if the footprints had more meaning
than the feet.
color after color,
designs that spin and sprout
were painted on the sky   75
but we were only confused
and turned our backs
and now we are trapped
inside our songlessness.

We are that kind of thing 80
that pushes away
the very song
keeping us alive
so the stories have been strong
and tell themselves 85
to this very day,
with or without us
it no longer matters.
The flower merges with the mud,
songs are hammered onto spirits 90
and spirits onto people;
every song is danced out loud
for we are the spirits,
we are the people,
descended from the ones 95
who circled the underworld
and return to circle again.

I feel the stories
rattle under my hand
like sun-dried greasy 100
gambling bones.

LESLIE MARMON SILKO   *(b. 1948)*

Story from Bear Country   *(1976)*

You will know
when you walk
in bear country
By the silence
flowing swiftly between the juniper trees 5
by the sundown colors of sandrock
all around you.

You may smell damp earth
scratched away
from yucca roots 10
You may hear snorts and growls
slow and massive sounds
from caves
in the cliffs high above you.

It is difficult to explain   15
how they call you
All but a few who went to them
left behind families
        grandparents
        and sons   20
        a good life.

The problem is
you will never want to return
Their beauty will overcome your memory
like winter sun   25
melting ice shadows from snow
And you will remain with them
locked forever inside yourself
        your eyes will see you
        dark shaggy and thick.   30

We can send bear priests
loping after you
their medicine bags
bouncing against their chests
Naked legs painted black   35
bear claw necklaces
rattling against
their capes of blue spruce.

They will follow your trail
into the narrow canyon   40
through the blue-gray mountain sage
to the clearing
where you stopped to look back
and saw only bear tracks
behind you.   45

When they call
faint memories
will writhe around your heart
and startle you with their distance.
But the others will listen   50
because bear priests
sing beautiful songs
They must
if they are ever to call you back.

They will try to bring you   55
step by step

back to the place you stopped
and found only bear prints in the sand
where your feet had been.

Whose voice is this?   60
You may wonder
hearing this story when
after all
you are alone
hiking in these canyons and hills   65
while your wife and sons are waiting
back at the car for you.

But you have been listening to me
for some time now
from the very beginning in fact   70
and you are alone in this canyon of stillness
not even cedar birds flutter.
See, the sun is going down now
the sandrock is washed in its colors
Don't be afraid   75
        we love you
        we've been calling you
        all this time
Go ahead
turn around   80
see the shape
of your footprints
in the sand.

SIMON ORTIZ   *(b. 1941)*

The Boy and the Coyote   *(1976)*

for a friend, Ed Theis, met
at VAH, Ft. Lyons,
Colorado, November and
December 1974

You can see the rippled sand rifts
shallow inches below the surface.
I walk on the alkalied sand.
Willows crowd the edges of sand banks
sloping to the Arkansas River.   5

I get lonesome for the young afternoons
of a boy growing at Acoma.
He listens to the river,
the slightest nuance of sound.

Breaking thin ice from a small still pool,   10
I find Coyote's footprints.
Coyote, he's always somewhere before you;
he knows you'll come along soon.
I smile at his tracks which are not fresh
except in memory and say a brief prayer   15
for good luck for him and for me and thanks.

All of a sudden, and not far away,
there are the reports of a shotgun,
muffled flat by saltcedar thickets.
Everything halts for several moments,   20
no sound; even the wind holds to itself.
The animal in me crouches, poised immobile,
eyes trained on the distance, waiting
for motion again. The sky is wide;
blue is depthless; and the animal   25
and I wait for breaks in the horizon.

Coyote's preference is for silence
broken only by the subtle wind,
uncanny bird sounds, saltcedar scraping,
and the desire to let that man free,   30
to listen for the motion of sound.

Making an Acquaintance   *(1976)*

I walk outside without my shoes
on searing hot asphalt front yard.
Howard, my new landlord, says,
"It's gonna be a bitch of a Summer."
Strange, I think, what words mean.   5
He has a tanned middle-aged face,
used to be in real estate in Ohio,
sold his business and moved West.
We get acquainted by talking
about the coming Summer.   10
"Yeah," I agree with him,
"it's gonna be a bitch."
My feet are burning for coolness.

Joy Harjo *(b. 1951)*

She Had Some Horses *(1983)*

She had some horses.

She had horses who were bodies of sand.
She had horses who were maps drawn of blood.
She had horses who were skins of ocean water.
She had horses who were the blue air of sky.   5
She had horses who were fur and teeth.
She had horses who were clay and would break.
She had horses who were splintered red cliff.

She had some horses.

She had horses with long, pointed breasts.   10
She had horses with full, brown thighs.
She had horses who laughed too much.
She had horses who threw rocks at glass houses.
She had horses who licked razor blades.

She had some horses.   15

She had horses who danced in their mothers' arms.
She had horses who thought they were the sun and their
bodies shone and burned like stars.
She had horses who waltzed nightly on the moon.
She had horses who were much too shy, and kept quiet   20
in stalls of their own making.

She had some horses.

She had horses who liked Creek Stomp Dance songs.
She had horses who cried in their beer.
She had horses who spit at male queens who made   25
them afraid of themselves.
She had horses who said they weren't afraid.
She had horses who lied.
She had horses who told the truth, who were stripped
bare of their tongues.   30

She had some horses.

She had horses who called themselves, "horse".
She had horses who called themselves, "spirit", and kept
their voices secret and to themselves.

She had horses who had no names.   35
She had horses who had books of names.

She had some horses.

She had horses who whispered in the dark, who were afraid to speak.
She had horses who screamed out of fear of the silence, who
carried knives to protect themselves from ghosts.   40
She had horses who waited for destruction.
She had horses who waited for resurrection.

She had some horses.

She had horses who got down on their knees for any saviour.
She had horses who thought their high price had saved them.   45
She had horses who tried to save her, who climbed in her
bed at night and prayed as they raped her.

She had some horses.

She had some horses she loved.
She had some horses she hated.   50

These were the same horses.

Call It Fear   *(1983)*

There is this edge where shadows
and bones of some of us walk
                              backwards.
Talk backwards. There is this edge
call it an ocean of fear of the dark. Or   5
name it with other songs. Under our ribs
our hearts are bloody stars. Shine on
shine on, and horses in their galloping flight
strike the curve of ribs.
                              Heartbeat   10
and breathe back sharply. Breathe
                              backwards.
There is this edge within me
                    I saw it once
an August Sunday morning when the heat hadn't   15
left this earth. And Goodluck
sat sleeping next to me in the truck.
We had never broken through the edge of the
singing at four a.m.
                    We had only wanted to talk, to hear   20

any other voice to stay alive with.
                 And there was this edge—
not the drop of sandy rock cliff
bones of volcanic earth into
                   Albuquerque.   25
Not that,
       but a string of shadow horses kicking
and pulling me out of my belly,
       not into the Rio Grande but into the music
barely coming through   30
               Sunday church singing
from the radio. Battery worn-down but the voices
talking backwards.

LINDA HOGAN   *(b. 1947)*

Heritage   *(1979)*

From my mother, the antique mirror
where I watch my face take on her lines.
She left me the smell of baking bread
to warm fine hairs in my nostrils,
she left the large white breasts that weigh down   5
my body.

From my father I take his brown eyes,
the plague of locusts that leveled our crops,
they flew in formation like buzzards.

From my uncle the whittled wood   10
that rattles like bones
and is white
and smells like all our old houses
that are no longer there. He was the man
who sang old chants to me, the words   15
my father was told not to remember.

From my grandfather who never spoke
I learned to fear silence.
I learned to kill a snake
when you're begging for rain.   20

And grandmother, blue-eyed woman
whose skin was brown,
she used snuff.

When her coffee can full of black saliva
spilled on me   25
it was like the brown cloud of grasshoppers
that leveled her fields.
It was the brown stain
that covered my white shirt,
my whiteness a shame.   30
That sweet black liquid like the food
she chewed up and spit into my father's mouth
when he was an infant.
It was the brown earth of Oklahoma
stained with oil.   35
She said tobacco would purge your body of poisons.
It has more medicine than stones and knives
against your enemies.

That tobacco is the dark night that covers me.

She said it is wise to eat the flesh of deer   40
so you will be swift and travel over many miles.
She told me how our tribe has always followed a stick
that pointed west
that pointed east.
From my family I have learned the secrets   45
of never having a home.

Blessings   *(1979)*

Blessed
are the injured animals
for they live in his cages.
But who will heal my father,
tape his old legs for him?   5

Here's the bird with the two broken wings
and her feathers are white as an angel
and she says goddamn stirring grains
in the kitchen. When the birds fly out
he leaves the cages open   10
and she kisses his brow for such
good works.

> Work he says
> all your life
> and at the end   15
> you don't own even a piece of land.

Blessed are the rich
for they eat meat every night.
They have already inherited the earth.

For the rest of us, may we just live   20
long enough
and unwrinkle our brows,
may we keep our good looks
and some of our teeth
and our bowels regular.   25

Perhaps we can go live places
a rich man can't inhabit,
in the sunfish and jackrabbits,
in the cinnamon colored soil,
the land of red grass   30
and red people
in the valley
of the shadow of Elk
who aren't there.

    He says the damned earth is so old   35
    and wobbles so hard
    you'd best hang on to everything.
    Your neighbors steal what little you got.

Blessed
are the rich   40
for they don't have the same old
Everyday to put up with
like my father
who's gotten old,
      Chickasaw   45
      chikkih asachi, which means
they left as a tribe not a very great while ago.
They are always leaving,
those people.

Blessed   50
are those who listen
when no one is left to speak.

Ray A. Young Bear   *(b. 1950)*

one chip of human bone   *(1980)*

one chip of human bone

it is almost fitting
to die on the railroad tracks.

i can easily understand
how they felt on their long   5
staggered walks back

grinning to the stars.

there is something about
trains, drinking, and being
an indian with nothing to lose.   10

morning-water train woman   *(1980)*

it didn't take much talk for her
to realize that her brother
was drunk
a couple of years ago
when the morning wind blew a train   5
into his sleep
spreading the muscles and fibers
of his body over the tracks
prematurely towards the sun
claiming another   10
after the long stillness of bells
now jingling with persistence in her ears.
maybe we convinced her
in accordance to time and place
about this life where we walk with but few friends,   15
feeling around for reception
at our presence
willing to exchange old familiar connections
with no forgiveness added to our partings.
perhaps she is still thinking of new methods   20
by which to end herself
this coming weekend or the next.
surely it won't be the same
as the last time she tried:
taking a bottle of aspirins   25

and downing them with a can of engine oil.
the people just laughed and said:
there are other ways, besides. . . .

one time before she went away
i dreamt of her   30
sitting on the tracks
attentive to the distant changing colors
of the signal post.
i knew what she thought and felt.
there were images of small black trains   35
circling around her teeth.
their wheels were throwing sparks
setting fire to her long stringy hair.
her eyes withdrew farther back inside
the skull of her head   40
afraid of the scars,
moving and shifting
across her ribs
like long silvery railroad tracks.

the seal   *(1980)*

in the corner of this
old woman's house,
sits another, of the same
age unable to speak
but able only to grunt   5
and moan like a seal,
doing a yes or a no
or a strange maybe.

people say when she
was inside her mother's   10
stomach, her mother
went to a circus, but
some also say it was while
swimming that she brushed
her body against a seal.   15
in time, the misfortune
is still here.

waiting to be fed   *(1980)*

she swam smiling in the river
thinking it was good that she

had come out here to be with the sun
going out into the air
and giving warmth to her sisters' faces   5
watching her from the sides
listening carefully for the hum
of human voices.
no one would show up here today
she thought. it was too hot   10
to swim with the sun
radiating on the wings of insects
flying in repetition
between shadow and sunlight
confused in their decisions   15
evident by the sound
of their open mouths everywhere.

through the years to now
she had known the river well.
sometimes she imagined herself   20
a rock under the water
surrounded by a landscape
that would bend the trees
through the sky
and then through the stars   25
reminding her of burnt holes
in cloth that protected
her hand from fire
while cooking for people
waiting to be fed.   30
she knew a place where
it was like this
where it suddenly became cool
and clear. this place
had often been mentioned   35
in her mother's constant warnings
about rivers.
like the insects and the sunlight
she released her thought
to a spiderweb drifting   40
across the river
breaking through the clouds
losing all revenge to the giants
lifting their heads in their watch
to her swimming over the cool   45
gushing spring
coming up from under the river
thinking of her stomach
and how it was growing fast.

the child swimming inside her: 50
the touching and speaking of two hearts
made her feel she could smell the sweetness
of the baby's skin in her breath.

in time she would be able to see
the face inside her stomach.   55
a dream indented on her body.
she took care of it
as if it were a god
as if the snow in winter
had already begun to take shape   60
in the hands of children
far from the staring foreheads
of their houses.
she knew it wasn't sacred
but everything in the land   65
seemed that way.
everyone took great interest
and care for her that she
could somehow make out visible
strips of gentleness gathering   70
around her body
streaming out from her family
a circle of suns.

she looked at her reflection
floating over the water.   75
it seemed as if the sound
of water was also the sound
of rustling leaves.
her sisters broke her thoughts
when they suddenly stopped   80
talking. she quickly asked
if there was anything wrong
but they remained motionless.
from a distance she could
not tell if they were playing.   85
it was a long time before
she found herself shouting
and hitting at the water
hoping they would start
moving. soon her sisters' hands   90
indicated a discussion.
she could not hear their words.
she felt her body drifting
away taken by the foam.
the water rippled to the banks.   95

seals crawled out from holes
she hadn't noticed before.
she could feel the cold
water as the seals swam by
brushing the bodies of her   100
sisters against her stomach.

she felt twisted in a dream.
there was talk around her
and she could sense by the words
being spoken that it was night   105
and that relatives were inside
the house being fed. each one
chewing and then
quietly nodding.
her mother's hand covered her head.   110
there was whisper from the root
telling her to be still.
she died as she gave birth.
the child lived without ever hearing
or speaking.   115
she lived in the shadows
of her keeper's house
and was taken care of all her life.
sometimes she would go out into
the daylight and rock her body   120
back and forth as she sat
on the porch.
a smile on her face.
her arms and legs folded to her body.
the sun deep inside her eyes   125
walking to the river.

TOPICS FOR CRITICAL THINKING

1. What is the point of Louise Erdrich's metaphoric comparison in "Dear John Wayne" of the Indian feathers of line 10 to ICBM or intercontinental ballistic missiles?
2. Discuss the relationships Rose draws among story, song, and spirituality in "Story Keeper."
3. Discuss Leslie Marmon Silko's mode of address to the reader in "Story from Bear Country." How does Silko involve the reader in the poem's movement from its literal opening to its closing's mythic frame?
4. Discuss Joy Harjo's technique of verbal repetition in "She Had Some Horses." What dramatic and emotive effects does repetition have in the poet's chanting in surreal catalogues of metaphoric horses?
5. Discuss Linda Hogan's use of figurative language to dramatize the lived intensities of her blood roots in "Heritage."

6. Compare and contrast the narrative point of view in Young Bear's "the seal" with the longer depiction of the myth of the seal in "waiting to be fed."

TOPICS FOR CRITICAL WRITING

1. Of the archetypal figure of the Trickster in Native American mythology, Kenneth Lincoln writes in *Native American Renaissance* (1983):

> Coyote, hare, raven, crow, jay, wolverine, loon, or spider: a recreant spirit masks as an animal wandering through hundreds of tribal Indian myths. He resists the boundaries of any given species and is likely to appear at any time in any image. Trickster goes his ways "undifferentiated," Paul Radin observes, a makeshift, unregenerate figure fomenting reality. He is less divine than bestial, more mythic than animal. This figure also known as Old Man, scavenges in and out of the tribal world a gamesman, glutton, amoralist, comic rapist, world transformer, and improvisational god. He steals wealth, devours game, breaks rules, seduces the princess, procreates plants and animals, and makes up reality as people unfortunately know it, full of surprises and twists, contrary, problematical.

In what ways does Wendy Rose identify the Trickster with language and poetry in "Trickster: 1977"?

2. In "If I Am Too Brown or Too White for You," consider Rose's metaphor of the garnet for her mixed Hopi, Miwok, English, Scottish, Irish, and German descent lines.

3. In "Call It Fear," how does Harjo's personification of fear and her address to death through apostrophe enable her to name and thereby master the traumatic heritage of Native American victimization?

4. In "Blessings," consider Hogan's appropriation of the Beatitudes of Christ's Sermon on the Mount in Matthew 5:1–2:

> (3) Blessed are the poor in spirit,
> for theirs is the kingdom of heaven.
> (4) Blessed are those who mourn,
> for they shall be comforted.
> (5) Blessed are the meek,
> for they shall inherit the earth.

How does Hogan recode such New Testament phrasings to muse on the ironies and contradictions of class difference?

5. Compare and contrast the stereotypical language of the "drunk Indian" train victim of "one chip of human bone" with Ray A. Young Bear's portrayal of how the trauma of the accident affects the victim's sister in "morning-water train woman."

19 Feminism and Representation

In the history of English verse, no female poets come down to us from the Old English period; few were recognized in the Middle Ages. Only in the late sixteenth century do women authors begin to enter the margins of the canon of valued poetic texts. Consequently, feminist representation **Web** in poetry faces at least two challenges. First, female poets must confront a literary tradition that, from the Old English period through the eighteenth century, largely silenced them. Second, they face the dilemma of writing in a genre whose conventions of gender have been linked to masculine narratives of epic heroism, warfare, and male civic governance, not to mention all the lyric stereotypes of romance and sexual seduction that objectify actual women. In this chapter, we explore two aspects of feminist poetics. The double task of feminist verse begins with critique, by exposing traditional stereotypes of women, but it doesn't stop there. Equally important, feminism conceives new modes of poetic representation beyond the imagination of men.

www

To help visualize women's place in traditional English letters, Virginia Woolf invites us to imagine the likely fate of a female author with the genius of Shakespeare living in the Elizabethan period. Shakespeare's "sister" would have been denied access to education, to the stage, and to most civic and cultural forums in the public sphere. In all likelihood, she would have experienced her gift for writing as a curse. Her dilemma might have driven her to madness, suicide, or both. Today, Woolf insists, we would have to read between the lines of the historical record, even to glimpse the plight of the woman poet in the premodern period:

> When, however, one reads of a witch being ducked, of a woman possessed by devils, of a wise woman selling herbs, or even of a very remarkable man who had a mother, then I think we are on the track of a lost novelist, a suppressed poet, of some mute and inglorious Jane Austen, some Emily Brontë who dashed her brains out on the moor or mopped and mowed about the highways crazed with the torture that her gift had put her to.

Not just a problem of the Elizabethan age, the marginalization of women from the centers of male civic power persists well into the twentieth century. As Simone de Beauvoir observed in her 1949 study *The Second Sex*, women's place in society until recently has been subordinated to man's. "Society," writes de Beauvoir, "has always been male; political power has always been in the hands of men." Thus feminist poetics starts with asserting women's voices in poetry across the categories of race, class, regional, national, and ethnic difference.

Paradoxically enough, while female poets have had very little social representation as authors before the nineteenth century, one of poetry's major subjects has been women's cultural representation. Woman as muse, courtly ideal, Angel of the House, and, conversely, as femme fatale, vamp, and monstrous "other" are deeply ingrained in the heritage of English verse. Such stereotypes of women not only have silenced real women but, equally important, have obscured the ways in which the voice of the male poet has been granted a universal authority to speak on behalf of both sexes. "Women have served all these centuries," writes Woolf, "as looking-glasses possessing the magic and delicious power of reflecting the figure of man at twice its natural size." However marginalized as writers, women have been represented at the center of poetry's subjects and themes that figure into the construction of male identity.

One way of empowering the masculine voice is to associate it with the forces of reason, argument, and potent rationality while identifying women with nature, the reproductive cycles of birth and death, and the passive embodiment of youth, beauty, and innocence. As contemporary feminist sociologists, anthropologists, historians, and political scientists have shown, biological differences between the sexes have served to "essentialize" and fix the roles men and women play in ancient and modern societies. Cultures typically assign separate spheres for women and men—the former associated with the domestic world, nature, and the social margins of public decision making versus the latter's privileged access to civic government, organized religious worship, the performative arts, and so on. Emphasizing women's maternal roles, this sexual politics divides nature and culture so as to identify the former as feminine and the latter as masculine.

Carpe Diem Verse and Feminist Critique

Insofar as the splitting of women's roles from men's tends to empower men over women, it has been the subject of feminist critique, especially in the twentieth century. Much of feminist inquiry examines the social construction of gender (see Chapter 20). One can see, for example, a stinging parody of the traditional message of women as the "second sex" in the feminist postmodern poster art of Barbara Kruger. Kruger's artwork combines image and text so as to explore and critique the relations of power that underlie male and female gender roles. A former designer for Conde Nast, Kruger's artwork has the look and feel of slick advertisements, but they question media stereotypes. *We Won't Play Nature to Your Culture* debunks and resists women's passive association with nature in **patriarchy.** A term drawn from the greek root *patriarkhes* and the Latin word *pater* or "father," patriarchy describes in feminist criticism the social and cultural relations that historically have empowered men at the expense of women.

A similar divide between nature and culture, mind and body, activity and passivity underwrites men's relation to women in the seductive conventions of **carpe diem** poetics. *Carpe diem* in Latin means "pluck, or seize, the day." The carpe diem theme of enjoying life in the moment as the cure for the specters of time and death has ancient roots in Egyptian and Babylonian cultures. Sexual metaphors that associate women's reproductive lives with flowers and seasonal change are a staple of the carpe diem tradition. Such floral images come into play when the seventeenth-century poet Robert Herrick persuades women to seize the day, writing "To the Virgins, to Make Much of Time."

ROBERT HERRICK   *(1591–1674)*

To the Virgins, to Make Much of Time   *(1648)*

Gather ye rosebuds while ye may,
    Old time is still a-flying;
And this same flower that smiles today,
    Tomorrow will be dying.

The glorious lamp of heaven, the sun,   5
    The higher he's a-getting;
The sooner will his race be run,
    And nearer he's to setting.

That age is best which is the first,
    When youth and blood are warmer;   10
But being spent, the worse, and worst
    Times still succeed the former.

Then be not coy, but use your time,
    And, while ye may, go marry;
For, having lost but once your prime,   15
    You may forever tarry.

TOPICS FOR CRITICAL THINKING

1. How do rosebuds, the rising sun, warm blood, and youth all conspire to define what virgins, according to Herrick, should value in themselves?
2. What assumptions about the course of women's lives form the basis of Herrick's advice to virgins?
3. The word *coy* signifies shyness or the teasing appearance of being shy. Compare Herrick's caveat against coyness with Andrew Marvell's argument in "To His Coy Mistress," which follows.

ANDREW MARVELL　　*(1621–1678)*

To His Coy Mistress　　　　　　　　　　　　　*(1681)*

Had we but world enough, and time,
This coyness, lady, were no crime.
We would sit down, and think which way
To walk, and pass our long love's day.
Thou by the Indian Ganges' side　　　　　　　　　　　　5
Shoudst rubies find; I by the tide
Of Humber would complain. I would
Love you ten years before the flood,
And you should, if you please, refuse
Till the conversion of the Jews.　　　　　　　　　　　　10
My vegetable love should grow
Vaster than empires, and more slow;
An hundred years should go to praise
Thine eyes, and on thy forehead gaze;
Two hundred to adore each breast,　　　　　　　　　　　15
But thirty thousand to the rest;
An age at least to every part,
And the last age should show your heart.
For, lady, you deserve this state,°
Nor would I love at lower rate.　　　　　　　　　　　　20
　　But at my back I always hear
Time's wingèd chariot hurrying near;
And yonder all before us lie
Deserts of vast eternity.
Thy beauty shall no more be found;　　　　　　　　　　25
Nor, in thy marble vault, shall sound
My echoing song; then worms shall try
That long-preserved virginity,
And your quaint honor turn to dust,
And into ashes all my lust:　　　　　　　　　　　　　30
The grave's a fine and private place,
But none, I think, do there embrace.
　　Now therefore, while the youthful hue
Sits on thy skin like morning dew,
And while thy willing soul transpires　　　　　　　　　　35
At every pore with instant fires,
Now let us sport us while we may,
And now, like amorous birds of prey,
Rather at once our time devour

----

19 *state:* Dignity.

Than languish in his slow-chapped power.
Let us roll all our strength and all
Our sweetness up into one ball,
And tear our pleasures with rough strife
Through the iron gates of life:
Thus, though we cannot make our sun   45
Stand still, yet we will make him run.

TOPICS FOR CRITICAL THINKING

1. Marvell parodies the conventions of the carpe diem tradition in presenting the theme of time. Discuss how Marvell employs **hyperbole,** or exaggeration, to dilate the time of seduction and foreplay to absurd lengths.
2. How does the poet also reinforce the urgency to "sport us while we may" through rather grisly, realistic images of the body's decomposition in the grave?

TOPIC FOR CRITICAL WRITING

Explore Marvell's figurative language in the poem. What kind of attitude, according to the poet, should the lovers have toward time, sexuality, and death?

   The modern American poet John Crowe Ransom similarly relies on the fact of aging to lend persuasive force to the carpe diem tradition in "Blue Girls."

JOHN CROWE RANSOM   *(1888–1974)*

Blue Girls   *(1927)*

Twirling your blue skirts, travelling the sward
Under the towers of your seminary,
Go listen to your teachers old and contrary
Without believing a word.

Tie the white fillets then about your hair   5
And think no more of what will come to pass
Than bluebirds that go walking on the grass
And chattering on the air.

Practise your beauty, blue girls, before it fail;
And I will cry with my loud lips and publish   10
Beauty which all our power shall never establish,
It is so frail.

For I could tell you a story which is true;
I know a woman with a terrible tongue,

Blear eyes fallen from blue,   15
All her perfections tarnished—yet it is not long
Since she was lovelier than any of you.

TOPICS FOR CRITICAL THINKING

1. Compare Ransom's representation of the blue girls' natural beauty with the carpe diem conventions that shape Herrick's depictions of the coy virgins.
2. Is there an irony in Ransom's assumption that the male poet knows the course of women's lives better than the blue girls?

TOPIC FOR CRITICAL WRITING

Contrast the blue girls' innocence or ignorance of the facts of aging with what the male poet knows about what will become of them. How does his knowledge give him a certain power and authority over the blue girls?

In his seductive "Elegy XIX. To His Mistress Going to Bed," John Donne likewise takes up, but also expands, the role of poet as instructor for an unknowing female addressee.

JOHN DONNE   *(1572–1631)*

Elegy XIX. To His Mistress Going to Bed   *(1669)*

Come, madam, come, all rest my powers defy,
Until I labor, I in labor lie.
The foe oft-times, having the foe in sight,
Is tired with standing though he never fight.
Off with that girdle, like heaven's zone glistering,   5
But a far fairer world encompassing.
Unpin that spangled breastplate which you wear,
That th' eyes of busy fools may be stopped there.
Unlace yourself, for that harmonious chime
Tells me from you that now it is bed time.   10
Off with that happy busk, which I envy,
That still can be, and still can stand so nigh.
Your gown going off such beauteous state reveals,
As when from flowery meads th'hill's shadow steals.
Off with that wiry coronet, and show   15
The hairy diadem which on you doth grow:
Now off with those shoes, and then safely tread
In this love's hallowed temple, this soft bed.
In such white robes, heaven's angels used to be
Received by men; thou, Angel, bring'st with thee   20
A heaven like Mahomet's Paradise; and though

Ill spirits walk in white, we easily know
By this these angels from an evil sprite:
Those set our hairs, but these our flesh upright.
    License my roving hands, and let them go   25
Before, behind, between, above, below.
O, my America! my new-found-land,
My kingdom, safeliest when with one man manned,
My mine of precious stones, my empery,
How blest am I in this discovering thee!   30
To enter in these bonds is to be free;
Then, where my hand is set, my seal shall be.
    Full nakedness! All joys are due to thee,
As souls unbodied, bodies unclothed must be,
To taste whole joys. Gems which you women use   35
Are like Atlanta's balls,° cast in men's views,
That when a fool's eye lighteth on a gem,
His earthly soul might covet theirs, not them:
Like pictures, or like books' gay coverings made
For lay-men, are all women thus arrayed.   40
Themselves are mystic books, which only we
(Whom their imputed grace will dignify)
Must see revealed. Then, since that I may know,
As liberally as to thy midwife, show
Thyself: cast all, yea, this white linen hence,   45
There is no penance due to innocence:
    To teach thee, I am naked first; why than,
What needst thou have more covering than a man?

Unlike Marvell's rhetorical strategy in "To His Coy Mistress," Donne's erotic argument to seize the day does not so much prey on the mistress's fears of aging and death. Rather, his seduction turns on tropes of mastery and surrender.

TOPICS FOR CRITICAL THINKING

1. Contrast the ways in which Donne imagines himself as a would-be lover in both male and female roles. Discuss Donne's childbirth imagery in the opening lines and contrast these conceits with his role as epic hero doing battle with the "foe" of his mistress's modesty.

2. Discuss Donne's simile that draws on conventions from nature to compare the lover's "beauteous state" with "flowery meads."

3. What gender relations of power are implied in Donne's self-presentation as colonizer of the lover figured as virgin land ("my America and my new-found-land")?

---

36 *Atlanta's balls:* While in a race with Atlanta, Hippomenes distracted her with gold balls in order to win and thereby marry her.

TOPIC FOR CRITICAL WRITING

To what extent does the lover—imagined as "kingdom, safeliest when with one man manned" and a "mine of precious stones"—embody value for male ownership, profit, and enjoyment?

Finally the question of whether a woman can know rather than embody history is likewise posed in W. B. Yeats's poem "Leda and the Swan."

W. B. YEATS *(1865–1939)*

Leda and the Swan *(1924)*

A sudden blow: the great wings beating still
Above the staggering girl, her thighs caressed
By the dark webs, her nape caught in his bill,
He holds her helpless breast upon his breast.

How can those terrified vague fingers push   5
The feathered glory from her loosening thighs?
And how can body, laid in that white rush,
But feel the strange heart beating where it lies?

A shudder in the loins engenders there
The broken wall, the burning roof and tower   10
And Agamemnon dead.
                 Being so caught up,
So mastered by the brute blood of the air,
Did she put on his knowledge with his power
Before the indifferent beak could let her drop?   15

In the ancient world, Leda was married to King Tyndareus of Sparta and gave birth to Clytemnestra. But she was also raped by Zeus in the incarnation of a swan. This union produced Helen of Troy and, according to some versions of the myth, the twins Castor and Pollux. The myth, depicted by such painters as Michelangelo (see color insert), Leonardo da Vinci, Correggio (Antonio Allegri) and François Boucher, was well known to Yeats, who had an active interest in the visual arts from his father, the painter John Yeats. As poet, however, Yeats gives the myth a new twist by focusing on this divine incarnation as the cause of the Trojan War. The synecdoches of "the broken wall, the burning roof and tower" refer to the destruction of Troy by the Greeks. The Greek campaign against Troy was in retaliation for Paris's abduction of Helen from her husband Menelaus, the king of Sparta. Brother to Menelaus and commander of the Greek forces, Agamemnon was the husband of Clytemnestra who murdered him in revenge for allowing the sacrifice of her daughter Iphigenia to the goddess Artemis to ensure safe passage of the Greek fleet to Troy.

"Leda and the Swan" foretells the violent history of the Trojan War and the family murders in the abrupt "sudden blow" that opens onto the poem's rape scene. That sexual assault is further dramatized in the hard *b* plosives that punctuate the opening quatrain of Yeats's sonnet. The estrangement of the poem's literal subject is further defamiliarized in the bizarre coupling of human and animal images ("her thighs caressed / By the dark webs, her nape caught in his bill"). The poem's crucial question—"Did she put on his knowledge with his power"?—asks whether Leda, as a mortal woman, was a full participant in knowing the significance of Zeus's incarnation. Was she, like the god, omniscient or all-knowing in that moment? Was she her own agent in history or merely the biological vehicle for destinies conceived by a patriarchal god for, and about, the world of men? Another question, which Yeats didn't anticipate explicitly in the poem, is whether the myth itself still has pertinence. That is, can this myth still serve as a source of memorable art glorifying, as it does, a rape narrative at the heart of history?

Poetry and Re-visionary Feminism

Part of the task of feminist poetics is to pose difficult questions to the received canon of great books. Such critical questioning happens, according to Adrienne Rich, through acts of poetic "re-vision":

> Re-vision—the act of looking back, of seeing with fresh eyes, of entering an old text from a new critical direction—is for women more than a chapter in cultural history: it is an act of survival. . . . A radical critique of literature, feminist in its impulse would take the work first of all as a clue to how we live, how we have been living, how we have been led to imagine ourselves, how our language has trapped as well as liberated us, how the very act of naming has been till now a male prerogative, and how we can begin to see and name—-and therefore live—afresh.

In undertaking a poetics of re-vision, feminist authors have written against the grain of patriarchal tradition—the Western heritage that values men over women. In the process, feminist poets have challenged the latter's foundational assumptions, its cultural logic and modes of representation, as well as its institutions of power. Emily Dickinson, for example, engages in just this kind of poetic re-vision, when she renames the patriarchal narratives underwriting the biblical authority of the Judeo-Christian tradition:

EMILY DICKINSON   *(1830–1886)*

Poem 1545 (The Bible is an antique Volume)   *(1882)*

The Bible is an antique Volume—
Written by faded Men
At the suggestion of Holy Spectres—

Subjects—Bethlehem—
Eden—the ancient Homestead—
Satan—the Brigadier—
Judas—the Great Defaulter—
David—the Troubadour—
Sin—a distinguished Precipice—
Others must resist—
Boys that "believe" are very lonesome—
Other Boys are "lost"—
Had but the Tale a warbling Teller—
All the Boys would come—
Orpheus' Sermon captivated—
It did not condemn—

In "Poem 1545," Dickinson substitutes "Orpheus' Sermon" for the biblical stories written by men "at the suggestion of Holy Spectres." Orpheus was the son of the god Apollo and Calliope, the muse of epic poetry. His parents blessed him with the arts of poetry and music. The special power of his lyre had the ability to enchant animals and change the course of nature. His music even "captivated" Pluto, the god of the underworld, persuading him to release Eurydice from death. Dickinson contrasts the aesthetic grace of the poet's art with, in her mind, the more coercive lessons of Eden, Satan, and Sin where "belief" is enforced by punishment, repression, and the slavish obedience of "Boys" to "faded Men." Although Dickinson led a deeply spiritual life, she shows a modern skepticism toward organized religion and the received authority of biblical narrative. Re-visioning the Bible in this way is fraught with controversy as it touches on religious truths that are held sacred in the Judeo-Christian tradition.

Equally challenging for the feminist poet is the critique of such foundational institutions as marriage. Historically, marriage and the traditional nuclear family unit have defined and reproduced women's place in the roles of wife and mother. Due in large part to the feminist liberation movements of the post-Vietnam era, those roles have become less restrictive than they once were. But in the conservative social milieu of the 1950s, the formal medium of poetry allowed Adrienne Rich to think critically about the plight of independent-minded women. She turned her attention to representing women who, however outwardly "normal," were nevertheless weighed down by the oppressive conditions of their married lives, as in "Aunt Jennifer's Tigers."

ADRIENNE RICH   *(b. 1929)*

Aunt Jennifer's Tigers   *(1951)*

Aunt Jennifer's tigers prance across a screen,
Bright topaz denizens of a world of green.

They do not fear the men beneath the tree;
They pace in sleek chivalric certainty.

Aunt Jennifer's fingers fluttering through her wool   5
Find even the ivory needle hard to pull.
The massive weight of Uncle's wedding band
Sits heavily upon Aunt Jennifer's hand.

When Aunt is dead, her terrified hands will lie
Still ringed with ordeals she was mastered by.   10
The tigers in the panel that she made
Will go on prancing, proud and unafraid.

The key details that clue us to Aunt Jennifer's oppression have to do with
her hands and fingers. The former are depicted as "terrified" and the latter are
arrested by the "massive weight of Uncle's wedding band"—a symbol for her
confinement in marriage. For, even in death, the "hands will lie / Still ringed
with ordeals she was mastered by." The ringed hands in Rich's subtle pun *lie* not
only are still in death but they also display the lie of Aunt Jennifer's marital identity as dutiful wife. The tigers of her artistry, however, tell a different story.
"Prancing, proud and unafraid," they are the opposite of Aunt Jennifer's "terrified" married life. Unlike Aunt Jennifer, "they do not fear the men beneath
the tree."

Verse writing allowed Rich to recognize quite early in her career the contradictions between one's creative life as an artist and the roles of wife and
mother that society demanded of women in the 1950s. Of her own dilemma
at that time, Rich writes:

> Looking back at poems I wrote before I was twenty-one, I'm startled because be-
> neath the conscious craft are glimpses of the split I even then experienced be-
> tween the girl who wrote poems, who defined herself in writing poems, and the
> girl who was to define herself by her relationships with men. "Aunt Jennifer's
> Tigers," written while I was a student, looks with deliberate detachment at this
> split. . . . In writing this poem, composed and apparently cool as it is, I thought I
> was creating a portrait of an imaginary woman. But this woman suffers from the
> opposition of her imagination, worked out in tapestry, and her life-style, "ringed
> with ordeals she was mastered by." It was important to me that Aunt Jennifer was
> a person as distinct from myself as possible—distanced by the formalism of the
> poem, by its objective, observant tone—even by putting the woman in a different
> generation. In those years formalism was part of the strategy—like asbestos
> gloves, it allowed me to handle materials I couldn't pick up bare handed.

Poetry begins for Rich as an unflinching encounter with, and buffer against,
the harsh realities of her experience as a woman.

Composed a decade later, Sylvia Plath's poem "Daddy" lends an urgency
and intensity to Rich's criticism of husbands and fathers: one whose confessional edge is far less distanced, less impersonal, and more intimate in its tone,
mode of address, and presentational style.

SYLVIA PLATH   *(1932–1963)*

Daddy   *(1962)*

You do not do, you do not do
Any more, black shoe
In which I have lived like a foot
For thirty years, poor and white,
Barely daring to breathe or Achoo.   5

Daddy, I have had to kill you.
You died before I had time—
Marble-heavy, a bag full of God,
Ghastly statue with one gray toe
Big as a Frisco seal   10

And a head in the freakish Atlantic
Where it pours bean green over blue
In the waters off the beautiful Nauset.
I used to pray to recover you.
Ach, du.°   15

In the German tongue, in the Polish town°
Scraped flat by the roller
Of wars, wars, wars.
But the name of the town is common.
My Polack friend   20

Says there are a dozen or two.
So I never could tell where you
Put your foot, your root,
I never could talk to you.
The tongue stuck in my jaw.   25

It stuck in a barb wire snare.
Ich, ich, ich, ich,°
I could hardly speak.
I thought every German was you.
And the language obscene   30

An engine, an engine
Chuffing me off like a Jew.

---

15 *Ach, du:* Ah, you.   16 *Polish town:* Grabów, birthplace of Otto Plath, the poet's father.
27 *ich:* I.

A Jew to Dachau, Auschwitz, Belsen.
I began to talk like a Jew.
I think I may well be a Jew.   35

The snows of the Tyrol,° the clear beer of Vienna
Are not very pure or true.
With my gypsy ancestress and my weird luck
And my Taroc pack and my Tarot pack°
I may be a bit of a Jew.   40

I have always been scared of *you*,
With your Luftwaffe,° your gobbledygoo.
And your neat mustache
And your Aryan eye, bright blue.
Panzer-man, panzer-man,° O You—   45

Not God but a swastika
So black no sky could squeak through.
Every woman adores a Fascist,
The boot in the face, the brute
Brute heart of a brute like you.   50

You stand at the blackboard, daddy,
In the picture I have of you,
A cleft in your chin instead of your foot
But no less a devil for that, no not
Any less the black man who   55

Bit my pretty red heart in two.
I was ten when they buried you.
At twenty I tried to die
And get back, back, back to you.
I thought even the bones would do.   60

But they pulled me out of the sack,
And they stuck me together with glue,
And then I knew what to do.
I made a model of you,
A man in black with a Meinkampf° look   65

---

36 *Tyrol:* Region of Austria.   39 *Tarot pack:* Pack of cards used to tell fortunes.   42 *Luft-waffe:* German airforce.   45 *panzer-man:* Tank-man.   65 *Meinkampf: My Struggle,* the title of Adolf Hitler's biography.

And a love of the rack and the screw.
And I said I do, I do.
So daddy, I'm finally through.
The black telephone's off at the root,
The voices just can't worm through.   70

If I've killed one man, I've killed two—
The vampire who said he was you
And drank my blood for a year,
Seven years, if you want to know.
Daddy, you can lie back now.   75

There's a stake in your fat black heart
And the villagers never liked you.
They are dancing and stamping on you.
They always *knew* it was you.
Daddy, daddy, you bastard, I'm through.   80

Sylvia Plath's father, Otto Plath, immigrated to America from Silesia and, although of German descent, had connections to neither Nazism nor Judaism. A Professor of Biology at Boston University, he published a book entitled *Bumblebees and Their Ways* in 1934, two years after Sylvia was born. Interrupting the normal course of Sylvia's girlhood, Otto suffered a traumatic illness involving the amputation of a gangrenous leg. He died in 1940 when Sylvia was just eight years old.

The poem's persona is angry and unforgiving toward the father; the entire poem performs a sustained tirade against him. The harsh tone of anger is symptomatic, paradoxically enough, of the poet's mourning process that would work through the traumatic loss of a loved one. But it is also driven by the breakup of her seven-year marriage to the English poet Ted Hughes. Plath's divorce was occasioned by Hughes's adultery in the summer of 1962 while they were living in Devon, England. In the poem, Plath is not unmindful of the connection between the two losses: of her own father as well as of Hughes, her husband and the "daddy" of her two young children. That first, childhood trauma and its return in the crisis of her marriage is evident in her lines "If I've killed one man, I've killed two— / The vampire who said he was you / And drank my blood for a year, / Seven years, if you want to know." But the poem is not just a confessional exploration of her personal losses. Rather, its feminist message would overthrow the father's authority and power as they shape women's place under patriarchy.

TOPICS FOR CRITICAL THINKING

1. Discuss the poet's use of apostrophe in its direct address to the father figure. How does Plath stage that address as a kind of declaration of independence in the decisive tone with which she at once judges and dismisses the father?

2. Consider how the poet's sing-song rhyme pattern of the opening stanza darkly invokes a childhood world of Mother Goose rhymes appropriate to the poet's regression back into the role of daughter to the dead patriarch.

3. How does Plath capture the ambiguity of her relation to the dead patriarch in her pun on the word *through* in the last lines of the poem?

4. The poem draws an analogy between women's oppression and that of the Jewish victims of the Nazi death camps. Do you think this analogy is appropriate?

TOPIC FOR CRITICAL WRITING

Is the poem a tirade against Plath's literal father? Or is it more concerned with criticizing the cultural role of father as patriarch represented, say, in God the Father, Führer, fascist, teacher, and vampire-husband? To what extent does Plath debunk the myth of the father as a composite figure whose authority extends throughout the fields of religion, state, classroom, and nuclear family?

Reversing men's power to represent women, Plath in "Daddy" appropriates patriarchy's power to name the "other" for her own purposes. In Plath's poetry, according to Adrienne Rich, "Man appears as, if not a dream, a fascination and a terror; and the source of the fascination and terror is, simply, Man's power—to dominate, tyrannize, choose, or reject the woman." Men's power to represent women is the subject of much of feminist verse, as in Christina Rossetti's "In an Artist's Studio."

CHRISTINA ROSSETTI   *(1830–1894)*

In an Artist's Studio   *(1856)*

One face looks out from all his canvases,
    One selfsame figure sits or walks or leans:
    We found her hidden just behind those screens,
That mirror gave back all her loveliness.
A queen in opal or in ruby dress,   5
    A nameless girl in freshest summer-greens,
    A saint, an angel—every canvas means
The same one meaning, neither more nor less.
He feeds upon her face by day and night,
    And she with true kind eyes looks back on him,   10
Fair as the moon and joyful as the light:
    Not wan with waiting, not with sorrow dim;
Not as she is, but was when hope shone bright;
    Not as she is, but as she fills his dream.

Born in 1830, Christina Rossetti was the sister to the famous Pre-Raphaelite painter Dante Gabriel Rossetti. She not only moved in Pre-Raphaelite circles—publishing in their journal *The Germ*—but she sat as a model for several of the Pre-Raphaelites and appears in many of their paintings, including her brother's *The Girlhood of Mary Virgin* (see color insert).

TOPICS FOR CRITICAL THINKING

1. How does Rossetti expose the ways in which the male artist's idealization of the "nameless girl" serves, paradoxically, as the source of her oppression?
2. Focus on the key terms through which the artist stereotypes his model in the poem. What qualities does he attribute to her?
3. How do the stereotypical representations of the poem's "selfsame figure" obscure the reality of the actual person who remains "hidden just behind those screens . . . / Not as she is, but as she fills his dream"?

TOPIC FOR CRITICAL WRITING

Compare the artist's representation of his female model in the poem to the presentation of women and girls in *The Girlhood of Mary Virgin* (see color insert).

A more overt criticism of man's power to represent woman is the subject of H. D.'s (Hilda Doolittle) lyric on "Helen."

H. D. (HILDA DOOLITTLE)   *(1886–1961)*

Helen   *(1924)*

All Greece hates
the still eyes in the white face,
the luster as of olives
where she stands,
And the white hands.   5

All Greece reviles
the wan face when she smiles,
hating it deeper still
when it grows wan and white,
remembering past enchantments   10
and past ills.

Greece sees, unmoved,
God's daughter, born of love,
the beauty of cool feet
and slenderest knees,   15
could love indeed the maid,
only if she were laid,
white ash amid funereal cypresses.

Helen's legendary charm and its effect on Paris and Menelaus led to the Trojan War. In H. D.'s portrait, it is Helen's subtle powers of seduction—her feminine "enchantments"—that "all Greece hates." H. D. insists on the fact of male misogyny—the hatred of women—implying that it stems from Helen's awesome beauty and her self-possession of character. "Unmoved, / God's daughter" is a threat to the power and authority of Greece's patriarchal order. Greece can only love "the maid" after she has been arrested by death. Greece's cure for her "past ills" is to transform the living face "growing wan and white" into "white ash amid funereal cypresses."

Feminist Verse

The work of feminist poetics, however, would move beyond the oppression of patriarchal representation to appropriate poetry's powers of re-vision. In this vein, "it is finally," for Adrienne Rich, "the woman's sense of *herself*—embattled, possessed—that gives the poetry its dynamic charge, its rhythms of struggle, need, will and female energy." Poetic re-vision of this kind, that recovers "female energy" out of the "embattled" condition of patriarchy, is at work in Muriel Rukeyser's reinterpretation of Botticelli's famous portrait of *The Birth of Venus* (see color insert).

MURIEL RUKEYSER   *(1913–1980)*

The Birth of Venus   *(1958)*

Risen in a
welter of waters.

Not as he saw her
standing upon a frayed and lovely surf
clean-riding the graceful leafy breezes   5
clean-poised and easy. Not yet.

But born in a
tidal wave of the father's overthrow,
the old rule killed and its mutilated sex.

The testicles of the father-god, father of fathers,   10
sickled off by his son, the next god Time.
Sickled off. Hurled into the ocean.
In all that blood and foam,
among raving and generation,
of semen and the sea born, the   15
great goddess rises.

However, possibly,
on the long worldward voyage flowing,
horror gone down in birth, the curse, being changed,
being used, is translated far at the margin into
our rose and saving image, curling toward a shore
early and April, with certainly shells, certainly blossoms.

And the girl, the wellborn goddess, human love—
young-known, new-knowing, mouth flickering, sure eyes—
rides shoreward, from death to us as we are at this moment, on
the crisp delightful Botticellian wave.

In revising Botticelli's serene depiction of Venus's birth, Rukeyser re-
stores the more violent context of her mythic origin based as it is in the age-
old struggle for patriarchal supremacy. The original Greek myth begins with
the "father's overthrow" in the castration of the god Uranus by his son, the
Titan Cronus. Venus or Aphrodite arises from the sea foam (aphros) fertilized
by Uranus's severed testicles. Rukeyser's version differs from the majestic images of Botticelli's portrait where Venus is blown to shore on a clam shell by
the West Wind Zephyr and Chloris. There she is met by one of the three
nymphs of the hours, or Horae, who will drape her in a regal purple robe.

TOPICS FOR CRITICAL THINKING

1. Why does Rukeyser refer to Venus as "our rose and saving image"?
2. How does Venus's birth in Rukeyser's representation serve to change and translate
   the violent history of patriarchal mythology?
3. In what ways does Rukeyser represent the new goddess in her final stanza? What
   qualities does she attribute to her?

TOPIC FOR CRITICAL WRITING

Contrast the tone and mood of Rukeyser's poem as conveyed through the key terms
of her diction with the depiction of the birth of Venus in Botticelli's painting (see
color insert).

Such re-visions of male representation take less mythic and more
everyday modes of expression in contemporary women's poetics as, say, when
Sharon Olds celebrates her daughter's math skills in "The One Girl at the
Boys Party."

SHARON OLDS   *(b. 1942)*

The One Girl at the Boys Party   *(1983)*

When I take my girl to the swimming party
I set her down among the boys. They tower and
bristle, she stands there smooth and sleek,
her math scores unfolding in the air around her.
They will strip to their suits, her body hard and   5
indivisible as a prime number,
they'll plunge in the deep end, she'll subtract
her height from ten feet, divide it into
hundreds of gallons of water, the numbers
bouncing in her mind like molecules of chlorine   10
in the bright blue pool. When they climb out,
her ponytail will hang its pencil lead
down her back, her narrow silk suit
with hamburgers and french fries printed on it
will glisten in the brilliant air, and they will   15
see her sweet face, solemn and
sealed, a factor of one, and she will
see their eyes, two each,
their legs, two each, and the curves of their sexes,
one each, and in her head she'll be doing her   20
wild multiplying, as the drops
sparkle and fall to the power of a thousand from her body.

TOPICS FOR CRITICAL THINKING

1. What stereotypes about girls does Sharon Olds write against in "The One Girl at the Boys Party"?

2. How does the pun on *wild multiplying* in the poem's next-to-last line add another dimension to Olds's portrait of her daughter?

TOPIC FOR CRITICAL WRITING

Discuss the ways in which Olds presents her daughter through the poem's mathematical tropes.

While Olds takes pride in her daughter's intellectual gifts, Lucille Clifton's "Homage to My Hips" celebrates the vitality of the feminine body.

LUCILLE CLIFTON *(b. 1936)*

Homage to My Hips *(1991)*

these hips are big hips.
they need space to
move around in.
they don't fit into little
petty places. these hips   5
are free hips.
they don't like to be held back.
these hips have never been enslaved,
they go where they want to go
they do what they want to do.   10
these hips are mighty hips.
these hips are magic hips.
i have known them
to put a spell on a man and
spin him like a top!   15

TOPICS FOR CRITICAL THINKING

1. In "Homage to My Hips" Clifton resists all of the cultural messages that would
   pressure women into the confining mold of what Mary Wollstonecraft in the eighteenth century criticized as women's "corporeal accomplishment." How does
   Clifton's poem resist the distorted body images that women receive from advertising, the media, and culture generally?
2. Explore the sexual politics of Clifton's erotic ending where she claims the power to
   "put a spell on a man and / spin him like a top!"

TOPIC FOR CRITICAL WRITING

The values of being slim, pert, lean, passive, demure, silent, and so on have no place in
Clifton's lexicon of feminine virtues. How does she link acceptance of her body to a
state of being "free" from "enslavement"?

Increasingly, contemporary women's poetry has complicated any acts of
poetic re-vision that would speak on behalf of all women. Instead, feminist
poetics has recognized the diversity of women's experiences across the borders of generational, ethnic, racial, national, sexual, and economic difference.
That social diversity reflects what critic Mary Louise Pratt describes as the
complex "contact zones" of difference that define contemporary multicultural
experience. Today, feminist verse explores new ways of representing "social
spaces where cultures meet, clash, and grapple with each other, often in contexts of highly asymmetrical relations of power, such as colonialism, slavery,
or their aftermaths as they are lived out in many parts of the world today."

This edgy world of clashing cultures and conflicted borders especially characterizes the situation of Native American women's poetry, as in Joy Harjo's "The Woman Hanging from the Thirteenth Floor Window."

JOY HARJO   *(b. 1951)*

The Woman Hanging from the Thirteenth Floor Window   *(1983)*

She is the woman hanging from the 13th floor
window. Her hands are pressed white against the
concrete moulding of the tenement building. She
hangs from the 13th floor window in east Chicago,
with a swirl of birds over her head. They could   5
be a halo, or a storm of glass waiting to crush her.

She thinks she will be set free.

The woman hanging from the 13th floor window
on the east side of Chicago is not alone.
She is a woman of children, of the baby, Carlos,   10
and of Margaret, and of Jimmy who is the oldest.
She is her mother's daughter and her father's son.
She is several pieces between the two husbands
she has had. She is all the women of the apartment
building who stand watching her, watching themselves.   15

When she was young she ate wild rice on scraped down
plates in warm wood rooms. It was in the farther
north and she was the baby then. They rocked her.

She sees Lake Michigan lapping at the shores of
herself. It is a dizzy hole of water and the rich   20
live in tall glass houses at the edge of it. In some
places Lake Michigan speaks softly, here, it just sputters
and butts itself against the asphalt. She sees
other buildings just like hers. She sees other
women hanging from many-floored windows   25
counting their lives in the palms of their hands
and in the palms of their children's hands.

She is the woman hanging from the 13th floor window
on the Indian side of town. Her belly is soft from
her children's births, her worn levis swing down below   30
her waist, and then her feet, and then her heart.
She is dangling.

The woman hanging from the 13th floor hears voices.
They come to her in the night when the lights have gone
dim. Sometimes they are little cats mewing and scratching   35
at the door, sometimes they are her grandmother's voice,
and sometimes they are gigantic men of light whispering
to her to get up, to get up, to get up. That's when she wants
to have another child to hold onto in the night, to be able
to fall back into dreams.   40

And the woman hanging from the 13th floor window
hears other voices. Some of them scream out from below
for her to jump, they would push her over. Others cry softly
from the sidewalks, pull their children up like flowers and gather
them into their arms. They would help her, like themselves.   45

But she is the woman hanging from the 13th floor window,
and she knows she is hanging by her own fingers, her
own skin, her own thread of indecision.

She thinks of Carlos, of Margaret, of Jimmy.
She thinks of her father, and of her mother.   50
She thinks of all the women she has been, of all
the men. She thinks of the color of her skin, and
of Chicago streets, and of waterfalls and pines.
She thinks of moonlight nights, and of cool spring storms.
Her mind chatters like neon and northside bars.   55
She thinks of the 4 a.m. lonelinesses that have folded
her up like death, discordant, without logical and
beautiful conclusion. Her teeth break off at the edges.
She would speak.

The woman hangs from the 13th floor window crying for   60
the lost beauty of her own life. She sees the
sun falling west over the grey plane of Chicago.
She thinks she remembers listening to her own life
break loose, as she falls from the 13th floor
window on the east side of Chicago, or as she   65
climbs back up to claim herself again.

"The Woman Hanging from the Thirteenth Floor Window" gives representation to the plight of urban Native American women who live with the daily extremity of social, cultural, and economic displacement. Harjo's hanging woman embodies in the contradictions of her precarious position the paradoxes of life in the "contact zone."

TOPICS FOR CRITICAL THINKING

1. Characterize how you imagine the life of the woman of Harjo's poem. What information does Harjo give us about her background?
2. In what ways is this woman both a hero and victim?
3. In what ways do the other women in the poem see themselves in her fate? Is she a representative figure, or is her story particular to her ethnic, class, or racial background?
4. How is she both connected to a network of parents and children, yet supremely alone?

TOPIC FOR CRITICAL WRITING

Describe your sense of what is at stake in the poem's last lines. Why do you think that Harjo presents two mutually exclusive endings to "The Woman Hanging from the Thirteenth Floor Window"?

Not insignificantly, Harjo leaves the woman who is hanging from the thirteenth floor window suspended between two contradictory fates. Similarly, Audre Lorde represents the irresolvable dilemma she faces as a contemporary woman of color. Her portrait of mother-daughter bonds in "From the House of Yemanjá" are inflected by her clashing identifications over race. Describing herself as a "black lesbian feminist warrior poet," Lorde internalizes the contradictions of her African American identity in the trope of having a mother with "two faces."

AUDRE LORDE   *(1934–1992)*

From the House of Yemanjá   *(1978)*

My mother had two faces and a frying pot
where she cooked up her daughters
into girls
before she fixed our dinner.
My mother had two faces   5
and a broken pot
where she hid out a perfect daughter
who was not me
I am the sun and moon and forever hungry
for her eyes.   10

I bear two women upon my back
one dark and rich and hidden
in the ivory hungers of the other
mother
pale as a witch   15

yet steady and familiar
brings me bread and terror
in my sleep
her breasts as huge exciting anchors
in the midnight storm.   20

All this has been
before
in my mother's bed
time has no sense
I have no brothers   25
and my sisters are cruel.

Mother I need
mother I need
mother I need your blackness now
as the august earth needs rain.   30

I am
the sun and moon and forever hungry
the sharpened edge
where day and night shall meet
and not be   35
one.

TOPICS FOR CRITICAL THINKING

1. How does Lorde complicate any simple notions of solidarity with other women in the poem?
2. In what sense might Lorde internalize Pratt's definition of the "contact zone" in the trope of the "sharpened edge" defining her personal identity?
3. Yemanjá, according to Lorde, is "mother of the other *Orisha* [gods and goddesses that belong to Western Nigeria and the Yoruba tribe]; Yemanjá is also the goddess of oceans. Rivers are said to flow from her breasts. One legend has it that a son tried to rape her. She fled until she collapsed, and from her breasts, the rivers flowed. Another legend says that a husband insulted Yemanjá's long breasts, and when she fled with her pots he knocked her down. From her breasts flowed the rivers, and from her body then sprang forth all the other *Orisha*. River-smooth stones are Yemanjá's symbol, and the sea is sacred to her followers. Those who please her are blessed with many children." Do you see any connections between these Yoruba myths of Yemanjá and how Lorde represents her in her poem?

TOPIC FOR CRITICAL WRITING

Discuss your interpretation of what the two faces signify in "From the House of Yemanjá." What other figures of doubling do you notice in the poem?

Poems for Further Reading and Critical Writing

Adrienne Rich published *Diving into the Wreck* in 1973, and the following year it won the National Book Award for Poetry. The title piece of the volume reflects on the "wreck" of her past and looks forward to the new evolution her career would take. Rich graduated Phi Beta Kappa in 1951 from Radcliffe College; that year her first volume of published verse *A Change of World* won the prestigious Yale Younger Poets Award. Rich went on to win a steady succession of awards and grants for her poetry at the same time that she married Alfred Conrad and gave birth to three boys between 1955–1960. Conrad took his life in 1970, which also coincided with Rich's commitment to lesbian poetics.

"Diving into the Wreck" reflects on these major transitions in the poet's life. Its open-form poetic style also marks a significant change from the fixed-form poetry, exemplified by "Aunt Jennifer's Tigers" in the early stages of her career.

ADRIENNE RICH   *(b. 1929)*

Diving into the Wreck   *(1973)*

First having read the book of myths,
and loaded the camera,
and checked the edge of the knife-blade,
I put on
the body-armor of black rubber   5
the absurd flippers
the grave and awkward mask.
I am having to do this
not like Cousteau° with his
assiduous team   10
aboard the sun-flooded schooner
but here alone.

There is a ladder.
The ladder is always there
hanging innocently   15
close to the side of the schooner.
We know what it is for,
we who have used it.

---

9 *Cousteau:* Jacques Cousteau (1910–1997), underwater explorer and inventor, with Emile Gagnan, of the aqualung.

Otherwise
it is a piece of maritime floss   20
some sundry equipment.

I go down.
Rung after rung and still
the oxygen immerses me
the blue light   25
the clear atoms
of our human air.
I go down.
My flippers cripple me,
I crawl like an insect down the ladder   30
and there is no one
to tell me when the ocean
will begin.

First the air is blue and then
it is bluer and then green and then   35
black I am blacking out and yet
my mask is powerful
it pumps my blood with power
the sea is another story
the sea is not a question of power   40
I have to learn alone
to turn my body without force
in the deep element.

And now: it is easy to forget
what I came for   45
among so many who have always
lived here
swaying their crenellated fans
between the reefs
and besides   50
you breathe differently down here.

I came to explore the wreck.
The words are purposes.
The words are maps.
I came to see the damage that was done   55
and the treasures that prevail.
I stroke the beam of my lamp
slowly along the flank
of something more permanent
than fish or weed   60

the thing I came for:
the wreck and not the story of the wreck
the thing itself and not the myth
the drowned face always staring
toward the sun   65
the evidence of damage
worn by salt and sway into this threadbare beauty
the ribs of the disaster
curving their assertion
among the tentative haunters.   70

This is the place.
And I am here, the mermaid whose dark hair
streams black, the merman in his armored body
We circle silently
about the wreck   75
we dive into the hold.
I am she: I am he

whose drowned face sleeps with open eyes
whose breasts still bear the stress
whose silver, copper, vermeil cargo lies   80
obscurely inside barrels
half-wedged and left to rot
we are the half-destroyed instruments
that once held to a course
the water-eaten log   85
the fouled compass

We are, I am, you are
by cowardice or courage
the one who find our way
back to this scene   90
carrying a knife, a camera
a book of myths
in which
our names do not appear.

TOPICS FOR CRITICAL THINKING

1. Describe the situation and setting that Rich presents in the opening lines of "Diving into the Wreck." What point is she making in contrasting her dive with those of Jacques Cousteau?

2. Of the writing process, Rich has said that "for a poem to coalesce . . . there has to be an imaginative transformation of reality which is in no way passive. And a certain freedom of the mind is needed—freedom to press on, to enter the currents of your thought like a glider pilot, knowing that your motion can be sustained, that

the buoyancy of your attention will not be suddenly snatched away." Compare this description to the empowered sense of buoyancy and freedom Rich discovers in her descent into the "deep element" of the dive.

3. What symbolic possibilities might the wreck stand for?

4. Discuss the mode of identity and address Rich projects in the final lines that shift the voice of the poem among the first-person singular and plural (*I* and *we*) and second-person (*you*) pronouns.

TOPIC FOR CRITICAL WRITING

Rich has written that she uses poetry as a "means of self-exploration." To what extent might the dive serve as an extended metaphor for such exploration of self?

Anne Killigrew was the daughter of the seventeenth-century dramatist Dr. Henry Killigrew, who gave her access to the court of the Duke and Duchess of York. John Donne wrote an elegy upon her untimely death from smallpox in 1885 entitled "To the Pious Memory of the Accomplished Young Lady Mrs. Anne Killigrew." Female authorship, however celebrated in this way, was not without its perils and frustration. The figure of the poetess was an easy mark for male criticism, as Killigrew relates in "Upon the Saying That My Verses Were Made by Another."

ANNE KILLIGREW   *(1660–1685)*

Upon the Saying That My Verses Were Made by Another

(1686)

Next Heaven, my Vows to thee (O Sacred *Muse!*)
I offer'd up, nor didst thou them refuse.

O Queen of Verse, said I, if thou'lt inspire,
And warm my Soul with thy Poetique Fire,
No love of gold shall share with thee my heart,   5
Or yet ambition in my brest have part,
More Rich, more Noble I will ever hold
The *Muse's* laurel, than a crown of gold.
An undivided sacrifice I'll lay
Upon thine altar, soul and body pay;   10
Thou shalt my pleasure, my employment be,
My all I'll make a holocaust° to thee.

The deity that ever does attend
Prayers so sincere, to mine did condescend.

---

12 *holocaust:* Burnt sacrifice.

I writ, and the judicious prais'd my pen: 15
Could any doubt ensuing Glory then?
What pleasing raptures fill'd my ravisht sense?
How strong, how sweet, fame, was thy influence?
And thine, false hope, that to my flatter'd sight
Did'st glories represent so near, and bright?!   20
By thee deceiv'd, methought, each verdant tree,
Apollos transform'd *Daphne* seem'd to be;
And ev'ry fresher branch, and ev'ry bough,
Appear'd as garlands to empale my brow.
The learn'd in Love say, thus the winged boy   25
Does first approach, drest up in welcome joy;
At first he to the cheated lover's sight
Nought represents but rapture and delight,
Alluring hopes, soft fears, which stronger bind
Their hearts, than when they more assurance find.   30

    Embolden'd thus, to fame I did commit,
By some few hands, my most unlucky wit.
But ah, the sad effects that from it came!
What ought t'have brought me honour, brought me shame!
Like Aesop's painted jay I seem'd to all,   35
Adorn'd in plumes, I not my own could call:
Rifl'd like her, each one my Feathers tore,
And, as they thought, unto the owner bore.
My laurels thus anothers brow adorn'd,
My Numbers they Admir'd, but me they scorn'd: 40
Anothers brow, that had so rich a store
Of sacred wreaths, that circled it before;
Where mine quite lost, (like a small stream that ran
Into a vast and boundless ocean)
Was swallow'd up, with what it joyn'd and drown'd.   45
And that Abyss yet no accession found.

    Orinda, (*Albions* and her sex's grace)
Ow'd not her glory to a beauteous face,
It was her radiant soul that shone within,
Which struck a lustre through her outward skin;   50
That did her lips and cheeks with roses dye,
Advanc't her Height, and Sparkled in her Eye.
Nor did her Sex at all obstruct her fame,
But higher 'mong the stars it fixt her name;
What she did write, not only all allow'd,   55
But ev'ry laurel, to her laurel, bowed!

    Th'envious age, only to Me alone,
Will not allow what I do write, my Own,

But let 'em rage, and 'gainst a maide conspire,
So deathless numbers from my tuneful lyre   60
Do ever flow; so *Phoebus* I by thee
Divinely inspired and possesed may be;
I willingly accept *Cassandra's* fate,
To speak the truth, although believed too late.

TOPICS FOR CRITICAL THINKING

1. Discuss Killigrew's use of simile in her complaint over the reception her writing received as she describes it in the fourth stanza.
2. How does Killigrew address her muse in the opening of the poem, and how does she set up the seriousness of her commitment to poetry?
3. How does the poet react to her initial fame in stanza three?

TOPIC FOR CRITICAL WRITING

Examine Killigrew's mythological allusions to Orinda, Phoebus, and Cassandra in her closing lines. What argument do they make about poetry's truth, however obscured by one's political circumstances?

A recipient of the Pulitzer Prize (1955) and National Book Award (1969), the widely traveled poet Elizabeth Bishop taught for many years at the University of Washington and Harvard. "In the Waiting Room" describes the crisis of identity she remembers from 1918 when she was seven years old.

ELIZABETH BISHOP   *(1911–1979)*

In the Waiting Room   *(1976)*

In Worcester, Massachusetts,
I went with Aunt Consuelo
to keep her dentist's appointment
and sat and waited for her
in the dentist's waiting room.   5
It was winter. It got dark
early. The waiting room
was full of grown-up people,
arctics and overcoats,
lamps and magazines.   10
My aunt was inside
what seemed like a long time
and while I waited and read
the *National Geographic*
(I could read) and carefully   15

studied the photographs:
the inside of a volcano,
black, and full of ashes;
then it was spilling over
in rivulets of fire.   20
Osa and Martin Johnson
dressed in riding breeches,
laced boots, and pith helmets.
A dead man slung on a pole
—"Long Pig,"° the caption said.   25
Babies with pointed heads
wound round and round with string;
black, naked women with necks
wound round and round with wire
like the necks of light bulbs.   30
Their breasts were horrifying.
I read it right straight through.
I was too shy to stop.
And then I looked at the cover:
the yellow margins, the date.   35

Suddenly, from inside,
came an *oh!* of pain
—Aunt Consuelo's voice—
not very loud or long.
I wasn't at all surprised;   40
even then I knew she was
a foolish, timid woman.
I might have been embarrassed,
but wasn't. What took me
completely by surprise   45
was that it was *me:*
my voice, in my mouth.
Without thinking at all
I was my foolish aunt,
I—we—were falling, falling,   50
our eyes glued to the cover
of the *National Geographic,*
February, 1918.

I said to myself: three days
and you'll be seven years old.   55
I was saying it to stop
the sensation of falling off
the round, turning world

---

25 *"Long Pig":* Melanesian slang term for human being; a victim of cannibalism.

into cold, blue-black space.   60
But I felt: you are an *I*,
you are an *Elizabeth*,
you are one of *them*.
Why should you be one, too?
I scarcely dared to look   65
to see what it was I was.
I gave a sidelong glance
—I couldn't look any higher—
at shadowy gray knees,
trousers and skirts and boots   70
and different pairs of hands
lying under the lamps.
I knew that nothing stranger
had ever happened, that nothing
stranger could ever happen.   75
Why should I be my aunt,
or me, or anyone?
What similarities—
boots, hands, the family voice
I felt in my throat, or even   80
the *National Geographic*
and those awful hanging breasts—
held us all together
or made us all just one?
How—I didn't know any   85
word for it—how "unlikely" . . .
How had I come to be here,
like them, and overhear
a cry of pain that could have
got loud and worse but hadn't?

                                                                90

The waiting room was bright
and too hot. It was sliding
beneath a big black wave,
another, and another.

Then I was back in it.   95
The War was on. Outside,
in Worcester, Massachusetts,
were night and slush and cold,
and it was still the fifth
of February, 1918.

TOPICS FOR CRITICAL THINKING

1. Discuss your sense of what kind of experience Bishop describes in her poem. What kind of ecstasy and what kind of empathy with others does Bishop's first-person narrator relate?
2. Examine closely the details from her reading in the February 1918 edition of *National Geographic*. Discuss the ways in which Bishop estranges our conventional images of the body in these passages.
3. What do you think the magazine representations have to do with her experience in the waiting room?
4. How significant is it that Bishop poses her revelations in the third stanza as questions rather than as statements?
5. What does her final reference to the poem's historical context of World War I have to do with the poem's action and events?

TOPIC FOR CRITICAL WRITING

How important is it that this event takes place in a waiting room? How crucial is the poem's setting to its situation and action?

Emily Brontë, the author of *Wuthering Heights*, is, like her sister Charlotte, known primarily as a novelist rather than a poet. Nevertheless, the Brontë sisters published a collection of verse entitled *Poems* under the male pseudonyms Currer, Ellis, and Acton Bell in 1846. Aside from a brief stint of study at the Roe Head, Law Hill, and Pensionnat Héger schools, Emily lived her life at her aunt's home at Haworth Parsonage in Yorkshire, whose surrounding moors comprise the settings of *Wuthering Heights*. Similar in some ways to Emily Dickinson, Emily Brontë chose, rather than succumbed to, a life of domestic seclusion. In fact, she had a strong sense of self, rooted in a romantic faith in the powers of the natural world as she describes them in "Stanzas."

EMILY BRONTË *(1818–1848)*

Stanzas   *(1846)*

Often rebuked, yet always back returning
    To those first feelings that were born with me,
And leaving busy chase of wealth and learning
    For idle dreams of things which cannot be;

To-day, I will seek not the shadowy region;   5
    Its unsustaining vastness waxes drear;
And visions rising, legion after legion,
    Bring the unreal world too strangely near.

I'll walk, but not in old heroic traces,
    And not in paths of high morality,   10
And not among the half-distinguished faces,
    The clouded forms of long-past history.

I'll walk where my own nature would be leading:
    It vexes me to choose another guide:
Where the gray flocks in ferny glens are feeding;   15
    Where the wild wind blows on the mountain side.

What have those lonely mountains worth revealing?
    More glory and more grief than I can tell:
The earth that wakes *one* human heart to feeling
    Can centre both the worlds of Heaven and Hell.   20

TOPICS FOR CRITICAL THINKING

1. Discuss the ways in which Brontë characterizes the public sphere of society in the first two stanzas. Why does she choose to turn away from it?
2. Consider her similar rejection of conventional history in stanza three. What, in your opinion, might account for why she takes this stance toward the recorded past?
3. If you have read *Wuthering Heights*, what kinds of thematic parallels do you find in the novel and her poem?

TOPIC FOR CRITICAL WRITING

Focus on the ways in which Brontë characterizes the landscapes around Haworth. What values does she find in that natural setting?

    A cousin to James Russell Lowell, Amy Lowell was raised in a prominent Boston family. Her father was on the board of the Massachusetts Institute of Technology and her brother Abbott Lowell was a president of Harvard University. Not insignificantly, Amy herself in 1912 founded *Poetry* magazine, one of the most important literary journals of the twentieth century. Two years later, she began to live with Ada Russell, her lifelong partner. In "Venus Transiens" she addresses her lover, comparing her to the goddess Venus.

AMY LOWELL   *(1847–1925)*

Venus Transiens   *(1919)*

Tell me,
Was Venus more beautiful
Than you are,

When she topped
The crinkled waves,   5
Drifting shoreward
On her plaited shell?
Was Botticelli's vision
Fairer than mine;
And were the painted rosebuds   10
He tossed his lady,
Of better worth
Than the words I blow about you
To cover your too great loveliness
As with a gauze   15
Of misted silver?
For me,
You stand poised
In the blue and buoyant air,
Cinctured by bright winds,   20
Treading the sunlight.
And the waves which precede you
Ripple and stir
The sands at my feet.

TOPIC FOR CRITICAL THINKING

Compare Lowell's poem to Botticelli's *The Birth of Venus* (see color insert), and discuss the ways in which the poem alludes to specific details in its verbal presentation.

TOPIC FOR CRITICAL WRITING

Contrast Lowell's use of Botticelli with that of Rukeyser above in "The Birth of Venus."

Critical Perspective: On Feminism and Re-vision

"Ibsen's *When We Dead Awaken* is a play about the use that the male artist and thinker—in the process of creating culture as we know it—has made of women, in his life and in his work; and about a woman's slow struggling awakening to the use to which her life has been put. Bernard Shaw wrote in 1900 of this play:

> [Ibsen] shows us that no degradation ever devized or permitted is as disastrous as this degradation; that through it women can die into luxuries for men and yet can kill them; that men and women are becoming conscious of this; and that what remains to be seen as perhaps the most interesting of all imminent social developments is what will happen "when we dead awaken."[1]

---

1. G. B. Shaw, *The Quintessence of Ibsenism* (New York: Hill & Wang, 1922), p. 139.

"It's exhilarating to be alive in a time of awakening consciousness; it can also be confusing, disorienting, and painful. This awakening of dead or sleeping consciousness has already affected the lives of millions of women, even those who don't know it yet. It is also affecting the lives of men, even those who deny its claims upon them. The argument will go on whether an oppressive economic class system is responsible for the oppressive nature of male/female relations, or whether, in fact, patriarchy—the domination of males—is the original model of oppression on which all others are based. But in the last few years the women's movement has drawn inescapable and illuminating connections between our sexual lives and our political institutions. The sleepwalkers are coming awake, and for the first time this awakening has a collective reality; it is no longer such a lonely thing to open one's eyes.

"Re-vision—the act of looking back, of seeing with fresh eyes, of entering an old text from a new critical direction—is for women more than a chapter in cultural history: it is an act of survival. Until we can understand the assumptions in which we are drenched we cannot know ourselves. And this drive to self-knowledge, for women, is more than a search for identity: it is part of our refusal of the self-destructiveness of male-dominated society. A radical critique of literature, feminist in its impulse, would take the work first of all as a clue to how we live, how we have been living, how we have been led to imagine ourselves, how our language has trapped as well as liberated us, how the very act of naming has been till now a male prerogative, and how we can begin to see and name—and therefore live—afresh. A change in the concept of sexual identity is essential if we are not going to see the old political order reassert itself in every new revolution. We need to know the writing of the past, and know it differently than we have ever known it; not to pass on a tradition but to break its hold over us.

"For writers, and at this moment for women writers in particular, there is the challenge and promise of a whole new psychic geography to be explored. But there is also a difficult and dangerous walking on the ice, as we try to find language and images for a consciousness we are just coming into, and with little in the past to support us."

—Adrienne Rich, from "When We Dead Awaken:
Writing as Re-vision" (1971)

Critical Perspective: On Sexual Difference

"For the woman artist is not privileged or mandated to find her self-in-world except by facing (affronting?) and mounting an enormous struggle with the cultural fictions—myths, narratives, iconographies, languages—which heretofore have delimited the representation of women. And which are culturally and psychically saturating.

"To define then. 'Female aesthetic': the production of formal, epistemological, and thematic strategies by members of the group Woman, strategies born in struggle with much of already existing culture, and overdetermined by two elements of sexual difference—by women's psychosocial experiences of gender asymmetry and by women's historical status in an (ambiguously) non-hegemonic group. . . .

"This both/and vision, the contradictory movement between the logically irreconcilable, must have several causes. Perhaps it is based on the bi-sexual oscillation within female psychosexual development. Nancy Chodorow shows how the Oedipal configuration occurs differently in girls and boys and that, because of the way the sexes are reproduced in the family, most women retain men as erotic objects and women as emotional objects. This oscillation between men and women, father and mother, pervades her emotional (and thus aesthetic) life. And do we also value the K-Mart version of this structure: conflict avoidance. Everybody is right. Feel like a chameleon, taking coloration—

"Insider-outsider social status will also help dissolve an either-or dualism. For the woman finds she is irreconcilable things: an outsider by her gender position, by her relation to power; may be an insider by her social position, her class. She can be both. Her ontological, her psychic, her class position all cause doubleness. Doubled consciousness. Doubled understandings. How then could she neglect to invent a form which produces this incessant, critical, splitting motion. To invent this form. To invent the theory for this form.

"Following, the 'female aesthetic' will produce artworks that incorporate contradiction and nonlinear movement into the heart of the text."
—Rachel Blau Du Plessis, from "For the Etruscans" (1981)

Featured Writer

Anne Sexton

ANNE SEXTON

Born on November 9, 1928, Anne Sexton was the third daughter of Ralph and Mary Gray Staples Harvey. Notable ancestors on her mother's side of the family included Nelson Dingley Jr., a governor of Maine and member of Congress, as well as Arthur Gray Staples, editor and publisher of the *Lewiston Evening Journal*. Sexton's paternal grandfather, Louis Harvey, was an influential member of the affluent Wellesley community and president of the Wellesley National Bank. Sexton's father, Ralph Churchill Harvey, was a successful traveling sales representative for the New England wool industry and became president of the R. C. Harvey Company. Bearing the literary influences of her maternal line, Anne shared her middle name with her mother and journalist grandfather. As a child, Anne also enjoyed a very close relationship to her maternal great-aunt Anna Ladd Dingley, or "Nana" as she called her, who was herself a journalist and part owner of her father's newspaper. Nana moved in with the Harvey family in 1939 when Anne was eleven; after a period of deteriorating mental health, Nana was removed to a nursing home five years later. The example of her great-aunt's mental illness, coupled with her parents' alcoholism, were powerful shaping forces in Sexton's troubled psychic development.

Brought up and educated in Wellesley and in Weston, Sexton graduated from the Rogers Hall preparatory school in 1947 and then attended the Garland School in Boston, where she met and later eloped with Alfred Muller Sexton II in 1948. Nicknamed Kayo, Anne's husband had been a premedical major at Colgate University but soon dropped out of college. After serving in the Navy during the Korean War, Kayo eventually went to work for his father-in-law, joining the R. C. Harvey Company as a traveling salesman. Meanwhile, Anne pursued a brief career as a fashion model for the Hart Agency in Boston before giving birth to her first daughter, Linda Gray Sexton, in 1953. After her great-aunt Nana died in 1954, Anne suffered her first hospitalization for anxiety in 1956, following the birth of her second daughter, Joyce Ladd Sexton, the previous year.

In 1956, Sexton began psychoanalytic treatment with Dr. Martin Orne. Over the next eight years, Orne would offer supportive encouragement for Sexton's emergence as a major poet. During his first consultation with Sexton, Orne suggested she write about her treatment, and poetry quickly became a vital aspect of her therapy. The following year, she enrolled in a poetry work-shop under the direction of John Holmes at the Boston Center for Adult Ed-ucation, where she met her lifelong friend and colleague poet Maxine Kumin. Sexton quickly found a receptive audience for her distinctive style of autobio-graphical verse. By the summer of 1958, she was placing her poems in such national journals as *Harpers*, *The New Yorker*, and *Christian Science Monitor*. Moreover, Sexton received a scholarship to study at the Antioch Writer's Conference with the "confessional" poet W. D. Snodgrass.

Through Snodgrass's influence, Sexton began studying creative writing with the poet Robert Lowell at Boston University, where she met the young poets George Starbuck and Sylvia Plath. During this time, Sexton continued to place her work in notable journals such as the *Hudson Review*, which pub-lished her entire 240-line poem "The Double Image." Soon she had enough material for her first book, *To Bedlam and Part Way Back*, but John Holmes, her first teacher, urged her not to publish it. Although Holmes was a support-ive mentor for Sexton's new life as a writer, he also discouraged her from writ-ing overt poems about her mental illness, especially her recurrent periods of hospitalization. Her verse response in "For John, Who Begs Me Not to En-quire Further" forcefully rejected his advice as it declared her independence and self-possession as a poet.

For John, Who Begs Me Not to Enquire Further   *(1960)*

Not that it was beautiful,
but that, in the end, there was
a certain sense of order there;
something worth learning
in that narrow diary of my mind,   5
in the commonplaces of the asylum
where the cracked mirror
or my own selfish death
outstared me.
And if I tried   10
to give you something else,
something outside of myself,
you would not know
that the worst of anyone
can be, finally,   15
an accident of hope.
I tapped my own head;
it was glass, an inverted bowl.
It is a small thing
to rage in your own bowl.   20
At first it was private.
Then it was more than myself;
it was you, or your house

or your kitchen.
And if you turn away   25
because there is no lesson here
I will hold my awkward bowl,
with all its cracked stars shining
like a complicated lie,
and fasten a new skin around it   30
as if I were dressing an orange
or a strange sun.
Not that it was beautiful,
but that I found some order there.
There ought to be something special   35
for someone
in this kind of hope.
This is something I would never find
in a lovelier place, my dear,
although your fear is anyone's fear,   40
like an invisible veil between us all . . .
and sometimes in private,
my kitchen, your kitchen,
my face, your face.

TOPICS FOR CRITICAL THINKING

1. Sexton rejects conventional beauty as her poetry's subject matter. What does she value in its place?

2. In exploring the terms of her own madness, Sexton writes, "At first it was private. / Then it was more than myself." In what ways does she invite Holmes and her extended audience to identify with her "cracked" mental states?

TOPIC FOR CRITICAL WRITING

Discuss the metaphors and similes through which Sexton describes her psychological condition in the poem.

Sexton's title alludes to Schopenhauer's famous letter to Goethe where he writes "Most of us carry in our heart the Jocasta who begs Oedipus for God's sake not to inquire further." Identifying with Oedipus, not Jocasta, Sexton chose this quote on fearless, though tragic, self-knowledge as the epigraph to her first volume of verse. As a psychoanalytic poet, Sexton insists on finding poetic material, paradoxically, in the antipoetic yet illuminating encounters with her psychic life, its "complicated lie." Although the settings, themes, and images of her chosen subject matter—"the common places of the asylum"— are not beautiful in any conventional sense, they communicate as she says "something I would never find / in a lovelier place." Although Sexton's poetry has been given the label of "confessional" verse, her materials, as she says here, are both personal and universal in scope. "At first it was private. / Then it was more than myself." The fear that she probes and that Holmes resists is "anyone's fear, / like an invisible veil between us all."

By the end of the 1950s, Sexton was on her way toward becoming a major poet, but she was also experiencing tragic, personal losses. On the one hand, she received the good news that Houghton Mifflin would publish *To Bedlam and Part Way Back*. On the other hand, she lost both her parents with her mother dying of cancer in March 1959 and the poet's father suffering a fatal cerebral hemorrhage that June. Sexton herself had begun the year with a breakdown and recuperation at the Westwood Lodge. Despite these personal setbacks, Sexton's career as an American poet was flourishing. She received a Robert Frost Fellowship at the Bread Loaf Writer's Conference followed by her first book's nomination for the National Book Award the next year.

The 1960s was Sexton's watershed decade as a poet, beginning with her appointment to the Radcliffe Institute for Independent Study in 1961 and followed by the Levinson Prize from *Poetry* magazine for her second book of poems *All My Pretty Ones* (1962). Soon she received a traveling fellowship from the American Academy of Arts and Letters (1963) and a Ford Foundation writers in residence grant with the Charles Playhouse in Boston (1964). The mid-1960s saw the publication of her third volume *Selected Poems* (1964), her election as a Fellow of the Royal Society of Literature (1965), another travel grant from the International Congress of Cultural Freedom (1965), culminating in the Pulitzer Prize and the Shelley Award from the Poetry Society of America for her 1967 volume *Live or Die*. Other honors followed in her award of a Guggenheim Fellowship (1969) for producing her play *Mercy Street* at the American Place Theater, an honorary doctor of letters from Tufts University (1970), her promotion to Full Professor at Boston University (1972), and her award of the Crashaw Chair in Literature at Colgate University (1972). Amidst this whirlwind of readings, award ceremonies, and teaching, Sexton also found time to make an adventurous tour of Kenya with Kayo during the summer of 1966.

Throughout her meteoric rise to worldwide prominence as a poet, lecturer, and educator, Sexton continued to be hospitalized for periodic bouts with mental illness and suicide attempts. Nevertheless, she mined these experiences as material for her verse and kept in touch with fellow patients by teaching poetry, for example, in 1968 at McLean Hospital. In that same year, Sexton also made forays into popular culture by performing her verse in a rock band she formed called Anne Sexton and Her Kind. Sexton based the name of her band on her poem "Her Kind" from *To Bedlam and Partway Back*. In fact, she considered "Her Kind" to be her signature poem. She usually opened her poetry readings with it, often inviting her audience to leave if they could not identify with her kind.

Her Kind   *(1960)*

I have gone out, a possessed witch,
haunting the black air, braver at night;

dreaming evil, I have done my hitch
over the plain houses, light by light:
lonely thing, twelve-fingered, out of mind.   5
A woman like that is not a woman, quite.
I have been her kind.

I have found the warm caves in the woods,
filled them with skillets, carvings, shelves,
closets, silks, innumerable goods;   10
fixed the suppers for the worms and the elves:
whining, rearranging the disaligned.
A woman like that is misunderstood.
I have been her kind.

I have ridden in your cart, driver,   15
waved my nude arms at villages going by,
learning the last bright routes, survivor
where your flames still bite my thigh
and my ribs crack where your wheels wind.
A woman like that is not ashamed to die.   20
I have been her kind.

TOPICS FOR CRITICAL THINKING

1. While "Her Kind" reflects on the phases of the poet's life, it is not strictly autobio-graphical. For one thing, the first-person *I* pronoun is not fixed but reflects at least three personae. How would you distinguish the differences among the various ver-sions of the self's experience in the three stanzas?

2. What unites the speakers?

3. Although the final stanza presents an image of martyrdom, perhaps for infidelity, how does it assert the poet's identity, nevertheless, as a "survivor" in luminous and ecstatic terms?

TOPIC FOR CRITICAL WRITING

How might the represented pronoun *I* in the poem differ from the poet's subject position as the one who witnesses, records, and performs what she has otherwise experienced?

Sexton ushered in the 1970s with a creative stint that produced the sev-enteen long poems of *Transformations* (1971) based on the fairy tales of the Brothers Grimm. She also made progress on two other volumes *The Book of Folly* (1972) and *The Death Notebooks* (1974). In the early part of 1973, Sexton divorced Kayo and was frequently accompanied by Lois Ames, Louise Co-nant, or Joan Smith on her reading tours. Moving beyond her roles of wife and mother in midlife, Sexton increasingly sought psychological and emo-tional support from other women. Toward the end of her life, Sexton gave one of her most powerful performances on March 7, 1974, reading at the Sanders Theater for the Harvard Literary Club. There she read what she archly declared as her "posthumous poems" from her recently published collection *The Death Notebooks* and her manuscript of *The Awful Rowing Toward God*. Indeed, as these titles implied, Sexton's obsession with death and suicide was something that was growing apace in middle age. While Sexton had attempted to take her life more than once in her career, she now began to contemplate suicide more deliberately. Setting her estate in order, Sexton amended her will to make her daughter Linda her literary executor. Finally, after making the last corrections to *The Awful Rowing Toward God* and at the height of her fame, Anne Sexton committed suicide by carbon monoxide poisoning in her garage on October 4, 1974.

Since her death, Sexton's notoriety as poet has continued to grow. The complete corpus of her eight books of verse and two volumes of posthumous verse were compiled by Linda Gray Sexton in *The Complete Poems* (1981). In addition, numerous critical studies and a major biography by Diane Middlebrook have examined her life and work. But equally important, Sexton remains a popular poet for the general reader. "Women poets in particular," writes poet Maxine Kumin, "owe a debt to Anne Sexton, who broke new ground, shattered taboos, and endured a barrage of attacks along the way because of the flamboyance of her subject matter. . . . Anne Sexton has earned her place in the canon."

Poems for Further Reading and Critical Writing

ANNE SEXTON *(1928–1974)*

The Moss of His Skin   *(1960)*

> *"Young girls in old Arabia were often buried alive next*
> *to their dead fathers, apparently as sacrifice to the*
> *goddesses of the tribes . . ."*
>   –HAROLD FELDMAN, "CHILDREN OF THE DESERT,"
>   PSYCHOANALYSIS AND PSYCHOANALYTIC REVIEW,
>   *Fall 1958*

It was only important
to smile and hold still,
to lie down beside him
and to rest awhile,
to be folded up together   5
as if we were silk,
to sink from the eyes of mother
and not to talk.
The black room took us
like a cave or a mouth   10
or an indoor belly.

I held my breath
and daddy was there,
his thumbs, his fat skull,
his teeth, his hair growing   15
like a field or a shawl.
I lay by the moss
of his skin until
it grew strange. My sisters
will never know that I fall   20
out of myself and pretend
that Allah will not see
how I hold my daddy
like an old stone tree.

TOPICS FOR CRITICAL THINKING

1. In her therapy sessions, Sexton often entered into trance states. In one of them she reported an incident of sexual molestation by her father Ralph Harvey. Although Sexton wrote several poems on the erotic connection between fathers and daughters, she never made up her mind whether this material was a memory of an actual encounter or something she had fantasized. How does the poem's epigraph set up a mythical frame for approaching the archetypal bond between daughters and fathers?

2. How would you describe the tone of the poem's opening lines?

3. What role, if any, does the mother play in the family drama the poet recounts?

4. How do you interpret the final lines? Do they maintain or break the mythic frame that sets up the poem in the epigraph? How are we to interpret the poem as a parable of the relationship between daughters and fathers?

5. Compare and contrast Sexton's mythic presentation of fathers and daughters in "The Moss of His Skin" with Sexton's use of the fairy tale narrative of Sleeping Beauty in "Briar Rose (Sleeping Beauty)," which follows.

TOPIC FOR CRITICAL WRITING

How does Sexton's language in "The Moss of His Skin" alternate realistic detail with more stylized descriptions that rely on figurative language?

Briar Rose (Sleeping Beauty)   *(1971)*

Consider
a girl who keeps slipping off,
arms limp as old carrots,
into the hypnotist's trance,
into a spirit world   5
speaking with the gift of tongues.
She is stuck in the time machine,
suddenly two years old sucking her thumb,
as inward as a snail,

learning to talk again.   10
She's on a voyage.
She is swimming further and further back,
up like a salmon,
struggling into her mother's pocketbook.
Little doll child,   15
come here to Papa.
Sit on my knee.
I have kisses for the back of your neck.
A penny for your thoughts, Princess.
I will hunt them like an emerald.   20

Come be my snooky
and I will give you a root.
That kind of voyage,
rank as honeysuckle.

Once   25
a king had a christening
for his daughter Briar Rose
and because he had only twelve gold plates
he asked only twelve fairies
to the grand event.   30
The thirteenth fairy,
her fingers as long and thin as straws,
her eyes burnt by cigarettes,
her uterus an empty teacup,
arrived with an evil gift.   35
She made this prophecy:
The princess shall prick herself
on a spinning wheel in her fifteenth year
and then fall down dead.
Kaputt!   40
The court fell silent.
The king looked like Munch's *Scream*°
Fairies' prophecies,
in times like those,
held water.   45
However the twelfth fairy
had a certain kind of eraser
and thus she mitigated the curse
changing that death
into a hundred-year sleep.   50

---

42 *Munch's* Scream: *The Scream* (1893) by Norwegian expressionist painter Edvard Munch (1863–1944).

The king ordered every spinning wheel
exterminated and exorcized.
Briar Rose grew to be a goddess
and each night the king
bit the hem of her gown   55
to keep her safe.
He fastened the moon up
with a safety pin
to give her perpetual light.
He forced every male in the court   60
to scour his tongue with Bab-o
lest they poison the air she dwelt in.
Thus she dwelt in his odor.
Rank as honeysuckle.

On her fifteenth birthday   65
she pricked her finger
on a charred spinning wheel
and the clocks stopped.
Yes indeed. She went to sleep.
The king and queen went to sleep,   70
the courtiers, the flies on the wall.
The fire in the hearth grew still
and the roast meat stopped crackling.
The trees turned into metal
and the dog became china.   75
They all lay in a trance,
each a catatonic
stuck in a time machine.
Even the frogs were zombies.
Only a bunch of briar roses grew   80
forming a great wall of tacks
around the castle.
Many princes
tried to get through the brambles
for they had heard much of Briar Rose   85
but they had not scoured their tongues
so they were held by the thorns
and thus were crucified.
In due time
a hundred years passed   90
and a prince got through.
The briars parted as if for Moses
and the prince found the tableau intact.
He kissed Briar Rose
and she woke up crying: 95
Daddy! Daddy!

Presto! She's out of prison!
She married the prince
and all went well
except for the fear—   100
the fear of sleep.

Briar Rose
was an insomniac . . .
She could not nap
or lie in sleep   105
without the court chemist
mixing her some knock-out drops
and never in the prince's presence.
If it is to come, she said,
sleep must take me unawares   110
while I am laughing or dancing
so that I do not know that brutal place
where I lie down with cattle prods,
the hole in my cheek open.
Further, I must not dream   115
for when I do I see the table set
and a faltering crone at my place,
her eyes burnt by cigarettes
as she eats betrayal like a slice of meat.

I must not sleep   120
for while asleep I'm ninety
and think I'm dying.
Death rattles in my throat
like a marble.
I wear tubes like earrings.   125
I lie as still as a bar of iron.
You can stick a needle
through my kneecap and I won't flinch.
I'm all shot up with Novocain.
This trance girl   130
is yours to do with.
You could lay her in a grave,
an awful package,
and shovel dirt on her face
and she'd never call back: Hello there!   135
But if you kissed her on the mouth
her eyes would spring open
and she'd call out: Daddy! Daddy!
Presto!
She's out of prison.   140

There was a theft.
That much I am told.
I was abandoned.
That much I know.
I was forced backward.   145
I was forced forward.
I was passed hand to hand
like a bowl of fruit.
Each night I am nailed into place
and forget who I am.   150
Daddy?
That's another kind of prison.
It's not the prince at all,
but my father
drunkenly bent over my bed,   155
circling the abyss like a shark,
my father thick upon me
like some sleeping jellyfish.
What voyage this, little girl?
This coming out of prison?   160
God help—
this life after death?

TOPICS FOR CRITICAL THINKING

1. Sleeping Beauty is a well-known Brothers Grimm fairy tale that has a central place in the popular imagination. Walt Disney Pictures, for example, adapted Tchaikovsky's "Sleeping Beauty" as the sound track for its 1959 cartoon version of the legend and won the Academy Award for Best Score for a Musical Picture that year. Recount what you know about the fairy tale of Sleeping Beauty. How faithful is Sexton to the original storyline?

2. Discuss Sexton's opening stanza in "Briar Rose (Sleeping Beauty)." How might it refer to the kind of regressions back to childhood that the poet experienced in psychoanalysis?

3. Sexton emphasizes the father's obsession with keeping Briar Rose safe from the curse of the thirteenth fairy. Why does Sexton then alter the original legend to have Briar Rose call out the name of "Daddy" when the prince awakens her with a kiss?

TOPIC FOR CRITICAL WRITING

How do you interpret the ending of the poem that moves from the distanced frame of fairy tale toward a more directly autobiographical statement? Discuss the presentation of Briar Rose as an insomniac in the poem. How do you read her final questions that end the poem?

from The Death of the Fathers   *(1972)*

4. *Santa*

Father,
the Santa Claus suit
you bought from Wolff Fording Theatrical Supplies,
back before I was born,
is dead.   5
The white beard you fooled me with
and the hair like Moses,
the thick crimpy wool
that used to buzz me on the neck,
is dead.   10
Yes, my busting rosy Santa,
ringing your bronze cowbell.
You with real soot on your nose
and snow (taken from the refrigerator some years)
on your big shoulder.   15
The room was like Florida.
You took so many oranges out of your bag
and threw them around the living room,
all the time laughing that North Pole laugh.
Mother would kiss you   20
for she was that tall.
Mother could hug you
for she was not afraid.
The reindeer pounded on the roof.
(It was my Nana with a hammer in the attic.   25
For *my* children it was my husband
with a crowbar breaking things up.)
The year I ceased to believe in you
is the year you were drunk.
My boozy red man,   30
your voice all slithery like soap,
you were a long way from Saint Nick
with Daddy's cocktail smell.
I cried and ran from the room
and you said, "Well, thank God that's over!"   35
And it was, until the grandchildren came.
Then I tied up your pillows
in the five A.M. Christ morning
and I adjusted the beard,
all yellow with age,   40
and applied rouge to your cheeks
and Chalk White to your eyebrows.
We were conspirators,

secret actors,
and I kissed you   45
because I was tall enough.
But that is over.
The era closes
and large children hang their stockings
and build a black memorial to you.   50
And you, you fade out of sight
like a lost signalman
wagging his lantern
for the train that comes no more.

TOPICS FOR CRITICAL THINKING

1. Compare and contrast the treatment of fathers in the previous two poems with "Santa."
2. How does Sexton as the mature speaker of the poem differ from the childhood memory of herself as daughter represented in the opening lines?
3. In what sense have she and her father become "conspirators" in restaging the myth of Santa for her own children?
4. What change is signaled in Sexton's blunt line "But that is over" in the poem's ending?

TOPIC FOR CRITICAL WRITING

How does Sexton use the legend of Santa Claus for her own symbolic purposes in the poem? What point is Sexton making about Santa as an imagined father figure and her father's impersonation of Santa?

Rapunzel   *(1971)*

A woman
who loves a woman
is forever young.
The mentor
and the student   5
feed off each other.
Many a girl
had an old aunt
who locked her in the study
to keep the boys away.   10
They would play rummy
or lie on the couch
and touch and touch.
Old breast against young breast . . .

Let your dress fall down your shoulder,   15
come touch a copy of you

for I am at the mercy of rain,
for I have left the three Christs of Ypsilanti,
for I have left the long naps of Ann Arbor
and the church spires have turned to stumps.   20
The sea bangs into my cloister
for the young politicians are dying,
and dying so hold me, my young dear,
hold me . . .

The yellow rose will turn to cinder   25
and New York City will fall in
before we are done so hold me,
my young dear, hold me.
Put your pale arms around my neck.
Let me hold your heart like a flower   30
lest it bloom and collapse.
Give me your skin
as sheer as a cobweb,
let me open it up
and listen in and scoop out the dark.   35
Give me your nether lips
all puffy with their art
and I will give you angel fire in return.
We are two clouds
glistening in the bottle glass.   40
We are two birds
washing in the same mirror.
We were fair game
but we have kept out of the cesspool.
We are strong.   45
We are the good ones.
Do not discover us
for we lie together all in green
like pond weeds.
Hold me, my young dear, hold me.   50

They touch their delicate watches
one at a time.
They dance to the lute
two at a time.
They are as tender as bog moss.   55
They play mother-me-do
all day.
A woman
who loves a woman
is forever young.   60

Once there was a witch's garden
more beautiful than Eve's
with carrots growing like little fish,
with many tomatoes rich as frogs,
onions as ingrown as hearts, 65
the squash singing like a dolphin
and one patch given over wholly, to magic—
rampion, a kind of salad root,
a kind of harebell more potent than penicillin,
growing leaf by leaf, skin by skin, 70
as rapt and as fluid as Isadora Duncan.
However the witch's garden was kept locked
and each day a woman who was with child
looked upon the rampion wildly,
fancying that she would die 75
if she could not have it.
Her husband feared for her welfare
and thus climbed into the garden
to fetch the life-giving tubers.

Ah ha, cried the witch, 80
whose proper name was Mother Gothel,
you are a thief and now you will die.
However they made a trade,
typical enough in those times.
He promised his child to Mother Gothel 85
so of course when it was born
she took the child away with her.
She gave the child the name Rapunzel,
another name for the life-giving rampion.
Because Rapunzel was a beautiful girl 90
Mother Gothel treasured her beyond all things.
As she grew older Mother Gothel thought:
None but I will ever see her or touch her.
She locked her in a tower without a door
or a staircase. It had only a high window. 95
When the witch wanted to enter she cried:
Rapunzel, Rapunzel, let down your hair.
Rapunzel's hair fell to the ground like a rainbow.
It was as yellow as a dandelion
and as strong as a dog leash. 100
Hand over hand she shinnied up
the hair like a sailor
and there in the stone-cold room,
as cold as a museum,
Mother Gothel cried: 105
Hold me, my young dear, hold me,
and thus they played mother-me-do.

Years later a prince came by
and heard Rapunzel singing in her loneliness.
That song pierced his heart like a valentine   110
but he could find no way to get to her.
Like a chameleon he hid himself among the trees
and watched the witch ascend the swinging hair.
The next day he himself called out:
Rapunzel, Rapunzel, let down your hair,   115
and thus they met and he declared his love.
What is this beast, she thought,
with muscles on his arms
like a bag of snakes?
What is this moss on his legs?   120
What prickly plant grows on his cheeks?
What is this voice as deep as a dog?
Yet he dazzled her with his answers.
Yet he dazzled her with his dancing stick.
They lay together upon the yellowy threads,   125
swimming through them
like minnows through kelp
and they sang out benedictions like the Pope.

Each day he brought her a skein of silk
to fashion a ladder so they could both escape.   130
But Mother Gothel discovered the plot
and cut off Rapunzel's hair to her ears
and took her into the forest to repent.
When the prince came the witch fastened
the hair to a hook and let it down.   135
When he saw Rapunzel had been banished
he flung himself out of the tower, a side of beef.
He was blinded by thorns that pricked him like tacks.
As blind as Oedipus he wandered for years
until he heard a song that pierced his heart   140
like that long-ago valentine.
As he kissed Rapunzel her tears fell on his eyes
and in the manner of such cure-alls
his sight was suddenly restored.

They lived happily as you might expect   145
proving that mother-me-do
can be outgrown,
just as the fish on Friday,
just as a tricycle.
The world, some say,   150
is made up of couples.
A rose must have a stem.

As for Mother Gothel,
her heart shrank to the size of a pin,
never again to say: Hold me, my young dear,   155
hold me,
and only as she dreamt of the yellow hair
did moonlight sift into her mouth.

TOPICS FOR CRITICAL THINKING

1. Recount what you know about the fairy tale Rapunzel.
2. Consider Sexton's narrative strategy of presenting a bonding between women before she begins the story line of "Rapunzel." How does this opening make a feminist difference in the story?
3. How does Sexton shift the narrative point of view to have us identify or at least sympathize with Mother Gothel?
4. Discuss Sexton's use of figurative language to describe Rapunzel's mixed feelings toward the prince when she first meets him.

TOPIC FOR CRITICAL WRITING

How significant is Sexton's allusion to Oedipus in the poem? What does that myth have to do with her rendering of Rapunzel?

The Abortion   (1962)

Somebody who should have been born
is gone.

Just as the earth puckered its mouth,
each bud puffing out from its knot,
I changed my shoes, and then drove south.   5

Up past the Blue Mountains, where
Pennsylvania humps on endlessly,
wearing, like a crayoned cat, its green hair,

its roads sunken in like a gray washboard;
where, in truth, the ground cracks evilly,   10
a dark socket from which the coal has poured,

Somebody who should have been born
is gone.

the grass as bristly and stout as chives,
and me wondering when the ground would break,   15
and me wondering how anything fragile survives;

up in Pennsylvania, I met a little man,
not Rumpelstiltskin, at all, at all . . .
he took the fullness that love began.

Returning north, even the sky grew thin   20
like a high window looking nowhere.
The road was as flat as a sheet of tin.

Somebody who should have been born
is gone.

Yes, woman, such logic will lead   25
to loss without death. Or say what you meant,
you coward . . . this baby that I bleed.

TOPICS FOR CRITICAL THINKING

1. Sexton had an abortion in the spring of 1960. How does her refrain line emphasize and mourn that fact through repetition?
2. Discuss Sexton's setting in the poem. How does landscape imagery contribute to her theme?
3. How does Sexton employ figurative language to depict the intensities of her abortion experience?
4. Discuss the poet's allusion to the Rumpelstiltskin fairy tale in the poem. Who was Rumpelstiltskin, and how might his story relate to Sexton's theme? Why does she insist that the little man she encounters is not Rumpelstiltskin?

TOPIC FOR CRITICAL WRITING

On January 22, 1973, the U.S. Supreme Court sided with Jane Roe in the case *Roe v. Wade* that struck down a Texas statute making abortion a crime in Texas. This legal precedent found that the right to privacy granted under the Constitution covered a woman's choice whether to terminate her pregnancy. Sexton's poem "The Abortion" was published a decade before *Roe v. Wade* guaranteed a woman's right to choose the course of her reproductive life. Does the poem project any stand on the ethics or politics of abortion? Does it criticize the adverse and illegal conditions under which Sexton had to pursue her abortion?

With Mercy for the Greedy   (1962)

For my friend, Ruth, who urges me to make an
appointment for the Sacrament of Confession

Concerning your letter in which you ask
me to call a priest and in which you ask
me to wear The Cross that you enclose;
your own cross,

your dog-bitten cross,   5
no larger than a thumb,
small and wooden, no thorns, this rose—

I pray to its shadow,
that gray place
where it lies on your letter . . . deep, deep.   10
I detest my sins and I try to believe
in The Cross. I touch its tender hips, its dark jawed face,
its solid neck, its brown sleep.

True. There is
a beautiful Jesus.   15
He is frozen to his bones like a chunk of beef.
How desperately he wanted to pull his arms in!
How desperately I touch his vertical and horizontal axes!
But I can't. Need is not quite belief.

All morning long   20
I have worn
your cross, hung with package string around my throat.
It tapped me lightly as a child's heart might,
tapping secondhand, softly waiting to be born.
Ruth, I cherish the letter you wrote.   25

My friend, my friend, I was born
doing reference work in sin, and born
confessing it. This is what poems are:
with mercy
for the greedy,   30
they are the tongue's wrangle,
the world's pottage, the rat's star.

TOPICS FOR CRITICAL THINKING

1. "With Mercy for the Greedy" is a companion piece to "The Abortion." Sexton addresses the poem to her friend Ruth Soter, who had recently converted to Catholicism. Ruth was also the only person that Sexton told about her abortion. In response, her friend sent her a cross and urged her to seek consolation and forgiveness in the church. How does Sexton negotiate the rhetorical dilemma of having to turn down a friend to whom she is, nevertheless, still devoted?

2. Though Sexton does not accept the sacraments of Catholicism, how does her poem assert a serious commitment to the life of the spirit?

3. In refusing to believe in Christ as her personal savior, Sexton declares that "Need is not the same as belief." What do you think she means here?

4. In what ways does poetry offer another kind of mercy than that held out by Jesus Christ?

5. "Rats live on no evil star" reads the same forwards and backwards, and it was Sexton's favorite **palindrome.** In claiming that poetry is the "rats star," she is alluding to the ways in which language can take on a life of its own beyond our intentions, expectations, or judgment. How might this transformative power of language be considered a source of redemption in the poem's context?

TOPIC FOR CRITICAL WRITING

Compare Sexton's linguistic credo in "With Mercy for the Greedy" with her declaration that "My business is words" in "Said the Poet to the Analyst," which follows.

Said the Poet to the Analyst   *(1960)*

My business is words. Words are like labels,
or coins, or better, like swarming bees.
I confess I am only broken by the sources of things;
as if words were counted like dead bees in the attic,
unbuckled from their yellow eyes and their dry wings.   5
I must always forget how one word is able to pick
out another, to manner another, until I have got
something I might have said . . .
but did not.

Your business is watching my words. But I   10
admit nothing. I work with my best, for instance,
when I can write my praise for a nickel machine,
that one night in Nevada: telling how the magic jackpot
came clacking three bells out, over the lucky screen.
But if you should say this is something it is not,   15
then I grow weak, remembering how my hands felt funny
and ridiculous and crowded with all
the believing money.

TOPICS FOR CRITICAL THINKING

1. Discuss Sexton's similes for words in the opening lines of "Said the Poet to the Analyst." How does language take on an agency of its own in the first stanza?
2. What do you make of the poem's ending metaphor of writing as slot machine gambling?

TOPIC FOR CRITICAL WRITING

How does the analyst's role and attitude toward language differ from those of the poet, according to Sexton?

For My Lover, Returning to His Wife

(1969)

She is all there.
She was melted carefully down for you
and cast up from your childhood,
cast up from your one hundred favorite aggies.

She has always been there, my darling.   5
She is, in fact, exquisite.
Fireworks in the dull middle of February
and as real as a cast-iron pot.

Let's face it, I have been momentary.
A luxury. A bright red sloop in the harbor.   10
My hair rising like smoke from the car window.
Littleneck clams out of season.

She is more than that. She is your have to have,
has grown you your practical your tropical growth.
This is not an experiment. She is all harmony.   15
She sees to oars and oarlocks for the dinghy,

has placed wild flowers at the window at breakfast,
sat by the potter's wheel at midday,
set forth three children under the moon,
three cherubs drawn by Michelangelo,   20

done this with her legs spread out
in the terrible months in the chapel.
If you glance up, the children are there
like delicate balloons resting on the ceiling.

She has also carried each one down the hall   25
after supper, their heads privately bent,
two legs protesting, person to person,
her face flushed with a song and their little sleep.

I give you back your heart.
I give you permission—   30

for the fuse inside her, throbbing
angrily in the dirt, for the bitch in her
and the burying of her wound—
for the burying of her small red wound alive—

for the pale flickering flare under her ribs,   35
for the drunken sailor who waits in her left pulse,

for the mother's knee, for the stockings,
for the garter belt, for the call—

the curious call
when you will burrow in arms and breasts   40
and tug at the orange ribbon in her hair
and answer the call, the curious call.

She is so naked and singular
She is the sum of yourself and your dream.
Climb her like a monument, step after step.   45
She is solid.

As for me, I am a watercolor.
I wash off.

TOPICS FOR CRITICAL THINKING

1. Discuss the ways in which Sexton contrasts herself with her lover's wife, to whom he has returned in the poem's situation.
2. Examine the tropes through which Sexton describes love as a kind of fine art.

TOPIC FOR CRITICAL WRITING

In breaking off her affair, she addresses her lover with the strange farewell: "I give you permission." In considering the surreal catalogue of images that follows this declaration, what kind of permission is Sexton granting the lover? How do you read the poet's tone and her attitude toward the end of the affair? Consider how she captures and focuses that attitude in the subtle turn of her final trope when she admits that "As for me, I am a watercolor. / I wash off."

Critical Perspective: On Poetry and the Unconscious

"In the beginning, what was the relationship between your poetry and your therapy?

"Sometimes, my doctors tell me that I understand something in a poem that I haven't integrated into my life. In fact, I may be concealing it from myself, while I was revealing it to the readers. The poetry is often more advanced, in terms of my unconscious, than I am. Poetry, after all, milks the unconscious. The unconscious is there to feed it little images, little symbols, the answers, the insights I know not of. In therapy, one seeks to hide sometimes. I'll give you a rather intimate example of this. About three or four years ago my analyst asked me what I thought of my parents having intercourse when I was young. I couldn't talk. I knew there was suddenly a poem there, and I selfishly guarded it from him. Two days later, I had a poem, entitled, 'In the Beach House,' which describes overhearing the primal scene. In it I say, 'Inside my prison of pine and bedspring, / over my window sill, under my knob, / it is plain that they are at / the royal strapping.' The point of this little story is the image, 'the royal strapping.' My analyst was quite impressed with that image and so was I, although I don't remember going any further with it then. About three weeks ago, he said to me, 'Were you ever beaten as a child?' I told him that I had been, when I was about nine. I had torn up a five-dollar bill that my father gave to my sister; my father took me into his bedroom, laid me down on his bed, pulled off my pants and beat me with a riding crop. As I related this to my doctor, he said, 'See, that was quite a royal strapping,' thus revealing to me, by way of my own image, the intensity of that moment, the sexuality of that beating, the little masochistic seizure—it's so classic, it's almost corny. Perhaps it's too intimate an example, but then both poetry and therapy are intimate.

"Are your poems still closely connected to your therapy as in the past?

"No. The subject of therapy was an early theme—the process itself as in 'Said the Poet to the Analyst,' the people of my past, admitting what my parents were really like, the whole Gothic New England story. I've had about eight doctors, but only two that count. I've written a poem for each of the two—'You, Doctor Martin' and 'Cripples and Other Stories.' And that will do. Those poems are about the two men as well as the strange process. One can say that my new poems, the love poems, come about as a result of new attitudes, an awareness of the possibly good as well as the possibly rotten. Inherent in the process is a rebirth of a sense of self, each time stripping away a dead self."
     —Anne Sexton, "Interview with Barbara Kevles" (1974)

Critical Perspective: On Anne Sexton's "Her Kind"

"Because Sexton's writing seems so personal she is often labeled a 'confessional' poet and grouped (to her disadvantage) with poets such as Lowell, Berryman, Roethke, and Plath. But Sexton resisted the label 'confessional'; she preferred to be regarded as a 'storyteller.' To emphasize that she considered the speaking 'I' in her poetry as a literary rather than a real identity, Sexton invariably opened her public performances by reading the early poem 'Her Kind.' . . . No matter what poetry she had on an evening's agenda, Sexton offered this persona as a point of entry to her art. 'I' in the poem is a disturbing, marginal female whose power is associated with disfigurement, sexuality, and magic. But at the end of each stanza, 'I' is displaced from sufferer onto storyteller. With the lines 'A woman like that . . . I have been her kind' Sexton conveys the terms on which she wishes to be understood: not victim, but witness and witch.

     "The witch-persona of Sexton's poetry is the voice Sexton invented to tell the story of her changing relationship to a severe, incurable, but apparently undiagnosable malady. She was born in 1928 in Wellesley, Massachusetts, and lived all her life in the suburbs of Boston. Married at age nineteen to a man in the wool business, Sexton had two daughters. Severe depression following the birth of her second child deepened into a permanent mental illness for which she was treated by psychiatrists for the rest of her life. She died by suicide of carbon monoxide poisoning in 1974. Her professional interest in poetry began during the first phase of her illness, in 1956. Intensified by the death of her parents in 1959, the illness was the fixed point of reference by which she measured the reality of love, the practice of poetry, and the possibility of spiritual redemption."

    —Diane Wood Middlebrook, from "Poet of Weird Abundance" (1985)

Critical Perspective: On Fathers and Daughters in Sexton's Verse

"Sexton's ablest critics have located the shift from personal to 'transpersonal' or 'cultural' in Sexton's work in her fourth volume, *Transformations*. While I agree that in *Transformations* such a shift is mythically embodied and newly garbed, there is within the 'narrow diary' of even the early poems a structural outline for the psychic biography of a gender, and particularly for what Phyllis Chesler calls 'woman's "dependent" and "incestuous" personality' in relation to her father—a pattern long known to and exploited by psychoanalysis, to the degree that therapeutic method colludes with patriarchy. If Anne Sexton learned about her own incestuous dependencies from Freud and his proxies during the early stages of her life as a career mental patient, hers was still the first contemporary voice outside of the psychoanalytic world to describe the normative relationship between father and daughter from the daughter's perspective. Sexton's early poetry both represents and dissects the subtle and pervasive psycho-social pattern that Phyllis Chesler would later discuss, and damn, in *Women and Madness*, and which now, in the wake of feminist inquiry, seems almost obvious: 'romantic' love in the western world is 'psychologically predicated on sexual union between Daughter and Father figures.'

    "The 'normal' woman in western society, whether or not she is a poet, and whether or not she is fully aware of the psychic dynamics, falls in love with her father, who delights her, despises her, seduces her, betrays her, and dies. The father who dies in 1959 in the poet's personal life undergoes a series of resurrections as man and imago—husband, doctor, lover, priest—and is finally reborn as the diety of *The Awful Rowing Toward God*. Burial and resurrection of the fathers becomes a central theme in Sexton's poetry, as it is in the personal lives of her contemporaries and the collective life of her culture. In all of his incarnations in Sexton's poetry, the father finally fails himself and his daughter, for he is a god not sufficiently omnipotent, a man not sufficiently human, a male principle not sufficiently able to accommodate feminine powers and desires. But this ultimate failure is never judged harshly in Sexton's poetry, never evoked without the empathy that always accompanies insight; for the shortcomings of the father-god in a patriarchy are nearly definitive of the failures of the human enterprise, one in which all men and all women engage."

—Diana Hume George, from "How We Danced:
Anne Sexton on Fathers and Daughters" (1986)

Critical Perspective: On Sexton and Confessional Verse

"In fact, surprisingly little has been written with any authority on the subject of confessionalism, which has become, under the rubric of 'sincerity,' an impulse behind many of the significant social movements and styles since 1960.

"One of the few studies available is Theodor Reik's *The Compulsion to Confess*, a work that, while hardly exhaustive, at least opens up a few theoretical approaches toward an understanding of the 'compulsion' and its results. Broadly, Reik defines a confession as 'a statement about impulses or drives which are felt or recognized as forbidden,' and their expression involves both the repressed tendency and the repressing forces. If this secular interpretation seems to exclude the usual religious (and even legal) sense of the term as narrowed to facts and intentions, they can easily be added to Reik's definition without any loss to the force of his point. The confessional situation—most obvious in analytical sessions—resides in 'the transformation of a primitive urge for expression into the compulsion to confess,' occasioned by social and psychic restraints and 'the reactive reinforcement which the intensity of the drive experiences through repression,' so that 'confession is a repetition of action or of certain behavior substituted by displacement and with different emotional material, as words must substitute for action.' This weakened repetition allows its own gratifications, indulging as it does both guilt and the need for punishment, even while the 'reproduction through narration' achieves 'the retroactive annulment of repression.' That is to say, confession is at once the process of exorcism and the plea for absolution. And the result, in Reik's view, is that 'the disintegrating of the personality is at least temporarily halted by the confession. The communication between the ego and that part of the ego from which it was estranged is restored.' . . .

"To some extent, then, the poetry is therapeutic; or as D. H. Lawrence said, 'One sheds one's sicknesses in books—repeats and presents again one's emotions, to be master of them.' Erik Erikson underscores this aspect of the situation by reminding that 'the individual's mastery over his neurosis begins where he is put in a position to accept the historical necessity which made him what he is.' Acceptance becomes survival. Anne Sexton: 'Writing, and especially having written, is evidence of survival—the books accumulate

ego-strength.' And so confessional poets are driven back to their losses, to that alienation—from self and others, from sanity and love—which is the thematic center of their vision and work. The betrayals in childhood, the family romance, the divorces and madnesses, the suicide attempts, the self-defeat and longing—the poets pursue them in their most intimate and painful detail."
   —J. D. McClatchy, from "Anne Sexton: Somehow to Endure" (1978)

20 Representations of Desire and Sexuality

"How do I love thee?" Elizabeth Barrett Browning muses in her widely read Sonnet 43, "Let me count the ways." Addressed to her husband, the poet Robert Browning, Elizabeth Browning's *Sonnets from the Portuguese* enumerates the many ways that love, admiration, and desire are experienced in marriage. Poetry has always given passionate utterance to the several ways love takes, ranging from friendship to passionate sexual desire.

ELIZABETH BARRETT BROWNING *(1806–1861)*

Sonnet 43 *(1850)*

How do I love thee? Let me count the ways.
I love thee to the depth and breadth and height
My soul can reach, when feeling out of sight
For the ends of Being and ideal Grace.
I love thee to the level of everyday's   5
Most quiet need, by sun and candle-light.
I love thee freely, as men strive for Right;
I love thee purely, as they turn from Praise.
I love thee with the passion put to use
In my old griefs, and with my childhood's faith.   10
I love thee with a love I seemed to lose
With my lost saints—I love thee with the breath,
Smiles, tears, of all my life!—and, if God choose,
I shall but love thee better after death.

TOPICS FOR CRITICAL THINKING

1. Discuss the ways in which Browning portrays the extent of her love through spatial figures in the sonnet's first quatrain.
2. In what ways does Browning project her love into a spiritual dimension in her final quatrain?

How does Browning ascribe wonder, passion, and moral qualities to her love?

While Browning's sonnet expresses an unwavering commitment to her soulmate, desire in much of love poetry from the medieval period through the present is represented as both a joyful and disruptive emotive force, as in Elizabeth I of England's "On Monsieur's Departure."

QUEEN ELIZABETH I   *(1533–1603)*

On Monsieur's Departure   *(c. 1570)*

I grieve and dare not show my discontent,
I love and yet am forced to seem to hate,
I do, yet dare not say I ever meant,
I seem stark mute but inwardly do prate.
   I am and not, I freeze and yet am burned,   5
   Since from myself another self I turned.

My care is like my shadow in the sun,
Follows me flying, flies when I pursue it,
Stands and lies by me, doth what I have done.
His too familiar care doth make me rue it.   10
   No means I find to rid him from my breast,
   Till by the end of things it be suppressed.

Some gentler passion slide into my mind,
For I am soft and made of melting snow;
Or be more cruel, love, and so be kind.   15
Let me or float or sink, be high or low.
   Or let me live with some more sweet content,
   Or die and so forget what love ere meant.

TOPICS FOR CRITICAL THINKING

1. At least two historical figures have been advanced as possible candidates for the identity of the "monsieur" of Queen Elizabeth's sonnet: the French Duc d'Anjou, who left England in 1582, and the courtier Robert Devereux, Earl of Essex. Whoever is the historical subject of the poem, Elizabeth's theme is her struggle to come to terms with the "care" that she feels but, because of her royal status, must not outwardly show. How does Elizabeth present the poem's speaker as divided on the issue of desire?

2. To *die* in the Elizabethan context has a double meaning. It can mean literally to perish, but it also has the sexual connotation of experiencing orgasm. Discuss how the poem puns on this key word in its conclusion.

TOPIC FOR CRITICAL WRITING

Discuss how Elizabeth presents her emotional dilemma in her figurative language.

Queen Elizabeth's musings on the paradoxes of love are hardly unique to her, as is plain to see in Dorothy Parker's modern poem "Somebody's Song."

DOROTHY PARKER   *(1893–1967)*

Somebody's Song   *(1926)*

This is what I vow:
He shall have my heart to keep;
Sweetly will we stir and sleep,
    All the years, as now.
Swift the measured sands may run;   5
Love like this is never done;
He and I are welded one:
    This is what I vow.

This is what I pray:
Keep him by me tenderly;
Keep him sweet in pride of me,   10
    Ever and a day;
Keep me from the old distress;
Let me, for our happiness,
Be the one to love the less: 15
    This is what I pray.

This is what I know:
Lovers' oaths are thin as rain;
Love's a harbinger of pain—
    Would it were not so!   20
Ever is my heart a-thirst,
Ever is my love accurst;
He is neither last nor first—
    This is what I know.

TOPICS FOR CRITICAL THINKING

1. Compare and contrast what, on the one hand, Parker vows and prays in the pursuit of love with what, on the other hand, she "knows" about love.
2. Contrast Parker's misgivings about love with Christina Rossetti's celebration of love as a rare gift in "A Birthday," which follows.

TOPIC FOR CRITICAL WRITING

Consider Parker's presentation of the differences between idealized hopes for love versus love's realities. Does either have the last word, or does the poem's irony suspend them in a contradictory tension?

CHRISTINA ROSSETTI *(1830–1894)*

A Birthday   *(1861)*

My heart is like a singing bird
 Whose nest is in a watered shoot;
My heart is like an apple-tree
 Whose boughs are bent with thickset fruit;
My heart is like a rainbow shell   5
 That paddles in a halcyon sea;
My heart is gladder than all these
 Because my love is come to me.

Raise me a dais of silk and down;
 Hang it with vair and purple dyes;   10
Carve it in doves and pomegranates,
 And peacocks with a hundred eyes;
Work it in gold and silver grapes,
 In leaves and silver fleurs-de-lys;
Because the birthday of my life   15
 Is come, my love is come to me.

Rossetti not only depicts love through the metaphor of the artful gift in the second stanza, but she also presents her heart through a series of similes taken from the natural world of birds, trees, shells, and sea. Much of traditional English love poetry represents desire by reaching back to the natural landscapes of Greek and Roman **pastoral** verse, as in the *Idylls* of Theocritus and lyric fragments of Sappho.

The pastoral tradition's rich repertoire of conventional tropes, images, and symbols has long served as a poetic resource for rendering idealized states of desire from ancient times through the present. Pastoral poetry takes love as its stock theme, grounded in the down-to-earth characters of rustics, herdsmen, and farmers. The bucolic simplicity of the pastoral world is presented in such canonical works as Edmund Spenser's *The Shepheardes Calendar*; William Shakespeare's sonnets, comedies, and romances; Christopher Marlowe's "The Passionate Shepherd to His Love"; Sir Walter Raleigh's "Nymph's Reply to the Shepherd"; John Milton's "L'Allegro" and "Lycidas"; Andrew Marvell's "The Garden," as well as his "mower" poems; Alexander Pope's "Discourse on Pastoral Poetry"; William Wordsworth's "Michael: A Pastoral Poem"; and Alfred, Lord Tennyson's *Dora*, among many others. In these works, the simplicity of pastoral desire contrasts with the social complexities, coded behaviors, and power politics that belong to court and city life.

Punning on the language and stock figures of pastoral love poetry, Theodore Roethke's contemporary poem "I Knew a Woman" celebrates the ecstatic joy of sexuality between men and women as a dance of natural sensuality.

THEODORE ROETHKE *(1908–1963)*

I Knew a Woman *(1958)*

I knew a woman, lovely in her bones,
When small birds sighed, she would sigh back at them;
Ah, when she moved, she moved more ways than one:
The shapes a bright container can contain!
Of her choice virtues only gods should speak,   5
Or English poets who grew up on Greek
(I'd have them sing in chorus, cheek to cheek).

How well her wishes went! She stroked my chin,
She taught me Turn, and Counter-turn, and Stand;
She taught me Touch, that undulant white skin;   10
I nibbled meekly from her proffered hand;
She was the sickle; I, poor I, the rake,
Coming behind her for her pretty sake
(But what prodigious mowing did we make).

Love likes a gander, and adores a goose: 15
Her full lips pursed, the errant note to seize;
She played it quick, she played it light and loose,
My eyes, they dazzled at her flowing knees;
Her several parts could keep a pure repose,
Or one hip quiver with a mobile nose   20
(She moved in circles, and those circles moved).

Let seed be grass, and grass turn into hay:
I'm martyr to a motion not my own;
What's freedom for? To know eternity.
I swear she cast a shadow white as stone.   25
But who would count eternity in days?
These old bones live to learn her wanton ways:
(I measure time by how a body sways).

Roethke's "I Knew a Woman" reflects on his passionate midlife marriage to Beatrice O'Connell in 1953. The poet's fervor is inscribed right at the beginning in the word play of the poem's title, which puns on the well-known double entendre of the word to *know*, signifying both familiarity and carnal knowledge. Other puns underscore the latter connotation in the Scots dialect word *mow* as a term for love-making. Eroticizing the tradition of love lyricism, Roethke portrays English poets who "grew up on Greek" singing "in chorus, cheek to cheek." The Hellenistic allusion is further picked up in the lover's sensual movements of "Turn, and Counter-turn, and Stand" that allude to both the literary terms of strophe, antistrophe, and epode of Greek verse and the sexual positionings the poet learns from the beloved's "wanton ways." Finally, when Roethke depicts himself in the metaphor of the "rake / Coming behind her," he is not just alluding to a garden tool. A rake is the kind of sexual libertine and "man of loose habits" that the eighteenth-century British artist William Hogarth satirizes in his series of engravings *The Rake's Progress*. Roethke adopts the persona of the rake in matching the lover's "wanton ways." The poem's situation of erotic instruction is set in a natural landscape whose birds, including the goose and gander, reflect in their sighs the "errant note" the lovers play "light and loose." The mirroring of natural and sexual fertility is aptly summed up in declarations like "Let seed be grass, and grass turn into hay."

The kind of frolicsome, pastoral representations we find in Roethke's love poetry achieve their effects through figures of naturalized sexuality. Roethke would give us the lesson the beloved taught him in ways that instruct us about the facts of life. Such naturalized metaphors of desire have broad currency in English love lyricism. To take just one more example, when Lord Byron pays

William Hogarth, *The Rake's Progress*, Plate III (1735)

tribute to one of his many lovers, he employs the naturalizing simile of the night sky in "She Walks in Beauty."

GEORGE GORDON, LORD BYRON *(1788–1824)*

She Walks in Beauty *(1815)*

She walks in beauty, like the night
   Of cloudless climes and starry skies;
And all that's best of dark and bright
   Meet in her aspect and her eyes:
Thus mellowed to that tender light   5
   Which heaven to gaudy day denies.

One shade the more, one ray the less,
   Had half impaired the nameless grace
Which waves in every raven tress,
   Or softly lightens o'er her face;   10
Where thoughts serenely sweet express
   How pure, how dear their dwelling place.

And on that cheek and o'er the brow,
   So soft, so calm, yet eloquent,
The smiles that win, the tints that glow,   15
   But tell of days in goodness spent,
A mind at peace with all below,
   A heart whose love is innocent!

TOPICS FOR CRITICAL THINKING

1. Discuss Byron's simile that captures the lover's beauty in tropes of light.
2. What key terms further portray what Byron admires in the lover's character?

TOPIC FOR CRITICAL WRITING

Compare and contrast the ways in which Byron describes the lover with Roethke's poetic representations in "I Knew a Woman." If Roethke depicts the lover as "wanton," how does Byron portray the lover as "innocent"?

In "I Knew a Woman" and "She Walks in Beauty," the male poet expresses his desire for the beloved woman through stylized tropes that locate desire in natural settings. Nevertheless, in both of these lyrics, the immediate essence and felt urgency of the poet's emotive utterance are posed in pastoral conventions that belie the artificial, or constructed, terms of desire. Both poems are not only passionate expressions of desire, but also highly stylized poetic performances that stage the traditional conventions of English love poetry. So familiar are these pastoral tropes that Shakespeare parodies them in his well-known Sonnet 18.

WILLIAM SHAKESPEARE   *(1564–1616)*

Sonnet 18   *(1609)*

Shall I compare thee to a summer's day?
Thou art more lovely and more temperate:
Rough winds do shake the darling buds of May,
And summer's lease hath all too short a date;
Sometimes too hot the eye of heaven shines,   5
And often is his gold complexion dimmed;
And every fair from fair sometime declines,
By chance or nature's changing course untrimmed;
But thy eternal summer shall not fade,
Nor lose possession of that fair thou ow'st;   10
Nor shall death brag thou wand'rest in his shade,
While in eternal lines to Time thou grow'st:
   So long as men can breathe, or eyes can see,
   So long live this, and this gives life to thee.

TOPICS FOR CRITICAL THINKING

1. How does Shakespeare's opening rhetorical question—"Shall I compare thee to a summer's day?"—reveal this conceit as already outworn and marked by cliché?
2. In what ways does poetry immortalize the lover beyond natural comparison?

TOPIC FOR CRITICAL WRITING

Examine how Shakespeare describes nature as subject to time, decay, and death. How does the lover's beauty transcend the "changing course" of nature's mutability?

In Sonnet 18, Shakespeare not only pokes fun at the natural conventions of the pastoral tradition but, equally important, he underscores the constructed, or artificial, aspect of desire. Passion is as much produced in language as it is experienced in the real world. As poet, he reveals the ways in which desire is mediated and even generated by our representations of it. The beloved becomes an object of our admiration only insofar as the poet's representations "give life" to her beauty.

In probing the constructed—rather than wholly natural—aspect of desire, it would be a mistake to assume that the conventions of the pastoral tradition have the last word in exhausting the query Elizabeth Barrett Browning puts to desire: "How do I love thee?" If desire is not only reflected in but also produced by its representation in language, then whom we love and what it is exactly that we love about them renders Browning's question truly open-ended. In fact, contemporary debate over sexual orientation makes Browning's query a difficult question to answer in any straightforward way.

Representations of Sexuality

In current discussions of sexuality **Web**, a controversy turns on the issue of *www* whether nature or nurture determines the sources and objects of our desire. Is there a natural, essential basis for sexual orientation and sexual object choice? Or is every form and expression of desire, to a greater or lesser extent, shaped by our cultural lives? Is one's particular sexual bent innate: a result of hormonal and genetic factors, or even brain structure? Or is sexual disposition acquired through environment, upbringing, and cultural background? Not surprisingly, there are no simple answers to these controversial questions and how they bear on one's identity, civil rights, and legal entitlements.

Much of modern psychoanalytic theory **Web**, beginning with Sigmund *www* Freud's *Three Essays on the Theory of Sexuality* (1905), distinguishes between biological needs and sexual drives. Freud located drives as "lying at the frontier between the mental and the physical." For example, a newborn baby has biological needs for basic sustenance in, say, breast-feeding. But in the absence of the breast and in excess of biological survival, the developing infant's drive for oral gratification will find a range of pleasurable substitute objects in bottles, cups, fingers, toys, candy, and pacifiers. Moreover, sexual orientation does not just serve the aims of biological reproduction. In fact, Freud hypothesized that the infantile drives are bisexual and polymorphous. Only through later social and cultural processes of nurture do these drives become identified with heterosexual object choices.

Contemporary psychoanalytic theorists typically define biological **sex** in terms of the embodied differences that distinguish women from men. In contrast, **gender** **Web** refers to the social construction of men's and women's roles *www* in everyday life. Today, the rigid stereotypes of men's and women's roles are largely things of the past. We no longer ascribe intelligence, rationality, and activity solely to men, nor do we necessarily attribute emotion, nurturing, and passivity to women. Furthermore, contemporary gender theorists have shown that masculine and feminine traits are neither universal across cultures and time periods nor fixed characteristics that distinguish men from women. Instead, how we define ourselves as men and women depends on an ensemble of local customs, rituals, and practices of everyday life that both reinforce and complicate basic anatomical differences. Contemporary culture affords us a fluid, not fixed, repertoire of gendered dispositions, outlooks, attitudes, and behaviors that cut across sexual difference.

Similarly, our understanding of sexual orientation has undergone a sea-change since the birth of the gay liberation era of the 1960s. In America, a profound cultural shift in national attitudes toward gays and lesbians **Web** *www* marks the twenty-year history between 1952 when the American Psychiatric Association (APA) added homosexuality to its list of mental disorders and 1973 when the APA removed the category of homosexuality from its *Diagnostic and Statistical Manual of Sexual Disorders* (DSM-III). Today, how we experience masculinity and femininity has less to do with simple anatomy. In addition to one's biological sex, several components of sexuality contribute to personal identity. These aspects include one's sexual orientation, one's gendered sense of being masculine or feminine, as well as one's social behavior: how one acts on or refrains from acting on that self-perception of gender.

Lesbian identity, according to poet Adrienne Rich, should not be simply reduced to sexual acts but includes a continuum of female identifications in everyday life. In her 1980 essay "Compulsory Heterosexuality and Lesbian Existence," Rich defines the "lesbian continuum" in terms of "woman-identified experience; not simply the fact that a woman has had or consciously desired genital sexual experience with another woman." Rich recommends that we extend our understanding of lesbianism so as to

> expand it to embrace many more forms of primary intensity between and among women, including the sharing of a rich inner life, the bonding against male tyranny, the giving and receiving of practical and political support; if we can also hear in it such associations as marriage resistance we begin to grasp breadths of female history and psychology which have lain out of reach as a consequence of limited, mostly clinical definitions of "lesbianism."

Such theoretical insights enable us to reread traditional English lyrics such as Anne Finch's "Friendship Between Ephelia and Ardelia" as expressing a feminist solidarity between women beyond the conventional norms of patriarchy.

ANNE FINCH, COUNTESS OF WINCHILSEA   *(1661–1720)*

Friendship Between Ephelia and Ardelia   *(1713)*

Eph. What Friendship is, Ardelia show.
Ard. 'Tis to love, as I love you.
Eph. This account, so short (tho' kind)
    Suits not my inquiring mind.
    Therefore farther now repeat: 5
    What is Friendship when complete?
Ard. 'Tis to share all joy and grief;
    'Tis to lend all due relief
    From the tongue, the heart, the hand;
    'Tis to mortgage house and land;   10
    For a friend be sold a slave;
    'Tis to die upon a grave,
    If a friend therein do lie.
Eph. This indeed, tho' carried high,
    This, tho' more than e'er was done   15
    Underneath the rolling sun,

This has all been said before.
Can Ardelia say no more?
Ard. Words indeed no more can show:
  But 'tis to love, as I love you.   20

TOPICS FOR CRITICAL THINKING

1. In Finch's dialogue, Ephelia asks Ardelia to show "what Friendship is." Even after Ardelia takes this invitation as an opening to announce her love for Ephelia, the latter presses her to "complete" her definition. How many times does Ephelia urge Ardelia to show what female friendship means? What is the point of Ephelia's repeated questioning?
2. Discuss the ways in which Ardelia actually defines her ideal of friendship.

TOPIC FOR CRITICAL WRITING

How does the poem's dialogue progress from defining friendship in the abstract to an actual pledge of love between the two women?

Poetry is a discourse that fashions as much as reflects masculine and feminine gender roles. Finch's "Friendship Between Ephelia and Ardelia" ends with Ardelia's underscored declaration of the simple fact of her love, which "words indeed no more can show." What Ephelia desires, however, is not just the fact of her friend's love but its seemingly endless construction through performative declaration. Love lyricism gives us the pleasure of rethinking and reexperiencing who we take ourselves to be as male and female desiring subjects as well as whom and what we desire. One way of altering traditional male and female roles is to perform them in language, but with a difference.

This strategy is obviously at work in same-sex appropriations of pastoral tropes that describe one's desire for the beloved as a natural fact. Adrienne Rich's Poem XI from *Twenty-One Love Poems* locates the loved one in a landscape of sensuous natural metaphors that rename the masculine conventions of pastoral literature.

ADRIENNE RICH   *(b. 1929)*

Poem XI, from Twenty-One Love Poems   *(1976)*

Every peak is a crater. This is the law of volcanoes,
making them eternally and visibly female.
No height without depth, without a burning core,
though our straw soles shred on the hardened lava.
I want to travel with you to every sacred mountain   5
smoking within like the sibyl stooped over his tripod,
I want to reach for your hand as we scale the path,
to feel your arteries glowing in my clasp,

never failing to note the small, jewel-like flower
unfamiliar to us, nameless till we rename her,   10
that clings to the slowly altering rock—
that detail outside ourselves that brings us to ourselves,
was here before us, knew we would come, and sees beyond us.

As in the romantic tradition of nature poetry, Rich finds natural objects
that present symbolic correspondences to her inward, psychic states of being.
Here she finds such symbolic correspondences for a distinctively feminine
gender identity in the figure of the volcano whose peak is also a crater. Not
unlike the metaphor that Emily Dickinson chooses for the psychic extremities
of women's experience—"Vesuvius at home"—Rich similarly dwells on the
intensities she experiences as a woman within the "law of volcanoes" that are
"eternally and visibly female. / No height without depth, without a burning
core." Similarly, in the "small, jewel-like flower," the poet encounters something unfamiliar that, paradoxically enough, returns her to herself. Moreover,
that rediscovery involves a same-sex identity shared with the beloved female
"other": a mutual identity achieved through the act of renaming. Just as the
flower is something partly discovered and partly invented through the poet's
power to "rename her," so Rich's love relation to her companion is both passionately affirmed in their heartfelt "clasp" and constructed through poetry's
power to rename that immediate experience.

The primary intensity of same-sex desire takes many forms for women,
and writing during the Harlem Renaissance, the African American poet
Mae V. Cowdery explores the terms of jealousy between a black woman and
her white lover.

Mae V. Cowdery *(1909–1953)*

Insatiate   *(1936)*

If my love were meat and bread
And sweet cool wine to drink,
They would not be enough,
For I must have a finer table spread
To sate my entity.   5

If her lips were rubies red,
Her eyes two sapphires blue,
Her fingers ten sticks of white jade,
Coral tipped . . . and her hair of purple hue
Hung down in a silken shawl . . .   10
They would not be enough
To fill the coffers of my need.

If her thoughts were arrows
Ever speeding true
Into the core of my mind,   15
And her voice round notes of melody
No nightingale or lark
Could ever hope to sing . . .
Not even these would be enough
To keep my constancy.   20

But if my love did whisper
Her song into another's ear
Or place the tip of one pink nail
Upon another's hand,
Then would I forever be   25
A willing prisoner . . .
Chained to her side by uncertainty!

TOPICS FOR CRITICAL THINKING

1. In what ways does Cowdery present desire as something that exceeds any object that could possibly satisfy it in her opening stanzas?
2. What images represent Cowdery's interracial, same-sex relationship to the lover?

TOPIC FOR CRITICAL WRITING

Examine the poem's assertion of desire for and commitment to the other, paradoxically enough, through the uncertainty concerning the lover's fidelity.

Not unlike Rich's project in *Twenty-One Love Poems*, the African American lesbian poet Audre Lorde also discovers the poet's power to rename her gender in relation to a same-sexed other in "Love Poem."

AUDRE LORDE   *(1924–1992)*

Love Poem   *(1971)*

Speak earth and bless me
with what is richest
make sky flow honey out of my hips
rigid as mountains
spread over a valley   5
carved out by the mouth of rain.

And I knew when I entered her I was
high wind in her forest's hollow

fingers whispering sound
honey flowed from the split cup   10
impaled on a lance of tongues
on the tips of her breasts on her navel
and my breath howling into her entrances
through lungs of pain.

Greedy as herring-gulls   15
or a child
I swung out over the earth
over and over again.

Beginning with her opening imperative, or command, verb—*speak*—Lorde
lays emphasis on the power of language to construct, as much as reflect, experience. Here she conjures the earth as her muse to "speak" and thereby "bless"
her as poet and lover.

TOPIC FOR CRITICAL THINKING

Discuss Lorde's use of synaesthesia—the blending of the senses—in such phrases as
"sky flow honey out of my hips" or "fingers whispering sound." How do these usages
add a level of surreal intensity to the already fervent metaphors and similes Lorde employs to depict her embrace of the beloved as a vital commingling of passionate forces?

TOPICS FOR CRITICAL WRITING

1. Examine the ways in which Lorde's figurative language adopts a hard and active
   masculinity in phrases such as "hips / rigid as mountains" or "split cup / impaled on
   a lance of tongues / on the tips of her breasts."
2. Consider the sexual role Lorde adopts in her figurative language, describing, say,
   her "breath / howling into her entrances" or such declarations as "And I knew when
   I entered her I was / high wind in her forests hollow."

Lorde adopts an assertive, masculine persona in relation to her same-sex
"other," but poets have always complicated the ways in which men and
women possess masculine and feminine gender characteristics. Of Shakespeare's 154 sonnets, the first 126 are devoted to a young man while the subsequent sonnets 127–152 are addressed to the sequence's "dark lady." His last
two sonnets dwell on the god Cupid and a maiden worshipper of the goddess
Diana. Some of the first group on the young man unsettle the differences that
traditionally distinguish men from women even as they explore modes of desire in excess of typical romantic conceits, as in Sonnet 20.

WILLIAM SHAKESPEARE   *(1564–1616)*

Sonnet 20   *(1609)*

A woman's face, with nature's own hand painted,
Hast thou, the master mistress of my passion;
A woman's gentle heart, but not acquainted
With shifting change as is false women's fashion;
An eye more bright than theirs, less false in rolling,   5
Gilding the object whereupon it gazeth;
A man in hue all hues in his controlling,
Which steals men's eyes and women's souls amazeth.
And for a woman wert thou first created,
Till Nature as she wrought thee fell a-doting,   10
And by addition me of thee defeated,
By adding one thing to my purpose nothing.
   But since she prick'd thee out for women's pleasure,
   Mine be thy love, and thy love's use their treasure.

TOPICS FOR CRITICAL THINKING

1. How does Shakespeare revise traditional differences between masculinity and femininity in his portrait of the poem's "master mistress"?
2. Discuss Shakespeare's personification of nature in the poem.

TOPIC FOR CRITICAL WRITING

"To prick out" is to select something or someone from a list, but as a noun, the word *prick* also has a sexual connotation. How does the sonnet explore the paradoxes of love and pleasure as they involve gender?

Not unlike Shakespeare, John Donne also complicates gender identifications in his prayer to God imagined as a male lover in his famous Holy Sonnet 14, "Batter My Heart, Three-Personed God."

JOHN DONNE   *(1572–1631)*

Batter My Heart, Three-Personed God   *(1633)*

Batter my heart, three-personed God; for You
As yet but knock, breathe, shine, and seek to mend;
That I may rise and stand, o'erthrow me, 'and bend
Your force to break, blow, burn, and make me new.

I, like an usurped town, to'another due,   5
Labor to'admit you, but O, to no end;
Reason, Your viceroy in me, me should defend,
But is captived, and proves weak or untrue.
Yet dearly I love you, 'and would be loved fain,
But am betrothed unto your enemy.   10
Divorce me, untie or break that knot again;
Take me to you, imprison me, for I,
Except you enthrall me, never shall be free,
Nor ever chaste, except you ravish me.

TOPICS FOR CRITICAL THINKING

1. In the opening quatrain unit of this holy sonnet, Donne alludes to the traditional image of Christ the bridegroom who knocks on the door of the heart. Donne presents that biblical figure, however, with a new and arresting violence. Consider how Donne dramatizes the violence of conversion through the poem's hard, plosive *b* sounds in the first quatrain of the poem.

2. Discuss the examples of Donne's figurative language in the poem's second quatrain in his simile of the "usurped town" and his personfication of his reason as a "viceroy." How do you interpret his argument here?

TOPIC FOR CRITICAL WRITING

Examine the paradox of Donne's final musings on divorce, chastity, and his desire that Christ "ravish" him in the poem.

In "Batter My Heart, Three-Personed God," Donne wants a "divorce" from Satan. But unwilling to wait for it, he implores the "three-personed God" to "untie" and even more forcefully "break" the marriage "knot" of his betrothal to the "enemy." By the end of Donne's holy sonnet, the poet has not only prayed for spiritual conversion but, equally important, has imagined masculine gender roles in a new, revolutionary way.

In the poem's final sestet, the third quatrain and concluding couplet introduce the speaker's plea to be made a soulmate to the conventional figure of Christ, the bridegroom. The last six lines turn on the irony set out in the couplet, namely that the speaker's spiritual chastity, paradoxically enough, depends on the force of Christ's masculinity to ravish, or rape, him. Critics generally read Donne's gender positioning here as necessarily feminine. The poet, that is, takes on the female gender role to reinstate the redemptive closure of his remarriage to the church personified in Christ, the ravishing bridegroom. Yet in his rereading of the poem, the Renaissance scholar Richard Rambuss asserts that there is nothing in the poem that warrants such a conventional albeit feminized reading of what remains a distinctively homoerotic sex act between men. Rambuss thus concludes that "it isn't remarriage that the poet says he then desires, but rather something that is, I think, meant to be felt as far more transgressive. For Donne says he wants to be ravished, and hence what is offered as the sonnet's devotional climax is his insistent solicitation that God would rape and enthrall this desirous devotee."

Although both Shakespeare's Sonnet 20 and Donne's "Batter My Heart, Three-Personed God" explore representations of desire between men, it would be a category error to read either as a homosexual lyric. Homosexual identity is a modern concept that emerged only in the nineteenth century. Renaissance scholars such as Alan Bray and Bruce R. Smith are clear on this point. According to Smith,

> No one in England during the sixteenth or seventeenth centuries would have thought of himself as "gay" or "homosexual" for the simple reason that those categories of self-definition did not exist. But that does not mean . . . that there were no men in early modern England whose sexual desires were turned primarily toward other men.

It is not until the nineteenth century with figures such as Walt Whitman that desire between men becomes the basis for identity. "Whitman," as Robert K. Martin reads him, "coincides with and defines a radical change in historical consciousness: the self-conscious awareness of homosexuality as an identity."

Today, the difficulty that some readers have in acknowledging gay identity is compounded, according to the critical theorist Eve Kosofsky Sedgwick, in accepting gay male effeminacy. This cultural resistance to the effeminate male is especially troubling for the gay child. "The crisis for the gay child," according to Professor David Bergman, "is in the tension between other people's views and expectations of him, and the views and expectations he has of himself." The tension in the child's recognition of same-sex desires that transgress traditional family values is the subject of Bergman's poem "Blueberry Man."

DAVID BERGMAN *(b. 1950)*

Blueberry Man   *(1985)*

I was never the one to spot him walking
slowly up the street, pulling his yellow
wagon. It was always a brother or sister
who'd race home with the news. Then everything
spun into action like gulls at low tide.   5

Mother would shoo the children from the yard
and hide us out of danger in the living room,
warning with harsh whispers not to peek
from the windows and knowing we would anyway,
tracking the blueberry man across the porch   10
to where he knocked at the kitchen door.

Grandfather greeted him. Mother said
she was afraid. But I think she was jealous.
For though I was five or six, I knew I'd
never see such beautiful hair again. Hair   15
like a storybook princess. Great golden skeins,
falling halfway down his back. And such eyes,
freaked like a robin's egg and bobbing
beneath mascara waves of lashes. I remember
the Victory Red lips unfurling like a flag   20
when he spoke and the frilly shirt.

                                            My brothers
giggled nervously. But I wasn't scared.
I wanted to pull the chiffon curtains back
and speak. But what would I say? That I knew   25
what it was to be alone? That I had heard
my own family scamper with trepidation
from my door when I was quarantined with
scarlet fever and no one but my mother was
allowed into my room?   30
                            I could have said:
I'm only a child but certain to end an outcast too.
Still, I said nothing, except once, a weak
goodby for which I was roundly scolded.
I used to ride my bike to his house, a tiny   35
cabin covered with angry brambles and
the hiss of intriguing bees, hoping we'd meet.
But he stayed inside during the day when he
wasn't peddling the wares he gathered at night.

One sleepless dawn I saw him coming home   40
with a kerosene lantern in one hand
and a silvery pail in the other.
Mother washed his berries twice to cleanse
them of his memory, as if he communicated
with his touch the fearful urge to dress   45
in women's clothing. For dessert she'd douse
the fruit with milk or pile them on peaks of
sour cream, chubby mountain climbers in the snow.
My brothers ate them greedily. But I
when everyone had left the table, would   50
still be seated, savoring the sweet juice
and the delicate flesh he had brought me.

    In the poem's opening lines, the blueberry man's coming stirs the poet's
whole family into a flurry of simultaneous desire and panic. Paradoxically
enough, he represents both a treat and a taboo. The blueberry vendor's obvi-

ous effeminacy marks him off as an abject figure of sexual transgression for
the poet's family.

TOPICS FOR CRITICAL THINKING

1. Examine the parents' attempts to "hide" their children "out of danger" away from
   the example of the blueberry man. To what extent is the mother's compulsive efforts to "cleanse" the fruit he sells a symptomatic attempt to sanitize and contain
   the blueberry man's feminized gender identification?
2. Discuss the visual details that feminize the blueberry man. How do these qualities
   make him a figure of jealousy for the poet's mother?

TOPIC FOR CRITICAL WRITING

How does the poem present the poet's identification with the blueberry man's "quarantined" status as a social outsider?

> In discussing gay identity, "the most significant term," writes Bergman,
>
> and the one from which the other differences derive is otherness. Although a
> sense of otherness affects us all, the otherness that affects the homosexual—or af-
> fects his sense of homosexuality—is more profound. For while otherness is an un-
> avoidable part of any self's awareness of its own subjectivity and its difference to
> other persons around it, the homosexual suffers a categorical, perhaps even onto-
> logical, otherness since he is made to feel his "unlikeness" to the heterosexual acts
> and persons who gave him being.

Same-sex desire in "Blueberry Man" happens not just as a sexual attraction
but, equally important, as a homoerotic identification with the blueberry
man's "otherness": his distinctive style of gender identification. But however
"other" the blueberry man appears to the poet's "normal" family, he brings
the dessert, paradoxically enough, that they all crave. In the poem's final erotic
turn, the poet takes sensuous pleasure in the "sweet" fruit, which, through
metaphor, is also the blueberry man's gift of "delicate flesh."

Poems for Further Reading and Critical Writing

ELIZABETH BISHOP *(1911–1979)*

Insomnia   *(1955)*

The moon in the bureau mirror
looks out a million miles
(and perhaps with pride, at herself,
but she never, never smiles)
far and away beyond sleep, or   5
perhaps she's a daytime sleeper.

By the Universe deserted,
she'd tell it to go to hell,
and she'd find a body of water,
or a mirror, on which to dwell.   10
So wrap up care in a cobweb
and drop it down the well

into that world inverted
where left is always right,
where the shadows are really the body,   15
where we stay awake all night,
where the heavens are shallow as the sea
is now deep, and you love me.

TOPICS FOR CRITICAL THINKING

1. Consider the ways in which Bishop's poem is set in a distinctively feminine landscape through her personification of the moon in stanzas one and two.
2. Describe the ways in which Bishop characterizes the moon. How does she assert an
   unconventional identity?

TOPIC FOR CRITICAL WRITING

In considering the title of Bishop's poem, what effect does love have on the world of
the speaker and her lover? How does love bestow a vision of the world that turns life
upside down? Examine the poem's tropes for that "world inverted."

APHRA BEHN   *(1640–1689)*

To the Fair Clarinda, Who Made Love
to Me, Imagined More Than Woman   *(1688)*

By Mrs. B

Fair lovely maid, or if that title be
Too weak, too feminine for nobler thee
Permit a name that more approaches truth:
And let me call thee lovely charming youth.
This last will justify my soft complaint,   5
While they may serve to lessen my constraint;
And without blushes I the youth pursue,
When so much beauteous woman is in view.
Against thy charms we struggle but in vain;
With thy deluding form thou giv'st us pain,   10
While the bright nymph betrays us to the swain.

In pity to our sex sure thou wer't sent,
That we might love, and yet be innocent:
For sure no crime with thee we can commit;
Or if we should—thy form excuses it.   15
For who, that gathers fairest flowers believes
A snake lies hid beneath the fragrant leaves.

Though beauteous wonder of a different kind,
Soft *Cloris* with the dear *Alexis* joined;
Whene'er the manly part of thee, would plead   20
Though tempts us with the image of the maid,
While we the noblest passions do extend
The love to *Hermes*, *Aphrodite* the friend.

The seventeenth-century playwright and poet Aphra Behn led an adventurous life with travels to Surinam in the West Indies and a stint as a spy for King Charles II. She wrote for a living after being widowed in 1666. Her published plays include *The Rover* (1677), *Sir Patient Fancy* (1678), *The Roundheads* (1681), and *The City Heiress* (1682). She also was an early experimenter with prose fiction in works such as *Love Letters between a Nobleman and his Sister* (1684–1666), *The Fair Jilt* (1688), *Agnes de Castro* (1688), and *Oroonoko* (1688). Writing in the liberal atmosphere of Restoration England, Behn's poetry demonstrates an unusually frank eroticism, particularly so for a woman writer of that era. Her playful "To the Fair Clarinda, Who Made Love to Me, Imagined More Than Woman" shows a very modern representation of the advantages of same-sex relationships.

TOPICS FOR CRITICAL THINKING

1. Discuss the ways in which Behn addresses Clarinda in the poem and in particular how Behn constructs an alternatively gendered identity for her—one less feminine—in the figure of the "charming youth."
2. How does this youth come to embody both feminine and masculine traits?
3. What, according to Behn, are some of the advantages of this same-sex bond over those one might have to the opposite sex?

TOPICS FOR CRITICAL WRITING

1. Compare Behn's representation of her relationship to Clarinda with Finch's dialogue between Ephelia and Ardelia. How would you contrast the latter's "friendship" with Behn's address to Clarinda?
2. Examine the splitting of Clarinda's gendered identity in the final classical allusions to Hermes and Aphrodite.

WALT WHITMAN   *(1819–1892)*

When I Heard at the Close of the Day   *(1881)*

When I heard at the close of the day how my name had been
   receiv'd with plaudits in the capitol, still it was not a
   happy night for me that follow'd,
And else when I carous'd, or when my plans were
   accomplish'd, still I was not happy,
But the day when I rose at dawn from the bed of perfect
   health, refresh'd, singing, inhaling the ripe breath of
   autumn,
When I saw the full moon in the west grow pale and
   disappear in the morning light,
When I wander'd alone over the beach, and undressing   5
   bathed, laughing with the cool waters, and saw the sun
   rise,
And when I thought how my dear friend my lover was on his
   way coming, O then I was happy,
O then each breath tasted sweeter, and all that day my food
   nourish'd me more, and the beautiful day pass'd well,
And the next came with equal joy, and with the next at
   evening came my friend,
And that night while all was still I heard the waters roll
   slowly continually up the shores,
I heard the hissing rustle of the liquid and sands as directed   10
   to me whispering to congratulate me,
For the one I love most lay sleeping by me under the same
   cover in the cool night,
In the stillness in the autumn moonbeams his face was
   inclined toward me,
And his arm lay lightly around my breast—and that night I
   was happy.

    The famous American nineteenth-century poet Walt Whitman had several relationships with men and even built his theories of democracy on the passionate "adhesion" among "loving comradeship," as he defines it in "Democratic Vistas":

> I confidently expect a time when there will be seen, running like a half-hid warp through all the myriad audible and visible worldly interests of America, threads of manly friendship, fond and loving, pure and sweet, strong and life-long, carried to degrees hitherto unknown . . . having the deepest relation to general politics. I say democracy infers such loving comradeship, as its most inevitable twin or counter part.

Beyond the many forms "manly friendship" took for Whitman, he enjoyed a long-term relationship with Peter Doyle that began after the Civil War and lasted until the poet's death in 1892. Whitman's most explicit musing on his same-sex identifications come in the "Calamus" section of *Leaves of Grass*, as in his passionate poem "When I Heard at the Close of the Day."

TOPICS FOR CRITICAL THINKING

1. Discuss the poet's opening situation and the catalog of outward successes that, nevertheless, bring him no lasting joy.
2. Contrast the poet's sense of dissatisfaction that opens the poem with the effect the thought of the lover has on Whitman's outlook.

TOPIC FOR CRITICAL WRITING

How does anticipating the lover's arrival change Whitman's perception of the physical world? What details does Whitman use to depict his more vivid participation in the life around him?

MINA LOY   *(1882–1966)*

Poems I, II, IX, from Songs to Joannes   *(1917)*

I

Spawn   of   Fantasies
Silting the appraisable
Pig Cupid   his rosy snout
Rooting erotic garbage
"Once upon a time"   5
Pulls a weed   white star-topped
Among wild oats   sown in mucous-membrane

I would   an   eye in a Bengal light°
Eternity in a sky-rocket
Constellations in an ocean   10
Whose rivers run no fresher
Than a trickle of saliva

These   are suspect places

I must live in my lantern
Trimming subliminal flicker   15
Virginal   to the bellows
Of Experience
                    Coloured   glass

---

8 *Bengal light:* A blue signal flare.

II

The skin-sack   20
In which a wanton duality
Packed
All the completion of my infructuous impulses
Something the shape of a man
To the casual vulgarity of the merely observant   25
More of a clock-work mechanism
Running down against time
To which I am not paced
  My finger-tips are numb from fretting your hair
A God's door-mat   30
  On the threshold of your mind

IX

When we lifted
Our eye-lids on Love
A cosmos   35
Of coloured voices
And laughing honey

And spermatozoa
At the core of Nothing
In the milk of the Moon   40

    The experimental modernist poet Mina Loy began her career as a visual
artist with a well-received exhibition at the reputable Salon d'Automne show
in Paris in 1905. One of the few women to affiliate with the Italian futurist
movement, Loy also had ties to dadaism and surrealism. Her lifestyle was as
radically modern as her poetry. Originally published under the title "Love
Songs" in the experimental modernist journal *Others*, the opening selections
of her *Songs to Joannes* (1917) depict frank, though highly stylized, scenes of
desire between men and women.

TOPICS FOR CRITICAL THINKING

1. Discuss Loy's blending of highly figurative language and realistic detail in her images of sexuality in the above selections from *Songs to Joannes*.
2. How does Loy capture the ironies of sexuality and desire in her oxymoronic figure
   of "Pig Cupid"?

TOPICS FOR CRITICAL WRITING

1. Compare Loy's imagery in stanza two of Poem I with that of Poem IX. What
   similarities and differences do you see in her depictions of the ecstatic intensities
   of sexuality?

2. Loy also depicts somewhat obscene images of sexuality's "suspect places" and "casual vulgarity." Discuss the forms these moments take in her poems.

ROBERT DUNCAN *(1919–1988)*

The Torso: Passages 18 *(1968)*

Most beautiful! the red-flowering eucalyptus
  the madrone, the yew

Is he . . .

So thou wouldst smile, and take me in thine arms
The sight of London to my exiled eyes   5
Is as Elysium to a new-come soul

  If he be Truth
  I would dwell in the illusion of him

His hands unlocking from chambers of my male body

    such an idea in man's image   10

rising tides that sweep me towards him

      . . . *homosexual?*

    and at the treasure of his mouth

  pour forth my soul

      his soul   commingling   15

I thought a Being more than vast, His body leading
  into Paradise,   his eyes

    quickening a fire in me,   a trembling

  hieroglyph: At the root of the neck

the clavicle, for the neck is the stem of the great artery   20
  upward into his head that is beautiful

    At the rise of the pectoral muscle,

the nipples, for the breasts are like sleeping fountains
  of feeling in man, waiting above the beat of his heart,

shielding the rise and fall of his breath, to be   25
   awakend

                    At the axis of his mid hriff

the navel, for in the pit of his stomach the chord from
   which first he was fed has its temple

                    At the root of the groin   30

the pubic hair, for the torso is the stem in which the man
   flowers forth and leads to the stamen of flesh in which
   his seed rises

a wave of need and desire over   taking me

                    cried out my name   35

(This was long ago; It was another life)

                    and said,

         What do you want of me?

I do not know, I said.   I have fallen in love.   He
      has brought me into heights and depths my heart   40
         would fear   without him.   His look

   pierces my side • fire eyes •

      I have been waiting for you, he said:
         I know what you desire

      you do not yet know   but through me •   45

And I am with you everywhere.   In your falling

I have fallen from a high place.   I have raised myself

      from darkness in your   rising

                    wherever you are

   my hand in your hand   seeking   the locks, the keys   50

I am there.   Gathering me, you gather

      your Self •

For my Other is not a woman but a man

the King upon whose bosom let me lie.

Robert Duncan was a celebrated avant-garde poet of the San Francisco Renaissance in the post–World War II era. During the 1950s, at the Black Mountain school in North Carolina, Duncan, along with Charles Olson and Robert Creeley, would experiment with serial-form long poems made up of encyclopedic details linked through repeated tropes, themes, and poetic motifs. In 1944 at the age of twenty-six, Duncan published "The Homosexual in Society," a pioneering essay propounding a gay civic and cultural politics. In his personal life, Duncan lived in a same-sex relationship with Jess Collins from 1951 until his death in 1988. Duncan's open-form poem "The Torso: Passages 18" celebrates a vision of homoerotic passion.

TOPICS FOR CRITICAL THINKING

1. The term *torso* derives from *thyrsus*, the Latin word for "stalk" or "stem." The *thyrsus* was also used as a phallic ceremonial object in Bacchanalian rites and rituals. How does Duncan inscribe the etymological origins of *torso* in his organic and floral images in the poem?

2. Male poets have long paid tribute to women in the traditional poetic form of the **blazon** that compliments the details of a lover's face and body. How does Duncan work within this convention to present a same-sex blazon of the male body?

3. The italicized third stanza and the last italicized line in the poem are quotes from Christopher Marlowe's *Edward the Second* that, in part, explores Edward's devotion to a young liege Gaveston. Describe the effect of placing this intertext after Duncan's ellipsis in posing the question "Is he . . . homosexual?"

TOPICS FOR CRITICAL WRITING

1. How does Duncan invent, not just reflect, his experience of same-sex desire in his response to the lover's claim to know him: "you do not yet know   but through me"?

2. What biblical tropes of crucifixion and resurrection can you detect in the poem?

OLGA BROUMAS   *(b. 1949)*

The Masseuse   *(1999)*

Always an angel rises from the figure
naked and safe between my towels
as before taboo. It's why I close
my eyes. A smell
precedes him as the heart   5
fills from his bowl. I bow
down to the riddle of the ear,
its embryonic sworl nested with nodes

that calm the uncurled spine,
a maypole among organs.   10
Each day a stranger or almost
crosses my heart to die
from the unsayable
into the thickened beating
of those wings and we are shy.   15
Or frightened as with clothes
on we forget
abysmally what heaven
shares with death: what gypsy vowels
unshackled from the lips   20
rush the impenetrable
mind and the atlas
clicks in my trowel hands.
Crocuses on the threshold's south
side then and now. It goes on   25
like an egret scaling the unruly bands
of atmosphere we have agreed on
by my palms'
erratic longing of the flesh
to try. Toes crack. Hips   30
soften and the spine,
a seaweed in the shallow spume,
undulates like a musical
string by the struck note,
helpless with harmonics.   35
Rock. Cradle the perceptible
scar of the compass, sensible
stigma in a poised blind
of trust angling for reentry,
and the rain, the wind   40
across its face like minnows in the dark
of love schooling the light
will speak to you and you will walk
home dizzy, grazed by the gloaming and the just
illumined stars.   45

Olga Broumas grew up in Greece and came to the United States on a Fulbright exchange program in Architecture and Modern Dance in 1967. A recipient of the prestigious Yale Younger Poets Award ten years later, she
combined her identity as a poet with a career in massage. In 1982 she became
licensed as a bodywork therapist, a vocation she depicts in "The Masseuse."

TOPICS FOR CRITICAL THINKING

1. Explore Broumas's primal tropes of life, death, and resurrection to depict her vocation of therapeutic bodywork.

2. Discuss how figurative language presents Broumas's experience of her physical contact with the bodies of her clients.

TOPIC FOR CRITICAL WRITING

In what ways does Broumas depict embodied desire in the poem? What is the effect of this bodywork on the one addressed at the end of the poem?

RICHARD HARTEIS *(b. 1946)*

Star Trek III *(1987)*

The fantasy spaceman
returning from death
greets his captain
gingerly: "Jim?"

Spock's Vulcan father explains   5
that only time will tell
if the priestess' magic
will bring him totally back.
Instead of "the end"
the film's last frames promise,   10
"the adventure continues."

I want to cry a little:
I grew up on these heroes—
to be as good as Kirk . . .

But life is a little closer now.   15
We watch the film together
and I explain the plot

the way one would talk to someone
trapped under ice. My manuals say
I mustn't convey anxiety.   20

I remember the day after
weeks at your bedside when
you said my name finally.

You were IN there,
KNEW me.   25

The same shock the cardiac nurse
felt the year before when she

randomly took the tape from
your sweet eyes and they flew open
as she called your name.   30

We've been in a few
tight spots lately.

All these months.
My loneliness deepens.
I cry in private   35
when you forget my name.

Still, you love me clearly,
whoever I am.

The adventure continues.
                                                                     40

    Richard Harteis has lived with the poet William Meredith since 1971
and, in addition to publishing several volumes of verse, has served in the
Peace Corps and pursued careers as a health care worker and teacher. His lu-
dic poem "Star Trek III" explores the frontiers of life and death, finding ways
to affirm desire in the face of terminal illness.

TOPICS FOR CRITICAL THINKING

1. How does Harteis, as he says, "explain the plot" of the popular TV and film series
   Star Trek?
2. In what ways does Harteis change the conventional relationship between Kirk and
   Spock have as colleagues aboard the *Enterprise?*

TOPICS FOR CRITICAL WRITING

1. How do you interpret his phrase "to be as good as Kirk . . ." in stanza three? How
   does Harteis reinterpret what Kirk should stand for as a role model?
2. How has Harteis's love relationship been compromised by illness, and how has it
   been deepened by that experience? Compare the final phrase "the adventure continues" with its earlier use in stanza two.

GREGORY CORSO   *(1930–2001)*

Marriage   *(1960)*

Should I get married? Should I be good?
Astound the girl next door with my velvet suit and faustus hood?
Don't take her to movies but to cemeteries
tell all about werewolf bathtubs and forked clarinets

then desire her and kiss her and all the preliminaries   5
and she going just so far and I understanding why
not getting angry saying You must feel! It's beautiful to feel!
Instead take her in my arms lean against an old crooked tombstone
and woo her the entire night the constellations in the sky—

When she introduces me to her parents   10
back straightened, hair finally combed, strangled by a tie,
should I sit with my knees together on their 3rd degree sofa
and not ask Where's the bathroom?
How else to feel other than I am,
often thinking Flash Gordon soap—   15
O how terrible it must be for a young man
seated before a family and the family thinking
We never saw him before! He wants our Mary Lou!
After tea and homemade cookies they ask What do you do for a living?

Should I tell them? Would they like me then?   20
Say All right get married, we're losing a daughter
but we're gaining a son—
And should I then ask Where's the bathroom?

 O God, and the wedding! All her family and her friends
and only a handful of mine all scroungy and bearded   25
just wait to get at the drinks and food—
And the priest! he looking at me as if I masturbated
asking me Do you take this woman for your lawful wedded wife?
And I trembling what to say say Pie Glue!
I kiss the bride all those corny men slapping me on the back   30
She's all yours, boy! Ha-ha-ha!
And in their eyes you could see some obscene honeymoon going on—
Then all that absurd rice and clanky cans and shoes
Niagara Falls! Hordes of us! Husbands! Wives! Flowers! Chocolates!
All streaming into cozy hotels   35
All going to do the same thing tonight
The indifferent clerk he knowing what was going to happen
The lobby zombies they knowing what
The whistling elevator man he knowing
The winking bellboy knowing   40
Everybody knowing! I'd almost be inclined not to do anything!
Stay up all night! Stare that hotel clerk in the eye!
Screaming: I deny honeymoon! I deny honeymoon!
running rampant into those almost climactic suites
yelling Radio belly! Cat shovel!   45
O I'd live in Niagara forever! in a dark cave beneath the Falls
I'd sit there the Mad Honeymooner
devising ways to break marriages, a scourge of bigamy
a saint of divorce—

But I should get married I should be good   50
How nice it'd be to come home to her
and sit by the fireplace and she in the kitchen
aproned young and lovely wanting my baby
and so happy about me she burns the roast beef
and comes crying to me and I get up from my big papa chair   55
saying Christmas teeth! Radiant brains! Apple deaf!
God what a husband I'd make! Yes, I should get married!
So much to do! like sneaking into Mr Jones' house late at night
and cover his golf clubs with 1920 Norwegian books
Like hanging a picture of Rimbaud° on the lawnmower   60
like pasting Tannu Tuva postage stamps all over the picket fence
like when Mrs Kindhead comes to collect for the Community Chest
grab her and tell her There are unfavorable omens in the sky!
And when the mayor comes to get my vote tell him
When are you going to stop people killing whales!   65
And when the milkman comes leave him a note in the bottle
Penguin dust, bring me penguin dust, I want penguin dust—

Yet if I should get married and it's Connecticut and snow
and she gives birth to a child and I am sleepless, worn,
up for nights, head bowed against a quiet window, the past behind me,   70
finding myself in the most common of situations a trembling man
knowledged with responsibility not twig-smear nor Roman coin soup—
O what would that be like!
Surely I'd give it for a nipple a rubber Tacitus°
For a rattle a bag of broken Bach records   75
Tack Della Francesca° all over its crib
Sew the Greek alphabet on its bib
And build for its playpen a roofless Parthenon

No, I doubt I'd be that kind of father
Not rural not snow no quiet window   80
but hot smelly tight New York City
seven flights up, roaches and rats in the walls
a fat Reichian° wife screeching over potatoes Get a job!
And five nose running brats in love with Batman
And the neighbors all toothless and dry haired   85
like those hag masses of the 18th century
all wanting to come in and watch TV
The landlord wants his rent

---

60 *Rimbaud:* Arthur Rimbaud (1854–1891), French symbolist poet.   74 *Tacitus:* Cornelius
Tacitus (A.D. 55–A.D. 117), Roman historian.   76 *Della Francesca:* Piero Della Francesca
(1420?–1492), Italian painter of the Renaissance.   83 *Reichian:* Wilhelm Reich (1897–1957),
psychological theorist of sexual pleasure.

Grocery store Blue Cross Gas & Electric Knights of Columbus
Impossible to lie back and dream Telephone snow, ghost parking—   90
No! I should not get married! I should never get married!
But—imagine if I were married to a beautiful sophisticated woman
tall and pale wearing an elegant black dress and long black gloves
holding a cigarette holder in one hand and a highball in the other
and we lived high up in a penthouse with a huge window   95
from which we could see all of New York and even farther on clearer days
No, can't imagine myself married to that pleasant prison dream—

O but what about love? I forget love
not that I am incapable of love
it's just that I see love as odd as wearing shoes—   100
I never wanted to marry a girl who was like my mother
And Ingrid Bergman was always impossible
And there's maybe a girl now but she's already married
And I don't like men and—
but there's got to be somebody!   105
Because what if I'm 60 years old and not married,
all alone in a furnished room with pee stains on my underwear
and everybody else is married! All the universe married but me!

Ah, yet well I know that were a woman possible as I am possible
then marriage would be possible—   110
Like SHE° in her lonely alien gaud waiting her Egyptian lover
so I wait—bereft of 2,000 years and the bath of life.

Gregory Corso was born in 1930 in Greenwich Village and was brought up in foster homes until he was arrested for petty theft at the age of sixteen. After spending three years in prison, he met the Beat poet Allen Ginsberg, who gave Corso encouragement as an emerging poet. Along with Ginsberg, Jack Kerouac, William S. Burroughs, and Gary Snyder, Corso became one of the more celebrated figures of the Beat generation. In his novel the *Subterraneans* (1958), Jack Kerouac based his character of Yuri Gregorovic on Gregory Corso. Corso's famous Beat poem "Marriage" presents an absurdist look at the conventions of married life in the postwar era.

TOPICS FOR CRITICAL THINKING

1. In Corso's opening lines he asks "Should I get married? Should I be good?" How might marriage be associated with success, "goodness," and normality in the cultural milieu of the late 1950s and early 1960s when Corso wrote "Marriage"?
2. "Marriage" depicts several stereotypical scenarios of courtship, marital vows, honeymooning, and so on. Discuss these scenes and Corso's parodies of them.

---

111 *SHE:* An 1887 novel by H. Rider Haggard.

TOPICS FOR CRITICAL WRITING

1. How does Corso use the institution of marriage to satirize the wider public sphere of society in the 1950s?

2. Corso employs language as a subversive medium for performing his sense of the absurdities of existence. Discuss his use of verbal non sequiturs such as "Radio belly" and "penguin dust." How do these and other comic phrases jar us out of conventional and habitual thinking?

Critical Perspective: On Sexual Representation in John Donne's Holy Sonnet 14

"Conversely, Achsah Guibbory reads 'Batter my heart' in terms that not only heterosexualize Donne's coupling of salvation and sexual violation, but thoroughly domesticate the poem as well. In her chapter on Donne for the *Cambridge Companion to English Poetry: Donne to Marvell*, Guibbory describes the sonnet's amorous scenario this way: the speaker, she writes, is 'like a woman who loves one man (God) but is betrothed to another (Satan), and wants to be rescued, even by force.' Thus, 'Christ is the bridegroom,' while the poet adopts the 'conventionally "feminine," passive role of bride.' Yet the connubial narrative Guibbory reads into 'Batter my heart,' while orthodox enough in form, is unwarranted by the sonnet itself, this critic taming Donne's poem of the very outrageousness that is surely its point. For although Donne sees himself as currently betrothed to the devil, he never asks God to intervene and make a proper 'bride' out of him. The sonnet, in other words, fails to end with the expected and complementary call for a re-betrothal to Christ as a more appropriate spouse for the Christian. Indeed, there is little that is proper about Donne's sonnet and its multiply metaphorized scheme of redemption, one that is predicated upon a series of violent and violative actions: the Godhead is to take a battering ram to a hard heart; to besiege and steal away a town that is 'due' to another; to provoke a divorce. And, after all this, it isn't remarriage that the poet says he then desires, but rather something that is, I think, meant to be felt as far more transgressive. For Donne says he wants to be ravished, and hence what is offered as the sonnet's devotional climax is his insistent solicitation that God would rape and enthrall this desirous devotee. . . .

"Similarly, nowhere in 'Batter my heart' does Donne apostrophize himself or his soul as 'she'; nor does he accord himself the position of a 'woman,' much less a bride, over the course of the poem's envisioned path to redemption. Instead, despite enduring cultural proscriptions that have tended generally, though not monolithically, to feminize any body subject to penetration, Donne's desire in view of divine ravishment remains bawdily assertive, even priapic: 'That I may rise, and stand, o'erthrow me' (line 3). Thus, to return to Fish's formulation, while the poet may be spreading his legs and his cheeks— 'I . . . / Labour to admit you, but oh, to no end' (lines 5–6)—being so taken here does not entail effeminization or castration. Indeed, it is as though Donne wants the Godhead to ravish him, 'to break that knot again,' *in order that* he will be rendered potent, erect. Moreover, if there is any taking on of a feminized subject position in 'Batter my heart,' it is one Donne looks to abjure in seeking severance from the devil: 'Divorce me, . . . / Take me to you' (lines 11–12). Satan is the one who has made a 'woman' of him, a rectifiable situation if only God would himself 'rise' (as Donne likewise urges him to do in 'As due by many titles') and finally take him as his own, ravish him, make more of a man of him."

—Richard Rambuss, from *Closet Devotions* (1998)

Critical Perspective: On Lesbian Existence and the Lesbian Continuum

"I have chosen to use the terms *lesbian existence* and *lesbian continuum* because the word *lesbianism* has a clinical and limiting ring. *Lesbian existence* suggests both the fact of the historical presence of lesbians and our continuing creation of the meaning of that existence. I mean the term *lesbian continuum* to include a range—through each woman's life and throughout history—of woman-identified experience, not simply the fact that a woman has had or consciously desired genital sexual experience with another woman. If we expand it to embrace many more forms of primary intensity between and among women, including the sharing of a rich inner life, the bonding against male tyranny, the giving and receiving of practical and political support, if we can also hear it in such associations as *marriage resistance* and the 'haggard' behavior identified by Mary Daly (obsolete meanings 'intractable,' 'willful,' 'wanton,' and 'unchaste,' 'a woman reluctant to yield to wooing'),[45] we begin to grasp breadths of female history and psychology which have lain out of reach as a consequence of limited, mostly clinical, definitions of *lesbianism*.

"Lesbian existence comprises both the breaking of a taboo and the rejection of a compulsory way of life. It is also a direct or indirect attack on male right of access to women. But it is more than these, although we may first begin to perceive it as a form of naysaying to patriarchy, an act of resistance. It has, of course, included isolation, self-hatred, breakdown, alcoholism, suicide, and intrawoman violence; we romanticize at our peril what it means to love and act against the grain, and under heavy penalties; and lesbian existence has been lived (unlike, say, Jewish or Catholic existence) without access to any knowledge of a tradition, a continuity, a social underpinning. The destruction of records and memorabilia and letters documenting the realities of lesbian existence must be taken very seriously as a means of keeping heterosexuality

---

45. Mary Daly, *Gyn/Ecology: The Metaethics of Radical Feminism* (Boston: Beacon Press, 1978), p 15.

compulsory for women, since what has been kept from our knowledge is joy, sensuality, courage, and community, as well as guilt, self-betrayal, and pain.[46] . . .

"As the term *lesbian* has been held to limiting clinical associations in its patriarchal definition, female friendship and comradeship have been set apart from the erotic, thus limiting the erotic itself. But as we deepen and broaden the range of what we define as lesbian existence, as we delineate a lesbian continuum, we begin to discover the erotic in female terms: as that which is unconfined to any single part of the body or solely to the body itself; as an energy not only diffuse but, as Audre Lorde has described it, omnipresent in 'the sharing of joy, whether physical, emotional, psychic,' and in the sharing of work; as the empowering joy which 'makes us less willing to accept powerlessness, or those other supplied states of being which are not native to me, such as resignation, despair, self-effacement, depression, self-denial.'"[48]

—Adrienne Rich, from "Compulsory Heterosexuality and Lesbian Existence" (1980)

Critical Perspective: On Sexual Knowledge, Power, and Ideology in Shakespeare's England

"Foucault's model of how sex is 'put into discourse' points us to the two things we need to look for: 'knowledge' and 'power.' Concerning 'knowledge,' the French language allows Foucault to make an important distinction that is sometimes lost in Robert Hurley's English translation. The 'special knowledges' that Foucault speaks of in connection with bodily pleasure, controls and resistances, and talk about sex are *connaissances*, knowledge in the sense of acquaintance, familiarity, experience. (Compare our borrowed term *connoisseur*.) The knowledge that Foucault allies with power is, on the other hand, *savoir*, knowledge in the sense of learning, erudition, ideas. In Foucault's formulation, experience (*connaissances*) is a function of ideology (*savoir*). The experience of sexual desire at a given moment in history is shaped by the ideas that people happen to entertain at that historical moment. To avoid confusing these two different senses of knowledge, we should perhaps prefer the term 'ideology' as a coordinate with power.

"'Ideology' is one aspect of sex put into discourse; 'power' is the other. The power implicit in a text is ideology put into action. It is a speaker exert-

---

46. "In a hostile world in which women are not supposed to survive except in relation with and in service to men, entire communities of women were simply erased. History tends to bury what it seeks to reject" (Blanche W. Cook, "'Women Alone Stir My Imagination': Lesbianism and the Cultural Tradition," *Signs: Journal of Women in Culture and Society* 4, no. 4 [Summer 1979]: 719–720). The Lesbian Herstory Archives in New York City is one attempt to preserve contemporary documents on lesbian existence—a project of enormous value and meaning, working against the continuing censorship and obliteration of relationships, networks, communities in other archives and elsewhere in the culture.

48. Audre Lorde, "Uses of the Erotic: The Erotic as Power," in *Sister Outsider* (Trumansburg, N.Y.: Crossing Press, 1984).

ing control over a listener, a writer exerting control over a reader. It is a listener or a reader internalizing the text and exerting control over himself. Power, in Foucault's view, is not just a matter of negative prohibitions, a central authority telling people what they may and may not do, what they may and may not feel. Power is also a matter of positive excitations: it is people, situations, and objects that a particular culture endows with erotic value. That is to say, sexuality is not simply *subject* to power; it *manifests* power. To understand homosexuality in early modern England we need to investigate not just what was prohibited but what was actively homoeroticized. What we discover is a startling ambiguity. The one salient fact about homosexuality in early modern England, as in early modern Europe generally, is the disparity that separates the extreme punishments prescribed by law and the apparent tolerance, even positive valuation, of homoerotic desire in the visual arts, in literature, and . . . in the political power structure. What are we to make of a culture that could consume popular prints of Apollo embracing Hyacinth and yet could order hanging for men who acted on the very feelings that inspire that embrace?"

—Bruce Smith, from *Homosexual Desire in Shakespeare's England* (1991)

21  Postcolonial Poetics

www The word *postcolonial* **Web** designates both a period term and a set of theoretical issues emerging from the literature and culture of Europe's former colonies. The rise of national and international independence movements of the twentieth century reflects the breakup of Europe's colonial powers that at the time of World War I ruled over some 85 percent of the globe. In the post-World War II era, much of world literature reflected shifting social and cultural arrangements that once defined the imperial centers of power against their colonial margins in India, Africa, the Middle East, Asia, and the Pacific rim. Thus, when poet and Nobel laureate Derek Walcott composed "A Far Cry from Africa," he not only wrote as a West Indian author in the context of world literature, but, equally important, he also expanded the frontiers of **postcolonial** literature.

DEREK WALCOTT *(b. 1930)*

A Far Cry from Africa *(1962)*

A wind is ruffling the tawny pelt
Of Africa. Kikuyu,° quick as flies,
Batten upon the bloodstreams of the veldt.
Corpses are scattered through a paradise.
Only the worm, colonel of carrion, cries: 5
"Waste no compassion on these separate dead!"
Statistics justify and scholars seize
The salients of colonial policy.
What is that to the white child hacked in bed?
To savages, expendable as Jews?   10

Threshed out by beaters, the long rushes break
In a white dust of ibises whose cries
Have wheeled since civilization's dawn
From the parched river or beast-teeming plain.
The violence of beast on beast is read   15
As natural law, but upright man

---

2 *Kikuyu:* Mau Mau secret society of the "burning spear."

Seeks his divinity by inflicting pain.
Delirious as these worried beasts, his wars
Dance to the tightened carcass of a drum,
While he calls courage still that native dread   20
Of the white peace contracted by the dead.

Again brutish necessity wipes its hands
Upon the napkin of a dirty cause, again
A waste of our compassion, as with Spain,°
The gorilla wrestles with the superman.   25
I who am poisoned with the blood of both,
Where shall I turn, divided to the vein?
I who have cursed
The drunken officer of British rule, how choose
Between this Africa and the English tongue I love?   30
Betray them both, or give back what they give?
How can I face such slaughter and be cool?
How can I turn from Africa and live?

Published in 1962, Walcott's poem addresses the disintegration of British rule over East Africa in Kenya. Specifically, Walcott probes the struggle of the Kikuyu tribesmen against the British government and settler population over such issues as land ownership, burdensome taxation, educational access, and civil rights concerns generally. This social conflict gave birth to the Kikuyu secret society of the "burning spear," or *Mau Mau*, which led a violent campaign against colonial rule beginning in 1952. Allegedly implicated in the Lari massacre of 1953, the *Mau Mau* became the object of British reprisals under a declared state of emergency. By 1956, more than 11,000 Kenyan rebels had been killed and another 20,000 arrested. Despite this colonial crackdown, the nationalist leader Jomo Kenyatta, who had been jailed in 1953, prevailed in ousting British rule, becoming prime minister over an independent Kenya the year after Walcott's poem was published.

"A Far Cry from Africa," however, does not just allude to colonial policy; equally important, it stages the distinctive dilemma of postcolonial **hybridity.** The *American Heritage Dictionary* defines a hybrid as the "offspring of genetically dissimilar parents or stock . . . [and, by implication] something of mixed origin or composition." Reflecting the lived relationship of imperial center and colonial margin, the term *hybridity* in postcolonial studies describes the hyphenated subject of colonial rule or, in Leela Gandhi's words from *Postcolonial Theory: A Critical Introduction* (1998), "the Janus-faced bearer of a split consciousness or a double vision." In "A Far Cry from Africa," Walcott's double vision begins with an ethical dilemma. He cannot wholly affirm either side of the conflict when both are implicated in the murder of innocents. What do statistics or colonial policy matter, he asks "to the white child hacked in bed? / To savages, expendable as Jews." In the poem, the dilemma of split loyalties is

24 *Spain:* Spanish Civil War, 1936–1939.

not just an intellectual abstraction but something played along the pulses. The poet does not have the luxury of choosing between colonial and post-colonial identities. "I," he realizes, "who am poisoned with the blood of both, / Where shall I turn, divided to the vein?"

For Walcott, the political clash in Kenya not only implicates him at the level of the divided self but alerts him, as poet, to his conflicted relation to colonial language. He awakens to a lived understanding of how identity is always already underwritten by a prior linguistic hybridity. The literary understanding of postcolonial discourse derives, in part, from the critical theory of the Russian formalist critic Mikhail Bakhtin. Specifically, Bakhtin views language usage in literature and in everyday life not as unitary or monolithic but "dialogic" in nature. Language comes to us as already marked by contradictory social usage. In *The Dialogic Imagination* (1981) he writes that each verbal coinage is "a mixture of two social languages within the limits of a single utterance, an encounter, within the arena of an utterance, between two different linguistic consciousnesses, separated from one another by an epoch, by social differentiation, or by some other factor." As poet, Walcott performs the dialogic utterance by simultaneously avowing and cursing his inherited language, steeped as it is in a history of colonial domination:

> I who have cursed
> The drunken officer of British rule, how choose
> Between this Africa and the English tongue I love?

In the poem's last four lines, which all end in questions, Walcott stages that impossibility of choice as the distinctive social position of the postcolonial subject. The hybrid, in-between space of postcolonial speaking, moreover, is inscribed from the beginning in the "cry" of the poem's title. Not insignificantly, the cry intones the dialogism of a split utterance. Here the syntax of the poem's title communicates a mixed message. It can be read either as a prepositional phrase or as a phrase of possession: as either a far-away cry addressing the poet "from Africa" (possession) or as the poet's cry voiced at a far distance away "from Africa" (preposition). It is the challenge of postcolonial hybridity to hear and utter each far cry at the same time.

The postcolonial acknowledgment of hybridity—the fact that one's language, art, and identity are already shaped by the discourse of imperial powers—is not necessarily a disabling recognition. Such influences, once mastered, can be voiced with a difference: in ways that subvert, parody, and baffle colonial rule. In his Introduction to *Poems of Black Africa* (1975), Nobel Prize laureate Wole Soyinka writes:

> A distinct quality in all great poets does exercise a ghostly influence in other writers, but this need not be cause for self-flagellation. The resulting work is judged by its capacity to move ahead or sideways, by the thoroughness of ingestion within a new organic mould, by the original strength of the new entity. Modern African poems which betray traces of an internal dialogue are often accused of alien affectation, but examination of traditional poetry reveals that it too is built on a densely packed matrix of references (and not, as is sometimes claimed to the contrary, on simplistic narrative).

One technique of presenting the "densely packed matrix" of postcolonial poetry is through a discursive mimicry. "The emerging consensus on post-colonial literary practice has it," writes Gandhi, "that the most radical anti-colonial writers are 'mimic men,' whose generic misappropriations constantly transgress the received and orthodox boundaries of 'literariness.' . . . Accordingly, the paradigmatic moment of anti-colonial counter-textuality is seen to begin with the first indecorous mixing of Western genres with local content."

Yambo Ouologuem, the Mali-born and Paris-educated African writer whose novel *Le Devoir de Violence (Bound to Violence)* won the Prix Renaudot in 1968, employs such mimicry in his ironic poem "Tomatoes." There, his poetic persona as "mimic man," parodies the colonial stereotypes of the African "other" as primitive cannibal and as sloganizing political nationalist.

YAMBO OUOLOGUEM   *(b. 1948)*

Tomatoes   *(1966)*

People think I'm a cannibal
But you know what people say

People say I've got red gums but who has
White ones
Up the tomatoes   5

People say there are not nearly so many tourists
Now
But you know
This isn't America and nobody
Has the money   10

People think it's my fault and are scared
But look
My teeth are white not red
I've not eaten anybody

People are rotten they say I scoff   15
Baked tourists
Or maybe grilled
Baked or grilled was my order
They don't say anything just keep looking uneasily at my gums
Up the tomatoes   20

Everyone knows that in an agricultural country there's agriculture
Up the vegetables

Everyone knows that vegetables
Well you can't live on the vegetables you grow
And that I'm quite well developed for someone underdeveloped   25
Miserable scum living off the tourists
Down with my teeth

People suddenly surrounded me
Tied me up
Threw me down   30
At the feet of justice
Cannibal or not cannibal
Answer

Ah you think you're so clever
So proud of yourself   35

Well we'll see I'm going to settle your account
Have you anything to say
Before you are sentenced to death

I shouted Up the tomatoes

People are rotten and women curious you know   40
There was one of these in the curious circle
In her rasping voice sort of bubbling like a saucepan
With a hole in it
Shrieked
Slit open his belly   45
I'm sure father is still inside

There weren't any knives
Naturally enough among the vegetarians
Of the western world
So they got a Gillette blade   50
And carefully
Slit
Slat
Plop
Slit open my belly   55

Inside flourishing rows of tomatoes
Watered by streams of palm wine
Up the tomatoes

TOPICS FOR CRITICAL THINKING

1. Describe the colonial stereotypes and attitudes that Ouologuem parodies in "Tomatoes."
2. How does he contrast America with conditions in his home state?

TOPIC FOR CRITICAL WRITING

How does the poet reveal the tourists as, in fact, more violent than the "natives" they fear? How does Ouologuem mimic colonial language in phrasings such as "settle your account"?

Colonial mimicry, according to postcolonial theorist Homi Bhabha, mines the sly contradictions between the discourses of deference toward and defiance of imperial authority: "Between the Western sign and its colonial signification," he writes in *The Location of Culture* (1994), "there emerges a map of misreading that embarrasses the righteousness of recordation and its certainty of good government . . . a range of differential knowledges and positionalities that both estrange its 'identity' [to] produce new forms of knowledge, new modes of differentiation, new sites of power."

Imperial representations of the colonial subject are not nearly as transparent as they were, say, in the 1950s thanks, in part, to such works of critical theory as Edward Said's pioneering book *Orientalism* (1978). In it, Said makes the point that the empire's knowledge of the colonies is a form of power exerted over colonial peoples. Going back to nineteenth-century European scholarship, Said reveals the ways in which its system of stereotyped representations and ideological assumptions projected a version of the Orient— Asia, India, the Middle East, and Far East—that was "other" to the imagined ideals of Western society. A set of ideological oppositions projected the West as active in relation to Oriental passivity, as masculine as opposed to feminine, normative versus exotic, intellectually superior versus culturally inferior, advanced versus backward, dominate versus subordinate, and so on.

Thinking critically about the ways in which the imperial center casts such negative stereotypes onto the colonial margins is the first step toward conceiving new forms of representational agency. Such emerging, cosmopolitan forms of identity are made possible by counter-discourses that will "write back" to the imperial centers of colonial power. These new, postcolonial forms of writing will belong neither wholly to the Euro-American first world nor to the third world of the former colonies but somewhere in-between, in the literature of postcolonial hybridity.

Poems for Further Reading and Critical Writing

HA JIN *(b. 1956)*

Ways of Talking *(1996)*

We used to like talking about grief.
Our journals and letters were packed
with losses, complaints, and sorrows.
Even if there was no grief

we wouldn't stop lamenting   5
as though longing for the charm
of a distressed face.

Then we couldn't help expressing grief.
So many things descended without warning:
labor wasted, loves lost, houses gone,   10
marriages broken, friends estranged,
ambitions worn away by immediate needs.
Words lined up in our throats
for a good whining.
Grief seemed like an endless river—   15
the only immortal flow of life.

After losing a land and then giving up a tongue,
we stopped talking of grief.
Smiles began to brighten our faces.
We laugh a lot, at our own mess.   20
Things become beautiful,
even hailstones in the strawberry fields.

LÉOPOLD SÉDAR SENGHOR   *(1906–2001)*

Prayer to the Masks   *(1964)*

Masks! O Masks!
Black mask, red mask, you white-and-black masks
Masks of the four cardinal points where the Spirit blows
I greet you in silence!
And you, not the least of all, Ancestor with the lion head.   5
You keep this place safe from women's laughter
And any wry, profane smiles
You exude the immortal air where I inhale
The breath of my Fathers.
Masks with faces without masks, stripped of every dimple   10
And every wrinkle
You created this portrait, my face leaning
On an altar of blank paper
And in your image, listen to me!
The Africa of empires is dying—it is the agony   15
Of a sorrowful princess
And Europe, too, tied to us at the navel.
Fix your steady eyes on your oppressed children
Who give their lives like the poor man his last garment.
Let us answer "present" at the rebirth of the World   20
As white flour cannot rise without the leaven.

Who else will teach rhythm to the world
Deadened by machines and cannons?
Who will sound the shout of joy at daybreak to wake
  orphans and the dead?   25
Tell me, who will bring back the memory of life
To the man of gutted hopes?
They call us men of cotton, coffee, and oil
They call us men of death.
But we are men of dance, whose feet get stronger 30
As we pound upon firm ground.

WOLE SOYINKA (b. 1934)

Telephone Conversation   *(1960)*

The price seemed reasonable, location
Indifferent. The landlady swore she lived
Off premises. Nothing remained
But self-confession. "Madam," I warned,
"I hate a wasted journey—I am African."   5
Silence. Silenced transmission of
Pressurized good-breeding. Voice, when it came,
Lipstick coated, long gold-rolled
Cigarette-holder pipped. Caught I was, foully.
"HOW DARK?" . . . I had not misheard . . . "ARE YOU LIGHT 10
OR VERY DARK?" Button B. Button A. Stench
Of rancid breath of public hide-and-speak.
Red booth. Red pillar box. Red double-tiered
Omnibus squelching tar. It *was* real! Shamed
By ill-mannered silence, surrender   15
Pushed dumbfoundment to beg simplification.
Considerate she was, varying the emphasis—
"ARE YOU DARK? OR VERY LIGHT?" Revelation came.
"You mean—like plain or milk chocolate?"
Her assent was clinical, crushing in its light 20
Impersonality. Rapidly, wave-length adjusted,
I chose, "West African sepia"—and as afterthought,
"Down in my passport." Silence for spectroscopic
Flight of fancy, till truthfulness clanged her accent
Hard on the mouthpiece. "WHAT'S THAT?" conceding 25
"DON'T KNOW WHAT THAT IS." "Like brunette."
"THAT'S DARK, ISN'T IT?" "Not altogether.
Facially, I am brunette, but madam, you should see
The rest of me. Palm of my hand, soles of my feet
Are a peroxide blonde. Friction, caused— 30
Foolishly, madam—by sitting down, has turned

My bottom raven black—One moment, madam!"—sensing
Her receiver rearing on the thunderclap
About my ears—"Madam," I pleaded, "wouldn't you rather
See for yourself?"   35

ADRIAN OKTENBERG   *(b. 1947)*

A Young Sniper   *(1997)*

A YOUNG sniper   A single sparrow
        A sparrow crosses the air
        in Sniper Alley   His eye
is briefly on the sparrow   magnified   in his lens
        He enjoys a pretty sight   5
He can see   anyone who moves   into the open
in search of food or water   or in search of a hasty death
as easily as if he were watching a film
        a thriller in which he is the shooter the hero the man with the gun
        his finger rests lightly on the trigger   ready to squeeze   10
        his own personal film and he can   shoot any one he likes
He is calm and happy   at ease   the city is at his feet
He knows he is free
His eye is on the sparrow   and I am here below
I know he is watching me   I live   15
a few blocks from Sniper Alley and I go   in order to live
        across the open space   there is no way to judge
the degree of safety or danger   in this topsy-turvy world
        you must go   this choice too has been taken from you
        by this war   20
the whole of the Balkans is but a mote   in God's glass eye
        a single slap   there is no noise   she doesn't hear a noise
sprawled on the pavement, skirt splayed above her waist, blood
        comes from somewhere, she doesn't know where
She has a daughter she thinks of her daughter she is unable to move   25

He knows he is free
His eye is on the sparrow
and I know he is watching me

FAIZ AHMED FAIZ   *(1911–1984)*

A Prison Evening   *(1991)*

Translated by Agha Shahid Ali

Each star a rung,
night comes down the spiral
staircase of the evening.
The breeze passes by so very close
as if someone just happened to speak of love.   5
In the courtyard,
the trees are absorbed refugees
embroidering maps of return on the sky.
On the roof,
the moon—lovingly, generously—   10
is turning the stars
into a dust of sheen.
From every corner, dark-green shadows,
in ripples, come towards me.
At any moment they may break over me,   15
like the waves of pain each time I remember
this separation from my lover.
This thought keeps consoling me:
though tyrants may command that lamps be smashed
in rooms where lovers are destined to meet,   20
they cannot snuff out the moon, so today,
nor tomorrow, no tyranny will succeed,
no poison of torture make me bitter,
if just one evening in prison
can be so strangely sweet,   25
if just one moment anywhere on this earth.

TASLIMA NASRIN   *(b. 1962)*

Border   *(1995)*

Translated by Carolyne Wright and Farida Sarkar

I'm going to move ahead.
Behind me my whole family is calling,
my child is pulling at my *sari*-end,
my husband stands blocking the door,
but I will go.   5
There's nothing ahead but a river

I will cross.
I know how to swim but they
won't let me swim, won't let me cross.

There's nothing on the other side of the river   10
            but a vast expanse of fields
but I'll touch this emptiness once
and run against the wind, whose whooshing sound
makes me want to dance. I'll dance someday
and then return.   15

I've not played keep-away for years
            as I did in childhood.
I'll raise a great commotion playing keep-away someday
and then return.

For years I haven't cried with my head   20
            in the lap of solitude.
I'll cry to my heart's content someday
and then return.

There's nothing ahead but a river
and I know how to swim.   25
Why shouldn't I go? I'll go.

JAYANTA MAHAPATRA   *(b. 1928)*

Main Temple Street, Puri   *(1987)*

Children, brown as earth, continue to laugh away
at cripples and mating mongrels.
Nobody ever bothers about them.

The temple points to unending rhythm.

On the dusty street the colour of shorn scalp   5
there are things moving all the time
and yet nothing seems to go away from sight.

Injuries drowsy with the heat.

And that sky there,
claimed by inviolable authority,   10
hanging on to its crutches of silence.

CHITRA BANERJEE DIVAKARUNI   *(b. 1957)*

Song of the Fisher Wife   *(1991)*

He pushes out the boat, black skeleton
against the pale east. His veins
are blue cords. Sun scours the ocean
with its red nails. I hand him
curds and rice wrapped in leaves. Sand   5
wells over my feet, rotting smell
of seaweed. I sing with the wives.

> *O husbands, muzzle the great wave,*
> *leap the dark. Bring back boats*
> *filled with fish like silver smiles,*   10
> *silver bracelets for our arms.*

All day I dry the fish, the upturned eyes,
the dead, grinning jaws. How stiff
flesh feels, the flaking layers
under my hand. Salt has cracked   15
my palms open. The odor crusts me.
My eyes are flecked with sand
and waiting. How well I learn
by the dryness in my mouth
to tell the coming storm.   20

> *O husbands, no fear*
> *though the sky's breath is black.*
> *We line the calling shore, faithful.*
> *Lip and eye and loin, we keep you*
> *from the jagged wind.*   25

They say all heard the crack and yell,
the boat exploding into splintered air.
Searched for hours. They strip
my widowed arms, shave off my hair.
Thrust me beyond the village walls.   30
Nights of no-moon they will come to me,
grunting, heaving, grinding
the damp sand into my naked back,
men with cloths over their faces.

> *O husband, sent by my evil luck*   35
> *into the great wave's jaw,*
> *do you ride the ocean's boiling back,*
> *eyes phosphorus, sea-lichen hair, gleam*

of shell-studded skin, to see
my forehead branded whore?   40

Note: In many coastal villages in India, it is believed that the wife's virtue keeps her husband safe at sea. Widows are often outcast and forced into becoming prostitutes in order to survive.

SHU TING   *(b. 1952)*

Assembly Line   *(1991)*

Translated by Carolyn Kizer

In time's assembly line
Night presses against night.
We come off the factory night-shift
In line as we march towards home.
Over our heads in a row   5
The assembly line of stars
Stretches across the sky.
Beside us, little trees
Stand numb in assembly lines.

The stars must be exhausted   10
After thousands of years
Of journeys which never change.
The little trees are all sick,
Choked on smog and monotony,
Stripped of their color and shape.   15
It's not hard to feel for them;
We share the same tempo and rhythm.

Yes, I'm numb to my own existence
As if, like the trees and stars
—perhaps just out of habit   20
—perhaps just out of sorrow,
I'm unable to show concern
For my own manufactured fate.

Bits of Reminiscence   *(1991)*

Translated by Carolyn Kizer

A toppled wine-cup,
A stone path floating beneath the moon
Where the grass was trampled:
One azalea branch left lying there . . .

Eucalyptus trees begin to spin 5
In a collage of stars
As I sit on the rusted anchor,
The dizzy sky reflected in my eyes.

A book held up to shut out candlelight;
Fingers lightly at your mouth; 10
In the fragile cup of silence
A dream, half-illumined, half-obscure.

Critical Perspective: On Postcolonial Resistance

"The emergence of anti-colonial and 'independent' nation-States after colonialism is frequently accompanied by a desire to forget the colonial past. This 'will-to-forget' takes a number of historical forms, and is impelled by a variety of cultural and political motivations. Principally, postcolonial amnesia is symptomatic of the urge for historical self-invention or the need to make a new start—to erase painful memories of colonial subordination. As it happens, histories, much as families, cannot be freely chosen by a simple act of will, and newly emergent postcolonial nation-States are often deluded and unsuccessful in their attempts to disown the burdens of their colonial inheritance. The mere repression of colonial memories is never, in itself, tantamount to a surpassing of or emancipation from the uncomfortable realities of the colonial encounter.

"In response, postcolonialism can be seen as a theoretical resistance to the mystifying amnesia of the colonial aftermath. It is a disciplinary project devoted to the academic task of revisiting, remembering and, crucially, interrogating the colonial past. The process of returning to the colonial scene discloses a relationship of reciprocal antagonism and desire between coloniser and colonised. And it is in the unfolding of this troubled and troubling relationship that we might start to discern the ambivalent prehistory of the postcolonial condition. If postcoloniality is to be reminded of its origins in colonial oppression, it must also be theoretically urged to recollect the compelling seductions of colonial power. The forgotten archive of the colonial encounter narrates multiple stories of contestation and its discomfiting other, complicity.

"In addition, the colonial archive preserves those versions of knowledge and agency produced in response to the particular pressures of the colonial encounter. The colonial past is not simply a reservoir of 'raw' political experiences and practices to be theorised from the detached and enlightened perspective of the present. It is also the scene of intense discursive and conceptual activity, characterised by a profusion of thought and writing about the cultural and political identities of colonised subjects. Thus, in its therapeutic retrieval of the colonial past, postcolonialism needs to define itself as an area of study which is willing not only to make, but also to gain, theoretical sense out of that past."

—Leela Gandhi, from *Postcolonial Theory* (1998)

Critical Perspective: On African Poets and the European Tradition

"There is a charge often raised against African poets, that of aping other models, particularly the European. This charge is of course frequently true, even to the extent of outright plagiarism, and covers the entire spectrum of stylistic development: twenty years ago it was quite possible to read poems (of serious intent) which began 'Gather ye hibiscus while ye may,' while today we are more commonly inundated with the re-creation of Waste Lands of tropical humidity. Dadaisms abound both in their founding innocence and in the revivalist adaptations hallowed by the 'beat' generation of America. Even the perverse phase of European decadence has not failed to diffuse its 'poisonous ecstasy' through situations clearly shaped in a far different clime, nurtured in the perpetual season of revolution.

"All this must be conceded and deplored. But then another question must be asked: whether this has not occurred in all other fields that make up the personalities of new nations. The excesses committed in a small part of the poetic output achieve an importance only for those who fail to see the poet's preoccupations as springing from the same source of creativity which activates the major technological developments: town-planning, sewage-disposal, hydro-electric power. None of these and others—including the making of war—has taken place or will ever again take place without the awareness of foreign thought and culture patterns, and their exploitation. To recommend, on the one hand, that the embattled general or the liberation fighter seek the most sophisticated weaponry from Europe, America or China, while, on the other, that the poet totally expunge from his consciousness all knowledge of a foreign tradition in his own craft, is an absurdity.

"A distinct quality in all great poets does exercise a ghostly influence in other writers, but this need not be cause for self-flagellation. The resulting work is judged by its capacity to move ahead or sideways, by the thoroughness of ingestion within a new organic mould, by the original strength of the new entity. Modern African poems which betray traces of an internal dialogue are often accused of alien affectation, but an examination of traditional poetry reveals that it too is built on a densely packed matrix of references (and not, as is sometimes claimed to the contrary, on simplistic narrative). This progression of linked allusions towards an elucidation of the experience of reality is the language of all poets."

—Wole Soyinka, from *Poems of Black Africa* (1975)

TOPICS FOR CRITICAL THINKING

1. Discuss the ways in which Senghor's "Prayer to the Masks" serves as a counter-discourse to the colonial representation of Africans as "men of cotton, coffee, and oil."

2. The Urdu poet Faiz Ahmed Faiz was born in Sialkot in the Punjab region in northern India in the 1930s during the reign of the British. Associated with the leftist Progressive Movement, he served in the Indian army during World War II and then moved to Pakistan after the partition and edited *The Pakistan Times*. During

the early 1950s, he was arrested in the Rawalpindi Conspiracy and served four years under a death sentence. In 1962, the former Soviet Union awarded him the Lenin Peace Prize. Consider the ways in which the natural world provides Faiz a sense of freedom in his poem "A Prison Evening." What role does figurative language play in his evocation of natural beauty?

3. The Indian poet Jayanta Mahapatra was born in Cuttack, Orissa. Contrast Mahapatra's representation of everyday life in "Main Temple Street, Puri" with the poet's more stylized personification of the sky.

4. Shu Ting was born in Fujian, China, and spent her formative years there until her father was exiled to the countryside for nonconformity with the party line during the Cultural Revolution. Sent to work in a cement factory and later a textile mill, Shu Ting began to write and then publish verse. Soon she was invited to become a member of the Chinese Writers' Association and won National Poetry Awards in 1981 and 1983. Discuss the images of uniformity and monotony that make up the poet's "manufactured fate" in "Assembly Line."

TOPICS FOR CRITICAL WRITING

1. After serving in the People's Army, Ha Jin studied English at Heilongjiang University in Harbin and later at Shandong University in the People's Republic of China. Some years later, he received a Ph.D. from Brandeis University and left China for good after the Tiananmen uprising. "Ways of Talking" meditates on grief and exile. How does the poem balance Jin's sense of loss with joy? How do you interpret the poet's image of the "beautiful" in the final image of "hail stones in the strawberry fields"?

2. Wole Soyinka is the first Nigerian writer to have won the Nobel Prize for Literature (1986). In addition to publishing poetry, novels, critical essays, plays for the stage, television, and radio, he was arrested as a political prisoner and jailed by the Federal Military Government of Nigeria from 1967–1969. Discuss the ways in which Soyinka mimics and parodies the discourse of racism so as to subvert its force in "Telephone Conversation."

3. Adrian Oktenberg's "A Young Sniper" alludes to the New Testament Book of Matthew 10:29–31, where Jesus affirms that God takes note of every creature in his kingdom, even the sparrows:

> Are not two sparrows sold for a cent?
> And yet not one of them will fall to the ground
> apart from your Father.
> But the very hairs of your head are all numbered.
> Therefore do not fear;
> you are of more value than many sparrows.

Examine the ways in the sniper attains a kind of godlike freedom through the power of his gaze. In what ways does his happiness come, paradoxically, through the ability to terrorize others? How does Oktenberg's first-person narrator experience his enjoyment as her oppression?

4. In her note to "Song of the Fisher Wife," Chitra Banerjee Divakaruni writes that "in many coastal villages in India, it is believed that the wife's virtue keeps her husband safe at sea. Widows are often outcast and forced into becoming prostitutes in order to survive." Contrast the poem's italicized passages with the speaker's narrative of her husband's shipwreck. How do you interpret the final question in the poem's last stanza?

22 Cultural Criticism

In an earlier era, cultural criticism referred to the study of what the British Victorian Matthew Arnold defined in his book *Culture and Anarchy* (1869) as "the best which has been thought and said in the world." Culture in this definition meant the canon of "great" works that had withstood the test of time. This definition lent a privileged status to high culture as distinct from the folkways, customs, and popular culture of everyday life. Writing a century later, the British Marxist critic Raymond Williams challenged Arnold's canonical values, and redefined culture in more anthropological terms. Culture in Williams's view describes "a particular way of life, whether of a people, a period or a group . . . a particular way of life which expresses certain meanings and values not only in art and learning, but also in institutions and ordinary behaviour." This social understanding of culture interprets literature in its relation to the world at large.

Cultural approaches to understanding literature move beyond a consideration of the work "on the page" to explore literature's economic, social, and political contexts. In this respect, cultural criticism differs from formalist criticism. Formalism limits its critical readings to poems, stories, plays, nonfictional prose, and so on. Cultural criticism, however, also reads literary tradition in relation *www* to nonliterary objects of study. **Web** For example, a cultural approach to T. S. Eliot's *The Waste Land* would consider not just how Eliot's modern verse epic alludes to canonical works such as, say, *The Satyricon* of Petronius, Virgil's *Aeneid*, Dante's *Purgatorio*, Shakespeare's *The Tempest*, or Wagner's *Tristan und Isolde*. But equally important, it also would take into account how *The Waste Land* weaves the canon of great literature with such "low" forms as the Ziegfeld Follies, other vaudeville and music hall comedies, popular song, ragtime, London street slang, and so on. Cultural criticism would explore how new combinations of meaning are created out of the relationship Eliot draws between, say, Marvell's "To His Coy Mistress" and a bawdy Australian military lyric.

Cultural criticism takes literature into what theorist Edward Said calls a more "worldly" register of interpretation. Its reading strategies are variously shaped by theories of gender, race, class, ethnicity, sexual orientation, nationalism, and so on. Cultural criticism also reflects not just on a work's cultural context or cultural themes but also on literature itself as a cultural institution. It analyzes the social relations among authors, readers, teachers, editors, publishers, critics, and others who have a stake in defining what we mean by literature and literary meaning. Such an approach to poetry would consider the different social meanings that a poem expresses at the time of its publication. But it would also go on to examine the later uses a poem serves in the expanded public sphere: that is, the several worlds of politics, government, religion, education, the arts and mass media that make up today's global information society. In this vein, cultural criticism also examines the process of how those meanings change over time depending on who reads that same poem as well as where and when and for what purpose it is read. For example, Claude McKay's famous sonnet "If We Must Die" was written in 1919 following a turbulent summer of urban race riots:

CLAUDE McKAY

If We Must Die *(1919)*

If we must die, let it not be like hogs
Hunted and penned in an inglorious spot,
While round us bark the mad and hungry dogs,
Making their mock at our accursed lot.
If we must die, O let us nobly die,
So that our precious blood may not be shed
In vain; then even the monsters we defy
Shall be constrained to honor us though dead!
O kinsmen we must meet the common foe!
Though far outnumbered let us show us brave,
And for their thousand blows deal one deathblow!
What though before us lies the open grave?
Like men we'll face the murderous, cowardly pack,
Pressed to the wall, dying, but fighting back!

"If We Must Die" was published in the 1919 issue of the radical, socialist magazine *The Liberator*. Originally, the sonnet protested the lynchings, shootings, and other violent threats to African Americans that defined the racial tensions of McKay's moment. The kind of cultural work "If We Must Die" did in the segregated conditions of Jim Crow America, however, differed radically from the rhetorical meanings it later assumed. For example, Prime Minister Winston Churchill read McKay's sonnet some twenty years later as part of a speech meant to stir British nationalist patriotism in the war against Nazi Germany. Those nationalist politics, in turn, were at odds with Mao Zedong's agenda when he used McKay's poem to defend Chinese communism.

How poetry reflects and actively shapes the social connotations of racial, national, sexual, class, and gender politics are vital concerns for cultural criticism. Moreover, cultural criticism explores literature's interactions with other media such as television, video, film, radio, the Web, hypertexts, performance art, and street rap. Cultural approaches to poetry investigate verse writing's dynamic relationship to a world of nonliterary objects of study drawn from TV and print journalism, advertising, talk shows, political broadsides, manifestos, travel guides, court testimony, documentary, and so on. Cultural criticism considers poetry's place within the rich array of products and consumables drawn from the popular culture of everyday life. Needless to say, the range of possible topics that would fit under the rubric of cultural criticism is as vast as

culture itself. One good place to begin understanding cultural criticism, however, is with the poetry of Langston Hughes and its cultural relation to jazz
and the blues. Beyond considering the influence of popular music on poetry,
cultural readings of Hughes's verse also includes its relation to social narratives of racial "double-consciousness" and to modern political movements.

Featured Writer

LANGSTON HUGHES

African American Culture

Langston Hughes

A midwesterner by birth, Langston Hughes
(1903–1967) grew up in Lawrence, Kansas,
with some time spent as well in Illinois,
Ohio, and Mexico. As an adolescent, Hughes
showed a passion for literature and for poetry in particular. Graduating from the
eighth grade in 1916, he was named class
poet. In high school, he showcased his
verse and short stories in the *Central High
Monthly Magazine*. Two of Hughes's favorite American poets were Walt Whitman
and Carl Sandburg, and their influence is apparent in Hughes's first major
poem "The Negro Speaks of Rivers." Hughes published this signature piece
in *The Crisis* in 1921, and it was later set to music by Margaret Bonds in 1942.

The Negro Speaks of Rivers   *(1926)*

(To W. E. B. Du Bois)

I've known rivers:
I've known rivers ancient as the world and older than the
     flow of human blood in human veins.
My soul has grown deep like the rivers.

I bathed in the Euphrates when dawns were young.
I built my hut near the Congo and it lulled me to sleep.
I looked upon the Nile and raised the pyramids above it.   5
I heard the singing of the Mississippi when Abe Lincoln
      went down to New Orleans, and I've seen its muddy
      bosom turn all golden in the sunset.

I've known rivers:
Ancient, dusky rivers.

My soul has grown deep like the rivers.   10

In his autobiography *The Big Sea*, Hughes tells of how he composed "The Negro Speaks of Rivers" on a train trip to visit his father in Mexico:

"The Negro Speaks of Rivers"
(1926)

I had been to dinner early that afternoon on the train. Now it was just sunset, and we crossed the Mississippi, slowly, over a long bridge. I looked out the window of the Pullman at the great muddy river flowing down toward the heart of the South, and I began to think what that river, the old Mississippi, had meant to Negroes in the past—how to be sold down the river was the worst fate that could overtake a slave in times of bondage. Then I remembered reading how Abraham Lincoln had made a trip down the Mississippi on a raft to New Orleans, and how he had seen slavery at its worst, and had decided within himself that it should be removed from American life. Then I began to think about other rivers in our past—the Congo, and the Niger, and the Nile in Africa—and the thought came to me: "I've known rivers," and I put it down on the back of an envelope I had in my pocket, and within the space of ten or fifteen minutes, as the train gathered speed in the dusk, I had written this poem, which I called "The Negro Speaks of Rivers."

TOPICS FOR CRITICAL THINKING

1. In his autobiographical statement on the poem, Hughes stresses the cultural meanings of the Mississippi, particularly as they are rooted in slavery. Does the poem allude to bondage at all? Where?

2. The poem's title presents the speaker in the third person generically as "the negro." The poem, however, is told from the first person point of view. What is the effect of that contradiction?

TOPIC FOR CRITICAL WRITING

In the autobiographical statement, Hughes speaks about himself both in the first-person singular *I* and in the first-person plural *our*. How does the poem's speaker voice a collective rather than individual persona? How does Hughes speak on behalf of a tradition of African American heritage rather than from his own, private experience?

As poet, Hughes viewed his personal experience through the lens of a broader, African American cultural inheritance. As Hughes relates in his celebrated autobiography, *The Big Sea*, his family background led him to write about a specifically African American cultural inheritance. Hughes's maternal grandmother, Mary Langston, was one of the first female African American students to attend Oberlin College. Her husband, the free African American

Lewis Sheridan Leary, had been killed in 1859 with John Brown at Harper's
Ferry. John Brown was an abolitionist who raided the federal arsenal at
Harper's Ferry in an attempt to secure weapons for a proposed colony of runaway slaves. Hughes's grandfather, Charles Howard Langston, was also an
abolitionist; he was imprisoned and fined for helping a fugitive slave escape to
Canada. On his mother's side, Hughes's great-grandfather Ralph Quarles was
a white Virginia planter and slaveholder. Moreover, both of Hughes's paternal
great-grandfathers were white and one of them, Silas Cushenberry, was a Jewish slave trader from Kentucky. This complex, double heritage of abolition
and slaveholding is something that Hughes narrates in *The Big Sea.*

In many of his poems Hughes plumbs the paradoxes of African American
cultural identity—what W. E. B. Du Bois defined as "double consciousness"
in *The Souls of Black Folk* (1903). Double-consciousness, as Du Bois defines it,
stems from the traumatic history of slavery beginning with the Middle Passage (see Chapter 16). As a black person, Du Bois argues, "[o]ne ever feels his
two-ness—an American, a Negro; two souls, two thoughts, two unreconciled
strivings; two warring ideals in one dark body, whose dogged strength alone
keeps it from being torn asunder." Hughes dramatizes such "unreconciled
strivings" in his widely anthologized 1949 poem "Theme for English B":

Theme for English B   *(1949)*

The instructor said,

> *Go home and write*
> *a page tonight.*
> *And let that page come out of you—*
> *Then, it will be true.*   5

I wonder if it's that simple?
I am twenty-two, colored, born in Winston-Salem.
I went to school there, then Durham, then here
to this college on the hill above Harlem.
I am the only colored student in my class.   10
The steps from the hill lead down into Harlem,
through a park, then I cross St. Nicholas,
Eighth Avenue, Seventh, and I come to the Y,
the Harlem Branch Y, where I take the elevator
up to my room, sit down, and write this page: 15

It's not easy to know what is true for you or me
at twenty-two, my age. But I guess I'm what
I feel and see and hear, Harlem, I hear you:
hear you, hear me—we two—you, me, talk on this page.
(I hear New York, too.) Me—who?   20
Well, I like to eat, sleep, drink, and be in love.
I like to work, read, learn, and understand life.

I like a pipe for a Christmas present,
or records—Bessie, bop, or Bach.
I guess being colored doesn't make me *not* like   25
the same things other folks like who are other races.
So will my page be colored that I write?
Being me, it will not be white.
But it will be
a part of you, instructor.   30
You are white—
yet a part of me, as I am a part of you.
That's American.
Sometimes perhaps you don't want to be a part of me.
Nor do I often want to be a part of you.   35
But we are, that's true!
As I learn from you,
I guess you learn from me—
although you're older—and white—
and somewhat more free.   40

   This is my page for English B.

TOPICS FOR CRITICAL THINKING

1. How does Hughes complicate any commonsense or "simple" notions of "just being oneself" assumed in the writing assignment he is given as a college student?

2. Discuss the poem's focus on setting and the lived experience that defines black double-consciousness in the poem. How does Hughes represent a new version of American national identity—one that embraces the cosmopolitan diversity of "Bessie, bop, or Bach"?

TOPIC FOR CRITICAL WRITING

Does the poem offer the hope of racial reconciliation in spite of racial difference?

   In "Theme for English B," Hughes muses on what he does and does not have in common with his white Columbia University instructor. If the poem is autobiographical, it also witnesses to the wider plight of double-consciousness that Hughes investigates in works such as "Cross"—a poem Hughes published in *The Crisis*, the official publication of the National Association for the Advancement of Colored People (NAACP), founded by Du Bois:

Cross   *(1925)*

My old man's a white old man
And my old mother's black.
If I ever cursed my white old man
I take my curses back.

If ever I cursed my black old mother   5
And wished she were in hell,
I'm sorry for that evil wish
And now I wish her well.

My old man died in a fine big house,
My ma died in a shack.   10
I wonder where I'm gonna die,
Being neither white nor black?

TOPICS FOR CRITICAL THINKING

1. Discuss what you know about the historical subject of "Cross," which deals with the legacy of sexual oppression under slavery.
2. Examine Hughes's representation of slavery's mixed lines of racial descent and the consequences of that heritage for modern African American identity in the poem.

TOPIC FOR CRITICAL WRITING

How does poetry attempt to cure slavery's abusive past in "Cross"? What does Hughes claim as an African American, and what remains unclaimed in the form of the poem's final question?

Langston Hughes, the Harlem Renaissance, and the Blues

Hughes's career as a poet was powerfully shaped by and had a powerful shaping influence on the Harlem Renaissance. After graduating from high school, Hughes's affinity for black cultural expression drew him to Harlem, where he studied at Columbia University. His father insisted that he train in a German engineering school, but, as Hughes relates in *The Big Sea*, "I had an overwhelming desire to see Harlem. More than Paris, or the Shakespeare country, or Berlin, or the Alps, I wanted to see Harlem, the greatest Negro city in the world. *Shuffle Along* had just burst into being, and I wanted to hear Florence Mills sing." Throughout the Roaring Twenties, the rebirth in African American cultural expression was celebrated in the salons, cabarets, and lecture halls of Washington, D.C., Atlanta, Hampton, Durham, Nashville, and especially in Harlem.

The cosmopolitan culture of the Harlem Renaissance was promoted in such important collections as Alain Locke's 1925 *The New Negro*. This edited book expanded on Locke's March 1925 "Harlem: Mecca of the New Negro" issue of *Survey Graphic*. Handsomely illustrated with drawings and decorations by Winold Reiss, Aaron Douglas, and Miguel Covarrubias, among others, *The New Negro* brought together new works of fiction, poetry, and drama, as well as essays on African American spirituals, jazz, and folk literature. Finally, *The New Negro* also explored the public culture of black America in sociological essays on such topics as "Harlem: The Culture Capital," "Howard: The National Negro University," "Durham: Capital of the Black Middle Class," and "The Task of Negro Womanhood." The Harlem Renaissance was further popularized for mainstream audiences in such novels as Carl Van Vechten's *Nigger Heaven* (1926) and Claude McKay's *Home to Harlem* (1928).

Van Vechten, in particular, contributed to the surge of interest in black culture at the mid-decade by publishing over a dozen articles and reviews of jazz and blues artists, black theater, and African American literature in such journals as *Vanity Fair, Theatre Magazine*, and *The Crisis*. But he also was a broker of black literature, promoting and reprinting James Weldon Johnson's *Autobiography of an Ex-Coloured Man* (1926) and securing publication for Langston Hughes's first two volumes of verse, *The Weary Blues* (1926) and *Fine Clothes to the Jew* (1927). Writing in *The Big Sea*, Hughes has described, better than any of the period's historians, what it was like to be young and full of creative fire at the peak of the Harlem Renaissance:

> The 1920s were the years of Manhattan's black Renaissance. It began with "Shuffle Along," "Running Wild," and the Charleston. Perhaps some people would say even with *The Emperor Jones*, Charles Gilpin, and the tom-toms at the Provincetown. But certainly it was the musical revue, "Shuffle Along," that gave a scintillating send-off to that Negro vogue in Manhattan, which reached its peak just before the crash of 1929, the crash that sent Negroes, white folks, and all rolling down the hill toward the Works Progress Administration.
>
> . . . Put down the 1920's for the rise of Roland Hayes, who packed Carnegie Hall, the rise of Paul Robeson in New York and London, of Florence Mills over two continents, of Rose McClendon in Broadway parts that never measured up to her, the booming voice of Bessie Smith and the low moan of Clara on thousands of records, and the rise of that grand comedienne of song, Ethel Waters, singing: "Charlie's elected now! He's in right for sure!" Put down the 1920's for Louis Armstrong and Gladys Bentley and Josephine Baker.

Harlem's fashionable visibility for white cosmopolitans, however, forced most black Harlemites out of high-profile establishments like the Cotton Club. House-rent parties replaced nightclubs as the centers of black social life in Harlem. Hughes's descriptions of these entertaining social venues capture the excitement of these urban soirées.

As noted earlier, Hughes witnessed the Harlem Renaissance firsthand as a Columbia University student during 1922. After a year at Columbia, Hughes became alienated from his father, who wanted him to abandon his interests in poetry. Cut off from his father's backing for his career at Columbia, Hughes supported himself during 1923 by working as a messman on a mothballed ship drydocked on the Hudson River. Leaving New York in June of that year, Hughes sailed on a steamship, the *West Hesseltine*, that traveled to the coast of West Africa. There Hughes visited ports in Senegal, Ghana, Nigeria, Congo, and Angola, where he witnessed the plight of oppressed African laborers that he would later record in his poem "The Same" and in *The Big Sea*.

The following year, he shipped out as a seaman to Europe. In France, Hughes reveled in the Parisian jazz scene. Working in the kitchen of the Le

Grand Duc nightclub in Montmartre, he captured the ambience of the Roaring Twenties in "Jazz Band in a Parisian Cabaret." From Paris, Hughes traveled to Genoa and then on to the United States to live for a year with his mother in Washington, D.C. In 1925, Hughes won *Opportunity* magazine's first prize in poetry for "The Weary Blues," which became the title piece for his first volume of verse, published the following January, the same month Hughes enrolled at Lincoln University, Pennsylvania.

The Weary Blues   *(1925)*

Droning a drowsy syncopated tune,
Rocking back and forth to a mellow croon,
   I heard a Negro play.
Down on Lenox Avenue the other night
By the pale dull pallor of an old gas light   5
   He did a lazy sway . . .
   He did a lazy sway . . .
To the tune o' those Weary Blues.
With his ebony hands on each ivory key
He made that poor piano moan with melody.   10
   O Blues!
Swaying to and fro on his rickety stool
He played that sad raggy tune like a musical
    fool.
   Sweet Blues!
Coming from a black man's soul.   15
   O Blues!

The Weary Blues (1926)

In a deep song voice with a melancholy tone
I heard that Negro sing, that old piano moan—
   "Ain't got nobody in all this world,
   Ain't got nobody but ma self.
   I's gwine to quit ma frownin'   20
   And put ma troubles on the shelf."
Thump, thump, thump, went his foot on the floor.
He played a few chords then he sang some more—
   "I got the Weary Blues   25
   And I can't be satisfied.
   Got the Weary Blues
   And can't be satisfied—
   I ain't happy no mo'
   And I wish that I had died."   30
And far into the night he crooned that tune.
The stars went out and so did the moon.
The singer stopped playing and went to bed
While the Weary Blues echoed through his head.
He slept like a rock or a man that's dead.   35

TOPICS FOR CRITICAL THINKING

1. What do you know about the blues as a musical tradition? Do you have favorite blues artists or blues songs? Who and what are they?

2. Describe your experience of the poem's performance of the blues through its repetitions, its rhythms, and its use of the blues refrain.

TOPIC FOR CRITICAL WRITING

Langston Hughes invokes and celebrates the "Sweet Blues! / Coming from a black man's soul." What, according to the poem, are the sources of that "soul" music? How does the poem define the condition of being "weary," and how does weariness, paradoxically, animate the blues artist's performance?

The Weary Blues (1926) boldly celebrates the everyday lives of ordinary black folk in a vernacular poetics based in the kind of blues lyricism, black sermon, spirituals, and other expressive forms that are rooted in African American culture. Hughes heard jazz and the blues idiom everywhere played upon the pulses of Harlem's vibrant urban scene. The blues form and the improvisational techniques of jazz inform many of Hughes's lyrics. Listening to the blues was a formative experience for Hughes while growing up in Kansas City, as he relates in a 1959 recording:

> [W]hen I was a kid in Kansas City very often I used to hear the blues. There were blind guitar players who would sing the blues on street corners. There were people plunking the blues on beat up old pianos. That was of course before the days of the jukebox and the radio. In those days, almost everybody who could afford to have a piano had one, and played them in their homes. And so you heard a lot of music. Well, at any rate, I was very much attracted to the blues. I remember even now some of the blues verses that I used to hear as a child in Kansas City. And so I, in my early beginnings at poetry writing, tried to weave the blues into my poetry.

Hughes's use of jazz and blues rhythms, however, was a source of cultural controversy in the 1920s. Writing in the February 1926 issue of the journal *Opportunity*, the poet Countée Cullen praised *The Weary Blues* as a whole but rejected Hughes's jazz-based poetics in particular.

In an important manifesto, "The Negro Artist and the Racial Mountain," Hughes asserted the cultural importance of African American art forms. There, he called jazz

> one of the inherent expressions of Negro life in America; the eternal tom-tom beating in the Negro soul—the tom-tom of revolt against weariness in a white world, a world of subway trains, and work, work, work; the tom-tom of joy and laughter, and pain swallowed in a smile. . . . Let the blare of Negro jazz bands and the bellowing voice of Bessie Smith singing blues penetrate the closed ears of the colored near-intellectuals until they listen and perhaps understand.

The title piece of *The Weary Blues* captures that "tom-tom of revolt against weariness" in its rhythms, repetitions, and variations on the blues vernacular.

Hughes published "The Negro Artist and the Racial Mountain" in *The Nation* magazine. Hughes's essay not only criticized the kind of Romantic poetic measures that shaped Countée Cullen's verse, but it also served as a defense against what black journalist George Schuyler had satirized a week earlier as "The Negro-Art Hokum." Hughes made a strong case for the significance of the new black cultural expression by resisting the idea that black artists should imitate traditional, European models of art, literature, and music. In Hughes's metaphor the "racial mountain" stood for the "urge within the race toward whiteness, the desire to pour racial individuality into the mold of American standardization, and to be as little Negro and as much American as possible."

The following year, Hughes published a second volume of verse, entitled *Fine Clothes to the Jew* (1927) whose blues-based lyrics met with even harsher criticism than *The Weary Blues*. That same year, Hughes was introduced by Alain Locke to the wealthy philanthropist Charlotte Mason, who would become the poet's patron until 1930. Mason, however, attempted to shape Hughes's writing to conform to her own "primitivist" stereotypes about people of color. "Concerning Negroes," Hughes would later write in *The Big Sea*, "she felt that they were America's great link with the primitive." Owing to irreconcilable differences in politics, taste, and personality, Hughes reached a parting of the ways with Mason when his first novel, *Not Without Laughter*, was published in 1930.

Langston Hughes and Social Activism

Like many writers during the Depression era, Hughes became a committed political activist on the Left and was involved in the worldwide struggle for social justice. During the early 1930s, Hughes applied to the Rosenwald Foundation to fund a reading tour of the American south. During this year of readings in the southern states, Hughes espoused the cause of the Scottsboro Boys, nine black youths who had been arrested on the trumped-up charge of raping two white girls, Victoria Price and Ruby Bates, aboard a freight train in Alabama. As it happened, physical evidence offered by medical examiners at the time actually refuted this charge. Moreover, testifying under oath, Bates later recanted the whole story as a lie in 1933. Hughes met with the Scottsboro Boys in their prison cells in Decatur, Alabama, the year of their arrest and contributed a poem on their behalf to the journal *Contempo*. Not insignificantly, the Scottsboro Boys were represented in court by the Communist-affiliated International Labor Defense.

Like many fellow travelers during the 1930s, Hughes increasingly aligned himself with the American Left during the Depression era. In 1932, Hughes published a play and four poems under the title *Scottsboro Limited*. That same year he joined twenty-two other African Americans to work on a film in Russia. Although the movie was never produced, the opportunity enabled the poet to travel extensively throughout the Soviet Union, where his works were widely translated.

At this time, his blues-based verse began to take on board a leftist political agenda that openly espoused the cause of international socialism. Poems such as "Good-Morning, Revolution," published in the socialist journal the

New Masses, and "The Same," and "Goodbye Christ," which appeared in the International Trade Unions Committee magazine *The Negro Worker,* offered a cultural critique of racial discrimination and class oppression under monopoly capitalism during the Depression era. Hughes was impressed by the socialist system he encountered in the Soviet Union, and in his poem "One More 'S' in the U.S.A.," published in the Communist newspaper *The Daily Worker,* he offered a vision of a Soviet America. In addition to writing radical Left poetry during the 1930s, Hughes published two books for children, *The Dream Keeper* (1932) and *Popo and Fifina: Children of Haiti* (1932). Moreover, Hughes authored a volume of short stories, *The Ways of White Folks* (1934), and the Broadway play *Mulatto* (1935), followed by other dramatic productions.

By 1937, Hughes had left the country again, this time to lend his support to the Internationalist cause in the Spanish Civil War (1936–1939). For Hughes as well as for many partisans of the Spanish cause, such as Ernest Hemingway, Edwin Rolfe, Steven Spender, and W. H. Auden, the battleground in Spain pitted the forces of fascism under Hitler, Mussolini, and Franco against the free world. In fact, Hughes considered the Spanish Civil War as a prelude to World War II. While in Madrid, Hughes described what he saw at stake there in an article written for *El Voluntario de la Libertad* (*The Volunteer for Liberty*), the official organ of the International Brigades:

> In Spain, there is no color prejudice. Here in Madrid, heroic and bravest of cities, Madrid where the shells of Franco plow through the roof-tops at night, Madrid where you can take a streetcar to the trenches, this Madrid to whose defense lovers of freedom and democracy all over the world have sent food and money and men—here to this Madrid have come Negroes from all over the world to offer help.
>
> On the opposite side of the trenches with Franco, in the company of the professional soldiers of Germany, and the illiterate troops of Italy, are the deluded and driven Moors of North Africa. An oppressed colonial people of color being used by Fascism to make a colony of Spain. And they are being used ruthlessly, without pity. Young boys, men from the desert, old men and even women, compose the Moorish hordes brought by the reactionaries from Africa to Europe in their attempt to crush the Spanish people.

While in Spain, Hughes employed his poetic talent as a witness to the devastation of war in works such as "Air Raid: Barcelona," "Moonlight in Valencia: Civil War," and "Madrid—1937." Returning once more to America, Hughes published an original collection of radical verse, entitled *A New Song,* the following year.

Langston Hughes and Contemporary African American Poetics

During World War II, Hughes continued to inveigh against racism, publishing the first volume of his autobiography, *The Big Sea* (1940), and verse collections such as *Shakespeare in Harlem* (1942) and *Jim Crow's Last Stand* (1943). As a member of the Writers War Committee, Hughes wrote a radio script celebrating black military heroism, entitled "Brothers," that had a national broadcast. He also wrote song lyrics to Earl Robinson's "We'll Hammer It Out Together," Emerson Harper's musical rendition of "Freedom Road," and "Carry On, America," among several others. It was at this time that Hughes reached a wide popular audience in his weekly column for an African American newspaper, the *Chicago Defender*. Over the next twenty years, Hughes entertained his readership with the wickedly ironic insights of his comic persona Jesse B. Semple. Following the war, Hughes continued to publish such volumes of verse as *Fields of Wonder* (1947), *One-Way Ticket* (1949), and *Montage of a Dream Deferred* (1951), as well as a collection of short stories, *Laughing to Keep from Crying* (1952). By 1953, however, his earlier politics made him a target of Senator Joseph McCarthy and his House Un-American Activities Committee hearings during the Red Scare. Forced to disavow his radical stances of the 1930s, Hughes nevertheless survived McCarthy's own loss of public credibility and went on to narrate his time in the Soviet Union in the second volume of his autobiography, *I Wonder as I Wander* (1956). A series of successful musical collaborations on oratorios, librettos, cantatas, gospels, and plays during the 1950s brought Hughes a measure of prosperity in his late career.

Music and verse composition were always closely associated in Hughes's mind. In the 1950s, Hughes followed the lead of African American be-bop and jazz artists such as Charlie Parker, Dizzy Gillespie, Dexter Gordon, Miles Davis, and John Coltrane. In rendering the complexity of the contemporary urban scene, Hughes found common ground between jazz and poetry, as he explains in the introduction to *Montage of a Dream Deferred*:

> In terms of current Afro-American popular music and the sources from which it has progressed—jazz, ragtime, swing, blues, boogie-woogie, and be-bop—this poem on contemporary Harlem, like be-bop, is marked by conflicting changes, sudden nuances, sharp and impudent interjections, broken rhythms, and passages sometimes in the manner of the jam session, sometimes the popular song, punctuated by the riffs, runs, breaks and distortions of the music of community in transition.

In 1958, Hughes began to perform his poetry with such notable jazz artists as Charles Mingus at the Village Vanguard club in Greenwich Village and Billy Taylor on the NBC television show *The Subject Is Jazz*. In 1959, Hughes published his *Selected Poems*, followed two years later by *Ask Your Mama: 12 Moods for Jazz* (1961). Hughes's reputation in the Pan-Africanist community culminated in his celebration at the 1966 First World Festival of Negro Arts in Dakar, Senegal. Hughes's final volume of verse, *The Panther and the Lash* (1967), recounted the racial struggles of the civil rights era of the 1960s and was posthumously published the year he died, 1967.

By making black gospel, black sermon, the blues, jazz, and other versions of African American vernacular culture legitimate forms of expression for poetry, Langston Hughes forwarded the poetic innovations of a subsequent generation of writers during the Black Arts Movement of the 1960s as well as rap and hip-hop artists of the post-Vietnam era. Hughes remains a highly influential figure for such writers as Amiri Baraka, Gwendolyn Brooks, Sonya Sanchez, Ted Joans, Bob Kaufman, Nikki Giovanni, Haki Madhubuti,

Etheridge Knight, A. B. Spellman, Calvin C. Hernton, Mari Evans, June Jordan, Jayne Cortez, Henry Dumas, Carolyn M. Rodgers, Lucille Clifton, Audre Lorde, Jay Wright, Yusef Komunyakaa, Natasha Trethewey, and Michael S. Harper, as well as contemporary performance and rap poets such as Ntozake Shange, Miguel Piñero, Reg E. Gaines, Paul Beatty, and Tracie Morris.

Poems for Further Reading and Discussion

Negro   *(1922)*

I am a Negro:
    Black as the night is black,
    Black like the depths of my Africa.

I've been a slave:
    Caesar told me to keep his door-steps clean.   5
    I brushed the boots of Washington.

I've been a worker:
    Under my hand the pyramids arose.
    I made mortar for the Woolworth building.

I've been a singer: 10
    All the way from Africa to Georgia
    I carried my sorrow songs.
    I made ragtime.

I've been a victim:
    The Belgians cut off my hands in the Congo.   15
    They lynch me still in Mississippi.

I am a Negro:
    Black as the night is black,
    Black like the depths of my Africa.

Jazz Band in a Parisian Cabaret   *(1925)*

Play that thing,
Jazz band!
Play it for the lords and ladies,
For the dukes and counts,
For the whores and gigolos,   5
And the American millionaires,
And the school teachers
Out for a spree.

Play it,
Jazz band!   10
You know that tune
That laughs and cries at the same time.
You know it.

    May I?
    Mais oui.   15
    Mein Gott!
    Parece una rumba.

Play it, jazz band!
You've got seven languages to speak in
And then some,   20
Even if you do come from Georgia.
    Can I go home wid yuh, sweetie?
    Sure.

Good-Morning Revolution   *(1932)*

Good-morning, Revolution:
    You're the very best friend
    I ever had.
We gonna pal around together from now on.
Say, listen, Revolution: 5
You know, the boss where I used to work,
The guy that gimme the air to cut down expenses,
He wrote a long letter to the paper about you:
Said you was a troublemaker, a alien-enemy,
In other words a son-of-a-bitch.   10
He called up the police
And told 'em to watch out for a guy
Named Revolution.

You see,
The boss knows we're hungry, and ragged,   15
And ain't got a damn thing in this world—
And are gonna do something about it.

The boss's got all he needs, certainly,
    Eats swell,
    Owns a lotta houses,   20
    Goes vacationin',
    Breaks strikes,
    Runs politics, bribes police,
    Pays off congress,
    And struts all over the earth—   25

But me, I ain't never had enough to eat.
Me, I ain't never been warm in winter.
Me, I ain't never known security—
All my life, been livin' hand to mouth,
    Hand to mouth.   30

Listen, Revolution,
    We're buddies, see—
    Together
    We can take everything:
    Factories, arsenals, houses, ships,   35
    Railroads, forests, fields, orchards,
    Bus lines, telegraphs, radios,
    (Jesus! Raise hell with radios!)
    Steel mills, coal mines, oil wells, gas,
    All the tools of production,   40
    (Great day in the morning!)
    Everything—
    And turn 'em over to the people who work.
    Rule and run 'em for us people who work.

Boy! Them radios—   45
Broadcasting that very first morning to USSR:
Another member the International Soviet's done come
Greetings to the Socialist Soviet Republics
Hey you rising workers everywhere greetings—
    And we'll sign it: *Germany*   50
    Sign it: *China*
    Sign it: *Africa*
    Sign it: *Poland*
    Sign it: *Italy*
    Sign it: *America*   55
    Sign it with my own name: *Worker*
On that day when no one will be hungry, cold, oppressed,
Anywhere in the world again.

    That's our job!

    I been starvin' too long,   60
    Ain't you?

    Let's go, Revolution!

The Same   (1932)

It is the same everywhere for me:
On the docks at Sierra Leone,
In the cotton fields of Alabama,

In the diamond mines of Kimberley,
On the coffee hills of Haiti,   5
The banana lands of Central America,
The streets of Harlem,
And the cities of Morocco and Tripoli.
Black:
Exploited, beaten and robbed,   10
Shot and killed.
Blood running into

    DOLLARS
    POUNDS
    FRANCS   15
    PESETAS
    LIRE

For the wealth of the exploiters—
Blood that never comes back to me again.
Better that my blood   20
Runs into the deep channels of Revolution,
Runs into the strong hands of Revolution,
Stains all flags red,
Drives me away from

    SIERRA LEONE   25
    KIMBERLEY
    ALABAMA
    HAITI
    CENTRAL AMERICA
    HARLEM   30
    MOROCCO
    TRIPOLI

And all the black lands everywhere.
The force that kills,
The power that robs,   35
And the greed that does not care.
Better that my blood makes one with the blood
Of all the struggling workers in the world—
Till every land is free of

    DOLLAR ROBBERS   40
    POUND ROBBERS
    FRANC ROBBERS
    PESETA ROBBERS
    LIRE ROBBERS
    LIFE ROBBERS—   45

Until the Red Armies of the International Proletariat
Their faces, black, white, olive, yellow, brown,
Unite to raise the blood-red flag that
Never will come down!

One More "S" in the U.S.A.   *(1934)*

Put one more s in the U.S.A.
To make it Soviet.
One more s in the U.S.A.
Oh, we'll have to see it yet.
When the land belongs to the farmers   5
And the factories to the working men—
The U.S.A. when we take control
Will be the U.S.S.A. then.

Now across the water in Russia
They have a big U.S.S.R.   10
The fatherland of the Soviets—
But that is mighty far
From New York, or Texas, or California, too.
So listen, fellow workers,
This is what we have to do.   15

Put one more S in the U.S.A.
    [Repeat Chorus]

But we can't win by just talking.
So let us take things in our hand.
Then down and away with the bosses' sway—
Hail Communistic land.   20
So stand up in battle and wave our flag on high,
And shout out fellow workers
Our new slogan in the sky:

Put one more S in the U.S.A.   25

But we can't join hands together
So long as whites are lynching black,
So black and white in one union fight
And get on the right track.
By Texas, or Georgia, or Alabama led   30
Come together, fellow workers
Black and white can all be red:

    Put one more S in the U.S.A.

Oh, the bankers they all are planning
For another great big war.   35
To make them rich from the worker's dead,
That's all the war is for.
So if you don't want to see bullets holding sway
Then come on, all you workers,
And join our fight today: 40

> Put one more S in the U.S.A.
> To make it Soviet.
> One more S in the U.S.A.
> Oh, we'll live to see it yet.
> When the land belongs to the farmers   45
> And the factories to the working men—
> The U.S.A. when we take control
> Will be the U.S.S.A. then.

Let America Be America Again   *(1934)*

Let America be America again.
Let it be the dream it used to be.
Let it be the pioneer on the plain
Seeking a home where he himself is free.

(America never was America to me.)   5

Let America be the dream the dreamers dreamed—
Let it be that great strong land of love
Where never kings connive not tyrants scheme
That any man be crushed by one above.

(It never was America to me.)   10

Air Raid: Barcelona   *(1938)*

Black smoke of sound Curls against the midnight sky.

Deeper than a whistle,
Louder than a cry,
Worse than a scream
Tangled in the wail   5
Of a nightmare dream,
  The siren
Of the air raid sounds.

Flames and bombs and
Death in the ear!
The siren announces   10
Planes drawing near.
Down from the bedrooms
Stumble women in gowns.
Men, half-dressed,   15
Carrying children rush down.

Up in the sky-lanes
Against the stars
A flock of death birds
Whose wings are steel bars   20
Fill the sky with a low dull roar
Of a plane,
          two planes,
                    three planes,
                              or more.   25
The anti-aircraft guns bark into space.
The searchlights make wounds
On the night's dark face.
The siren's wild cry
Like a hollow scream   30
Echoes out of hell in a nightmare dream.
     Then the BOMBS fall!
All other noises are nothing at all
     When the first BOMBS fall.
All other noises are suddenly still   35
     When the bombs fall.
All other noises are deathly still
As blood spatters the wall
And the whirling sound
Of the iron star of death   40
Comes hurtling down.
No other noises can be heard
As a child's life goes up
In the night like a bird.
Swift pursuit planes   45
Dart over the town,
Steel bullets fly
Slitting the starry silk
     Of the sky:
A bomber's brought down   50
In flames orange and blue,
All the night's all red
Like blood, too.
The last BOMB falls.

The death birds wheel East   55
To their lairs again
Leaving iron eggs
In the streets in Spain.
With wings like black cubes
Against the far dawn,   60
The stench of their passage
Remains when they're gone.
In what was a courtyard
A child weeps alone.

Men uncover bodies   65
From ruins of stones.

Ballad of the Fortune Teller   *(1942)*

Madam could look in your hand—
Never seen you before—
And tell you more than
You'd want to know.

She could tell you about love,   5
And money, and such.
And she wouldn't
Charge you much.

A fellow came one day.
Madam took him in.   10
She treated him like
He was her kin.

Gave him money to gamble.
She gave him bread,
And let him sleep in her   15
Walnut bed.

Friends tried to tell her
Dave meant her no good.
Looks like she could've knowed it
If she only would.   20

He mistreated her terrible,
Beat her up bad.
Then went off and left her.
Stole all she had.

She tried to find out   25
What road he took.

There wasn't a trace
No way she looked.

That woman who could foresee
What *your* future meant,　　　　　　　　　　　30
Couldn't tell, to save her,
Where Dave went.

Too Blue　　　　　　　　　　　　　　　　*(1943)*

I got those sad old weary blues.
I don't know where to turn.
I don't know where to go.
Nobody cares about you
When you sink so low.　　　　　　　　　　　　5

What shall I do?
What shall I say?
Shall I take a gun
And put myself away?

I wonder if　　　　　　　　　　　　　　　　10
One bullet would do?
As hard as my head is,
I would probably take two.

But I ain't got
Neither bullet nor gun—
And I'm too blue　　　　　　　　　　　　　15
To look for one.

Blues at Dawn　　　　　　　　　　　　*(1951)*

I don't dare start thinking in the morning.
I don't dare start thinking in the morning.
　　If I thought thoughts in bed,
　　Them thoughts would bust my head—
So I don't dare start thinking in the morning.　　　5

I don't remember in the morning
Don't dare remember in the morning.
　　If I recall the day before,
　　I wouldn't get up no more—
So I don't dare remember in the morning.　　　10

Consider Me   *(1951)*

Consider me,
A colored boy,
Once sixteen,
Once five, once three
Once nobody,   5
Now me.
Before me
Papa, mama,
Grandpa, grandma,
So on back   10
To original
Pa.

    (A capital letter there,
    He
    Being Mystery.)   15

Consider me,
Colored boy,
Downtown at eight,
Sometimes working late,
Overtime pay   20
To sport away,
Or save,
Or give my Sugar
For the things
She needs.   25

My Sugar,
Consider her
Who works, too—
Has to.
One don't make enough   30
For all this stuff
It takes to live.
Forgive me
What I lack,
Black,   35
Caught in a crack
That splits the world in two
From China
By way of Arkansas
To Lenox Avenue.   40

Consider me,
On Friday the eagle flies.

Saturday laughter, a bar, a bed.
Sunday prayers syncopate glory.
Monday comes,   45
To work at eight,
Late,
Maybe.

Consider me,
Descended also   50
From the
Mystery.

Critical Perspective: On Racial Heritage

"You see, unfortunately, I am not black. There are lots of different kinds of blood in our family. But here in the United States, the word Negro is used to mean anyone who has *any* Negro blood at all in his veins. In Africa, the word is more pure. It means *all* Negro, therefore *black*.

"I am brown. My father was a darker brown. My mother an olive-yellow. On my father's side, the white blood in his family came from a Jewish slave trader in Kentucky, Silas Cushenberry, of Clark County, who was his mother's father; and Sam Clay, a distiller of Scotch descent, living in Henry County, who was his father's father. So on my father's side both male great-grandparents were white, and Sam Clay was said to be a relative of the great statesman, Henry Clay, his contemporary.

"On my mother's side, I had a paternal great-grandfather named Quarles— Captain Ralph Quarles—who was white and who lived in Louisa County, Virginia, before the Civil War, and who had several colored children by a colored housekeeper, who was his slave. The Quarles traced their ancestry back to Francis Quarles, famous Jacobean poet, who wrote *A Feast for Wormes*.

"On my maternal grandmother's side, there was French and Indian blood. My grandmother looked like any Indian—with very long black hair. She said she could lay claim to Indian land, but that she never wanted the government (or anybody else) to give her anything. She said there had been a French trader who came down the St. Lawrence, then on foot to the Carolinas, and mated with her grandmother, who was a Cherokee—so all her people were free. During slavery, she had free papers in North Carolina, and traveled about free, at will. Her name was Mary Sampson Patterson, and in Oberlin, Ohio, where she went to college, she married a free man named Sheridan Leary.

"She was with child in Oberlin when Sheridan Leary went away, and nobody knew where he had gone, except that he told her he was going on a trip. A few weeks later his shawl came back to her full of bullet holes. He had been killed following John Brown in that historic raid at Harper's Ferry. They did not hang him. He had been killed that first night in the raid—shot attacking, believing in John Brown. My grandmother said Sheridan Leary always did believe people should be free.

"She married another man who believed the same thing. His name was Charles Langston, my grandfather. And in the '70's the Langstons came out to Kansas where my mother was born on a farm near Lawrence.

"My grandfather never made much money. But he went into politics, looking for a bigger freedom than the Emancipation Proclamation had provided. He let his farm and his grocery store in Lawrence run along, and didn't much care about making money. But he left some fine speeches behind him.

"His brother, John Mercer Langston, left a book of speeches, too, and an autobiography, *From a Virginia Plantation to the National Capital.* But he was much better than Charles at making money, so he left a big house as well, and I guess some stocks and bonds. When I was small, we had cousins in Washington, who lived a lot better than we did in Kansas. But my grandmother never wrote them for anything. John Mercer Langston had been a Congressman from Virginia, and later United States Minister to Haiti, and Dean of the first Law School at Howard University. He had held many high positions— very high positions for a Negro in his day, or any day in this rather difficult country. And his descendants are still in society."

—Langston Hughes, from *The Big Sea: An Autobiography* (1940)

Critical Perspective: On the Harlem Renaissance

"The 1920's were the years of Manhattan's black Renaissance. It began with *Shuffle Along, Running Wild,* and the Charleston. Perhaps some people would say even with *The Emperor Jones,* Charles Gilpin, and the tom-toms at the Provincetown. But certainly it was the musical revue, *Shuffle Along,* that gave a scintillating send-off to that Negro vogue in Manhattan, which reached its peak just before the crash of 1929, the crash that sent Negroes, white folks, and all rolling down the hill toward the Works Progress Administration. . . .

"Put down the 1920's for the rise of Roland Hayes, who packed Carnegie Hall, the rise of Paul Robeson in New York and London, of Florence Mills over two continents, of Rose McClendon in Broadway parts that never measured up to her, the booming voice of Bessie Smith and the low moan of Clara on thousands of records, and the rise of that grand comedienne of song, Ethel Waters, singing: 'Charlie's elected now! He's in right for sure!' Put down the 1920's for Louis Armstrong and Gladys Bentley and Josephine Baker.

"White people began to come to Harlem in droves. For several years they packed the expensive Cotton Club on Lenox Avenue. But I was never there, because the Cotton Club was a Jim Crow club for gangsters and monied whites. They were not cordial to Negro patronage, unless you were a celebrity like Bojangles. So Harlem Negroes did not like the Cotton Club and never appreciated its Jim Crow policy in the very heart of their dark community. Nor did ordinary Negroes like the growing influx of whites toward Harlem after sundown, flooding the little cabarets and bars where formerly only colored people laughed and sang, and where now the strangers were given the best ringside tables to sit and stare at the Negro customers—like amusing animals in a zoo."

—Langston Hughes, *The Big Sea: An Autobiography* (1940)

Critical Perspective: On House-Rent Parties

"The Saturday night rent parties that I attended were often more amusing than any night club, in small apartments where God knows who lived—because the guests seldom did—but where the piano would often be augmented by a guitar, or an odd cornet, or somebody with a pair of drums walking in off the street. And where awful bootleg whiskey and good fried fish or steaming chitterling were sold at very low prices. And the dancing and singing and impromptu entertaining went on until dawn came in at the windows.

"These parties often termed whist parties or dances, were usually announced by brightly colored cards stuck in the grille of apartment house elevators. Some of the cards were highly entertaining in themselves. . . .

"Almost every Saturday night when I was in Harlem I went to a house-rent party. I wrote lots of poems about house-rent parties, and ate thereat many a fried fish and pig's foot—with liquid refreshments on the side. I met ladies' maids and truck drivers, laundry workers and shoe shine boys, seamstresses and porters. I can still hear their laughter in my ears, hear the soft slow music, and feel the floor shaking as the dancers danced."

—Langston Hughes, *The Big Sea: An Autobiography* (1940)

Critical Perspective: On the Mahogany Harvest

"They were of the Kru tribe, those Africans. And they proved very useful, working, loading, and cleaning all day long. They had one very dangerous job. They had to load the mahogany logs. These logs, some of them weighing tons, were dragged by human beings driven like mules, from the forests to the beaches. There they were floated out to our ship, at anchor offshore. Bouncing and bobbing in the waves, they had to be secured with great iron chains so that the cranes could lift them into the hold of the ship. To chain them was the job!

A dozen black Kru boys would dive into the water, swimming under and about the log until the chains were tight around the great bobbing hulk of wood. If a boy was caught between the floating black logs, or between a log and the ship, death would often result. Or if the sharks came, death would come, too. Watching them, I had somewhat the same feeling I had had in Mexico, watching Sanchez Mejias turning his red cape so gracefully before a bull's horns. It was beautiful and dangerous work, those black boys swimming there in the tossing waves among the iron chains and the great rolling logs, that would perhaps someday be somebody's grand piano or chest of drawers made of wood and life, energy and death out of Africa."

—Langston Hughes, *The Big Sea: An Autobiography* (1940)

Critical Perspective: On *The Weary Blues*

"Never having been one to think all subjects and forms proper for poetic consideration, I regard these jazz poems as interlopers in the company of the
truly beautiful poems in other sections of the book. They move along with the
frenzy and electric heat of a Methodist or Baptist revival meeting, and affect
me in much the same manner. The revival meeting excites me, cooling and
flushing me with alternate chills and fevers of emotion; so do these poems.
But when the storm is over, I wonder if the quiet way of communing is not
more spiritual for the Godseeking heart; and in the light of reflection I wonder if jazz poems really belong to that dignified company, that select and austere circle of high literary expression which we call poetry. . . .

"Taken as a group the selections in this book seem one-sided to me. They
tend to hurl this poet into the gaping pit that lies before all Negro writers in
the confines of which they become racial artists instead of artists pure and
simple. There is too much emphasis here on strictly Negro themes; and this
is probably an added reason for my coldness toward the jazz poems—they
seem to set a too definite limit upon an already limited field."

—Countee Cullen, from a review of *The Weary Blues*,
Opportunity (February 1926)

Critical Perspective: On the Black Arts Movement

"For the publication of Black Arts creative literature, no magazine was more
important than the Chicago-based Johnson publication *Negro Digest/Black
World*. Johnson published America's most popular Black magazines, *Jet* and
Ebony. Hoyt Fuller, who became the editor in 1961, was a Black intellectual
with near-encyclopedic knowledge of Black literature and seemingly inexhaustible contacts. . . . The two major Black Arts presses were poet Dudley
Randall's Broadside Press in Detroit and Haki Madhubuti's Third World
Press in Chicago. From a literary standpoint, Broadside Press, which concen-
trated almost exclusively on poetry, was by far the more important. Founded
in 1965, Broadside published more than four hundred poets in more than one
hundred books or recordings and was singularly responsible for presenting
older Black poets (Gwendolyn Brooks, Sterling A. Brown, and Margaret
Walker) to a new audience and introducing emerging poets (Nikki Giovanni,
Etheridge Knight, Don L. Lee/Haki Madhubuti, and Sonia Sanchez) who
would go on to become major voices for the movement. In 1976, strapped by
economic restrictions and with a severely overworked and overwhelmed
three-person staff, Broadside Press went into serious decline. Although it
functions mainly on its back catalog, Broadside Press is still alive.

"A number of poets (e.g., Amiri Baraka, Nikki Giovanni, Haki Madhubuti, and Sonia Sanchez), playwrights (e.g., Ed Bullins and Ron Milner),
and spoken-word artists (e.g., the Last Poets and Gil Scott-Heron, both of
whom were extremely popular and influential although often overlooked by
literary critics) are indelibly associated with the Black Arts movement. Rather

than focusing on their individual work, however, one gets a much stronger and much more accurate impression of the movement by reading seven anthologies focusing on the 1960s and the 1970s.

"*Black Fire* (1968), edited by Baraka and Neal, is a massive collection of essays, poetry, fiction, and drama featuring the first wave of Black Arts writers and thinkers. . . . For *Malcolm X, Poems on the Life and the Death of Malcolm X* (1969), edited by Dudley Randall and Margaret Taylor Goss Burroughs, demonstrates the political thrust of the movement and the specific influence of Malcolm X. . . . *The Black Woman* (1970), edited by Toni Cade Bambara, is the first major Black feminist anthology and features work by Jean Bond, Nikki Giovanni, Abbey Lincoln, Audre Lorde, Paule Marshall, Gwen Patton, Pat Robinson, Alice Walker, Shirley Williams, and others. . . . Edited by Addison Gayle, Jr., *The Black Aesthetic* (1971) is significant because it both articulates and contextualizes Black Arts theory. The work of writers such as Alain Locke, W. E. B. Du Bois, Langston Hughes, and J. A. Rogers showcases the movement's roots in an earlier era into sections on theory, music, fiction, poetry, and drama. Gayle's seminal anthology features a broad array of writers who are regarded as the chief Black Arts theorists-practitioners.

"Stephen Henderson's *Understanding the New Black Poetry* (1972) is important not only because of the poets included but also because of Henderson's insightful and unparalleled sixty-seven page overview. . . . *New Black Voices* (1972), edited by Abraham Chapman, is significant because its focus is specifically on the emerging voices in addition to new work by established voices who were active in the Black Arts movement. . . . The seventh book, Eugene Redmond's *Drumvoices, The Mission of Afro-American Poetry: A Critical History* (1976), is a surprisingly thorough survey that has been unjustly neglected."

—Kaluma ya Salaam, from "The Black Arts Movement," *The Oxford Companion to African American Literature* (1997)

TOPICS FOR CRITICAL THINKING

1. How does Langston Hughes claim multiple roles as an African American in "Negro"? What is his point about black identity and history in "Negro"?
2. In what ways does "Good-Morning Revolution" present a social alternative to the oppressive histories of "Negro"?
3. Discuss Hughes's critique of organized religion in "Goodbye Christ."
4. Consider the ways in which Hughes links class and race oppressions in "One More 'S' in the U.S.A."
5. Discuss the role that irony plays in Langston Hughes's "Ballad of the Fortune Teller."
6. Explore the role of comedy and self-parody in Hughes's blues lyrics "Too Blue" and "Blues at Dawn." How does that comic attitude cure the despair otherwise registered in both poems?

TOPICS FOR CRITICAL THINKING

1. Research the historical contexts that Langston Hughes alludes to in "Negro." Compare Hughes's social critique in "Negro" to the scenes of exploitation in "The Same."

2. Explore Hughes's apostrophe to "Revolution" and the role personification plays in visualizing social change in "Good-Morning, Revolution."

3. Write an essay that contrasts Hughes's hopeful vision of America with his own sense of American discrimination in "Let America Be America Again."

4. Research the role Barcelona played in the Spanish Civil War, and write an essay on the ways in which Hughes represents the trauma of war in "Air Raid: Barcelona." What role does figurative language play in Hughes's depiction of the air raids?

5. Write an essay that discusses Hughes's line lengths in "Consider Me." What does Hughes gain from his minimalist presentation of language in the poem? What role does white space play in the poem's compositional design?

23 Poems for Further Reading

Ai *(b. 1947)*

The Mother's Tale

(1986)

Once when I was young, Juanito,
there was a ballroom in Lima
where Hernán, your father,
danced with another woman
and I cut him across the cheek   5
with a pocketknife.
Oh, the pitch of the music sometimes,
the smoke and rustle of crinoline.
But what things to remember now
on your wedding day.   10
I pour a kettle of hot water
into the wooden tub where you are sitting.
I was young, free.
But Juanito, how free is a woman?—
born with Eve's sin between her legs,   15
and inside her,
Lucifer sits on a throne of abalone shells,
his staff with the head of John the Baptist
skewered on it.
And in judgment, son, in judgment he says   20
that women will bear the fruit of the tree
we wished so much to eat
and that fruit will devour us
generation by generation,
so my son,   25
you must beat Rosita often.
She must know the weight of a man's hand,
the bruises that are like the wounds of Christ.
Her blood that is black at the heart
must flow until it is as red and pure as His.   30
And she must be pregnant always
if not with child
then with the knowledge
that she is alive because of you.

That you can take her life   35
more easily than she creates it,
that suffering is her inheritance from you
and through you, from Christ,
who walked on his mother's body
to be the King of Heaven.   40

JOHN ASHBERY   *(b. 1927)*

The Painter   *(1956)*

Sitting between the sea and the buildings
He enjoyed painting the sea's portrait.
But just as children imagine a prayer
Is merely silence, he expected his subject
To rush up the sand, and, seizing a brush,   5
Plaster its own portrait on the canvas.

So there was never any paint on his canvas
Until the people who lived in the buildings
Put him to work: "Try using the brush
As a means to an end. Select, for a portrait,   10
Something less angry and large, and more subject
To a painter's moods, or, perhaps, to a prayer."

How could he explain to them his prayer
That nature, not art, might usurp the canvas?
He chose his wife for a new subject,   15
Making her vast, like ruined buildings,
As if, forgetting itself, the portrait
Had expressed itself without a brush.

Slightly encouraged, he dipped his brush
In the sea, murmuring a heartfelt prayer: 20
"My soul, when I paint this next portrait
Let it be you who wrecks the canvas."
The news spread like wildfire through the buildings:
He had gone back to the sea for his subject.

Imagine a painter crucified by his subject!   25
Too exhausted even to lift his brush,
He provoked some artists leaning from the buildings
To malicious mirth: "We haven't a prayer
Now, of puffing ourselves on canvas,
Or getting the sea to sit for a portrait!"   30

Others declared it a self-portrait.
Finally all indications of a subject
Began to fade, leaving the canvas
Perfectly white. He put down the brush.
At once a howl, that was also a prayer,   35
Arose from the overcrowded buildings.

They tossed him, the portrait, from the tallest of the buildings;
And the sea devoured the canvas and the brush
As though his subject had decided to remain a prayer.

W. H. Auden   *(1907–1973)*

The Shield of Achilles°   *(1955)*

> She looked over his shoulder
>   For vines and olive trees,
> Marble well-governed cities
>   And ships upon untamed seas,
> But there on the shining metal   5
>   His hands had put instead
> An artificial wilderness
>   And a sky like lead.

A plain without a feature, bare and brown,
    No blade of grass, no sign of neighbourhood,   10
Nothing to eat and nowhere to sit down,
    Yet, congregated on its blankness, stood
    An unintelligible multitude,
A million eyes, a million boots in line,
Without expression, waiting for a sign.   15

Out of the air a voice without a face
    Proved by statistics that some cause was just
In tones as dry and level as the place:
    No one was cheered and nothing was discussed;
    Column by column in a cloud of dust   20
They marched away enduring a belief
Whose logic brought them, somewhere else, to grief.

> She looked over his shoulder
>   For ritual pieties,

Shield of Achilles: Mythic shield forged by Hephaestos, the god of fire, for Achilles in Book 18 of Homer's *Iliad*.

White flower-garlanded heifers,   25
   Libation and sacrifice,
But there on the shining metal
   Where the altar should have been,
She saw by his flickering forge-light
   Quite another scene.   30

Barbed wire enclosed an arbitrary spot
   Where bored officials lounged (one cracked a joke)
And sentries sweated for the day was hot:
   A crowd of ordinary decent folk
   Watched from without and neither moved nor spoke   35
As three pale figures were led forth and bound
To three posts driven upright in the ground.

The mass and majesty of this world, all
   That carries weight and always weighs the same
Lay in the hands of others; they were small   40
   And could not hope for help and no help came:
   What their foes liked to do was done, their shame
Was all the worst could wish; they lost their pride
And died as men before their bodies died.

   She looked over his shoulder   45
      For athletes at their games,
   Men and women in a dance
      Moving their sweet limbs
   Quick, quick, to music,
      But there on the shining shield   50
   His hands had set no dancing-floor
      But a weed-choked field.

A ragged urchin, aimless and alone,
   Loitered about that vacancy, a bird
Flew up to safety from his well-aimed stone: 55
   That girls are raped, that two boys knife a third,
   Were axioms to him, who'd never heard
Of any world where promises were kept,
Or one could weep because another wept.

   The thin-lipped armourer,   60
      Hephaestos hobbled away,
   Thetis of the shining breasts
      Cried out in dismay
   At what the god had wrought
      To please her son, the strong   65
   Iron-hearted man-slaying Achilles
      Who would not live long.

Lullaby   *(1940)*

Lay your sleeping head, my love,
Human on my faithless arm;
Time and fevers burn away
Individual beauty from
Thoughtful children, and the grave   5
Proves the child ephemeral:
But in my arms till break of day
Let the living creature lie,
Mortal, guilty, but to me
The entirely beautiful.   10

Soul and body have no bounds:
To lovers as they lie upon
Her tolerant enchanted slope
In their ordinary swoon,
Grave the vision Venus sends   15
Of supernatural sympathy,
Universal love and hope;
While an abstract insight wakes
Among the glaciers and the rocks
The hermit's carnal ecstasy.   20

Certainty, fidelity
On the stroke of midnight pass
Like vibrations of a bell
And fashionable madmen raise
Their pedantic boring cry: 25
Every farthing of the cost,
All the dreaded cards foretell,
Shall be paid, but from this night
Not a whisper, not a thought,
Not a kiss nor look be lost.   30

Beauty, midnight, vision dies:
Let the winds of dawn that blow
Softly round your dreaming head
Such a day of welcome show
Eye and knocking heart may bless,   35
Find our mortal world enough;
Noons of dryness find you fed
By the involuntary powers,
Nights of insult let you pass
Watched by every human love.   40

Peter Balakian   *(b. 1951)*

After the Survivors Are Gone   *(1996)*

I tried to imagine the Vilna ghetto,
to see a persimmon tree after the flash at Nagasaki.
Because my own tree had been hacked,
I tried to kiss the lips of Armenia.

At the table and the altar   5
we said some words written ages ago.
Have we settled for just the wine and bread,
for candles lit and snuffed?

Let us remember how the law has failed us.
Let us remember the child naked,   10
waiting to be shot on a bright day
with tulips blooming around the ditch.

We shall not forget the earth,
the artifact, the particular song,
the dirt of an idiom—   15
things that stick in the ear.

from *Beowulf*   *(700–900)*

[The Last Survivor's Speech]

"Now earth hold fast, since heroes have failed to,
The riches of the race! Was it not from you
That good men once won it? Battle-death, evil
Mortal and terrible has taken every man   5
Of this folk of mine that has left life and time,
That has gazed its last on feast and gladness.
No one I have to be sword-bearer or burnisher
Of the beaten-gold goblet, the dearly-loved drinking-cup:
That chivalry has slipped away. Hard helmet must shed   10
Its flashing furnishing, its plating of gold;
Burnishers sleep who should sheen the battle-mask;
So too the mail-coat that has met the biting
Of iron war-blades above clashed shields
Crumbles after its wearer; nor can this chain-armor   15
Follow the fight's commander into far-off regions

At the heroes' side. There is no harp-pleasure
And no happy minstrelsy, there is no good hawk
To swoop through the hall, there is no swift horse
With hoofbeats in the courtyard. Hatred and death   20
Have driven out on their voyage the hosts of the living!"
So one sad-minded spoke out the misery
He felt for all, moving unconsoled
Restless day and night, till the tidewater of death
Rose touching his heart.   25

[The Last Survivor's Speech in Old English]

"Heald þu nu, hruse,   nu hæleð ne mostan,
eorla æhte!   Hwæt, hyt ær on ðe
gode begeaton.   Guþ-deað fornam,
feorh-bealo frecne   fyra gehwylcne   30
leoda minra,   þare ðe þis lif ofgeaf,
gesawon sele-dreamas.   Nah hwa sweord wege
oððe feormie   fæted wæge,
drync-fæt deore;   duguð ellor scoc.
Sceal se hearda helm   hyrsted golde   35
fætum befeallen;   feormynd swefað,
þa ðe beado-griman   bywan sceoldon;
ge swylce seo here-pad,   sio æt hilde gebad
ofer borda gebræc   bite irena,
brosnað æfter beorne;   ne mæg byrnan hring   40
æfter wig-fruman   wide feran
hæleðum be healfe.   Næs hearpan wyn
gomen gleo-beames,   ne god hafoc
geond sæl swingeð,   ne se swifta mearh
burh-stede beateð.   Bealo-cwealm hafað   45
fela feorh-cynna   forð onsended!"

Elizabeth Bishop   *(1911–1979)*

One Art   *(1976)*

The art of losing isn't hard to master;
so many things seem filled with the intent
to be lost that their loss is no disaster.

Lose something every day. Accept the fluster
of lost door keys, the hour badly spent.   5
The art of losing isn't hard to master.

Then practice losing farther, losing faster:
places, and names, and where it was you meant
to travel. None of these will bring disaster.

I lost my mother's watch. And look! my last, or   10
next-to-last, of three loved houses went.
The art of losing isn't hard to master.

I lost two cities, lovely ones. And, vaster,
some realms I owned, two rivers, a continent.
I miss them, but it wasn't a disaster.   15

—Even losing you (the joking voice, a gesture
I love) I shan't have lied. It's evident
the art of losing's not too hard to master
though it may look like (*Write it!*) like disaster.

WILLIAM BLAKE   *(1757–1827)*

The Divine Image   *(1789)*

To Mercy, Pity, Peace, and Love,
All pray in their distress:
And to these virtues of delight
Return their thankfulness.

For Mercy, Pity, Peace, and Love,   5
Is God, our father dear:
And Mercy, Pity, Peace, and Love,
Is Man, his child and care.

For Mercy has a human heart,
Pity, a human face: 10
And Love, the human form divine,
And Peace, the human dress.

Then every man of every clime,
That prays in his distress,
Prays to the human form divine,   15
Love, Mercy, Pity, Peace.

And all must love the human form,
In heathen, Turk, or Jew.
Where Mercy, Love, & Pity dwell,
There God is dwelling too.   20

A Divine Image   *(1790–1791)*

Cruelty has a Human heart
And Jealousy a Human Face,
Terror, the Human Form Divine,
And Secrecy, the Human Dress.

The Human Dress is forgéd Iron,   5
The Human Form, a fiery Forge,
The Human Face, a Furnace seal'd,
The Human Heart, its hungry Gorge.

A Poison Tree   *(1794)*

I was angry with my friend:
I told my wrath, my wrath did end.
I was angry with my foe:
I told it not, my wrath did grow.

And I waterd it in fears,   5
Night & morning with my tears;
And I sunnéd it with smiles,
And with soft deceitful wiles.

And it grew both day and night,
Till it bore an apple bright.   10
And my foe beheld it shine,
And he knew that it was mine,

And into my garden stole,
When the night had veild the pole;
In the morning glad I see   15
My foe outstretchd beneath the tree.

The Tyger   *(1794)*

Tyger! Tyger! burning bright
In the forests of the night,
What immortal hand or eye
Could frame thy fearful symmetry?

In what distant deeps or skies   5
Burnt the fire of thine eyes?
On what wings dare he aspire?
What the hand, dare seize the fire?

And what shoulder, & what art,
Could twist the sinews of thy heart?   10
And when thy heart began to beat,
What dread hand? & what dread feet?

What the hammer? what the chain?
In what furnace was thy brain?
What the anvil? what dread grasp   15
Dare its deadly terrors clasp?

When the stars threw down their spears,
And water'd heaven with their tears,
Did he smile his work to see?
Did he who made the Lamb make thee?   20

Tyger! Tyger! burning bright
In the forests of the night,
What immortal hand or eye
Dare frame thy fearful symmetry?

Louise Bogan   *(1897–1970)*

Medusa   *(1923)*

I had come to the house, in a cave of trees,
Facing a sheer sky.
Everything moved,—a bell hung ready to strike,
Sun and reflection wheeled by.

When the bare eyes were before me   5
And the hissing hair,
Held up at a window, seen through a door.
The stiff bald eyes, the serpents on the forehead
Formed in the air.

This is a dead scene forever now.   10
Nothing will ever stir.
The end will never brighten it more than this,
Nor the rain blur.

The water will always fall, and will not fall,
And the tipped bell make no sound.   15
The grass will always be growing for hay
Deep on the ground.

And I shall stand here like a shadow
Under the great balanced day,
My eyes on the yellow dust, that was lifting in the wind,   20
And does not drift away.

EAVAN BOLAND   *(b. 1944)*

The Pomegranate   *(1994)*

The only legend I have ever loved is
the story of a daughter lost in hell.
And found and rescued there.
Love and blackmail are the gist of it.
Ceres and Persephone the names.   5
And the best thing about the legend is
I can enter it anywhere. And have.
As a child in exile in
a city of fogs and strange consonants,
I read it first and at first I was   10
an exiled child in the crackling dusk of
the underworld, the stars blighted. Later
I walked out in a summer twilight
searching for my daughter at bed-time.
When she came running I was ready   15
to make any bargain to keep her.
I carried her back past whitebeams
and wasps and honey-scented buddleias.
But I was Ceres then and I knew
winter was in store for every leaf   20
on every tree on that road.
Was inescapable for each one we passed.
And for me.
            It is winter
and the stars are hidden.   25
I climb the stairs and stand where I can see
my child asleep beside her teen magazines,
her can of Coke, her plate of uncut fruit.
The pomegranate! How did I forget it?
She could have come home and been safe   30
and ended the story and all
our heart-broken searching but she reached
out a hand and plucked a pomegranate.
She put out her hand and pulled down
the French sound for apple and   35
the noise of stone and the proof

that even in the place of death,
at the heart of legend, in the midst
of rocks full of unshed tears
ready to be diamonds by the time   40
the story was told, a child can be
hungry. I could warn her. There is still a chance.
The rain is cold. The road is flint-coloured.
The suburb has cars and cable television.
The veiled stars are above ground.   45
It is another world. But what else
can a mother give her daughter but such
beautiful rifts in time?
If I defer the grief I will diminish the gift.
The legend will be hers as well as mine.   50
She will enter it. As I have.
She will wake up. She will hold
the papery flushed skin in her hand.
And to her lips. I will say nothing.

ANNE BRADSTREET   *(c. 1612–1672)*

To My Dear and Loving Husband   *(1678)*

If ever two were one, then surely we.
If ever man were loved by wife, then thee;
If ever wife was happy in a man,
Compare with me ye women if you can.
I prize thy love more than whole mines of gold,   5
Or all the riches that the East doth hold.
My love is such that Rivers cannot quench,
Nor ought but love from thee, give recompence.
Thy love is such I can no way repay,
The heavens reward thee manifold, I pray.   10
Then while we live, in love lets so persever,
That when we live no more we may live ever.

EMILY BRONTË   *(1818–1848)*

[Long Neglect Has Worn Away]   *(1837)*

Long neglect has worn away
Half the sweet enchanting smile;
Time has turned the bloom to gray;
Mold and damp the face defile.

But that lock of silky hair,   5
Still beneath the picture twined,
Tells what once those features were,
Paints their image on the mind.

Fair the hand that traced that line,
"Dearest, ever deem me true";   10
Swiftly flew the fingers fine
When the pen that motto drew.

STERLING A. BROWN   *(1901–1989)*

Slim in Atlanta   *(1932)*

Down in Atlanta,
    De whitefolks got laws
For to keep all de niggers
    From laughin' outdoors.

        Hope to Gawd I may die   5
            If I ain't speakin' truth
        Make de niggers do deir laughin'
            In a telefoam booth.

Slim Greer hit de town
    An' de rebs got him told,—   10
"Dontcha laugh on de street,
    If you want to die old."

        Den dey showed him de booth,
            An' a hundred shines
        In front of it, waitin'   15
            In double lines.

Slim thought his sides
    Would bust in two,
Yelled, "Lookout, everybody,
    I'm coming through!"   20

        Pulled de other man out,
            An' bust in de box,
        An' laughed four hours
            By de Georgia clocks.

Den he peeked through de door,   25
    An' what did he see?

Three hundred niggers there
   In misery.—

     Some holdin' deir sides,
       Some holdin' deir jaws,   30
     To keep from breakin'
       De Georgia laws.

An' Slim gave a holler,
   An' started again;
An' from three hundred throats   35
   Come a moan of pain.

     An' everytime Slim
       Saw what was outside,
     Got to whoopin' again
       Till he nearly died.   40

An' while de poor critters
   Was waitin' deir chance,
Slim laughed till dey sent
   Fo' de ambulance.

     De state paid de railroad   45
       To take him away;
     Den, things was as usural
       In Atlanta, Gee A.

Elizabeth Barrett Browning   *(1806–1861)*

To George Sand   *(1844)*

A Desire

Thou large-brained woman and large-hearted man,
Self-called George Sand! whose soul, amid the lions
Of thy tumultuous senses, moans defiance
And answers roar for roar, as spirits can:
I would some mild miraculous thunder ran   5
Above the applauded circus, in appliance
Of thine own nobler nature's strength and science,
Drawing two pinions, white as wings of swan,
From thy strong shoulders, to amaze the place
With holier light! that thou to woman's claim   10
And man's mightest join beside the angel's grace
Of a pure genius sanctified from blame,

Till child and maiden pressed to thine embrace
To kiss upon thy lips a stainless fame.

Sonnet 14, from Sonnets from the Portuguese   *(1850)*

If thou must love me, let it be for nought
Except for love's sake only. Do not say,
"I love her for her smile—her look—her way
Of speaking gently,—for a trick of thought
That falls in well with mine, and certes brought   5
A sense of pleasant ease on such a day"—
For these things in themselves, Belovèd, may
Be changed, or change for thee,—and love, so wrought,
May be unwrought so. Neither love me for
Thine own dear pity's wiping my cheeks dry,—   10
A creature might forget to weep, who bore
Thy comfort long, and lose thy love thereby!
But love me for love's sake, that evermore
Thou may'st love on, through love's eternity.

ROBERT BROWNING   *(1812–1889)*

My Last Duchess°   *(1842)*

Ferrara

That's my last duchess painted on the wall,
Looking as if she were alive. I call
That piece a wonder, now: Frà Pandolf's hands
Worked busily a day, and there she stands.
Will't please you sit and look at her? I said   5
"Frà Pandolf" by design, for never read
Strangers like you that pictured countenance,
The depth and passion of its earnest glance,
But to myself they turned (since none puts by
The curtain I have drawn for you, but I)   10
And seemed as they would ask me, if they durst,
How such a glance came there; so, not the first
Are you to turn and ask thus. Sir, 'twas not
Her husband's presence only, called the spot
Of joy into the Duchess' cheek: perhaps   15
Frà Pandolf chanced to say "Her mantle laps

Duchess: Daughter of Cosimo I de Medici, duke of Florence, and wife of Alfonso II d'Este, duke
of Ferrera who is the speaker in Browning's dramatic monologue.

"Over my lady's wrist too much," or "Paint
"Must never hope to reproduce the faint
"Half-flush that dies along her throat": such stuff
Was courtesy, she thought, and cause enough   20
For calling up that spot of joy. She had
A heart—how shall I say?—too soon made glad,
Too easily impressed; she liked whate'er
She looked on, and her looks went everywhere.
Sir, 'twas all one! My favor at her breast,   25
The dropping of the daylight in the West,
The bough of cherries some officious fool
Broke in the orchard for her, the white mule
She rode with round the terrace—all and each
Would draw from her alike the approving speech,   30
Or blush, at least. She thanked men—good! but thanked
Somehow—I know not how—as if she ranked
My gift of a nine-hundred-years-old name
With anybody's gift. Who'd stoop to blame
This sort of trifling? Even had you skill   35
In speech—which I have not—to make your will
Quite clear to such an one, and say, "Just this
"Or that in you disgusts me; here you miss,
"Or there exceed the mark"—and if she let
Herself be lessoned so, nor plainly set   40
Her wits to yours, forsooth, and made excuse,
—E'en then would be some stooping; and I choose
Never to stoop. Oh sir, she smiled, no doubt,
Whene'er I passed her; but who passed without
Much the same smile? This grew; I gave commands;   45
Then all smiles stopped together. There she stands
As if alive. Will 't please you rise? We'll meet
The company below, then. I repeat,
The Count your master's known munificence
Is ample warrant that no just pretense   50
Of mine for dowry will be disallowed;
Though his fair daughter's self, as I avowed
At starting, is my object. Nay, we'll go
Together down, sir. Notice Neptune, though,
Taming a sea-horse, thought a rarity,   55
Which Claus of Innsbruck cast in bronze for me!

GEORGE GORDON, LORD BYRON   *(1788–1824)*

The Destruction of Sennacherib   *(1815)*

The Assyrian came down like the wolf on the fold,
And his cohorts were gleaming in purple and gold;
And the sheen of their spears was like stars on the sea,
When the blue wave rolls nightly on deep Galilee.

Like the leaves of the forest when summer is green,   5
That host with their banners at sunset were seen:
Like the leaves of the forest when autumn hath blown,
That host on the morrow lay wither'd and strown.

For the Angel of Death spread his wings on the blast,
And breathed in the face of the foe as he passed   10
And the eyes of the sleepers wax'd deadly and chill,
And their hearts but once heaved, and forever grew still!

And there lay the steed with his nostril all wide,
But through it there roll'd not the breath of his pride;
And the foam of his gasping lay white on the turf,   15
And cold as the spray of the rock-beating surf.

And there lay the rider distorted and pale,
With the dew on his brow, and the rust on his mail:
And the tents were all silent, the banners alone,
The lances uplifted, the trumpet unblown.   20

And the widows of Ashur are loud in their wail,
And the idols are broke in the temple of Baal;
And the might of the Gentile, unsmote by the sword,
Hath melted like snow in the glance of the Lord!

LEWIS CARROLL   *(1832–1898)*

Jabberwocky   *(1871)*

'Twas brillig, and the slithy toves
    Did gyre and gimble in the wabe;
All mimsy were the borogoves,
    And the mome raths outgrabe.

"Beware the Jabberwock, my son!   5
    The jaws that bite, the claws that catch!
Beware the Jubjub bird, and shun
    The frumious Bandersnatch!"

He took his vorpal sword in hand;
    Long time the manxome foe he sought—   10
So rested he by the Tumtum tree,
    And stood awhile in thought.

And, as in uffish thought he stood,
    The Jabberwock, with eyes of flame,
Came whiffling through the tulgey wood,   15
    And burbled as it came!

One, two! One, two! And through and through
    The vorpal blade went snicker-snack!
He left it dead, and with its head
    He went galumphing back.   20

"And hast thou slain the Jabberwock?
    Come to my arms, my beamish boy!
O frabjous day! Callooh! Callay!"
    He chortled in his joy.

'Twas brillig, and the slithy toves   25
    Did gyre and gimble in the wabe:
All mimsy were the borogoves,
    And the mome raths outgrabe.

MARGARET CAVENDISH   *(1623–1673)*

An Apology for Writing So Much upon This Book   *(1653)*

Condemn me not, I make so much ado
About this book, it is my child, you know.
Just like a bird, when her young are in nest,
Goes in, and out, and hops, and takes no rest:
But when their young are fledg'd, their heads out-peep,   5
Lord! What a chirping does the old one keep!
So I, for fear my strengthless child should fall
Against a door, or stool, aloud I call;
Bid have a care of such a dangerous place:
Thus write I much, to hinder all disgrace.   10

GEOFFREY CHAUCER   *(c. 1343–1400)*

from *The Canterbury Tales*   *(1387–1400)*

The General Prologue

Whan that April with his° showres soote°
The droughte of March hath perced to the roote,
And bathed every veine° in swich licour,°
Of which vertu° engendred is the flowr;
Whan Zephyrus° eek° with his sweete breeth   5
Inspired° hath in every holt° and heeth°
The tendre croppes,° and the yonge sonne°
Hath in the Ram his halve cours yronne,
And smale fowles° maken melodye
That sleepen al the night with open yë°—   10
So priketh hem° Nature in hir corages°—
Thanne longen folk to goon° on pilgrimages,
And palmeres° for to seeken straunge strondes°
To ferne halwes,° couthe° in sondry° londes;
And specially from every shires ende   15
Of Engelond to Canterbury they wende,
The holy blisful martyr° for to seeke
That hem hath holpen° whan that they were seke.°
    Bifel° that in that seson on a day,
In Southwerk° at the Tabard as I lay,   20
Redy to wenden on my pilgrimage
To Canterbury with ful° devout corage,
At night was come into that hostelrye
Wel nine and twenty in a compaignye
Of sondry folk, by aventure° yfalle   25
In felaweshipe, and pilgrimes were they alle
That toward Canterbury wolden° ride.
The chambres and the stables weren wide,
And wel we weren esed° at the beste.°

---

1 *his:* Its. *soote:* Fresh.   3 *every veine:* I.e., in plants. *in swich licour:* In such liquid.   4 *Of which vertu:* By the power of which.   5 *Zephyrus:* The west wind. *eek:* Also.   6 *Inspired:* Breathed into. *holt:* Grove. *heeth:* Field.   7 *croppes:* Shoots. *yonge sonne:* The sun is young because it has run only halfway through its course in Aries, the Ram—the first sign of the zodiac in the solar year.   9 *fowles:* Birds.   10 *yë:* Eye.   11 *hem:* Them. *hir corages:* Their hearts.   12 *goon:* Go.   13 *palmeres:* Pilgrims, especially to the Holy Land. *straunge strondes:* Foreign shores.   14 *ferne halwes:* Far-off shrines. *couthe:* Known. *sondry:* Various.   17 *martyr:* Thomas à Becket, archbishop murdered in Canterbury Cathedral in 1170; his shrine was associated with healing.   18 *holpen:* Helped. *seke:* Sick.   19 *Bifel:* It happened.   20 *Southwerk:* Then a suburb of London, south of the Thames River, that was the site of the Southwerk Inn.   22 *ful:* Very.   25 *aventure:* Chance.   27 *wolden:* Would.   29 *esed:* Accommodated. *beste:* In the best possible way.

And shortly, whan the sonne was to reste,°   30
So hadde I spoken with hem everichoon°
That I was of hir felaweshipe anoon,°
And made forward° erly for to rise,
To take oure way ther as° I you devise.°
    But nathelees,° whil I have time and space,°   35
Er° that I ferther in this tale pace,°
Me thinketh it accordant to resoun°
To telle you al the condicioun
Of eech of hem, so as it seemed me,
And whiche they were, and of what degree,°   40
And eek in what array that they were inne:
And at a knight thanne° wol I first biginne.
    A Knight ther was, and that a worthy man,
That fro the time that he first bigan
To riden out, he loved chivalrye,   45
Trouthe and honour, freedom and curteisye.°
Ful worthy was he in his lordes werre,°
And therto hadde he riden, no man ferre,°
As wel in Cristendom as hethenesse,°
And evere honoured for his worthinesse.   50
    At Alisandre° he was whan it was wonne;
Ful ofte time he hadde the boord bigonne°
Aboven alle nacions in Pruce;
In Lettou had he reised,° and in Ruce,
No Cristen man so ofte of his degree;   55
In Gernade° at the sege eek hadde he be
Of Algezir, and riden in Belmarye;
At Lyeis was he, and at Satalye,
Whan they were wonne; and in the Grete See°
At many a noble arivee° hadde he be.   60
    At mortal batailes° hadde he been fifteene,
And foughten for oure faith at Tramissene
In listes° thries,° and ay° slain his fo.

---

30 *was to reste:* Had set.   31 *everichoon:* Every one.   32 *anoon:* At once.   33 *made forward:* Made an agreement.   34 *as:* Where. *devise:* Describe.   35 *natheless:* Nevertheless. *time and space:* Opportunity.   36 *Er:* Before. *pace:* Proceed.   37 *Me . . . resoun:* It seems to me according to reason.   40 *degree:* Social rank.   42 *thanne:* Them. 46 *Trouthe . . . curteisye:* Integrity, honor, generosity of spirit, courtesy.   47 *werre:* War. 48 *ferre:* Further.   49 *hethenesse:* Heathen lands.   51 *At Alisandre:* The Knight has taken part in campaigns fought against three groups who threatened Christian Europe during the fourteenth century: the Moslems in the Near East, from whom Alexandria was seized after a famous siege; the northern barbarians in Prussia, Lithuania, and Russia; and the Moors in North Africa. The place names in the following lines refer to battlegrounds in these continuing wars.   52 *hadde the boord bigonne:* Sat in the seat of honor at military feasts.   54 *reised:* Campaigned. 56 *Gernade:* Granada.   59 *Grete See:* The Mediterranean.   60 *noble arivee:* Military landing.   61 *mortal batailes:* Tournaments fought to the death.   63 *listes:* Lists, tournament grounds. *thries:* Thrice. *ay:* Always.

This ilke° worthy Knight hadde been also
Somtime with the lord of Palatye°   65
Again° another hethen in Turkye;
And everemore he hadde a soverein pris.°
And though that he were worthy, he was wis,°
And of his port° as meeke as is a maide.
He nevere yit no vilainye° ne saide   70
In al his lif unto no manere wight:°
He was a verray,° parfit,° gentil° knight.
But for to tellen you of his array,
His hors° were goode, but he was nat gay.°
Of fustian° he wered° a gipoun°   75
Al bismotered with his haubergeoun,°
For he was late° come from his viage,°
And wente for to doon his pilgrimage.

LADY MARY CHUDLEIGH *(1656–1710)*

To the Ladies   *(1703)*

Wife and Servant are the same,
But only differ in the Name:
For when that fatal Knot is ty'd,
Which nothing, nothing can divide:
When she the word *obey* has said,   5
And Man by Law supreme has made,
Then all that's kind is laid aside,
And nothing left but State and Pride:
Fierce as an Eastern Prince he grows,
And all his innate Rigor shows: 10
Then but to look, to laugh, or speak,
Will the Nuptial Contract break.
Like Mutes she Signs alone must make,
And never any Freedom take:
But still be govern'd by a Nod,   15
And fear her Husband as her God:
Him still must serve, him still obey,

---

64 *ilke:* Same.   65 *lord of Palatye:* A Moslem. Alliances of convenience were often made during
the Crusades between Christians and Moslems.   66 *Again:* Against.   67 *pris:* Reputation.
68 *he was wis:* He was wise as well as bold.   69 *port:* Deportment, demeanor.   70 *vilainye:*
Nudeness.   71 *no manere wight:* Any sort of person. In Middle English, negatives are multiplied for emphasis, as in these two lines: "nevere," "no," "ne," "no."   72 *verray:* True. *parfit:*
Perfect. *gentil:* Noble.   74 *hors:* Horses. *gay:* Gaily dressed.   75 *fustian:* Thick cloth.
wered: Wore. *gipouni:* Tunic worn underneath the coat of mail.   76 *Al . . . haubergeoun:* All
rust-stained from his hauberk (coat of mail).   77 *late:* Lately. *viage:* Expedition.

And nothing act, and nothing say,
But what her haughty Lord thinks fit,
Who with the Pow'r, has all the Wit.   20
Then shun, oh! shun that wretched State,
And all the fawning Flatt'rers hate:
Value your selves, and Men despise,
You must be proud, if you'll be wise.

SAMUEL TAYLOR COLERIDGE   *(1772–1834)*

Frost at Midnight   *(1798)*

  The Frost performs its secret ministry,
Unhelped by any wind. The owlet's cry
Came loud—and hark, again! loud as before.
The inmates of my cottage, all at rest,
Have left me to that solitude, which suits   5
Abstruser musings: save that at my side
My cradled infant° slumbers peacefully.
'Tis calm indeed! so calm, that it disturbs
And vexes meditation with its strange
And extreme silentness. Sea, hill, and wood,   10
This populous village! Sea, and hill, and wood,
With all the numberless goings-on of life,
Inaudible as dreams! the thin blue flame
Lies on my low-burnt fire, and quivers not;
Only that film,° which fluttered on the grate,   15
Still flutters there, the sole unquiet thing.
Methinks its motion in this hush of nature
Gives it dim sympathies with me who live,
Making it a companionable form,
Whose puny flaps and freaks the idling Spirit   20
By its own moods interprets, everywhere
Echo or mirror seeking of itself,
And makes a toy of Thought.

                            But O! how oft,
How oft, at school, with most believing mind,
Presageful, have I gazed upon the bars,   25
To watch that fluttering *stranger!* and as oft
With unclosed lids, already had I dreamt
Of my sweet birthplace, and the old church tower,

---

7 *infant:* Hartley Coleridge.   15 *film:* Soot: in popular folk lore thought to foreshadow a
guest's visit.

Whose bells, the poor man's only music, rang
From morn to evening, all the hot Fair-day,   30
So sweetly, that they stirred and haunted me
With a wild pleasure, falling on mine ear
Most like articulate sounds of things to come!
So gazed I, till the soothing things, I dreamt,
Lulled me to sleep, and sleep prolonged my dreams!   35
And so I brooded all the following morn,
Awed by the stern preceptor's° face, mine eye
Fixed with mock study on my swimming book:
Save if the door half opened, and I snatched
A hasty glance, and still my heart leaped up,   40
For still I hoped to see the *stranger's* face,
Townsman, or aunt, or sister more beloved,
My playmate when we both were clothed alike!

   Dear Babe, that sleepest cradled by my side,
Whose gentle breathings, heard in this deep calm,   45
Fill up the interspersèd vacancies
And momentary pauses of the thought!
My babe so beautiful! it thrills my heart
With tender gladness, thus to look at thee,
And think that thou shalt learn far other lore,   50
And in far other scenes! For I was reared
In the great city, pent 'mid cloisters dim,
And saw nought lovely but the sky and stars.
But *thou*, my babe! shalt wander like a breeze
By lakes and sandy shores, beneath the crags   55
Of ancient mountain, and beneath the clouds,
Which image in their bulk both lakes and shores
And mountain crags: so shalt thou see and hear
The lovely shapes and sounds intelligible
Of that eternal language, which thy God   60
Utters, who from eternity doth teach
Himself in all, and all things in himself.
Great universal Teacher! he shall mold
Thy spirit, and by giving make it ask.

   Therefore all seasons shall be sweet to thee,   65
Whether the summer clothe the general earth
With greenness, or the redbreast sit and sing
Betwixt the tufts of snow on the bare branch
Of mossy apple tree, while the nigh thatch
Smokes in the sun-thaw; whether the eave-drops fall   70
Heard only in the trances of the blast,

---

37 *preceptor:* Teacher.

Or if the secret ministry of frost
Shall hang them up in silent icicles,
Quietly shining to the quiet Moon.

HART CRANE   *(1899–1932)*

Proem: To Brooklyn Bridge   *(1930)*

How many dawns, chill from his rippling rest
The seagull's wings shall dip and pivot him,
Shedding white rings of tumult, building high
Over the chained bay waters Liberty—

Then, with inviolate curve, forsake our eyes   5
As apparitional as sails that cross
Some page of figures to be filed away;
—Till elevators drop us from our day . . .

I think of cinemas, panoramic sleights
With multitudes bent toward some flashing scene   10
Never disclosed, but hastened to again,
Foretold to other eyes on the same screen;

And Thee, across the harbor, silver-paced
As though the sun took step of thee, yet left
Some motion ever unspent in thy stride,—   15
Implicitly thy freedom staying thee!

Out of some subway scuttle, cell or loft
A bedlamite° speeds to thy parapets,
Tilting there momently, shrill shirt ballooning,
A jest falls from the speechless caravan.   20

Down Wall, from girder into street noon leaks,
A rip-tooth of the sky's acetylene;
All afternoon the cloud-flown derricks turn . . .
Thy cables breathe the North Atlantic still.

And obscure as that heaven of the Jews,   25
Thy guerdon . . . Accolade thou dost bestow
Of anonymity time cannot raise;
Vibrant reprieve and pardon thou dost show.

———
18 *Bedlamite:* Mad person.

O harp and altar, of the fury fused,
(How could mere toil align thy choiring strings!)   30
Terrific threshold of the prophet's pledge,
Prayer of pariah, and the lover's cry,—

Again the traffic lights that skim thy swift
Unfractioned idiom, immaculate sigh of stars,
Beading thy path—condense eternity: 35
And we have seen night lifted in thine arms.

Under thy shadow by the piers I waited;
Only in darkness is thy shadow clear.
The City's fiery parcels all undone,
Already snow submerges an iron year . . .   40

O Sleepless as the river under thee,
Vaulting the sea, the prairies' dreaming sod,
Unto us lowliest sometime sweep, descend
And of the curveship lend a myth to God.

ROBERT CREELEY   *(b. 1926)*

I Know a Man   *(1957)*

As I sd to my
friend, because I am
always talking,—John, I

sd, which was not his
name, the darkness sur-   5
rounds us, what

can we do against
it, or else, shall we &
why not, buy a goddam big car,

drive, he sd, for   10
christ's sake, look
out where yr going.

COUNTÉE CULLEN   *(1903–1946)*

Incident   *(1925)*

Once riding in old Baltimore,
   Heart-filled, head-filled with glee,
I saw a Baltimorean
   Keep looking straight at me.

Now I was eight and very small,   5
   And he was no whit bigger,
And so I smiled, but he poked out
   His tongue and called me, "Nigger."

I saw the whole of Baltimore
   From May until December;   10
Of all the things that happened there
   That's all that I remember.

E. E. CUMMINGS   *(1894–1962)*

in Just-   *(1923)*

in Just-
spring   when the world is mud-
luscious the little
lame balloonman

whistles   far   and wee   5

and eddieandbill come
running from marbles and
piracies and it's
spring

when the world is puddle-wonderful   10

the queer
old balloonman whistles
far   and   wee
and bettyandisbel come dancing

from hop-scotch and jump-rope and   15

it's
spring
and
    the

        goat-footed   20
balloonMan   whistles
far
and
wee

JAMES DICKEY   *(1923–1997)*

The Performance   *(1967)*

The last time I saw Donald Armstrong
He was staggering oddly off into the sun,
Going down, off the Philippine Islands.
I let my shovel fall, and put that hand
Above my eyes, and moved some way to one side   5
That his body might pass through the sun,

And I saw how well he was not
Standing there on his hands,
On his spindle-shanked forearms balanced,
Unbalanced, with his big feet looming and waving   10
In the great, untrustworthy air
He flew in each night, when it darkened.

Dust fanned in scraped puffs from the earth
Between his arms, and blood turned his face inside out,
To demonstrate its suppleness   15
Of veins, as he perfected his role.
Next day, he toppled his head off
On an island beach to the south,

And the enemy's two-handed sword
Did not fall from anyone's hands   20
At that miraculous sight,
As the head rolled over upon
Its wide-eyed face, and fell
Into the inadequate grave

He had dug for himself, under pressure.   25
Yet I put my flat hand to my eyebrows

Months later, to see him again
In the sun, when I learned how he died,
And imagined him, there,
Come, judged, before his small captors,   30

Doing all his lean tricks to amaze them—
The back somersault, the kip-up—
And at last, the stand on his hands,
Perfect, with his feet together,
His head down, evenly breathing,   35
As the sun poured up from the sea

And the headsmen broke down
In a blaze of tears, in that light
Of the thin, long human frame
Upside down in its own strange joy,   40
And, if some other one had not told him,
Would have cut off the feet

Instead of the head,
And if Armstrong had not presently risen
In kingly, round-shouldered attendance,   45
And then knelt down in himself
Beside his hacked, glittering grave, having done
All things in this life that he could.

EMILY DICKINSON   *(1830–1886)*

Poem 67 (Success is counted sweetest)   *(1878)*

Success is counted sweetest
By those who ne'er succeed.
To comprehend a nectar
Requires sorest need.

Not one of all the purple Host   5
Who took the Flag today
Can tell the definition
So clear of Victory

As he defeated — dying —
On whose forbidden ear   10
The distant strains of triumph
Burst agonized and clear!

Poem 216 (Safe in their Alabaster Chambers)   *(1861)*

Safe in their Alabaster Chambers —
Untouched by Morning —
And untouched by Noon —
Lie the meek members of the Resurrection —
Rafter of Satin — and Roof of Stone!   5

Grand go the Years — in the Crescent — above them —
Worlds scoop their Arcs —
And Firmaments — row —
Diadems — drop — and Doges — surrender —
Soundless as dots — on a Disc of Snow —   10

Poem 241 (I like a look of Agony)   *(1861)*

I like a look of Agony,
Because I know it's true —
Men do not sham Convulsion,
Nor simulate, a Throe —

The Eyes glaze once — and that is Death —   5
Impossible to feign
The Beads upon the Forehead
By homely Anguish strung.

Poem 280 (I felt a Funeral, in my Brain)   *(c. 1861)*

I felt a Funeral, in my Brain,
And Mourners to and fro
Kept treading — treading — till it seemed
That Sense was breaking through —

And when they all were seated,   5
A Service, like a Drum —
Kept beating — beating — till I thought
My Mind was going numb —

And then I heard them lift a Box
And creak across my Soul   10
With those same Boots of Lead, again,
Then Space — began to toll,

As all the Heavens were a Bell,
And Being, but an Ear,
And I, and Silence, some strange Race   15
Wrecked, solitary, here —

And then a Plank in Reason, broke,
And I dropped down, and down —
And hit a World, at every plunge,
And Finished knowing — then —   20

Poem 303 (The Soul selects her own Society)   *(c. 1862)*

The Soul selects her own Society —
Then — shuts the Door —
To her divine Majority —
Present no more —

Unmoved — she notes the Chariots — pausing —   5
At her low Gate —
Unmoved — an Emperor be kneeling
Upon her Mat —

I've known her — from an ample nation —
Choose One —   10
Then — close the Valves of her attention —
Like Stone —

Poem 341 (After great pain, a formal feeling comes)   *(c. 1862)*

After great pain, a formal feeling comes —
The Nerves sit ceremonious, like Tombs —
The stiff Heart questions was it He, that bore,
And Yesterday, or Centuries before?

The Feet, mechanical, go round —   5
Of Ground, or Air, or Ought —
A Wooden way
Regardless grown,
A Quartz contentment, like a stone —

This is the Hour of Lead —   10
Remembered, if outlived,
As Freezing persons, recollect the Snow —
First — Chill — then Stupor — then the letting go —

Poem 435 (Much Madness is divinest Sense)   *(c. 1862)*

Much Madness is divinest Sense —
To a discerning Eye —
Much Sense — the starkest Madness —
'Tis the Majority
In this, as All, prevail —   5
Assent — and you are sane —
Demur — you're straightway dangerous —
And handled with a Chain —

Poem 528 (Mine–by the Right of the White Election)   *(c. 1862)*

Mine — by the Right of the White Election!
Mine — by the Royal Seal!
Mine — by the Sign in the Scarlet prison —
Bars — cannot conceal!

Mine — here — in Vision — and in Veto!   5
Mine — by the Grave's Repeal —
Titled — Confirmed —
Delirious Charter!
Mine — long as Ages steal!

Poem 754 (My Life had stood– a Loaded Gun)   *(c. 1863)*

My Life had stood — a Loaded Gun —
In Corners — till a Day
The Owner passed — identified —
And carried Me away —

And now We roam in Sovereign Woods —   5
And now We hunt the Doe —
And every time I speak for Him —
The Mountains straight reply —

And do I smile, such cordial light
Upon the Valley glow —   10
It is as a Vesuvian face
Had let its pleasure through —

And when at Night — Our good Day done —
I guard My Master's Head —
'Tis better than the Eider-Duck's   15
Deep Pillow — to have shared —

To foe of His — I'm deadly foe —
None stir the second time —
On whom I lay a Yellow Eye —
Or an emphatic Thumb —   20

Though I than He — may longer live
He longer must — than I —
For I have but the power to kill,
Without — the power to die —

Poem 1129 (Tell all the Truth but tell it slant)   *(c. 1868)*

Tell all the Truth but tell it slant —
Success in Circuit lies
Too bright for our infirm Delight
The Truth's superb surprise

As Lightning to the Children eased   5
With explanation kind
The Truth must dazzle gradually
Or every man be blind —

Poem 1763 (Fame is a bee)   *(1898)*

Fame is a bee.
    It has a song —
It has a sting —
    Ah, too, it has a wing.

JOHN DONNE   *(1572–1631)*

The Sun Rising   *(1633)*

    Busy old fool, unruly sun,
        Why dost thou thus
Through windows and through curtains call on us?
Must to thy motions lovers' seasons run?

Saucy, pedantic wretch, go chide   5
   Late schoolboys and sour 'prentices,
  Go tell court huntsmen that the king will ride,
  Call country ants to harvest offices.
Love, all alike, no season knows nor clime,
Nor hours, days, months, which are the rags of time.   10

   Thy beams, so reverend and strong
    Why shouldst thou think?
I could eclipse and cloud them with a wink,
But that I would not lose her sight so long.
   If her eyes have not blinded thine,   15
   Look, and tomorrow late tell me
  Whether both th' Indias of spice and mine
  Be where thou left'st them, or lie here with me;
Ask for those kings whom thou saw'st yesterday,
And thou shalt hear: All here in one bed lay.   20

   She's all states, and all princes I;
    Nothing else is.
Princes do but play us; compared to this,
All honor's mimic, all wealth alchemy.
   Thou, sun, art half as happy as we,   25
   In that the world's contracted thus;
  Thine age asks ease, and since thy duties be
  To warm the world, that's done in warming us.
Shine here to us, and thou art everywhere;
This bed thy center is, these walls thy sphere.   30

from Holy Sonnets   *(1633)*

Sonnet 10

Death, be not proud, though some have callèd thee
Mighty and dreadful, for thou art not so;
For those whom thou think'st thou dost overthrow
Die not, poor Death, nor yet canst thou kill me.
From rest and sleep, which but thy pictures be,   5
Much pleasure; then from thee much more must flow;
And soonest our best men with thee do go,
Rest of their bones and soul's delivery.
Thou'rt slave to fate, chance, kings, and desperate men,
And dost with poison, war, and sickness dwell;   10
And poppy or charms can make us sleep as well
And better than thy stroke; why swell'st thou then?
One short sleep past, we wake eternally,
And Death shall be no more: death, thou shalt die.

RITA DOVE   *(b. 1952)*

Parsley°   *(1983)*

1. The Cane Fields

There is a parrot imitating spring
in the palace, its feathers parsley green.
Out of the swamp the cane appears

to haunt us, and we cut it down. El General
searches for a word; he is all the world   5
there is. Like a parrot imitating spring,

we lie down screaming as rain punches through
and we come up green. We cannot speak an R—
out of the swamp, the cane appears

and then the mountain we call in whispers *Katalina.*   10
The children gnaw their teeth to arrowheads.
There is a parrot imitating spring.

El General has found his word: *perejil.*
Who says it, lives. He laughs, teeth shining
out of the swamp. The cane appears   15

in our dreams, lashed by wind and streaming.
And we lie down. For every drop of blood
there is a parrot imitating spring.
Out of the swamp the cane appears.

2. The Palace

The word the general's chosen is parsley.   20
It is fall, when thoughts turn
to love and death; the general thinks
of his mother, how she died in the fall
and he planted her walking cane at the grave
and it flowered, each spring stolidly forming   25
four-star blossoms. The general

pulls on his boots, he stomps to
her room in the palace, the one without
curtains, the one with a parrot
in a brass ring. As he paces he wonders   30

Parsley: According to Dove, On October 2, 1957, Rafael Trujillo (1891–1961), dictator of the
Dominican Republic, ordered 20,000 blacks killed because they could not pronounce the letter r
in *perejil,* the Spanish word for "parsley."

Who can I kill today. And for a moment
the little knot of screams
is still. The parrot, who has traveled

all the way from Australia in an ivory
cage, is, coy as a widow, practising   35
spring. Ever since the morning
his mother collapsed in the kitchen
while baking skull-shaped candies
for the Day of the Dead, the general
has hated sweets. He orders pastries   40
brought up for the bird; they arrive

dusted with sugar on a bed of lace.
The knot in his throat starts to twitch;
he sees his boots the first day in battle
splashed with mud and urine   45
as a soldier falls at his feet amazed—
how stupid he looked!—at the sound
of artillery. *I never thought it would sing*
the soldier said, and died. Now

the general sees the fields of sugar   50
cane, lashed by rain and streaming.
He sees his mother's smile, the teeth
gnawed to arrowheads. He hears
the Haitians sing without R's
as they swing the great machetes: 55
Katalina, they sing, *Katalina,*

mi madle, mi amol en muelte. God knows
his mother was no stupid woman; she
could roll an R like a queen. Even
a parrot can roll an R! In the bare room   60
the bright feathers arch in a parody
of greenery, as the last pale crumbs
disappear under the blackened tongue. Someone

calls out his name in a voice
so like his mother's, a startled tear   65
splashes the tip of his right boot.
My mother, my love in death.
The general remembers the tiny green sprigs
men of his village wore in their capes
to honor the birth of a son. He will   70
order many, this time, to be killed

for a single, beautiful word.

PAUL LAURENCE DUNBAR   *(1872–1906)*

Sympathy   *(1899)*

I know what the caged bird feels, alas!
　When the sun is bright on the upland slopes;
When the wind stirs soft through the springing grass,
And the river flows like a stream of glass;
　When the first bird sings and the first bud opes,   5
And the faint perfume from its chalice steals—
I know what the caged bird feels!

I know why the caged bird beats his wing
　Till its blood is red on the cruel bars;
For he must fly back to his perch and cling   10
When he fain would be on the bough a-swing;
　And a pain still throbs in the old, old scars
And they pulse again with a keener sting—
I know why he beats his wing!

I know why the caged bird sings, ah me,   15
　When his wing is bruised and his bosom sore,—
When he beats his bars and he would be free;
It is not a carol of joy or glee,
　But a prayer that he sends from his heart's deep core,
But a plea, that upward to Heaven he flings—   20
I know why the caged bird sings!

ROBERT DUNCAN   *(1919–1988)*

Often I Am Permitted to Return to a Meadow   *(1960)*

as if it were a scene made-up by the mind,
that is not mine, but is a made place,

that is mine, it is so near to the heart,
an eternal pasture folded in all thought
so that there is a hall therein   5

that is a made place, created by light
wherefrom the shadows that are forms fall.

Wherefrom fall all architectures I am
I say are likenesses of the First Beloved
whose flowers are flames lit to the Lady.   10

She it is Queen Under The Hill
whose hosts are a disturbance of words within words
that is a field folded.

It is only a dream of the grass blowing
east against the source of the sun   15
in an hour before the sun's going down

whose secret we see in a children's game
of ring a round of roses told.

Often I am permitted to return to a meadow
as if it were a given property of the mind   20
that certain bounds hold against chaos,

that is a place of first permission,
everlasting omen of what is.

T. S. Eliot *(1888–1965)*

The Love Song of J. Alfred Prufrock   *(1917)*

S'io credesse che mia risposta fosse
A persona che mai tornasse al mondo,
Questa fiamma staria senza piu scosse.
Ma perciocche giammai di questo fondo
Non torno vivo alcun, s'i'odo il vero,
Senza tema d'infamia ti rispondo.

Let us go then, you and I,
When the evening is spread out against the sky
Like a patient etherized upon a table;
Let us go, through certain half-deserted streets,
The muttering retreats   5
Of restless nights in one-night cheap hotels
And sawdust restaurants with oyster-shells:
Streets that follow like a tedious argument
Of insidious intent
To lead you to an overwhelming question . . .   10
Oh, do not ask, "What is it?"
Let us go and make our visit.

In the room the women come and go
Talking of Michelangelo.

The yellow fog that rubs its back upon the window-panes   15
The yellow smoke that rubs its muzzle on the window-panes

Licked its tongue into the corners of the evening,
Lingered upon the pools that stand in drains,
Let fall upon its back the soot that falls from chimneys,
Slipped by the terrace, made a sudden leap,   20
And seeing that it was a soft October night,
Curled once about the house, and fell asleep.

And indeed there will be time
For the yellow smoke that slides along the street,
Rubbing its back upon the window-panes;   25
There will be time, there will be time
To prepare a face to meet the faces that you meet;
There will be time to murder and create,
And time for all the works and days of hands
That lift and drop a question on your plate;   30
Time for you and time for me,
And time yet for a hundred indecisions,
And for a hundred visions and revisions,
Before the taking of a toast and tea.

In the room the women come and go   35
Talking of Michelangelo.

And indeed there will be time
To wonder, "Do I dare?" and, "Do I dare?"
Time to turn back and descend the stair,
With a bald spot in the middle of my hair—   40
[They will say: "How his hair is growing thin!"]
My morning coat, my collar mounting firmly to the chin,
My necktie rich and modest, but asserted by a simple pin—
[They will say: "But how his arms and legs are thin!"]
Do I dare   45
Disturb the universe?
In a minute there is time
For decisions and revisions which a minute will reverse.

For I have known them all already, known them all—
Have know the evenings, mornings, afternoons,   50
I have measured out my life with coffee spoons;
I know the voices dying with a dying fall
Beneath the music from a farther room.
    So how should I presume?

And I have known the eyes already, known them all—   55
The eyes that fix you in a formulated phrase,
And when I am formulated, sprawling on a pin,
When I am pinned and wriggling on the wall,

Then how should I begin
To spit out all the butt-ends of my days and ways?   60
    And how should I presume?

And I have known the arms already, known them all—
Arms that are braceleted and white and bare
[But in the lamplight, downed with light brown hair!]
Is it perfume from a dress   65
That makes me so digress?
Arms that lie along a table, or wrap about a shawl.
    And should I then presume?
    And how should I begin?

*   *   *   *

Shall I say, I have gone at dusk through narrow streets   70
And watched the smoke the rises from the pipes
Of lonely men in shirt-sleeves, leaning out of windows? . . .

I should have been a pair of ragged claws
Scuttling across the floors of silent seas.

*   *   *   *

And the afternoon, the evening, sleeps so peacefully!   75
Smoothed by long fingers,
Asleep . . . tired . . . or it malingers,
Stretched on the floor, here beside you and me.
Should I, after tea and cakes and ices,
Have the strength to force the moment to its crisis?   80
But though I have wept and fasted, wept and prayed,
Though I have seen my head [grown slightly bald] brought in upon a
    platter,
I am no prophet—and here's no great matter;
I have seen the moment of my greatness flicker,
And I have seen the eternal Footman hold my coat, and snicker,   85
And in short, I was afraid.

And would it have been worth it, after all,
After the cups, the marmalade, the tea,
Among the porcelain, among some talk of you and me,
Would it have been worth while,   90
To have bitten off the matter with a smile,
To have squeezed the universe into a ball
To roll it toward some overwhelming question,
To say: "I am Lazarus, come from the dead,
Come back to tell you all, I shall tell you all"—   95
If one, settling a pillow by her head,
    Should say: "That is not what I meant at all.
    That is not it, at all."

And would it have been worth it, after all,
Would it have been worth while,   100
After the sunsets and the dooryards and the sprinkled streets,
After the novels, after the teacups, after the skirts that trail along the floor—
And this, and so much more?—
It is impossible to say just what I mean!
But as if a magic lantern threw the nerves in patterns on a screen: 105
Would it have been worth while
If one, settling a pillow or throwing off a shawl,
And turning toward the window, should say:
        "That is not it at all,
        That is not what I meant, at all."   110

*   *   *   *

No! I am not Prince Hamlet, nor was meant to be;
Am an attendant lord, one that will do
To swell a progress, start a scene or two,
Advise the prince; no doubt, an easy tool,
Deferential, glad to be of use,   115
Politic, cautious, and meticulous;
Full of high sentence, but a bit obtuse;
At times, indeed, almost ridiculous—
Almost at times, the Fool.

I grow old . . . I grow old . . .   120
I shall wear the bottoms of my trousers rolled.

Shall I part my hair behind? Do I dare to eat a peach?
I shall wear white flannel trousers, and walk upon the beach.
I have heard the mermaids singing, each to each.

I do not think that they will sing to me.   125

I have seen them riding seaward on the waves
Combing the white hair of the waves blown back
When the wind blows the water white and black.

We have lingered in the chambers of the sea
By sea-girls wreathed with seaweed red and brown   130
Till human voices wake us, and we drown.

Queen Elizabeth I   *(1533–1603)*

When I Was Fair and Young   *(c. 1585)*

When I was fair and young, then favor graced me.
Of many was I sought their mistress for to be,

But I did scorn them all and answered them therefore:
Go, go, go, seek some other where, importune me no more.

How many weeping eyes I made to pine in woe,   5
How many sighing hearts I have not skill to show,
But I the prouder grew and still this spake therefore:
Go, go, go, seek some other where, importune me no more.

Then spake fair Venus' son°, that proud victorious boy,
Saying: You dainty dame, for that you be so coy,   10
I will so pluck your plumes as you shall say no more:
Go, go, go, seek some other where, importune me no more.

As soon as he had said, such change grew in my breast
That neither night nor day I could take any rest.
Wherefore I did repent that I had said before: 15
Go, go, go, seek some other where, importune me no more.

RALPH WALDO EMERSON   *(1803–1882)*

Concord Hymn   *(1837)*

> Sung at the completion of the Battle Monument, July 4, 1837

By the rude bridge that arched the flood,
   Their flag to April's breeze unfurled,
Here once the embattled farmers stood
   And fired the shot heard round the world.

The foe long since in silence slept;   5
   Alike the conqueror silent sleeps;
And Time the ruined bridge has swept
   Down the dark stream which seaward creeps.

On this green bank, by this soft stream,
   We set to-day a votive stone;   10
That memory may their deed redeem,
   When, like our sires, our sons are gone.

Spirit, that made those heroes dare
   To die, and leave their children free,
Bid Time and Nature gently spare   15
   That shaft we raise to them and thee.

---

9 *Venus' son:* Cupid.

CAROLYN FORCHÉ   *(b. 1950)*

The Testimony of Light   *(1994)*

Our life is a fire dampened, or a fire shut up in stone.
          –JACOB BOEHME, DE INCARNATIONE VERBI

Outside everything visible and invisible a blazing maple.
Daybreak: a seam at the curve of the world. The trousered legs of the
     women shimmered.
They held their arms in front of them like ghosts.

The coal bones of the house clinked in a kimono of smoke.   5
An attention hovered over the dream where the world had been.

For if Hiroshima in the morning, after the bomb has fallen,
     is like a dream, one must ask whose dream it is.

Must understand how not to speak would carry it with us.
With bones put into rice bowls.   10
While the baby crawled over its dead mother seeking milk.

Muga-muchu: without self, without center. Thrown up in the sky by a wind.

The way back is lost, the one obsession.
The worst is over.
The worst is yet to come.   15

ROBERT FROST   *(1874–1963)*

The Road Not Taken   *(1916)*

Two roads diverged in a yellow wood,
And sorry I could not travel both
And be one traveler, long I stood
And looked down one as far as I could
To where it bent in the undergrowth;   5

Then took the other, as just as fair,
And having perhaps the better claim,
Because it was grassy and wanted wear;
Though as for that, the passing there
Had worn them really about the same,   10

And both that morning equally lay
In leaves no step had trodden black.
Oh, I kept the first for another day!
Yet knowing how way leads on to way,
I doubted if I should ever come back.   15

I shall be telling this with a sigh
Somewhere ages and ages hence:
Two roads diverged in a wood, and I—
I took the one less traveled by,
And that has made all the difference.   20

Stopping by Woods on a Snowy Evening   *(1923)*

Whose woods these are I think I know.
His house is in the village, though;
He will not see me stopping here
To watch his woods fill up with snow.

My little horse must think it queer   5
To stop without a farmhouse near
Between the woods and frozen lake
The darkest evening of the year.

He gives his harness bells a shake
To ask if there is some mistake.   10
The only other sound's the sweep
Of easy wind and downy flake.

The woods are lovely, dark, and deep,
But I have promises to keep,
And miles to go before I sleep,   15
And miles to go before I sleep.

Design   *(1936)*

I found a dimpled spider, fat and white,
On a white heal-all, holding up a moth
Like a white piece of rigid satin cloth—
Assorted characters of death and blight
Mixed ready to begin the morning right,   5
Like the ingredients of a witches' broth—
A snow-drop spider, a flower like a froth,
And dead wings carried like a paper kite.

What had that flower to do with being white,
The wayside blue and innocent heal-all?   10
What brought the kindred spider to that height,
Then steered the white moth thither in the night?
What but design of darkness to appall?—
If design govern in a thing so small.

Robert Graves   *(1895–1985)*

The White Goddess   *(1948)*

All saints revile her, and all sober men
Ruled by the God Apollo's golden mean—
In scorn of which we sailed to find her
In distant regions likeliest to hold her
Whom we desired above all things to know,   5
Sister of the mirage and echo.

It was a virtue not to stay,
To go our headstrong and heroic way
Seeking her out at the volcano's head,
Among pack ice, or where the track had faded   10
Beyond the cavern of the seven sleepers:
Whose broad high brow was white as any leper's,
Whose eyes were blue, with rowan-berry lips,
With hair curled honey-coloured to white hips.

Green sap of Spring in the young wood a-stir   15
Will celebrate the Mountain Mother,
And every song-bird shout awhile for her;
But we are gifted, even in November
Rawest of seasons, with so huge a sense
Of her nakedly worn magnificence   20
We forget cruelty and past betrayal,
Heedless of where the next bright bolt may fall.

Thomas Hardy   *(1840–1928)*

Channel Firing   *(1914)*

That night your great guns, unawares,
Shook all our coffins as we lay,

And broke the chancel window-squares,
We thought it was the Judgment-day

And sat upright. While drearisome   5
Arose the howl of wakened hounds:
The mouse let fall the altar-crumb,
The worms drew back into the mounds,

The glebe cow drooled. Till God called "No;
It's gunnery practice out at sea   10
Just as before you went below;
The world is as it used to be:

"All nations striving strong to make
Red war yet redder. Mad as hatters
They do no more for Christés sake   15
Than you who are helpless in such matters.

"That this is not the judgment-hour
For some of them's a blessed thing,
For if it were they'd have to scour
Hell's floor for so much threatening . . .   20

"Ha, ha. It will be warmer when
I blow the trumpet (if indeed
I ever do; for you are men,
And rest eternal sorely need)."

So down we lay again. "I wonder,   25
Will the world ever saner be,"
Said, one "than when He sent us under
In our indifferent century!"

And many a skeleton shook his head.
"Instead of preaching forty year,"   30
My neighbor Parson Thirdly said,
"I wish I had stuck to pipes and beer."

Again the guns disturbed the hour,
Roaring their readiness to avenge,
As far inland as Stourton Tower,   35
And Camelot, and starlit Stonehenge.

ROBERT HAYDEN   *(1913–1980)*

Those Winter Sundays   *(1962)*

Sundays too my father got up early
and put his clothes on in the blueblack cold,
then with cracked hands that ached
from labor in the weekday weather made
banked fires blaze. No one ever thanked him.   5

I'd wake and hear the cold splintering, breaking.
When the rooms were warm, he'd call,
and slowly I would rise and dress,
fearing the chronic angers of that house,

Speaking indifferently to him,   10
who had driven out the cold
and polished my good shoes as well.
What did I know, what did I know
of love's austere and lonely offices?

Paul Laurence Dunbar   *(1978)*

For Herbert Martin

   We lay red roses on his grave,
speak sorrowfully of him
as if he were but newly dead

   And so it seems to us
this raw spring day, though years   5
before we two were born he was
   a young poet dead.

   Poet of our youth—
his "cri du coeur" our own,
his verses "in a broken tongue"   10

   beguiling as an elder
brother's antic lore.
Their sad blackface lilt and croon
   survive him like

   The happy look (subliminal   15
of victim, dying man)
a summer's tintypes hold.

The roses flutter in the wind;
we weight their stems
with stones, then drive away.   20

GEORGE HERBERT   *(1593–1633)*

The Altar   *(1633)*

A broken ALTAR, Lord, thy servant rears,
Made of a heart, and cemented with tears:
   Whose parts are as thy hand did frame;
   No workman's tool hath touched the same.
      A   HEART   alone   5
      Is such a stone,
      As   nothing but
      Thy power doth cut.
      Wherefore each part
      Of my hard heart   10
      Meets in this frame,
      To praise thy Name:
   That, if I chance to hold my peace,
   These stones to praise thee may not cease.
Oh let thy blessed SACRIFICE be mine,   15
And sanctify this ALTAR to be thine.

ROBERT HERRICK   *(1591–1674)*

The Vine   *(1648)*

I dreamed this mortal part of mine
Was metamorphosed to a vine,
Which crawling one and every way
Enthralled my dainty Lucia.
Methought her long small legs and thighs   5
I with my tendrils did surprise;
Her belly, buttocks, and her waist
By my soft nervelets were embraced.
About her head I writhing hung,
And with rich clusters (hid among   10
The leaves) her temples I behung,
So that my Lucia seemed to me
Young Bacchus ravished by his tree.
My curls about her neck did crawl,

And arms and hands they did enthrall,   15
So that she could not freely stir
(All parts there made one prisoner).
But when I crept with leaves to hide
Those parts which maids keep unespied,
Such fleeting pleasures there I took   20
That with the fancy I awoke;
And found (ah me!) this flesh of mine
More like a stock than like a vine.

The Pillar of Fame   *(1648)*

Fame's pillar here at last we set,
Out-during marble, brass or jet;
   Charmed and enchanted so
   As to withstand the blow
      O f   o v e r t h r o w ;   5
      Nor   shall   the   seas,
      O r   o u t r a g e s
      Of storms, o'erbear
      What   we   uprear;
      Tho' kingdoms fall,   10
   This pillar never shall
   Decline or waste at all;
But stand for ever by his own
Firm and well-fixed foundation.

GARRETT KAORU HONGO   *(b. 1951)*

Yellow Light   *(1982)*

One arm hooked around the frayed strap
of a tar-black patent-leather purse,
the other cradling something for dinner:
fresh bunches of spinach from a J-Town *yaoya*,
sides of split Spanish mackerel from Alviso's,   5
maybe a loaf of Langendorf; she steps
off the hissing bus at Olympic and Fig,
begins the three-block climb up the hill,
passing gangs of schoolboys playing war,
Japs against Japs, Chicanas chalking sidewalks   10
with the holy double-yoked crosses of hopscotch,
and the Korean grocer's wife out for a stroll
around this neighborhood of Hawaiian apartments

just starting to steam with cooking
and the anger of young couples coming home   15
from work, yelling at kids, flicking on
TV sets for the Wednesday Night Fights.

If it were May, hydrangeas and jacaranda
flowers in the streetside trees would be
blooming through the smog of late spring.   20
Wisteria in Masuda's front yard would be
shaking out the long tresses of its purple hair.
Maybe mosquitoes, moths, a few orange butterflies
settling on the lattice of monkey flowers
tangled in chain-link fences by the trash.   25

But this is October, and Los Angeles
seethes like a billboard under twilight.
From used-car lots and the movie houses uptown,
long silver sticks of light probe the sky.
From the Miracle Mile, whole freeways away,   30
a brilliant fluorescence breaks out
and makes war with the dim squares
of yellow kitchen light winking on
in all the side streets of the Barrio.

She climbs up the two flights of flagstone   35
stairs to 201-B, the spikes of her high heels
clicking like kitchen knives on a cutting board,
props the groceries against the door,
fishes through memo pads, a compact,
empty packs of chewing gum, and finds her keys.   40

The moon then, cruising from behind
a screen of eucalyptus across the street,
covers everything, everything in sight,
in a heavy light like yellow onions.

GERARD MANLEY HOPKINS *(1844–1889)*

Pied Beauty   *(1877)*

Glory be to God for dappled things—
    For skies of couple-color as a brinded cow;
        For rose-moles all in stipple upon trout that swim;
Fresh-firecoal chestnut-falls; finches' wings;
    Landscape plotted and pieced—fold, fallow, and plough;   5
        And áll trádes, their gear and tackle and trim.

All things counter, original, spare, strange;
   Whatever is fickle, freckled (who knows how?)
     With swift, slow; sweet, sour; adazzle, dim;
He fathers-forth whose beauty is past change: 10
            Praise him.

Thou Art Indeed Just, Lord   (1889)

Justus quidem tu es, Domine, si disputem tecum:
verum justa loquar ad te: Quare
via impiorum prosperatur?

Thou art indeed just, Lord, if I contend
With thee; but, sir, so what I plead is just.
Why do sinners' ways prosper? and why must
Disappointment all I endeavour end?
   Wert thou my enemy, O thou my friend,   5
How wouldst thou worse, I wonder, than thou dost
Defeat, thwart me? Oh, the sots and thralls of lust
Do in spare hours more thrive than I that spend,
Sir, life upon thy cause. See, banks and brakes
Now, leavèd how thick! lacèd they are again   10
With fretty chervil,° look, and fresh wind shakes
Them; birds build—but not I build; no, but strain,
Time's eunuch, and not breed one work that wakes.
Mine, O thou lord of life, send my roots rain.

A. E. HOUSMAN   *(1859–1936)*

To an Athlete Dying Young   (1896)

The time you won your town the race
We chaired you through the market-place;
Man and boy stood cheering by,
And home we brought you shoulder-high.

To-day, the road all runners come,   5
Shoulder-high we bring you home,
And set you at your threshold down,
Townsman of a stiller town.

Smart lad, to slip betimes away
From fields where glory does not stay   10

---

11 *chervil:* Herb, parsley.

And early though the laurel grows
It withers quicker than the rose.

Eyes the shady night has shut
Cannot see the record cut,
And silence sounds no worse than cheers   15
After earth has stopped the ears:

Now you will not swell the rout
Of lads that wore their honors out,
Runners whom renown outran
And the name died before the man.   20

So set, before its echoes fade,
The fleet foot on the sill of shade,
And hold to the low lintel up
The still-defended challenge-cup.

And round that early-laurelled head   25
Will flock to gaze the strengthless dead,
And find unwithered on its curls
The garland briefer than a girl's.

ANDREW HUDGINS   *(b. 1951)*

Supper   *(1998)*

We shared our supper with the flames,
or the shadow of the flames—each candle
in the light of the other casting shadows
across the table, dark flickers of a brilliant flicker,
and the grain of rubbed pine swirled with light   5
and shadow, shoaled and deepened in the soft
inconstancy of candlelight.
                            With every gesture
the bright flames flinched and then corrected.
Your shrug, my laugh,   10
                        my nod, your tilting head
—conveyed on air—invited their response.
They bowed their heads, then snapped upright—
a ripple in the gases' fluted yellow silk,
blue silk, transparent silk. I yearned   15
to touch the rich untouchable fabric, and finger
the sheen beneath its scorching,

but when I reached, it leaned away
decorously, and I did not pursue it, knowing.

But the dark flames reached out, licked the meat,   20
licked the plate, the fork, and the knife edge.
They licked our faces and our lips—a dry unfelt tongue,
the shadow of the flame consuming nothing,
but stroking everything as if it could
grasp, hold, take, devour. How ardently it hungers   25
because it cannot have us.
How chaste the bright flame, because it can.

LANGSTON HUGHES *(1902–1967)* `CD-ROM`

Bad Luck Card   *(1927)*

Cause you don't love me
Is awful, awful hard.
Gypsy done showed me
My bad luck card.

There ain't no good left   5
In this world for me.
Gypsy done tole me—
Unlucky as can be.

I don't know what
Po' weary me can do.
Gypsy says I'd kill my self   10
If I was you.

Harlem Sweeties   *(1942)*

Have you dug the spill
Of Sugar Hill?
Cast your gims
On this sepia thrill:
Brown sugar lassie,   5
Caramel treat,
Honey-gold baby
Sweet enough to eat.
Peach-skinned girlie,
Coffee and cream,   10

Chocolate darling
Out of a dream.
Walnut tinted
Or cocoa brown,
Pomegranate-lipped   15
Pride of the town.
Rich cream-colored
To plum-tinted black,
Feminine sweetness
In Harlem's no lack.   20
Glow of the quince
To blush of the rose.
Persimmon bronze
To cinnamon toes.
Blackberry cordial,   25
Virginia Dare wine—
All those sweet colors
Flavor Harlem of mine!
Walnut or cocoa,
Let me repeat: 30
Caramel, brown sugar,
A chocolate treat.
Molasses taffy,
Coffee and cream,
Licorice, clove, cinnamon   35
To a honey-brown dream.
Ginger, wine-gold,
Persimmon, blackberry,
All through the spectrum
Harlem girls vary—   40
So if you want to know beauty's
Rainbow-sweet thrill,
Stroll down luscious,
Delicious, *fine* Sugar Hill.

Harlem   *(1951)*

What happens to a dream deferred?

Does it dry up
like a raisin in the sun?
Or fester like a sore—
And then run?   5
Does it stink like rotten meat?
Or crust and sugar over—
like a syrupy sweet?

Maybe it just sags
like a heavy load.   10

Or does it explode?

Café: 3 A.M.   *(1951)*

Detectives from the vice squad
with weary sadistic eyes
spotting fairies.
   Degenerates,
   some folks say.   5

   But God, Nature,
   or somebody
   made them that way.

Police lady or Lesbian
over there?   10
   Where?

RANDALL JARRELL   *(1914–1965)*

The Death of the Ball Turret Gunner   *(1945)*

From my mother's sleep I fell into the State,
And I hunched in its belly till my wet fur froze.
Six miles from earth, loosed from its dream of life,
I woke to black flak and the nightmare fighters.
When I died they washed me out of the turret with a hose.   5

HA JIN   *(b. 1956)*

In New York City   *(1996)*

In the golden rain
I plod along Madison Avenue,
loaded with words.
They are from a page
that shows the insignificance   5
of a person to a tribe,
just as a hive keeps thriving
while a bee is lost.

On my back the words
are gnawing and gnawing   10
till they enter into my bones—
I become another man,
alone, wandering,
no longer dreaming of luck
or meeting a friend.   15

No wisdom shines
like the neon and traffic lights,
but there are words as true as
the money eyes, the yellow cabs,
the fat pigeons on the sills.   20

BEN JONSON   *(1572–1637)*

Song: To Celia (II)   *(1616)*

Drink to me only with thine eyes,
And I will pledge with mine;
Or leave a kiss but in the cup,
And I'll not look for wine.
The thirst that from the soul doth rise,   5
Doth ask a drink divine:
But might I of Jove's nectar sup,
I would not change for thine.
I sent thee late a rosy wreath,
Not so much honoring thee,   10
As giving it a hope, that there
It could not withered be.
But thou thereon did'st only breathe,
And sent'st it back to me;
Since when it grows and smells, I swear,   15
Not of itself, but thee.

Slow, Slow, Fresh Fount°   *(1600)*

Slow, slow, fresh fount, keep time with my salt tears;
Yet slower, yet, O faintly, gentle springs!
List to the heavy part the music bears,
Woe weeps out her division, when she sings.
    Droop herbs and flowers;   5
    Fall grief in showers;

Slow, Slow, Fresh Fount: Spoken by Echo for Narcissus in Jonson's play *Cynthia's Revels* (1600).

Our beauties are not ours. O, I could still,
   Like melting snow upon some craggy hill,
      Drop, drop, drop, drop,
Since nature's pride is now a withered daffodil.   10

CAROLYN KIZER   *(b. 1925)*

Semele° Recycled   *(1984)*

After you left me forever,
I was broken into pieces,
and all the pieces flung into the river.
Then the legs crawled ashore
and aimlessly wandered the dusty cow-track.   5
They became, for a while, a simple roadside shrine:
A tiny table set up between the thighs
held a dusty candle, weed, and field flower chains
placed reverently there by children and old women.
My knees were hung with tin triangular medals   10
to cure all forms of hysterical disease.

After I died forever in the river,
my torso floated, bloated in the stream,
catching on logs or stones among the eddies.
White water foamed around it, then dislodged it;   15
after a whirlwind trip, it bumped ashore.
A grizzled old man who scavenged along the banks
had already rescued my arms and put them by,
knowing everything has its uses, sooner or later.

When he found my torso, he called it his canoe,   20
and, using my arms as paddles,
he rowed me up and down the scummy river.
When catfish nibbled my fingers, he scooped them up
and blessed his reusable bait.
Clumsy but serviceable, that canoe!   25
The trail of blood that was its wake
attracted the carp and eels, and the river turtle,
easily landed, dazed by my tasty red.

A young lad found my head among the rushes
and placed it on a dry stone.   30
He carefully combed my hair with a bit of shell

Semele: Mother of Dionysus and beloved of Zeus.

and set small offerings before it
which the birds and rats obligingly stole at night,
so it seemed I ate.
And the breeze wound through my mouth and empty sockets   35
so my lungs would sigh, and my dead tongue mutter.

Attached to my throat like a sacred necklace
was a circlet of small snails.
Soon the villagers came to consult my oracular head
with its waterweed crown.   40
Seers found occupation, interpreting sighs,
and their papyrus rolls accumulated.

Meanwhile, young boys retrieved my eyes
they used for marbles in a simple game
—till somebody's pretty sister snatched at them   45
and set them, for luck, in her bridal diadem.
Poor girl! When her future groom caught sight of her,
all eyes, he crossed himself in horror,
and stumbled away in haste
through her dowered meadows.   50

What then of my heart and organs,
my sacred slit
which loved you best of all?
They were caught in a fisherman's net
and tossed at night into a pen for swine.   55
But they shone so by moonlight that the sows stampeded,
trampled one another in fear, to get away.
And the fisherman's wife, who had thirteen living children
and was contemptuous of holy love,
raked the rest of me onto the compost heap.   60

Then in their various places and helpful functions,
the altar, oracle, offal, canoe and oars
learned the wild rumor of your return.
The altar leapt up, and ran to the canoe,
scattering candle grease and wilted grasses.   65
Arms sprang to their sockets, blind hands with nibbled nails
groped their way, aided by loud lamentation,
to the bed of the bride, snatched up those unlucky eyes
from her discarded veil and diadem,
and rammed them home. Oh, what a bright day it was!   70
This empty body danced on the riverbank.
Hollow, it called and searched among the fields
for those parts that steamed and simmered in the sun,
and never would have found them.

But then your great voice rang out under the skies   75
my name!—and all those private names
for the parts and places that had loved you best.
And they stirred in their nest of hay and dung.
The distraught old ladies chasing their lost altar,
and the seers pursuing my skull, their lost employment,   80
and the tumbling boys, who wanted the magic marbles,
and the runaway groom, and the fisherman's thirteen children
set up such a clamor, with their cries of "Miracle!"
that our two bodies met like a thunderclap
in midday—right at the corner of that wretched field   85
with its broken fenceposts and startled, skinny cattle.
We fell in a heap on the compost heap
and all our loving parts made love at once,
while the bystanders cheered and prayed and hid their eyes
and then went decently about their business.   90

And here it is, moonlight again; we've bathed in the river
and are sweet and wholesome once more.
We kneel side by side in the sand;
we worship each other in whispers.
But the inner parts remember fermenting hay,   95
the comfortable odor of dung, the animal incense,
and passion, its bloody labor,
its birth and rebirth and decay.

YUSEF KOMUNYAKAA   *(b. 1947)*

Blackberries   *(1989)*

They left my hands like a printer's
Or thief's before a police blotter
& pulled me into early morning's
Terrestrial sweetness, so thick
The damp ground was consecrated   5
Where they fell among a garland of thorns.

Although I could smell old lime-covered
History, at ten I'd still hold out my hands
& berries fell into them. Eating from one
& filling a half gallon with the other,   10
I ate the mythology & dreamt
Of pies & cobbler, almost

Needful as forgiveness. My bird dog Spot
Eyed blue jays & thrashers. The mud frogs

In rich blackness, hid from daylight. 15
An hour later, beside City Limits Road
I balanced a gleaming can in each hand,
Limboed between worlds, repeating *one dollar*.

The big blue car made me sweat.
Wintertime crawled out of the windows. 20
When I leaned closer I saw the boy
& girl my age, in the wide back seat
Smirking, & it was then I remembered my fingers
Burning with thorns among berries too ripe to touch.

MAXINE KUMIN *(b. 1925)*

Woodchucks *(1972)*

Gassing the woodchucks didn't turn out right.
The knockout bomb from the Feed and Grain Exchange
was featured as merciful, quick at the bone
and the case we had against them was airtight,
both exits shoehorned shut with puddingstone, 5
but they had a sub-sub-basement out of range.

Next morning they turned up again, no worse
for the cyanide than we for our cigarettes
and state-store Scotch, all of us up to scratch.
They brought down the marigolds as a matter of course 10
and then took over the vegetable patch
nipping the broccoli shoots, beheading the carrots.

The food from our mouths, I said, righteously thrilling
to the feel of the .22, the bullets' neat noses.
I, a lapsed pacifist fallen from grace 15
puffed with Darwinian pieties for killing,
now drew a bead on the littlest woodchuck's face.
He died down in the everbearing roses.

Ten minutes later I dropped the mother. She
flipflopped in the air and fell, her needle teeth 20
still hooked in a leaf of early Swiss chard.
Another baby next. O one-two-three
the murderer inside me rose up hard,
the hawkeye killer came on stage forthwith.

There's one chuck left. Old wily fellow, he keeps 25
me cocked and ready day after day after day.

All night I hunt his humped-up form. I dream
I sight along the barrel in my sleep.
If only they'd all consented to die unseen
gassed underground the quiet Nazi way.   30

Philip Larkin   *(1922–1985)*

Talking in Bed   *(1964)*

Talking in bed ought to be easiest,
Lying together there goes back so far,
An emblem of two people being honest.

Yet more and more time passes silently.
Outside, the wind's incomplete unrest   5
Builds and disperses clouds about the sky,

And dark towns heap up on the horizon.
None of this cares for us. Nothing shows why
At this unique distance from isolation

It becomes still more difficult to find   10
Words at once true and kind,
Or not untrue and not unkind.

D. H. Lawrence   *(1885–1930)*

Bavarian Gentians   *(1932)*

Not every man has gentians in his house
in Soft September, at slow, sad Michaelmas.

Bavarian gentians, big and dark, only dark
darkening the daytime, torch-like with the smoking blueness of Pluto's
     gloom,
ribbed and torch-like, with their blaze of darkness spread blue   5
down flattening into points, flattened under the sweep of white day
torch-flower of the blue-smoking darkness, Pluto's dark-blue daze,
black lamps from the halls of Dis,° burning dark blue,
giving off darkness, blue darkness, as Demeter's pale lamps give off light,
lead me then, lead the way.   10

---

8 *Dis:* Hades.

Reach me a gentian, give me a torch!
let me guide myself with the blue, forked torch of this flower
down the darker and darker stairs, where blue is darkened on blueness
even where Persephone goes, just now, from the frosted September
to the sightless realm where darkness is awake upon the dark　　　　15
and Persephone herself is but a voice
or a darkness invisible enfolded in the deeper dark
of the arms Plutonic, and pierced with the passion of dense gloom,
among the splendour of torches of darkness, shedding darkness on the
　　lost bride and her groom.

EMMA LAZARUS *(1849–1887)*

The New Colossus°　　　　　　　　　　　　　　*(1888)*

Not like the brazen giant of Greek fame,
With conquering limbs astride from land to land;
Here at our sea-washed, sunset gates shall stand
A mighty woman with a torch, whose flame
Is the imprisoned lightning, and her name　　　　5
Mother of Exiles. From her beacon-hand
Glows world-wide welcome; her mild eyes command
The air-bridged harbor that twin cities frame.
"Keep, ancient lands, your storied pomp!" cries she
With silent lips. "Give me your tired, your poor,　　　　10
Your huddled masses yearning to breathe free,
The wretched refuse of your teeming shore.
Send these, the homeless, tempest-tost to me,
I lift my lamp beside the golden door!"

MICHAEL LONGLEY *(b. 1939)*

The Linen Industry　　　　　　　　　　　　　　*(1979)*

Pulling up flax after the blue flowers have fallen
And laying our handfuls in the peaty water
To rot these grasses to the bone, or building stooks
That recall the skirts of an invisible dancer,

We become a part of the linen industry　　　　5
And follow its processes to the grubby town

The New Colossus: Engraved on the pedestal of the Statue of Liberty.

Where fields are compacted into window-boxes
And there is little room among the big machines.

But even in our attic under the skylight
We make love on a bleach green, the whole meadow   10
Draped with material turning white in the sun
As though snow reluctant to melt were our attire.

What's passion but a battering of stubborn stalks,
Then a gentle combing out of fibres like hair
And a weaving of these into christening robes,   15
Into garments for a marriage or funeral?

Since it's like a bereavement once the labour's done
To find ourselves last workers in a dying trade,
Let flax be our matchmaker, our undertaker,
The provider of sheets for whatever the bed—   20

And be shy of your breasts in the presence of death,
Say that you look more beautiful in linen
Wearing white petticoats, the bow on your bodice
A butterfly attending the embroidered flowers.

Audre Lorde   *(1934–1992)*

Coal   *(1976)*

I
is the total black, being spoken
from the earth's inside.
There are many kinds of open
how a diamond comes into a knot of flame   5
how sound comes into a word, colored
by who pays what for speaking.

Some words are open like a diamond
on glass windows
singing out within the passing crash of sun   10
Then there are words like stapled wagers
in a perforated book—buy and sign and tear apart—
and come whatever wills all chances
the stub remains
and ill-pulled tooth with a ragged edge.   15
Some words live in my throat

breeding like adders. Others know sun
seeking like gypsies over my tongue
to explode through my lips
like young sparrows bursting from shell.   20
Some words
bedevil me.

Love is a word, another kind of open.
As the diamond comes into a knot of flame
I am Black because I come from the earth's inside   25
now take my word for jewel in the open light.

ROBERT LOWELL   *(1917–1977)*

For the Union Dead   *(1964)*

"Relinquunt Omnia Servare Rem Publicam."°

The old South Boston Aquarium stands
in a Sahara of snow now. Its broken windows are boarded.
The bronze weathervane cod has lost half its scales.
The airy tanks are dry.

Once my nose crawled like a snail on the glass;   5
my hand tingled
to burst the bubbles
drifting from the noses of the cowed, compliant fish.

My hand draws back. I often sigh still
for the dark downward and vegetating kingdom   10
of the fish and reptile. One morning last March,
I pressed against the new barbed and galvanized

fence on the Boston Common. Behind their cage,
yellow dinosaur steamshovels were grunting
as they cropped up tons of mush and grass   15
to gouge their underworld garage.

Parking spaces luxuriate like civic
sandpiles in the heart of Boston.
A girdle of orange, Puritan-pumpkin colored girders
braces the tingling Statehouse,   20

"Relinquunt . . . Publicam": "They give up everything to serve the Republic."

shaking over the excavations, as it faces Colonel Shaw°
and his bell-cheeked Negro infantry
on St. Gaudens'° shaking Civil War relief,
propped by a plank splint against the garage's earthquake.

Two months after marching through Boston,   25
half the regiment was dead;
at the dedication,
William James could almost hear the bronze Negroes breathe.

Their monument sticks like a fishbone
in the city's throat.   30
Its Colonel is as lean
as a compass-needle.

He has an angry wrenlike vigilance,
a greyhound's gentle tautness;
he seems to wince at pleasure,   35
and suffocate for privacy.

He is out of bounds now. He rejoices in man's lovely,
peculiar power to choose life and die—
when he leads his black soldiers to death,
he cannot bend his back.   40

On a thousand small town New England greens,
the old white churches hold their air
of sparse, sincere rebellion; frayed flags
quilt the graveyards of the Grand Army of the Republic.

The stone statues of the abstract Union Soldier   45
grow slimmer and younger each year—
wasp-waisted, they doze over muskets
and muse through their sideburns . . .

Shaw's father wanted no monument
except the ditch,   50
where his son's body was thrown
and lost with his "niggers."

The ditch is nearer.
There are no statues for the last war here;

---

21 *Colonel Shaw:* Colonel Robert Gould Shaw (1837–1863), killed with several of his troops in a battle at Fort Wagner, South Carolina.   23 *St. Gaudens:* August Saint-Gaudens (1848–1907), sculptor.

on Boylston Street, a commercial photograph   55
shows Hiroshima boiling

over a Mosler Safe, the "Rock of Ages"
that survived the blast. Space is nearer.
When I crouch to my television set,
the drained faces of Negro school-children rise like balloons.   60

Colonel Shaw
is riding on his bubble,
he waits
for the blessèd break.

The Aquarium is gone. Everywhere,   65
giant finned cars nose forward like fish;
a savage servility
slides by on grease.

ANDREW MARVELL   *(1621–1678)*

The Garden   *(1681)*

How vainly men themselves amaze
To win the palm, the oak, or bays,
And their incessant labors see
Crowned from some single herb, or tree,
Whose short and narrow-vergèd shade   5
Does prudently their toils upbraid;
While all flowers and all trees do close
To weave the garlands of repose!

Fair Quiet, have I found thee here,
And Innocence, thy sister dear?   10
Mistaken long, I sought you then
In busy companies of men.
Your sacred plants, if here below,
Only among the plants will grow;
Society is all but rude   15
To this delicious solitude.

No white nor red was ever seen
So amorous as this lovely green.
Fond lovers, cruel as their flame,
Cut in these trees their mistress' name: 20
Little, alas, they know or heed

How far these beauties hers exceed!
Fair trees, wheresoe'er your barks I wound,
No name shall but your own be found.

  When we have run our passion's heat,   25
Love hither makes his best retreat.
The gods, that mortal beauty chase,
Still in a tree did end their race:
Apollo hunted Daphne so,
Only that she might laurel grow;   30
And Pan did after Syrinx speed,
Not as a nymph, but for a reed.

  What wondrous life is this I lead!
Ripe apples drop about my head;
The luscious clusters of the vine   35
Upon my mouth do crush their wine;
The nectarine and curious peach
Into my hands themselves do reach;
Stumbling on melons, as I pass,
Insnared with flowers, I fall on grass.   40

  Meanwhile the mind, from pleasure less,
Withdraws into its happiness;
The mind, that ocean where each kind
Does straight its own resemblance find;
Yet it creates, transcending these,   45
Far other worlds and other seas,
Annihilating all that's made
To a green thought in a green shade.

  Here at the fountain's sliding foot,
Or at some fruit tree's mossy root,   50
Casting the body's vest aside,
My soul into the boughs does glide:
There, like a bird, it sits and sings,
Then whets and combs its silver wings,
And, till prepared for longer flight,   55
Waves in its plumes the various light.

  Such was that happy garden-state,
While man there walked without a mate:
After a place so pure and sweet,
What other help could yet be meet!   60
But 'twas beyond a mortal's share
To wander solitary there:
Two paradises 'twere in one
To live in paradise alone.

How well the skillful gardener drew   65
Of flowers and herbs this dial new,
Where, from above, the milder sun
Does through a fragrant zodiac run;
And as it works, th' industrious bee
Computes its time as well as we!   70
How could such sweet and wholesome hours
Be reckoned but with herbs and flowers?

HERMAN MELVILLE   *(1819–1891)*

The Maldive Shark   *(1888)*

About the Shark, phlegmatical one,
Pale sot of the Maldive sea,
The sleek little pilot-fish, azure and slim,
How alert in attendance be.
From his saw-pit of mouth, from his charnel of maw,   5
They have nothing of harm to dread
But liquidly glide on his ghastly flank
Or before his Gorgonian head;
Or lurk in the port of serrated teeth
In white triple tiers of glittering gates,   10
And there find a haven when peril's abroad,
An asylum in jaws of the Fates!

They are friends; and friendly they guide him to prey,
Yet never partake of the treat—
Eyes and brains to the dotard lethargic and dull,   15
Pale ravener of horrible meat.

GEORGE MEREDITH   *(1828–1909)*

Lucifer in Starlight   *(1883)*

On a starred night Prince Lucifer uprose.
Tired of his dark dominion, swung the fiend
Above the rolling ball, in cloud part screened,
Where sinners hugged their specter of repose.
Poor prey to his hot fit of pride were those.   5
And now upon his western wing he leaned,
Now his huge bulk o'er Afric's sands careened,
Now the black planet shadowed Arctic snows.
Soaring through wider zones that pricked his scars

With memory of the old revolt from Awe,   10
He reached a middle height, and at the stars,
Which are the brain of heaven, he looked, and sank.
Around the ancient track marched, rank on rank,
The army of unalterable law.

W. S. MERWIN   *(b. 1927)*

The Drunk in the Furnace   *(1960)*

        For a good decade
The furnace stood in the naked gully, fireless
And vacant as any hat. Then when it was
No more to them than a hulking black fossil
To erode unnoticed with the rest of the junk-hill   5
By the poisonous creek, and rapidly to be added
        To their ignorance.

        They were afterwards astonished
To confirm, one morning, a twist of smoke like a pale
Resurrection, staggering out of its chewed hole,   10
And to remark then other tokens that someone,
Cozily bolted behind the eye-holed iron
Door of the drafty burner, had there established
        His bad castle.

        Where he gets his spirits   15
It's a mystery. But the stuff keeps him musical:
Hammer-and-anviling with poker and bottle
To his jugged bellowings, till the last groaning clang
As he collapses onto the rioting
Springs of a litter of car-seats ranged on the grates,   20
        To sleep like an iron pig.

        In their tar-paper church
On a text about stoke-holes that are sated never
Their Reverend lingers. They nod and hate trespassers.
When the furnace wakes, though, all afternoon   25
Their witless offspring flock like piped rats to its siren
Crescendo, and agape on the crumbling ridge
        Stand in a row and learn.

Chord   *(1988)*

While Keats wrote they were cutting down the sandalwood forests
while he listened to the nightingale they heard their own axes
    echoing through the forests
while he sat in the walled garden on the hill outside the city they
    thought of their gardens dying far away on the mountain
while the sound of the words clawed at him they thought of their wives
while the tip of his pen travelled the iron they had coveted was
    hateful to them   5
while he thought of the Grecian woods they bled under red flowers
while he dreamed of wine the trees were falling from the trees
while he felt his heart they were hungry and their faith was sick
while the song broke over him they were in a secret place and they
    were cutting it forever
while he coughed they carried the trunks to the hole in the forest
    the size of a foreign ship   10
while he groaned on the voyage to Italy they fell on the trails and
    were broken
when he lay with the odes behind him the wood was sold for cannons
when he lay watching the window they came home and lay down
and an age arrived when everything was explained in another language

EDNA ST. VINCENT MILLAY   *(1892–1950)*

Spring   *(1920)*

To what purpose, April, do you return again?
Beauty is not enough.
You can no longer quiet me with the redness
Of little leaves opening stickily.
I know what I know.   5
The sun is hot on my neck as I observe
The spikes of the crocus.
The smell of the earth is good.
It is apparent that there is no death.
But what does that signify?   10
Not only under ground are the brains of men
Eaten by maggots.
Life in itself
Is nothing,
An empty cup, a flight of uncarpeted stairs.   15
It is not enough that yearly, down this hill,
April
Comes like an idiot, babbling and strewing flowers.

JOHN MILTON   *(1608–1674)*

On the Late Massacre in Piedmont°   *(1673)*

Avenge, O Lord, thy slaughtered saints, whose bones
Lie scattered on the Alpine mountains cold;
Even them who kept thy truth so pure of old
When all our fathers worshipped stocks and stones,
Forget not: in thy book record their groans   5
Who were thy sheep and in their ancient fold
Slain by the bloody Piedmontese, that rolled
Mother with infant down the rocks. Their moans
The vales redoubled to the hills, and they
To heaven. Their martyred blood and ashes sow   10
O'er all the Italian fields where still doth sway
The triple tyrant; that from these may grow
A hundredfold, who, having learnt thy way,
Early may fly the Babylonian woe.°

JANICE MIRIKITANI   *(b. 1942)*

Desert Flowers   *(1978)*

Flowers
faded
in the desert wind.
No flowers grow
where dust winds blow   5
and rain is like
a dry heave moan.

        Mama, did you dream about that
        beau who would take you
        away from it all,   10
        who would show you
        in his '41 ford
        and tell you how soft
        your hands
        like the silk kimono   15
        you folded for the wedding?

Piedmont: On Easter 1655, the duke of Savoy killed seventeen hundred members of the Protestant Waldensian sect in northern Italy.   **14** *Babylonian woe:* A refernce to the papal court.

Make you forget
about That place,
the back bending
wind that fell like a wall,   20
drowned all your geraniums
and flooded the shed
where you tried to sleep
away hyenas?
And mama,   25
bending in the candlelight,
after lights out in barracks,
an ageless shadow
grows victory flowers
made from crepe paper,   30
shaping those petals
like the tears
your eyes bled.

Your fingers
knotted at knuckles   35
wounded, winding around wire stems
the tiny, sloganed banner:

"america for americans".

Did you dream
of the shiny ford   40
(only always a dream)
ride your youth
like the wind
in the headless night?

Flowers   45
2 ¢ a dozen,
flowers for American Legions
worn like a badge
on america's lapel
made in post-concentration camps   50
by candlelight.
Flowers
watered
by the spit
of "no japs wanted here",   55
planted in poverty
of postwar relocations,
plucked by
victory's veterans.

Mama, do you dream   60
of the wall of wind
that falls
on your limbless desert,
on stems
brimming with petals/crushed   65
crepepaper
growing
from the crippled
mouth of your hand?

Your tears, mama,   70
have nourished us.
Your children
like pollen
scatter in the wind.

MARIANNE MOORE   *(1887–1972)*

The Fish   *(1921)*

wade
through black jade.
   Of the crow-blue mussel-shells, one keeps
   adjusting the ash-heaps;
       opening and shutting itself like   5

an
injured fan.
   The barnacles which encrust the side
   of the wave, cannot hide
       there for the submerged shafts of the   10

sun,
split like spun
   glass, move themselves with spotlight swiftness
into the crevices—
   in and out, illuminating   15

the
turquoise sea
   of bodies. The water drives a wedge
   of iron through the iron edge
       of the cliff; whereupon the stars,   20

pink
rice-grains, ink-
    bespattered jelly-fish, crabs like green
    lilies, and submarine
        toadstools, slide each on the other.   25

All
external
    marks of abuse are present on this
    defiant edifice—
        all the physical features of   30

ac-
cident—lack
    of cornice, dynamite grooves, burns, and
    hatchet strokes, these things stand
        out on it; the chasm-side is   35

dead.
Repeated
    evidence has proved that it can live
    on what can not revive
        its youth. The sea grows old in it.   40

PAUL MULDOON   *(b. 1951)*

Milkweed and Monarch   *(1994)*

As he knelt by the grave of his mother and father
the taste of dill, or tarragon—
he could barely tell one from the other—

filled his mouth. It seemed as if he might smother.
Why should he be stricken   5
with grief, not for his mother and father,

but a woman slinking from the fur of a sea-otter
in Portland, Maine, or, yes, Portland, Oregon—
he could barely tell one from the other—

and why should he now savour   10
the tang of her, her little pickled gherkin,
as he knelt by the grave of his mother and father?

*

He looked about. He remembered her palaver
on how both earth and sky would darken—
"You could barely tell one from the other"—   15

while the Monarch butterflies passed over
in their milkweed-hunger: "A wing-beat, some reckon,
may trigger off the mother and father

of all storms, striking your Irish Cliffs of Moher
with the force of a hurricane."   20
Then: "Milkweed and Monarch 'invented' each other."

*

He looked about. Cow's-parsley in a samovar.
He'd mistaken his mother's name, "Regan", for "Anger":
as he knelt by the grave of his mother and father
he could barely tell one from the other.   25

FRANK O'HARA   *(1926–1966)*

The Day Lady° Died   *(1964)*

It is 12:20 in New York a Friday
three days after Bastille day, yes
it is 1959 and I go get a shoeshine
because I will get off the 4:19 in Easthampton
at 7:15 and then go straight to dinner   5
and I don't know the people who will feed me

I walk up the muggy street beginning to sun
and have a hamburger and a malted and buy
an ugly NEW WORLD WRITING to see what the poets
in Ghana are doing these days   10
        I go on to the bank
and Miss Stillwagon (first name Linda I once heard)
doesn't even look up my balance for once in her life
and in the GOLDEN GRIFFIN° I get a little Verlaine
for Patsy with drawings by Bonnard although I do   15
think of Hesiod, trans. Richmond Lattimore or
Brendan Behan's new play or *Le Balcon or Les Nègres*

Lady: Billie Holiday (1915–1959), legendary jazz singer.   14 *GOLDEN GRIFFIN:* Bookstore in
New York City.

of Genet, but I don't, I stick with Verlaine
after practically going to sleep with quandariness
and for Mike I just stroll into the PARK LANE   20
Liquor Store and ask for a bottle of Strega and
then I go back where I came from to 6th Avenue
and the tobacconist in the Ziegfeld Theatre and
casually ask for a carton of Gauloises and a carton
of Picayunes, and a NEW YORK POST with her face on it   25

and I am sweating a lot by now and thinking of
leaning on the john door in the 5 SPOT°
while she whispered a song along the keyboard
to Mal Wandron° and everyone and I stopped breathing

WILFRED OWEN *(1893–1918)*

Dulce et Decorum Est°   *(1920)*

Bent double, like old beggars under sacks,
Knock-kneed, coughing like hags, we cursed through sludge,
Till on the haunting flares we turned our backs
And towards our distant rest began to trudge.
Men marched asleep. Many had lost their boots   5
But limped on, blood-shod. All went lame; all blind;
Drunk with fatigue; deaf even to the hoots
Of tired, outstripped Five-Nines° that dropped behind.

Gas! Gas! Quick, boys!—An ecstasy of fumbling,
Fitting the clumsy helmets just in time;   10
But someone still was yelling out and stumbling,
And flound'ring like a man in fire or lime . . .
Dim, through the misty panes and thick green light,
As under a green sea, I saw him drowning.

In all my dreams, before my helpless sight,   15
He plunges at me, guttering, choking, drowning.

If in smothering dreams you too could pace
Behind the wagon that we flung him in,
And watch the white eyes writhing in his face,
His hanging face, like a devil's sick of sin;   20

---

27 *5 SPOT:* A New York jazz club.   29 *Mal Wandron:* Pianist and composer (b. 1935) who accompanied Billie Holiday from 1957–1959.   *Dulce et Decorum Est:* From Horace, *Odes* 3.2.13, "It is sweet and proper to die for one's country."   8 *Five-Nines:* 5.9-inch caliber cannon shells.

If you could hear, at every jolt, the blood
Come gargling from the froth-corrupted lungs,
Obscene as cancer, bitter as the cud
Of vile, incurable sores on innocent tongues,—
My friend,° you would not tell with such high zest   25
To children ardent for some desperate glory,
The old Lie: Dulce et decorum est
Pro patria mori.

SYLVIA PLATH   *(1932–1963)*

The Colossus°   *(1960)*

I shall never get you put together entirely,
Pieced, glued, and properly jointed.
Mule-bray, pig-grunt and bawdy cackles
Proceed from your great lips.
It's worse than a barnyard.   5

Perhaps you consider yourself an oracle,
Mouthpiece of the dead, or of some god or other.
Thirty years now I have labored
To dredge the silt from your throat.
I am none the wiser.   10

Scaling little ladders with gluepots and pails of lysol
I crawl like an ant in mourning
Over the weedy acres of your brow
To mend the immense skull plates and clear
The bald, white tumuli of your eyes.   15

A blue sky out of the Oresteia°
Arches above us. O father, all by yourself
You are pithy and historical as the Roman Forum.
I open my lunch on a hill of black cypress.
Your fluted bones and acanthine hair are littered   20

In their old anarchy to the horizon-line.
It would take more than a lightning-stroke
To create such a ruin.
Nights, I squat in the cornucopia
Of your left ear, out of the wind,   25

---

25 *My friend:* Jessie Pope, author of *Jessie Pope's War Poems* (1915).   *Colossus:* Third-century
B.C. statue that once stood in the harbor entrance to Rhodes, Greece.   16 *Oresteia:* Dramatic
trilogy by Aeschylus (525–456 B.C.) that presents a cycle of family murders.

Counting the red stars and those of plum-color.
The sun rises under the pillar of your tongue.
My hours are married to shadow.
No longer do I listen for the scrape of a keel
On the blank stones of the landing.　　30

Witch Burning　　*(1959)*

In the marketplace they are piling the dry sticks.
A thicket of shadows is a poor coat. I inhabit
The wax image of myself, a doll's body.
Sickness begins here: I am a dartboard for witches.
Only the devil can eat the devil out.　　5
In the month of red leaves I climb to a bed of fire.

It is easy to blame the dark: the mouth of a door,
The cellar's belly. They've blown my sparkler out.
A black-sharded lady keeps me in a parrot cage.
What large eyes the dead have!　　10
I am intimate with a hairy spirit.
Smoke wheels from the beak of this empty jar.

If I am a little one, I can do no harm.
If I don't move about, I'll knock nothing over. So I said,
Sitting under a potlid, tiny and inert as a rice grain.　　15
They are turning the burners up, ring after ring.
We are full of starch, my small white fellows. We grow.
It hurts at first. The red tongues will teach the truth.

Mother of beetles, only unclench your hand:
I'll fly through the candle's mouth like a singeless moth.　　20
Give me back my shape. I am ready to construe the days
I coupled with dust in the shadow of a stone.
My ankles brighten. Brightness ascends my thighs.
I am lost, I am lost, in the robes of all this light.

EDGAR ALLAN POE　*(1809–1849)*

The Raven　　*(1845)*

Once upon a midnight dreary, while I pondered, weak and weary,
Over many a quaint and curious volume of forgotten lore—
While I nodded, nearly napping, suddenly there came a tapping,
As of some one gently rapping, rapping at my chamber door.

"'Tis some visiter," I muttered, "tapping at my chamber door—   5
          Only this and nothing more."

Ah, distinctly I remember it was in the bleak December;
And each separate dying ember wrought its ghost upon the floor.
Eagerly I wished the morrow;—vainly I had sought to borrow
From my books surcease of sorrow—sorrow for the lost Lenore—   10
For the rare and radiant maiden whom the angels name Lenore—
          Nameless *here* for evermore.

And the silken, sad, uncertain rustling of each purple curtain
Thrilled me—filled me with fantastic terrors never felt before;
So that now, to still the beating of my heart, I stood repeating   15
"'Tis some visiter entreating entrance at my chamber door—
Some late visiter entreating entrance at my chamber door;—
          This it is and nothing more."

Presently my soul grew stronger; hesitating then no longer,
"Sir," said I, "or Madam, truly your forgiveness I implore;   20
But the fact is I was napping, and so gently you came rapping,
And so faintly you came tapping, tapping at my chamber door,
That I scarce was sure I heard you"—here I opened wide the door;—
          Darkness there and nothing more.

Deep into that darkness peering, long I stood there wondering, fearing,   25
Doubting, dreaming dreams no mortal ever dared to dream before;
But the silence was unbroken, and the stillness gave no token,
And the only word there spoken was the whispered word, "Lenore?"
This I whispered, and an echo murmured back the word "Lenore!"—
          Merely this and nothing more.   30

Back into the chamber turning, all my soul within me burning,
Soon again I heard a tapping somewhat louder than before.
"Surely," said I, "surely that is something at my window lattice;
Let me see, then, what thereat is, and this mystery explore—
Let my heart be still a moment and this mystery explore;—   35
          'Tis the wind and nothing more!"

Open here I flung the shutter, when, with many a flirt and flutter,
In there stepped a stately Raven of the saintly days of yore;
Not the least obeisance made he; not a minute stopped or stayed he;
But, when mien of lord or lady, perched above my chamber door—   40
Perched upon a bust of Pallas just above my chamber door—
          Perched, and sat, and nothing more.

Then this ebony bird beguiling my sad fancy into smiling,
By the grave and stern decorum of the countenance it wore,

"Though thy crest be short and shaven, thou," I said, "art sure no craven,   45
Ghastly grim and ancient Raven wandering from the Nightly shore—
Tell me what thy lordly name is on the Night's Plutonian shore!"
                         Quoth the Raven "Nevermore."

Much I marvelled this ungainly fowl to hear discourse so plainly,
Though its answer little meaning—little relevancy bore;   50
For we cannot help agreeing that no living human being
Ever yet blessed with seeing bird above this chamber door—
Bird or beast upon the sculptured bust above his chamber door,
                         With such name as "Nevermore."

But the Raven, sitting lonely on the placid bust, spoke only   55
That one word, as if his soul in that one word he did outpour.
Nothing farther then he uttered—not a feather then he fluttered—
Till I scarcely more than muttered "Other friends have flown before—
On the morrow *he* will leave me, as my Hopes have flown before."
                         Then the bird said "Nevermore."   60

Startled at the stillness broken by reply so aptly spoken,
"Doubtless," said I, "what it utters is its only stock and store
Caught from some unhappy master whom unmerciful Disaster
Followed fast and followed faster till his songs one burden bore—
Till the dirges of his Hope that melancholy burden bore   65
                         Of 'Never-nevermore.'"

But the Raven still beguiling all my fancy into smiling,
Straight I wheeled a cushioned seat in front of bird, and bust and door;
Then, upon the velvet sinking, I betook myself to linking
Fancy unto fancy, thinking what this ominous bird of yore—   70
What this grim, ungainly, ghastly, gaunt, and ominous bird of yore
                         Meant in croaking "Nevermore."

This I sat engaged in guessing, but no syllable expressing
To the fowl whose fiery eyes now burned into my bosom's core;
This and more I sat divining, with my head at ease reclining   75
On the cushion's velvet lining that the lamp light gloated o'er,
But whose velvet-violet lining with the lamp-light gloating o'er,
                         She shall press, ah, nevermore!

Then, methought, the air grew denser, perfumed from an unseen censer
Swung by Seraphim whose foot-falls tinkled on the tufted floor.   80
"Wretch," I cried, "thy God hath lent thee—by these angels he hath sent
    thee
Respite—respite and nepenthe from thy memories of Lenore;
Quaff, of quaff this kind nepenthe and forget this lost Lenore!"
                         Quoth the Raven "Nevermore."

"Prophet!" said I, "thing of evil!—prophet still, if bird or devil!—   85
Whether Tempter sent, or whether tempest tossed thee here ashore,
Desolate yet all undaunted, on this desert land enchanted—
On this home by Horror haunted—tell me truly, I implore—
Is there—*is* there balm in Gilead?—tell me—tell me, I implore!"
                    Quoth the Raven "Nevermore."   90

"Prophet!" said I, "thing of evil!—prophet still, if bird or devil!
By that Heaven that bends above us—by that God we both adore!—
Tell this soul with sorrow laden if, within the distant Aidenn,
It shall clasp a sainted maiden whom the angels name Lenore—
Clasp a rare and radiant maiden whom the angels name Lenore."   95
                    Quoth the Raven "Nevermore."

"Be that word our sign of parting, bird or fiend!" I shrieked, upstarting—
"Get thee back into the tempest and the Night's Plutonian shore!
Leave no black plume as a token of that lie thy soul hath spoken!
Leave my loneliness unbroken!—quit the bust above my door!   100
Take thy beak from out my heart, and take thy form from off my door!"
                    Quoth the Raven "Nevermore."

And the Raven, never flitting, still is sitting, *still* is sitting
On the pallid bust of Pallas just above my chamber door;
And his eyes have all the seeming of a demon's that is dreaming,   105
And the lamp-light o'er him streaming throws his shadow on the floor;
And my soul from out that shadow that lies floating on the floor
                    Shall be lifted—nevermore!

ALEXANDER POPE   *(1688–1744)*

from Epistle II. Of the Nature and State of Man With Respect to Himself, as an Individual   *(1733)*

Know then thyself, presume not God to scan;
The proper study of mankind is man.
Placed on this isthmus of a middle state,
A being darkly wise, and rudely great:
With too much knowledge for the skeptic side,   5
With too much weakness for the Stoic's pride,
He hangs between; in doubt to act, or rest,
In doubt to deem himself a god, or beast;
In doubt his mind or body to prefer;
Born but to die, and reasoning but to err;   10
Alike in ignorance, his reason such,
Whether he thinks too little, or too much:

Chaos of thought and passion, all confused;
Still by himself abused, or disabused;
Created half to rise, and half to fall;   15
Great lord of all things, yet a prey to all;
Sole judge of truth, in endless error hurled:
The glory, jest, and riddle of the world!

EZRA POUND   *(1885–1972)*

from The Cantos   *(1921, 1930)*

I

And then went down to the ship,
Set keel to breakers, forth on the godly sea, and
We set up mast and sail on that swart ship,
Bore sheep aboard her, and our bodies also
Heavy with weeping, and winds from sternward   5
Bore us out onward with bellying canvas,
Circe's° this craft, the trim-coifed goddess.
Then sat we amidships, wind jamming the tiller,
Thus with stretched sail, we went over sea till day's end.
Sun to his slumber, shadows o'er all the ocean,   10
Came we then to the bounds of deepest water,
To the Kimmerian lands, and peopled cities
Covered with close-webbed mist, unpierced ever
With glitter of sun-rays
Nor with stars stretched, nor looking back from heaven   15
Swartest night stretched over wretched men there.
The ocean flowing backward, came we then to the place
Aforesaid by Circe.
Here did they rites, Perimedes and Eurylochus,°
And drawing sword from my hip   20
I dug the ell-square pitkin;
Poured we libations unto each the dead,
First mead and then sweet wine, water mixed with white flour.
Then prayed I many a prayer to the sickly death's-heads;
As set in Ithaca, sterile bulls of the best   25
For sacrifice, heaping the pyre with goods,
A sheep to Tiresias only, black and a bell-sheep.
Dark blood flowed in the fosse,
Souls out of Erebus, cadaverous dead, of brides
Of youths and of the old who had borne much;   30
Souls stained with recent tears, girls tender,

---

7 *Circe:* Enchantress and mistress of Odysseus.   19 *Perimedes and Eurylochus:* Companions of
Odysseus.

Men many, mauled with bronze lance heads,
Battle spoil, bearing yet dreory° arms,
These many crowded about me; with shouting,
Pallor upon me, cried to my men for more beasts;   35
Slaughtered the herds, sheep slain of bronze;
Poured ointment, cried to the gods,
To Pluto° the strong, and praised Proserpine;°
Unsheathed the narrow sword,
I sat to keep off the impetuous impotent dead,   40
Till I should hear Tiresias.
But first Elpenor came, our friend Elpenor,
Unburied, cast on the wide earth,
Limbs that we left in the house of Circe,
Unwept, unwrapped in sepulchre, since toils urged other.   45
Pitiful spirit. And I cried in hurried speech:
"Elpenor, how art thou come to this dark coast?
"Cam'st thou afoot, outstripping seamen?"
        And he in heavy speech:
"Ill fate and abundant wine. I slept in Circe's ingle.   50
"Going down the long ladder unguarded,
"I fell against the buttress,
"Shattered the nape-nerve, the soul sought Avernus.°
"But thou, O King, I bid remember me, unwept, unburied,
"Heap up mine arms, be tomb by sea-bord, and inscribed: 55
"*A man of no fortune, and with a name to come.*
"And set my oar up, that I swung mid fellows."

And Anticlea° came, whom I beat off, and then Tiresias Theban,
Holding his golden wand, knew me, and spoke first:
"A second time? why? man of ill star,   60
"Facing the sunless dead and this joyless region?
"Stand from the fosse, leave me my bloody bever
"For soothsay."
        And I stepped back,
And he strong with the blood, said then: "Odysseus   65
"Shalt return through spiteful Neptune, over dark seas,
"Lose all companions." And then Anticlea came.
Lie quiet Divus. I mean, that is Andreas Divus,°
In officina Wecheli, 1538, out of Homer.
And he sailed, by Sirens and thence outward and away   70
And unto Circe.
        Venerandam,°
In the Cretan's phrase, with the golden crown, Aphrodite,

---

33 *dreory:* Bloody.   38 *Pluto:* Latin name for god of the underworld. *Proserpine:* Pluto's queen.   53 *Avernus:* Lake and entrance to the underworld.   58 *Anticlea:* Mother of Odysseus.   68 *Andreas Divus:* Sixteenth-century Italian translator of the *Odyssey.*   72 *Venerandum:* "Worthy of worship."

Cypri munimenta sortita est, mirthful, orichalchi, with golden
Girdles and breast bands, thou with dark eyelids　　　　　　　　　75
Bearing the golden bough of Argicida.° So that:

JOHN CROWE RANSOM　　(1888–1974)

Piazza Piece　　　　　　　　　　　　　　　　　　　　*(1925)*

—I am a gentleman in a dustcoat trying
To make you hear. Your ears are soft and small
And listen to an old man not at all,
They want the young men's whispering and sighing.
But see the roses on your trellis dying　　　　　　　　　　　5
And hear the spectral singing of the moon;
For I must have my lovely lady soon,
I am a gentleman in a dustcoat trying.

—I am a lady young in beauty waiting
Until my truelove comes, and then we kiss.　　　　　　　　10
But what grey man among the vines is this
Whose words are dry and faint as in a dream?
Back from my trellis, Sir, before I scream!
I am a lady young in beauty waiting.

EDWIN ARLINGTON ROBINSON　　(1869–1935)

Richard Cory　　　　　　　　　　　　　　　　　*(1896–1897)*

Whenever Richard Cory went down town,
　　We people on the pavement looked at him:
He was a gentleman from sole to crown,
　　Clean favored, and imperially slim.

And he was always quietly arrayed,　　　　　　　　　　　5
　　And he was always human when he talked;
But still he fluttered pulses when he said,
　　"Good-morning," and he glittered when he walked.

And he was rich—yes, richer than a king,
　　And admirably schooled in every grace:　　　　　　　　10
In fine, we thought that he was everything
　　To make us wish that we were in his place.

———
76 *Argicida:* A reference to the god Hermes.

So on we worked, and waited for the light,
   And went without the meat, and cursed the bread;
And Richard Cory, one calm summer night,   15
   Went home and put a bullet through his head.

Theodore Roethke   *(1908–1963)*

Root Cellar   *(1948)*

Nothing would sleep in that cellar, dank as a ditch,
Bulbs broke out of boxes hunting for chinks in the dark,
Shoots dangled and drooped,
Lolling obscenely from mildewed crates,
Hung down long yellow evil necks, like tropical snakes.   5
And what a congress of stinks!
Roots ripe as old bait,
Pulpy stems, rank, silo-rich,
Leaf-mold, manure, lime, piled against slippery planks.
Nothing would give up life: 10
Even the dirt kept breathing a small breath.

In a Dark Time   *(1960)*

In a dark time, the eye begins to see,
I meet my shadow in the deepening shade;
I hear my echo in the echoing wood—
A lord of nature weeping to a tree.
I live between the heron and the wren,   5
Beasts of the hill and serpents of the den.

What's madness but nobility of soul
At odds with circumstance? The day's on fire!
I know the purity of pure despair,
My shadow pinned against a sweating wall.   10
That place among the rocks—is it a cave,
Or winding path? The edge is what I have.

A steady storm of correspondences!
A night flowing with birds, a ragged moon,
And in broad day the midnight come again!   15
A man goes far to find out what he is—
Death of the self in a long, tearless night,
All natural shapes blazing unnatural light.

Dark, dark my light, and darker my desire.
My soul, like some heat-maddened summer fly,   20
Keeps buzzing at the sill. Which I is *I?*
A fallen man, I climb out of my fear.
The mind enters itself, and God the mind,
And one is One, free in the tearing wind.

CHRISTINA ROSSETTI *(1830–1894)*

After Death   *(1862)*

The curtains were half drawn, the floor was swept
   And strewn with rushes, rosemary and may
   Lay thick upon the bed on which I lay,
Where through the lattice ivy-shadows crept.
He leaned above me, thinking that I slept   5
   And could not hear him, but I heard him say,
   'Poor child, poor child': and as he turned away
Came a deep silence, and I knew he wept.
He did not touch the shroud, or raise the fold
   That hid my face, or take my hand in his,   10
      Or ruffle the smooth pillows for my head;
        He did not love me living; but once dead
   He pitied me; and very sweet it is
To know that he is warm though I am cold.

DANTE GABRIEL ROSSETTI *(1828–1882)*

The Woodspurge   *(1870)*

The wind flapped loose, the wind was still,
Shaken out dead from tree and hill:
I had walked on at the wind's will—
I sat now, for the wind was still.

Between my knees my forehead was—   5
My lips, drawn in, said not Alas!
My hair was over in the grass,
My naked ears heard the day pass.

My eyes, wide open, had the run
Of some ten weeds to fix upon;   10
Among those few, out of the sun,
The woodspurge flowered, three cups in one.

From perfect grief there need not be
Wisdom or even memory:
One thing then learnt remains to me—   15
The woodspurge has a cup of three.

CARL SANDBURG   *(1878–1967)*

Chicago   *(1916)*

Hog Butcher for the World,
Tool Maker, Stacker of Wheat,
Player with Railroads and the Nation's Freight Handler;
Stormy, husky, brawling,
City of the Big Shoulders: 5

They tell me you are wicked and I believe them, for I have seen your painted
    women under the gas lamps luring the farm boys.
And they tell me you are crooked and I answer: Yes, it is true I have seen the
    gunman kill and go free to kill again.
And they tell me you are brutal and my reply is: On the faces of women and
    children I have seen the marks of wanton hunger.
And having answered so I turn once more to those who sneer at this my city,
    and I give them back the sneer and say to them:
Come and show me another city with lifted head singing so proud to be
    alive and coarse and strong and cunning.   10
Flinging magnetic curses amid the toil of piling job on job, here is a tall bold
    slugger set vivid against the little soft cities;
Fierce as a dog with tongue lapping for action, cunning as a savage pitted
    against the wilderness,
        Bareheaded,
        Shoveling,
        Wrecking,   15
        Planning,
        Building, breaking, rebuilding,
Under the smoke, dust all over his mouth, laughing with white teeth,
Under the terrible burden of destiny laughing as a young man laughs,
Laughing even as an ignorant fighter laughs who has never lost a battle,   20
Bragging and laughing that under his wrist is the pulse, and under his ribs
    the heart of the people,
            Laughing!
Laughing the stormy, husky, brawling laughter of Youth, half-naked, sweat-
    ing, proud to be Hog Butcher, Tool Maker, Stacker of Wheat, Player
    with Railroads and Freight Handler to the Nation.

Grass   *(1918)*

Pile the bodies high at Austerlitz and Waterloo.
Shovel them under and let me work—
        I am the grass; I cover all.

And pile them high at Gettysburg
And pile them high at Ypres and Verdun.   5
Shovel them under and let me work.
Two years, ten years, and passengers ask the conductor:
        What place is this?
        Where are we now?

        I am the grass.   10
        Let me work.

SIEGFRIED SASSOON   *(1886–1967)*

Christ and the Soldier   *(1916)*

I

The straggled soldier halted—stared at Him—
Then clumsily dumped down upon his knees,
Gasping, "O blessed crucifix, I'm beat!"
And Christ, still sentried by the seraphim,
Near the front-line, between two splintered trees,   5
Spoke him: "My son, behold these hands and feet."

The soldier eyed Him upward, limb by limb,
Paused at the Face; then muttered, "Wounds like these
Would shift a bloke to Blighty° just a treat!"
Christ, gazing downward, grieving and ungrim,   10
Whispered, "I made for you the mysteries,
Beyond all battles moves the Paraclete."°

II

The soldier chucked his rifle in the dust,
And slipped his pack, and wiped his neck, and said—
"O Christ Almighty, stop this bleeding fight!"   15
Above that hill the sky was stained like rust
With smoke. In sullen daybreak flaring red
The guns were thundering bombardment's blight.

---

9 *Blighty:* Britain.   12 *Paraclete:* Holy Ghost.

The soldier cried, "I was born full of lust,
With hunger, thirst, and wishfulness to wed.   20
Who cares today if I done wrong or right?"
Christ asked all pitying, "Can you put no trust
In my known word that shrives each faithful head?
Am I not resurrection, life and light?"

III

Machine-guns rattled from below the hill;   25
High bullets flicked and whistled through the leaves;
And smoke came drifting from exploding shells.
Christ said, "Believe; and I can cleanse your ill.
I have not died in vain between two thieves;
Nor made a fruitless gift of miracles."   30

The soldier answered, "Heal me if you will,
Maybe there's comfort when a soul believes
In mercy, and we need it in these hells.
But be you for both sides? I'm paid to kill
And if I shoot a man his mother grieves.   35
Does that come into what your teaching tells?"

A bird lit on the Christ and twittered gay;
Then a breeze passed and shook the ripening corn.
A Red Cross waggon bumped along the track.
Forsaken Jesus dreamed in the desolate day—   40
Uplifted Jesus, Prince of Peace forsworn—
An observation post for the attack.

"Lord Jesus, ain't you got no more to say?"
Bowed hung that head below the crown of thorns.
The soldier shifted, and picked up his pack,   45
And slung his gun, and stumbled on his way.
"O God," he groaned, "why ever was I born?" . . .
The battle boomed, and no reply came back.
a thousand cranes curtain the window,
fly up in a sudden breeze.   50

WILLIAM SHAKESPEARE   *(1564–1616)*

Sonnet 129   *(1609)*

Th' expense of spirit in a waste of shame
Is lust in action; and, till action, lust
Is perjured, murd'rous, bloody, full of blame,

Savage, extreme, rude, cruel, not to trust;
Enjoyed no sooner but despisèd straight;   5
Past reason hunted, and no sooner had,
Past reason hated, as a swallowed bait
On purpose laid to make the taker mad:
Mad in pursuit, and in possession so;
Had, having, and in quest to have, extreme;   10
A bliss in proof, and proved, a very woe;
Before, a joy proposed; behind, a dream.
    All this the world well knows; yet none knows well
    To shun the heaven that leads men to this hell.

Sonnet 130   *(1609)*

My mistress' eyes are nothing like the sun;
Coral is far more red than her lips' red;
If snow be white, why then her breasts are dun;
If hairs be wires, black wires grow on her head.
I have seen roses damasked, red and white,   5
But no such roses see I in her cheeks;
And in some perfumes is there more delight
Than in the breath that from my mistress reeks.
I love to hear her speak, yet well I know
That music hath a far more pleasing sound.   10
I grant I never saw a goddess go;
My mistress, when she walks, treads on the ground.
    And yet, by heaven, I think my love as rare
    As any she belied with false compare.

PERCY BYSSHE SHELLEY   *(1792–1822)*

Ozymandias°   *(1818)*

I met a traveler from an antique land
Who said: Two vast and trunkless legs of stone
Stand in the desert . . . Near them, on the sand,
Half sunk, a shattered visage lies, whose frown,
And wrinkled lip, and sneer of cold command,   5
Tell that its sculptor well those passions read
Which yet survive, stamped on these lifeless things,
The hand that mocked them, and the heart that fed:
And on the pedestal these words appear:

Ozymandias: Egyptian King Ramses II.

"My name is Ozymandias, king of kings: 10
Look on my works, ye Mighty, and despair!"
Nothing beside remains. Round the decay
Of that colossal wreck, boundless and bare
The lone and level sands stretch far away.

Sir Philip Sidney   *(1554–1586)*

What Length of Verse?   *(1593)*

What length of verse can serve brave Mopsa's good to show,
Whose virtues strange, and beauties such, as no man them may
    know?
Thus shrewdly burden, then, how can my Muse escape?
The gods must help, and precious things must serve to show her
    shape.

Like great god Saturn, fair, and like fair Venus, chaste;   5
As smooth as Pan, as Juno mild, like goddess Iris fast.
With Cupid she foresees, and goes god Vulcan's pace;
And for a taste of all these gifts, she borrows Momus' grace.

Her forehead jacinth-like, her cheeks of opal hue,
Her twinkling eyes bedecked with pearl, her lips of sapphire blue,   10
Her hair pure crapall stone, her mouth, O heavenly wide,
Her skin like burnished gold, her hands like silver ore untried.

As for those parts unknown, which hidden sure are best,
Happy be they which will believe, and never seek the rest.

Charlotte Smith   *(1749–1806)*

XXXVIII   *(1784)*

When welcome slumber sets my spirit free,
    Forth to fictitious happiness it flies,
    And where Elysian bowers of bliss arise,
I seem, my Emmeline—to meet with thee!
Ah! Fancy then, dissolving human ties,   5
    Gives me the wishes of my soul to see;
Tears of fond pity fill thy soften'd eyes:
    In heavenly harmony—our hearts agree.
Alas! these joys are mine in dreams alone,
When cruel Reason abdicates her throne!   10

Her harsh return condemns me to complain
Thro' life unpitied, unrelieved, unknown!
   And as the dear delusions leave my brain,
   She bids the truth recur—with aggravated pain!

CATHY SONG *(b. 1955)*

The Youngest Daughter   *(1983)*

The sky has been dark
for many years.
My skin has become as damp
and pale as rice paper
and feels the way   5
mother's used to before the drying sun
parched it out there in the fields.

   Lately, when I touch my eyelids,
my hands react as if
I had just touched something   10
hot enough to burn.
My skin, aspirin colored,
tingles with migraine. Mother
has been massaging the left side of my face
especially in the evenings   15
when the pain flares up.

This morning
her breathing was graveled,
her voice gruff with affection
when I wheeled her into the bath.   20
She was in a good humor,
making jokes about her great breasts,
floating in the milky water
like two walruses,
flaccid and whiskered around the nipples.   25
I scrubbed them with a sour taste
in my mouth, thinking:
six children and an old man
have sucked from these brown nipples.

I was almost tender   30
when I came to the blue bruises
that freckle her body,
places where she has been injecting insulin
for thirty years. I soaped her slowly,

she sighed deeply, her eyes closed.   35
It seems it has always
been like this: the two of us
in this sunless room,
the splashing of the bathwater.

In the afternoons   40
when she has rested,
she prepares our ritual of tea and rice,
garnished with a shred of gingered fish,
a slice of pickled turnip,
a token for my white body.   45
We eat in the familiar silence.
She knows I am not to be trusted,
even now planning my escape.
As I toast to her health
with the tea she has poured,   50
a thousand cranes curtain the window,
fly up in a sudden breeze.

GERTRUDE STEIN   *(1874–1946)*

from Lifting Belly   *(1915–1917)*

I have been heavy and had much selecting. I saw a star which was low. It
was so low it twinkled. Breath was in it. Little pieces are stupid.

I want to tell about fire. Fire is that which we have when we have olive.
Olive is a wood. We like linen. Linen is ordered. We are going to order linen.

All belly belly well.

Bed of coals made out of wood.

I think this one may be an expression. We can understand heating and   5
burning composition. Heating with wood.

Sometimes we readily decide upon wind we decide that there will be stars
and perhaps thunder and perhaps rain and perhaps no moon. Sometimes we
decide that there will be a storm and rain. Sometimes we look at the boats.
When we read about a boat we know that it has been sunk. Not by the waves
but by the sails. Any one knows that rowing is dangerous. Be alright. Be careful. Be angry. Say what you think. Believe in there being the same kind of a
dog. Jerk. Jerk him away. Answer that you do not care to think so.

We quarreled with him. We quarreled with him then. Do not forget that
I showed you the road. Do not forget that I showed you the road. We will forget it because he does not oblige himself to thank me. Ask him to thank me.

The next time that he came we offered him something to read. There is a
great difference of opinion as to whether cooking in oil is or is not healthful.

I don't pardon him. I find him objectionable.

What is it when it's upset. It isn't in the room. Moonlight and darkness. 10
Sleep and not sleep. We sleep every night.
  What was it.
  I said lifting belly.
  You didn't say it.
  I said it I mean lifting belly.
  Don't misunderstand me.   15
  Do you.
  Do you lift everybody in that way.
  No.
  You are to say No.
  Lifting belly.   20
  How are you.
  Lifting belly how are you lifting belly.
  We like a fire and we don't mind if it smokes.
  Do you.
  How do you do. The Englishmen are coming. Not here. No an English- 25
woman. An Englishman and an Englishwoman.
  What did you say lifting belly. I did not understand you correctly. It is not
well said. For lifting belly. For lifting belly not to lifting belly.
  Did you say, oh lifting belly.
  What is my another name.
  Representative.
  Of what.   30
  Of the evils of eating.
  What are they then.
  They are sweet and figs.
  Do not send them.
  Yes we will it will be very easy.   35

Part II

Lifting belly. Are you. Lifting.
Oh dear I said I was tender, fierce and tender.
Do it. What a splendid example of carelessness.
It gives me a great deal of pleasure to say yes.
Why do I always smile.   40
I don't know.
It pleases me.
You are easily pleased.
I am very pleased.
Thank you I am scarcely sunny.   45
I wish the sun would come out.
Yes.
Do you lift it.
High.
Yes sir I helped to do it.   50
Did you.

WALLACE STEVENS   *(1879–1955)*

The Snow Man   *(1923)*

One must have a mind of winter
To regard the frost and the boughs
Of the pine-trees crusted with snow;

And have been cold a long time
To behold the junipers shagged with ice,   5
The spruces rough in the distant glitter

Of the January sun; and not to think
Of any misery in the sound of the wind,
In the sound of a few leaves,

Which is the sound of the land   10
Full of the same wind
That is blowing in the same bare place

For the listener, who listens in the snow,
And, nothing himself, beholds
Nothing that is not there and the nothing that is.   15

The Emperor of Ice-Cream   *(1923)*

Call the roller of big cigars,
The muscular one, and bid him whip
In kitchen cups concupiscent curds.
Let the wenches dawdle in such dress
As they are used to wear, and let the boys   5
Bring flowers in last month's newspapers.
Let be be finale of seem.
The only emperor is the emperor of ice-cream.

Take from the dresser of deal.°
Lacking the three glass knobs, that sheet   10
On which she embroidered fantails once
And spread it so as to cover her face.
If her horny feet protrude, they come
To show how cold she is, and dumb.
Let the lamp affix its beam.   15
The only emperor is the emperor of ice-cream.

---

9 *deal*: Pinewood.

Anecdote of the Jar (1937)

I placed a jar in Tennessee,
And round it was, upon a hill.
It made the slovenly wilderness
Surround that hill.

The wilderness rose up to it,   5
And sprawled around, no longer wild.
The jar was round upon the ground
And tall and of a port in air.

It took dominion everywhere.
The jar was gray and bare.   10
It did not give of bird or bush,
Like nothing else in Tennessee.

MAY SWENSON   (1913–1989)

Poet to Tiger (1991)

THE HAIR

You went downstairs
saw a hair in the sink
and squeezed my toothpaste by the neck.
You roared. My ribs are sore.
This morning even my pencil's got your toothmarks.   5
Big Cat Eye cocked on me you see bird bones.
Snuggled in the rug of your belly
your breath so warm
I smell delicious fear.
Come breathe on me rough pard   10
put soft paws here.

THE SALT

You don't put salt on anything
so I'm eating without.
Honey on the eggs is all right
mustard on the toast.   15
I'm not complaining I'm saying I'm
living with *you*.
You like your meat raw
don't care if it's cold.

Your stomach must have tastebuds   20
you swallow so fast.
Night falls early. It's foggy. Just now

I found another of your bite marks in the cheese.
I'm hungry. Please
come bounding home   25
I'll hand you the wine to open
with your teeth.
Scorched me a steak unsalted
boil my coffee twice
say the blessing to a jingle on the blue TV.   30
Under the lap robe on our chilly couch
look behind my ears "for welps"
and hug me.

THE SAND

You're right I brought a grain
or two of sand   35
into bed I guess in my socks.
But it was you pushed them off
along with everything else.

Asleep you flip
over roll   40
everything under
you and off
me. I'm always grabbing
for my share of the sheets.

Or else you wake me every hour with sudden   45
growled I-love-yous
trapping my face between those plushy
shoulders. All my float-dreams turn spins
and never finish. I'm thinner
now. My watch keeps running fast.   50
But best is when we're riding pillion
my hips within your lap. You let me steer.
Your hand and arm go clear
around my ribs your moist
dream teeth fastened on my nape.   55

A grain of sand in the bed upsets you or
a hair on the floor.
But you'll get
in slick and wet from the shower if I let
you. Or with your wool cap   60

and skiing jacket on
if it's cold.
Tiger don't scold me
don't make me comb my hair outdoors.
Cuff me careful. Lick don't   65
crunch. Make last what's yours.

THE DREAM

You get into the tub holding *The Naked Ape*
in your teeth. You wet that blond
three-cornered pelt lie back wide
chest afloat. You're reading   70
in the rising steam and I'm
drinking coffee from your tiger cup.
You say you dreamed
I had your baby book
and it was pink and blue.   75
I pointed to a page and there
was your face with a cub grin.

You put your paws in your armpits
make a tiger-moo.
Then you say: "Come here   80
Poet and take
this hair
off me." I do.
It's one of mine. I carefully
kill it and carry   85
it outside. And stamp on it
and bury it.

In the begonia bed.
And then take off my shoes
not to bring a grain   90
of sand in to get
into our bed.
I'm going to
do the cooking
now instead   95
of you.
And sneak some salt in
when you're not looking.

ALFRED, LORD TENNYSON   *(1809–1892)*

Break, Break, Break   *(1834)*

Break, break, break,
   On thy cold gray stones, O Sea!
And I would that my tongue could utter
   The thoughts that arise in me.

O well for the fisherman's boy,   5
   That he shouts with his sister at play!
O well for the sailor lad,
   That he sings in his boat on the bay!

And the stately ships go on
   To their haven under the hill;   10
But O for the touch of a vanished hand,
   And the sound of a voice that is still!

Break, break, break
   At the foot of thy crags, O Sea!
But the tender grace of a day that is dead   15
   Will never come back to me.

Crossing the Bar   *(1889)*

Sunset and evening star,
   And one clear call for me!
And may there be no moaning of the bar,
   When I put out to sea,

But such a tide as moving seems asleep,   5
   Too full for sound and foam,
When that which drew from out the boundless deep
   Turns again home.

Twilight and evening bell,
   And after that the dark!   10
And may there be no sadness of farewell,
   When I embark;

For though from out our bourne of Time and Place
   The flood may bear me far,
I hope to see my Pilot face to face   15
   When I have crossed that bar.

DYLAN THOMAS   *(1914–1953)*

In My Craft or Sullen Art   *(1946)*

In my craft or sullen art
Exercised in the still night
When only the moon rages
And the lovers lie abed
With all their griefs in their arms,   5
I labor by singing light
Not for ambition or bread
Or the strut and trade of charms
On the ivory stages
But for the common wages   10
Of their most secret heart.

Not for the proud man apart
From the raging moon I write
On these spindrift pages
Nor for the towering dead   15
With their nightingales and psalms
But for the lovers, their arms
Round the griefs of the ages,
Who pay no praise or wages
Nor heed my craft or art.   20

Do Not Go Gentle into That Good Night   *(1952)*

Do not go gentle into that good night,
Old age should burn and rave at close of day;
Rage, rage against the dying of the light.

Though wise men at their end know dark is right,
Because their words had forked no lightning they   5
Do not go gentle into that good night.

Good men, the last wave by, crying how bright
Their frail deeds might have danced in a green bay,
Rage, rage against the dying of the light.

Wild men who caught and sang the sun in flight,   10
And learn, too late, they grieved it on its way,
Do not go gentle into that good night.

Grave men, near death, who see with blinding sight
Blind eyes could blaze like meteors and be gay,
Rage, rage against the dying of the light.   15

And you, my father, there on the sad height,
Curse, bless, me now with your fierce tears, I pray.
Do not go gentle into that good night.
Rage, rage against the dying of the light.

EDWARD THOMAS   *(1878–1917)*

The Owl   *(1917)*

Downhill I came, hungry, and yet not starved;
Cold, yet had heat within me that was proof
Against the North wind; tired, yet so that rest
Had seemed the sweetest thing under a roof.

Then at the inn I had food, fire, and rest,   5
Knowing how hungry, cold, and tired was I.
All of the night was quite barred out except
An owl's cry, a most melancholy cry

Shaken out long and clear upon the hill,
No merry note, nor cause of merriment,   10
But one telling me plain what I escaped
And others could not, that night, as in I went.

And salted was my food, and my repose,
Salted and sobered, too, by the bird's voice
Speaking for all who lay under the stars,   15
Soldiers and poor, unable to rejoice.

HENRY DAVID THOREAU   *(1817–1862)*

I Am a Parcel of Vain Strivings Tied   *(1841)*

I am a parcel of vain strivings tied
    By a chance bond together,
  Dangling this way and that, their links
      Were made so loose and wide,
            Methinks,   5
        For milder weather.

A bunch of violets without their roots,
    And sorrel intermixed,
    Encircled by a wisp of straw
       Once coiled about their shoots,   10
          The law
          By which I'm fixed.

A nosegay which Time clutched from out
    Those fair Elysian fields,°
    With weeds and broken stems, in haste,   15
       Doth make the rabble rout
          That waste
          The day he yields.

And here I bloom for a short hour unseen,
    Drinking my juices up,   20
    With no root in the land
       To keep my branches green,
          But stand
          In a bare cup.

JEAN TOOMER   *(1894–1967)*

Georgia Dusk   *(1923)*

The sky, lazily disdaining to pursue
    The setting sun, too indolent to hold
    A lengthened tournament for flashing gold,
Passively darkens for night's barbecue,

A feast of moon and men and barking hounds,   5
    An orgy for some genius of the South
    With blood-hot eyes and cane-lipped scented mouth,
Surprised in making folksongs from soul sounds.

The sawmill blows its whistle, buzz-saws stop,
    And silence breaks the bud of knoll and hill,   10
    Soft settling pollen where plowed lands fulfill
Their early promise of a bumper crop.

Smoke from the pyramidal sawdust pile
    Curls up, blue ghosts of trees, tarrying low

---

14 *Elysian fields:* After life of the blessed in Greek and Roman mythology.

Where only chips and stumps are left to show   15
The solid proof of former domicile.

Meanwhile, the men, with vestiges of pomp,
   Race memories of king and caravan,
   High-priests, an ostrich, and a juju-man,
Go singing through the footpaths of the swamp.   20

Their voices rise . . the pine trees are guitars,
   Strumming, pine-needles fall like sheets of rain . .
   Their voices rise . . the chorus of the cane
Is caroling a vesper to the stars. .

O singers, resinous and soft your songs   25
   Above the sacred whisper of the pines,
   Give virgin lips to cornfield concubines,
Bring dreams of Christ to dusky cane-lipped throngs.

Margaret Walker *(1915–1998)*

Childhood   *(1942)*

When I was a child I knew red miners
dressed raggedly and wearing carbide lamps.
I saw them come down red hills to their camps
dyed with red dust from old Ishkooda mines.°
Night after night I met them on the roads,   5
or on the streets in town I caught their glance;
the swing of dinner buckets in their hands,
and grumbling undermining all their words.

I also lived in low cotton country
where moonlight hovered over ripe haystacks,   10
or stumps of trees, and croppers' rotting shacks
with famine, terror, flood, and plague near by;
where sentiment and hatred still held sway
and only bitter land was washed away.

---

4 *Ishkooda mines:* Located south of Birmingham, Alabama.

PHILLIS WHEATLEY   *(1753–1784)*

On Being Brought from Africa to America°   *(1773)*

'Twas mercy brought me from my pagan land,
Taught my benighted soul to understand
That there's a God, that there's a Savior too:
Once I redemption neither sought nor knew.
Some view our sable race with scornful eye,   5
"Their color is a diabolic die."°
Remember, Christians, Negros, black as Cain,
May be refined, and join th' angelic train.

WALT WHITMAN   *(1819–1892)*

from Song of Myself   *(1855, 1881)*

1

I celebrate myself, and sing myself,
And what I assume you shall assume,
For every atom belonging to me as good belongs to you.

I loafe and invite my soul,
I lean and loafe at my ease observing a spear of summer grass.   5

My tongue, every atom of my blood, form'd from this soil, this air,
Born here of parents born here from parents the same, and their
     parents the same,
I, now thirty-seven years old in perfect health begin,
Hoping to cease not till death.

Creeds and schools in abeyance,   10
Retiring back a while sufficed at what they are, but never forgotten,
I harbor for good or bad, I permit to speak at every hazard,
Nature without check with original energy.

11

Twenty-eight young men bathe by the shore,
Twenty-eight young men and all so friendly;   15
Twenty-eight years of womanly life and all so lonesome.

---

from Africa to America: Wheatley arrived in Boston from Africa in 1761 at the age of eight.
6 *die:* Dye.

She owns the fine house by the rise of the bank,
She hides handsome and richly drest aft the blinds of the window.

Which of the young men does she like the best?
Ah the homeliest of them is beautiful to her.   20

Where are you off to, lady? for I see you,
You splash in the water there, yet stay stock still in your room.

Dancing and laughing along the beach came the twenty-ninth bather,
The rest did not see her, but she saw them and loved them.

The beards of the young men glisten'd with wet, it ran from their long   25
    hair,
Little streams, pass'd all over their bodies.
An unseen hand also pass'd over their bodies,
It descended tremblingly from their temples and ribs.

The young men float on their backs, their white bellies bulge to the
    sun, they do not ask who seizes fast to them,
They do not know who puffs and declines with pendant and bending   30
    arch,
They do not think whom they souse with spray.

52

The spotted hawk swoops by and accuses me, he complains of my gab
    and my loitering.

I too am not a bit tamed, I too am untranslatable,
I sound my barbaric yawp over the roofs of the world.

The last scud of day holds back for me,
It flings my likeness after the rest and true as any on the shadow'd wilds,   35
It coaxes me to the vapor and the dusk.

I depart as air, I shake my white locks at the runaway sun,
I effuse my flesh in eddies, and drift it in lacy jags.

I bequeath myself to the dirt to grow from the grass I love,
If you want me again look for me under your boot-soles.   40

You will hardly know who I am or what I mean,
But I shall be good health to you nevertheless,
And filter and fibre your blood.

Failing to fetch me at first keep encouraged,
Missing me one place search another,   45
I stop somewhere waiting for you.

When I Heard the Learn'd Astronomer   *(1865)*

When I heard the learn'd astronomer,
When the proofs, the figures, were ranged in columns before me,
When I was shown the charts and diagrams, to add, divide, and measure
    them,
When I sitting heard the astronomer where he lectured with much applause in
    the lecture-room,
How soon unaccountable I became tired and sick,   5
Till rising and gliding out I wander'd off by myself,
In the mystical moist night-air, and from time to time,
Look'd up in perfect silence at the stars.

By the Bivouac's Fitful Flame   *(1867)*

By the bivouac's fitful flame,
A procession winding around me, solemn and sweet and slow—but
    first I note,
The tents of the sleeping army, the fields' and woods' dim outline,
The darkness lit by spots of kindled fire, the silence,
Like a phantom far or near an occasional figure moving,   5
The shrubs and trees, (as I lift my eyes they seem to be stealthily
    watching me,)
While wind in procession thoughts, O tender and wondrous thoughts,
Of life and death, of home and the past and loved, and of those that
    are far away;
A solemn and slow procession there as I sit on the ground,
By the bivouac's fitful flame.   10

Cavalry Crossing a Ford   *(1871)*

A line in long array where they wind betwixt green islands,
They take a serpentine course, their arms flash in the sun—hark to
    the musical clank,
Behold the silvery river, in it the splashing horses loitering stop to
    drink,   5
Behold the brown-faced men, each group, each person a picture, the
    negligent rest on the saddles,
Some emerge on the opposite bank, others are just entering the
    ford—while,
Scarlet and blue and snowy white,   10
The guidon flags° flutter gayly in the wind.

---

11 *guidon flags:* Military banners.

A Noiseless Patient Spider   *(1868)*

A noiseless patient spider,
I mark'd where on a little promontory it stood isolated,
Mark'd how to explore the vacant vast surrounding,
It launch'd forth filament, filament, filament, out of itself,
Ever unreeling them, ever tirelessly speeding them.   5

And you O my soul where you stand,
Surrounded, detached, in measureless oceans of space,
Ceaselessly musing, venturing, throwing, seeking the spheres to connect
    them,
Till the bridge you will need be form'd, till the ductile anchor hold,
Till the gossamer thread you fling catch somewhere, O my soul.   10

RICHARD WILBUR   *(b. 1921)*

The Death of a Toad   *(1950)*

    A toad the power mower caught,
Chewed and clipped off a leg, with a hobbling hop has got
    To the garden verge, and sanctuaried him
    Under the cineraria leaves, in the shade
        Of the ashen heartshaped leaves, in a dim,   5
            Low, and a final glade.

    The rare original heartsblood goes,
Spends on the earthen hide, in the folds and wizening, flows
    In the gutters of the banked and staring eyes. He lies
    As still as if he would return to stone,   10
        And soundlessly attending, dies
            Toward some deep monotone,

    Toward misted and ebullient seas
And cooling shores, toward lost Amphibia's emperies.
    Day dwindles, drowning, and at length is gone   15
    In the wide and antique eyes, which still appear
        To watch, across the castrate lawn,
            The haggard daylight steer.

Junk   *(1961)*

Huru Welandes
                    worc ne geswiceð
monna ænigum
                    ðara ðe Mimming can
heardne gehealdan.
                         —WALDERE°

An axe angles
                    from my neighbor's ashcan;
It is hell's handiwork,
                         the wood not hickory,
The flow of the grain   5
                         not faithfully followed.
The shivered shaft
                    rises from a shellheap
Of plastic playthings,
                         paper plates,   10
And the sheer shards
                         of shattered tumblers
That were not annealed
                         for the time needful.
At the same curbside,   15
                         a cast-off cabinet
Of wavily-warped
                    unseasoned wood
Waits to be trundled
                         in the trash-man's truck.   20
Haul them off! Hide them!
                         The heart winces
For junk and gimcrack,
                         for jerrybuilt things
And the men who make them   25
                         for a little money,
Bartering pride
                    like the bought boxer
Who pulls his punches,
                         or the paid-off jockey   30
Who in the home stretch
                         holds in his horse.
Yet the things themselves
                         in thoughtless honor

Waldere: Old English poem, "The handiwork of Weland will not betray any man who knows how to wield [the sword] mimming."

Have kept composure,   35
                    like captives who would not
Talk under torture.
                    Tossed from a tailgate
Where the dump displays
                              its random dolmens,   40
Its black barrows
                    and blazing valleys,
They shall waste in the weather
                              toward what they were.
The sun shall glory   45
                    in the glitter of glass-chips,
Foreseeing the salvage
                              of the prisoned sand,
And the blistering paint
                              peel off in patches,   50
That the good grain
                    be discovered again.
Then burnt, bulldozed,
                    they shall all be buried
To the depth of diamonds,   55
                    in the making dark
Where halt Hephaestus
                    keeps his hammer
And Wayland's work
                    is worn away.   60

WILLIAM CARLOS WILLIAMS   *(1883–1963)*

Danse Russe   *(1916)*

If when my wife is sleeping
and the baby and Kathleen
are sleeping
and the sun is a flame-white disc
in silken mists   5
above shining trees,—
if I in my north room
dance naked, grotesquely
before my mirror
waving my shirt round my head   10
and singing softly to myself:
"I am lonely, lonely.
I was born to be lonely,
I am best so!"

If I admire my arms, my face,   15
my shoulders, flanks, buttocks
against the yellow drawn shades,—

Who shall say I am not
the happy genius of my household?

This Is Just to Say   *(1934)*

I have eaten
the plums
that were in
the icebox

and which   5
you were probably
saving
for breakfast

Forgive me
they were delicious   10
so sweet
and so cold

The Dance   *(1944)*

In Breughel's° great picture, The Kermess,
the dancers go round, they go round and
around, the squeal and the blare and the
tweedle of bagpipes, a bugle and fiddles
tipping their bellies (round as the thick-   5
sided glasses whose wash they impound)
their hips and their bellies off balance
to turn them. Kicking and rolling about
the Fair Grounds, swinging their butts, those
shanks must be sound to bear up under such   10
rollicking measures, prance as they dance
in Breughel's great picture, The Kermess.

---

1 *Breughel:* Pieter Brueghel, the Elder (1525–1569), Flemish painter.

The Descent   *(1954)*

The descent beckons
         as the ascent beckoned.
                 Memory is a kind
of accomplishment,
         a sort of renewal   5
even
an initiation, since the spaces it opens are new places
         inhabited by hordes
                 heretofore unrealized,

of new kinds—   10
         since their movements
                 are toward new objectives
(even though formerly they were abandoned).

No defeat is made up entirely of defeat—since
the world it opens is always a place   15
         formerly
                 unsuspected. A
world lost,
         a world unsuspected,
                 beckons to new places   20
and no whiteness (lost) is so white as the memory
of whiteness.

With evening, love wakens
         though its shadows
                 which are alive by reason   25
of the sun shining—
         grow sleepy now and drop away
                 from desire.

Love without shadows stirs now
         beginning to awaken   30
         as night
advances.

The descent
         made up of despairs
                 and without accomplishment   35
realizes a new awakening:
         which is a reversal
of despair.
         For what we cannot accomplish, what

is denied to love, 40
what we have lost in the anticipation—
    a descent follows,
        endless and indestructible.

WILLIAM WORDSWORTH *(1770–1850)*

She Dwelt Among the Untrodden Ways *(1800)*

She dwelt among the untrodden ways
   Beside the springs of Dove.
A Maid whom there were none to praise
   And very few to love;

A violet by a mossy stone 5
   Half hidden from the eye!
—Fair as a star, when only one
   Is shining in the sky.

She lived unknown, and few could know
   When Lucy ceased to be; 10
But she is in her grave, and, oh,
   The difference to me!

It Is a Beauteous Evening *(1807)*

It is a beauteous evening, calm and free,
The holy time is quiet as a Nun
Breathless with adoration; the broad sun
Is sinking down in its tranquility;
The gentleness of heaven broods o'er the Sea: 5
Listen! the mighty Being is awake,
And doth with his eternal motion make
A sound like thunder—everlastingly.
Dear Child! dear Girl! that walkest with me here,
If thou appear untouched by solemn thought, 10
Thy nature is not therefore less divine:
Thou livest in Abraham's bosom all the year;
And worshipp'st at the Temple's inner shrine,
God being with thee when we know it not.

London, 1802   *(1807)*

Milton! thou shouldst be living at this hour:
England hath need of thee: she is a fen
Of stagnant waters: altar, sword, and pen,
Fireside, the heroic wealth of hall and bower,
Have forfeited their ancient English dower   5
Of inward happiness. We are selfish men;
Oh! raise us up, return to us again;
And give us manners, virtue, freedom, power.
Thy soul was like a Star, and dwelt apart;
Thou hadst a voice whose sound was like the sea: 10
Pure as the naked heavens, majestic, free,
So didst thou travel on life's common way,
In cheerful godliness; and yet thy heart
The lowliest duties on herself did lay.

My Heart Leaps Up   *(1807)*

My heart leaps up when I behold
    A rainbow in the sky:
So was it when my life began;
So is it now I am a man;
So be it when I shall grow old,   5
    Or let me die!
The Child is father of the Man;
And I could wish my days to be
Bound each to each by natural piety.

JAMES WRIGHT   *(1927–1980)*

The Journey   *(1982)*

Anghiari is medieval, a sleeve sloping down
A steep hill, suddenly sweeping out
To the edge of a cliff, and dwindling.
But far up the mountain, behind the town,
We too were swept out, out by the wind,   5
Alone with the Tuscan grass.

Wind had been blowing across the hills
For days, and everything now was graying gold
With dust, everything we saw, even
Some small children scampering along a road,   10

Twittering Italian to a small caged bird.
We sat beside them to rest in some brushwood,
And I leaned down to rinse the dust from my face.

I found the spider web there, whose hinges
Reeled heavily and crazily with the dust, 15
Whole mounds and cemeteries of it, sagging
And scattering shadows among shells and wings.
And then she stepped into the center of air
Slender and fastidious, the golden hair
Of daylight along her shoulders, she poised there, 20
While ruins crumbled on every side of her.
Free of the dust, as though a moment before
She had stepped inside the earth, to bathe herself.

I gazed, close to her, till at last she stepped
Away in her own good time. 25

Many men
Have searched all over Tuscany and never found
What I found there, the heart of the light
Itself shelled and leaved, balancing
On filaments themselves falling. The secret 30
Of this journey is to let the wind
Blow its dust all over your body,
To let it go on blowing, to step lightly, lightly
All the way through your ruins, and not to lose
Any sleep over the dead, who surely 35
Will bury their own, don't worry.

SIR THOMAS WYATT   *(1503–1542)*

They Flee from Me   *(1557)*

They flee from me that sometime did me seek
   With naked foot stalking in my chamber.
I have seen them gentle tame and meek
   That now are wild and do not remember
   That sometime they put themselves in danger 5
To take bread at my hand; and now they range
Busily seeking with a continual change.

Thanked be fortune it hath been otherwise
   Twenty times better; but once in special,
In thin array after a pleasant guise, 10

When her loose gown from her shoulders did fall,
  And she me caught in her arms long and small;
And therewithall sweetly did me kiss,
And softly said, "Dear heart, how like you this?"

It was no dream: I lay broad waking.   15
  But all is turned thorough my gentleness
Into a strange fashion of forsaking;
  And I have leave to go of her goodness,
  And she also to use newfangleness.
But since that I so kindely am served,   20
I fain would know what she hath deserved.

W. B. Yeats   *(1865–1939)*

The Second Coming   *(1921)*

Turning and turning in the widening gyre°
The falcon cannot hear the falconer;
Things fall apart; the centre cannot hold;
Mere anarchy is loosed upon the world,
The blood-dimmed tide is loosed, and everywhere   5
The ceremony of innocence is drowned;
The best lack all conviction, while the worst
Are full of passionate intensity.

Surely some revelation is at hand;
Surely the Second Coming is at hand: 10
The Second Coming! Hardly are those words out
When a vast image out of *Spiritus Mundi*°
Troubles my sight: somewhere in sands of the desert
A shape with lion body and the head of a man,
A gaze blank and pitiless as the sun,   15
Is moving its slow thighs, while all about it
Reel shadows of the indignant desert birds.
The darkness drops again; but now I know
That twenty centuries of stony sleep
Were vexed to nightmare by a rocking cradle,   20
And what rough beast, its hour come round at last,
Slouches toward Bethlehem to be born?

---

1 *gyre:* Conical spiral that Yeats understood as a "fundamental symbol" for cycles of history that distinguish the Greco-Roman from the Christian epoch.   12 *Spiritus Mundi:* Spirit of the world, or what Yeats described as the "great memory" of the collective unconscious.

Sailing to Byzantium°   *(1927)*

1

That is no country for old men. The young
In one another's arms, birds in the trees
—Those dying generations—at their song,
The salmon-falls, the mackerel-crowded seas,
Fish, flesh, or fowl, commend all summer long   5
Whatever is begotten, born, and dies.
Caught in that sensual music all neglect
Monuments of unaging intellect.

2

An aged man is but a paltry thing,
A tattered coat upon a stick, unless   10
Soul clap its hands and sing, and louder sing
For every tatter in its mortal dress,
Nor is there singing school but studying
Monuments of its own magnificence;
And therefore I have sailed the seas and come   15
To the holy city of Byzantium.

3

O sages standing in God's holy fire
As in the gold mosaic of a wall,
Come from the holy fire, perne in a gyre,°
And be the singing-masters of my soul.   20
Consume my heart away; sick with desire
And fastened to a dying animal
It knows not what it is; and gather me
Into the artifice of eternity.

4

Once out of nature I shall never take   25
My bodily form from any natural thing,
But such a form as Grecian goldsmiths make
Of hammered gold and gold enamelling
To keep a drowsy Emperor awake;
Or set upon a golden bough to sing   30
To lords and ladies of Byzantium
Of what is past, or passing, or to come.

———

Byzantium: Modern Istanbul. Yeats considered Byzantium and its fifth- and sixth-century mosaics as symbols for the "unity of being" where "religious, aesthetic, and practical life were one." 19 *perne in a gyre:* Spin a bobbin in a spiral motion. Yeats implies here that the holy fire spins forth the sages in a spiral to purge the poet's soul.

24 Biographical Sketches of Selected Poets

John Ashbery (b. 1927)

Born and raised in Rochester, New York, John Ashbery attended Harvard University and Columbia University. Three years after publishing his first volume *Turandot and Other Poems* (1953), Ashbery's *Some Trees* (1956) was selected by W. H. Auden for the prestigious Yale Younger Poets Series award. Of his subject matter, Ashbery has written that "the particular experience is of lesser interest to me than the way it filters through to me. I believe this is the way in which it happens with most people, and I'm trying to record a kind of generalized transcript of what's really going on in our minds all day long." Ashbery has published more than twenty books of verse and prose poems including *The Tennis Court Oath* (1962), *Rivers and Mountains* (1966), *The Double Dream of Spring* (1970), *Three Poems* (1972), *Self-Portrait in a Convex Mirror* (1975), *Houseboat Days* (1977), *As We Know* (1979), *Shadow Train* (1981), *Flow Chart* (1991), *Hotel Lautramont* (1994), *And the Stars Were Shining* (1994), *Can You Hear, Bird* (1995), *Wakefulness* (1998), *Girls on the Run: A Poem* (1999), *Your Name Here* (2000). He is a recipient of the Pulitzer Prize for Poetry, the National Book Critics Circle Award, and the National Book Award for *Self-Portrait in a Convex Mirror*. He teaches at Brooklyn College.

Matthew Arnold (1822–1888)

The Victorian English poet Matthew Arnold was born at Laleham on the Thames, Middlesex. He received his education at Winchester, Rugby, and Balliol College, Oxford. Early on, Arnold showed promise as a poet, winning prizes for his poem "Alaric at Rome" at Rugby and the Newdigate Prize at Oxford for "Cromwell, A Prize Poem." Before becoming private secretary to Lord Lanscowne in 1847, Arnold traveled in France where he met the novelist George Sand. In 1851 Arnold was appointed inspector of schools, which became a lifelong vocation and enabled him to marry Frances Lucy Wightman. Arnold's literary career began in 1849 with his first volume of verse, *The Strayed Reveller and Other Poems*, followed by *Empedocles on Etna and Other Poems* (1852), *Poems, Second Series* (1855), and *New Poems* (1867). Arnold's reputation rests as much on his work as a literary and cultural critic as on his published poetry. Throughout his career in volumes such as *Essays in Criticism* (1865) and *Culture and Anarchy* (1869), Arnold sought what he described as "the pursuit of total perfection by means of getting to know, on all the matters which most concern us, the best which has been thought and said in the world." This version of high culture was later disputed in cultural criticism by critics such as Raymond Williams, who redefined culture in terms of a "particular way of life" which, he said, "expresses certain meanings and values not only in art and learning, but also in institutions and ordinary behaviour." Beginning in 1883, Arnold received an annual pension of 250 pounds per year conferred by William Gladstone which allowed him to travel widely including a lecture tour to the United States. He returned for another visit in 1886 to visit his daughter, who had married an American. Matthew Arnold died two years later in Liverpool.

Margaret Atwood (b. 1939)

A Canadian author, Margaret Atwood was born in 1939 in Ottawa, Ontario and received her education first at Victoria College, and later the University of Toronto, and Harvard University. In 1962, she published her first volume of verse, entitled *Double Persephone*, followed by *The Circle Game* (1964), which received the Governor's General Award. In addition, she has published three other compilations of her verse in *Selected Poems* (1976), *Selected Poems II* (1986), and *Eating Fire: Selected Poems 1965–1998*). In addition to her work as a published poet, Margaret Atwood is more widely known as a prose writer of short stories, children's literature and nonfiction as well as novels, including *The Edible Woman* (1969), *Surfacing* (1972), and *Cat's Eye* (1988), among others. Since 1990 when Atwood's 1985 novel *The Handmaid's Tale* was made into a Hollywood film, Atwood has enjoyed a broad, popular readership. A writer of literary distinction, Atwood has won several major awards, including the Booker Prize for *The Blind Assassin* (2000).

W. H. Auden (1907–1973)

The British modernist author W. H. Auden was born in York, England. As a student at St. Edmund's preparatory school, he first met Christopher Isherwood with whom he would share a rich literary collaboration. Auden later studied at Christ Church, Oxford, and was a leader of a new circle of British poets that included Stephen Spender, C. Day-Lewis, and Louis MacNeice. Auden's early poetry in *Poems* (1930) and *Look Stranger!* (1936) was inspired by Freudian psychology, social Marxism, and a commitment to the leftist international community that led him to participate in the Spanish Civil War, where he served the Republican cause as an ambulance driver. In 1939 Auden emigrated to the United States and became a citizen in 1946. During the 1940s, Auden turned toward Christianity and became a convert to the Anglican church. By 1956, Auden assumed the position of professor of poetry at Oxford and led a cosmopolitan life in England, New York, Italy, and Austria, where he died in 1973. Throughout his life, Auden authored more than twenty-five volumes of verse. In addition to his career as a poet, Auden composed with his long-time companion, Chester Kallman, several opera librettos, including one for Igor Stravinsky's *The Rake's Progress* (1951); he also wrote discerning literary criticism collected in *The Dyer's Hand* (1962).

Elizabeth Bishop (1911–1979)

Elizabeth Bishop was born in Worcester, Massachusetts, in 1911, and her father passed away before her first birthday. By the time she turned five, her mother had suffered a series of breakdowns and become institutionalized for mental illness. As a result, Bishop was raised by her maternal grandparents in Nova Scotia before moving to Worcester at the age of six to live with her father's family. At age sixteen, Bishop enrolled at Walnut Hill boarding school, later followed by her undergraduate studies at Vassar College. At Vassar, she met Mary McCarthy, with whom she would share a literary collaboration. The poems she wrote while at Vassar drew the notice of the modernist poet Marianne Moore, who became an important mentor and a lifelong friend. Elizabeth Bishop was a cosmopolitan citizen of the world and traveled widely in France, Mexico, and Key West. For fifteen years she lived in Brazil with her longtime companion, Lota de Macedo Soares. This broad, international experience is reflected in such volume titles as *North and South* (1946), *A Cold Spring* (1955), *Questions of Travel* (1965), and *Geography III* (1976), all of which are compiled in *The Complete Poems 1927–1979* (1983). Bishop had a pronounced influence on a number of her contemporaries, including Robert Lowell, who dedicated his widely read poem "Skunk Hour" to Bishop. Following the suicide of Lota de Macedo Soares, Bishop left Brazil and took a teaching position at the University of Washington in 1966 and then at Harvard University from 1969 through her retirement in 1977, two years before her death in 1979. Among her numerous awards and honors, Bishop is a recipient of the Pulitzer Prize and the National Book Award.

William Blake (1757–1827)

The son of a London hosier, William Blake was home schooled due in part to his tendency even in childhood toward visionary experience. Not just a visionary, however, Blake showed early talent for the visual arts. After attending drawing school, he apprenticed to an engraver for seven years, after which he briefly attended the Royal Academy. In 1782, Blake married Catherine Boucher and taught her to read and write. She assisted Blake with the illustrations for his poetic manuscripts. Blake's first published volume, *Poetical Sketches* (1783), took a stance of protest against King George III and his policies toward the American colonies. As an independent-minded thinker, Blake also criticized the institutions of rational science, the church, and state in *Songs of Innocence* (1789) and *Songs of Experience* (1794). Blake's famous nonconformist slogan—"I must create a system or be enslaved by another man's"—reflected his philosophical resistance to neoclassical rationalism. In the 1790s Blake's long poems—such as "The French Revolution" (1791), "America, a Prophecy" (1793), and "Europe, a Prophecy" (1791)—engaged imaginatively with the revolutionary contexts of his age. Theological parody and critique of religious orthodoxy and utilitarian thought characterize works from this decade including "The Book of Urizen" (1794) and "The Marriage of Heaven and Hell" (1790–1793). In addition to his income from professional engraving, Blake also received the patronage of William Hayley, which allowed him to move to Felpham where he learned classical languages and Hebrew and cultivated the kind of visionary mysticism that informs his major epics: *Milton* (1804–1808), *Vala, or The Four Zoas* (1797, 1800), and *Jerusalem* (1804–1820). Although reduced to poverty in later life, Blake mentored a new generation of artists, including John Linnell who commissioned Blake's last work, illustrations for Dante's *Divine Comedy*, which Blake worked on until he passed away in 1827.

Robert Bly (b. 1926)

A native Minnesotan, Robert Bly was brought up on a farm in Madison, Minnesota, and later served in the U.S. Navy during World War II. He then attended St. Olaf College and graduated from Harvard University in 1950. In college and while living for a time in New York City, Bly composed the poems that would make up his first volume, *The Lute of Three Loudnesses*. In 1958 he founded the influential and provocative literary magazine *The Fifties* that later evolved into *The Sixties, The Seventies,* and so on down to the present. Bly's poetry of the so-called deep image, which he explored in collaboration with Robert Kelly and James Wright, was influenced by the archetypal psychology of Carl Jung. Another poetic influence has come from translating Spanish and South American surrealist poets such as César Vallejo, Pablo Neruda, and Antonio Machado as well as the Swedish poet Tomas Transtromer. In explaining his understanding of the poetic symbol, Bly has employed the key word *entangle* from the Irish modernist poet W. B. Yeats: "I'll use Yeats's marvellous word *entangle*; he suggested that the symbolist poem entangles some substance from the divine world in its words." Bly's role as a poet has also entangled forms of social and political advocacy as in his founding (with David Ray) of American Writers Against the Vietnam War and his controversial promotion of a male spiritualist movement theorized in his 1990 best-selling book of prose, *Iron John*. In addition to numerous translations, volumes of prose, and prose poems, Bly's major books of poetry include *Silence in the Snowy Fields* (1962), *The Light Around the Body* (1967), *The Morning Glory* (1969), *The Teeth Mother Naked at Last* (1970), *Sleepers Joining Hands* (1973), *Old Man Rubbing His Eyes* (1975), *This Tree Will Be Here for a Thousand Years* (1979), *The Man in the Black Coat Turns* (1981), and *Eating the Honey of Words: New and Selected Poems* (1999). Never having held a permanent academic position, Bly supports himself from his writing, residing in rural Minnesota.

Louise Bogan (1897–1970)

A native of Maine, Louise Bogan grew up in an unsettled household owing, in part, to her mother's marital infidelity. After her education at Boston Girls' Latin School, Bogan attended Boston University in 1915 and 1916, when she married Curt Alexander, an army officer, with whom she had a daughter. Four years later, Alexander's death left her a single parent with uncertain means. Moving to New York City, Bogan began her life as a writer in earnest, collaborating with such major modernist writers as William Carlos Williams, Malcolm Cowley, Lola Ridge, John Reed, Marianne Moore, and Edmund Wilson, who coached Bogan in professional reviewing that gave her an income. Her first volume of verse, *Body of This Death* (1923), mined the resources of formal lyricism in exploring the terms of her artistic survival that ranged from depression to joy. Poetry and psychoanalysis sustained Bogan during these years through her troubled marriage to writer Raymond Holden. Her turmoil is reflected in such titles as *Dark Summer* (1929) and *The Sleeping Fury* (1937). *A Poet's Alphabet: Reflections on the Literary Art and Vocation*, later published in 1970, collects the pieces Bogan wrote as a poetry reviewer for *The New Yorker* magazine. Her visibility as a reviewer and teacher of poetry is also reflected in her critical history *American Poetry, 1900–1950*. Bogan's achievement as a poet, however, did not go unrecognized, and she received a Bollingen Prize in 1955 and awards from the Academy of American Poets (1959) and the National Endowment for the Arts (1967). Following her *Collected Poems, 1923–1953*, her last volume of verse is *Estuaries: Poems 1923–1968*.

Gwendolyn Brooks (1917–2000). *See Chapter 16.*

Elizabeth Barrett Browning (1806–1861)

Born in Durham, England, Elizabeth Barrett Browning had an affluent childhood due to the wealth her father accumulated from his sugar plantations in Jamaica. In 1821, she began to suffer from a nervous disorder which was aggravated further by the death of her mother in that year. This trauma, according to her critics, left its trace in her poem "Aurora Leigh." Browning had a passion for classical learning and taught herself Hebrew in order to read the Old Testament. Hugh Stuart Boyd encouraged her in her studies of Greek authors. Her own major volume of accomplished verse appeared in 1838 under the title *The Seraphim and Other Poems*. That same year, however, the trauma of her brother Edward's drowning off the coast of Devon left her an invalid and recluse for the next five years. Nevertheless, her next volume, entitled simply *Poems*, in 1844 drew the attention of Robert Browning, and although six years younger than Elizabeth and in far better health, he courted her over the period of two years. During this time, she composed the poetry that would later make up her *Sonnets from the Portuguese*. Following the example of Percy Shelley and Mary Godwin, the couple eloped to Italy in 1846 and three years later became parents of a son, Robert, in Florence. In 1850, Elizabeth published a second edition of *Poems* including the *Sonnets from the Portuguese*. With the death of William Wordsworth that same year, she became a serious contender for the Laureateship which passed, however, to Tennyson. Her publication of the verse-novel *Aurora Leigh* in 1857 consolidated her popular readership. Toward the end of her life, her political commitment to Italian independence was reflected in *Casa Guidi Windows* (1851) and *Poems before Congress* (1860). In 1861, Robert Browning took Elizabeth to the south in an attempt to treat the disease that would nevertheless take her life that year.

Robert Browning (1812–1889)

Browning's father was a nonconformist who gave up a fortune rather than manage his family's West Indies sugar plantation. Nevertheless, as a bank clerk, Robert senior provided his son with an extensive library collection, which whetted his appetite for a life of letters. Although he attended the University of London in 1828, Browning was largely self-taught and undertook his own studies in Latin, Greek, French, and Italian authors. The eccentricity of his education, however, crept into the obscure references in his early volumes of verse such as *Pauline* (1833), *Paracelsus* (1834), and *Bells and Pomegranates* (1841–1846), which were not particularly well received by critics. It was only through the influence of the theater and such actors as William Macready that Browning turned to the dramatic monologue verse which proved to be his signature form in the *Collected Poems* (1862) and *Dramatis Persone* (1863). By then, his passionate marriage to Elizabeth Barrett Browning, begun in 1846, had been cut short by her death in 1861. Returning from Florence to London, Browning devoted the next decade to his major oeuvre *The Ring and the Book* (1869). After his death in 1889, Browning's poetic craft in such memorable dramatic monologues as "My Last Duchess" and "Soliloquy of the Spanish Cloister" had a lasting influence on the course of modern verse and particularly in the careers of its major practitioners such as T. S. Eliot and Ezra Pound.

George Gordon, Lord Byron (1788–1824)

A contemporary of English romantic poets Percy Bysshe Shelley and John Keats, Lord Byron cut an unconventional and at times heroic character. His mother's family traced its aristocratic roots back to the aristocratic Scottish Gordons. James I. Byron's father, the infamous captain "Mad Jack" Byron, abandoned the family to escape his creditors when the poet was three years old. Raised by his mother in Scotland, Byron at age ten inherited his great-uncle's title and estates. Returning to England, Byron was tutored in Nottingham and in 1801 attended Harrow and later Trinity College, where he published in 1807 two verse volumes: *Fugitive Pieces* and *Hours of Idleness*. Assuming his seat in the House of Lords in 1809, Byron responded to his harsh critics by publishing an anonymous satire, *English Bards and Scotch Reviewers*. A tour of Portugal, Spain, Malta, Albania, and Greece provided material for his autobiographical poem *Childe Harold's Pilgrimage*, which won Byron a broad readership when it was published in 1812. Of his newfound popularity, he later remarked, "I awoke one morning and found myself famous." A series of affairs culminated in Byron's troubled marriage to Anabella Milbanke in 1815. Due to mounting debt and temperamental differences, Byron left England for Europe, never to return. Touring with Percy and Mary Shelley, Byron began an affair with the stepdaughter of William Godwin, Claire

Clairmont, who would later give birth to Byron's daughter. The type of brooding romantic hero that Byron came to represent was captured in his poetic drama *Manfred* (1817), who describes mankind as "half dust, half deity, alike unfit to sink or soar." By 1818 Byron was composing his great work *Don Juan*, inspired, in part, by his affairs with Marianna Segati, a Venetian draper's wife, then Margarita Cogni, and finally Countess Teresa Guicciolo. Following the Countess to Ravenna, Byron was inducted by her father into the revolutionary secret society of the Carbonari. After Shelley's tragic drowning in 1821, Byron became a committed partisan in the Greek war of independence from Turkey. Traveling to Greece, Byron financed and participated in the planning for the assault on the Turkish fortress of Lepanto. In 1824, however, after a year spent in Greece, Byron's health steadily declined and after slipping into a coma, he died on April 19, 1824.

Lewis Carroll (1832–1898)

Charles Lutwidge Dodgson, or "Lewis Carroll," was born into a north English family in 1832. From Cheshire the family moved to Yorkshire when Charles was eleven. Home schooled early on, Charles was enrolled in Yorkshire Grammar School and the Rugby School. For his advanced study, Carroll attended his father's alma mater, Christ Chruch of Oxford. A gifted mathematician, on graduation Dodgson assumed a Christ Church mathematical lectureship and held it for the next twenty-six years. In addition to his mathematical genius, by the mid-1850s he had published several comical and satirical poems and short stories in such national journals as *The Comic Times*, and by 1856 he had also become a skilled photographer. It was also in this year that he published his first poem, "Solitude," under the pseudonym "Lewis Carroll." The genesis for his famous publication *Alice's Adventures under Ground, or Alice in Wonderland* (1865) came in 1862 in stories he invented to entertain the children of Henry Liddell, the dean of Christ Church. At the urging of Alice Liddell, Dodgson wrote out what would become *Alice in Wonderland*, which brought him his lasting reputation as an author, publishing the sequels *Through the Looking-Glass* and *What Alice Found There* (1871), as well as *The Hunting of The Snark* (1876).

Sandra Cisneros (b. 1954)

Born to a Mexican American mother and a Mexican father, Sandra Cisneros spent her early life moving between Mexico City and Chicago. When she studied creative writing as a college student in 1974, she became an active writer. After earning a degree from Chicago's Loyola University, Cisneros earned an M.A. from the creative writing program at the University of Iowa. During the late 1970s, she worked as a teacher in the Chicago barrio, where she found ample material for her writing. Cisneros's rootedness in the Chicano community is reflected in her first volume of poetry, *Bad Boys* (1980), published in a series edited by the Chicano poet Gary Soto. Her first published book of fiction, *The House on Mango Street* (1983), mixed her gift for poetic expression with fictional forms depicting, she has said, "those ghosts inside that haunt me, that will not let me sleep." Two years later, her first book won the Before Columbus American Book Award, followed in 1987 by the publication of her first volume of verse, the widely acclaimed *My Wicked Wicked Ways*. In addition, Cisneros has continued to balance her fictional and poetic forms in publishing *Woman Hollering Creek and Other Stories* (1991) and *Loose Woman: Poems* (1994).

Samuel Taylor Coleridge (1772–1834)

The youngest of fourteen children in the household of the parish vicar and master of the grammar school in Devonshire, England, Coleridge was born in 1772. Following the death of his father in 1781, Coleridge studied at Christ's Hospital School, London, and ten years later entered Jesus College, University of Cambridge. It was here that Coleridge both became an independent-minded philosopher and also where he began to accumulate the debts that would dog him throughout his life. In 1794, Coleridge met Robert Southey and for a time the two planned to emigrate to America to found a commune in Pennsylvania. This utopian scheme fell through when Southey became engaged to Edith Fricker and Coleridge met and married Sarah Fricker, Edith's younger sister. The next year Coleridge began his poetic collaboration with William Wordsworth who encouraged Coleridge to write in a more direct, natural, and colloquial form in such so-called conversation poems as "The Eolian Harp," "This Lime-Tree Bower My Prison" and other works collected in his first volume, *Poems on Various Subjects* (1796). From 1797, Coleridge lived near Wordsworth and his sister, Dorothy, in Somersetshire. Here, the two poets coauthored *Lyrical Ballads* with the famous manifesto on Romantic poetics laid out in its "Preface." Coleridge not only pioneered new colloquial forms of poetry but also worked in traditional forms such as the ode and most notably the ballad in *The Rime of the Ancient Mariner*. Subsequently, Coleridge and Wordsworth toured Europe, with Coleridge spending most of his time in Germany engaged in philosophical study of Immmanuel Kant, Jakob Boehme, A. W. Schlegel, and G. E. Lessing. After settling in Keswick in 1800, Coleridge increasingly was prone to the kind of depression recounted in his 1802 "Dejection: An Ode." Despite personal turmoil that led to his separation from his wife Sarah in 1808 and his break with Wordsworth in 1810, he turned his powers to literary criticism, philosophy, theology, and political theory until his ill health and his addiction to opium took his life in 1834. During his final decades, Coleridge published his magnum opus, *Biographica Literaria* (1817), *Sibyline Leaves* (1817), *Aids to Reflection* (1825), and *Church and State* (1830).

Countée Cullen (1903–1946)

In the 1920s, Countée Cullen became a primary figure of the Harlem Renaissance and one of its major poetic talents. Born in 1903, he was adopted by the Reverend Frederick A. and Carolyn Belle Cullen and brought up in New York

City in what the poet later described as "the conservative atmosphere of a Methodist parsonage." Such early religious influences, however ambivalently portrayed, are pronounced in Cullen's signature poem "Heritage" and in the lyrics included in *The Black Christ and Other Poems* (1929). After graduating at the top of his class at DeWitt Clinton High School in 1921, Cullen attended New York University, graduating Phi Beta Kappa in 1925. While at NYU, Cullen wrote poetry prolifically and showed an early mastery of traditional English measures in ballad stanzas, sonnets, and other fixed forms. In the mid-1920s, many of these works would appear in his early volumes of verse: *Color* (1925), *Copper Sun* (1927), and *The Ballad of the Brown Girl* (1927) which brought him the recognition of the modern literary world in such awards as the Witter Bynner Poetry Prize, *Poetry* magazine's prestigious John Reed Memorial Prize, *Crisis* magazine's Amy Spingarn Award, and a Guggenheim Fellowship. His literary fame was further capped in his highly publicized New York marriage to Yolande Du Bois, the daughter of noted black intellectual W. E. B. Du Bois. Their union proved short-lived, however, and they were divorced two years later. Cullen's productivity as a writer fell off somewhat in the 1930s owing to his teaching responsibilities as a French instructor at Frederick Douglass Junior High School, but he published a retrospective parody of the Harlem Renaissance in his novel *One Way to Heaven* (1932) and another volume of verse *The Media and Other Poems* (1935) that included a major translation of Euripides' tragedy. In 1940, Cullen married Ida Mae Roberson, and at the time of his death six years later he was collaborating with Arna Bontemps on the play *St. Louis Woman* (1946).

E. E. Cummings (1894–1962)

Poet and painter, Edward Estlin Cummings was born into the household of Unitarian minister and former Harvard professor Edward Cummings who, along with his wife, Rebecca Haswell Clarke Cummings, encouraged Cummings to pursue his creativity especially in poetry. Cummings graduated from Harvard College in 1915 and received an M.A. from Harvard the next year. His early verse was included in the collection *Eight Harvard Poets* published in 1917, the year Cummings also volunteered for the Ambulance Corps serving in France during World War I. Arrested with his friend William Slater Brown on suspicion of espionage, owing to some of Brown's pacifist letters, Cummings was held in detention at a concentration camp at La Ferté-Macé for four months, which he writes about in his autobiographical book *The Enormous Room* (1922). After serving in the 73rd Infantry until November 1918, Cummings lived in New York and exhibited his artwork modeled on cubist prinicples that also shaped the new compositional innovations to modern poetry. Making dynamic use of the page as a compositonal space, Cummings subverted the authenticity of the speaking voice in favor of visual manipulations of punctuation and typography, unusual and playful phrasings, disruption of syntax, and other unconventional formal techniques. Such early experimentation appeared in three volumes—*Tulips and Chimneys* (1923), *XLI Poems* (1925), and *&* (1925). The youthful exuberance of these first volumes was tempered by two failed marriages, the first to Elaine Orr from 1924 to 1925 and the second to Anne Barton from 1929 to 1932. A new critical temper entered his verse in the volumes *5* (1926), *ViVa* (1931), and *No Thanks* (1935). A six-week trip to the Soviet Union in 1931 provided the impetus for Cummings's parody, modeled on Dante's *Inferno, Purgatorio,* and *Paradiso,* of bureaucratic communism in *Eimi* (1933). In 1934, Cummings's entered into a relationship with Marion Morehouse that would last the rest of his life, much of which was spent at the poet's summer house "Joy Farm" in Madison, New Hampshire. A new optimism is evident in *50 Poems* (1940), *1 X 1* (1944), and *Xaipe* (1950) that reflects, in part, Cummings's reunion with the daughter of his first marriage, Nancy. She had lost contact with her father when Elaine Orr left Cummings, taking Nancy with her to Ireland in 1925. In his final years, Cummings received broad recognition for his poetic achievement both as a public reader of his work and in the awards of a special citation from the National Book Award Committee (1955), a Bollingen Prize (1958), and a Ford Foundation grant. Four years after his final volume of verse *95 poems* was published, Cummings died in New Hampshire after suffering a stroke at Joy Farm.

Emily Dickinson (1830–1886)

Born in 1830, Emily Dickinson grew up in a prominent nineteenth-century New England family. Her grandfather, Samuel Fowler Dickinson, founded Amherst Academy in 1814 in western Massachusetts and Amherst College seven years later. Dickinson's father was a successful Amherst lawyer who served as treasurer of the college and was elected a member of the U.S. House of Representatives. The Dickinson family home was the annual site of the Amherst College commencement receptions and a center of the community. At the heart of Amherst's social life, however, Emily Dickinson chose a life largely devoted to the solitary cultivation of her poetic imagination, becoming, in the words of her friend and editor Samuel Bowles, "the Queen Recluse." Rather than define herself through the available roles of dutiful daughter, attentive wife, devoted mother, or even devout Christian, she largely turned her back on the Amherst community in favor of an existence where, as she writes in Poem 303, the "Soul selects her own Society."

As capable as any of the great Dickinson patriarchs, Emily excelled as a student, first at Amherst Academy, where she studied under Edward Hitchcock, and later during the year she spent at Mount Holyoke Female Seminary in 1847 to 1848. It was at Holyoke that her radical independence asserted itself as she became the only student in her class not to profess a belief in Christ by the end of her year there. Similarly, by age thirty she stopped attending church services, largely cutting her ties with Amherst public life. Instead, she cultivated a rich inner spirituality and intense creative life that would produce some 1,147 poems and thousands of letters to her select circle of correspondents. Of her large corpus of poetry, however, only ten were published by the time of her death from Bright's disease in 1886. Although she courted literary editors, she was skeptical of literary fame in her own lifetime and was extremely guarded in her literary negotiations with such editors as Samuel Bowles and Thomas Wentworth Higginson. Stitched together into packets or "fascicles," Dickinson's verse in its formal innovations parts company with the conventional writing of her age and remains an important precursor for modernist poetics and also for twentieth-century feminist verse. Her use of experimental punctuation and dashes, her typographical capitalizations of key words, her unconventional phrasings and syntax, her penchant for paradox (captured in striking oxymorons such as "Heavenly Hurt" in Poem 258), the composed quality of the poem on the page, and the intertextual relations enter into the fascicle format together and broke new ground for lyric expression.

John Donne (1572–1631)

Born in London to a Roman Catholic family, John Donne lived at a time when Catholics were persecuted in England. Although Donne studied at Oxford and Cambridge, he did not receive a degree from either university because of his refusal to subscribe to Anglicanism. After his brother was convicted of Catholic loyalties and died in prison, Donne converted to avoid his brother's fate. Donne emerged as a spokesperson for a new poetic style that Samuel Johnson would later characterize, writing in the eighteenth-century, as "metaphysical poetry"—a poetics that also defines the work of George Herbert, Richard Crashaw, Andrew Marvell, and John Cleveland. Through highly ironic, extended metaphors—or metaphysical "conceits"—such verse possessed wit in the use of puns, fresh and arresting insights from sharply conceived paradoxes, subtle turns of argument, and startling insights drawn from the everyday world of things observed close at hand. Donne composed much of his metaphysical love lyrics and erotic poetry during the 1590s before becoming Sir Thomas Edgarton's private secretary in 1598. In 1601, Donne secretly married the sixteen-year-old niece of Lady Edgarton, Anne More. Disapproving of the marriage when it became public, Edgarton imprisoned Donne briefly and withheld his dowry, leaving the poet to struggle in raising what would become a large household of children. After the death of Anne during childbirth in 1617, Donne was appointed four years later by King James to the post of dean of St. Paul's Cathedral, a position he would hold until he died in 1631. In addition to breaking fresh ground in the metaphysical love lyric, Donne also explored the theological and existential implications of death and spirituality in the *Holy Sonnets* and *Devotions upon Emergent Occasions* (1624).

H. D. (Hilda Doolittle) (1886–1961)

A pioneeering figure in feminist poetics, H. D. was raised in Upper Darby, a Philadelphia suburb near the University of Pennsylvania, where her father, Charles Doolittle, an astronomer, directed the Flower Observatory. H. D. was encouraged in her creative and artistic pursuits by her mother Helen (Wolle), who was a musician. An early influence on her poetry and identity was the modernist poet Ezra Pound, to whom she was twice engaged. Her attachment to Pound was complicated by her attraction to Frances Josepha Gregg, a student enrolled at the Pennsylvania Academy of Fine Arts. Throughout her life, Doolittle would pursue a bisexual lifestyle beginning with her lifelong relationship to the shipping heiress Winifred Ellerman, who called herself Bryher. Following the failure of Doolittle's marriage to Richard Aldington and affairs with the British author D. H. Lawrence and the painter Cecil Grey (the father of Doolittle's daughter Perdita), Doolittle had a close relationship to Bryher that lasted until the poet's death in 1961. In fact, her connection to Bryher persisted through Bryher's marriages to the author Robert McAlmon and the filmmaker Kenneth Macpherson, who was also Doolittle's lover. She received her nom du plume from Ezra Pound who in 1913 sent her poems to Harriet Monroe, the editor of *Poetry Magazine,* adding the signature "H. D., Imagiste." H. D. became forever identified thereafter with the imagist movement, which stressed a concise, straightforward, and direct "treatment of the thing" at hand. Such an imagist style characterized H. D.'s first collection of verse *Sea Garden* (1916). Increasingly, however, in such mature works as *Trilogy* (1946), *Helen in Egypt* (1961), and *Hermetic Definition* (1972), H. D. devoted herself to developing a modernist "women's mythology": one that, in its epic scope, revisited and rewrote classical Greek myth. H. D.'s interest in Greek literature extended to the several translations she undertook of Sappho, Meleager, and Euripides, among others. H. D. also wrote an important and provocative memoir of her time as an analysand with Sigmund Freud, entitled *Tribute to Freud* (written in 1944 and published between 1945 and 1985). Other prose works include *End to Torment* (1979) and *The Gift* (1982), as well as *Pilate's Wife, Asphodel,* and *Her,* collected in *Hermione* (1981).

Rita Dove (b. 1952)

Born and raised in Akron, Ohio, Rita Dove grew up in an African American middle-class family headed by her father, who worked as a research chemist in the Akron tire industry. In 1970, Dove received a Presidential Scholar award to study at Miami University, where she later graduated Phi Beta Kappa in 1973. Following college, Dove received a Fulbright scholarship to pursue two semesters of advanced study at the Universtät Tübingen in Germany, where she met and married the German writer Fred Viebahn. Returning to the United States, Dove received an M.F.A. from the prestigious creative writing program at the University of Iowa. Her first collection of poetry was entitled *The Yellow House on the Corner* (1980), followed by *Museum* (1983). With her next volume of verse, *Thomas and Beulah* (1986), Dove became the second African American poet, after Gwendolyn Brooks, to win a Pulitzer Prize. Her subsequent volumes include *Grace Notes* (1989), *Selected Poems* (1993), *Mother Love* (1995), *On the Bus with Rosa Parks* (1999), as well as a book of short stories *Fifth Sunday* (1985) and a novel *Through the Ivory Gate* (1992), plus a book of essays entitled *The Poet's World* (1995). Her 1996 play *The Darker Face of the Earth* premiered at the Oregon Shakespeare Festival and was staged at the Kennedy Center in Washington, D.C., and the Royal National Theatre in

London. In addition to editing *Best American Poetry 2000*, she also writes a column entitled "Poet's Choice" for the *Washington Post*. In 1993, Rita Dove was the first African American to be named as Poet Laureate of the United States and consultant in poetry at the Library of Congress. Over the course of her career, Rita Dove has received numerous honorary doctorates as well as several prestigious prizes, and she is currently the Commonwealth Professor of English at the University of Virginia, Charlottesville.

T. S. Eliot (1888–1965)

Although born into a New England family, Thomas Stearns Eliot grew up in St. Louis, where his father was the president of the Hydraulic-Press Brick Company. Entering Harvard University as a freshman in 1906, Eliot studied under George Santayana and Irving Babbitt, and by 1908, he had begun studying the French symbolist verse of Jules LaForgue, who became a major modernist influence on Eliot's early poetry. Following his graduation from Harvard, Eliot lived for a year in Paris, where he met Jean Verdenal, a medical student who was later killed in the battle of the Dardenelles during World War I. Influenced by the dramatic monologue forms of Robert Browning, Eliot soon, according to the poet Ezra Pound, "trained himself and modernized himself on his own," writing his famous interior monologue "The Love Song of J. Alfred Prufrock" while in Paris in the early 1910s. By 1914, Eliot traveled to Marburg, Germany, and had intended to study at Merton College, Oxford, but soon entered into what soon would become a very difficult marriage to Vivien Haigh-Wood the following year. By 1917, Eliot had established himself in the London literary scene with the publication of *Prufrock and Other Observations* while he supported himself by working in the foreign section of Lloyds Bank. Moving in the same international literary circles as noted writers W. B. Yeats, James Joyce, Wyndham Lewis, and Filippo Tommaso Marinetti, among others, Eliot published what soon became the definitive modernist long poem, *The Waste Land* (1922). As the editor of the influential journal *The Criterion*, Eliot moved to the center of London intellectual life, becoming a literary editor at Faber and Gwyer in the mid-twenties. Not insignificantly, it was at this time that Eliot converted to the Church of England and by 1928 had famously declared himself in a book of essays called *For Lancelot Andrewes*, a "classicist in literature, royalist in politics, and anglo-catholic in religion." Eliot had already arrived as a highly influential literary critic in early 1919 with his foundational essay "Tradition and the Individual Talent." He sustained and amplified that influence in subsequent volumes of prose and authored a series of popular plays including *The Family Reunion* (1939), *The Cocktail Party* (1949), *The Confidential Clerk* (1953), and *The Elder Statesman* (1958). Among the most reputable writers of the twentieth century, Eliot was invited to deliver the Clark Lectures at Cambridge University, and the Norton Lectures at Harvard, and while a Fellow at Princeton's Institute for Advanced Study, he was awarded the Nobel Prize in literature in 1948. His late suite of poems, *Four Quartets* (1943), crowned his career as poet. In 1957,

Eliot married Valerie Fletcher and enjoyed the remainder of his life with her until his death in 1965.

Anne Finch (1661–1720)

The third child born to Sir William Kingsmill and Anne Haslewood, Anne Kingsmill Finch was five months old when her father died in 1661. Following her mother's death three years later, Anne was brought up by her grandmother, Bridget, Lady Kingsmill. After Lady Kingsmill's death in 1672, Anne was raised in the household of William Haslewood, where she studied French and Italian, Greek and Roman mythology, the Bible, and the humanities. Ten years later, Anne became a maid of honor to Mary of Modena, the wife of James, Duke of York. In 1684, Anne married Heneage Finch, who was a courtier to James. Finch retained his status at the Stuart court after the coronation of the Duke of York as King James II. After the revolution of 1688 and the coronation of William of Orange, Heneage Finch was arrested for a short period for his continuing allegiance to James II. In the 1690s, the couple lived at the estate of Charles Finch, Earl of Winchilsea. Following the succession of James II's daughter, Queen Anne, to the throne in the early 1700s, the Finches returned to London, where Anne Finch began to publish her poetry. *Miscellany Poems, on Several Occasions* appeared in 1713 and comprised eighty-six poems and Finch's play *Aristomenes: Or, The Royal Shepherd*. The previous year, her husband had become the Earl of Winchilsea. Continuing political and financial stresses, however, took their toll on Anne Finch, countess of Winchilsea, as reflected in her last poems, written during her latter years up to her death in 1720.

Robert Frost (1874–1963)

Although considered a New England poet, Robert Frost was actually born in San Francisco and lived there until the age of eleven when, after the death of his father, he moved with his mother and sister to Salem, New Hampshire. Although he graduated as a high school valedictorian, an honor he shared with future wife, Elinor White, Frost could not adjust to college life at Dartmouth and, years later, dropped out of Harvard as well. While living in Derry, New Hampshire, on the farm bequeathed to him by his grandfather, Frost split his time between farming and teaching at the Pinkerton Academy. During the decade he lived in Derry, Frost composed most of the poems that would go into his first volumes—*A Boy's Will* (1913) and *North of Boston* (1914)—which he published in England after selling the family farm and moving there in 1912. Living outside of London, Frost struck important literary friendships with the British poet Edward Thomas and the American expatriate Ezra Pound, both of whom wrote important reviews of Frost's early work and introduced him to the Irish poet W. B. Yeats. Frost returned to America in 1915 and was greeted by literary success for his next volume, *Mountain Interval* (1916), and his Pulitzer Prize–winning book *New Hampshire*

(1924). Frost would go on to win three more Pulitzers as his verse gained force and he became a leading poet of the twentieth century. Despite the steady growth of his literary reputation during the 1930s, Frost suffered domestic tragedy in the deaths of his daughter Marjorie in 1934, his wife's death in 1938, the suicide of his son Carol in 1940, and his daughter Irma's affliction with mental disorders. Several of Frost's later critics such as Randall Jarrell and Lionel Trilling would point out the tragic dimensions of his poetic vision beneath the outgoing demeanor of the good, grey New England poet. Although becoming something of an American institution culminating in his reading at President John F. Kennedy's presidential inaugural ceremony, Frost's public image further shifted after his death in 1963 owing to Lawrence Thompson's 1970 biography *Robert Frost: The Years of Triumph, 1915–1937* that depicted him as, in the critic Helen Vendler's words, a "monster of egotism." In other biographies and criticism, however, Frost received a more fairminded reception in such works as W. H. Pritchard's *A Literary Life Reconsidered* (1984) and Stanley Burnshaw's *Robert Frost Himself* (1986).

Allen Ginsberg (1926–1997)

Like Walt Whitman and William Carlos Williams, Allen Ginsberg was a New Jersey poet. Born in Newark, New Jersey, Ginsberg was introduced to literature early on by his father, Louis, himself a poet and high school English teacher. The other major influence in Ginsberg's formative years was his mother Naomi, who was a Communist Party member and also suffered from bouts of acute paranoia and mental illness, which Ginsberg records in his long poem *Kaddish*. Growing up in Paterson, New Jersey, Ginsberg took the modernist American poet William Carlos Williams as a poetic mentor, and his letters to Williams appear in the latter's long poem, *Paterson*. Ginsberg went on to study at Columbia University with such famous critics of the time as Lionel Trilling, Mark Van Doren, and Raymond Weaver. But it was also at Columbia and in New York City generally where Ginsberg met through Lucien Carr those who would become the inner core of the beat movement: William S. Burroughs, Jack Kerouac, and Neal Cassady, who all appear in Kerouac's celebrated novel *On the Road* (1957). The paradoxical connotations of the "beat" generation signified both what was down and out and spiritually beatified. That contradictory mix of urban destitution and visionary experience was memorably captured in Ginsberg's ground-breaking volume of verse, *Howl and Other Poems* (1956). Part of this book records not only Ginsberg's subterranean lifestyle but also his hospitalization in the Columbia Presbyterian Psychiatric Institute, where he met the young writer Carl Solomon. Not just a poet, Ginsberg became a cultural icon and his memorable poetry readings—including his celebrated 1955 reading at the Six Gallery in San Francisco with fellow San Francisco Renaissance poets Kenneth Rexroth, Gary Snyder, Michael McClure, Philip Whalen, and Philip LaMantia—amount to performance art. Published by Lawrence Ferlinghetti's City Lights Pocket Poets series, *Howl and Other Poems* was quickly confiscated by the San Francisco police. By the end of 1957, however, the American Civil Liberties Union successfully defended the book, convincing Judge Clayton Horn that the work had aesthetic and social value that exceeded the charges of pornography. Reviving the long line and poetic catalogue forms of Walt Whitman, whom the poet addresses in "Supermarket in California," Ginsberg went on to publish an elegy for his mother, *Kaddish and Other Poems* (1961), followed by such major volumes as *Reality Sandwiches* (1963), *Planet News, 1961–1967* (1968), *The Fall of America: Poems of These States, 1965–1971* (1973), *Plutonium Ode: Poems 1977–1980* (1982), and *Death and Fame: Last Poems 1993–1997* (1999). A winner of the National Book Award in 1974, Ginsberg combined the roles of poet and prophet in the visionary mode of William Blake, but he also was an outspoken social critic, political activist, and a distinguished professor at Brooklyn College. He died of liver cancer in New York City at the age of seventy.

Thomas Hardy (1840–1928)

Born in the rural village of Higher Bockhampton in Dorset, Thomas Hardy was the son of a stonemason. Early on, his mother encouraged his reading, and at age sixteen he apprenticed to study architecture, later traveling to London to pursue that trade at twenty-two. Although he considered taking holy orders, in London he gradually adopted a more modern skepticism toward religion owing, in part, to his reading of Charles Darwin, Herbert Spencer, and John Stuart Mill. Hardy began life as a writer by returning to Dorchester in 1867, where he worked on an unpublished novel, *The Poor Man and the Lady*. In the 1870s he emerged as a novelist with a popular following for such works of fiction as *Desperate Remedies* (1871), *Under the Greenwood Tree* (1872), *A Pair of Blue Eyes* (1873), and *Far from the Madding Crowd* (1874). Following on this successful run of fiction, he entered into a difficult marriage to Emma Gifford. His troubles with Gifford are apparent in the increasing pessimism of his themes from *The Return of the Native* (1878) followed by *The Mayor of Casterbridge* (1886), *Tess of the D'Urbervilles* (1891), and *Jude the Obscure* (1895). The latter two, in particular, were so harshly criticized by Hardy's contemporaries that he gave up fiction and turned to writing poetry, producing such notable volumes as *Wessex Poems and Other Verses* (1898), *Poems of the Past and Present* (1902), and *Satires of Circumstance, Lyrics and Reveries* (1914). Following the death of wife Emma in 1912, Hardy remarried Florence Emily Dugdale two years later. The many honors bestowed on Hardy during the final years of his life included the Order of Merit awarded by King George V, the presidency of the Society of Authors, a Nobel Prize nomination, the Gold Medal of the Royal Society of Literature, and numerous honorary degrees. Hardy died in his native Dorchester in 1928, and, after cremation, his ashes were buried in the Poet's Corner in Westminster Abbey.

Robert Hayden (1913–1980)

Robert Hayden was born in the "Paradise Valley" ghetto of Detroit to Ruth and Asa Sheffey who separated after his birth. Adopted by William and Ruth Hayden, the poet grew up in a troubled household filled with what he later described as "chronic angers." Attending Detroit City College until 1936, he then joined the Federal Writer's project, where for two years he researched African American history and folklore. Hayden married Erma Morris in 1940, which was also the year of his first publication, *Heart-Shape in the Dust*. The following year he attended the University of Michigan, where he studied with the modernist poet W. H. Auden. Graduating in 1942, Hayden remained there until 1946, when he joined the faculty of Fisk University. After he went on to enjoy a twenty-three-year career, publishing such major volumes as *The Lion and the Archer* (1948), *Figures of Time: Poems* (1955), *Night-Blooming Cereus* (1972), *Angle of Ascent* (1975), *American Journal* (1978, 1982), and his posthumous *Collected Poems* (1985). "His poetry," according to critic Mark A. Sanders, "posits race as a means through which one contemplates the expansive possibilities of language, and the transformative power of art." A master of poetic craft and modernist experimentation, Robert Hayden remains a seminal voice in American literature, and his verse spans the course of African American poetics reaching from the Harlem Renaissance through the black aesthetic movement and beyond.

Seamus Heaney (b. 1939)

Seamus Heaney has the distinction of being the only Irish poet since W. B. Yeats to have won the Nobel Prize in literature. Born and raised north of Belfast in Mossbawn, County Derry, he attended Queen's College from 1957 to 1961 and then went on to receive a teacher's certificate in English at St. Joseph's College, Belfast, where he became a lecturer while pursuing literary collaboration with such poets as Philip Hobsbaum, Derek Mahon, and Michael Longley. Four years later, he married Marie Devlin and published *Eleven Poems*, followed the next year by *Death of a Naturalist*, which brought him much recognition and such prizes as the E. C. Gregory Award, the Cholmondeley Award, Somerset Maugham Award, and Geoffrey Faber Memorial Prize. His next volume, *Door into the Dark*, became the Poetry Book Society Choice for 1969. Following a brief appointment at the University of California, Berkeley, Heaney gave up his lectureship at Queens College and took up residence in Glanmore, County Wicklow. During the 1970s, Heaney alternated giving poetry readings with a teaching position at Carysfort, publishing *North* (1975) and *Field Work* (1979), which presented the rural settings of his earlier volumes through a deeper attention to Irish history and politics. With his publication of *Station Island* in 1984, Heaney became the Boylston Professor of Rhetoric and Oratory at Harvard and in 1989 professor of poetry at Oxford University. He was awarded the Nobel Prize for literature in 1995. His recent volumes include *Seeing Things* (1991) and *The Spirit Level* (1996).

George Herbert (1593–1633)

A cousin of the Earl of Pembroke, George Herbert was born into a prominent Welsh family. His mother was a patron of the metaphysical poet John Donne, who dedicated his *Holy Sonnets* to her. Following the death of his father, Herbert attended Westminster School at age ten and then took a B.A. (1613) and an M.A. (1616) at Trinity College, Cambridge, where he later became the public orator of the University and was elected a representative to Parliament in 1624 and 1625. Herbert also received the patronage of King James I until the latter's death in 1625. After resigning his position as orator in 1627, Herbert married Jane Danvers in 1629. The following year, he took holy orders in the Church of England and assumed the duties of vicar and rector of the Bemerton parish near Salisbury. For the next three years until his death in 1633, Herbert composed the poems that would be posthumously published as *The Temple* (1633). The enormous success of this work established George Herbert's reputation among the metaphysical poets and he remains one of the major voices in seventeenth-century verse.

Robert Herrick (1591–1674)

The son of a London goldsmith, Robert Herrick apprenticed to his uncle, also in the same trade, for six years between the ages of sixteen and twenty-two before entering Saint John's College, Cambridge. After graduating in 1617, Herrick was a protégé to Ben Jonson to whom he wrote five poems. Not just a poet, Herrick took holy orders in the Church of England in 1623 and served as vicar at Dean Prior in Devonshire until 1647, when, owing to his Royalist allegiances, he was removed during the Great Rebellion. That same year, Herrick published his first volume of verse, *Noble Numbers*, which was collected in his *Herperides; or, the Works Both Human and Divine of Robert Herrick, Esq.* (1648). This major book of more than 1,200 poems includes carpe diem love lyrics, epigrams, elegies, and epistles. From his studies of Horace, Catullus, and other authors of classical antiquity, Herrick adapted the conventions of the Roman pastoral tradition to the English eclogue tradition in order to celebrate British village life and customs. With the restoration of Charles II, Herrick resumed his office of vicar at Dean Prior from 1662 until his death in 1674.

Gerard Manley Hopkins (1844–1889)

The first of nine children born to Manley and Catherine Hopkins, Gerard Manley Hopkins grew up in a household of high church Anglicans. He was not, however, the only poet in his family; the year before Gerard's birth, his father, a marine insurance adjuster, had published a volume of verse. Following in his father's footsteps, Gerard showed early promise as a poet by winning a poetry prize at Highgate, his grammar school, before going on to win a scholarship to Balliol College, Oxford, where he studied with such tutors as the famous English "Art-for-Art's-Sake" writer, Walter Pater. Another powerful mentor at Oxford was John Henry Newman, whose conversion from the Anglican church to Catholicism was an example that Hopkins followed in 1866. The following year he graduated with a "double-first" degree from Balliol and entered the Society of Jesus in 1868, eventually becoming ordained as a Jesuit priest in 1877. Although he turned away from poetry to pursue his religious vocation initally, his studies of the medieval Catholic philosopher Duns Scotus allowed him to find parallels between what the medievalist emphasized as the vivid uniqueness or haecceitas ("thisness") of experience and what Hopkins himself depicted as the perceptual intensity of poetic "inscape" in later works such as "God's Grandeur," "Pied Beauty," and "The Windhover." History, however, drew Hopkins back into poetry in the 1875 loss of the ship *Deutschland*, whose passenger list included five Franciscan nuns. Hopkins wrote his must challenging long poem, *The Wreck of the Deutschland*, in commemoration of this tragedy, although the rector who had commissioned this work actually rejected it for final publication. During the late 1870s, Hopkins served briefly in Sheffield, Oxford, as a preacher and in the early 1880s became parish priest, ministering to the working poor of Manchester, Liverpool, and Glasgow. In the late 1880s, while teaching Latin and Greek at Stonyhurst College, Hopkins wrestled with modern, religious doubt that produced the so-called terrible sonnets before his death from typhoid fever in 1889. Hopkins's major poetry did not appear in print in his lifetime, but thanks to Robert Bridges, the Poet Laureate in 1913 and Hopkins's friend from Oxford, his work was published posthumously in 1918. Subsequently, the freshness of Hopkins's experiments in language, "sprung" rhythm, as well as poetic "inscape" and "instress" became a major influence in modern verse.

Langston Hughes (1903–1967)

A Midwesterner by birth, Hughes grew up in Lawrence, Kansas, with additional time spent in Illinois, Ohio, and Mexico. Hughes received some of his impetus to write about the specific experience of African Americans, in part, from his maternal grandmother, Mary Langston, whose husband had been killed with John Brown at Harper's Ferry. Even before attending Columbia University, Hughes had published in the prestigious *Crisis* magazine what would become a signature poem, "The Negro Speaks of Rivers." After a year at Columbia, Hughes left in 1922 to work and to travel to such destinations as the West Coast of Africa and Paris. Returning to the United States in 1924, he received notoriety as the most talented and original poet of the Harlem Renaissance. His first book, *The Weary Blues* (1926), boldly celebrated the everyday lives of ordinary black folk in a vernacular poetics influenced by such American forerunners as Walt Whitman and Carl Sandburg but also based in the kind of blues lyricism, black sermon, and other expressive forms rooted in African American culture that he espoused in an important manifesto published in *The Nation* magazine: "The Negro Artist and the Racial Mountain" (1926). The following year Hughes published his second volume *Fine Clothes to the Jew* and as a student at Lincoln University received financial support from Mrs. Charlotte Mason, Hughes's patron in the arts during the next two years. Owing to irreconcilable differences in politics, taste, and personality, Hughes reached a parting of the ways with Mason when his first novel, *Not Without Laughter*, was published in 1930. Like many writers during the Depression era, Hughes became a committed political activist on the left and was involved in the worldwide struggle for social justice. During the early thirties Hughes traveled to the Soviet Union, and in addition to publishing radical left poetry, he authored a volume of short stories, *The Ways of White Folks* (1934), and the Broadway play *Mulatto* (1935), followed other dramatic productions. By 1937, Hughes had left the country again, this time to lend his support to the Internationalist cause in the Spanish Civil War, where he wrote his moving war poem "Madrid." Returning once more to America, Hughes published an original collection of radical verse entitled "A New Song" the following year. During World War II, Hughes continued to inveigh against racism, publishing the first volume of his autobiography *The Big Sea* (1940) and verse collections such as *Shakespeare in Harlem* (1942) and *Jim Crow's Last Stand* (1943). It was at this time that Hughes reached a wide popular audience in his weekly column for the *Chicago Defender* that over the next twenty years would follow the ironic insights of Hughes's comic persona, Jesse B. Semple. Following the war, Hughes continued to publish such volumes of verse as *Fields of Wonder* (1947), *One-Way Ticket* (1949), and *Montage of a Dream Deferred* (1951). By 1953, however, his earlier politics made him a target of Senator Joseph McCarthy and his House Un-American Activities Committee hearings during the Red Scare. Forced to disavow his radical stances of the 1930s, Hughes nevertheless survived McCarthy's own loss of public credibility and went on to narrate his time in the Soviet Union in the second volume of his autobiography, *I Wonder as I Wander* (1956). A series of successful musical collaborations during the 1950s brought Hughes a measure of prosperity in his late career. His reputation in the Pan-Africanist community culminated in his celebration at the 1966 First World Festival of Negro Arts in Dakar, Senegal. Hughes's final volume of verse, *The Panther and the Lash* (1967), recounted the racial struggles of the civil rights era of the 1960s and was posthumously published the year he died in 1967.

Kobayashi Issa [Yataro Nobuyuki] (1763–1827)

Born in the small town Kashiwabara in the mountainous central region of Japan, Issa lived there until the age of thirteen when he left to live in Edo (present-day Tokyo). Under the patronage of Seibi Natsume, Issa began writing Haiku poetry at the age of twenty-five after studying under his teachers Genmu and Chiku-a. Although he was elected to take the place of his teacher on the latter's death, Issa chose instead to live the life of a wanderer until 1801, when his father died. Owing to a dispute with his stepmother and half brother over his father's estate, Issa continued to travel to Kyoto, Osaka, Nagasaki, and Matsuyama until the age of fifty-one when he married a much younger woman. Tragedy marked his married life, however, with the death of each of his four children in infancy and, finally, the death of his wife from yet another childbirth. Moreover, his house burned to the ground. Nevertheless, during the last four years, Issa married again and fathered a girl who was born shortly after his death. Issa composed plainspoken haiku lyrics that reflect on the difficult circumstances of his private life, influenced as it was by Buddhist philosophy. Among Issa's most famous literary works are "The Diary at My Father's

Death" (1801) and "My Springtime" (1819). His poetry is ranked among the best haiku verse produced by such Japanese masters of the genre as Basho Matsuo, Buson Yosa, and Shiki Masaoka.

Randall Jarrell (1914–1965)

Randall Jarrell grew up in Los Angeles until his parents' divorce, when he returned to Nashville, the city of his birth. Tellingly, his Los Angeles experiences, especially his visit with his grandparents at the age of twelve, would be represented in the title piece of his last book of verse, *The Lost World.* Supported in part by a National Youth Administration scholarship, Jarrell later attended college at Vanderbilt University, where he was mentored by Robert Penn Warren, who published Jarrell's first poems, and John Crowe Ransom, who later hired Jarrell to teach freshman composition and to coach tennis at Kenyon College. At Kenyon, Jarrell befriended the emerging fiction writer Peter Taylor and, more important, the young student Robert Lowell, whose poetry Jarrell helped to encourage through his personal and professional criticism. After his time at Kenyon, Jarrell combined careers as poet, critic, and teacher. At the University of Texas, he married Mackie Langham in 1940 and then served in the U.S. Army Air Force teaching celestial navigation. Meanwhile, he published his first book of verse, *Blood for a Stranger* (1942), and had success placing poems in *The New Republic* through his connection to the critic and editor Edmund Wilson. Jarrell's air force experience would form the basis of two volumes of verse, *Little Friend, Little Friend* (1945) and *Losses* (1948). In the postwar years, Jarrell served for a year as the literary editor of *The Nation* magzine and then taught at Sarah Lawrence College. His teaching experience there would be the subject of his humorous best-selling novel lampooning the fictional Benton College in *Pictures from an Institution* (1954). Two years previously, Jarrell married his second wife, Mary von Shrader, and moved to the University of North Carolina at Greensboro. At the same time, Jarrell was making a name for himself as an incisive and influential critic of modern American poetry with his best work collected in the volume *Poetry and the Age* (1953). His reputation as a poet, however, flowered later in the sixties when he won the National Book Award for *The Woman at the Washington Zoo* (1960) and *The Lost World* (1965). Jarrell was also a translator of Goethe's *Faust, Part I,* several of Grimm's fairy tales, and Chekhov's *The Three Sisters.* In addition, he published four books of children's stories. Toward the end of his life Jarrell suffered from depression and attempted suicide by slashing his wrist. In the fall of 1965, he received treatment at a hospital in Chapel Hill, and while walking on a highway he was struck and killed by a car.

Ben Jonson (1572–1637)

The son of a minister, who died before the poet was born, Jonson was brought up by his mother and a stepfather, who was a bricklayer by trade. Raised in Westminster, Jonson attended St. Martin's parish school, where he was mentored by the classicist William Camden. After a brief stint working in his stepfather's vocation, Jonson served in the military. He returned to London in 1592 and two years later married Anne Lewis, with whom he would have two sons. In 1598, Jonson wrote his first successful play, *Every Man in His Humor,* and its 1616 production included the famous dramatist William Shakespeare in the cast. The year it opened, however, Jonson killed actor Gabriel Spencer in a duel and barely escaped the gallows for murder by pleading "benefit of clergy" owing to his ability to read and write Latin. During the first decade of the seventeenth century, Jonson enjoyed the patronage of James I and produced a number of entertaining and witty court masques such as the *Masque of Blacknesse* (1605) and the *Masque of Queens* (1608) in addition to such popular masterpieces as *Volpone* (1606) and *The Alchemist* (1610). At this time, he also presided— mainly at the Mermaid Tavern in Fleet Street and later at the Devil's Tavern— over a circle of protégés and admirers who became known as the "Tribe of Ben" and counted among its numbers such writers as Thomas Carew, Richard Lovelace, and Robert Herrick. Jonson was appointed Poet Laureate in 1616 and wrote lyric verse, odes, and epigrams in a classical mode. Among his other offices was his appointment in 1628 to City Chronologer of London. That same year, Jonson suffered a debilitating stroke; he died nine years later and was buried in Westminster Abbey under a tombstone whose epitaph "O Rare Ben Jonson!" testifies to his unique place in English letters. His final, unfinished play, *Sad Shepherd's Tale,* was published posthmously in 1641.

John Keats (1795–1821). *See Chapter 9.*

Denise Levertov (1923–1997)

Born in Ilford, Essex, England, Denise Levertov benefited from her family's rich cultural heritage. A descendant of Shneour Zalman, a Russian founder of the Habad branch of Hasidism, Levertov's father, Paul Levertoff, converted from Judaism to become an Anglican priest. The poet's mother, Beatrice Spooner-Jones Levertoff, claimed an ancestry that included the mystical teacher Angell Jones of Mold, whose son sponsored a Welch intellectual salon in the 1870s. Educated largely at home, Levertov combined a love of literature with an eclectic spirituality. Like her mother, who undertook humanitarian causes for the League of Nations Union, Denise Levertov was an activist in the cause of peace during the antiwar movements from Vietnam onwards. During World War II, Levertov served the cause of healing as a nurse in London. In 1946 she published a first volume of verse and then emigrated to America two years later. Through her husband, Mitchell Goodman, she met poets in the Black Mountain school, including Robert Creeley and Cid Corman, who published her verse in the avant-garde journal *Origin.* Her new style parted company with the formalist measures of her early poetry in favor of the free-verse forms of William Carlos Williams, Charles Olson, and Robert Duncan. In 1955 Levertov became an American citizen and during the subsequent decades in her several roles as poet, critic, and teacher, she had an important influence on a younger generation of American experimental poets. In addition to publishing fifteen volumes of verse, including her representative collection *Selected Poems* (1986), she authored two volumes of prose criticism, *The Poet in The World* (1973) and *Light Up the Cave* (1981). After teaching variously in the Boston area at Brandeis, MIT, and Tufts University, she moved to Seattle in 1989, where she combined lecturing at the University of Washington with her appointment as professor at Stanford University from 1982 to 1993. Until her death in 1997, she pursued an active schedule of public readings and carried on a dynamic correspondence with a network of other writers. A deeply sacramental author, Levertov believed, as she wrote in "Poetry, Prophecy, Survival," that her special vocation as poet was "to live with the door of one's life open to the transcendent, the numinous."

Audre Lorde (1934–1992)

The youngest of three daughters born to the West Indian immigrants Frederic Byron and Linda Belmar Lorde, Audre Lorde was raised in Manhattan during the Depression era. She attended Catholic grammar schools, St. Mark's School and St. Catherine's School, and from the eighth grade onward, she wrote poetry and identified herself as a poet. From 1954 through 1959, Audre Lorde attended Hunter College, graduating with a B.A. In 1961, she earned an M.A. in library science from Columbia University. Working as a librarian at Mount Vernon Public Library, she married lawyer Edward Ashley Rollins, and the couple had two children before divorcing in 1970. By 1966, Lorde had assumed the position of head librarian at Town School Library in New York City. Throughout the 1960s, Lorde divided her time between writing, publishing her poetry, working, raising a family, and becoming an activist in the civil rights, antiwar, and feminist movements. In 1968 she was awarded a National Endowment for the Arts grant that funded her poet-in-residence position at Tougaloo College in Mississippi. It was at Tougaloo that Lorde met her longtime companion, Frances Clayton. That year, her inaugural volume of poetry, *The First Cities*, was published by Poets Press. Two years later, she published *Cables to Rage*, depicting her lesbian identity in a poem entitled "Martha" based on her relationship with Clayton. Three years later, Broadside Press published *From a Land Where Other People Live*, which was nominated for the National Book Award for 1973. The following year, Lorde's poetry took a decidedly more political turn in *New York Head Shop and Museum*, followed in 1976 by *Coal*, which collected poetry from the first two volumes and was published by W. W. Norton. Much of Lorde's lyric poetry explores women's erotic lives. "The erotic," she has commented, "is a resource within each of us that lies in a deeply female and spiritual plane, firmly rooted in the power of our unexpressed or unrecognized feeling." *The Black Unicorn* (1978) moved beyond her earlier verse by reading Lorde's contemporary experience as a black lesbian feminist through African mythology. In addition to her poetry of the 1970s, Lorde wrote a series of essays based on her experience as an African American intellectual and as a survivor of breast cancer. "The Transformation of Silence into Language and Action," "A Black Lesbian Feminist Experience," and "Breast Cancer: Power vs. Prosthesis" were collected in her 1980 volume, *The Cancer Journals*, which won the American Library Association Gay Caucus Book of the Year Award for 1981. Lorde's cultural study of her own mastectomy was followed by what she called her "biomythography" in *Zami: A New Spelling of My Name* (1982). Six years later, in *A Burst of Light*, Lorde reflected on her diagnosis of liver cancer, the disease that would eventually take her life in 1992. In her last years, Lorde lived on St. Croix, U.S. Virgin Islands, and took the African name Gamba Adisa, which translates as "Warrior, She Who Makes Her Meaning Known." Her last publications include *Undersong: Chosen Poems Old and New* (1992) and *The Marvelous Arithmetics of Distance* (1993). In addition to receiving several awards throughout her life, Audre Lorde was Poet Laureate of New York in 1991 and a recipient of the Walt Whitman Citation of Merit.

Robert Lowell (1917–1977)

Born into an elite Boston family, Robert Lowell claimed as distant relatives both the fireside poet, James Russell Lowell, and the modern imagist poet, Amy Lowell. At St. Marks School, Lowell benefited from studying with the poet Richard Eberhart. After graduating from St. Marks, Lowell went to Harvard but stayed there for only a year before transfering to Kenyon College to study with John Crowe Ransom and Allen Tate. In 1940 Lowell graduated from Kenyon, converted to Roman Catholicism, and married the novelist Jean Stafford. Lowell would further his connections to the American New Critics by studying with Robert Penn Warren and Cleanth Brooks at Louisiana State University. Such connections helped secure a powerful critical reception for his early volumes such as the *Land of Unlikeness* (1944) and *Lord Weary's Castle* (1946), which won a Pulitzer Prize for poetry in 1947. Meanwhile, his antiwar stance as a conscientious objector to World War II had earned him in 1943 a year of jail time in New York's West Street prison, which he would later commemorate in his poem "Memories of West Street and Lepke." His stormy marriage to Stafford lasted eight years, and following his divorce, the poet met writer and editor Elizabeth (Lizzie) Hardwick at the Yaddo writer's institute. The two married the following year in 1949. Lowell went by the nickname Cal, which signified both on the cruelty of the Roman emporer Caligula and the wildness of Shakespeare's monstrous character Caliban from *The Tempest*. Lowell suffered from manic depression and was periodically institutionalized for mental illness throughout his life. Like other contemporaneous poets such as John Berryman, Theodore Roethke, and Anne Sexton, Lowell exploited his bouts of madness as material for his verse, which took on more intimate and less formal qualities in the so-called confessional poetry of *Life Studies* (1959), which received the National Book Award in 1960. Lowell's poetry during the 1960s became more politically engaged with public history as in the titlepiece of his 1964 collection *For the Union Dead*. His translations of Rilke and Rimbaud among others collected in *Imitations* (1961) won the prestigious Bollingen Prize in 1962. Later in the decade, Lowell became a vocal critic of the Vietnam War and participated in antiwar rallies, which he would record in such poems as "The March I" and "The March II" from his volume *Notebook* (1970). Lowell expanded on the work in *Notebook* in three volumes published in 1973: *History, For Lizzie and Harriet,* and *The Dolphin.* These books record his divorce from Hardwick, its effects on his daughter, Harriet, and his remarriage to Caroline Blackwood in 1972. Although critics were divided on Lowell's use of private letters in the intimate confessional verse of *The Dolphin,* this volume won the poet another Pulitzer Prize. Four years after this success, Lowell died of a heart attack in a taxi cab while enroute to Lizzie and Harriet in New York City.

Mina Loy (1882–1966)

The daughter of a second-generation Hungarian Jewish father and an English mother, Mina Gertrude Lowry was born in London and began her career as a visual artist, exhibiting her paintings in the Salon d'Automne show in Paris, 1905. A cosmopolitan modernist, she spent time in England, Paris, and Florence before moving to the United States. In 1903, at the time she married the photographer and writer Stephen Haweis, she shortened the spelling of her name to become Mina Loy. Between 1904 and 1907 she had three children and was an active friend to fellow modernists Gertrude Stein and Mabel Dodge, in whose salons she met such figures as the cubist painter Pablo Picasso, John Reed, and Carl Van Vechten. By 1913, Loy was emerging as a modern artist in her own right, in part through her connections to Italian futurists such as Filippo Tommaso Marinetti and through her published verse in Alfred Steiglitz's stylish journal *Camera Work* and in Carl Van Vechten's *Trend.* Her publication of the experimental verse collection "Love Songs" in the avant-garde magazine *Others* created a literary stir. In 1916, Loy moved to New York to take the lead role in Alfred Kreymbourg's play *Lima Beans,* and the following year met and married the surreal poet and professional boxer Alfred Cravan. Her marriage was shortlived, however, owing to Cravan's disappearance in Mexico. Returning to England, Loy gave birth to Cravan's daughter, Fabienne, in 1919 and later moved to Florence. Leaving her children there, she sailed for New York, where she became a member of the Provincetown Players. With the financial support of Peggy Guggenheim, Loy traveled to Paris three years later with Fabienne and opened a lampshade business. In that same year, Robert McAlmon's Contact Press published her book of verse *Lunar Baedecker* (1923). By 1930 Loy had given up her business in Paris and was working as the Paris agent for a New York gallery managed by Julien Levy, her son-in-law. Her last creative project of Bowery "constructions" was documented in her New York gallery exhibition and involved a series of poems and experimental artworks based on the street life of the lower Bowery, where she lived until the age of seventy-one. Loy spent the remaining decade of her life with her daughters in Colorado, where she died in Aspen at the age of eighty-four.

Andrew Marvell (1621–1678)

The son of a minister, Andrew Marvell was born in the Yorkshire town of Hull and at age twelve attended Trinity College, Cambridge. At the age of sixteen, he published poems written in Latin and Greek in an anthology of Cambridge poets. Graduating with a B.A. in 1639, Marvell began his studies toward an M.A. degree, but his advanced degree work was interrupted when his father drowned in the Hull estuary. During the 1640s, Marvell traveled on the Continent and became a tutor in the 1650s, the decade that he most likely wrote his most enduring lyrics. Owing to his friendship with the poet John Milton, Marvell was appointed his Latin secretary from 1657 to 1660, when Marvell was elected to Parliament. A consummate politician, Marvell held office under Cromwell as well as during the Restoration. His posthumously published satires present sharp and witty criticisms of loyalists of both the Royalist and Republican causes. Not just a closet satirist, however, Marvell used his political influence to free Milton from jail after the Restoration and served on diplomatic journeys to Holland, Russia, Sweden, and Denmark. Although now remembered for such masterful carpe diem lyrics as "To His Coy Mistress," pastoral lyrics such as "The Garden," and political odes such as "An Horation Ode upon Cromwell's Return from Ireland," Marvell published very little during his lifetime. It was not until 1681, three years after his death, that his nephew published Marvell's verse under the title *Miscellaneous Poems.*

Claude McKay (1889–1948)

Born into a Jamaican farm family, Festus Claudius McKay received an education at first from his oldest brother, a schoolteacher. McKay began to write poetry as early as age ten before he entered into an apprenticeship to a cabinetmaker. At eighteen, he was encouraged to write dialect poetry by an expatriate English gentleman living in Jamaica, Walter Jekyll, who later set McKay's verse to music. When he immigrated to the United States in 1912, McKay had already published two volumes of dialect verse that drew on native folkloric motifs, *Songs of Jamaica* (1912) and *Constab Ballads* (1912). On his arrival in America, McKay studied briefly at Tuskegee Institute before leaving for Kansas State College. By 1914, he had moved to New York through Jekyll's patronage, where he was briefly married to Eulalie Imelda Lewars. In 1917 he published "Invocation" and "The Harlem Dancer," which drew the attention of Max Eastman, the editor of the socialist little magazine *The Liberator.* Through his collaboration with Eastman, McKay came to edit *The Liberator* and emerged as a leading voice in the Harlem Renaissance. In 1919 he published several protest poems that showed a mastery of the sonnet form including "If We Must Die," "Baptism," "The White House," and "The Lynching." For the next three years, McKay lived in England where he worked for the *Workers' Drednought,* a British socialist magazine. The year 1922 marked the publication of two volumes of verse, *Spring in New Hampshire* and *Harlem Shadows.* For the following twelve years, McKay traveled in Europe, the Soviet Union, and Africa, during which time he published *Home to Harlem* (1928), his first widely read novel, followed by *Banjo: A Story without a Plot* (1929), *Gingertown* (1932), and *Banana Bottom* (1933). Living in France, he became a major influence on Léopold Sédar Senghor, Aimé Cesaire, and others in the Negritude movement of French West Africa and the West Indies.

Returning to the United States in 1934, McKay worked for the Federal Writers Project in 1936, finishing *A Long Way from Home*, his autobiography. Four years later, he became a citizen of the United States and later converted to Catholicism, working for the Chicago-based Catholic Youth Organization. After suffering chronic coronary disease for several years, McKay died of congestive heart failure in 1948. Remembered not just as one of the seminal voices of the Harlem Renaissance, McKay's masterful fusion of the sonnet tradition with the rhetoric of social commitment remains an important example for a subsequent generation of formalist writers including Gwendolyn Brooks and for later poets of the black aesthetic movement.

Edna St. Vincent Millay (1892–1950)

Millay was born in Rockland, Maine, to Henry Tollman Millay, a schoolteacher, and Cora Millay, who became a nurse after divorcing her husband in 1900 and moving her family to Camden, Maine. In her teen years, Millay showed early literary talent in editing her school magazine and publishing in *St. Nicholas Magazine*. Based in part on her poem "Renascence," published in *The Lyric Year*, Millay received a scholarship from the National Training School of the YWCA to attend Vassar College, where she studied literature and was active in the Vassar drama department. In 1917, the year of her graduation, she published *Renascence and Other Poems*, and became a part of the lively Bohemian community of Greenwich Village. As a member of the Provincetown Players, she befriended such notable modernist intellectuals as Edmund Wilson, Floyd Dell, and Susan Glaspell. In 1920, Millay published *A Few Figs from Thistles* followed by her Pulitzer Prize–winning volume, *The Harp Weaver* in 1923. That year Millay married Eugen Boissevain, who encouraged Millay's literary career as well as her unconventional bisexual orientation in her extramarital relations with others. Boissevain helped to promote Millay's literary career by managing her reading schedule in the mid-1920s. In 1927 Millay published a libretto for *The King's Henchman*, which had a successful premier at New York's Metropolitan Opera. That same year, Millay became committed to the leftist struggle over the murder conviction of two Italian labor agitators, Nicola Sacco and Bartolomeo Vanzetti. Millay's protest of the Sacco-Vanzetti case reflected her socialist commitments, which are evident in her 1927 poem, "Justice Denied in Massachusetts." Two years later Millay was elected to the National Institute of Arts and Letters, followed by a similar accolade in 1940 from the American Academy of Arts and Letters. Millay's antifascist stances in the Spanish Civil War and her protest of Nazism are featured in such volumes of verse as *Huntsman, What Quarry?* (1939), *Make Bright the Arrows* (1940), and *The Murder of Lidice* (1942). Owing in part to her chronic alcoholism, Millay suffered a nervous breakdown in 1944; her husband died of cancer in 1949. A year later, Millay also passed away, leaving behind a rich corpus of verse gathered in her *Collected Lyrics* (1943) and *Collected Poems* (1949, 1956).

John Milton (1609–1674)

Born in London and educated at St. Paul's School, John Milton entered Christ's College of Cambridge University in 1625. Milton received a bachelor's degree in 1629 and a master's degree three years later. Publishing his essay "On Shakespeare" in the Second Folio of Shakespeare's works, Milton went on to read widely in his family homes at Hammersmith and Horton. In 1634, his play *Comus* was performed in honor of Thomas Egerton, and it was published three years later. In 1637, Milton's mother died, and he also lost his friend and fellow student at Christ's College, Edward King, who is the subject of Milton's great elegy "Lycidas," published the following year. For 1638, Milton traveled in France and throughout Italy, returning to London the following year. During the next three years, Milton sided with Parliament against Charles I's claim to monarchical power and published such essays as "Of Reformation" and "The Reason of Church Government." In 1642, Milton married Mary Powell, who then separated from the poet during the next three years owing to her family's sympathy for the Royalist cause. By 1645, Milton had emerged as a major poet with the publication of his *Poems.* Mary returned to him that year at the time of the Battle of Naseby, which marked Charles I's decisive military defeat. In 1649, following the public execution of King Charles I, Milton was appointed to the diplomatic post of Secretary of Foreign Tongues. During the next two years, Milton wrote defenses of Charles's execution in works such as his 1651 *Defensio pro populo Anglicano* (a "defense of the English people"). The following year was marked by the death of Milton's first wife and the loss of his eyesight, most likely due to glaucoma. Curtailing his diplomatic work, Milton undertook a Latin dictionary and Greek lexicon in the mid-1650s and in 1657 married Katharine Woodcock, who died two years later. Following the death of Oliver Cromwell in 1658, Milton went into hiding from the loyalist supporters of Charles II and was arrested and imprisoned in the fall of the following year. Defended by Andrew Marvell, however, Milton was fined and released at the time of the restoration of Charles II in 1660. During the 1660s, Milton worked on the composition of *Paradise Lost,* which was published as a ten-book volume in 1667, four years after Milton had married his third wife, Elizabeth Minshully. In 1671, Milton published *Paradise Regain'd* and *Samson Agonistes,* followed by the expanded, twelve-book edition of *Paradise Lost,* published in 1674, the year Milton died.

Marianne Moore (1887–1972)

Raised by her grandfather, a Presbyterian minister, Marianne Moore moved to Carlisle, Pennsylvania in 1896 two years after his death. Moore graduated from Bryn Mawr College with a B.A. degree in 1909 and, after studying typing at the Carlisle Commercial College for a year, worked as a teacher of "commerical subjects" at the Carlisle Indian School through 1915. That year, Moore published in the little magazine *The Egoist* and moved with her mother to Chatham, New Jersey, and later to an apartment at St. Luke's Place in Greenwich Village. The 1920s marked the ascent of Moore as a poet in her collaboration with such modernists as William Carlos Williams, Wallace Stevens, and Kenneth Burke. While working as an assistant at the Hudson Park branch of the New York Public Library, she published a volume entitled *Poems* in 1920 and from 1925 through 1932 served as the editor of the influential modernist journal *The Dial*. In the 1930s, Moore won the Helen Haire Levinson Prize for Poetry (1932), published her *Selected Poems* (1935), received the Ernst Harstock Memorial Prize, and published a volume entitled *The Pangolin and Other Verse* (1936). Beginning the next decade with the Shelley Memorial Award (1940), Moore also won *Contemporary Poetry*'s Patrons Prize (1944), the Harriet Monroe Poetry Prize (1944), and a Guggenheim Fellowship (1945). During this period, Moore published *What Are Years?* (1941) and *Nevertheless* (1944), followed by her *Collected Poems* (1951), which received the Pulitzer Prize, National Book Award, and the Bollingen Prize (1953). In 1955, Moore was elected to the Academy of Arts and Letters, and the National Institute of Arts and Letters observed her seventy-fifth birthday in 1962. By the end of that decade, Moore had become a popular celebrity and in addition to throwing out the first baseball of the 1968 season at Yankee Stadium at age eighty, she was named "Senior Citizen of the Year" for 1969. The following year she received an honorary degree from Harvard and published her final poems before her death in 1972 at age eighty-four.

Pat Mora (b. 1942)

A native of El Paso, Texas, Pat Mora is a Mexican American writer whose grandparents emigrated to the United States at the beginning of the twentieth century. The poet's father, an optician, was born in Chihuahua, and her mother came from El Paso. After completing her bachelor's degree in 1963 from Texas Western College—now the University of Texas, El Paso—Mora went on to receive a master's degree, also from UTEP (1967). While working as a secondary school teacher and college-level instructor, she also hosted a radio program entitled *Voices: The Mexican-American Perspective*. The mother of three children, Mora is an author of poetry and of children's literature. Mora's numerous awards include the Creative Writing Award of the National Association for Chicano Studies (1983), Women Artists and Writers of the Southwest poetry award (1984), and the Tomas Rivera Mexican American Children's Book Award (1997). In the fall of 1999, she was named Garrey Carruthers Chair in Honors, Distinguished Visiting Professor at the University of New Mexico. A self-proclaimed "daughter of the desert," Mora has explored in such works as *Chants* (1984), *Borders* (1986), *Communion* (1991), *Nepantla: Essays from the Land in the Middle* (1993), *House of Houses* (1997), and *My Own True Name: New and Selected Poems for Young Adults, 1984–1999* (2000) what Gloria Anzaldua has characterized as the "border land" of bilingual and bicultural identity as a Mexican American woman.

Sharon Olds (b. 1942)

Born and raised in San Francisco, Sharon Olds received a B.A. at Stanford and pursued graduate work in English at Columbia University. Her first volume of verse, *Satan Says* (1980), won the San Francisco Poetry Center Award for its intense and candid portrayals of desire and domestic turmoil. Influenced by the example of such precursor poets as Robert Lowell, Sylvia Plath, and Anne Sexton, Olds continued to explore the psychic terrain of family experience in her second book, *The Dead and the Living*, which received the 1983 Lamont Poetry Prize and the National Book Critics Circle Award. On the question of whether her poetry presents autobiographical or invented personae, Olds is somewhat ambiguous and compares her work with that of Emily Dickinson. "I guess," she has said, "I'm trying to lead two lives, the life of art and the life of life, and to keep them as separate as possible from each other. Emily Dickinson talks somewhere about the 'someone' in her poems. That seems to me a useful way to think about it." Olds's subsequent volumes similarly have paid unflinching attention to the sources of her desire, grief, rage, and joy in *The Gold Cell* (1987), *The Father* (1992) (a finalist for the National Book Critics' Circle Award), *The Wellspring* (1996), and *Blood, Tin, Straw* (1999). Olds's poetry is widely anthologized and translated. She is a faculty member of the graduate creative writing program at New York University. Olds was also the New York State Poet Laureate from 1998 to 2000.

Wilfred Owen (1893–1918)

The son of a railway clerk, Wilfred Owen showed early talent as a poet but, despite his mother's encouragement of his love for literature, failed in 1912 to win a scholarship to London University. Instead, he taught English the following year at a Berlitz School in Bordeaux. After the start of the Great War, Owen returned to England in 1915, where he lived for a time at the Poetry Bookshop managed by Harold Monro. Two years later, Owen joined the 2nd Manchesters Regiment, where, on the Somme, he was exposed to the trauma of trench warfare. In 1917, Owen suffered a concussion and after prolonged exposure to the violence of war on the front lines was blown into the air by a shell blast. Diagnosed with shell-shock, he recuperated near Edinburgh at Craiglockhart Hospital, where he met Siegfried Sassoon, who helped clarify Owen's poetic aims and introduced him to the author Robert Graves. By the end of 1917, Owen had received a promotion to the rank of lieutenant and published poems in *The Nation* and *The Bookman*. The next year, Owen returned to the front, where he was awarded the Military Cross a month before he was killed while leading his command across the Sambre Canal. Of his work as a poet, Owen wrote, "My subject is War, and the pity of War. The Poetry is in the pity."

Sylvia Plath (1932–1963)

Of German American descent, Sylvia Plath was born in Jamaica Plain, Massachusetts, to Otto and Aurelia Schoeber Plath. Having immigrated to America from Silesia, Otto Plath was a professor of Biology at Boston University and the author of *Bumblebees and Their Ways* published in 1934, two years after Sylvia was born. Interrupting the normal course of Sylvia's girlhood, Otto suffered a traumatic illness involving the amputation of a gangrenous leg. He died in 1940, when Sylvia was eight years old. A creative writer herself, Aurelia Plath encouraged Sylvia's interest in poetry and literature. Sylvia Plath attended Smith College on scholarship and was appointed to the College Board of *Mademoiselle* magazine in 1953. That year, Plath suffered from depression and received bipolar electroconvulsive shock treatment. In August, she attempted suicide for the first time. But after six months of therapy, she was able to return to Smith, where she graduated summa cum laude in English and won a Fulbright fellowship to Newnham College, Cambridge in 1955. There she met the British poet Ted Hughes, whom she married in June 1956. The following year, the Hugheses sailed to the United States, where Plath taught in the Smith College English Department for a year. During 1958 and 1959, Sylvia and Ted lived in Boston and, while Ted's first volume *The Hawk* received much notoriety, Sylvia attended Robert Lowell's poetry seminar at Boston University, where she met Anne Sexton and George Starbuck. After spending the fall at the writer's colony at Yaddo, New York, Plath gave birth to her daughter Frieda in April 1960. That spring the Hugheses moved from London to Devon, where Plath studied beekeeping and entered into her most creative phase as a poet. In the fall of 1960, Plath published *The Colossus and Other Poems*, and the following year, Plath authored her autobiographical novel *The Bell Jar*. Meanwhile, Ted Hughes moved to the center of England's literary world through his contacts with the BBC and T. S. Eliot. Plath's son Nicholas was born in January 1962, but Ted Hughes's infidelity led Plath to separate from her husband that fall. It was at this time that she wrote her so-called October poems, which would appear in her posthumously published volume, *Ariel* (1965). Returning to London as a single mother with two children, Plath suffered from depression and chronic flu-like symptoms in December of that year. Overwhelmed by the return of her depression, compounded by her isolation and ill health, Plath committed suicide on February 11, 1963, two weeks before the publication of *The Bell Jar*. With the publication of *Ariel*, Plath became a central poet of her generation and was awarded a Pulitzer Prize for poetry in 1982 for her posthumous volume of *Collected Poems*.

Edgar Allan Poe (1809–1847)

Poe's parents, the traveling actors David and Elizabeth Poe, died before Edgar Allan Poe reached the age of three. The poet's foster parents, John and Frances Allan, traveled with him to England, where between the age of six and eleven Poe studied in a boarding school. In 1826, Poe attended the University of Virginia, but gambling debts caused him to drop out of college. He traveled to Boston, where he published his first book of verse, *Tamerlane and Other Poems* (1827), and then had a brief appointment to West Point. Poe's second book of poems, *Al Aaraaf, Tamerlane, and Minor Poems*, appeared in 1829 before the publication of *Poems* (1831), which included such famous works as "To Helen" and "Israfel." In 1832, Poe was living in Baltimore with his aunt Maria Clemm and her daughter, Virginia. That year, he published five stories followed in 1833 by the award of a prize from the *Baltimore Satur-*

day Visitor for "Ms. Found in a Bottle." Two years later, Poe moved to Richmond, Virginia, where he assumed the position of editor of the *Southern Literary Messenger* and married Virginia Clemm in 1836. The following year, Poe moved his family to New York, where he published *The Narrative of Arthur Gordon Pym*. During the next decade—from his time in Philadelphia between 1838 and 1844 and then in New York from 1844 through 1849—Poe sought to consolidate his reputation as a journalist, poet, and fiction writer, publishing such masterpieces as "Ligeia" (1838), "The Fall of the House of Usher" (1839), "The Murders in the Rue Morgue" (1841), "The Raven" (1845), and "The Bells" (1849). Two years after the death of Virginia from tuberculosis in 1847, Poe returned to Richmond for a lecture tour, but traveling north en route to New York, Poe died in Baltimore of "acute congestion of the brain."

Alexander Pope (1688–1744)

Born to a Catholic cloth merchant in London, Pope grew up in an era of anti-Catholic prejudice and was denied a university education. Consequently, he studied under independent teachers such as the Catholic convert and former Oxford don, Thomas Deane. Pope also was a victim of tuberculosis, which left him, in the words of Sir Joshua Reynolds, "about four feet six high; very humpbacked and deformed." Nevertheless, through the encouragement he received from William Wycherley, among others, Pope grew in stature as a poet and writer with the publication of *Pastorals* in 1709, his neoclassical *Essay on Criticism* (1711), and his bawdy mock epic *The Rape of the Lock* (1712). A translator of the *Iliad* and the *Odyssey*, Pope emerged as the preeminent man of letters with his 1717 publication of his *Collected Works*. With his move to Twickenham, Pope shared an interest in horticulture with Lady Mary Wortley before entering into a lasting companionship with Martha Blount. In 1728, he published *The Dunciad*, a satiric reponse to an attack of his edition of Shakespeare, followed by his *Moral Essays* (1731) and *Essay on Man* (1733–1734). During his remaining years, Pope hosted the major literary figures of his age at his villa where he died on May 21, 1744.

Ezra Pound (1885–1972)

Born in Hailey, Idaho, Pound studied at the University of Pennsylvania for two years before graduating from Hamilton College in 1905. Following a two-year teaching stint at Wabash College, Pound traveled to Europe in 1908, where he met W. B. Yeats. By 1911, Pound had published six volumes of verse whose style reflected Pound's interests in Provençal and Italian literary models. Influenced by such modernists as Ford Madox Ford and T. E. Hulme, Pound founded the imagist movement in 1912 and later propounded the more dynamic compositional style of vorticism. Reflecting his study of Ernest Fenollosa and the Chinese written character, Pound published *Cathay* in 1915, the year after his marriage to Dorothy Shakespear. Moving to the center of London's international literary scene, Pound became the editor of the *Little Review* in 1917. Deeply troubled by the events of the First World War, Pound wrote "Homage to Sextus Propertius" (1919) and "Hugh Selwyn Mauberley" (1921), which protested what Pound criticized as the cultural decadence and wasted promise of the war generation. At this time, Pound was also editing T. S. Eliot's *The Waste Land* (1922), leading Eliot to name him as *il miglior fabbro* or "the better craftsman." By 1924, Pound had left London to settle in Rapallo, where he began to compose a long "poem including history" that would evolve into *The Cantos*. Following the publication of the first section of *The Cantos* in 1925, Pound expanded them with the release of *A Draft of XXX Cantos* (1930), followed by Cantos 31 to 70 published between 1934 and 1940. Throughout the 1930s, Pound became increasingly involved with Italian fascism, which culminated in his infamous Rome Radio addresses that promoted the dictatorship of Benito Mussolini and anti-Semitism. After Pound's six-month detention in the Disciplinary Training Centre near Pisa, he was deemed mentally unfit to stand trial for treason in 1945. Instead, Pound was diagnosed as insane and became an inmate at St. Elizabeth's Hospital in Washington, D.C. from 1946 to 1958. He continued on as poet, publishing *The Pisan Cantos* (1948), *Section: Rock-Drill* (1955), *Thrones* (1959), and *Drafts and Fragments of Cantos CX–CXVII* (1969). On his release from St. Elizabeth's, Pound lived out his remaining years in Italy, eventually settling in Venice, where he died in 1972.

Edwin Arlington Robinson (1869–1935)

Born in Head Tide, Maine, Robinson was the son of Edward Robinson, a timber merchant, and Mary Elizabeth Palmer. He grew up in the town of Gardiner, which is the setting for his poems on life in "Tilbury Town." The third of three sons, Robinson pursued poetry as early as age eleven before attending Harvard University from 1891 through 1893. During this time, Robinson's father died in 1892, and the Robinsons plummeted into bankruptcy over the next seven years, forcing the poet to leave Harvard. Robinson published *The Torrent and the Night Before*, in 1896, also the year his mother died. The next year he brought out a revised version of this volume entitled *The Children of the Night*. Poems such as "Richard Cory," "Luke Havergal," and "Aaron Stark" witness to the bleak social lives and tragic circumstances of Robinson's "Tilbury Town" characters. In 1897, Robinson left Gardiner for New York City, where he lived in poverty owing to the collapse of his family finances. After publishing *Captain Craig* in 1902, Robinson made a sporatic living from temporary work, eventually receiving, through Kermit Roosevelt, a New York Customs House job in 1905 that allowed him to sustain himself while writing. In 1909, Robinson published *The Town Down the River* and quit the Customs House, spending summers at the MacDowell Colony in New Hampshire after 1911. His literary reputation grew with the publication in 1916 of *The Man Against the Sky* and with Amy Lowell's favorable chapter on his work in her book of essays entitled *Tendencies in Modern American Poetry* (1917). By 1921, he had won the first Pulitzer Prize for poetry for his *Collected Poems* followed by a second Pulitzer for *The Man Who Died Twice* (1924). Throughout the 1920s, Robinson published actively with such major volumes as *Avon's Harvest* (1921), *Roman Bartholow* (1925), *Dionysus in Doubt* (1925), *Cavender's House* (1929), *Matthias at the Door* (1931), a collection of shorter poems called *Nicodemus* (1932), *Talifer* (1933), and *Amaranth* (1934). His last volume, *King Jasper*, was published posthumously in 1935.

Theodore Roethke (1908–1963)

As a youth, Roethke literally grew up in the garden world of his parents' greenhouse business before becoming a student at Saginaw's Arthur Hill High School, where he showed early promise in a speech on the Junior Red Cross that was subsequently published in twenty-six languages. The poet's adolescent years were jarred, however, by the death of his father from cancer in 1923, a loss that would powerfully shape Roethke's psychic and creative lives. From 1925 to 1929 Roethke distinguished himself at the University of Michigan at Ann Arbor, graduating magna cum laude. Resisting family pressure to pursue a legal career, he quit law school after one semester and, from 1929 to 1931, took graduate courses at the University of Michigan and later the Harvard Graduate School, where he worked closely with the poet Robert Hillyer. The hard economic times of the Great Depression forced Roethke to leave Harvard and to take up a teaching career at Lafayette College from 1931 to 1935. Here he met Rolfe Humphries, who introduced him to Louise Bogan; during these years Roethke also found a powerful supporter, colleague, and friend in the poet Stanley Kunitz. In the fall of 1935 Roethke assumed his second teaching post, at Michigan State College at Lansing, but was soon hospitalized for what would prove to be recurring bouts of mental illness. Throughout his subsequent career Roethke used these periodic incidents of depression for creative self-exploration. During the remainder of the decade Roethke enjoyed a growing reputation as a poet. He taught at Pennsylvania State University from 1936 to 1943, publishing in such prestigious journals as *Poetry*, the *New Republic*, the *Saturday Review*, and *Sewanee Review*. He brought out his first volume of verse, *Open House*, in 1941. The year after *Open House* was published, Roethke was invited to deliver one of the prestigious Morris Gray lectures at Harvard University, and in 1943 he left Penn State to teach at Bennington College, where he joined such luminaries as Léonie Adams and Kenneth Burke. His collaboration with Burke, in particular, was crucial to the development of the second, and pivotal, volume of Roethke's career, *The Lost Son and Other Poems* (1948). The descent into the organic life of things themselves dramatized the theme of regression that is explored in psychoanalytic terms in the book's title piece. In his next volume, *Praise to the End!* (1951), Roethke's regressive aesthetic continued to explore further the prerational experience of early childhood and sexual discoveries of adolescence. The volume's title, as an allusion to Wordsworth's *The Prelude*, signaled the work's romantic celebration of the child's unity of being in the natural world. *Praise to the End!* was composed after the poet's move to the University of Washington. The early 1950s augured Roethke's growing stature with the award of a Guggenheim fellowship (1950), *Poetry* magazine's Levinson Prize

(1951), and major grants from the Ford Foundation and the National Institute of Arts and Letters in 1952. The following year Roethke married Beatrice O'Connell, whom he had met during his earlier stint at Bennington. The two spent the following spring at W. H. Auden's villa at Ischia, off the coast of Italy, where Roethke edited the galley proofs for *The Waking: Poems 1933–1953* (1953), a seminal volume that won the Pulitzer Prize the next year. Although thematically akin to Roethke's work of the late 1940s, this volume's title piece marked the poet's return to formalist verse, composed as it is in the complex villanelle pattern. Throughout 1955 and 1956 the Roethkes traveled in Italy, Europe, and England on a Fulbright grant. The following year he published a collection of works that included forty-three new poems entitled *Words for the Wind* (1957), which won the Bollingen Prize, the National Book Award, the Edna St. Vincent Millay Prize, the Longview Foundation Award, and the Pacific Northwest Writer's Award. Now at the height of his popularity and fame, Roethke balanced his teaching career with reading tours in New York and Europe, underwritten by another Ford Foundation grant. While visiting with friends at Bainbridge Island, Washington, Roethke suffered a fatal heart attack in 1963. During the last years of his life he had composed the sixty-one new poems that were published posthumously in *The Far Field* (1964)—which received the National Book Award—and in *The Collected Poems* (1966).

Christina Rossetti (1830–1894)

The daughter of Gabriele and Frances Rossetti, Christina Rossetti was also the sister of the famous Pre-Raphelite painter and sculptor Dante Gabriel Rossetti, for whom she posed as a model. At the age of eighteen, she became engaged to James Collinson, a member of Dante's Pre-Raphelite circle. After the death of her father, Christina led a reclusive life owing to her poor health that may have been a result of angina or tuberculosis. During the 1860s, Rossetti had a relationship with Charles Cayley, but she never married him due, most likely, to the fact that he was not a professed Christian. Nevertheless, Christina had a close circle of friends and admirers that included such figures as Charles Dodgson (Lewis Carroll), James Abbott McNeill Whistler, and Algernon Charles Swinburne. Moreover, she was an active member of the Society for Promoting Christian Knowedge before her death in 1894.

Carl Sandburg (1878–1967)

A native of Illinois, Carl Sandburg was born into a working-class family of Swedish immigrants. After finishing the eighth grade, Sandburg labored at a series of odd jobs before riding the rails in search of work at the age of nineteen. In 1898, he joined Company C of the Sixth Infantry Regiment of the Illinois Volunteers and was assigned to Puerto Rico during the Spanish-American War. That same year he was admitted to Lombard College on a veteran's scholarship. After leaving Lombard in 1902, Sandburg worked as a journalist in Chicago. For five years beginning in 1907, he served as a Social-Democratic Party organizer in Wisconsin, returning to journalism as a staff member for the *Chicago Evening World* in 1912. Significantly, two years later he emerged as a poet when Harriet Monroe published six of his poems in the Chicago-based journal *Poetry: A Magazine of Verse*. In 1916, Henry Holt and Company published his *Chicago Poems* followed by *Cornhuskers* two years later. The next year, he left Holt to publish later volumes such as *Smoke and Steel* (1920), *Good Morning, America* (1928), and *The People, Yes* (1936) with Harcourt, Brace & Howe. Sandburg reported on the First World War for the Newspaper Enterprise Association and became an investigative journalist for the *Chicago Daily News* thereafter until he covered World War II as a syndicated columnist. In 1950, Sandburg was awarded the Pulitzer Prize in poetry for his *Complete Poems*. He was also a collector and performer of American folk songs and published many of them in *The American Songbag* (1927). Moreover, he was a prolific author of children's books as well as a major biographer of Abraham Lincoln, publishing *Abraham Lincoln: The Prairie Years* in 1926, followed by a four-volume sequel, *Abraham Lincoln: The War Years* (1939), which was awarded the Pulitzer Prize for history. In 1952, Sandburg received the American Academy of Arts and Letters gold medal in biography and history and a year later published his own autobiography, *Always the Young Strangers*. In 1955 he collaborated with his brother-in-law, the photographer Edward Steichen, on *The Family of Man*. In 1964, Sandburg received the Presidential Medal of Freedom and his achievement as a man of American letters was celebrated by President Lyndon B. Johnson, among many others, at the Lincoln Memorial shortly after the poet's death in 1967.

Anne Sexton (1928–1974). *See Chapter 19.*

William Shakespeare (1564–1616)

The third of eight children born to the leather merchant John Shakespeare, William Shakespeare most likely was educated at Stratford Grammar School. What little is known about Shakespeare's life must be gleaned from church and legal documents as well as his writing. Shakespeare did not receive a university education, and, according to Ben Jonson, he possessed "small Latine, and less Greeke." There is almost no information on his early life until his marriage at age eighteen to Anne Hathaway, who was then twenty-six. Between 1588 and 1592, Shakespeare had left Stratford for London. The year 1593 marked his emergence as a poet with "Venus and Adonis," and "The Rape of Lucrece" was published the next year. By 1594, Shakespeare was acting as one of the Lord Chamberlain's Men (better known as the King's Men following the ascension of James I in 1603), and during the mid-1590s, Shakespeare became a proprietor of the Globe Theatre and a part owner of Blackfriar's Theatre. Shakespeare began his career as a playwright in 1595. In 1609, the Sonnets and "A Lover's Complaint" were published in *Shake-speares Sonnets*. During his lifetime eighteen of his plays were published in the quarto editions. Thirty-six of the Shakespeare canon of thirty-eight plays appeared in the 1623 *First Folio* of the collected works published by two of Shakespeare's colleagues in the King's Men, John Heminges and Henry Condell. Shakespeare retired from his writing career in 1611, returning to Stratford. Although Shakespeare's son Hamnet and his twin sister Judith both died during the bard's lifetime, his other daughter, Susanna, outlived him to marry John Hall. Shakespeare died in 1616 and was buried in the Church of the Holy Trinity, where he had been baptized fifty-two years earlier.

Percy Bysshe Shelley (1792–1822)

As the eldest son born to Elizabeth Shelley and Timothy Shelley (a member of the House of Commons), Percy Bysshe Shelley came from a venerable family whose roots reached back to the era of William of Normandy. From 1804 to 1810, Shelley was a student at Eton College and then entered Oxford University. A prolific essayist and poet, Shelley was nevertheless expelled early on from Oxford owing to an essay he coauthored with a fellow student, Thomas Jefferson Hogg, entitled "The Necessity of Atheism." At the age of nineteen, Shelley eloped to Scotland with Harriet Westbrook, three years his junior. During this time Shelley met Wordsworth, Southey, De Quincey, and Wilson, who encouraged Shelley's literary ambitions. Over the next three years, Shelley and Harriet had two children before the poet abandoned his young family. While living in the Lake District, Shelley had befriended William Godwin and Mary Wollstonecraft and eloped to Europe with their daughter, Mary Godwin, in 1814. In January 1815, Mary Godwin bore Shelley a son, and the following May, Shelley and Godwin moved to Lake Geneva, where the poet composed his allegorical poem *Alastor, or The Spirit of Solitude* while spending time with George Gordon, Lord Byron. In 1816 Harriet Shelley committed suicide by drowning herself in the Serpentine River. Although Shelley and Mary Godwin soon married thereafter, he nevertheless lost custody of his two children conceived with Harriet. Two years later, Shelley left England for good and published *The Revolt of Islam*. During the next four years, Shelley traveled in Italy and befriended Leigh Hunt and others. During this period, he produced the major works of his canon including "Prometheus Unbound," "Hellas," "The Witch of Atlas," "Adonais," and "Epipsychidion." Sailing under stormy conditions from Leghorn in 1822, Shelley drowned after his small schooner the *Don Juan* sank in the Bay of Spezia.

Gary Snyder (b. 1930)

Born in San Francisco, Gary Snyder grew up in rural Oregon and Washington. After earning a B.A. degree in anthropology from Reed College, he worked variously on logging crews and as a forest-fire lookout in Baker National Forest in the early 1950s. During this time, he pursued graduate studies in Asian languages at the University of California, Berkeley. By the decade's end, he would become a culture hero in the Beat movement, appearing as the character of Japphy Rider in Jack Kerouac's celebrated novel *The Dharma Bums*. Snyder's commitment to Asian studies extended beyond his time at Berkeley, and later in the 1960s he became a student of Buddhism in

Kyoto, Japan, under the Zen master Oda Sesso Roshi. Similar to Ezra Pound's collaborative work with Ernest Fenollosa in *The Chinese Written Character as a Medium for Poetry*, Snyder's spare imagist style in his short lyrics, such as "Mid-August at Sourdough Mountain Lookout," reflects the poet's work as a translator of classical Chinese verse and Japanese haiku poetry. Included among his numerous awards are a Guggenehim fellowship (1968) and the Pulitzer Prize for poetry (1975) for *Turtle Island* (1974). In addition to this volume, Snyder's other major books of poetry include *Riprap* (1958), *The Back Country* (1968), *Earth House Hold* (1969), *Regarding Wave* (1970), *Axe Handles* (1983), and *Mountains and Rivers without End* (1997).

Cathy Song (b. 1955)

A native of Wahiawa, Hawaii, Cathy Song was born in Honolulu to a Chinese American mother and Korean American father. At the age of seven, she moved with her family to the Waialae Kahala district of Honolulu. She began writing poetry at Kalani High School before attending the University of Hawaii at Manoa for two years, where she studied with the poet John Unterecker. In 1977, Song graduated from Wellesley College with a B.A. in English and then earned an M.A. in creative writing from Boston University in 1981. Two years later, she published her first volume of poetry, *Picture Bride*, which won the prestigious Yale Younger Poets Award. In 1987, she returned to Hawaii with her husband, Douglas Davenport, and the following year she published *Frameless Windows, Squares of Light* (1988) followed by *School Figures* (1994). She divides her time between teaching at the University of Hawaii at Manoa and working as an editor for the Bamboo Ridge Press, which is devoted to publishing the literature of Hawaii.

Gary Soto (b. 1952)

A native of Fresno, California, Gary Soto was born into a Mexican American family of farm workers. At the age of five, Soto lost his twenty-seven-year-old father in a factory accident. Soto returns to the barrio of his childhood for the setting of many of his poems. "It's important to me," he has said "to create and share new stories about my heritage. . . . That's why I write so much about growing up in the barrio. It allows me to use specific memories that are vivid for me." After graduating high school in 1970, Soto began studying geology at Fresno City College where he received an A.A. degree in 1972. Two years later, he earned a B.A. in English studying under the poet Philip Levine at California State University at Fresno. The following year, he married and received the Discovery-Nation Prize for his writing. In 1976, Soto earned an M.F.A. degree in creative writing from the University of California and won the U.S. Award of the International Poetry Forum. The following year, he published his first book of verse, *The Elements of San Joaquin*. Two years later, he published *The Tale of Sunlight* in 1978. During the 1980s and 1990s, Soto emerged as one of the most prolific poets and children's authors of his generation in such works as *Where Sparrows Work Hard* (1981), *Black Hair* (1985),

Who Will Know Us? (1990), *Home Course in Religion* (1991), *Neighborhood Odes* (1992), *Canto Familiar/Familiar Song* (1994), and *Selected Poems* (1995). He lives in Berkeley and is a Distinguished Professor at the University of California at Riverside.

Wole Soyinka (b. 1934)

Oluwole Akinwande Soyinka was born in Ijebu Isara, Western Nigeria, to a school supervisor. From 1940 through 1952, Soyinka attended primary school in Abeokuta and secondary school at the Government College, Ibadan. From 1952 through 1954, he was enrolled at University College, Ibadan, which has an affiliation with the University of London. In 1957, Soyinka received his honors degree in English literature from the University of Leeds followed by work toward an M.A. that same year; in 1973 he completed his doctorate there. The year 1958 marked the debut of Soyinka's career as a dramatist with the production of *The Swamp Dwellers* for the University of London Drama Festival followed by a run of *The Swamp Dwellers* and *The Lion and the Jewel* the next year in Ibadan. In 1959, Soyinka wrote, produced, and acted in *An Evening with Décor* at the Royal Court Theatre, London. In 1960, Soyinka was awarded a Rockefeller bursary to study African drama in Nigeria, and he also founded the theater group The 1960 Masks followed four years later by the Orisun Theatre Company. In 1965, Soyinka published the novel *The Interpreters* and recorded *The Detainee* for the BBC in London. In the mid-sixties, Soyinka became increasingly critical of dictatorships in Africa, and in 1967, he was arrested for conspiring with the Biafra rebels and detained as a political prisoner for twenty-two months. In 1971, Soyinka published a volume of poems entitled *A Shuttle in the Crypt* and gave testimony concerning the violation of student rights to the Kazeem Enquiry. The next year he published his prison memoir, *The Man Died*, followed by a second novel, *Season of Anomy* (1973). In addition to earlier volumes of verse, including *Idanre, and Other Poems* (1967) and *Poems from Prison* (1969), he edited *Poems of Black Africa* in 1975. He would go on to publish such books of poetry as *Ogun Abibiman* (1976) and *Mandela's Earth and Other Poems* (1988). Since winning the Nobel Prize for literature in 1986, Soyinka has continued to publish steadily in all genres and is the author of over forty works of literature. During this time he has also led an active, cosmopolitan life as an educator and social activitist, holding several professorships at such prestigious universities as Cambridge, Sheffield, Yale, and Emory.

William Stafford (1914–1993)

Born in Hutchinson, Kansas, to Ruby Mayher and Earl Ingersoll Stafford, William Stafford grew up in a working-class family and graduated from high school in 1933 during the middle of the Depression era. After passing through two junior colleges, Stafford earned a bachelor's degree from the University of Kansas in 1937. Over the next three years, he studied for a master's degree in English, but World War II cut short his graduate education. As a conscientious objector to the war, Stafford spent 1942 through 1946 doing community service in such areas as soil conservation, fire fighting, road maintenance, and other forms of manual labor in Arkansas, California, and Illinois. During this period, in California he married Dorothy Frantz in 1944. After the war, Stafford taught high school and worked for the Church World Service before earning his master's degree from the University of Kansas in 1947. That year, the poet's memoir of his war experiences as a conscientious objector, *Down in My Heart*, was published by Brethren Publish House. The next year Stafford moved to Portland, Oregon, to accept a teaching position at Lewis and Clark College, where he would remain for the rest of his professional career until 1980. In 1954, he earned a Ph.D. from the University of Iowa. Stafford's first volume of verse, *Traveling through the Dark*, was not published until the poet was forty-eight, but it won him the National Book Award in 1963. Other awards followed, including the Award in Literature by the American Academy and Institute of Arts and Letters, Shelley Memorial Award, a Guggenheim Fellowship, and a Western States Lifetime Achievement Award, among numerous other prizes. In 1970, he served as the consultant in poetry to the Library of Congress. Before his death at the age of seventy-nine in 1993, he had published more than sixty-five volumes of poetry, including *The Rescued Year* (1966), *Stories That Could Be True: New and Collected Poems* (1977), *Writing the Australian Crawl: Views on the Writer's Vocation* (1978), and *An Oregon Message* (1987).

Wallace Stevens (1879–1955)

Born in Reading, Pennsylvania, Wallace Stevens attended Harvard University as a special student for three years between 1897 and 1900 without graduating. Three years later, he graduated from New York law school and passed the New York bar exam the following year. During the next five years, he courted a Reading woman, Elsie Kachel, and married her in 1909. Making his way in New York as an attorney, Stevens worked as a bond lawyer, rising to the position of vice president of the New York office of the Equitable Surety Co. of St. Louis in 1914. Two years later, he joined the Hartford Accident and Indemnity Co. and moved to Hartford, Connecticut, where he lived for the rest of his life. Although Stevens began writing poetry while a student at Harvard, he did not publish his first volume, *Harmonium*, until 1923, the year before the birth of his only child, Holly Bight. It was not until 1931 that he published a second edition of *Harmonium*, which included only eight new poems. Meanwhile, Stevens advanced his professional career and assumed the position of vice president of the Hartford in 1934. Stevens's career as a poet also picked up speed in the mid-thirties with the publication of *Ideas of Order* (1935), *The Man with the Blue Guitar* (1937), and *Owl's Clover* (1937). Throughout the 1940s, Stevens would achieve a major reputation as a modern American poet based, in part, on his long, philosophical poems in such works as *Parts of a World* (1942), *Notes toward a Supreme Fiction* (1942), "Esthetique du Mal" (1945), "The Auroras of Autumn" (1947), and "An Ordinary Evening in New Haven" (1950). In 1951, Stevens published an important book of essays on modernist aesthetics entitled *The Necessary Angel*. In it, he defined the imagination as "A violence from within that protects us from a violence without. It is the imagination pressing back against the pressure of reality." By the time of his death in 1955, Stevens was recognized as one of the foremost poets of his generation.

May Swenson (1913–1989)

Born in Logan, Utah, May Swenson received a bachelor's degree from Utah State University in 1939. It was not until 1954, however, that she published her first volume of poetry, entitled *Another Animal*, followed by two more books: *A Cage of Spines* (1958) and *To Mix with Time, New and Selected Poems* (1963). During this time, from 1959 through 1966, she served as editor at New Directions and held a number of teaching positions at Bryn Mawr, the University of North Carolina, the University of California, Riverside, Purdue University, and Utah State University. She also published a volume of translations of contemporary Swedish poetry entitled *Iconographs* (1970). Poetry, for Swenson, allowed access to what she described as "the vastness of the unknown beyond [one's] consciousness." Until her death in 1989, she remained a prolific writer whose books of poetry include *Poems to Solve* (1966), *Half Sun Half Sleep* (1967), *More Poems to Solve* (1968), *New & Selected Things Taking Place* (1978), and *In Other Words* (1987). She is a recipient of the American Introductions Prize, the Longview Foundation Award, a National Instititute of Arts and Letters Award, Shelley Award, a Bollingen Prize for poetry, and the MacArthur Fellowship, among other numerous awards.

Alfred, Lord Tennyson (1809–1892)

The fourth of twelve children born to George and Elizabeth Tennyson, Alfred Tennyson was raised in Lincolnshire before he entered Trinity College, Cambridge, in 1827 to study under William Whewell. There, like his brothers, Tennyson distinguished himself as a poet and won the Chancellor's Gold Medal in 1828 for *Timbuctoo*. At Cambridge, he joined a group of student intellectuals who called themselves "The Apostles" and included Arthur Henry Hallam, who was Tennyson's closest friend. Hallam became engaged to Emily Tennyson, but at the age of twenty-two he died suddenly from illness. This trauma had a formative influence on Tennyson in such major works as *In Memoriam*, "The Passing of Arthur," "Ulysses," and "Tithonus." Although Tennyson's 1832 volume *Poems* met a mixed critical reception, he had success ten years later with his 1842 *Poems*. By 1850, Tennyson was named Poet Laureate and at the time of his death in 1892 was the most popular poet of the Victorian age.

Dylan Thomas (1914–1953)

Named after the medieval Welsh word for the "sea," Dylan Thomas was born in Swansea, Wales. At the age of twenty, he moved to London, where in 1934 he published his first book of poetry, *Eighteen Poems*. Two years later, Thomas published *Twenty-five Poems* and met Caitlin MacNamara, whom he married the following year. In 1938, the couple moved to Laugharne, Wales, and soon had a son, Llewelyn Edouard Thomas, born in 1939, the year Thomas also published *The Map of Love* and *The World I Breathe*. In 1940, Thomas published *Portrait of the Artist as a Young Dog* and began work for Strand Films, where he would stay on throughout World War II. Thomas would have two more children during the 1940s, Aeronwyn Bryn Thomas born in 1943, followed by Colm Garan Hart Thomas in 1949. During these years, Thomas published *Deaths and Entrances* (1946), *In Country Sleep* (1951), followed by his final book *Collected Poems, 1934–1952*. A charismatic public reader of his own verse, Thomas gave a series of popular reading tours in the United States. Chronic alcoholism took its toll on the poet's health, and during his fourth tour, accompanied by a physician, Thomas collapsed in his New York hotel room and died at St. Vincent's Hospital at the age of thirty-nine. *Under Milk Wood*, a play scripted for radio broadcast and Thomas's unfinished novel, *Adventures in the Skin Trade*, were published posthumously in 1954.

Phillis Wheatley (1753–1784)

A native of West Africa, Phillis Wheatley was kidnapped at the age of seven and sold to John Wheatley, a Boston tailor, in 1761. Although Phillis Wheatley did not attend school, she received her education from Mrs. John Wheatley. According to John Wheatley, Phillis learned to read English in only sixteen months. Just four years later in 1765, Phillis also had become a proficient writer, addressing a letter to the Reverend Mr. Occom. She also learned Latin and began publishing poetry with "On Messrs. Hussey and Coffin" in 1767. Three years later, her poem "On the Death of the Rev. Mr. George Whitefield, 1770" had a broad circulation in England and in such northern cities as Boston, Newport, and Philadelphia. While traveling to England as part of her treatment for severe asthma, Phillis Wheatley identified a publisher for her first book of verse, entitled *Poems on Various Subjects, Religious and Moral* (1773). To put to rest the suspicion that Wheatly was not the sole author of her book, her publishers included a statement verifying her as the author, witnessed by a group of distinguished New England civic leaders including the governor and lieutenant-governor of Massachusettes—Thomas Hutchinson and Andrew Oliver. Wheatley's poetry reflected the major strands of her New England education in terms of its focus on religious and classical themes. On returning to Boston in 1773, John Wheatley freed Phillis although she nevertheless continued to live with Wheatley as his caretaker. During the Revolutionary period, Phillis corresponded with George Washington and wrote a poem in his honor in 1776. Two years later, John Wheatley died, and Phillis, herself now free, married John Peters, who was also a freed former slave. Living in a squalid New England boarding house, the couple fell into poverty. In these adverse circumstances, Phillis gave birth to three children, all of whom died in childhood. In 1784, the year of her death at the age of thirty-one, Phillis Wheatley published a number of poems, including "To Mr. And Mrs.——, on the Death of Their Infant Son," under the name of Phillis Peters. Her poetry, however, survived her tragic end and, by the Abolitionist period of the 1830s, had achieved a recognized place in the canon of American literature.

Walt Whitman (1819–1892)

The second son in a family of nine children, Walt Whitman grew up on Long Island in a troubled household headed by the poet's alcoholic father. After failing as a carpenter and farmer, Walter Whitman Sr. moved his family to Brooklyn in 1823. After attending school in Brooklyn, Whitman worked at the age of eleven as a clerk before apprenticing as a printer at the *Patriot* and *Star* newspapers in Brooklyn. At the age of seventeen, Whitman began teaching in one-room schoolhouses on Long Island until 1841, when he turned to journalism and founded the weekly paper, *The Long Islander.* For the next seven years, he would work on a number of New York papers, including the *Aurora, Tatler,* the *Democrat,* and the *Brooklyn Daily Eagle.* In 1848, he traveled to New Orleans to become the editor of the *New Orleans Crescent.* Returning to Brooklyn that year, Whitman became the founding editor of the *Brooklyn Freeman.* By 1855, Whitman had composed and published the first edition of *Leaves of Grass,* sending a copy to Ralph Waldo Emerson, who responded with the famous reply, "I greet you at the beginning of a great career." During the American Civil War, Whitman traveled to Washington, D.C., to care for his wounded brother. Whitman's role as caregiver to the wounded and dying in the area hospitals became the basis for his "Drum Taps" section of *Leaves of Grass.* During the next eleven years, Whitman lived in Washington. For part of that time, Whitman worked as a Department of Interior clerk until he was fired by Secretary James Harlan, who was offended by the explicit sexuality of *Leaves of Grass.* At the age of forty-four in 1873, Whitman suffered a stroke from which he never fully recovered. Nevertheless, he continued to add poems to *Leaves of Grass* over the course of eight editions. In 1884, the poet bought a small house in Camden, New Jersey, and four years later another major stroke left him immobilized. By 1891, his health was failing completely, but he managed to finish *Good-Bye, My Fancy* (1891) and revise the so-called death-bed edition of *Leaves of Grass* before he died in 1892.

William Carlos Williams (1883–1963)

Born and raised in Rutherford, New Jersey, William Carlos Williams was the son of William George Williams, a New York businessman, and Raquel Hélène Hoheb, who was a native of Puerto Rico. From 1897 through 1899, Williams studied in Europe and began writing verse while attending the Horace Mann High School in New York City. Williams studied medicine and received his M.D. from the University of Pennsylvania. While there he met the painter Charles Demuth and the modernist poets Hilda Doolittle and Ezra Pound. After studying pediatrics in Leipzig, Germany, Williams returned to Rutherford in 1910 where he set up his private practice, married Flossie Herman two years later, and over time became the head pediatrician of Paterson General Hospital. At the same time, Williams also had a parallel career as poet, publishing his first volume *Poems* in 1909, followed by *The Tempers* in 1913, which he published in London largely through the efforts of Ezra Pound. Influenced by the artistic tendencies that he saw in the 1913 Armory show in New York, Williams was an active member of the New York avant-garde, publishing in such little magazines as *Others*. Williams's third volume of verse, *Al Que Quiere!* (1917), reflected his Spanish American inheritance from his mother's family. Throughout his career, Williams composed a poetry in search of an original American idiom. Influenced by the tight verbal economy of the Imagist movement, Williams's new poetic style examined the subtle life of things rooted in native place. Williams demonstrated his famous dictum "no ideas but in things" in such volumes as *Kora in Hell: Improvisations* (1920) and in his 1923 volume *Spring and All*. In addition to these significant books of poems, Williams also wrote the important essay collection *In the American Grain* (1925). Moreover, in 1926 Williams won the Dial Award for his short story "Paterson." During the Depression era, Williams would publish several short stories in such little magazines as *New Masses, Anvil, Little Review*, and other journals. These works were then collected in his 1938 book of short stories, *Life Along the Passaic*. Throughout the thirties, Williams continued to write verse, publishing in 1934 his *Complete Poems, 1921–1931* followed by *Adam & Eve & the City* in 1936, and *The Complete Collected Poems* two years later. During World War II, Williams published his collection *The Wedge* in 1944 but turned his efforts as poet to the composition of his long poem *Paterson*, whose first section *Paterson I* he published in 1946, followed by *Paterson, A Dream of Love* two years later, and *Selected Poems and Paterson III* in 1949, which won the National Book Award the next year. In 1951, Williams's career as a writer culminated in the publication of *Paterson IV*, the *Autobiography of William Carlos Williams*, and *The Collected Earlier Poems*. Despite suffering strokes in 1951 and 1952, Williams was named consultant in poetry to the Library of Congress and won the Bollingen Prize the following year. In *Desert Music* (1954), he adopted a new poetic style of composition based in what he called the "triadic line," followed the next year by his poignant love poem "Asphodel, That Greeny Flower" written for his wife Flossie. In October 1955 Williams suffered another, devastating stroke that left him partially paralyzed. Nevertheless, he published his *Selected Letters* in 1957 and *Paterson V* in 1958. A series of strokes followed during the composition of *Pictures from Brueghel and Other Poems* (1962), which was awarded a posthumous Pulitzer Prize in 1963, the year of the poet's death.

William Wordsworth (1770–1850)

The second of five children born to John and Anne Wordsworth, William Wordsworth was sent to the reputable Hawkshead Grammar School after the death of his mother in 1778. While at Hawkshead, Wordsworth became an orphan with the death of his father. After Hawkshead, Wordsworth entered St. John's College, Cambridge in 1787, the next summer he became a prodigious walker in the English countryside, and two years later he went on his famous walking tour of France, Switzerland, and Germany. After graduating from Cambridge, Wordsworth returned to France in 1791. At this time, Wordsworth entered into a relationship with Annette Vallon, with whom he fathered a daughter, Caroline, in 1792. Returning to England at the time of France's Reign of Terror, Wordsworth would not return to France for another nine years. Meanwhile, Wordsworth kept company with his sister Dorothy and met Samuel Taylor Coleridge in 1795, with whom he would collaborate on the 1798 volume *Lyrical Ballads*, whose famous "Preface" advocated a Romantic poetics based on the "common speech" of vernacular English. With the Peace of Amiens in 1802, Wordsworth returned briefly to France before marrying Mary Hutchinson. *Poems in Two Volumes* (1807) increased Wordsworth's reputation as poet, and in 1813 Wordsworth was appointed Distributor of Stamps for Westmorland, which gave him a modicum of financial security while he lived in the Lake District's Rydal Mount. With the death of Robert Southey in 1843, Wordsworth became Poet Laureate. Although completed in earlier drafts as early as 1805, Wordsworth's greatest work *The Prelude* was published posthumously the year of his death in 1850.

W. B. Yeats (1865–1939)

The son of the famous Irish painter John Butler Yeats, William Butler Yeats was born in Dublin and raised in Western Ireland. At the age of fifteen, W. B. Yeats studied in Dublin and, after following his father's painterly art, pursued the vocation of poet and man of letters. Yeats began his career as a supporter of the celtic revival that promulgated Irish art, literature, and drama against the cultural influences of England. Yeats published his first volume of verse in 1887, but he wrote drama rather than poetry in his early career. With Lady Gregory, Yeats founded the Irish Theatre in 1902 and two years later moved to the Abbey Theatre in Dublin. His early plays include *The Countess Cathleen* (1892), *The Land of Heart's Desire* (1894), *Cathleen ni Houlihan* (1902), *The King's Threshold* (1904), and *Deirdre* (1907). During these years, Yeats also met the Irish political revolutionary Maud Gonne in 1889 and was involved in a relationship with her until her marriage to another in 1903. Having met and collaborated with Ezra Pound in London, Yeats's poetry began to take on a decidedly modern style after 1910, although he still composed his verse in traditional fixed forms involving rhyme and rhythm. At the height of his powers as poet, Yeats also played a role in Irish nationalist politics through his election to the Irish Senate in 1922. Two years later, he received the Nobel Prize. In addition to Yeats's participation in the Irish literary revival, he also was a student of spiritualism and occult traditions as a member of the Theosophical Society of London and the Hermetic Order of the Golden Dawn. Reflecting these esoteric pursuits, Yeats's evolving philosophical themes and major symbols found powerful poetic expression in such volumes of verse as *The Wilde Swans at Coole* (1919), *Michael Robartes and the Dancer* (1921), *The Tower* (1928), and *The Winding Stair and Other Poems* (1933). His final volume, *Last Poems and Plays* (1940), was published posthumously a year following his death in 1939.

Ray A. Young Bear (b. 1950)

Born in Marshalltown, Iowa, Ray A. Young Bear is a member of the Mesquakie Tribal community; Mesquakie translated means "People of the Red Earth." Young Bear is the great-great-grandson of the Mesquakie Okima (or tribal chief) Maminwanike. After the tribe had been removed to Kansas, the elder Young Bear negotiated the purchase of the tribe's sacred lands, returning in 1856 to Tama, Iowa, on the Iowa River. From early on, Ray Young Bear had a close relationship to Native American culture, and he received inspiration in storytelling from his maternal grandmother Ada Kapayou Old Bear. "I'm grateful for my grandmother," he has said. "She is all of everything to me." In addition, he received an introduction to contemporary poetry writing through participating in an Upward Bound program at Luther College in Decorah in 1968. Between 1969 and 1971, Young Bear attended Pomona College and went on to study creative writing at the University of Iowa (1971), Grinnell College (1973), Northern Iowa University (1975–1976), and at Iowa State University (1980). Since completing his education, Young Bear has taught creative writing at The Institute of American Indian Art (1984), Eastern Washington University (1987), Mesquakie Indian Elementary School (1988–1989), the University of Iowa (1989), and Iowa State University (1993 and 1998). Since 1975, the year he published his first volme *Waiting to Be Fed*, Young Bear has also published *Winter of the Salamander: The Keeper of Importance* (1980), *The Invisible Musician* (1990), *Black Eagle Child* (1992), and *Remnants of the First Earth* (1996). Young Bear views his poetry as an art of connection among the various dimensions of how the Native American heritage is lived in the present. "The most interesting facet in all of this," he says, "has been the artistic interlacing of ethereality, past and present. As such there are considerations of visions, traditional healing, supernaturalism, and hallucinogen-based sacraments interposed with centuries-old philosophies and customs." In addition to his books of poetry, Young Bear is also the cofounder with his wife of the Woodland Song and Dance Troupe.

Part IV
Writing about Literature

25 Writing about Literature

A well-known writer was once asked his opinion about a topic. He responded by saying that he could not possibly answer the question until he saw what he had written about it. The point is a particularly cogent one and very relevant to the composition of papers on literary topics: Essay-writing affords a reader the opportunity to organize ideas or responses, and to meditate deeply on the text or texts under consideration. Writing clarifies not only what is important about a text, illuminating what really matters to its construction, language, or meaning, but also what is important to the reader herself.

An essay, true to its origin in the French verb *essayer*, meaning "to try or attempt," communicates its author's efforts to convey his or her reflections about a text or group of texts. At the same time, these reflections constitute an attempt to persuade an audience of their interpretive validity and explanatory power. Writing about literature, therefore, is also writing about reading. But how to begin? What plan of attack will be most effective in conveying your ideas?

Getting Ready, Making Decisions

As your instructor will explain a writer needs to consider a number of questions before typing the first word: What audience am I addressing? What do they know about the text I want to discuss? What language will be most effective or appropriate in communicating to this audience? In other words, what assumptions should I make about the *rhetorical situation?* A writer always weighs these and other questions carefully before beginning, considering each point of the triangle below.

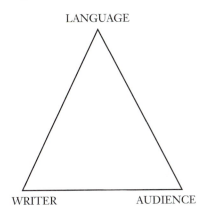

LANGUAGE

WRITER   AUDIENCE

719

In preparing to write essays on literary topics, you should consider, among other things, who will read the paper and why. Assume that your audience is already familiar with the work you intend to discuss; thus, there is little reason to summarize the plot. What kind of language and evidence will be most effective in addressing this audience? What role do you as writer play? Generally, the answer is none at all. You are not a professor or academician, nor are you talking to a personal friend. You aren't in a locker room either, so select terms appropriate both to the occasion of the composition and the audience. This is especially true when crafting your thesis, the most significant aspect of your essay that your audience does *not* know.

The thesis embodies your purpose in writing the paper in the first place. Unlike, say, the occupation of a drama or film reviewer in a newspaper, your job in writing about literature is to persuade your audience of the significance of your topic to an understanding of the text you are discussing. The single statement most crucial to this enterprise is your *thesis statement*.

Thesis Statements

The thesis statement provides focus and purpose for the entire essay. Because it represents the most direct expression of your "big idea" about the literature you have read, the thesis statement may take longer to formulate than any other sentence you prepare. And it may take some time, some experimentation, and some trial-and-error before you arrive at the precise point you want to make. As we discuss in detail in Chapter 26, "Writing about Poetry," you may want to try such techniques as *freewriting* or *brainstorming*, where you put down on paper as quickly as you can whatever thoughts enter your mind about a topic. Don't stop to worry about punctuation or spelling—these can be corrected later. In a freewriting exercise, sometimes called "automatic writing," simply transcribe your thoughts into words on a page or screen, revising them later into more precise and compelling statements. The purpose of this exercise is invention: You are trying to purge your mind of thoughts on a topic, one of which may be refined later into a thesis statement.

You might also consider the thesis statement as the culmination of a process that narrows the topic: from a text to discuss, to a topic in or about the text, to a specific issue or reading. So, for example, if the text is William Blake's poem "London," the subject or topic might be the poem's imagery and image patterns; the thesis might argue for the importance of images of confinement, regulation, or imprisonment. Same poem, different subject and thesis, and the same process of narrowing the scope of what will become your *argument*.

Argument in this context *is* the correct term. You should select a topic that you can develop into a persuasive argument, which begins with articulating a coherent, concise, and arguable thesis statement. Thesis statements have several distinctive features or criteria, as the following six points summarize. Test the thesis statement for your paper against these characteristics: Does your thesis meet all of the following? If not, what adjustments will make the statement more specific, more forceful, or more significant?

1. Thesis statements are statements of opinion, not statements of fact or intention.

Statement of Fact

> In William Shakespeare's tragedy *Othello*, Iago does a number of evil, reprehensible things.

As any reader of *Othello* will readily concede, Iago *does* act maliciously and destructively. Consequently, a research paper cannot be organized around a statement of this fact. Iago is an evil man, Boston is located in Massachusetts, the Beatles are still popular—these facts do not require discussion or the presentation of evidence. They are self-evident.

Statement of Intention

> In my essay, I want to show you that Iago commits evil deeds.

This sentence is no better than the first one. It not only fails to advance an opinion, but also is wordier than the statement of fact: "In my essay, I want to show you that" is particularly ineffective and verbose.

Statement of Opinion

> Since the plot of *Othello* is Iago's plot, improvisation by Iago constitutes the tragedy's heart and center.

This sentence, taken from Harold Bloom's popular and controversial book *Shakespeare: The Invention of the Human* (1998), actually contains two opinions: that Iago drives the plot of *Othello* and that the play's structure results largely from his improvised manipulations. The latter assertion in particular is one with which a number of readers of the play might disagree, locating the "heart" of the tragedy in jealousy, racism, cultural sexism, and so on. Often, abstract terms like *heart* and *center* in thesis statements spark disagreement or simple confusion, so be careful when inserting abstractions into theses. Nonetheless, Bloom's assertion fits the first criterion of an effective thesis statement by stating an opinion, not a fact or intention.

2. A thesis statement advances an opinion about which informed and reasonable people might disagree.

As is the case with Bloom's reading of Iago as a figure of universal evil, a thesis furthers an understanding about which informed readers might disagree. What would be the point of researching a topic about which everyone already possesses the same opinion? What would a reader of the paper learn that he or she does not know already? Thus, one way of testing a thesis is to present it to your classmates and determine if they all share your view. If they do, you need to keep working.

3. A thesis statement often contains an underlying rhetorical premise.

By *rhetorical premise* we mean a concept or mode of understanding that implicitly structures or organizes the rest of the paper. In the 1960s, the rhetorician

Randall Decker published a widely used textbook called *Patterns of Exposition*, which included chapters on comparison, process analysis, causality, definition, classification, and other rhetorical modes or premises. Such premises are frequently imbedded in the articulation of theses: "Willy Loman's collapse in Arthur Miller's *Death of a Salesman* progresses through three distinct stages" (this essay will follow the organizational strategy of process analysis); "The young boy's sudden insight at the end of James Joyce's 'Araby' is caused by the deflation of his fantasy" (this essay uses the organizational strategy of causality), and so on.

4. A thesis statement predicts, obligates, and controls what follows it. Rhetorician William Irmscher once made this point in a composition textbook, and its implications are still relevant today. Much like the title, a thesis suggests to a reader what course a research paper—or any essay, for that matter—will take. It *predicts*. It also *obligates* the writer to present evidence and discussion of the evidence consistent with the assertion; a writer cannot begin by claiming that Willy Loman experiences three distinct stages of psychological collapse and then later argue that there are, in fact, five stages to his downfall. Finally, a thesis *controls* the kinds of evidence relevant to the essay's purpose. If the thesis addresses Willy's troubled psychology, then long diagnoses of his wife's or sons' emotional problems would seem digressive unless they can be shown to affect his emotional state and decline.

5. A thesis statement takes on a topic of significance, often the answer to an implicit question. Many graduate students we know, parodying a well-known Victorian writer's phrases the "Everlasting Yea" and the "Everlasting Nay," talk about the "The Everlasting So What?" This means, simply, that a thesis should argue a point of importance. "Willy's decline progresses through three distinct stages"—so what? Why is this important? Notice, too, that all the examples we have used answer an unasked or implicit question, a "how" or "why" question: Why is the young boy in "Araby" so self-critical at the story's conclusion?

6. A thesis statement reflects theoretical or other assumptions that underlie your reading and, finally, the argument of the essay. All of the sample theses so far are based more or less on *formalist* premises: How is the plot constructed? How might a character's actions be explained? Why or how is an image, scene, or even a single word important to our understanding? Such questions quite properly involve close reading of the literary text, as they address one or more aspects of literary form. But, of course, as many of the chapters of *Understanding Poetry* outline, other kinds of readings—and other premises for thesis statements—exist. They arise, in part, by asking different questions of the text: How is race or sexuality represented? How is social class or capitalism depicted? How does psychoanalytic theory, Marx's social theory, or feminist thought help explain a character's action or predicament? In other words, literature is more than a self-contained aesthetic object—or, to borrow a metaphor—it is more than an exceptionally "well-wrought urn." A literary text is also a social text, a historical artifact, a product made in a specific place, time, and culture. It can tell us much about these cultures and times as well.

These are, admittedly, difficult concepts that often lead to difficult questions and challenging thesis statements. But they must be asked and answered, because no writer—or reader—wants to waste his or her time on a topic of little consequence. If your paper addresses the actions of an important character, the implications of a major event or a significant *motif* (repetition in a poem, play, or story), then this close reading is likely to be important enough to make. If your essay concerns a matter of representation—how Africans are portrayed in Joseph Conrad's *Heart of Darkness*, how the city is represented in modernist fiction, how women are portrayed in Shakespeare's plays—the chances are you can focus this interest into a significant thesis statement and thus respond effectively to the "Everlasting So What?"

And there's one other bit of good news, too—you're probably ready to write.

Writing

But how do you begin? If you're at all like the authors of this textbook, then you've probably asked yourself this very question scores of times. A thesis statement might be introduced in any number of ways, but it is actually easier to identify ways *not* to begin. The advice of rhetorician William Irmscher is again helpful in explaining three opening strategies to avoid at all costs.

1. The "Panoramic" Historical Gesture. We've all read sentences like this one and tried to suppress our groans: "Since the dawn of time, man has pondered the nature of _____." This sentence is so trite and predictable that you can fill in the blank with any number of terms: *love, men, women, life,* and so on. But if it really is true that humans have puzzled over such weighty and complex matters for millennia, what chance do you have of resolving the matter in three to five pages? Obviously, this opening strategy—and that's what we are discussing, a strategy or tactic to present the thesis—has now lapsed into a parody of a profound utterance more likely to elicit laughter than respect.

The problem is, when you've stared into a blank computer screen for an hour, a sentence like this one starts to sound better and better—better than nothing. It isn't.

2. The Appeal to Mr. Webster. Whenever a writer is really strapped for an opening gambit, this sentence starts to sound better as well: "According to *Webster's Dictionary*, tragedy is defined as . . . " Like the "panoramic" opener—and the "fact" that grandparents tend to die on the very day papers are due in a class like this one—this strategy has been overused. More important, the dictionary provides only a basic understanding of a term, its common meanings or denotations. Literary perceptions of a term like *tragedy* are far more complex and historically contingent than the definitions in most dictionaries.

3. Irrelevant Biographical Detail.   Young writers sometimes feel that literary understanding always begins with the biography of the author; consequently, they begin essays with hackneyed sentences: "Langston Hughes was born in Joplin, Missouri, in 1902." Fine. But save in the specific instance in which biography impinges directly upon reading, such a fact is not only superfluous, but irrelevant.

This was not always the case, which perhaps explains why the appeal to biography remains an attractive option for some students. In early twentieth-century British and American literary criticism, for example, biography often comprised the center around which interpretation revolved. In *The Human Approach to Literature* (1933), for example, William Freeman began a discussion of Chaucer's *Canterbury Tales* this way: "Geoffrey Chaucer, the sturdily-built man with the friendly brown eyes, was not merely a widely traveled Englishman who had passionately preserved his nationality, but a Londoner by birth and breeding."

Today, such opening strategies fail to introduce the real purpose of the essay and seem, well, almost silly. Chaucer's buff physique might be interesting, but surely it is not pertinent to a reading of his work. So why go there?

Fortunately, some devices *are* effective in introducing a thesis. You might begin with an epigraph, a brief quotation that encapsulates issues you feel are important to the text, and return to it in your opening paragraph (and later). You might start with a sensational detail, an anecdote, or a brief exchange of dialogue when discussing a play. Or, you might follow the instructions of countless composition texts by replicating the narrowing process discussed earlier, moving from a general subject, to a topic, to a specific statement.

The point is this: Thesis statements require introductions. The background of your "big idea" needs to be elaborated early in the essay and then, after your thesis is stated, you are ready to build a support structure for it. This is the body or argument of the essay.

Arguments and Admissible Evidence: Paraphrase and Quotation

Much like a lawyer in a criminal case who introduces materials into evidence and then "reads" the evidence in an attempt to persuade a judge or jury, writers of literary criticism marshal evidence carefully and discuss its implications. Persuasive arguments rely on well-chosen pieces of evidence and incisive analysis. The best kind of evidence is located in the literary text itself, parts of which will need to be summarized and paraphrased in the argument.

But perhaps the most difficult task facing writers of all ages and experience is quoting from the text; that is, there will be occasions when a paraphrase or summary will not serve your needs. You will need to quote the original. But when? How much should you quote? What are the most graceful methods of integrating quoted excerpts into your own prose?

Let's take up this last question. In general, the same formula that makes for a good legal argument—evidence + analysis = guilt or innocence—applies in writing essays about literature. A prosecutor, for example, doesn't throw a weapon on a table and claim, "You see—that proves the defendant is guilty." Rather, a prosecutor examines the evidence, then builds an argument about it: Forensic analysis proves this is the murder weapon; the gun is registered to the defendant, who had a motive to kill the victim; the defendant was witnessed at the scene of the murder minutes before, and so on. If the lawyer is lucky, she might have eyewitnesses to depose, hair fibers or DNA evidence to present and discuss, and more: evidence + analysis = case. The same is true of building literary arguments: textual evidence (quotations or paraphrases) + your analysis = an argument.

To bring this to an even smaller, more precise case, consider the following:

> your writing + quoted excerpts = complete sentence.

In other words, when quoting from a literary text don't simply drop a quotation between sentences; work to incorporate it into your sentence just as you attempt to integrate the piece of evidence into a larger argument. A citation should appear at the end of a quoted passage of any length (over a phrase or two), and usually this means that the citation appears at the end of a sentence. That is, try not to interrupt the sense of the sentence by placing page citations in the middle of clauses.

There are at least three proven ways of quoting effectively from a literary text.

1. Identification of the speaker + quotation.   This method is employed in both popular and academic writing, usually for passages of four lines or less. Example: In Margaret Edson's *Wit*, Vivian Bearing explains, "I have cancer, insidious cancer, with pernicious side effects—no the *treatment* has pernicious side effects" (12). The positioning of the identification may be manipulated in any way that reads smoothly, for example: "I have cancer," Vivian Bearing explains in *Wit*, "insidious cancer, with pernicious side effects—no the *treatment* has pernicious side effects" (12). Again, variety of structure will enhance the readability of your essay. Don't begin every quotation with "Vivian says" or "Iago says."

Because the introduction of the quotation specifies the origin of the passage, there is no need to identify it a second time by citing the author's name or the work's title in parenthesis. If, however, the identification fails to make this clear, then the author's name should appear in the citation. A full bibliographic entry should appear at the end of your paper in a section entitled "Works Cited."

2. The "block quotation" for longer excerpts.   Any passage greater than four lines should be set off from the paragraph by indenting on the left side, a method that renders quotation marks themselves superfluous. Lines taken from poems should be quoted exactly as they appear in the original—line by line—as should dialogue in blank verse from plays like Shakespeare's. Line numbers, not page numbers, should be cited for poems; and it is conventional to cite act, scene, and line numbers from plays edited with line numbers. For example:

> Toward the end of *The Tempest*, Prospero reveals to his visitors both the magical qualities of his island and his penchant for philosophy:
>
> Our revels now are ended. These our actors
> (As I foretold you) were all spirits, and
> Are melted into air, into thin air,
> And like the baseless fabric of this vision,
> The cloud-capp'd towers, the gorgeous palaces,
> The solemn temples, the great globe itself,
> Yea, all which it inherit, shall dissolve,
> And like this insubstantial pageant faded
> Leave not a rack behind. (4.1.148–56)

Or, to take another example, here is a passage from John Milton's elegy "Lycidas," written in memory of a friend who had drowned. Note that, as in the above cases, you must introduce the quotation, not simply "drop" it in the sentence.

> In "Lycidas," Milton's speaker searches for consolation in the sudden death of his friend and finds it, in part, in his faith:
>
> So Lycidas sunk low, but mounted high,
> Through the dear might of Him that walked the waves;
> Where other groves, and other streams along,
> With nectar pure his oozy locks he laves,
> And hears the unexpressive nuptial song,
> In the blest kingdoms meek of joy and love. (172–77)

In all of these examples, longer quotations are introduced by a complete sentence. But your responsibilities do not end here, because the quotation needs to be considered or "unpacked" thoroughly. After all, if the passage did not contain specific language that supports your argument, you would not have introduced it into evidence in the first place. Here, again, a balance between admissible evidence and your analysis is important. Remember: Quoting at length generally means discussing at length. This is entirely consistent with the logic that should inform your selection of the passage to quote: The very issues that led you to select the passage need to be conveyed to your reader.

3. Quoted phrases or "sound bites."   Often you may want to quote only a word or phrase from the original. No problem. In these instances, take bits or "bites" of texts and work them smoothly into the syntax of your sentence. One suggestion might help: After quoting the bites, pretend that the quotation marks aren't there—that the bits are merely words in your sentence. Does it read smoothly and clearly as a sentence? If so, you have probably integrated the quoted excerpts well into your prose.

Examples

> Since the late 1950s, Bruce Conner has been an "important but shadowy" figure in the world of American art and film, a kind of "home-grown" artist with strong connections to California (Boswell 26).

> Recalling the orthodox mores that Beat culture attempted to overthrow, Joyce Johnson describes sex in the 1950s as a "serious and anxious act" (89).

> In *M. Butterfly*, Gallimard describes Butterfly in Puccini's opera as a "feminine ideal," and later he expresses his dismay that such an ideal could be debased by a "womanizing cad" (7, 9).

Note here that all three examples, in addition to crafting sentences that accommodate the quotations, employ different strategies of citation. The first example includes both a name and page number because the context does not identify the author of the quotation. The second example includes only a page number because the author's name—Joyce Johnson—is specified. The citation for the third example explains that the two phrases appear on different pages in the original.

In conclusion, select evidence carefully and present it in a meaningful pattern or logical order: Have you arranged it chronologically, in the order events occur in the literature you are discussing? Or have you elected to present the evidence in another way: from the least compelling example to the most compelling? From the easiest point to prove to the most difficult? In some other way? Paraphrase or summarize events as part of your argument—relevant events that provide a background or context for the specific argument you hope to build. When the language of the original is striking or so perfectly stated for your argument that you want to introduce it into evidence, follow the instructions we have just outlined. Last but not least, make certain that you have quoted *accurately*: word for word, punctuation mark for punctuation mark. Also, use the quotation fairly; in other words, make sure that it represents what you take to be the intent of the original.

If you do all of these things, there is an excellent chance the argument of your essay—your attempt at persuading your reader of the validity and importance of your thesis—will be successful.

Concluding

Like the creation of an effective introduction, the drafting of effective conclusions often poses a challenge. And, like trite introductions, ineffective conclusions are fairly easy to describe. Here's the worst:

> And, in conclusion, I have just shown you that John Milton's speaker in "Lycidas" derives consolation from his religious beliefs.

Why is this such a weak statement? For several reasons. First, in a brief paper of three to five pages, it's fairly easy to determine that you are heading for a conclusion; you don't need to announce this. Second, the reader will decide whether you've made the case or not; the statement "I have just shown you" may in fact be inaccurate, because you might *not* have succeeded in making the case persuasively. Last, other than bringing the argument to a close, what is gained by this kind of sentence?

Fortunately, better concluding strategies exist. You might restate the thesis and offer a brief suggestion of its implications—or of matters related to the thesis that could not be admitted into your argument. Why is the thesis significant? What intellectual purchase or insight does it allow your reader? Such a tactic should not lead to a lengthy digression; rather, a strong thesis possesses a quality of interpretive richness that often exceeds the limits of the essay. Thus, in your conclusion you might outline briefly what other kinds of issues will be better understood because of your thesis statement. You might return to the epigraph or startling fact with which your essay began (assuming you employed one of these strategies). Or you might speculate briefly on how the field of evidence might have been expanded had you been afforded the opportunity of doing so.

Whatever strategy you use, remember that, like introductions, your conclusion for a short essay need not be overly elaborate. But you *do* need to bring the argument to closure.

Revision and Final Thoughts

Be sure to leave ample time to proofread your essay, which—we know—is advice easier to give than follow. Procrastination is the great enemy of revision. If you wait to begin your paper the night before it is due, the revision process will inevitably be compromised—or just totally nuked! So, get started early.

Then, after you have produced a rough draft, begin your revision process strategically. Does your essay satisfy the requirement of the assignment your instructor gave you? Is the title effective? Next, proceed to the largest elements of composition: arguments and paragraphs. Is the argument delineated in a logical and persuasive order? Are the paragraphs coherent, with immediately relevant topic sentences, evidence, and analysis? Is there an effective balance between evidence and discussion? Have you varied the lengths of quotations and your methods of introducing them? Have you created effective transitions between paragraphs and points of the argument?

Then, move to smaller matters, beginning with the problems your instructor has identified in previous essays. These differ from one writer to the next. Some have difficulty with sentence construction, others with phrasing and word choice, still others with spelling and punctuation. Recognize those areas of composition that have caused you difficulty in the past and revise them carefully. When writing on literary topics, again, accuracy is a crucial matter: Check every quotation against the original and make certain the citations are accurate. Also, be sure that you have followed your instructor's requirements in terms of pagination, presentation, and so on.

With any luck, this essay will prove a learning experience for you. How will you know what you think until you've seen what you have written?

26   Writing about Poetry

Thomas Edison—the modern inventor of the wireless telegraph, phonograph, and the light bulb (with Joseph Swan)—once remarked that "thinking is hard work." "Genius," he famously quipped, "is one percent inspiration and ninety-nine percent perspiration." We might want to modify this truism for the composition process to say that good writing is 40 percent invention and 60 percent presentation—give or take a few percentage points.

From the very beginning of your writing process, invention is your first step toward finished modes of rhetorical presentation. There is no presentation without invention because the stuff of writing—language—is not just a static vehicle or tool for thought. Instead, the very act of working with language, as a discursive practice, is a way of thinking. The British empiricist philosopher John Locke asserted as much in his *Essay Concerning Human Understanding* (1690) when he said, "there is so close a connection between ideas and WORDS . . . that it is impossible to speak clearly and distinctly of our knowledge, which all consists of propositions, without considering, first, the nature, use, and signification of Language."

If thinking always already takes place in language, then you can use that linguistic process to help you arrive at your "idea" or thesis and its proper presentational format for the essay assignment. Your completed essay might purposefully present a comparison/contrast pattern of development; it might define and classify a poem's key tropes and how they function together. You might even explain how particular combinations of alliteration and assonance cause certain sound effects based on, say, **onomatopoeia.** But in each case—whether you use the rhetorical modes of comparison/contrast, or classification, or cause/effect—your essay's presentation, ideally, will emerge from your engagement with the poem at hand in a prior process of invention.

Invention is, arguably, even more crucial to writing successfully about poetry than other literary genres. For one thing, there is less information on the page when we are reading a poem than, say, a Charles Dickens novel or Shakespearean romance. Moreover, what information is there often denies its status as information. "A poem," as Archibald MacLeish has it, "should not mean / But be." A poem's mode of being is defined, in part, not through its communication of meaning but, rather, through its artful resistance to paraphrased meaning.

The poet will almost never lay out a poem's message in the straightforward mode of the journalist's questions: who? what? when? where? how? and why? The poet's job, in fact, contradicts that of the newspaper reporter. "Do not forget," the philosopher Ludwig Wittgenstein once said, "that a poem, even though it is composed in the language of information, is not used in the language-game of giving information." Poetry, W. H. Auden wrote in his famous elegy "In Memory Of W. B. Yeats," "survives / In the valley of its making where executives / Would never want to tamper." So, if we are to analyze a poem—to tamper with its form, meaning, techniques, mode of address, and so on—we must first arrive "in the valley of its making": We must make an imaginative effort to understand the poem in its unique mode of utterance.

Two things that distinguish writing about poetry from writing about short stories or plays are length and arrangement. Take, for example, a fourteen-line sonnet like, say, Shakespeare's Sonnet 73: "That time of year thou mayst in me behold." It comprises 121 words. By contrast, Nathaniel Hawthorne's "Young Goodman Brown," a relatively brief short story, has over 5,000 words. Nevertheless, your instructor may ask you to write the same amount of material— say, anywhere from 750 to 1000 words of your own—regardless of whether it's on a 100-word poem or a 100,000-word novel. The artful presentation of language is important in both of these genres. Obviously, however, the individual words and their particular arrangement will matter in your analysis of the sonnet in ways that are far more crucial than in your reading of the novel. Poetry entails an incredibly compressed use of language when compared to a story, play, or novel. In poetry, then, less is more.

Second, whether composed in a fixed form like a sonnet, villanelle, sestina, ballad stanza, or even in free verse, a poem involves a highly stylized arrangement of language on the page. William Carlos Williams defined a poem as a "machine made out of words." The mechanics of a poem's visual presentation—its spacings, its line lengths, its pattern of enjambment, its typography, and so on—all go into the makeup of the kind of verbal mechanisms that Williams had in mind. Moreover, the ways in which the grammatical syntax and punctuation play against and across the line length in patterns of end-stopped utterances or in the artful use of enjambment further complicate a poem's presentation. Add to this the sonic dimension of poetry's rhyme scheme, alliteration, assonance, and onomatopoeia—not to mention the musical qualities of its meter and rhythm—and you confront a very different reading experience and interpretive situation when approaching a poem rather than, say, a newspaper article.

One way of understanding a poem—of entering into "the valley of its making"—is to read it aloud. Some practicing poets will tell you that they often compose poems out loud first by intoning certain unconscious rhythms and sounds orally even before the conscious sense of a particular line or composed stanza takes shape later on the page. Moreover, most poets will test their poems "on the air" by performing them at poetry readings before they are actually published in a magazine, anthology, or book. Reading the poem out loud several times will help you appreciate the cadences, sounds, and music of the work. Memorizing a short lyric will also give you a special sense of ownership of a poem that may help you later in interpreting it with confidence and care.

An analogous technique to reading verse aloud is to copy your poem out on the page or computer screen. In closely comparing your copy to the original, you may find discrepancies where you "got it wrong" or assumed a particular phrasing that wasn't exactly how the poet had it. This process, again, will attune you to a poem's particular verbal character and its formal arrangement as such. Copying the poem out may help you assume a greater sense of mastery over the material. That is, such close attention to the poem's crafted details may help you in the writing situation of dealing with the poem's language, imagery, form, and themes in the more advanced stages of your composing process later on.

If you are a writer who can effortlessly compose complete and polished sentences, consider yourself very unique. Most of us aren't this lucky; we typically don't write this way or at least for very long. Composition theorists agree that for the vast majority of authors, writing is a repetitive and recursive process full of fits and starts, blockages and flows, blindnesses and insights. Trying to "get it right" in composing phrases, sentences, paragraphs, or entire essay formats is seldom easy. Moreover, there is no final arbiter of successful writing. W. S. Merwin, in a poem about his former mentor John Berryman, recalls asking him how you could tell if a poem you wrote was actually "any good at all":

> . . . and he said you can't
> you can't you can never be sure
> you die without knowing
> whether anything you wrote was any good
> if you have to be sure don't write

The point here is not to agonize over the quality of your prose up front but to prime the compositional process by simply beginning to write, even if it's not your best writing. As it happens, there are several generative methods that can help you get material out on the page for later revision, arrangement, and polishing.

To begin with, you might photocopy the poem and annotate it. That is, circle key words and jot down in the margins any thoughts you have on their significance or on their relationships to other significant details and phrasings. In poetry especially, the compression and brevity of the poem's utterance, its gaps, line lengths, and sound patterning together suggest rather than insist on particular meanings. The reader has a greater collaborative role to play in the act of interpreting a poem. This is not to say that "anything goes" in responding to a poem. To be plausible, our interpretations must be rhetorically coherent, well argued, and pragmatically convincing for other readers. But before your reading of a poem arrives at that level of interpretive competence, you should give yourself time to experience the poem psychically. In this regard, you may want to take into account any of the following in generating your theme and organizational plan.

- Pay attention, perhaps in a journal, to your personal encounter with the particulars of the poem and to how your interpretative reading changes over time.
- Explore the differences between your historical moment and that of the poem. Are you coming from a very different historical moment than the time period in which the poem is written? Would it be helpful for your understanding to research that period difference?

- Does the poem address a particular gender or a particular race or class position and, if so, to what extent can you relate or empathize with the poem's take on these markers of identity? To what extent are you alienated by the work's assumption about audience?
- Are there significant language barriers—say, Old English, Middle English, or Shakespearean dialogue, modern experimental uses of syntax, or contemporary performative slang terms—that get in the way of your reading experience? Allow yourself extra time to look up difficult terms in a reference resource such as the *Oxford English Dictionary*. What role does etymology play in enriching your reading experience of a poem's particular diction choices and its unique idiom?
- How might you rewrite the poem and to what effect?
- What questions would you put to the poem?

Once you have generated your freewriting and brainstormed the relations that you see among key phrasings, you are ready to begin shaping your essay's thematic focus.

One way to start is to take some of the questions that you generated about the work and begin to answer them in sentence units. Here you can also build into your sentences some of the phrasings that you generated from your freewriting. Using these sentence openers, expand them into larger units, gradually assuming paragraph length based perhaps on the major ideas that you generated through your cluster map. Go on to develop your paragraph units with supporting illustration and evidence drawn from the text of the poem. In addition, you may find that quoted material from the author, historical and/or biographical contexts, secondary criticism, and so on may also lend themselves to the developing plan of your essay. Consult with your instructor on how much material beyond the text of the poem would be appropriate for your topic. Remember to document any primary or secondary summaries, paraphrases, or direct quotes that helped you develop your essay (see documentation under "Writing a Research Paper").

Handling Quotations

Handling quotes in writing about poetry entails special considerations that are unique to this genre. When quoting fewer than four lines of verse, format the quote in the body of your essay, indicating the line breaks with space followed by forward slash (/) and another space moving into the next line. In the student essay below, Jamie uses this technique:

> Man is constantly thrown into unpleasant situations. By climbing ". . . up a snow-white trunk / *Toward* heaven, till the tree could bear no more, / But dipped me [Frost] down again" (55–57), he would be able to escape briefly from life's difficulties and return unharmed. The tree represents an elevation away from complications, bringing the ascender closer to divinity for a moment yet without him having to die.

Always provide line numbers for your quoted excerpts of poetry. Notice that Jane gives the line numbers for her quote in her lead into the excerpt.

> In line 13, Dickinson combines onomatopoeia and synaesthesia to portray the fly "With Blue—uncertain stumbling Buzz—."

An alternative format for providing the line numbers is to present them in parentheses at the end of the quote. To indicate a stanza break while quoting in the body of your text, use two forward slashes (//) as in this example:

> In describing the ecstasy of horseback riding in her poem "Ariel," Plath depicts how "The furrow, // Splits and passes, sister to / The brown arc" (6–8).

For quotes of four or more lines, set the quote up in block format by indenting it ten spaces from the left-hand margin. Format the lines exactly as they appear in the original and double-space them. Cite the line numbers, again, in parentheses at the end of the quote. If you decide to leave certain lines out, indicate these omissions with a running line of spaced periods approximating the length of the lines you are quoting as follows:

> In the first and fourth stanzas of Theodore Roethke's poem "My Papa's Waltz," the poet employs an extra syllable to the iambic trimeter meter in the second and fourth lines of each stanza:

The whiskey on your breath
Could make a small boy dizzy;
But I hung on like death:
Such waltzing was not easy.
. . . .
The hand that held my wrist
Was battered on one knuckle;
At every step you missed
My right ear scraped a buckle. (1–4, 9–12)

As you revise subsequent drafts of your essay, continue to go over the recursive stages of revision to refine your essay's

- Overall arrangement
- Paragraph order and modes of paragraph development
- Thesis statement and conclusion strategy
- Integration of quoted material
- Exactness of quoted material
- Diction choices and phrasing
- Syntax and grammar
- Punctuation
- Spelling
- Formatting mechanics (margins, line spacings, title, name, course, date, and so on)

Naturally, to carry out all—or even some—of the steps outlined above will demand your most precious resource: time. Writing, as we have seen, is hard work that like, say, power-lifting cannot be attained overnight. Any weight trainer will tell you that you need to wait at least twenty-four hours between lifting sessions to give your muscles enough time to grow and strengthen. No one starts out by bench pressing his or her body weight, but over time, you can get there. Similarly, in writing, give yourself the time to make discoveries, to formulate your thesis, to draft successive revisions, to get to the next level. Successful writing takes practice.

Best Advice: Don't try to write your paper the night before it's due.

Sample Student Essay

To assist you further in drafting your essay, the following section provides a student essay with commentary from the instructor. The student chose to interpret Robert Frost's "Birches" through an **explication** of the poem's developing drama and argument. Literally meaning an "unfolding," an explication accounts for the significant features of a poem allowing the poet's narrative presentation of the work from beginning to middle to end to dictate the paper's order of arrangement. But an explication will not just restate the poem's meaning and themes in the manner of a paraphrase. More importantly, it will consider how significant formal features of the work perform that meaning in original ways at the level of poetic technique. Depending on the work at hand, explication could take into account such elements as a poem's rhyme scheme, its meter and rhythm, its figurative language (metaphor, simile, personification, metonymy, and synecdoche), its symbolism, alliteration, assonance, internal rhyme, onomatopoeia, and so on.

☙☙

ROBERT FROST *(1874–1963)*

Birches *(1916)*

When I see birches bend to left and right
Across the lines of straighter darker trees,
I like to think some boy's been swinging them.
But swinging doesn't bend them down to stay
As ice-storms do. Often you must have seen them   5
Loaded with ice a sunny winter morning
After a rain. They click upon themselves
As the breeze rises, and turn many-colored
As the stir cracks and crazes their enamel.
Soon the sun's warmth makes them shed crystal shells   10
Shattering and avalanching on the snowcrust—
Such heaps of broken glass to sweep away
You'd think the inner dome of heaven had fallen.
They are dragged to the withered bracken by the load,
And they seem not to break; though once they are bowed   15

So low for long, they never right themselves:
You may see their trunks arching in the woods
Years afterwards, trailing their leaves on the ground
Like girls on hands and knees that throw their hair
Before them over their heads to dry in the sun.   20
But I was going to say when Truth broke in
With all her matter-of-fact about the ice-storm,
I should prefer to have some boy bend them
As he went out and in to fetch the cows—
Some boy too far from town to learn baseball,   25
Whose only play was what he found himself,
Summer or winter, and could play alone.
One by one he subdued his father's trees
By riding them down over and over again
Until he took the stiffness out of them,   30
And not one but hung limp, not one was left
For him to conquer. He learned all there was
To learn about not launching out too soon
And so not carrying the tree away
Clear to the ground. He always kept his poise   35
To the top branches, climbing carefully
With the same pains you use to fill a cup
Up to the brim, and even above the brim.
Then he flung outward, feet first, with a swish,
Kicking his way down through the air to the ground.   40
So was I once myself a swinger of birches.
And so I dream of going back to be.
It's when I'm weary of considerations,
And life is too much like a pathless wood
Where your face burns and tickles with the cobwebs   45
Broken across it, and one eye is weeping
From a twig's having lashed across it open.
I'd like to get away from earth awhile
And then come back to it and begin over.
May no fate willfully misunderstand me   50
And half grant what I wish and snatch me away
Not to return. Earth's the right place for love:
I don't know where it's likely to go better.
I'd like to go by climbing a birch tree,
And climb black branches up a snow-white trunk,   55
Toward heaven, till the tree could bear no more,
But dipped its top and set me down again.
That would be good both going and coming back.
One could do worse than be a swinger of birches.

Jamie Stein

English 101

Prof. Kalaidjian

April 10, 2002

Frost's "Birches"

Robert Frost opens his poem "Birches" by
describing crippled birch trees bent against a set of
straighter neighbors. He then thinks of a hypothetical
boy swinging down from birch trees as he used to in
his earlier days. For a moment, in fact, he allows
himself to believe the child's vitality has been the
cause of the misshapen trees, but he remembers that
children do not have so much force. Time and winter
ice are the ultimate causes of the warped birches,
and Frost finds this tragic. Through the violent and
dissonant descriptions of the harmful ice, Frost
demonstrates his wish that the trees be altered in
some other method. The poem quickly shifts, however,
away from the ice and back again to the image of
swinging boys. Frost informs the reader of his former
childhood occupation as a birch swinger, and how he
wishes he could still perform such an act of youth.
Frost's masterful use of figurative language and setting transforms the tree from an amusement to a means
of rebirth. If he could, he would climb the tree to
escape from life when reality becomes too harsh. The
tree carries one towards heaven, yet transports one
back to the ground when the height becomes too great.
The climb provides a brief apotheosis, yet most important, one that is free of death.

Frost organizes his poem in an interesting manner. Speaking entirely in the first person, he decides
not to break the poem in stanzas. Thus, the poem reads
like a monologue. It has a "spoken" quality to it,
giving Frost much versatility in the various

Stein 2

directions he takes. Within the first twenty lines, it
seems as if Frost's main theme will be the destructive
force of winter and life's ultimate deference to the
coldness. Frost masterfully employs cacophonous language to describe the destructive ice that eternally
handicaps the tree. Listening to the birches, Frost
notices how:

> . . . They click upon themselves
>
> As the breeze rises, and turn many-colored
>
> As the stir cracks and crazes their enamel.
>
> Soon the sun's warmth makes them shed crystal
>   shells
>
> Shattering and avalanching on the snow crust—
>   (7–11)

Fricatives and plosives in this quote give the reader
a strong sense of sound. The hard consonants of the
words "cracks," "crazes," and "click," along with the
words "shattering" and "avalanching," fill the reader's
ears with the onomatopoeia of fracturing ice. These
words are loud and violent, perfectly imitating ice's
crashing sound; Frost's diction is masterful. He goes
on to describe that the "glass," figurative for ice,
upon the ground is so plentiful that one would "think
the inner dome of heaven had fallen." It is appropriate that he likens the ice from the trees to glass
from heaven, for later in the poem the tree acts as a
means for becoming closer to heaven. These slightly
divine trees have "fallen" from their heights (like
the "heavenly dome") and are now forever bowed to the
ground along with the "glass."

Frost, however, unexpectedly breaks his discus-

sion of the ice storm and recedes back to his original
thought of boys swinging from birches:

> But I was going to say when Truth broke in
>
> With all her matter-of-fact about the ice-storm
>
> I should prefer to have some boy bend them (21-23)

It is strange that Frost wonderfully describes the
deadly ice only to return to the image of a swinging
boy. His poem goes in a circle. Frost personifies
"Truth" and blames her for the break in discussion.
Ironically, *he* is the one to blame. The "Truth" is an
abstraction that Frost chooses to address; no one
forces him to discuss life's tendency to grow frail
during the winter. Thus, there must be a purpose in
including the "ice" section—for if it is only a side
track, as implied from the previous passage, why discuss it in such detail?

Frost is a master of his craft, and the
relevance of the ice is revealed later in the poem,
but first he must revisit the theme of boyhood vitality
within a natural setting:

> I should prefer to have some boy bend them
>
> . . . .
>
> By riding them down over and over again
>
> Until he took the stiffness out of them,
>
> And not one but hung limp, not one was left
>
> For him to conquer. . . . (23, 29-31)

Frost would rather a boy bend the trees than the ice.
In his mind, an energetic boy with the ambition and
persistence to humble a birch tree is more pleasing

Stein 4

than winter's harsh "Truth" causing the deformity. Instead of the tree being a symbol of life's frailty,
the bent birch would be a testament to the human
spirit.

    Frost, after giving an account on the skills of
birch swinging, recalls his former adventures with
such trees:

> So I was once myself a swinger of birches.
> And so I dream of going back to be.
> It's when I'm weary of considerations,
> And life's too much like a pathless wood
> Where your face burns and tickles with cobwebs
> . . . .
> I'd like to get away from earth awhile
> And then come back to it and begin over. (41-45,
>   48-49)

It is finally within this passage where the reader begins to understand Frost's purpose in describing the
ice storm. Frost explains that from time to time, he
would like to go back to his youth when he could climb
trees and swoop down from them. This desire only occurs, however, when he is "weary of life's considerations." Observing crippled and bent birch trees and
realizing that an icy and deadly storm has stripped
the tree of its magnificence is exactly one of those
"considerations" that lead to weariness. By
understanding the depressing "Truth," Frost does not
allow himself to believe that an innocent and
energetic boy caused the trees' deformities. Death and
coldness are instead the explanations.

    Life's sad realities, as documented by bent

birches, inevitably lead to times of frustration,
which Frost periodically wishes to escape. Earth can
be seen as difficult and agonizing. Frost analogizes
the more painful aspects of life to a directionless
wood filled with "pain" and "confusion." The pathless
wood, which symbolizes existence in a most disturbing
and chaotic setting, gives the reader insight as to why
Frost wishes to return to his youthful birch swinging
days. Humanity is constantly thrown into unpleasant
situations. By climbing ". . . up a snow-white trunk /
Toward heaven, till the tree could bear no more, / But
dipped me [Frost] down again" (55–57), he would be
able to escape briefly from life's difficulties and return unharmed. The tree represents an elevation away
from complications, bringing the ascender closer to
divinity for a moment yet without him having to die.
In fact, the key to this poem is that, despite the
hardships, Frost in no way wants to escape the world:

> May no fate willfully misunderstand me
>
> And half grant what I wish and snatch me away
>
> Not to return. Earth's the right place for love:
>
> I don't know where it's likely to go better
>
> (50–53)

Even with the imperfections, life is good to him, and
he does not wish to leave but instead to transcend
earth from time to time. "Fate" is of course figurative
for death, and death is not appealing. Love invokes a
desire to stay, and there is no telling if love exists
past the grave. These few lines shift the poem from
one that critiques life to one that celebrates it. The
pains of earth are by no means cause enough to forfeit

Stein 6

existence. The reader finally realizes from these few
lines that Frost does not wish to return to childhood
merely to bask in endless innocence; nor does he wish
to stop time altogether. He just wants to escape sometimes by getting close to the uncomplicated heavens,
like he could do as a boy by climbing a birch and then
swinging down. Atop the tree, one achieves godlike
status, observing the world from up high, detached and
safe from dangers. Upon return, life's gifts are much
easier to appreciate; one feels renewed. Unfortunately,
Frost is now too old to perform the rebirth that birch
swinging could provide.

    Frost fully understands the paradox of life. The
earth is saturated with pain and hardship, yet it is
also "the right place for love." He knows that the
earth is a beautiful place to live; the only problem
is that sometimes hardships seem to outweigh the joy.
These are the times when Frost wishes he could return
to his state of youthful vitality, but there is no way
to reverse time. Frost accepts this as a fact of life,
and he is willing to follow the rules. Ice may cause
some birches to hunch forever, but there will always
be some trees somewhere that a boy will find climbable,
and he will swing from these branches as Frost once
did. Thus, the world trudges forward. Life is
ultimately a sweet and enjoyable journey if approached
correctly. As stated at the end of the poem, "One
could do worse than be a swinger of birches" (59).

Commentary

In "Frost's Birches," Jamie Stein begins with a general explication of the poem's setting and situation in paragraph one. In it, he captures the thematic oscillation the poem stages between signs of life's tragedy and nature's violence versus moments and memories of ascent and escape from reality. In getting to the point of the essay's thesis, however, Jamie could compress this paragraph somewhat by editing down the opening paraphrase of the poem's plot narrative. Jamie should assume that his reader already knows the general story line of the poem. The second paragraph notes the poem's first-person, dramatic monologue format and makes a transition to Frost's onomatopoeia in capturing the cacophonous sound of breaking ice. Notice that Jamie does not just use the block quote for illustration but also explicates the sound elements he quotes at some length. The fourth paragraph focuses on the poem's personification of Truth that voices the reality of nature's violence that has broken the tree. The fifth paragraph makes a transition from the personified figure of Truth to the tree itself as a symbol both of "life's frailty" and the resistant "human spirit" depending on the poet's point of view. The sixth paragraph further probes the tension between truth and fiction in Frost's digression to childhood memory.

Notice in the next two paragraphs how Jamie mixes his presentational format both to incorporate quotes into the syntax of his own sentences and to set off key passages in block quote formats. The conclusion paragraph returns to the level of thematic generality that begins the essay but also frames the poem's central paradox through a new insistence that, however hard, earth is nevertheless "the right place for love." In this manner, then, the essay's overall rhetorical strategy follows the poem's unfolding narrative. Along the way, Jamie signals the key techniques of alliteration and assonance, personification, symbolism, and paradox as they shape and perform Frost's musings in "Birches."

27   Writing a Research Paper

This epigraph from Italo Calvino's novel, one chapter of which appears earlier in this book, seems uncannily accurate. For many of the phenomena we encounter in everyday life, however subtly, demand interpretation: menus, clothing styles, even the facial expressions of people we meet, to name just three. The interpretive process begins with reading, then moves to larger speculations, and, in the best of cases, leads to the formulation of answers to specific questions. What salad would go well with this entree? Why is this person frowning at me? What image does this suit or jacket and slacks ensemble project? In fact, many popular styles or recent "subcultures"—the Beat Movement, "Goth" culture, or the so-called punk rock movement of the 1970s—comprise a larger text to be read and interpreted. How is this music connected to that fashion, hairstyle, or lifestyle? What larger social or political statement is this subculture making, or not making? Consider, for example, all the things a term like *hip-hop* or *heavy metal* means. The list of things that might be interpreted is potentially endless.

Calvino's character Mr. Palomar, a compulsive reader and interpreter, knows this all too well. He contemplates waves, bodies on beaches, stellar constellations, the flight patterns of migrating birds—just about everything. Therein resides his problem: He has no rules to limit his interpretive activities; as a consequence, he drives himself to distraction by "reading" everything from the blades of grass and sea of weeds in his lawn to the kind of cheese he buys at a store. He is, in other words, both obsessed and adrift, a player immersed in a readerly game devoid of any organizing rules. And a game without rules quickly leads to chaos, which is one of the inferences *Mr. Palomar* seems to promote.

Fortunately, writing research papers on literature is a highly "ruleful" enterprise. Unlike Mr. Palomar's chaotic lawn, topics selected for research papers need to have clearly marked limits. Setting these boundaries, however, often poses one of the most difficult problems a writer faces, and this is merely one of the many decisions a research project demands. Some of these are relatively large, potentially complicated matters like "what is my topic?" and, even more central to most kinds of research papers, "what is my thesis statement?" Other decisions, like the one we just made about whether to quote directly or paraphrase a line from Calvino's novel, concern the smaller issues of a single sentence or paragraph. What would a paraphrase of this sentence sound like, and how should it be cited? Would it be more effective to render the passage as it appeared in the original?

This essay considers all of these questions and more. Throughout, however, as is the case in writing about literature without the benefit of research, we want to emphasize that at each step of the process—during the prewriting, writing, and revision stages—the composition of successful research papers depends on the writer's thoughtful decision making, the careful organization of reference materials, and a sincere effort to use these materials accurately. The best research writing is driven by the writer's intellectual curiosity about a subject, for writing based on research should result in increased knowledge for both the writer and reader of the paper.

As we described in Chapter 25, "Writing about Literature," the decisions that most influence the purpose and ultimate structure of a research paper are made during prewriting, before the first sentence is even drafted.

Prewriting

After being informed about the length of the assignment and its due date, the first question to be answered about a research project is this: What kind of essay am I being asked to write, a *review* or an interpretive *argument*? Most instructors will assign the latter, and the distinction between the two is crucial because it helps define your purpose in researching and writing about a topic, it determines who you are as a writer, and it suggests the kind of audience your paper is addressing. As in virtually every writing situation, from letters home to papers written for courses to portions of typical job applications, a writer at the prewriting stage needs to define as specifically as possible the purpose of the writing and the audience to whom it is directed.

The author of a *review*, a film review for example, regards his or her audience as *uninformed*. Because the audience has not seen the movie, the reviewer's job is largely descriptive and, finally, evaluative. For this reason, a reviewer of a feature film will almost always summarize the central plot or action, mention such features as the central characters, the actors' performances, and maybe even the film's musical score before rendering an opinion. And this opinion almost always pertains to the film's quality, its goodness or badness. That's the purpose of a review. The most influential reviewers, like Roger Ebert and the late Gene Siskel, can either breathe life into a movie's financial future or sound its death knell by giving it a "thumb's up" or a "thumb's down" verdict.

Reviewers, like all writers, make other decisions as well. What is the reading level of my audience? What language will most effectively communicate ideas to such readers? What other elements of my essay, such as the length and complexity of sentences or paragraphs, ought to be shaped for this particular group of readers? What kinds of evidence will be most persuasive in this particular rhetorical situation, and how should this evidence be presented?

By contrast, writers of critical essays define their audiences and purpose for writing quite differently. Such essays are addressed to *informed* readers, and the writer's task does not generally include commentary on a text's good- ness or badness—indications of whether the writer liked it or not—but rather develops an idea, an opinion, about the text or texts under discussion. Because the reader of the essay, by definition, is familiar with the text, knows who the characters are and so on, the writers of research papers—and, indeed, most papers on literary topics—are not required to provide long summaries of the plot or action, descriptions of the central characters, and other features of the text. Instead, the paper attempts to advance a *reading*, an interpretation, of some aspect or aspects of the play, story, or poem by making a case for the va- lidity of a particular understanding or intellectual "purchase" of the topic. This means that a research paper has to have a thesis statement.

Thesis Statements

The sentence that conveys the thrust of the writer's purpose—and, in fact, or- ganizes the entire essay—is called the *thesis statement*. And while it is often the case that a precise thesis statement is formulated after a rough draft is pro- duced, all research writing begins with at least some ideas about the topic to be undertaken and the direction the paper will take. But, as every writer also knows, finding that topic and refining the thesis are among the most difficult jobs a writer undertakes during prewriting.

By way of a brief review, here are the characteristics of a good thesis statement.

- A thesis statement is a statement of opinion, not a fact or statement of intention.
- A thesis statement offers an opinion about which reasonable people might disagree.
- A thesis statement usually possesses a rhetorical premise (comparison, process, classification, definition, and so on).
- A thesis statement predicts the progress of the paper and controls the evi- dence to be admitted.
- A thesis statement addresses a topic of interpretive significance, not a minor point.
- A thesis statement relies on theoretical or aesthetic assumptions.

All of these issues are described in greater detail in Chapter 25, "Writing about Literature." But when writing an essay based on research, one other component of thesis statements becomes relevant.

- A thesis statement enters its author into a critical conversation with other readers.

Unlike papers written solely from your own experience of a poem, short story, film, or play, a research paper inevitably leads to your consultation of other opinions. How have other readers before you understood Shakespeare's sonnets, T. S. Eliot's imagery, or Sylvia Plath's symbols? In some ways, this quality of a thesis statement becomes the most intimidating because, after all, if something is published in a book or academic journal, it must be correct. Right?

Wrong. A published essay or chapter of a book that analyzes the topic you want to explore need not be regarded as unimpeachable or exhaustive. In the case of materials printed on non-refereed Web sites, it may not even be any good. But such readings *do* exist and, as we will see, if you borrow anything from them—in any form—your indebtedness must be cited appropriately. The thesis of a research paper, in fact, responds in part to what "outside" sources you have found. But the best papers achieve more than a reiteration of source materials. They add to them, modify them, refocus them, even refute them. The sources you uncover during your research are much like the voices in a conversation into which your voice—your thesis statement—enters.

But how do you find this conversation in the first place? You start the research process by heading for the library.

Finding and Evaluating Sources

Your instructor will most likely stipulate the number of sources you need to consult for this assignment and may also restrict the kinds of materials you may use. One of the most controversial sources of information, whatever might be said of its convenience, is the World Wide Web, which can be "surfed" on topics ranging from Sophocles to Emily Dickinson, Edgar Allan Poe to performance artist Karen Finley. Several realities make information taken from the Web potentially problematic: the possibility that it has not been "refereed," for instance, and the fact that information on Web sites may exist in cyberspace today and be gone tomorrow. By "refereed," we mean that an essay appearing in most academic books and journals has undergone "peer review": It has been evaluated and approved by experts in the field before being published. In the case of most academic presses, a book has not only been recommended for publication by experts, but also endorsed by a review board at the press. Unfortunately, most Web sites cannot guarantee such quality in the materials they post, with the exception of such refereed online publications as *Postmodern Culture* and *Workplace: The Journal of Academic Labor.*

In general, at least two factors can help you decide the quality of the material you have found: its date of publication and the reputation of the publisher. Journals and books published at reputable institutions (that is, colleges and universities you have heard of) have undergone peer review, as have books accepted by such major publishers as Houghton Mifflin, Norton, Macmillan, John Wiley, Harcourt Brace, and others. When in doubt about a potential source, ask your instructor.

Also, it is generally advisable—not to mention, efficient—to begin your search with recently published books and journal articles. Not because the last thing written is necessarily the best thing written, but because the bibliographies in these publications will lead you to potential sources published earlier. Obviously, starting your research with earlier materials will not be similarly enhancing of your bibliography. Here, again, exceptions exist. If, for example, you are interested in how reviewers in the 1890s responded to several of Thomas Hardy's poems, then your investigation would most likely begin with the review of materials published then.

Finally, a number of indexes and bibliographies are helpful both in leading you to sources and in evaluating the sources you find. For example, the Modern Language Association (MLA) publishes the annual *MLA International Bibliography*, which lists works published about most American, British, and Western European authors during a given year. The *Reader's Guide to Periodical Literature* is similarly useful, because it indexes the contents of popular magazines, and the gateway site *Voice of the Shuttle: Web Page for Humanities Research* (if Internet sources are permissible for your assignment) can assist you in locating relevant materials on the Web. Most major city newspapers like the *New York Times* and the *Washington Post* are indexed and can prove indispensable sources for such materials as theater and film reviews. The *MLA Handbook for Writers of Research Papers*, 5th ed. (1999), whose documentation system we will summarize below, also recommends the *Book Review Index* and *Book Review Digest* as places you can go to find reviews of books you might want to consult. If you are preparing a research paper on a topic in American literature or culture, the annual volume *American Literary Scholarship* (*ALS*) could also prove valuable to you.

All of these reference books and much, much more are available in college and university libraries. And reference librarians are there to make your search for materials as painless and productive as possible; if you need assistance, don't hesitate to ask one for help.

Taking Notes from Sources

Remember that whatever sources you decide to use, it is your responsibility to paraphrase or quote from them accurately. Accuracy down to the last word or punctuation mark sounds like an easy enough goal to achieve, but it isn't. Imagine taking notes from a source when the phone rings, or when your roommate comes in and invites you to a party, or when someone next door puts on Eminem or Jimi Hendrix at high volume—any of these distractions could compromise your ability to record information accurately from a source. Further, after a week, a month, or more of reviewing and evaluating sources, it's easy to get confused about where certain material originated. If essential information from and about a source is not written down—and checked carefully—the possibilities of making mistakes increase dramatically. Of course, factors beyond your control may complicate your research: a book you are relying on may be called back to the library; a journal issue you found easily today may be missing tomorrow; and, as we have already mentioned, the Web site you discovered today may be quite different tomorrow.

For all of these reasons, it is essential that your note-taking system include at least the following information.

1. A *full* citation for every source. This means the author's complete name, title, publication information and, for articles or chapters of collected books, the full page run of the essay you intend to cite.
2. An indication for each entry that reminds you whether the information is a brief summary, an extended paraphrase of the original, or a direct quotation. The distinction between a paraphrase and a direct quotation is a crucial one and is discussed in the next section below.
3. A page number—or paragraph number for some Internet sites—for each note you take.
4. A note to yourself of exactly where you found the source, just in case you need to consult it later.

Quoting, Paraphrasing, and Avoiding Plagiarism

Once you have found sources relevant to your project and begin note-taking, you will need to decide whether to make a brief summary of the material, write a more extended paraphrase, or quote directly. Of course, you will probably do a combination of all three for many of the sources you find. The decision to quote or paraphrase involves several factors. Is the language of the original so striking that its precise phrasing is nearly as striking as its content? A sentence commonly found in histories of British drama like "The public theatre in England began in the later 1570s" might convey significant information, but its wording is hardly exceptional and need not be quoted. Whereas, Hamlet's famous soliloquy that begins "To be, or not to be, that is the question" (3.1.57) might prove awkward to restate and ineffective as well. "Should I, like, kill myself or maybe I shouldn't is what I'm trying to figure out" fails to capture the elegance of Shakespeare's line. Some passages, like the opening sentence of Samuel Beckett's novel *Murphy* (1957), are too cleverly phrased to be reduced to paraphrase: "The sun shone, having no alternative, on the nothing new." Others, like Salman Rushdie's description of the shame of colonized peoples from his novel *Shame* (1983), contain such vivid metaphors that you will probably want to quote it directly:

> Imagine shame as a liquid, let's say a sweet fizzy tooth-rotting drink stored in a vending machine. Push the right button and a cup plops down under a pissing stream of the liquid. How to push the button? Nothing to it. Tell a lie, sleep with a white boy, get born the wrong sex. (125)

You decide how best to use the material you find. Whether you quote or paraphrase, remember that you are obliged to explain the implications of this material when you write your paper.

When paraphrasing a passage, make certain that you not only convey its meaning accurately, but that you also restate it in your own words. This means, at the very least, revising the descriptive language of the original into your own prose. If you consciously recall taking a paraphrase from a source and using it in your essay, it must be cited, just as you would cite a direct quotation. Consider the following example, taken from Terry Eagleton's book *Crazy John and the Bishop and Other Essays on Irish Culture* (1998), which discusses the changing forms of modern art after World War II. Pay particular attention to the language Eagleton employs at the end of the excerpt to define aesthetic innovations and their origins.

Original Passage

> It is as though we can now recognize that, for example, simply because of the sharpening contradictions of naturalistic drama, there would have been a thrust beyond such theatrical realism, even if its names had not turned out to be Beckett or Pirandello or Ionesco. Someone, we feel, would have had to come up with free verse or musical dissonance or showing a face from five different angles simultaneously, just as once you have a variety of liquors it is hard not to think that cocktails were somehow preordained. Every cultural period provides us with a [host] of possibilities. . . . In post-war Europe, there were those authors gripped by a sense of spiritual exhaustion, writers who carved out a niche of anti-heroic debunkery, artistic exiles adrift between languages, and avant-garde experimenters in theatrical form. (Eagleton 297)

Paraphrase

> Naturalistic or realistic drama at the beginning of the twentieth century contained a number of ever-sharpening contradictions, so some innovative playwright inevitably would have gone beyond theatrical realism in terms of dramatic form. The same is true of all art in the period; someone would have had to come up with free verse in poetry, musical dissonance in composition, or showing a face from five different angles in filmmaking. Lots of aesthetic possibilities exist in every period. This is particularly true of Europe after World War II, where many authors, gripped by a sense of spiritual exhaustion, felt adrift between languages and led avant-garde experimentation, especially in a new theatre of anti-heroic debunkery.

Although this paraphrase accurately summarizes the original, it verges on *plagiarism* for at least two reasons: Highly descriptive phrases from the original appear without quotations marks, and no citation at the end identifies the source of these ideas. Notice that the quotation is followed by "(Eagleton 297)," signaling the origin of this material. If previous sentences clarified that Eagleton's book was the source, then only "(297)" would be necessary. But, again, *any material that you consciously recall taking from a source must be accompanied by a citation.* And, of course, fuller information about the source should appear in the "Works Cited" section at the end of the paper.

But this is only half of the problem with the above paraphrase. An equally significant failing is the writer's inability to rephrase important descriptions in Eagleton's paragraph: "sharpening contradictions," "gripped by a sense of spiritual exhaustion," "anti-heroic debunkery" and so on. Again, some language is, by its very nature, so basic and colorless that it really cannot be paraphrased. For example, "Abraham Lincoln was born in Kentucky and moved to Illinois when he was a small child" contains little descriptive language to rephrase. You cannot replace "born" with "came into this world" without risking verbosity; "moved" need not be changed to "migrated" or "transported." But phrases like "gripped by a sense of spiritual exhaustion" or "anti-heroic debunkery" in the original must be restated in your own words. The following paraphrase suggests one way to do this.

Paraphrase

> Contemporary scholars like Terry Eagleton emphasize the decline of dramatic realism in the early decades of the twentieth century, and the aesthetic experimentation that eventually took place not only in play writing, but in such other areas as poetry, musical composition, and filmmaking as well. So-called "free verse" in poetry and "musical dissonance" in musical composition were followed, in the years of soul-searching in Europe after World War II, by a variety of formal experiments in drama such as the writing of plays around anti-heroes and the creation of a dramatic mood on stage that matched the pessimism of the times. (297)

You may elect, as we have in the above paraphrase, to quote and paraphrase in the same paragraph. No problem—so long as the quoted portions are identified and are integrated smoothly into the syntax of your sentence. If you are at all confused about methods of quoting from the original, please review "Arguments and Admissible Evidence: Paraphrase and Quotation" in Chapter 25, "Writing about Literature."

Once you have formulated a thesis, however tentative and subject to refinement or tweaking; have found, evaluated, and taken notes from sources; and have made preliminary decisions about paraphrasing and quoting, you are probably ready to begin a rough draft. Of course, this stage of the research writing process means making more decisions, some of which are outlined in the following section.

Writing

Your trips to the library have helped you refine a thesis in which you feel confident; you have tested it against the criteria listed above and have asked informed readers (your classmates or instructor) to comment on its potential. After consulting the card catalogue at the library, indexes and bibliographies, and—perhaps—online sources, you have assembled a set of high-quality sources and taken accurate notes from them. You have read carefully the literary text or texts you intend to discuss, deciding what passages to incorporate into your argument; you have even made some preliminary decisions about which excerpts might be paraphrased and which should be quoted. Most important, you have allowed yourself sufficient time to write, rewrite, and revise some more. You are aware of the citation system you are supposed to follow and any other formal requirements outlined by your instructor: the recommended length of the essay, the placement of page numbers, and so on. You are well rested and comfortable.

You're ready to go! Well, almost.

Before you begin, reconsider the basic equation formulated in Chapter 25 and the ways in which your research will modify it. Here's the previous equation:

Your "reading" + textual evidence (paraphrase + quotation) = argument.

Writing that includes research material extends this equation as follows:

Your "reading" + textual evidence (paraphrase + quotation) + research (paraphrase + quotation) = argument.

Note that in both cases *your* analysis comes first, supported by concrete textual evidence. As we remarked earlier, a *balance* between your analysis and the evidence is crucial to the success of your paper. An argument with no evidence is no argument; an argument with only pieces of evidence left unexplained amounts to a mere patchwork of quotations and paraphrases. Effective arguments require both your organization and explanation of evidence—and, of course, the evidence itself must be presented clearly and concisely.

Most important, remember that the research you conduct only *supplements* your argument. That is to say, as is the case in writing any essay on a literary topic, your argument rests on your abilities to articulate a thesis statement and mount a convincing evidentiary case for it. Part of this evidence originates in the references you have consulted, but only a part and not necessarily the major part. And this prompts one more question:

What is your attitude toward this research and how does this affect your presentation of it in your argument?

As we mentioned earlier, not everything you read will be of equal quality, and you may not agree with everything you read. Fine. The question is, how do you present this information in your paper? The first answer is "with respect" and verbal grace.

After that, a number of possibilities exist. One common rhetorical tactic, for example, is called the "straw man" or "straw critic" approach in which a writer repeats a critical assertion only to modify or refute it. The purpose of the strategy is to create a "space" for the thesis or point of the argument by way of negation. Professional literary critics employ this strategy all the time, as the following passage from Richard H. Rodino's essay ("Authors, Characters, and Readers in *Gulliver's Travels*," *PMLA* 106 [October 1991]: 1054–70) on conflicting interpretations of Jonathan Swift's *Gulliver's Travels* suggests. Here, Rodino cites another scholar whose reading of the book, while incisive and useful, needs to be extended:

> Even a preliminary exploration of [conflicting views of *Gulliver's Travels*] requires an unusually complex understanding of the rhetorical relations involved. We must, for instance, go beyond Everett Zimmerman's pioneering description of the *Travels* as "a book not about a man who undergoes certain experiences but about a man who writes a book about experiences he has undergone"—a view that regards the reader simply as a receiver of meaning. . . . (1057)

In this passage Rodino expresses his admiration of Zimmerman's work ("pioneering description"), while at the same time insisting that his conception of the reader ought to be revised ("go beyond," "reader simply as a receiver"). The result is a respectful, yet strong statement of interpretive difference, which Rodino elaborates in his close reading of Swift's text.

On other occasions, broad critical agreement might exist, yet this consensus does not consider a text in which you are interested. Or, if it has been considered in such conversations, its significance hasn't been properly assessed. In such instances, you might indicate the principal parties in the conversation and then "clear a space" for your participation in the dialogue. This is the strategy Megan Sullivan uses to introduce her essay on recent women's films in Northern Ireland ("Orla Walsh's *The Visit* (1992): Incarceration and Feminist Cinema in Northern Ireland," *New Hibernia Review* 2 [Summer 1998]: 85–99):

> Following Pat Murphy, Anne Crilly, Margo Harkin, and Orla Walsh each have used film to critique nationalism and women's place in it. They also have taken great pains to suggest that nationalism itself is no longer women's primary concern; rather, they are concerned with day-to-day or material problems: censorship, the women's movement, class structure, and reproductive choice. Importantly, Crilly, Harkin, and Walsh invoke the site of the prison to suggest these concerns, and Murphy herself relies on the trope of incarceration to signal a young woman's emerging feminist consciousness.... Because her twenty-two minute film *The Visit* centers on the protagonist's physical and mental journey to visit her husband in prison, Walsh's film progresses furthest to argue for the significance of incarceration for nationalist women in Northern Ireland. (85)

This excerpt accomplishes several things at once. By alluding to several examples, it lends a sense of authority to the argument, suggesting that the writer really knows her subject. Like the "straw critic" approach, this more positive tactic also clears a discursive space for the writer's thesis. And, by returning to key terms in the essay's title, this passage reiterates elements crucial to the progress of the argument: "feminist cinema," Northern Ireland, and the importance of images of incarceration in these films.

However you choose to weave critical opinions into the fabric of your argument, do not let them overwhelm your presentation and analysis of textual detail. Introduce and enunciate the thesis statement, develop the evidence, and conclude—much as you would any other essay.

Revision

One unfortunate reality of research assignments is that while writers may spend weeks researching a topic and writing, many devote too little time to revising the argument, polishing the prose, and proofreading for mistakes. The revision stage, in fact, seems almost doomed to be given short shrift in most varieties of writing, yet its importance to the quality of the final product is indisputable. This is especially true of research papers.

Why? Because, as we have implied above, the process of conducting and writing a research paper is particularly vulnerable to human error. It isn't hard to understand why. Research writing includes more documents to read than most other kinds of writing, more material to process and organize, more quotations and decisions, more citations to foul up.

Our advice, consistent with that we have given earlier, is to read your draft carefully, checking in particular for some of the writing problems that have surfaced in earlier essays. This could mean checking all the transitions or topic sentences of paragraphs, sharpening the precision of your word selection, looking for spelling errors, and so on. By the time you write your research paper, you should have a fairly clear idea of the things you do well and those elements of your writing that need improvement. Remember that the root of word *revise* comes from the Latin meaning "look again," not "glance again" or "hurry through again." The very word, therefore, denotes a careful review of the entire project.

Research papers also add two significant elements to your list of "things to do" at the revision stage: Check the accuracy of every quotation in the essay—word by word, punctuation mark by punctuation mark—and verify that each entry in your "Notes" and "Works Cited" sections follow the *exact* format specified by your instructor. We are following the documentation system outlined in the *MLA Handbook for Writers of Research Papers,* 5th edition. If questions arise at any time in the process of researching or writing your paper, the *MLA Handbook* probably contains an answer. It is generally available in the reference section of college libraries or may be purchased from the Modern Language Association of America.

Because "Notes" and Works Cited" generally appear at the end of research papers, we will conclude with a brief discussion of their function and a listing of citation formats for the most common kinds of sources.

Notes and Works Cited

In the MLA citation system, "footnotes" and "endnotes" are greatly simplified. Why? Because instead of supplying a superscripted number for each citation and then listing each of these at the foot of the page or at the end of the essay, in the MLA system each reference in the text is followed by a parenthesis identifying the source and page number. So, to take the paraphrase from Terry Eagleton's book mentioned earlier, if the author of the excerpt is clear from the context—or if his name is specifically mentioned—you need only supply the page number at the end of the excerpt: thus, "(297)." If the source is *not* made clear by the context, then you must cite the author's last name and the page number: thus, "(Eagleton 297)." And, in cases in which you refer to two or more works by the same author, and the context does not specify the source of the excerpt, you must include the author's last name, an abbreviated title, and a page number: thus, "(Eagleton, *Crazy John* 297)."

That's about it. In this system of parenthetical or "internal" citation, the "Notes" section includes only extra information or brief asides—comments you might wish to make about a point raised in the essay that, in your judgment, is not important enough to include in the body of the argument. So, for example, suppose you had consulted several sources on literary experimentation after World War II, good sources but ones not so effective as Eagleton in explaining the topic. You might place a superscript after the passage from Eagleton and in your "Notes" section at the end of the paper direct your reader to these sources: thus,

Notes

[1]For further discussion of the origins of late modernist aesthetics and mid-twentieth-century "exhaustion," see Esslin and Miller.

You might even want to add a sentence or two to this entry distinguishing one source from another. Whatever the case, even if you only mention their names in one note, full information on Esslin and Miller must appear in the "Works Cited."

In the MLA documentation system of parenthetical citations, therefore, it is entirely possible to write a fine research paper without any notes at all. Not so with "Works Cited." Every work mentioned in notes, paraphrased or quoted in the body of the essay—and, of course, this includes the literary texts that form the nexus of your argument—must appear in the "Works Cited" at the end of the paper. Entries should be organized in alphabetical order by the author's last name (for a book written or edited by more than one person, you should use the last name of the first person listed on the title page). If an author is not listed for an article or essay, the first letter of the first major word in the title dictates its position in your "Works Cited."

Citation forms for the most commonly used kinds of sources follows.

A SINGLE-AUTHORED BOOK

Chávez, John R. *The Lost Land: The Chicano Image of the Southwest.* Albuquerque: U of New Mexico P, 1984.

TWO OR MORE BOOKS BY THE SAME AUTHOR

Jameson, Fredric. *The Political Unconscious: Narrative as a Socially Symbolic Act.* Ithaca: Cornell UP, 1981.

———. *Postmodernism, or, The Cultural Logic of Late Capitalism.* Durham, NC: Duke UP, 1991.

AN EDITED BOOK BY TWO OR MORE AUTHORS

Bérubé, Michael, and Cary Nelson, eds. *Higher Education Under Fire: Politics, Economics, and the Crisis of the Humanities.* New York: Routledge, 1995.

A TRANSLATED BOOK

Baudrillard, Jean. *Fatal Strategies.* Trans. Philip
     Beitchman and W. G. J. Niesluchowski. Ed. Jim Flem-
     ing. New York/London: Semiotext(e)/Pluto, 1990.

AN ARTICLE IN A SCHOLARLY JOURNAL

Newman, Karen. "Portia's Ring: Unruly Women and Struc-
     tures of Exchange in *The Merchant of Venice."*
     Shakespeare Quarterly 38 (1987): 19-33.

AN ARTICLE IN A MAGAZINE

Schlosser, Eric. "The Taking of the Presidency 2000."
     Rolling Stone 1 Feb. 2001: 36-38, 64.

AN ESSAY IN AN ANTHOLOGY

Onkey, Lauren. "The Passion Machine Theatre Company's
     Everyday Life." *A Century of Irish Drama: Widening
     the Stage.* Ed. Stephen Watt, Eileen Morgan, and
     Shakir Mustafa. Bloomington: Indiana UP, 2000.
     223-35.

A MULTIVOLUME WORK

Lauter, Paul, et al., eds. *The Heath Anthology of Ameri-
     can Literature.* 4th ed. 2 vols. Boston: Houghton
     Mifflin, 2002.

A FILM

North by Northwest. Dir. Alfred Hitchcock. Perf. Cary
     Grant, Eva Marie Saint, James Mason, Martin Landau,
     and Leo G. Carroll. MGM, 1959.

A LECTURE

Burke, Cynthia. "Tomorrow's English Majors." MLA Conven-
     tion. Hynes Auditorium, Boston. 25 Apr. 2002.

AN INTERVIEW

Harold Bloom. Interview with Anthony Perro. *Weekend
     Edition.* Natl. Public Radio. WBUR, Boston. 10
     June 1995.

AN E-MAIL

Tuttle, Robert. E-mail to the author. 2 May 2002.

CD-ROM

"Dickinson, Emily." *Discovering Authors*. Vers. 2.0. CD-
    ROM. Detroit: Gale, 1999.

A DOCUMENT WITHIN A DATABASE

"City Profile: San Francisco." *CNN Interactive*. 19 June
    1998. Cable News Network. 19 June 1998.<http://
    www.cnn.com>

WEB SITE

Internet Public Library. 1 May 2002. 6 July 2002.
    <http://www.ipl.org/>.

Glossary

accentual meter   The strong stress meter characteristic of Old English poetry.

accentual syllabic meter   Reaching back to the fourteenth century, this tradition of versification is based on the number of accents and syllables per line.

allegory   A symbolic representation of a character for a concept, position, or one aspect of personality. The term comes from the Greek words meaning "other" (*allos*) and "to speak" (*agoreuein*)—to speak in terms of something other.

allegorical   Pertaining to an allegory.

allusion   A reference in a text to a passage or figure from literary, popular, or religious traditions.

analepsis   A literary term for shifts in chronology from the present to the past. In film, this practice is called a *flashback*.

anapest   A poetic foot comprising two unaccented syllables followed by an accented syllable.

antagonist   A character who opposes the protagonist or whose actions conflict with the protagonist's aims or desires.

antistrophe   The second part of a choral ode.

apostrophe   A special performative instance of *prosopopoeia* (addressing an inanimate thing or a person who is absent or deceased).

archetype   The basic model for a particular character in a myth. Stemming from the Greek word *archetypos*, meaning "original pattern," an archetype in literature describes a symbolic image that is basic to the human experience of birth, death, fertility, disease, war, quest, and so on.

Black Arts Movement   A radically separatist cultural movement in the 1960s, led by such figures as Amiri Baraka, that advocated a negation of white aesthetics and the embrace of more authentic African and African American forms. Baraka founded the Black Arts Repertory Theatre School in Harlem in 1965.

blank verse   Unrhymed iambic pentameter.

blazon   A traditional poetic form where a male poet pays tribute to a woman by complimenting the details of her face or body.

cacophony   A sound that is unpleasant and grating.

caesura   A pause. From the Latin *caedere*, meaning "to cut."

catharsis   The expurgation of pity and fear. Taken from Aristotle's *Poetics*, this term describes the audience response that is appropriate to tragedy.

climax   The moment of greatest emotional tension in a narrative. Usually, after events lead up to this point, they are resolved in the *denouement*.

close reading   An engaged analysis and interpretation of a literary text that moves beyond a simple summary of the ideas or actions expressed in the work. A close reading often focuses on the specific words or figurative language used in a passage.

cognate   A word that has the same root as a word from a different language.

concrete poetry   Poetry that explores the visual possibilities of pattern in calligraphy, typewriter art, stamp art, and typographical design. The concrete poetry movement began in the 1950s.

connotation   The values, qualities, associations, and shades of meaning that a word acquires in contextual usage over time.

consonance   A similarity in beginning or ending consonant sounds but different vowel sounds.

couplet   A pair of rhyming lines.

dactyl   A poetic foot comprising one accented syllable followed by two unaccented syllables.

deconstruction   The examination of how structures, language, and imagery work against or contradict themselves or other aspects of a story's expression.

denotation   The literal meaning of a word or group of words rather than additional meanings those words might suggest (see *connotation*).

denouement   The final resolution of a plot's conflict, generally occurring after the *climax* of the narrative.

deus ex machina   God from the machine (Latin). An artificial device or character introduced to resolve a plot issue. It refers to the machinery that carried a Roman or Greek god to the stage to "save the day" at the last moment.

dialogism   A method of interpreting culture as responsive, as individuals act in a particular time and space and react to the past and to the expected future. Key words can be examined for their open-ended rather than closed nature. It is a key concept that New Historicism takes from the Russian thinker Mikhail Bakhtin (1895–1975).

dialogue   The conversation between two or more characters.

diction   The choice of words in prose, fiction, poetry, and drama.

diegesis   The world of the story.

dimeter   A line of verse consisting of two metrical feet.

drama   A composition that is intended for representation by one or more performers to an audience.

dramatic irony   The disparity created when readers (or viewers) know more than the characters.

end rhyme   A rhyme that comes at the end of a line of verse.

enjambment   The movement of syntactic phrasing from the end of one line to the beginning of the next.

epiphany   A sudden and overwhelming insight or recognition of a truth.

euphony   The impression of sounds that are pleasing to the ear.

explication   A critical interpretation of a text.

exposition   The beginning of a story or drama in which the characters and circumstances of the narrative are introduced.

expressionism   An early twentieth-century movement in the arts that attempted to express subjective or psychological realities. In German drama and silent film of the 1910s and 1920s, for example, expressionist techniques included distorted make-up or camera angles, slanted stages and settings, and other means to represent an interior or psychological reality.

feminine rhyme   A rhyming of words of two or more syllables where the final syllable is unstressed.

feminist criticism   The criticism that focuses on the politics and aesthetics of female experience and representation, as well as of gender generally.

figurative language   Words and descriptions, including metaphor, simile, and personification, that differ from purely denotative, or literal, meanings to suggest comparisons between two or more terms or things.

first-person narrator   See *narrator.*

foot   A unit of poetic meter consisting of stressed and unstressed syllables.

formalism   A kind of literary analysis that emphasizes using elements of form to interpret meaning.

frame narrator   See *narrator.*

free verse   A kind of poetry that varies in length, typography, rhythms, and stanza patterns to fit the particular style and content of the work at hand.

gay and lesbian criticism   Analysis that focuses on issues of sexuality or the politics and aesthetics of gay experience and representation. It is part of a larger investigation of sexuality and gender called *queer theory.*

half rhyme   Rhymes that have minor or dissonant tonalities.

hamartia   Tragic flaw or error (Greek). The tragic error leads to the protagonist's downfall. In his *Poetics,* Aristotle describes the downfall of a character brought about not by the character's vice or depravity but by some error or frailty.

hemistich   A half line of poetry.

heptameter   A metrical unit consisting of seven feet.

heroic couplet   In poetry, rhyming couplets composed in iambic pentameter. These couplets were a popular form in the eighteenth century.

hexameter   A metrical unit consisting of six feet.

hybridity   The multicultural reality of contemporary America. As discussed by Guillermo Goméz-Peña and other commentators on contemporary culture, identity and culture are now composed of different national and ethnic phenomena, as once firm cultural borders topple or disappear.

hyperbole   A figure of speech using exaggeration for emphasis or effect. An example is Andrew Marvell's pledge to his lover that "An hundred years should go to praise / Thine eyes, and on thy forehead gaze; / Two hundred to adore each breast."

hypertext   Internet-based writing that contains links to other resources. Hypertext is performative because it requires readers to engage in a constant process of selection and arrangement that produces narrative.

iambic foot   A metrical unit of verse based on the iamb, which comprises an unaccented syllable followed by an accented one.

iambic pentameter   The most typical metrical line in English constructed of five iambic feet per line.

image   A suggestion of sensory phenomena.

imagery   The use of language to evoke sensory experience.

in medias res   In the middle of the thing (Latin). This term refers to starting a narrative in the middle of events rather than at the beginning.

internal rhyme   A pair of words that rhyme within and across adjacent lines.

intertextuality   The various ways that texts refer to other texts.

irony   A situation (dramatic irony) or phrasing (verbal irony) that performs something contrary to expectation. Dramatic irony occurs when the audience knows more about an incident than a character in a play does.

literary movement   A set of ideas formulated by authors and critics about what literature should do and how it should be done.

low comedy   In drama, the kind of humor generated by characters noted for their physical dexterity, linguistic ineptitude, and ability to make an audience laugh; for example, the antics of a clown or jester. Some critics call this physical comedy.

Marxist criticism   A form of analysis that studies representations of class, the ways literature enacts the effects of economic disparity, and the material conditions and contexts in which literature is produced. It is based on a labor theory of value advanced by the nineteenth-century German philosopher, historian, social scientist, and revolutionary Karl Marx.

masculine rhyme   A rhyme made on a masculine ending. Masculine rhyme describes rhyming words of more than one syllable when the rhyming sound falls on the final, unstressed syllable.

metanarrative   A story that draws attention to the mechanisms of telling stories.

metaphor   Figurative language that compares one word or thing in terms of another word or thing by way of direct transference.

metonymy   Figurative language that describes a word substituted for another word associated with it. For instance, the metonymy of "the crown" is often used to refer to the regal authority of the king or queen who wears it. See also *synecdoche*.

mimesis   An imitation.

modernism   A term used to describe various aesthetic movements in the late nineteenth and twentieth centuries, especially those prior to World War II. Modernism reacted against realistic representations of nineteenth-century literature as well as the conformity of commercial culture, in part by emphasizing stylistic experimentation.

monologue   The spoken thoughts of a single character.

monometer   A verse consisting of a single metrical foot.

mood   The atmosphere or feeling produced in a text, usually through descriptive language of places, people, and events.

motif   Any significant repetition of images, symbols, language, actions, or other elements of a literary work.

myth criticism   An approach to literary studies that analyzes characters and events as representative parts of archetypal, mythical patterns.

narrative   A structure by which we make sense out of events by ordering them in a chain of cause-and-effect relations that play out in space and time.

narrator   The voice of the person telling the story. Typically, the author selects a dominant narrative mode for each literary work, though some works may include multiple narrators and multiple narrative modes. A *first-person narrator* is a participating character in the work identified through the narrator's use of *I* or occasionally *we*. A *third-person narrator* is not explicitly present in the work but appears to recount events from a position outside the work, which is not explained or accounted for by the story. A *third-person omniscient narrator* is a narrator who has a complete, nearly godlike range of knowledge, including the thoughts and emotions of all characters. A *third-person limited narrator* is a narrator whose implied knowledge is limited to his or her subjective experiences. If a work involves more than one narrator, the first narrator is called the *frame narrator*.

naturalism   A literary movement in which writers sought to render a realistic or scientific view of the human species.

near rhyme   Rhymes with minor or dissonant tonalities.

New Criticism   An approach to literary criticism that was followed by a group of American critics of the early and middle twentieth century who believed that analyzing the elements of a work was all that was necessary to understand it.

New Historicism   An approach to literary analysis that focuses on the historical and cultural aspects of a text, asserting the importance of context and treating the text as a cultural document, not a literary icon.

octameter   A unit of verse having eight feet per poetic line.

octave   The first eight lines of a sonnet.

onomatopoeia   The verbal sounds or words that are meant to mimic things imaginatively heard in the world, such as *buzz* and *plop*.

open form verse   Poetry that varies in length, typography, rhythms, and stanza patterns to fit the particular style and content of the work at hand.

Orientalism   An approach to cultural analysis that stereotypes Eastern or Asian peoples and rationalizes Western values as superior. Based on Edward Said's *Orientalism*. See D. H. Hwang's play *M. Butterfly*.

Other   The different. In both race and postcolonial criticism, the other is often constructed as a negation of white, European values. At times, the other is also made into an exotic or alluring figure of desire.

ottava rima   The eight-line stanza pattern rhyming *abababcc* (Italian).

oxymoron   A rhetorical figure that combines contradictory terms—a blending of opposites. It is derived from the Greek roots meaning sharp (*oxus*) and foolish (*moros*).

paradigms   The models or patterns that make up the events in a story.

paradox   A contradictory experience, insight, or truth that cuts across the grain of our conventional expectations. It is derived from the Greek root words meaning beyond (*para*) and opinion (*doxos*).

paraphrase A restatement in your own words of the main ideas, arguments, and thematic elements of a poem.

parataxis A technique in which images are set directly side by side. In experimental film, this might be a quick cut from one scene or image to another; in poetry, setting phrases side by side without an obvious or logical connection.

pastoral Relating to the natural landscapes of Greece and Rome, found in much of traditional English love poetry representing desire.

patriarchy The social and cultural relations that have historically empowered men at the expense of women. It is drawn from the Greek root *patriarkhes* and the Latin word *pater* or father.

pattern poetry A version of fixed form verse that presents the typography and arrangement of lines on the page as a visual icon for its subject matter.

pentameter A metrical measure of verse made up of five feet per line, as in the iambic pentameter measure of Shakespeare's sonnets.

personification A figure of speech in which nonhuman objects or creatures are endowed with human characteristics.

plot The purposeful arrangement of events in a work and the order in which they are presented. This arrangement of events may not necessarily follow the sequence in which they occurred but are usually presented for affective or causal reasons.

poetic foot A unit of verse measurement based on a metrical pattern of accented and unaccented syllables.

point of view The perspective from which people, events, and other details of a literary work are described.

popular culture The attitudes, customs, and folkways of ordinary, everyday people.

postcolonial criticism A set of theoretical issues emerging from the literature and culture of Europe's former colonies as they rebelled against colonial rule and asserted their own cultural and political independence, often by appropriating and recoding colonial discourse, national symbols, and other linguistic conventions of social distinction (see *hybridity*).

postmodernism A term used variously to characterize sets of aesthetic practices that break up any idea of unity, consistency, or singularity or that employs pastiche or other modes of borrowing. This term may also refer to postmodernist aesthetic practices or textual features.

prolepsis A flashforward.

prosopopoeia The figurative rhetoric that attributes human aspects to what are otherwise inanimate objects, abstractions, or nonhuman animals.

protagonist A character that serves as the primary actor in a literary work and with whom readers are often invited to sympathize.

psychoanalytic criticism A critical approach that investigates the ways literary texts embody, enact, or illustrate dynamic relations within or among characters using concepts taken from psychoanalysis, particularly the work of Sigmund Freud and Jacques Lacan.

psychological criticism A critical approach that focuses on interpreting the psychological motivations of characters. Such an approach may adopt vocabularies from any of several psychological "schools" of thought such as the work of Sigmund Freud, Carl Jung, or D. W. Winnicott.

pure rhyme　The heard likeness and differences linking two or more words.

pyrrhic　A metrical foot comprising two unaccented syllables.

quatrain　A four-line stanza unit.

queer theory　See *gay and lesbian theory*.

race criticism　An approach to literary analysis that focuses on how racial difference is represented in the themes, characterizations, symbolism, settings, diction, and formal properties of literary texts.

reader response criticism　An approach to literary analysis that focuses on the individual's response to literary texts and investigates the social conventions of reading that make up broader interpretive communities.

realism　A literary movement and style that focuses on reproducing objective portraits of normal life through the use of a rigorous observation of human behavior in its social and material contexts.

reliability　The degree to which readers can trust representations made by a narrator.

representation　The act of using a word, image or pictorial sign to stand for something else. Representations have a shaping role in society insofar as they communicate perceptions, influence opinions, and build consensus, as well as determine attitudes and beliefs.

rhyme royal　A seven-stanza rhyming unit patterned *ababbcc*.

romance　A kind of play known for bordering on the seriousness of tragedy even as its central conflicts are resolved happily. Shakespeare's later plays are often referred to as romances. The term is also used to describe medieval narratives in prose or verse—and written in Middle English or a Romance language such as French—that feature the adventures of knights or other heroes (*Sir Gawain and the Green Knight*, for example).

romantic comedy　A comic plot in which young lovers wish to be married and are prevented from doing so, usually by an intervening father or a harsh law. The conflict is brought to closure almost by accident, often by an unexpected twist that allows the conflicts driving the action to be settled happily.

satire　A literary work in which a person or group's vices, hypocrisies, or vanities are held up for ridicule or other comic criticism.

scansion　The process of noting the metrics of a line by counting the number of feet it contains and by charting both accents and syllables.

Scottish stanza　A six-line rhyming unit patterned *aaabab* that was popularized by Robert Burns.

script　The written text of a play, including the dialogue, stage directions, notes from the director, and so on.

semiotics　The study of how various signs (or signifiers) relate to one another in complex webs of meaning.

sestet　The last six lines of a sonnet.

setting The physical, environmental, social, historical, and cultural contexts described in a story as the scene of its action.

simile A figure of speech that makes an explicit comparison between two things by using words such as *like* or *as*. For instance, "She sings like a bird" is a simile.

slant rhyme A rhyme with minor or dissonant tonalities.

soliloquy A speech or lines in a drama in which an actor is alone, revealing his innermost thoughts to the audience.

sonnet The most widely written and read fixed form of poetry, which came into English from the Italian influence of Petrarch.

Spenserian stanza A distinctive nine-line stanza of poetry named after Spenser's "The Faerie Queen."

spondee A metrical foot of poetry consisting of two long or stressed syllables.

stanza A unit or grouping of poetry lines that have the same or similar patterns of meter, rhythm, and end rhyme.

stereotypes A character who represents a familiar type.

stock character A character that fills a predictable role that is conventional to certain kinds of drama. Westerns, for example, predictably offer readers and viewers a hero, a bad guy, a kind-hearted woman who either gambles or works in a saloon, and stereotypes of Native Americans.

story The collection of events that belong to the space and time of the world created by the text as well as events that are only suggested or implied in the text.

strophe A choral song in classical Greek drama accompanied by a movement from the right to the left of the stage.

structuralist criticism Criticism that focuses on a story's structure as a way to understand how the story works.

style The distinctive manner of expression an author uses in a literary text.

symbol A concrete image, word, or thing, that refers to an abstract idea or condition. For instance, a wedding ring is a symbol of marriage.

synaesthesia A literary device that uses one of the perceptual senses (sight, hearing, smell, taste, and touch) to portray figuratively another perceptual sense. For example, Dylan Thomas describes smoke as "tunes from the chimneys."

synecdoche A type of metonymy that substitutes a part of something for the whole designated. "Counting heads" is a synecdoche for taking attendance in a classroom.

tercet A group of three lines of verse, often rhyming together or with another triplet.

terza rima A well-known tercet pattern that takes the middle rhyme of each stanza and uses it as the envelope frame for the next stanza unit to rhyme (Italian).

tetrameter A line of verse consisting of four metrical feet.

theme The central idea or ideas suggested by a literary work.

third-person limited narrator See *narrator.*

third-person narrator See *narrator.*

third-person omniscient narrator See *narrator.*

tone   A literary concept analogous to the tone of voice in spoken language.

tragedy   A narrative in which the central character or protagonist suffers a fall, often death.

tragic hero   The protagonist of a tragedy.

trimeter   A line of poetry made up of three feet.

trochee   A metrical foot of poetry having two syllables where the accent falls on the first syllable rather than on the second, as it does in the iamb.

unity of action   An element of a tragedy privileged by Aristotle in *Poetics*. A unified plot has a beginning, middle, and end, the events of which are linked together by probability and necessity.

unreliability   The adjective applies to narrators whom readers may not trust to deliver unbiased information.

vers libre   Free verse (French). Verse that varies in length, typography, rhythms and stanza patterns to fit the particular style and content of the work at hand.

TEXT CREDITS

Ai, "The Mother's Tale," From *Vice*. Copyright © 1999 by Ai. Used by permission of W. W. Norton & Company, Inc.

Ashbery, John, "The Painter": From *Some Trees* by John Ashbery. Copyright © 1956 by John Ashbery. Reprinted by permission of George Borchardt, Inc., on behalf of the author.

Atwood, Margaret, "Habitation": From *Selected Poems, 1965–1975* by Margaret Atwood. Copyright © 1976 by Margaret Atwood. Reprinted by permission of Houghton Mifflin Company. All rights reserved.

Auden, W. H., "A Lullaby" copyright 1940, 1968 by W. H. Auden; "Musée des Beaux Arts" copyright 1940 and renewed 1968 by W. H. Auden; "Shield of Achilles" copyright 1956 by W. H. Auden: From *Collected Poems* by W. H. Auden. Used by permission of Random House, Inc.

Baca, Jimmy Santiago, "Bells," "Choices," "Dust-Bowl Memory," and "Mi Tío Baca El Poeta De Socorro": From *Black Mesa Poems*, copyright © 1989 by Jimmy Santiago Baca. Reprinted by permission of New Directions Publishing Corporation.

Balakian, Peter, "After the Survivors Are Gone": From *June-Tree: New and Selected Poems*, HarperCollins, 2001. Copyright © 2001 by Peter Balakian. Reprinted by permission of the author.

Baraka, Amiri, "Black Dada Nihilismus" from *The Dead Lecturer*, 1964; "Ka 'Ba" and "Three Modes of History and Culture" from *Black Magic*, 1969. Copyright © Amiri Baraka. Reprinted by permission of the author.

Beatty, Paul, "A Three Point Shot from Andromeda" and "Darryl Strawberry Asleep in a Field of Dreams": From *Big Bank Take Little Bank*. Copyright © 1991 by Paul Beatty. Reprinted by permission of The Wylie Agency, Inc.

Bennett, Gwendolyn B., "Heritage" and "To a Dark Girl:" From *The Book of American Negro Poetry*, edited by James Weldon Johnson, 1931.

Bergman, David, "Blueberry Man": From *Cracking the Code*, 1985. Reprinted by permission of the author.

Bernstein, Charles, "The Kiwi Bird in the Kiwi Tree," "Ear Shot," and "House of Formaldehyde": From *Rough Trades*. Copyright © 1991 by Charles Bernstein. Reprinted with the permission of Green Integer Books, Los Angeles.

Bishop, Elizabeth, "Insomnia," "In the Waiting Room" and "One Art": From *Complete Poems: 1927–1979* by Elizabeth Bishop. Copyright © 1979, 1983 by Alice Helen Methfessel. Reprinted by permission of Farrar, Straus and Giroux, LLC.

Bly, Robert, "Waking from Sleep": From *Silence in the Snowy Fields* © 1962 by Robert Bly and reprinted by permission of Wesleyan University Press.

Bogan, Louise, "Didactic Piece" and "Medusa": From *The Blue Estuaries: Poems 1923–1968* by Louise Bogan. Copyright © 1968 by Louise Bogan. Copyright renewed 1996 by Ruth Limmer. Reprinted by permission of Farrar, Straus and Giroux, LLC.

Boland, Eavan, "The Pomegranate": From *In a Time of Violence* by Eavan Boland. Copyright © 1994 by Eavan Boland. Used by permission of W. W. Norton & Company, Inc.

Brooks, Gwendolyn, "Ballad of Pearl May Lee," "Boy Breaking Glass," "A Bronzeville Mother Loiters in Mississippi. Meanwhile a Mississippi Mother Burns Bacon," "Gang Girls," "Jessie Mitchell's Mother," "kitchenette building," "the mother," "piano after war," "the rites for cousin vic," "Sadie and Maud," "a song in the front yard," "Ulysses," and "We Real Cool": From *Blacks*. Copyright © 1945. Reprinted by permission of the Estate of Gwendolyn Brooks.

Broumas, Olga, "The Masseuse": From *Rave: Poems 1975–1999*. Copyright © 1999 by Olga Broumas. Reprinted with the permission of Copper Canyon Press, P.O. Box 271, Port Townsend, WA 98368-0271.

Brown, Sterling A., "Slim in Atlanta": From *The Collected Poems of Sterling A. Brown*, edited by Michael S. Harper. Copyright © 1980 by Sterling A. Brown. Reprinted by permission of HarperCollins Publishers, Inc.

Celan, Paul, "Deathfugue": From *Selected Poems and Prose of Paul Celan*, translated by John Felstiner. Copyright © 2001 by John Felstiner. Used by permission of W. W. Norton & Company, Inc.

Cisneros, Sandra, "Little Clown, My Heart": From *Loose Woman*. Copyright © 1994 by Sandra Cisneros. Published by Vintage Books, a division of Random House, Inc., and originally in hardcover by

Zamora, Bernice, "Notes from a Chicana 'COED'": by Bernice Zamora from Mara Sanchez, ed., *Contemporary Chicana Poetry*. Copyright © 1985 The Regents of the University of California. Reprinted by permission of The University of California Press.

PHOTO CREDITS

Opener: page 1, Houghton Library, Harvard University. **Chapter 2:** page 18, Archivo Iconografico, S.A./Corbis #CS005031. **Chapter 3:** page 31, John Suiter. **Chapter 5:** page 68, Chris Dewitt. **Chapter 9:** page 140, Cover of "Love, Vortex, Vertigo" 1969 edited by Steward Baker; page 145, Keats–Shelley Museum, Rome; page 147, SEF/Art Resource, NY. **Chapter 11:** page 187, *The Masses*, May, 1912; page 188, National Archives Photo #NWDNS-102-LH-462. **Chapter 12:** page 242, Yad Vashem, The Holocaust Martyrs' and Heroes' Remembrance Authority #FA-268/35. **Chapter 13:** page 245, © by Fred W. McDarrah; page 246, © by Fred W. McDarrah; page 252, Ted Streshinsky/Corbis #TS001980; page 254, AP/Wide World Photos. **Chapter 14:** page 269, Solomon R. Guggenheim Museum, NY. **Chapter 15:** page 288, Metal wheel mounted on painted wooden stool. Gift of the Sidney & Harriet Janis Collection. Museum of Modern Art, NY, Art Resource, NY, © ARS, NY. **Chapter 16:** page 322, Leonard de Salva/Corbis #DS001446; page 323, Wisconsin State Historical Society; page 324, *left and right*, The Albert & Shirley Small Special Collections Library, University of Virginia; page 342, AP Photo #5813504. **Chapter 19:** page 447, Gwendolyn Stewart. **Chapter 20:** page 478, Burstein Collection/Corbis #BE007129. **Chapter 22:** page 528, Carl Van Vechten's portrait of Langston Hughes, © 1939 negative, Estate of Carl Van Vechten; © 1983 photogravure, Eakins Press Foundation/National Portrait Gallery, Smithsonian Institution/Art Resource, New York; page 529, "The Negro Speaks of Rivers," words by Langston Hughes and music by Margaret Bonds, © Handy Brothers Music Co., Inc., New York, with permission of Tele Cinema Music, Inc.; page 534, Collection: Cary Nelson; **Insert:** page 1, *top left*, Erich Lessing/Art Resource, NY #S0107605; *top right*, The Metropolitan Museum of Art, Alfred Stieglitz Collection, 1949. Photo © The Metropolitan Museum of Art; *bottom left*, © Copyright The Andy Warhol Foundation for the Visual Arts/ARS, NY/Art Resource, NY; *bottom right*, Chicago Women's Graphics Collective; page 2, *top*, Scala/Art Resource, NY #S0060943, *bottom*, Erich Lessing/Art Resource, NY #S0143011; page 3, *top*, National Gallery, London. All rights reserved #NG213; *bottom*, National Gallery, London. All rights reserved #NG1868; page 4, *top left*, Lessing J. Rosenwald Collection/The Library of Congress #PR4144.S6 1789b; *top right*, Copyright Tate Gallery, London/Art Resource, NY #S0086530; *bottom left and right*, Courtesy of the Yed Vashem Art Museum, Jerusalem.

Index of Literary Terms

Index of First Lines

Index of Authors and Titles